McGraw-Hill

netw⊙rks™

A Social Studies Learning System

MEETS YOU ANYWHERE —
TAKES YOU EVERYWHERE

McGraw-Hill networks™

MEETS YOU ANYWHERE — TAKES YOU EVERYWHERE

GO online

1. Go to *connected.mcgraw-hill.com.*

2. Get your User Name and Password from your teacher and enter them.

3. Click on your **Networks** book.

4. Select your chapter and lesson.

HOW do you learn?

Read • Reflect • Watch • Listen • Connect • Discover • Interact

start **netw rk**ing

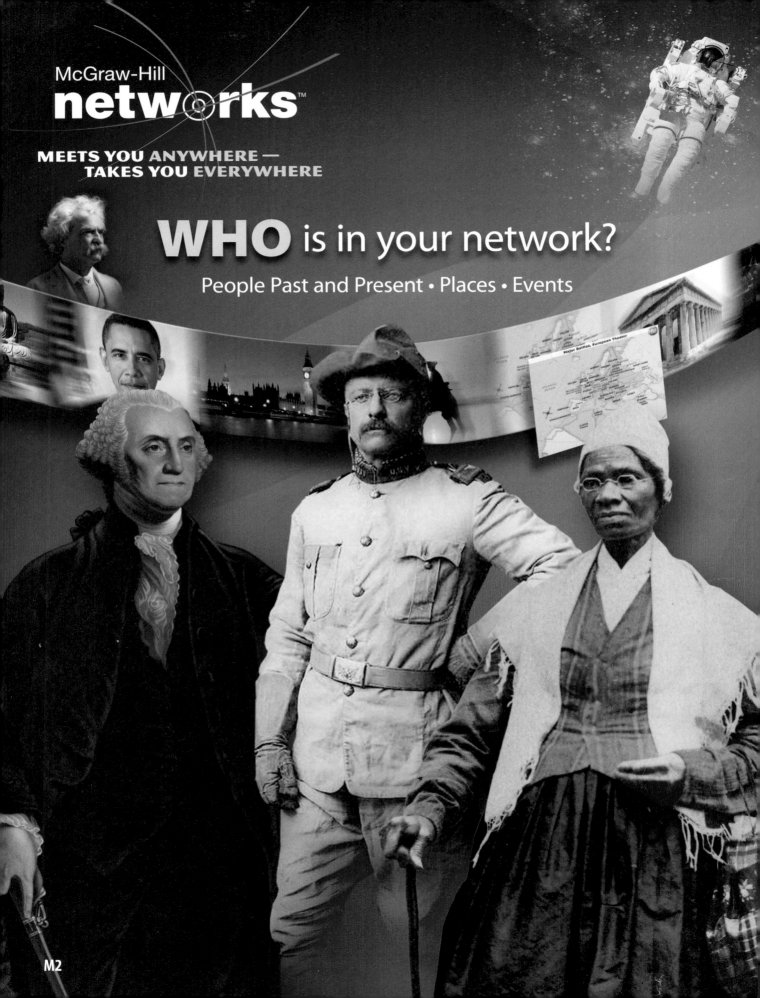

McGraw-Hill networks™

MEETS YOU ANYWHERE — TAKES YOU EVERYWHERE

WHO is in your network?

People Past and Present • Places • Events

WHAT do you learn?

History • Geography • Economics • Government • Culture

start **network**ing

McGraw-Hill networks™

MEETS YOU ANYWHERE — TAKES YOU EVERYWHERE

HOW do you make Networks yours?

Organize • Take Notes • Study • Submit • Message

M4

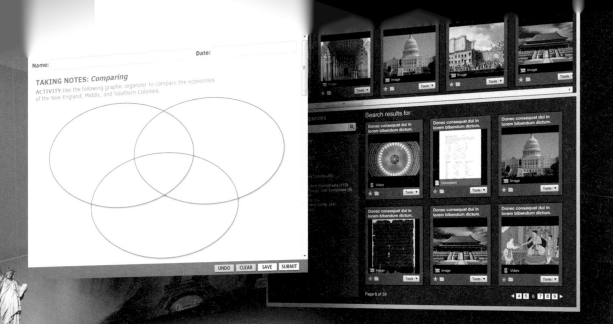

WHAT do you use?

Graphic Organizers • Primary Sources • Videos • Games • Photos

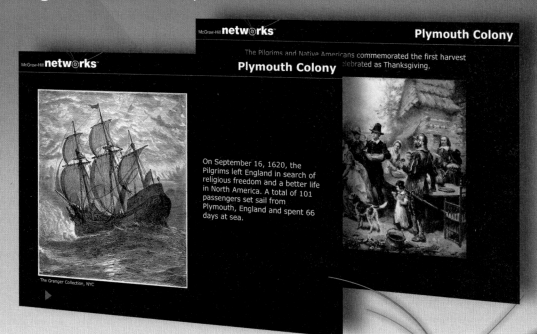

start**networking**

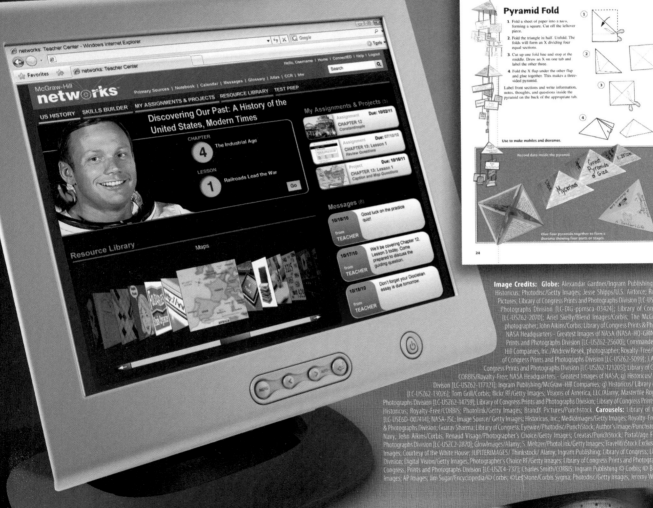

net**w**orks™

MEETS YOU ANYWHERE — TAKES YOU EVERYWHERE

HOW do you show what you know?

Hands-On Projects • Foldables® • Print or Online Assessments

start net**w**orking

connected.mcgraw-hill.com

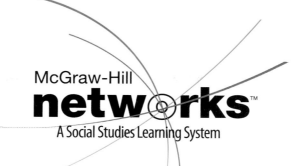

McGraw-Hill

networks™

A Social Studies Learning System

DISCOVERING OUR PAST

A HISTORY of the UNITED STATES

Modern Times

Joyce Appleby, Ph.D.

Alan Brinkley, Ph.D.

Albert S. Broussard, Ph.D.

James M. McPherson, Ph.D.

Donald A. Ritchie, Ph.D.

Mc Graw Hill Education

Bothell, WA • Chicago, IL • Columbus, OH • New York, NY

connected.mcgraw-hill.com

Copyright © 2014 McGraw-Hill Education

All rights reserved. No part of this publication may be reproduced or distributed in any form or by any means, or stored in a database or retrieval system, without the prior written consent of McGraw-Hill Education, including, but not limited to, network storage or transmission, or broadcast for distance learning.

Send all inquiries to:
McGraw-Hill Education
8787 Orion Place
Columbus, OH 43240

ISBN: 978-0-07-659729-1
MHID: 0-07-659729-6
Printed in the United States of America.

3 4 5 6 7 8 9 10 DOW 16 15 14 13

AUTHORS

Joyce Appleby, Ph.D., is Professor Emerita of History at UCLA. She is the author of several books, including her most recent, *The Relentless Revolution: A History of Capitalism*. She served as president of the Organization of American Historians and the American Historical Association, and she chaired the Council of the Institute of Early American History and Culture at Williamsburg. Appleby has been elected to the American Philosophical Society and the American Academy of Arts and Sciences, and she is a Corresponding Fellow of the British Academy.

Alan Brinkley, Ph.D., is Allan Nevins Professor of American History at Columbia University. His published works include *Voices of Protest: Huey Long, Father Coughlin, and the Great Depression,* which won the 1983 National Book Award. Other titles include *The End of Reform: New Deal Liberalism in Recession and War* and *Liberalism and Its Discontents*. Brinkley received the Levenson Memorial Teaching Prize at Harvard University.

Albert S. Broussard, Ph.D., is Professor of History at Texas A&M University, where he was selected as the Distinguished Faculty Lecturer for 1999–2000. He also served as the Langston Hughes Professor of American Studies at the University of Kansas in 2005. Before joining the Texas A&M faculty, Broussard was Assistant Professor of History and Director of the African American Studies Program at Southern Methodist University. Among the books he has published are *Black San Francisco: The Struggle for Racial Equality in the West, 1900–1954* and *African American Odyssey: The Stewarts, 1853–1963*. Broussard has also served as president of the Oral History Association.

James M. McPherson, Ph.D., is George Henry Davis Professor Emeritus of American History at Princeton University. He is the author of 11 books about the Civil War era, including *Tried by War: Abraham Lincoln as Commander in Chief*, for which he won a second Lincoln Prize in 2009. McPherson is a member of many professional historical associations, including the Civil War Preservation Trust.

Donald A. Ritchie, Ph.D., is Historian of the United States Senate. Ritchie received his doctorate in American history from the University of Maryland after service in the U.S. Marine Corps. He has taught American history at various levels, from high school to university. He edits the Historical Series of the Senate Foreign Relations Committee and is the author of several books, including *Press Gallery: Congress and the Washington Correspondents*, which received the Organization of American Historians' Richard W. Leopold Prize. Ritchie has served as president of the Oral History Association and as a council member of the American Historical Association.

Contributing Authors

Jay McTighe has published articles in a number of leading educational journals and has coauthored 10 books, including the best-selling *Understanding by Design* series with Grant Wiggins. McTighe also has an extensive background in professional development and is a featured speaker at national, state, and district conferences and workshops. He received his undergraduate degree from The College of William and Mary, earned a Masters degree from the University of Maryland, and completed post-graduate studies at the Johns Hopkins University.

Dinah Zike, M.Ed., is an award-winning author, educator, and inventor recognized for designing three-dimensional, hands-on manipulatives and graphic organizers known as Foldables®. Foldables are used nationally and internationally by teachers, parents, and other professionals in the education field. Zike has developed more than 150 supplemental educational books and materials. Her two latest books, *Notebook Foldables®* and *Foldables®, Notebook Foldables®, & VKV®s for Spelling and Vocabulary 4th–12th* were each awarded *Learning Magazine's* Teachers' Choice Award for 2011. In 2004, Zike was honored with the CESI Science Advocacy Award. She received her M.Ed. from Texas A&M, College Station, Texas.

Doug Fisher, Ph.D., and Nancy Frey, Ph.D., are professors in the School of Teacher Education at San Diego State University. Fisher's focus is on literacy and language, with an emphasis on students who are English Learners. Frey's focus is on literacy and learning, with a concentration in how students acquire content knowledge. Both teach elementary and secondary teacher preparation courses, in addition to their work with graduate and doctoral programs. Their shared interests include supporting students with diverse learning needs, instructional design, and curriculum development. They are coauthors of numerous articles and books, including *Better Learning Through Structured Teaching, Checking for Understanding, Background Knowledge,* and *Improving Adolescent Literacy*. They are coeditors (with Diane Lapp) of the NCTE journal *Voices from the Middle*.

CONSULTANTS AND REVIEWERS

ACADEMIC CONSULTANTS

David Berger, Ph.D.
Ruth and I. Lewis Gordon
  Professor of Jewish History
Dean, Bernard Revel Graduate
  School
Yeshiva University
New York, New York

Stephen Cunha, Ph.D.
Professor of Geography
Humboldt State University
Arcata, California

Tom Daccord
Educational Technology Specialist
Co-Director, EdTechTeacher
Boston, Massachusetts

Sylvia Kniest
Social Studies Teacher
Tucson Unified School District
Tucson, Arizona

Bernard Reich, Ph.D.
Professor of Political Science and
  International Affairs
George Washington University
Washington, D.C.

Justin Reich
Educational Technology Specialist
Co-Director, EdTechTeacher
Boston, Massachusetts

TEACHER REVIEWERS

Laura Abundes
Jefferson Middle School
Waukegan, Illinois

Debbie Clay
Brink Junior High
Moore, Oklahoma

Wendy Blanton
Berkeley Middle School
St. Louis, Missouri

Michael Frint
Fort Riley Middle School
Fort Riley, Kansas

Brian M. Gibson
Highland East Junior High School
Moore, Oklahoma

Carol V. Gimondo
Jefferson Middle School
Waukegan, Illinois

Mark Hamann
Perrysburg Junior High School
Perrysburg, Ohio

Norman Jackson
Frontier Middle School
O'Fallon, Missouri

Connie K. Simmonds
Ferguson Middle School
Ferguson, Missouri

Mary Beth Whaley
Highland West Junior High School
Moore, Oklahoma

CONTENTS

Bettmann/CORBIS

CHAPTER 1

This icon indicates where reading skills and writing skills from the *Common Core State Standards for English Language Arts & Literacy in History/Social Studies, Science, and Technical Subjects* are practiced and reinforced.

Bettmann/CORBIS

CHAPTER 2

PoodlesRock/Corbis

CHAPTER 3

CONTENTS

The Granger Collection, NYC

CHAPTER 4

The Industrial Age 95

Essential Question

How does technology change the way people live and work?

The Granger Collection, NYC

CHAPTER 5

An Urban Society 121

Essential Questions

Why do people move? • How do new ideas change the way people live?

CORBIS

CHAPTER 6

The Progressive Era 147

Essential Questions

Why do societies change? • What are the causes and consequences of prejudice and injustice?

The Granger Collection, New York

The Granger Collection, New York

The Granger Collection, NYC

CONTENTS

Library of Congress/LC-USF34-009058-C

CHAPTER 10

The Granger Collection, New York

CHA... 11

Bettmann/CORBIS

CHAPTER **12**

The Granger Collection, NYC

CHAPTER **13**

CONTENTS

Bettmann/CORBIS

CHAPTER **14**

CORBIS

CHAPTER **15**

U.S. Air Force

CHAPTER 16

New Challenges 447

Essential Questions

What are the consequences when cultures interact? • How do governments change? • Why does conflict develop? • How do new ideas change the way people live?

FEATURES

Thinking Like a HISTORIAN

Connections to TODAY

THEN AND NOW

ECONOMICS SKILLS

MAPS, CHARTS, AND GRAPHS

CHARTS AND GRAPHS

ONLINE RESOURCES

 Videos

Interactive Graphs and Charts

Slide Shows

networks ONLINE RESOURCES

Interactive Graphic Organizers

Chapter 1 Historian's Tools
Types of Maps
Economic Systems
Types of Government Systems

Chapter 2 Reconstruction Plans
The Fourteenth and Fifteenth Amendments
Improvements in Education
The New South

Chapter 3 Effects of Mining Booms
Settlement of the Great Plains
Government Actions
National Grange, Farmers' Alliances, Populist Party

Chapter 4 Effects of Railroad Expansion
Effects of Major Inventions
The Oil and Steel Industries
Strikes: Causes and Effects

Chapter 5 Immigration Laws Time Line
Growth of Cities
Individuals' Achievements

Chapter 6 Impact of the Seventeenth Amendment
The Eighteenth and Nineteenth Amendments
Comparing Roosevelt and Taft
Comparing Washington and DuBois

Chapter 7 U.S. Influence Expands
Relations Between U.S. and Japan
Land Acquired after Spanish-American War
Policies and Principles of U.S. Foreign Policy

Chapter 8 Causes of Tensions Leading to World War I
Events Causing U.S. Entry Into War
Signing the Armistice
Controlling Public Opinion
Conditions of the Treaty of Versailles

Chapter 9 Drop in Union Membership
The Harding and Coolidge Presidencies
Changes in Business Practices
Themes in the Arts During the 1920s

Chapter 10 Stock Market Crash Time Line
Roosevelt's New Deal
Groups Affected by the Depression
New Deal Complaints and Suggestions

Chapter 11 International Parties
Allied and Axis Powers
Role of Men and Women During WWII
Allied Victory in North Africa
Pacific Front Time Line

Chapter 12 Postwar Organizations
Postwar Changes
Nations in Korean War
Changes to American Society

Chapter 13 Equal Rights Time Line
New Frontier and Great Society
Freedom Riders
Civil Rights Movements

Chapter 14 Identifying Main Ideas
American Involvement in Vietnam
Events of 1968
Vietnam War Results

Chapter 15 Nixon's Foreign Policy
Watergate Time Line
Issues of the Carter Presidency

Chapter 16 Principles of Conservation
End of the Cold War
Clinton Legislation
Effects of September 11
Global Challenges

Maps

All maps that appear in your printed textbook are also available in an interactive format in your Online Student Edition.

REFERENCE ATLAS

ATLAS KEY

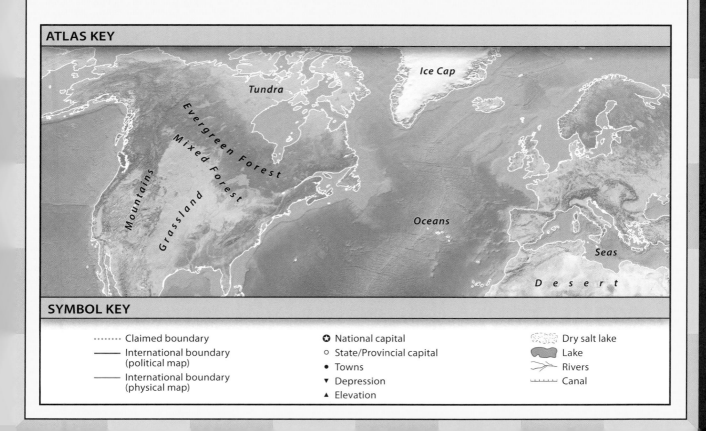

Ice Cap

Tundra

Evergreen Forest

Mixed Forest

Mountains

Grassland

Oceans

Seas

Desert

SYMBOL KEY

········· Claimed boundary	✪ National capital	Dry salt lake
——— International boundary (political map)	○ State/Provincial capital	Lake
——— International boundary (physical map)	● Towns	Rivers
	▼ Depression	Canal
	▲ Elevation	

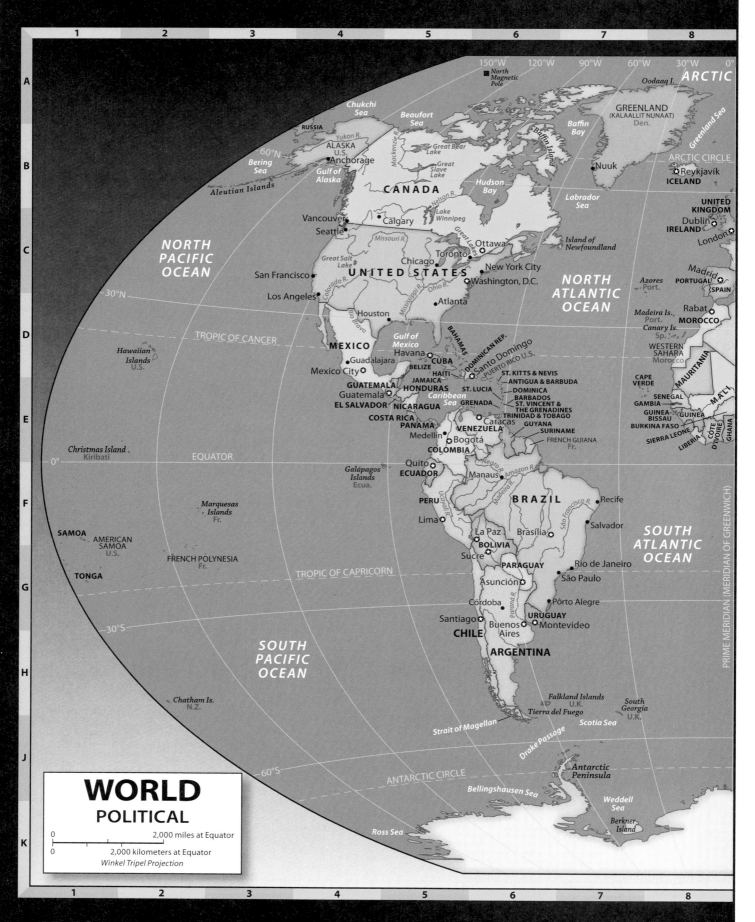

WORLD
POLITICAL

0   2,000 miles at Equator

0   2,000 kilometers at Equator

Winkel Tripel Projection

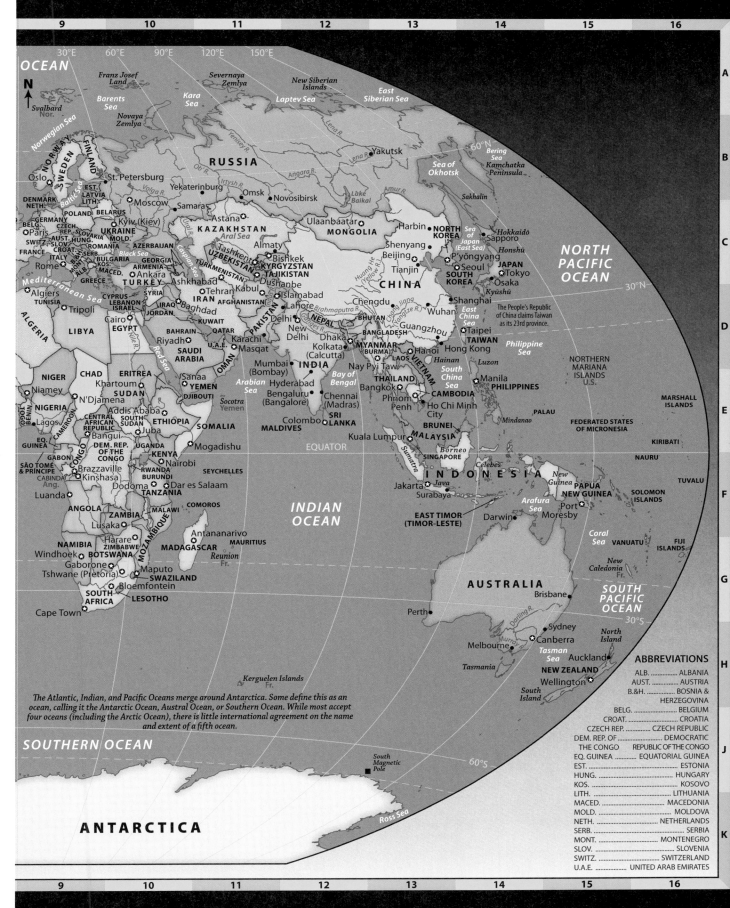

OCEAN

N

30°E 60°E 90°E 120°E 150°E

Svalbard
Nor.

Franz Josef
Land

Severnaya
Zemlya

New Siberian
Islands

East
Siberian Sea

Barents
Sea

Kara
Sea

Laptev Sea

Novaya
Zemlya

Norwegian Sea

NORWAY SWEDEN FINLAND

Oslo St. Petersburg

RUSSIA

Yakutsk

60°N

Bering
Sea

Kamchatka
Peninsula

Sea of
Okhotsk

DENMARK
NETH.

EST.
LATVIA
LITH.

Yekaterinburg Omsk Novosibirsk

Ob. R.

Irtysh R.

Angara R.

Lake
Baikal

Amur R.

Lena R.

Sakhalin

Baltic Sea

GERMANY
BELG. POLAND BELARUS
Paris CZECH
REP. SLOVAKIA
SWITZ. AUST. HUNG.
FRANCE SLOV. ROMANIA
CROAT. MOLD.
ITALY SERB. BULGARIA
Rome MONT. ALB. MACED.
GREECE KOS.

Moscow Samara

Volga R.

Astana

Ural R.

KAZAKHSTAN

Aral Sea

Almaty

Ulaanbaatar

MONGOLIA

Harbin NORTH
KOREA

Shenyang

Beijing

Sea
of
Japan
(East Sea)

Hokkaidō
Sapporo

Honshū

JAPAN
Tokyo

Mediterranean Sea
Algiers TUNISIA
Tripoli

AZERBAIJAN
Tashkent
UZBEKISTAN Bishkek KYRGYZSTAN
TURKMENISTAN TAJIKISTAN
Ashkhabad Dushanbe

Black Sea
GEORGIA
ARMENIA
Ankara TURKEY
CYPRUS
LEBANON SYRIA
ISRAEL IRAQ
JORDAN Baghdad

Caspian Sea

Tehran IRAN

Kabul
AFGHANISTAN

Islamabad
Lahore
PAKISTAN
Delhi
New
Delhi

Tianjin

CHINA

Chengdu

Huang He
(Yellow R.)

Chang Jiang
(Yangtze R.)

SOUTH
KOREA
Seoul
P'yǒngyang

Osaka
Kyūshū

Shanghai

Wuhan

Guangzhou

Taipei
TAIWAN

East
China
Sea

NORTH
PACIFIC
OCEAN

30°N

The People's Republic
of China claims Taiwan
as its 23rd province.

Cairo
EGYPT

LIBYA

Nile R.

Red Sea

BAHRAIN
QATAR
Riyadh U.A.E.
SAUDI
ARABIA
OMAN
Masqat

KUWAIT

Karachi

Brahmaputra R.

NEPAL BHUTAN
Ganges R.

Dhaka
Kolkata
(Calcutta)
BANGLADESH

MYANMAR
(BURMA) Hanoi

Hong Kong

Hainan

South
China
Sea

Luzon

Philippine
Sea

NORTHERN
MARIANA
ISLANDS
U.S.

ALGERIA

NIGER

CHAD

ERITREA
Khartoum
SUDAN
N'Djamena

Sanaa
YEMEN
DJIBOUTI

Socotra
Yemen

Arabian
Sea

Mumbai
(Bombay)

INDIA
Hyderabad
Bengaluru
(Bangalore)

Bay of
Bengal

Nay Pyi Taw

LAOS
THAILAND
Bangkok

VIETNAM

Manila
PHILIPPINES

MARSHALL
ISLANDS

NIGERIA

CAMEROON
CENTRAL
AFRICAN
REPUBLIC

SOUTH
SUDAN
Juba

ETHIOPIA

SOMALIA

Chennai
(Madras)
Colombo SRI
LANKA
MALDIVES

CAMBODIA
Phnom
Penh
Ho Chi Minh
City
BRUNEI
MALAYSIA

PALAU

Mindanao

FEDERATED STATES
OF MICRONESIA

KIRIBATI

Niamey
BENIN

Lagos
EQ.
GUINEA GABON
SÃO TOMÉ
& PRÍNCIPE
CABINDA
Ang.
Luanda

Bangui
CONGO
DEM. REP.
OF THE
CONGO
Brazzaville
Kinshasa

UGANDA
RWANDA
BURUNDI

KENYA
Nairobi
Dodoma
TANZANIA

Mogadishu

SEYCHELLES

Dar es Salaam

EQUATOR

Kuala Lumpur
SINGAPORE

Borneo

Celebes

INDONESIA
Jakarta Java
Surabaya

Sumatra

New
Guinea

PAPUA
NEW GUINEA

SOLOMON
ISLANDS

NAURU

TUVALU

ANGOLA
ZAMBIA
Lusaka
NAMIBIA
Windhoek BOTSWANA
Gaborone

MALAWI
MOZAMBIQUE
Harare
ZIMBABWE

COMOROS

Antananarivo
MADAGASCAR

MAURITIUS

Reunion
Fr.

INDIAN
OCEAN

EAST TIMOR
(TIMOR-LESTE)

Darwin

Arafura
Sea

Port
Moresby

Coral
Sea

VANUATU

New
Caledonia
Fr.

FIJI
ISLANDS

Tshwane (Pretoria)
Maputo
SWAZILAND
Bloemfontein
SOUTH
AFRICA LESOTHO

AUSTRALIA

Brisbane

SOUTH
PACIFIC
OCEAN

30°S

Cape Town

Kerguelen Islands
Fr.

The Atlantic, Indian, and Pacific Oceans merge around Antarctica. Some define this as an
ocean, calling it the Antarctic Ocean, Austral Ocean, or Southern Ocean. While most accept
four oceans (including the Arctic Ocean), there is little international agreement on the name
and extent of a fifth ocean.

SOUTHERN OCEAN

South
Magnetic
Pole

60°S

Perth

Darling R.

Melbourne
Murray R.
Canberra
Sydney

Tasman
Sea

Tasmania

North
Island
Auckland

NEW ZEALAND
Wellington
South
Island

ANTARCTICA

Ross Sea

ABBREVIATIONS

ALB.	ALBANIA
AUST.	AUSTRIA
B.&H.	BOSNIA & HERZEGOVINA
BELG.	BELGIUM
CROAT.	CROATIA
CZECH REP.	CZECH REPUBLIC
DEM. REP. OF THE CONGO	DEMOCRATIC REPUBLIC OF THE CONGO
EQ. GUINEA	EQUATORIAL GUINEA
EST.	ESTONIA
HUNG.	HUNGARY
KOS.	KOSOVO
LITH.	LITHUANIA
MACED.	MACEDONIA
MOLD.	MOLDOVA
NETH.	NETHERLANDS
SERB.	SERBIA
MONT.	MONTENEGRO
SLOV.	SLOVENIA
SWITZ.	SWITZERLAND
U.A.E.	UNITED ARAB EMIRATES

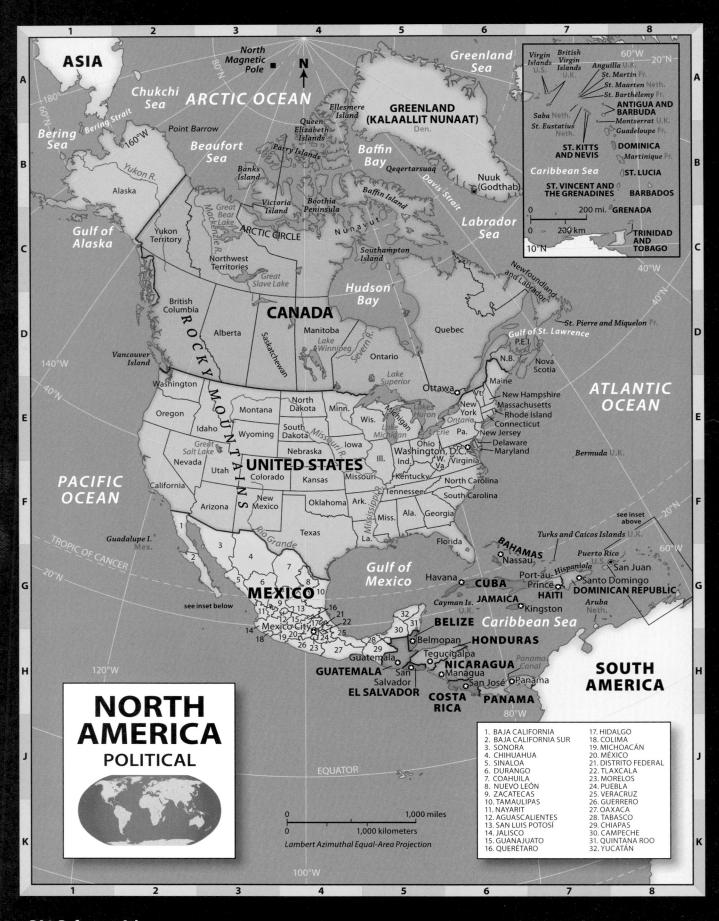

NORTH AMERICA

POLITICAL

ASIA

Chukchi Sea

North Magnetic Pole

N

ARCTIC OCEAN

Greenland Sea

Ellesmere Island

GREENLAND (KALAALLIT NUNAAT)
Den.

Bering Sea

Bering Strait

Point Barrow

Beaufort Sea

Alaska

Yukon R.

Parry Islands

Queen Elizabeth Islands

Baffin Bay

Qeqertarsuaq

Nuuk (Godthåb)

Gulf of Alaska

Yukon Territory

Banks Island

Victoria Island

Great Bear Lake

Mackenzie R.

Boothia Peninsula

ARCTIC CIRCLE

Baffin Island

Nunavut

Davis Strait

Labrador Sea

British Columbia

Northwest Territories

Great Slave Lake

Southampton Island

Newfoundland and Labrador

40°W

Vancouver Island

Alberta

Saskatchewan

Manitoba

Lake Winnipeg

Severn R.

Ontario

CANADA

Hudson Bay

Quebec

Ottawa

Gulf of St. Lawrence

St. Pierre and Miquelon Fr.

P.E.I.

N.B.

Nova Scotia

Maine

ATLANTIC OCEAN

Washington

Oregon

Idaho

Montana

Wyoming

North Dakota

South Dakota

Minn.

Wis.

Lake Superior

Lakes Huron

Michigan

Lake Michigan

L. Ontario

L. Erie

Pa.

New York

Vt.

New Hampshire

Massachusetts

Rhode Island

Connecticut

New Jersey

Delaware

Maryland

Bermuda U.K.

PACIFIC OCEAN

Nevada

Utah

Great Salt Lake

Colorado

Nebraska

Iowa

Missouri R.

UNITED STATES

Ill.

Ind.

Ohio

Washington, D.C.

W. Va.

Virginia

California

Arizona

New Mexico

Kansas

Missouri

Kentucky

Tennessee

North Carolina

South Carolina

Guadalupe I. Mex.

TROPIC OF CANCER

Rio Grande

1

2

3

4

5

6

7

8

9

10

11

12

13

14

15

16

17

18

19

20

21

22

23

24

25

26

27

28

29

30

31

32

Oklahoma

Ark.

Miss.

Ala.

Georgia

La.

Texas

Florida

Mississippi R.

Gulf of Mexico

Havana

CUBA

Cayman Is. U.K.

JAMAICA

Kingston

BAHAMAS

Nassau

Turks and Caicos Islands U.K.

see inset above

Puerto Rico U.S.

San Juan

Hispaniola

Port-au-Prince

HAITI

Santo Domingo

DOMINICAN REPUBLIC

Aruba Neth.

MEXICO

see inset below

Mexico City

Caribbean Sea

BELIZE

Belmopan

HONDURAS

Tegucigalpa

GUATEMALA

Guatemala

San Salvador

EL SALVADOR

Managua

NICARAGUA

San José

COSTA RICA

Panama Canal

Panama

PANAMA

SOUTH AMERICA

Caribbean inset

Virgin Islands U.S.

British Virgin Islands U.K.

60°W

20°N

Anguilla U.K.

St. Martin Fr.

St. Maarten Neth.

St. Barthélemy Fr.

Saba Neth.

St. Eustatius Neth.

ANTIGUA AND BARBUDA

Montserrat U.K.

Guadeloupe Fr.

ST. KITTS AND NEVIS

DOMINICA

Martinique Fr.

ST. LUCIA

Caribbean Sea

ST. VINCENT AND THE GRENADINES

BARBADOS

0 — 200 mi.

GRENADA

0 — 200 km

10°N

TRINIDAD AND TOBAGO

40°W

Mexican states legend

1. BAJA CALIFORNIA
2. BAJA CALIFORNIA SUR
3. SONORA
4. CHIHUAHUA
5. SINALOA
6. DURANGO
7. COAHUILA
8. NUEVO LEÓN
9. ZACATECAS
10. TAMAULIPAS
11. NAYARIT
12. AGUASCALIENTES
13. SAN LUIS POTOSÍ
14. JALISCO
15. GUANAJUATO
16. QUERÉTARO
17. HIDALGO
18. COLIMA
19. MICHOACÁN
20. MÉXICO
21. DISTRITO FEDERAL
22. TLAXCALA
23. MORELOS
24. PUEBLA
25. VERACRUZ
26. GUERRERO
27. OAXACA
28. TABASCO
29. CHIAPAS
30. CAMPECHE
31. QUINTANA ROO
32. YUCATÁN

0 — 1,000 miles

0 — 1,000 kilometers

Lambert Azimuthal Equal-Area Projection

EQUATOR

100°W

120°W

140°W

160°W

180°

80°N

60°N

40°N

20°N

80°W

60°W

20°N

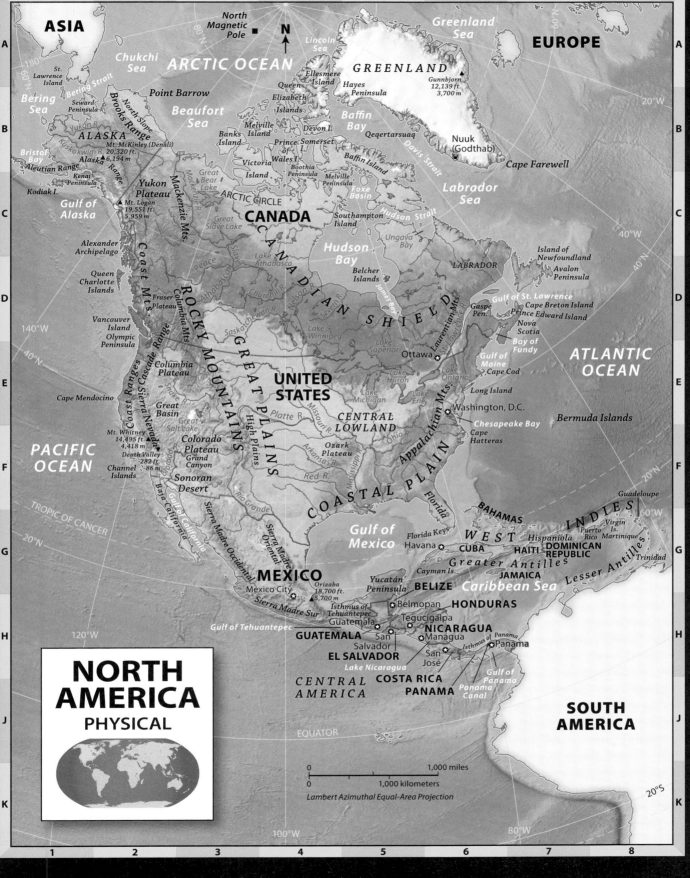

NORTH AMERICA
PHYSICAL

ASIA

EUROPE

North Magnetic Pole

N

ARCTIC OCEAN

Chukchi Sea

Lincoln Sea

Greenland Sea

GREENLAND

Ellesmere Island

Queen Elizabeth Islands

Gunnbjorn 12,139 ft. 3,700 m

Hayes Peninsula

Point Barrow

Beaufort Sea

Baffin Bay

Qeqertarsuaq

Nuuk (Godthab)

St. Lawrence Island

Bering Strait

Seward Peninsula

North Slope

Brooks Range

ALASKA

Mt. McKinley (Denali) 20,320 ft. 6,194 m

Melville Island

Banks Island

Victoria Island

Prince of Wales I.

Somerset I.

Boothia Peninsula

Devon I.

Melville Peninsula

Baffin Island

Foxe Basin

Davis Strait

Labrador Sea

Cape Farewell

Bristol Bay

Aleutian Range

Kenai Peninsula

Kodiak I.

Yukon R.

Kuskokwim R.

Alaska Range

Yukon Plateau

Mackenzie Mts.

Mt. Logan 19,551 ft. 5,959 m

ARCTIC CIRCLE

Great Bear Lake

CANADA

Hudson Strait

Southampton Island

Ungava Bay

Gulf of Alaska

Alexander Archipelago

Coast Mts.

Fraser Plateau

Columbia Plateau

Peace R.

Slave R.

Great Slave Lake

Athabasca R.

Lake Athabasca

C A N A D I A N   S H I E L D

Hudson Bay

Belcher Islands

James Bay

LABRADOR

Island of Newfoundland

Avalon Peninsula

Queen Charlotte Islands

Vancouver Island

Olympic Peninsula

ROCKY MOUNTAINS

Columbia Mts.

Cascade Range

Saskatchewan R.

Lake Winnipeg

Nelson R.

Severn R.

Churchill R.

Gulf of St. Lawrence

Cape Breton Island

Prince Edward Island

Gaspe Pen.

Laurentian Mts.

Nova Scotia

Bay of Fundy

ATLANTIC OCEAN

Cape Mendocino

Coast Ranges

Sierra Nevada

GREAT PLAINS

Great Basin

Columbia Plateau

Snake R.

Great Salt Lake

High Plains

Platte R.

Missouri R.

Lake Superior

UNITED STATES

Lake Michigan

Lake Huron

Lake Erie

Lake Ontario

Ottawa

St. Lawrence R.

Gulf of Maine

Cape Cod

Long Island

Washington, D.C.

Chesapeake Bay

Cape Hatteras

Bermuda Islands

PACIFIC OCEAN

Mt. Whitney 14,495 ft. 4,418 m

Death Valley -282 ft. -86 m

Channel Islands

Colorado Plateau

Grand Canyon

CENTRAL LOWLAND

Ozark Plateau

Arkansas R.

Ohio R.

Appalachian Mts.

COASTAL PLAIN

Sonoran Desert

Baja California

Gulf of California

Rio Grande

Sierra Madre Occidental

Red R.

Mississippi R.

Gulf of Mexico

Florida

TROPIC OF CANCER

MEXICO

Mexico City

Orizaba 18,700 ft. 5,700 m

Sierra Madre Oriental

Sierra Madre Sur

Gulf of Tehuantepec

Yucatán Peninsula

Florida Keys

Havana

CUBA

Cayman Is.

BAHAMAS

Greater Antilles

JAMAICA

W E S T

I N D I E S

Hispaniola

HAITI

DOMINICAN REPUBLIC

Puerto Rico

Virgin Is.

Martinique

Guadeloupe

Lesser Antilles

Trinidad

Isthmus of Tehuantepec

BELIZE

Belmopan

Guatemala

GUATEMALA

San Salvador

EL SALVADOR

HONDURAS

Tegucigalpa

NICARAGUA

Managua

Caribbean Sea

Isthmus of Panama

Panama

Gulf of Panama

CENTRAL AMERICA

Lake Nicaragua

COSTA RICA

San José

PANAMA

Panama Canal

SOUTH AMERICA

EQUATOR

0   1,000 miles

0   1,000 kilometers

Lambert Azimuthal Equal-Area Projection

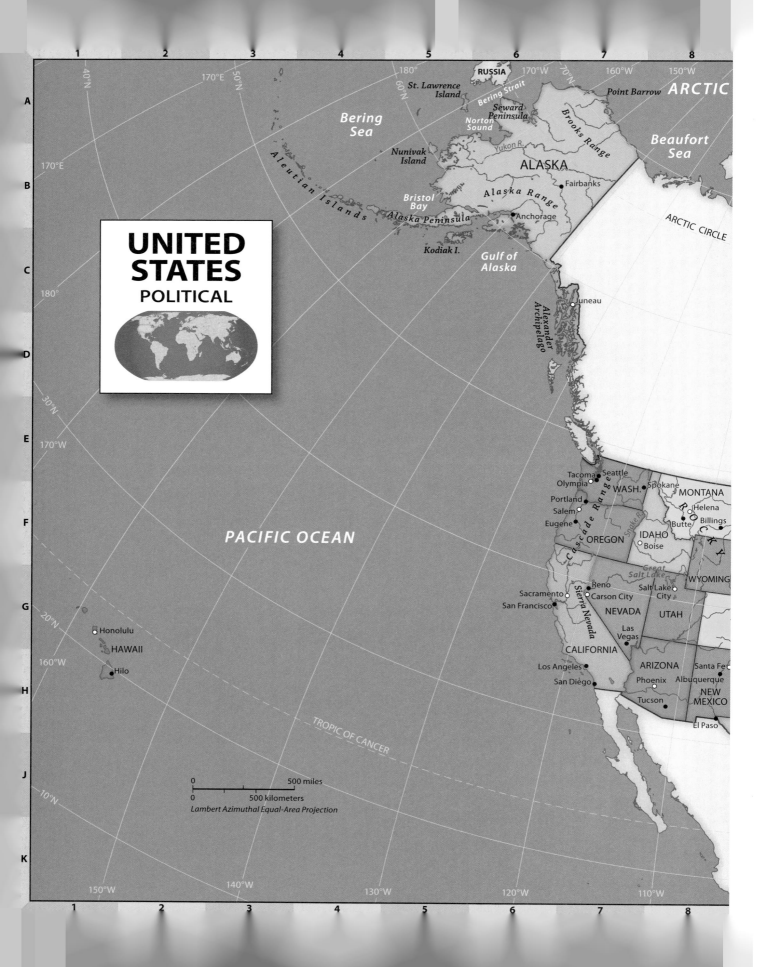

UNITED STATES
POLITICAL

RUSSIA

ARCTIC

St. Lawrence Island

Bering Strait

Point Barrow

Bering Sea

Seward Peninsula

Norton Sound

Brooks Range

Beaufort Sea

Nunivak Island

Fairbanks

ALASKA

Alaska Range

ARCTIC CIRCLE

Bristol Bay

Aleutian Islands

Alaska Peninsula

Anchorage

Kodiak I.

Gulf of Alaska

Juneau

Alexander Archipelago

PACIFIC OCEAN

Tacoma Seattle
Olympia
WASH. Spokane MONTANA
Portland Helena
Salem Butte Billings
Eugene ROCKY
OREGON IDAHO
Boise Snake R.
Cascade Range
Great Salt Lake WYOMING

Sacramento Reno
Carson City Salt Lake City
San Francisco Sierra Nevada NEVADA UTAH
Las Vegas
Honolulu CALIFORNIA ARIZONA Santa Fe
HAWAII Los Angeles Phoenix Albuquerque
Hilo San Diego Tucson NEW MEXICO
El Paso

TROPIC OF CANCER

0   500 miles
0   500 kilometers
Lambert Azimuthal Equal-Area Projection

40°N
170°E
50°N
60°N
180°
170°W
70°N
160°W
150°W
170°E
180°
30°N
170°W
20°N
160°W
10°N
150°W
140°W
130°W
120°W
110°W

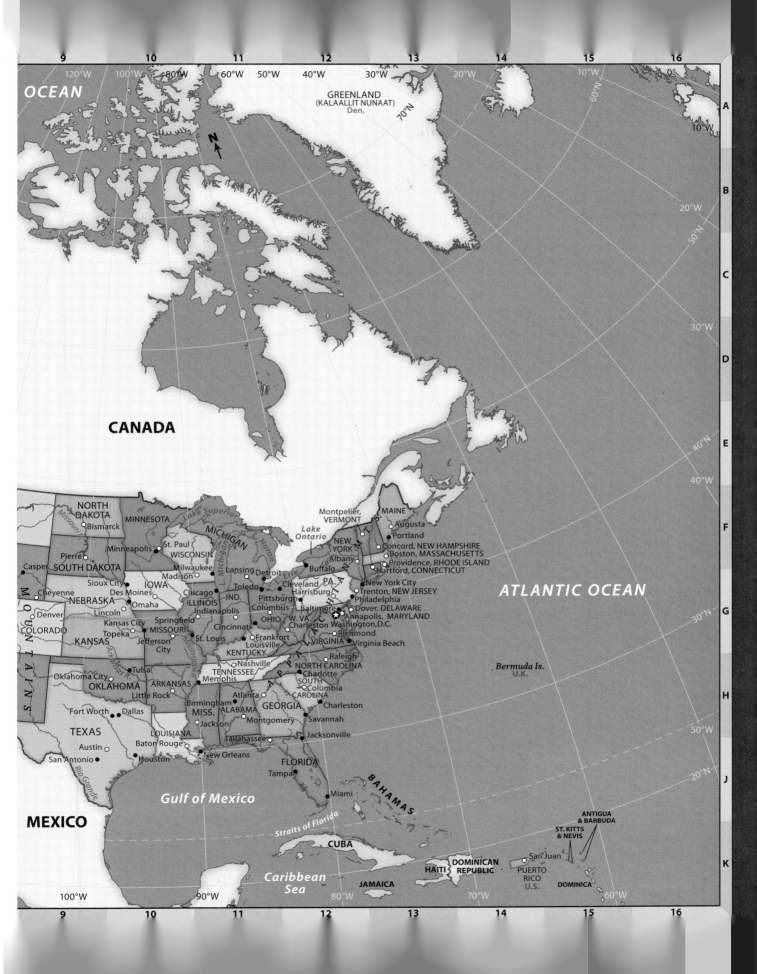

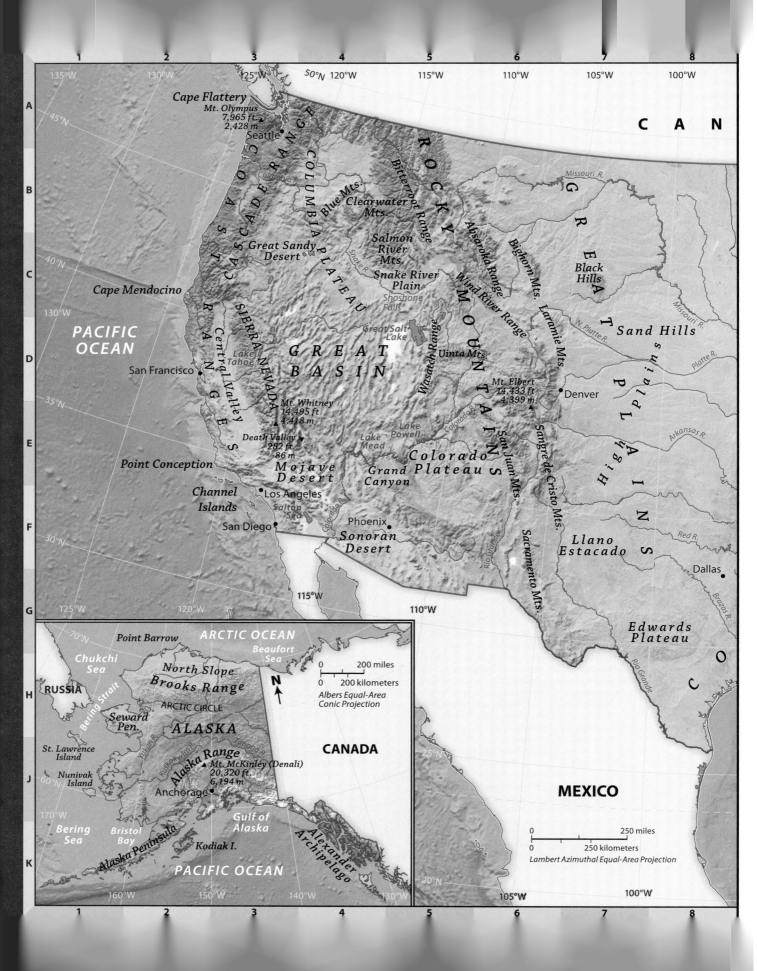

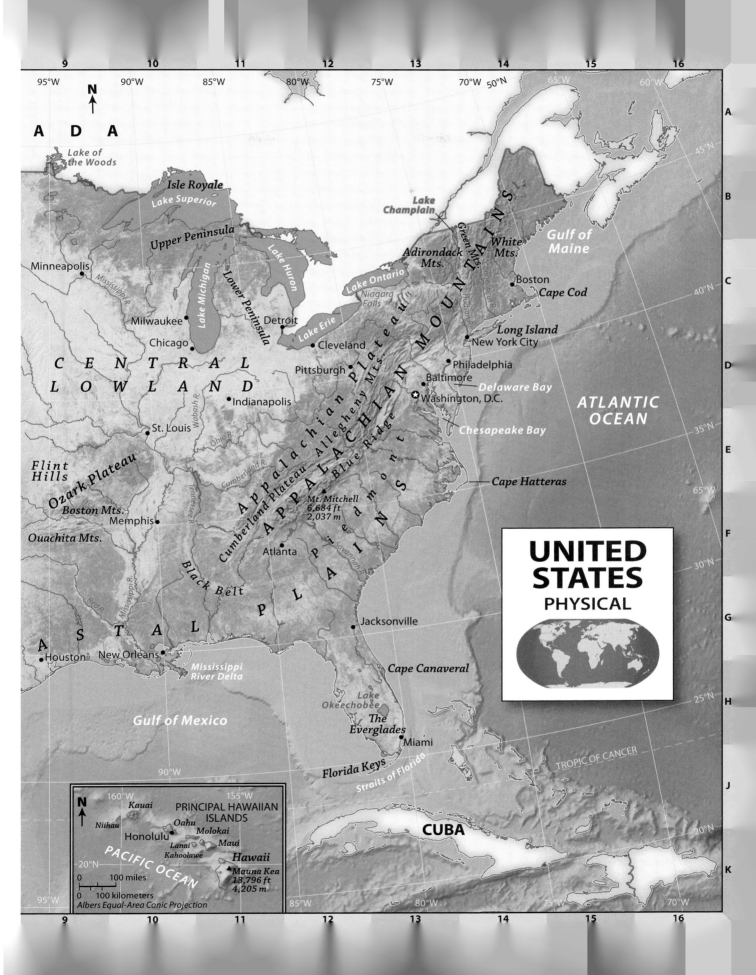

9   10   11   12   13   14   15   16

95°W   90°W   85°W   80°W   75°W   70°W   50°N   65°W   60°W

N

A D A

Lake of the Woods

Isle Royale

Lake Superior

Upper Peninsula

Minneapolis

Lower Peninsula

Lake Michigan

Lake Huron

Milwaukee

Chicago

Detroit

Lake Erie

Cleveland

Lake Ontario

Niagara Falls

Lake Champlain

Green Mts.

Adirondack Mts.

White Mts.

APPALACHIAN MOUNTAINS

Boston

Cape Cod

Gulf of Maine

Long Island

New York City

Pittsburgh

Philadelphia

Baltimore

Delaware Bay

Washington, D.C.

Mississippi R.

C E N T R A L

L O W L A N D

Wabash R.

Indianapolis

Ohio R.

St. Louis

Appalachian Plateau

Allegheny Mts.

Cumberland Plateau

Blue Ridge

Chesapeake Bay

Cape Hatteras

ATLANTIC OCEAN

Flint Hills

Ozark Plateau

Cumberland R.

Boston Mts.

Memphis

Tennessee R.

Ouachita Mts.

Mt. Mitchell
6,684 ft
2,037 m

Piedmont

Savannah R.

Atlanta

Black Belt

Red R.

Mississippi R.

C O A S T A L   P L A I N

Houston

New Orleans

Mississippi River Delta

Jacksonville

Cape Canaveral

Gulf of Mexico

Lake Okeechobee

The Everglades

Miami

Florida Keys

Straits of Florida

TROPIC OF CANCER

CUBA

UNITED STATES
PHYSICAL

65°W

45°N

40°N

35°N

30°N

25°N

20°N

A
B
C
D
E
F
G
H
J
K

N

160°W   155°W

Kauai

Niihau

PRINCIPAL HAWAIIAN ISLANDS

Oahu

Honolulu

Molokai

Lanai

Maui

Kahoolawe

Hawaii

▲ *Mauna Kea*
18,796 ft
4,205 m

20°N

PACIFIC OCEAN

0   100 miles

0   100 kilometers

Albers Equal-Area Conic Projection

95°W   90°W   85°W   80°W   75°W   70°W

9   10   11   12   13   14   15   16

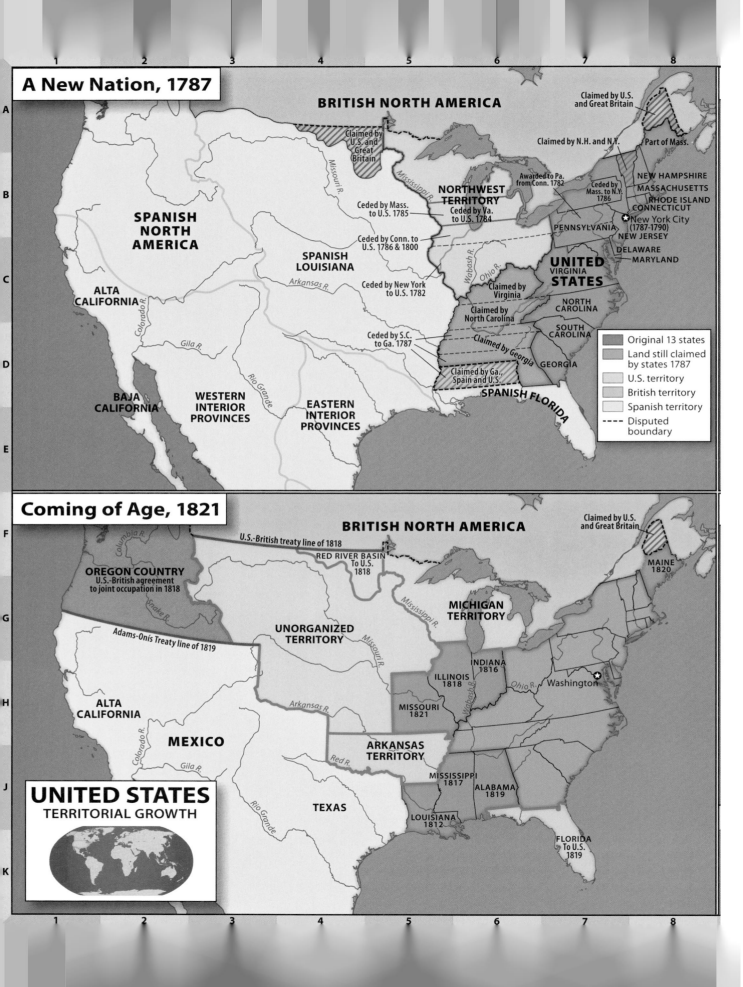

A New Nation, 1787

BRITISH NORTH AMERICA

Claimed by U.S. and Great Britain

Claimed by U.S. and Great Britain

Claimed by N.H. and N.Y.

Part of Mass.

SPANISH NORTH AMERICA

Missouri R.

Claimed by U.S. and Great Britain

NORTHWEST TERRITORY

Awarded to Pa. from Conn. 1782

Ceded by Mass. to N.Y. 1786

NEW HAMPSHIRE

MASSACHUSETTS

RHODE ISLAND

Ceded by Mass. to U.S. 1785

Ceded by Va. to U.S. 1784

CONNECTICUT

SPANISH LOUISIANA

Ceded by Conn. to U.S. 1786 & 1800

Wabash R.

Ohio R.

PENNSYLVANIA

NEW YORK CITY (1787-1790)

NEW JERSEY

DELAWARE

MARYLAND

ALTA CALIFORNIA

Arkansas R.

Ceded by New York to U.S. 1782

Claimed by Virginia

UNITED STATES

VIRGINIA

Colorado R.

Gila R.

Claimed by North Carolina

NORTH CAROLINA

SOUTH CAROLINA

Ceded by S.C. to Ga. 1787

Claimed by Georgia

GEORGIA

BAJA CALIFORNIA

WESTERN INTERIOR PROVINCES

Rio Grande

EASTERN INTERIOR PROVINCES

Claimed by Ga., Spain and U.S.

SPANISH FLORIDA

Original 13 states

Land still claimed by states 1787

U.S. territory

British territory

Spanish territory

- - - Disputed boundary

Coming of Age, 1821

BRITISH NORTH AMERICA

Claimed by U.S. and Great Britain

Columbia R.

U.S.-British treaty line of 1818

RED RIVER BASIN To U.S. 1818

MAINE 1820

OREGON COUNTRY
U.S.-British agreement to joint occupation in 1818

Snake R.

Mississippi R.

MICHIGAN TERRITORY

UNORGANIZED TERRITORY

Missouri R.

Adams-Onís Treaty line of 1819

INDIANA 1816

ALTA CALIFORNIA

Arkansas R.

ILLINOIS 1818

Wabash R.

Ohio R.

Washington

MEXICO

MISSOURI 1821

Colorado R.

Gila R.

ARKANSAS TERRITORY

Red R.

MISSISSIPPI 1817

ALABAMA 1819

UNITED STATES
TERRITORIAL GROWTH

Rio Grande

TEXAS

LOUISIANA 1812

FLORIDA To U.S. 1819

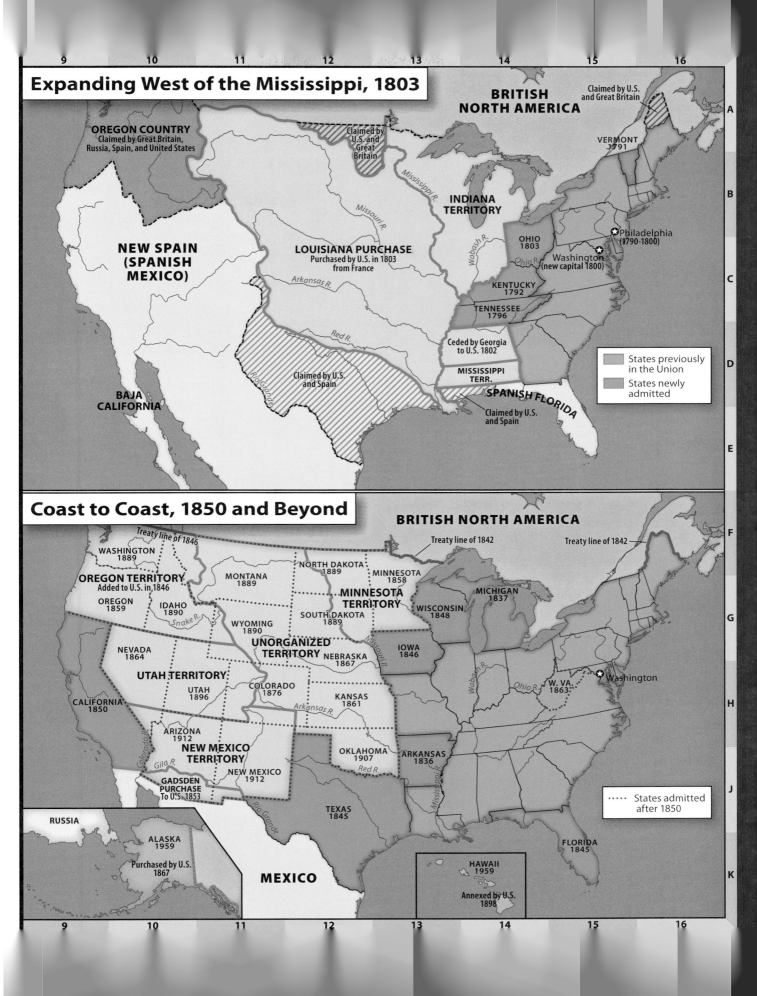

Expanding West of the Mississippi, 1803

BRITISH NORTH AMERICA

Claimed by U.S. and Great Britain

OREGON COUNTRY
Claimed by Great Britain, Russia, Spain, and United States

VERMONT 1791

Claimed by U.S. and Great Britain

Mississippi R.

INDIANA TERRITORY

Missouri R.

NEW SPAIN (SPANISH MEXICO)

LOUISIANA PURCHASE
Purchased by U.S. in 1803 from France

Arkansas R.

OHIO 1803

Wabash R.

Ohio R.

Philadelphia (1790-1800)

Washington (new capital 1800)

KENTUCKY 1792

TENNESSEE 1796

Red R.

Rio Grande

Claimed by U.S. and Spain

Ceded by Georgia to U.S. 1802

MISSISSIPPI TERR.

BAJA CALIFORNIA

Claimed by U.S. and Spain

SPANISH FLORIDA

Claimed by U.S. and Spain

States previously in the Union

States newly admitted

Coast to Coast, 1850 and Beyond

BRITISH NORTH AMERICA

Treaty line of 1846

Treaty line of 1842

Treaty line of 1842

WASHINGTON 1889

NORTH DAKOTA 1889

MINNESOTA 1858

OREGON TERRITORY
Added to U.S. in 1846

MONTANA 1889

MINNESOTA TERRITORY

MICHIGAN 1837

OREGON 1859

IDAHO 1890

Snake R.

WYOMING 1890

SOUTH DAKOTA 1889

WISCONSIN 1848

NEVADA 1864

UNORGANIZED TERRITORY

Missouri R.

IOWA 1846

UTAH TERRITORY

UTAH 1896

COLORADO 1876

NEBRASKA 1867

W. VA. 1863

Washington

CALIFORNIA 1850

Arkansas R.

KANSAS 1861

Wabash R.

Ohio R.

Colorado R.

ARIZONA 1912

NEW MEXICO TERRITORY

GADSDEN PURCHASE
To U.S. 1853

Gila R.

NEW MEXICO 1912

OKLAHOMA 1907

ARKANSAS 1836

Red R.

Mississippi R.

RUSSIA

Rio Grande

TEXAS 1845

ALASKA 1959

Purchased by U.S. 1867

MEXICO

HAWAII 1959

FLORIDA 1845

Annexed by U.S. 1898

States admitted after 1850

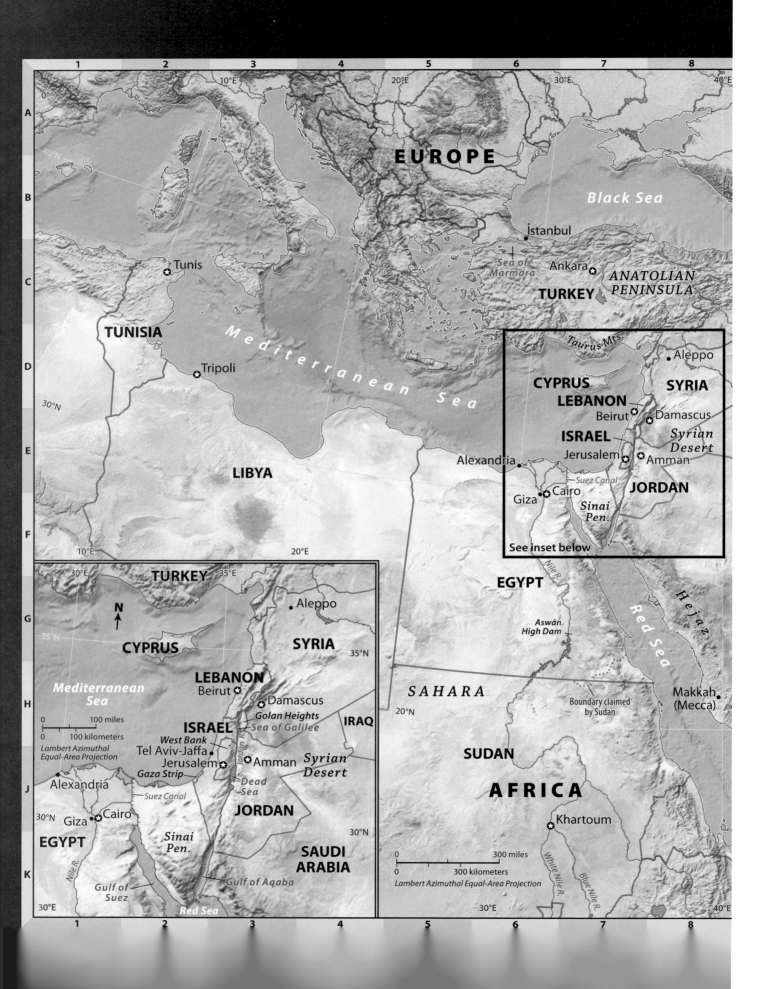

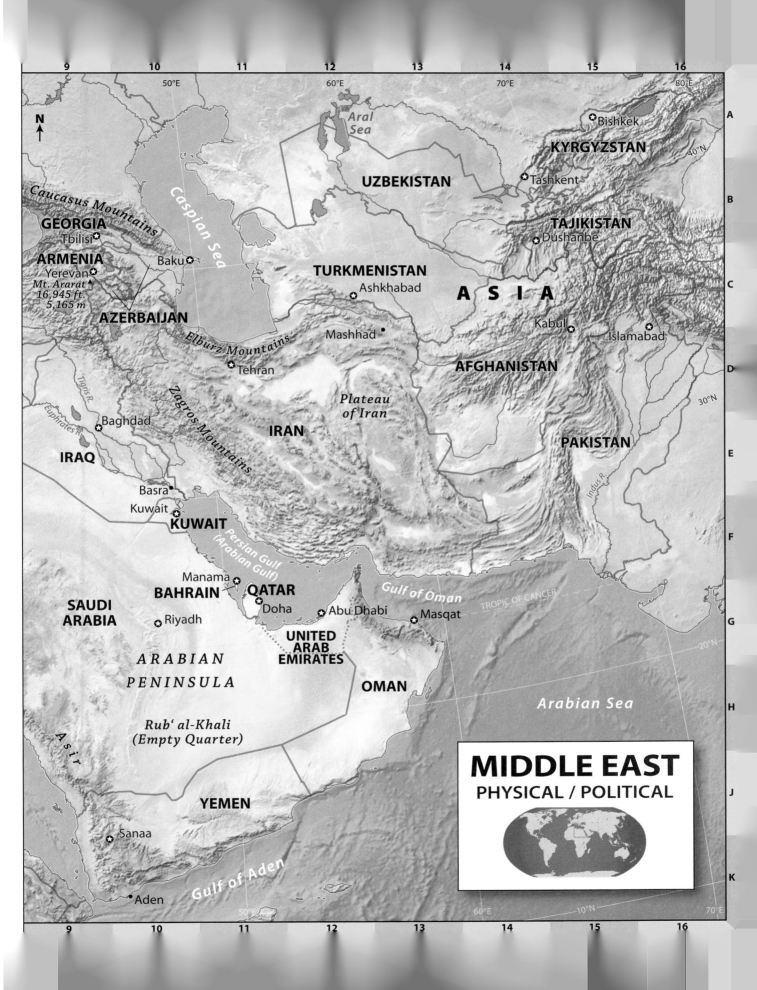

SCAVENGER HUNT

NETWORKS contains a wealth of information. The trick is to know where to look to access all the information in the book. If you complete this scavenger hunt exercise with your teachers or parents, you will see how the textbook is organized and how to get the most out of your reading and studying time. Let's get started!

1 How many chapters are in this book?

2 Where in the front of the book can you find a physical map of the United States?

3 What time period does Chapter 6 cover?

4 What is the 21st Century Skills Activity for Chapter 5?

5 Where can you find the *Thinking Like a Historian* activity in each chapter?

6 What is the title of Chapter 9?

7 What Essential Questions will you answer in Chapter 10?

8 What are the Academic Vocabulary words in Lesson 3, Chapter 12?

9 Where in the back of the book can you find the meaning of vocabulary words such as *imperialism*?

10 Where in the back of the book can you find page numbers for information about Franklin D. Roosevelt?

Exploring Social Studies

Beginnings to Today

ESSENTIAL QUESTIONS • *Why is history important?* • *How does geography influence the way we live?* • *Why do people make economic choices?* • *What makes a responsible citizen?*

The Story Matters . . .

Photographs like this can tell rich and vivid stories about the past. To uncover these stories, we ask questions: Who is this woman? Where is she from? When did she live? How did she come to appear in this photograph? Who took the picture, and for what purpose?

Learning about social studies helps us gain the skills we need to ask the right questions and to find the answers. As we learn about social studies, we will learn about the world of information and ideas waiting behind the words and images—in this book and beyond.

◄ *Rosa Parks was often referred to as the "first lady of civil rights."*

© Bettmann/CORBIS

1

Place and Time: United States Beginnings to Today

The story of the United States is an exciting one. In exploring this story, you will use many tools to help you understand people's actions. You will also gain and employ knowledge of geography, economics, and civics and government to help you learn about the past.

Step Into the Place

MAP FOCUS This map is a physical map. Like all physical maps, it focuses on the physical features—landforms, waterways, and ecosystems.

1 PLACE Look at the map. Which lake appears to be the largest?

2 PLACE Which area of the country has the highest mountains?

3 CRITICAL THINKING
Identifying What are five different types of landforms or waterways on this physical map?

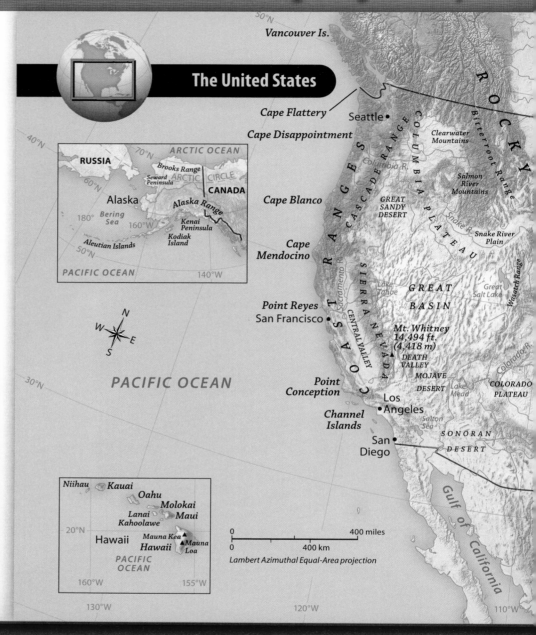

The United States

Step Into the Time

TIME LINE Look at the time line. It shows different eras in American history. An era is a time period known for a certain feature. How might a time line that shows specific events differ from one showing eras?

HISTORICAL ERAS

1400   1500   1600

1492–1607
European Exploration

Beginnings to 1492
Early America

1565–1763
Colonial America

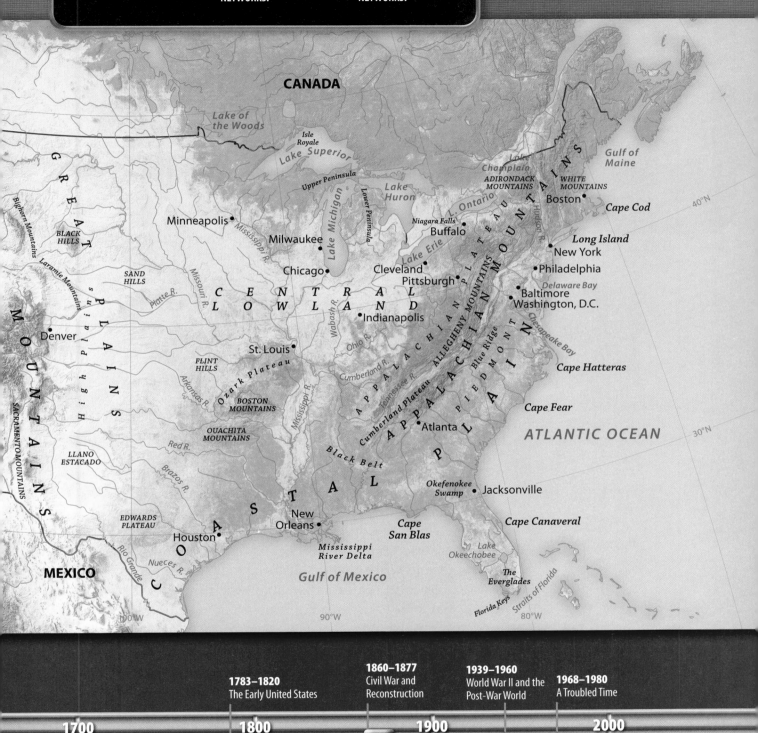

CANADA

Lake of the Woods

Isle Royale

Lake Superior

Upper Peninsula

Lower Peninsula

Lake Huron

Lake Champlain

Gulf of Maine

ADIRONDACK MOUNTAINS

WHITE MOUNTAINS

GREAT

Bighorn Mountains

BLACK HILLS

Laramie Mountains

SAND HILLS

PLAINS

Missouri R.

Mississippi R.

Minneapolis

Milwaukee

Chicago

Lake Michigan

Cleveland

Pittsburgh

L. Ontario

Niagara Falls

Buffalo

Lake Erie

ALLEGHENY MOUNTAINS

APPALACHIAN PLATEAU

Hudson R.

Boston

Cape Cod

40°N

Long Island

New York

Philadelphia

Delaware Bay

Baltimore

Washington, D.C.

MOUNTAINS

Denver

Platte R.

High Plains

CENTRAL

LOWLAND

Indianapolis

Wabash R.

St. Louis

Ohio R.

Cumberland R.

Tennessee R.

Cumberland Plateau

Blue Ridge

APPALACHIAN MOUNTAINS

PIEDMONT

Chesapeake Bay

Cape Hatteras

SACRAMENTO MOUNTAINS

Arkansas R.

FLINT HILLS

Ozark Plateau

BOSTON MOUNTAINS

Mississippi R.

Atlanta

Cape Fear

ATLANTIC OCEAN

30°N

LLANO ESTACADO

OUACHITA MOUNTAINS

Red R.

Black Belt

COASTAL

PLAIN

Okefenokee Swamp

Jacksonville

MEXICO

EDWARDS PLATEAU

Brazos R.

Houston

Nueces R.

Rio Grande

New Orleans

Mississippi River Delta

Cape San Blas

Gulf of Mexico

90°W

Lake Okeechobee

Cape Canaveral

The Everglades

Florida Keys

Straits of Florida

80°W

100°W

1783–1820
The Early United States

1860–1877
Civil War and Reconstruction

1939–1960
World War II and the Post-War World

1968–1980
A Troubled Time

1700

1800

1900

2000

1763–1783
Revolution and Independence

1820–1860
Expansion, Sectionalism, and Reform

1865–1918
Expansion, Industrialization, and World War

1918–1939
Prosperity and Depression

1954–1973
Civil Rights and Vietnam

1980–Present
New Challenges in a Global Age

networks
There's More Online!

☑ **GRAPHIC ORGANIZER**
Describing the Tools of
the Historian

☑ **GRAPH**
• Bar Graph
• Circle Graph
• Line Graph

☑ **TIME LINE** Life of
Benjamin Franklin

☑ **VIDEO**

Lesson 1
Thinking Like a Historian

ESSENTIAL QUESTION *Why is history important?*

IT MATTERS BECAUSE
History teaches us what has been important to others in the past and helps us to understand what to expect for the future.

What Does a Historian Do?

GUIDING QUESTION *Why do we study history?*

A historian is a person who studies and writes about the people and events of the past. Historians find out how people lived, what happened to them, and what happened around them. They look for the causes of events and the effects of those events.

We study history so we can understand what happened in the past. Understanding what happened to others can help us make sense of current events—things taking place today. It can also help us to predict what might happen in the future so that we can make better decisions about today and tomorrow.

Have you ever wondered if you could be a historian? To answer that question, you will need to find out how historians **research** and write history. Historians use a number of tools to research, or collect information about their subjects. They also use special tools to organize information. You will learn about these tools in the next few pages. You will also use these tools throughout this textbook.

☑ **PROGRESS CHECK**

Explaining How do you think studying the past can help us predict the future?

Reading **HELP**DESK **CCSS**

Taking Notes: *Describing*

As you read, use a table like this one to describe the different tools historians use. Use as many rows as needed.

Tools	Description

Content Vocabulary
• **calendar**
• **chronology**

Measuring Time

GUIDING QUESTION *What tools do we use to measure time?*

One **challenge** when studying history is knowing when events took place. Which event happened first? How far apart in time did events take place? We use different tools to measure time.

Throughout history, different cultures have developed different calendars. This calendar helped the Aztec people, who lived in what is now Mexico, keep track of both a 260-day-long religious year and a 365-day year used for planning farming and other nonreligious activities.

Calendars

A **calendar** is a system for breaking time into units and keeping track of those units. With a calendar, you can measure how much time has passed between events. You can describe that time, for example, in months and years.

The dates in this book are based on the Western calendar. In the Western calendar, a year is 365 days. The calendar begins at the birth of Jesus. The years before this date are known as "B.C.," or "before Christ." Years after are called "A.D.," or *anno domini*, Latin for "in the year of the Lord." Some people also use C.E., or "common era," and B.C.E., or "before common era."

To date events that took place before B.C., historians count backward from A.D. 1. There is no year "0." The year before A.D. 1 is 1 B.C. To date events after "A.D.," historians count forward. The year after A.D. 1 is A.D. 2.

Reading a Time Line

Historians are interested in **chronology,** or the order in which events happen. An easy way to keep track of chronology is to use or make a time line. A *time line* is a diagram showing the order of events within a period of time.

Along a time line, each section represents a period of time. A time line also has labels for events. The labels appear near the dates on the time line when the events took place.

✔ PROGRESS CHECK

Identifying What are two tools historians use for keeping track of time?

Thinking Like a
HISTORIAN

Reading a Time Line

To read a time line:
1. Find the time span—how long a period does the time line cover?
2. Study the order in which events occur.
3. Analyze relationships among events and look for trends. For example, the order of events may suggest how one event caused another.

INFOGRAPHIC

Look over the time line below.

1 **DESCRIBING** What is the title? When does the time line begin and end?

2 **CRITICAL THINKING** *Identifying* What feature shows a comparison between U.S. and world events?

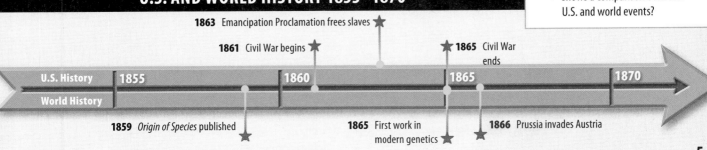

U.S. AND WORLD HISTORY 1855–1870

1863 Emancipation Proclamation frees slaves ⭐

1861 Civil War begins ⭐

⭐ **1865** Civil War ends

U.S. History	1855	1860	1865	1870
World History				

1859 *Origin of Species* published ⭐

1865 First work in modern genetics ⭐

1866 Prussia invades Austria

5

Analyzing Sources

GUIDING QUESTION *What is a primary source?*

Suppose a teacher has asked you to write a paper about the space program. Where would you get the information you need to begin writing? You would look for two types of information— primary and secondary sources.

Primary sources are descriptions or pictures of an event by someone who actually saw or lived through that event. In other words, if you see a rocket launch in person and then write about it, you are creating a primary source. Written impressions of any others who watched at the same time are primary sources, too. Diaries, journals, photographs, and eyewitness reports are examples of primary sources.

Secondary sources usually come from people who were not present at an event. A book about the history of the space program is a secondary source. The author of the book collected information from many sources. He or she then combined this information into something new. Textbooks, biographies, and histories are secondary sources.

Note that a secondary source may use primary sources. In this textbook, you will see and read many primary sources. The book itself, however, is a secondary source.

When analyzing primary sources, ask the five "W" questions:

1. **Who** created the primary source?
2. **Why** was the source created—what was its purpose and its intended audience?
3. **What** is the source about?
4. **Where** was the source created?
5. **When** was the source created?

Answering these questions can help you find the historical significance of a primary source. Ask yourself these questions as you look at the following primary sources.

CLASSIFYING PRIMARY SOURCES

- **Printed publications** include newspapers, magazines, or books. Web sites and e-mails are also printed publications that appear in electronic format.
- **Songs and poems** are often good sources of information because they describe events and reactions to them.
- **Visual materials** include original paintings, drawings, photographs, films, and maps. Political cartoons and other types of cartoons are also visual primary sources.
- **Oral histories** are interviews that are recorded to collect people's memories and observations about their lives and experiences.
- **Personal records** include diaries, journals, and letters.
- **Artifacts** are tools or ornaments that were used by people in the past.

✓ PROGRESS CHECK

Contrasting What is the difference between a primary and secondary source?

Reading **HELP**DESK (CCSS)

calendar a system for breaking time into units and keeping track of those units
chronology order of dates in which events happen

Academic Vocabulary

research the careful collection of information
challenge something that is difficult

Build Vocabulary: *Word Origins*

Primary comes from the Latin word *primus* which means *first*. It is also the source for other English words such as *primitive*, *prime*, and *primarily*.

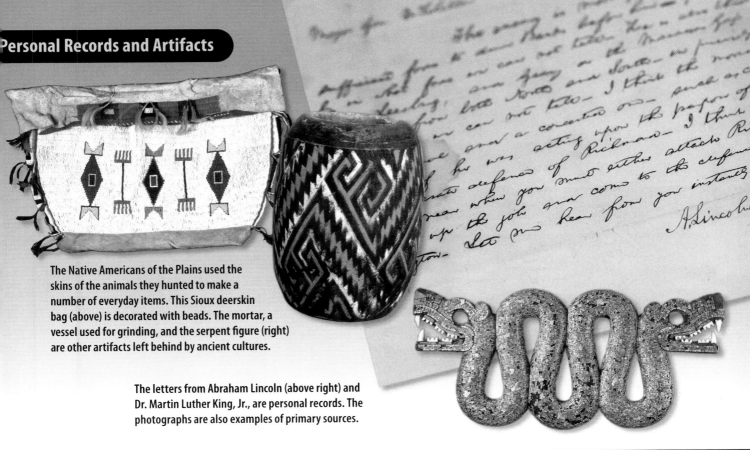

The Native Americans of the Plains used the skins of the animals they hunted to make a number of everyday items. This Sioux deerskin bag (above) is decorated with beads. The mortar, a vessel used for grinding, and the serpent figure (right) are other artifacts left behind by ancient cultures.

The letters from Abraham Lincoln (above right) and Dr. Martin Luther King, Jr., are personal records. The photographs are also examples of primary sources.

Letters and Visual Materials

❝ We have waited for more than 340 years for our constitutional and God-given rights. . . . [W]e still creep at horse and buggy pace toward gaining a cup of coffee at a lunch counter. Perhaps it is easy for those who have never felt the stinging darts of segregation to say, 'Wait.' . . . Let us all hope that the dark clouds of racial prejudice will soon pass away. **❞**

—Dr. Martin Luther King, Jr., "Letter from Birmingham Jail," April 1963

As Dr. Martin Luther King, Jr., sat in an Alabama jail, he wrote his famous "Letter from Birmingham Jail."

During the Great Depression of the 1930s, people struggled to survive. This photo shows one example of people affected by tough economic times.

Charts, Diagrams, and Graphs

GUIDING QUESTION *What types of information can be shown in charts, diagrams, and graphs?*

Graphs, charts, and diagrams are all ways of displaying types of information such as percentages, numbers, and amounts. They help organize this information and make it easier to read.

Chart Skill

Rank	Civil War	World War II 1942	Vietnam War 1965	Iraq War 2007
Private	*$13	$50	$85	$1,203–1,543
Corporal	$14	$66	$210	$1,700
Sergeant	$17	$78	$261	$1,854–2,339
Sergeant Major	$21	$138	$486	$4,110

*Until 1864, African Americans in the Civil War were paid only $7 per month

Source: Bureau of Economic Analysis; *Princeton Review*; www.militaryfactory.com

This chart shows information about monthly army salaries.

▶ **CRITICAL THINKING**

Comparing What two types of comparisons are possible using this chart?

Diagram Skill

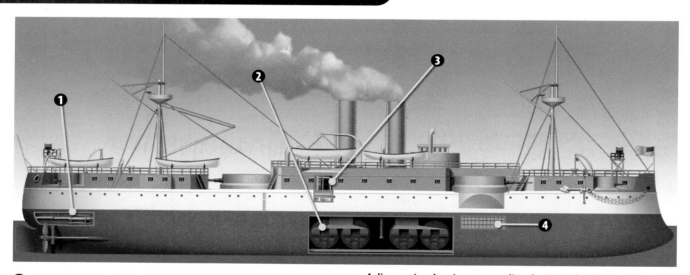

❶ **Torpedo tubes** are devices to launch torpedoes.

❷ **Steam boilers** power the engines.

❸ **Munitions** are stored in the magazine.

❹ **Cowls** provide fresh air below deck.

A diagram is a drawing or an outline that is used to show how things work or to show how parts relate to each other. This diagram shows an old U.S. warship, the USS *Maine* (1895).

▶ **CRITICAL THINKING**

Analyzing Why is a diagram a better choice for displaying this information compared to a chart?

Reading **HELP**DESK (CCSS)

Build Vocabulary: *Word Origins*

Latin and Greek words use the root *graph* to refer to a painting or drawing. A *graphic formula* is a drawing with numbers, a *graph* for short.

Reading in the Content Area: *Graphs, Charts, and Diagrams*

When you're presenting information for others, it is important to use the right type of graph, chart, or diagram. For example, if you wanted to show the number of Republicans and Democrats in the U.S. House of Representatives, would you use a graph, a diagram, or a chart? A chart or bar graph would be the best choice.

Charts

Charts present facts and numbers in an organized way. One type of chart is a table. A table arranges data, especially numbers, in rows and columns for easy reference. People also use charts to summarize ideas or main points of broader topics. This allows you to review material and compare main ideas easily.

Diagrams

Diagrams are drawings that show steps in a process, point out the parts of an object, or explain how something works. Diagrams are sometimes called "infographics."

Graphs

Graphs present numbers visually. This makes the numbers easier to understand. The types of graphs you will find in this textbook are described and displayed below:

- Circle graphs show how the whole of something is divided.
- Bar graphs use bars to compare numbers visually. Bar graphs compare different items or groups. Bar graphs can also compare items at different points in time.
- Line graphs can also show how something changes over time. Rather than showing data just for specific points in time, line graphs show a continuous line of data.

✔ **PROGRESS CHECK**

Problem Solving Which visual would best be used for presenting the price of a movie ticket from 2000 to 2010?

Graph Skill

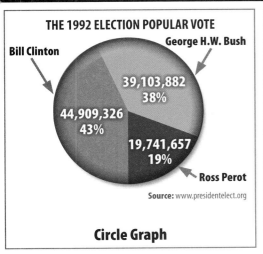

Circle Graph

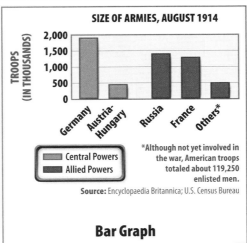

Bar Graph

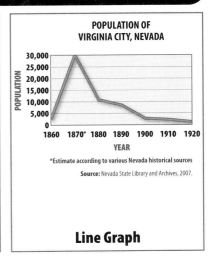

Line Graph

Different types of graphs are useful for presenting different types of information. What type of graph would you use to:

- compare the parts of a whole?
- compare amounts side-by-side?
- track how something—for example population or temperature—changes over time?

Critical Thinking Skills

GUIDING QUESTION *What types of thinking skills does a historian need?*

Studying history is about more than reading sources and viewing pictures or graphs. Historians use many thinking skills.

Understanding Cause and Effect

A *cause* is an action or situation that produces an event. What happens as a result of a cause is an *effect*. Understanding cause and effect means thinking about *why* an event occurred. It helps you see how one thing can lead to another. That can help you plan to encourage or prevent the same event in the future.

Predicting Consequences

Predicting future events is difficult. Sometimes, though, you can use knowledge of how certain causes led to certain effects in the past to make a prediction. For example, if you know that conflicts over borders have often led to war, you may be able to predict the outcome of a current border dispute.

Distinguishing Fact from Opinion

To determine the validity of sources and find answers in a text, you need to distinguish facts from opinions. You can check facts using reliable sources to determine whether or not they are accurate. They answer specific questions such as: What happened? Who did it?

Opinions are based on values and beliefs. They are not true, and they are not false. Opinions often begin with phrases such as *I believe . . .* or contain words such as *should, ought, best, worst,* or *greatest*.

Drawing Inferences and Conclusions

When you make an *inference*, you "read between the lines" to figure something out that is not stated directly. A *conclusion* is an understanding based on details or facts you read or hear.

Follow these steps to draw inferences and conclusions from a piece of writing:

- Read carefully for key facts and ideas, and list them.
- Summarize the information.
- Recall what you already know about the topic.
- Use your knowledge and insight to develop some inferences and conclusions about the passage.

Reading **HELP**DESK **CCSS**

Visual Vocabulary

A **diagram** is an illustration for organizing and presenting complex information.

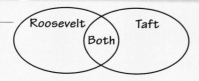

Reading Strategy: *Comparing and Contrasting*

A Venn diagram is a good tool for comparing and contrasting. Where the circles overlap, you can record the way the items compare. Create a Venn diagram to compare and contrast the images shown on the next page.

MAKING COMPARISONS

When making comparisons, you examine two or more things. Among the things to compare are documents, events, and images. Compare these two photographs.

▶ **CRITICAL THINKING**

Comparing and Contrasting What similarities do you see? How are the images different?

Making Comparisons

To make comparisons and contrasts, examine the two photographs and follow these steps:

1. Describe exactly what you see in the photos.
2. Ask and answer questions, such as
   - Who are the people in the pictures, and what is happening?
   - Why do you think the photographs were taken?
   - What questions do the photographs raise in your mind, and where could you find answers to these questions?
   - What story does each photo tell?
3. Summarize what you already know about the situations and the time period.

 PROGRESS CHECK

Summarizing What is the difference between a cause and an effect?

(l) Hulton Archive/Getty Images,
(r) Pfc. James Cox/CORBIS

LESSON 1 REVIEW (CCSS)

Review Vocabulary

1. Use the terms *calendar* and *chronology* in a sentence that explains their role in the study of history.

Answer the Guiding Questions

2. *Describing* Describe the role and purpose of the historian.

3. *Explaining* Why is it important to understand the order in which events occurred?

4. *Defining* Give three examples of primary sources.

5. *Describing* What is the purpose of graphs, charts, and diagrams?

6. NARRATIVE Write a short essay in which you express why you think it is important to read about, study, and understand the past.

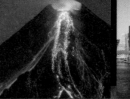

netwærks
There's More Online!

- ☑ **CHART/GRAPH**
  Miami's Latino Population
- ☑ **GRAPHIC ORGANIZER**
  Describing Different Types of Maps
- ☑ **MAPS**
  - United States Population Density
  - Physical Map: Florida
  - Political Map: Florida
  - Regions of the United States
- ☑ **VIDEO**

Lesson 2
Studying Geography

ESSENTIAL QUESTION *How does geography influence the way we live?*

IT MATTERS BECAUSE
Geography helps us to understand where we live and where others live.

What Is Geography?

GUIDING QUESTION *What are the five themes of geography?*

Geography is the study of the Earth and its people. A geographer tries to understand a place—not just where it is, but what it is like, what takes place there, and how the people there live.

To help them build this understanding, geographers organize their study into themes, or subjects. For example, geographers often speak of the five themes of geography: location, place, regions, movement, and human-environment interaction.

- **Location** describes where something is. Absolute location is the exact position on Earth where a geographic feature, such as a city or mountain, is found. Relative location expresses where a geographic feature is located in relation to another feature.

- **Place** explores the physical and human features that make a city, state, or country unique. The Grand Canyon and Hoover Dam are examples of features that make Arizona a special place.

- **Regions** are areas that share common features. A region may be land, water, or a specific area in a city or state. For instance, New England is a region in the northeastern

(l) Getty Images, (cl) NASA/CORBIS,
(cr) ROMEO RANOCO/Reuters/Corbis,
(r) Thomas Jackson/The Image Bank/Getty Images

Reading **HELP**DESK (CCSS)

Taking Notes: *Describing*

As you read, use a graphic organizer like this one to describe the different types of maps.

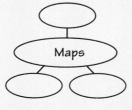

Maps

Content Vocabulary
- **globe**
- **map**
- **landform**
- **relief**
- **elevation**
- **ecosystem**

12 *Exploring Social Studies*

United States. The West Coast is a region bordering the Pacific Ocean and includes the states of California, Oregon, and Washington.

- **Movement** explains how and why people, things, and ideas move. For instance, a group of people may move for various reasons. Ideas spread from one place to another. Both types of movement lead to change.

- **Human-environment interaction** explores the relationship between people and their environments. For example, early Native Americans in the southwestern United States used materials from plants, animals, and the land to build their homes and to clothe and feed themselves.

✅ **PROGRESS CHECK**

Applying If you were describing the town where you live—its people, its sights—which theme would you be using?

Geography explores different places and the people who live in those places.

George Rose/Getty Images Entertainment/Getty Images

Build Vocabulary: *Word Parts*

Interaction uses the prefix *inter-*, meaning "between or among," to indicate actions between two groups or things.

Maps and Globes

GUIDING QUESTION *What stories do maps and globes tell?*

The tools of the geographer include maps and globes. These help us to learn more about the Earth.

Globes and maps serve different purposes, and each has its advantages and disadvantages.

A **globe** is a round model of the Earth. It shows the Earth's shape and its lands. The shapes, sizes, and locations of the lands are accurate.

A **map** is a flat drawing of all or part of the Earth's surface. Cartographers, or mapmakers, use complex mathematics to transfer shapes from the round globe to a flat map. Still, all maps change the shapes of the places they show.

Maps can show small areas such as a college campus. They can show the streets in a city. Or, they can show whole continents or even the entire world. They can show places as they exist now. There are also historical maps, which show the features of a place at some time in the past.

Understanding Parts of a Map

Maps can contain a large amount of information in a small space. In order to get at this information, however, you need to know how to read a map. You need to understand the different parts, what they represent, and how they work together. The map on the next page shows some of the most basic map parts.

Physical and Political Maps

Maps are very useful tools. You can use them to show information and make connections between different facts, such as how the location of cities relates to the location of waterways.

Geographers use many different kinds of maps. Maps that show a wide range of information about an area are known as general purpose maps. Two of the most common general purpose maps are physical maps and political maps.

Studying geography helps us to understand the Earth—its people, its natural features, and the ways they interact with each other.

NASA/Corbis

Reading **HELP**DESK **CCSS**

globe a round model of the Earth
map a flat drawing of all or part of the Earth's surface

landform natural feature of the Earth's land surface
relief ups and downs of the Earth's surface
elevation the height of an area above sea level

Physical maps show **landforms** and water features. Landforms are natural features on the Earth such as deserts, mountains, plains, or plateaus. Physical maps may also show **relief,** or ups and downs of the Earth's surface, and **elevation,** the height of an area above sea level.

Political maps show the names and political boundary lines, or borders, of a place. Political maps may also show human-made features, such as cities or transportation routes.

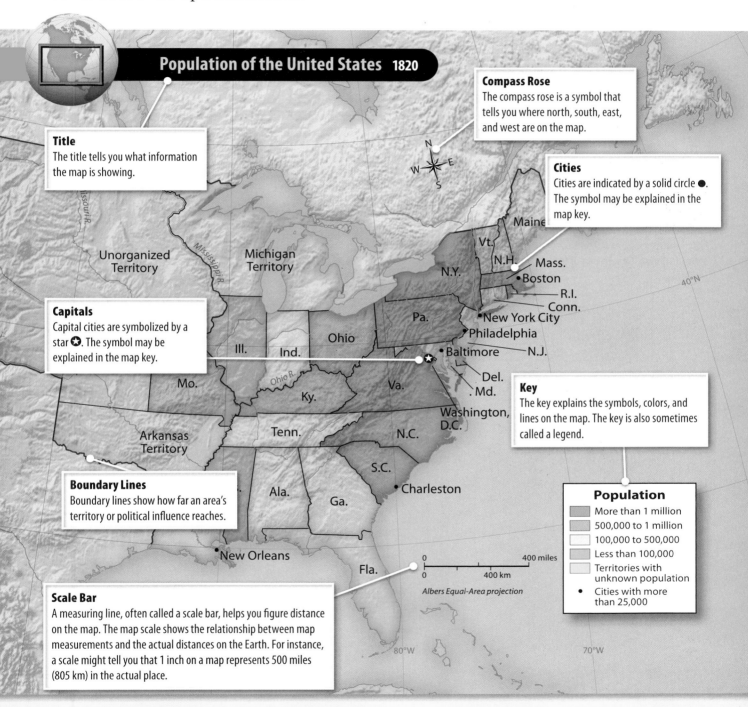

Population of the United States 1820

Compass Rose
The compass rose is a symbol that tells you where north, south, east, and west are on the map.

Title
The title tells you what information the map is showing.

Cities
Cities are indicated by a solid circle ●. The symbol may be explained in the map key.

Capitals
Capital cities are symbolized by a star ✪. The symbol may be explained in the map key.

Key
The key explains the symbols, colors, and lines on the map. The key is also sometimes called a legend.

Boundary Lines
Boundary lines show how far an area's territory or political influence reaches.

Population
- More than 1 million
- 500,000 to 1 million
- 100,000 to 500,000
- Less than 100,000
- Territories with unknown population
- • Cities with more than 25,000

Albers Equal-Area projection

Scale Bar
A measuring line, often called a scale bar, helps you figure distance on the map. The map scale shows the relationship between map measurements and the actual distances on the Earth. For instance, a scale might tell you that 1 inch on a map represents 500 miles (805 km) in the actual place.

Reading in the Content Area: *Map Scale*

To use the map scale to measure distances, use a ruler to measure the distance between two points on a map. Then, measure the map scale. Figure out how many times the length of the scale will "fit" within the distance between the two points you measured. Multiply that number times the number of miles or kilometers the scale represents. This number will be the actual distance between the two places.

Special Purpose Maps

Some maps present specific kinds of information. These are called thematic or special purpose maps. They usually show themes or patterns, or emphasize one subject. For example, special purpose maps may present information on climate or natural resources. They may display where different Native American languages are spoken, what industries are found in an area, or what kind of vegetation grows there.

One type of special purpose map shows population density. A population density map appears below. Population density refers to how thickly a place is settled—how many people live in each square mile. Cities have a high population density. Rural areas have a low population density. These maps use different colors or dots to show this.

Special purpose maps may also display events that occurred over time. Maps that display historical information, such as migration and changes in boundaries, are called historical maps. In this textbook, you will study many historical maps.

✓ PROGRESS CHECK

Identifying What are some examples of landforms?

The special purpose map explores a specific theme. It uses red dots to show the population density of the United States.

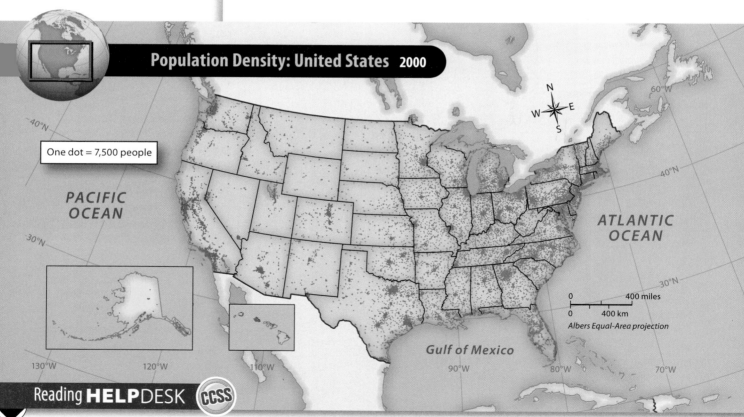

Population Density: United States 2000

One dot = 7,500 people

PACIFIC OCEAN

ATLANTIC OCEAN

Gulf of Mexico

0   400 miles
0   400 km

Albers Equal-Area projection

Reading **HELP**DESK   CCSS

Reading Strategy: *Differentiating*

When you differentiate, you highlight and describe the differences between two related people, events, or concepts. Read about the three types of maps, and write a few sentences that differentiate the maps.

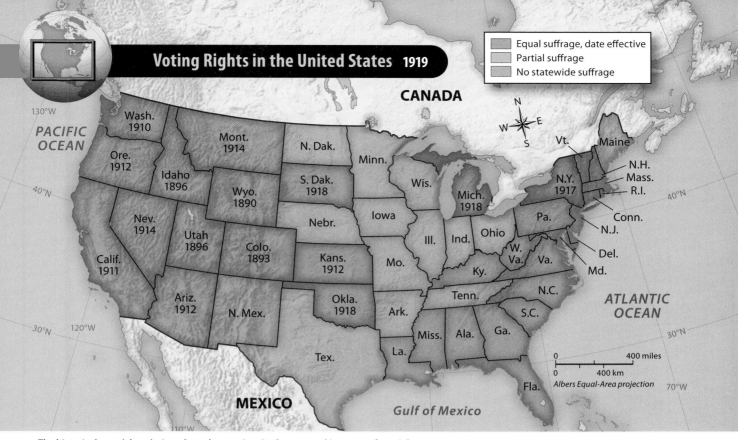

Voting Rights in the United States 1919

Legend:
- Equal suffrage, date effective
- Partial suffrage
- No statewide suffrage

CANADA

PACIFIC OCEAN

Wash. 1910
Ore. 1912
Mont. 1914
Idaho 1896
N. Dak.
Minn.
Wis.
Mich. 1918
Vt.
Maine
N.H.
Mass.
R.I.
N.Y. 1917
Nev. 1914
Wyo. 1890
S. Dak. 1918
Iowa
Ill.
Ind.
Ohio
Pa.
Conn.
N.J.
Calif. 1911
Utah 1896
Colo. 1893
Nebr.
Mo.
Ky.
W. Va.
Va.
Del.
Md.
Ariz. 1912
N. Mex.
Kans. 1912
Okla. 1918
Ark.
Tenn.
N.C.
S.C.
ATLANTIC OCEAN
Miss.
Ala.
Ga.
La.
Tex.
MEXICO
Fla.
Gulf of Mexico

0 — 400 miles
0 — 400 km
Albers Equal-Area projection

The historical map (above) gives data about a time in the past and is a type of special purpose map. This map also includes political information about state borders in 1919.

A physical map (below) calls out landforms and water features.

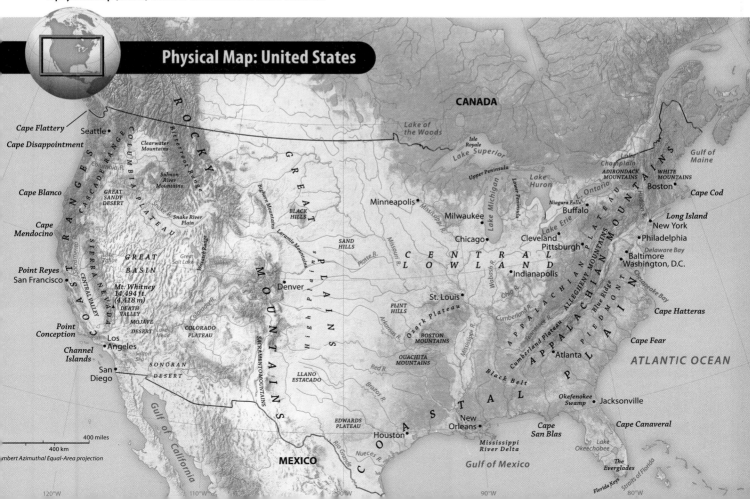

Physical Map: United States

CANADA

Cape Flattery
Cape Disappointment
Seattle
Clearwater Mountains
ROCKY
Bitterroot Range
Columbia R.
Columbia Plateau
GREAT SANDY DESERT
Salmon River Mountains
Snake River Plain
GREAT
Lake of the Woods
Lake Superior
Isle Royale
Upper Peninsula
Lake Michigan
Lake Huron
Lower Peninsula
Lake Ontario
Lake Champlain
ADIRONDACK MOUNTAINS
WHITE MOUNTAINS
Gulf of Maine
Cape Cod
Boston
Cape Blanco
CASCADE RANGE
Snake R.
Bighorn Mountains
BLACK HILLS
Lake Erie
Niagara Falls
Buffalo
Cleveland
Pittsburgh
Long Island
New York
Philadelphia
Cape Mendocino
SIERRA NEVADA
Wasatch Range
Great Salt Lake
Lake Tahoe
GREAT BASIN
PLAINS
SAND HILLS
Laramie Mountains
Platte R.
Minneapolis
Mississippi R.
Milwaukee
Chicago
CENTRAL LOWLAND
Wabash R.
Indianapolis
APPALACHIAN PLATEAU
ALLEGHENY MOUNTAINS
Baltimore
Washington, D.C.
Delaware Bay
Chesapeake Bay
Point Reyes
San Francisco
CENTRAL VALLEY
Mt. Whitney 14,494 ft. (4,418 m)
DEATH VALLEY
Colorado R.
MOUNTAINS
High Plains
Denver
St. Louis
Ohio R.
FLINT HILLS
Ozark Plateau
Missouri R.
Mississippi R.
Cumberland R.
Tennessee R.
APPALACHIAN
Blue Ridge
PIEDMONT
Cape Hatteras
Point Conception
MOJAVE DESERT
Lake Mead
COLORADO PLATEAU
Arkansas R.
BOSTON MOUNTAINS
Cumberland Plateau
APPALACHIAN MOUNTAINS
Cape Fear
Channel Islands
Los Angeles
Salton Sea
SONORAN DESERT
SACRAMENTO MOUNTAINS
LLANO ESTACADO
Red R.
OUACHITA MOUNTAINS
Atlanta
Black Belt
ATLANTIC OCEAN
San Diego
EDWARDS PLATEAU
Brazos R.
COASTAL
New Orleans
Okefenokee Swamp
Jacksonville
Rio Grande
Nueces R.
Houston
Mississippi River Delta
Cape San Blas
Lake Okeechobee
Cape Canaveral
PLAIN
The Everglades
Gulf of California
MEXICO
Gulf of Mexico
Florida Keys
Straits of Florida

0 — 400 miles
0 — 400 km
Lambert Azimuthal Equal-Area projection

The Elements of Geography

GUIDING QUESTION *What are the six essential elements of geography?*

You have read about the five themes of geography. Geographers have also broken down the study of their subject into six essential elements. Thinking about these six elements is another good way to organize your study and understanding of geography.

Tampa's Ybor City shows the influence of its Cuban population. Florida's location, not far from the island of Cuba, helps explain the strong Cuban influence in the state.

The World in Spatial Terms

When studying a place, geographers are interested in where it is located. Every place has an absolute location and a relative location. *Absolute location* refers to the exact spot of a place on the Earth's surface. For example, the city of Montgomery, Alabama, is located at a specific spot on the Earth—33°22' N latitude and 86°18' W longitude. No other place on Earth has the same absolute location as Montgomery.

Relative location tells where a place is compared with one or more other places. Miami is southeast of Tampa, west of the Atlantic Ocean, and about 228 miles (367 km) north of the capital city of Havana on the island of Cuba. Knowing a place's relative location may help a historian understand how it was settled and how its culture developed. For example, Miami is the closest large U.S. city to Cuba. This fact helps explain why Miami and the surrounding area is home to such a large population of Cuban Americans.

Places and Regions

Place describes all of the characteristics that give an area its own special quality. These can be physical features such as mountains, waterways, climate, and plant or animal life. Places can also be described by human features. These include language, religion, and architecture. If you were trying to tell someone about the town where you live, you would be describing place.

John Coletti/JAI/Corbis

Reading **HELP**DESK (CCSS)

ecosystem a community of living things and the surroundings in which they live

Each place is unique. Still, many places share features in common with others. A *region* is a group of places that share common features.

Physical features, such as a type of landform or plant life, can define regions. Human features, such as religion, language, or industry, also shape regions. For example, the South during the early 1800s was a largely agricultural region. The economy was based on trading agricultural products. The widespread practice of slavery also defined the region.

Physical Systems

Have you ever wondered where mountains come from or how the oceans formed? What are the factors that cause storms? The planet Earth is subject to powerful forces. These physical systems have shaped the planet.

Physical systems include the complex forces that create weather—wind, rain, snow, and storms. These, of course, can change the Earth. There are also physical systems that make the surface of the Earth move and change shape. These forces build mountain ranges, cause earthquakes, and form volcanoes.

Physical systems affect where and how humans live. For example, people may decide not to live on the slopes of an active volcano that could erupt at any time. Almost every place that people choose to live feels some sort of impact from storms, earthquakes, fires, or other physical systems.

Ecosystems are a type of physical system. An **ecosystem** is a community of living beings and the surroundings in which they live. A lake is an example of an ecosystem. The ecosystem includes the plants, animals, water, and everything that lives beneath the water. Other major ecosystems in the United States include forests, wetlands, grasslands, and deserts.

In an ecosystem, all the creatures and features are connected. A change to one part can affect other parts.

Human Systems

Geographers are also interested in human systems. A human system includes all the things humans create as they build their lives together on Earth. It includes all the people and their settlements, as well as the cultures they form. It also includes the way different groups of people

Volcanoes show the powerful impact of physical systems.

ROMEO RANOCO/Reuters/Corbis

Cities like New York City are one form of human system that affects the world. The city has grown significantly over its history.

interact with each other, how they work to get along—and how they settle conflicts when they occur.

Human systems are always changing. Movements of people, ideas, and goods also shape the world. At all times of day, people are flying across oceans and continents, delivering goods to distant cities or supermarkets. They are piloting boats filled with goods across the ocean or learning about other cultures through textbooks and the Internet. People move to new places and take up new lives. Cultures spread into new areas.

Environment and Society

People shape the world in which they live. In turn, the world shapes them. People settle in certain places and change their **environment** to suit them. For example, people create cities with buildings, streets, and homes. People tunnel through mountains to create roads, and they use nonrenewable resources such as coal to make electricity. People also adapt to the world around them. For example, they use renewable energy sources.

The relationship between people and their surroundings is an important one. Landforms, waterways, climate, and natural resources have all helped and hindered human activities.

People have responded to their surroundings in different ways. Sometimes they have adjusted to them. At other times, people have changed their environment to meet their needs.

Human beings tend to have a great impact on the ecosystem they live in. For instance, your school is a building that took a great amount of time and energy to build. The ground had to be leveled. Workers built walls with wood and concrete. Roads were laid down to allow people to come and go from the school.

Thomas Jackson/The Image Bank/Getty Images

All of these actions affected the environment, causing plants to be destroyed and forcing animals to find new places to live.

In April 2010, an explosion on an oil-drilling platform in the Gulf of Mexico killed 11 workers. The blast also triggered the worst oil spill—and the worst human-made environmental disaster—in the nation's history. The spill fouled shorelines from Louisiana to the Florida Panhandle.

Even before the spill, pollution, overexploitation, natural disasters, and environmental changes had taxed the Gulf's ecosystems. These factors impacted the region's environment, marine life, and wildlife, as well as the health and well-being of residents. The disaster added to these effects and threatened the people who relied on the Gulf for their livelihood. Jobs and industry in fishing, agriculture, oil, and trade are at risk. Restoration efforts continue, but long-term effects are still unknown.

The Uses of Geography

Knowledge of geography helps people understand the relationships between people, places, and the environment. Just as Native Americans and European explorers used knowledge of geography to live in and explore our land, your ability to understand geography and tools and technology available for its study will equip you for life in our modern world.

☑ **PROGRESS CHECK**

Defining What are ecosystems?

LESSON 2 REVIEW (CCSS)

Review Vocabulary

1. Use the following terms in a sentence that explains the relationship between the terms.

   a. globe   **b.** map

2. Use the following terms in a sentence that explains the relationship among the terms.

   a. landforms   **b.** relief   **c.** elevation

Answer the Guiding Questions

3. *Identifying* What are the five themes of geography? Why are they important?

4. *Listing* What are the different disadvantages of globes and maps?

5. *Applying* What is the absolute location of your community? What is the relative location?

6. *Assessing* How do physical systems affect humans?

7. *Speculating* What are two examples of ways that people shape the world they live in? Why do you think people do this?

8. *Explaining* Why is it important to protect our ecosystems?

9. **INFORMATIVE/EXPLANATORY** What is the definition of a place? Give two examples of places that you are familiar with.

netwrks
There's More Online!

☑ **CHART**
Economics Vocabulary

☑ **GAME**
Goods and Services

☑ **GRAPHIC ORGANIZER**
Economic Systems

Lesson 3
Studying Economics

ESSENTIAL QUESTION *Why do people make economic choices?*

IT MATTERS BECAUSE
Understanding economic systems also helps us understand the reasons for many actions by people and governments throughout history.

What Is Economics?

GUIDING QUESTION *What makes up an economy?*

Economics is the study of how people and nations make choices about using scarce resources to fill their needs and wants. Economics is also the study of how things are made, bought, sold, and used. The economic concepts you will read about here have played a role in the development of the United States.

Scarcity and Choice

Goods are things that people buy, like peanut butter or pencils. Services are things that people do for one another. The person who cuts hair or grooms dogs performs a service. People or businesses that produce goods or services are known as producers. People who consume, or use, goods or services are known as consumers.

A key economic concept is the idea of scarcity. Scarcity means there are not enough resources to produce everything people want and need. Because of scarcity, people and societies must make choices about how to use resources. They must decide:
- what to produce.
- how to produce.
- for whom to produce.

Reading **HELP**DESK **CCSS**

Taking Notes: *Summarizing*
As you read, use a graphic organizer like this one to list and summarize the different economic systems.

Economic Systems
1.
2.
3.
4.

Content Vocabulary
- **opportunity cost**
- **capital**
- **entrepreneur**
- **market economy**
- **free enterprise system**
- **tariff**

22 *Exploring Social Studies*

Scarcity is a challenge all societies face. The choices people make in response to it play a key role in how people live and how societies interact with each other.

The Cost of Choices

Remember, scarcity forces people to make choices. For example, when you buy a song online, you are making a choice. You could instead choose to save your money. Your decision to buy the song costs you the opportunity to save the money. In other words, there is a cost involved in your choice. This is called the **opportunity cost**—the chance you pass up when you make a choice. The opportunity cost of buying a song is the lost chance to save the money. The opportunity cost of saving the money is not having a song you want. Every decision comes with an opportunity cost.

Factors of Production

Economists call the resources needed to produce goods and services factors of production. The factors of production include land, labor, and capital.

Land refers to the natural resources people use to make products. Examples include farmland and forests.

A nation's workforce is called labor. These human resources include anyone who works to produce goods and services.

These workers are examples of labor. Do these workers produce goods or provide a service?

Another factor of production is capital. **Capital** refers to human-made goods that people use to produce other goods and services. Examples include machines, buildings, and tools. Economists often think of money as a form of capital.

Many experts also think of **entrepreneurs** (ahn·truh·pruh·NUHRZ) as a factor of production. An entrepreneur is a person who organizes and manages a business. He or she brings together the other factors of production. The entrepreneur takes economic risks to make a profit.

☑ PROGRESS CHECK

Explaining What is the difference between goods and services?

opportunity cost the cost of passing up the second choice when making a decision
capital human-made goods that people use to produce goods and services; also, money

entrepreneur a person who starts and runs a business

Most nations have a mixed economy, a combination of a market and a command economy. For many years, China had a strictly command economy, but today it allows some features of a market economy. The United States has, in general, had a market economy with some government involvement.

Market Economy

GUIDING QUESTION *How do people decide what to produce?*

Every country has an economic system. Economic systems explain the ways people produce and trade goods and services.

A few places in the world have a "traditional economy." In this system, what people do and make is based on tradition— "the way it's always been done." Traditional economies are still found in our world today. An example might be a Native American group living in far northern Canada. Such people live much as they have for hundreds of years.

Some places have a command economy. Here, the government controls most economic activity. Government leaders tell people what to make and sell.

The United States has a market economy. Market, in this sense, means a system of buying and selling things. In a **market economy,** buyers and sellers freely choose to buy or make whatever they want. Government takes little role in these decisions. People are free to act in their own interests.

This freedom leads to competition. Producers try to win customers. Customers seek the best deal. Producers win customers by making a good product at lower prices than others. So, competition keeps prices down and quality high.

In a market system, the forces of supply and demand help set prices. *Supply* is the amount of a good or service available at a certain price. *Demand* is how much consumers will buy at a certain price. Price is affected by supply and demand.

Think of a video-game company. It decides to make 10,000 copies of its newest game. This is a risk because it costs money to make each game. However, the company thinks it can sell 10,000 copies for $50. The game sells out quickly. The company then decides to make 5,000 more—and to charge $60. It sells only 3,000 copies at this price. To sell the rest, the company cuts its price to $55. That is where supply and demand have met.

Sometimes, there is a shift in supply or demand. Suppose the new video game gets a great review in a magazine. Suddenly everyone wants to buy the game. The demand goes way up. The price may go up, too, if consumers are willing to pay more.

✓ **PROGRESS CHECK**

Listing What are the three basic economic systems?

Reading **HELP**DESK (CCSS)

market economy economic system in which buyers and sellers choose to do business with those who satisfy their needs and wants best

free enterprise system economic system in which people are free to control and own the means of production

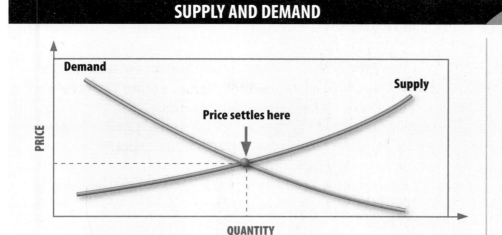

Demand

Supply

Price settles here

PRICE

QUANTITY

The supply of a product a business produces and consumers' demand for the product work together to affect the price.

1 **DESCRIBING** How large of a supply is a producer willing to make if the price is very low?

2 **CRITICAL THINKING** *Explaining* How do supply and demand work together to help set price?

National Economy

GUIDING QUESTION *What determines the strength or weakness of a nation's economy?*

The American economy is also called a **free enterprise system.** This means individuals are free to control and own the means of production. For example, if you decide to go into business, you will freely choose what goods or services to produce and how to produce them. Of course, there is some regulation of the free enterprise system on the state and federal levels. Laws protect consumers from unfair or unsafe business practices. Regulations also prevent businesses from taking over all their competitors and becoming monopolies.

With freedom of choice, buyers control businesses through their buying decisions. For instance, if a movie theater's service is poor or its prices are high, people won't go to movies there. The theater will eventually close. Once again, competition is the key to buyer decisions.

Businesses, of course, sell goods and services. They receive money in return. From this money they pay the costs of creating the goods and services. Anything leftover is called a profit. The desire to make a profit is called the profit motive. It motivates people to make things that others want to buy. It leads businesses to lower their prices to attract customers. No business can survive selling something for less than it costs to make it.

Private property is anything owned by individuals or groups rather than by the government. The right to own private property is guaranteed by the United States Constitution. As an individual, you are free to buy whatever you can afford. You also control how, when, and by whom your property is used.

Thinking Like a
HISTORIAN

Analyzing Graphs

The graph above provides a picture of what is actually a mathematics problem. The two lines plot the relationship between quantity and price. The point where the lines cross represents that price at which the market tends to settle. It is the one solution that works for both equations. For more about analyzing graphs, review Lesson 1 "Thinking Like a Historian."

☑ **PROGRESS CHECK**

Defining What is the profit motive?

As trade takes place, the trading partners become interdependent. Each trading partner depends on the other to help provide his or her wants and needs. This interdependence occurs between international trading partners, and also between partners within countries such as the United States. For more about understanding cause and effect, review Lesson 1 "Thinking Like a Historian."

International Economy

GUIDING QUESTION *How do nations trade with each other?*

No country produces all the goods and services it needs. Because most countries have more than they need of some things and not enough of others, trade is important.

International trade is the exchange of goods and services across national borders. Every country imports, or buys, goods and services from other countries, and exports, or sells, goods and services to other countries. This interdependence links the countries of the world together. It also links the states of the United States.

Voluntary Exchange

Trade is based on the principle of voluntary exchange. Neither the buyer nor the seller is forced to trade. A buyer voluntarily trades money for goods or services. The seller voluntarily trades goods or services for money.

Specialization

Trade allows for specialization. Nations use their scarce resources to focus on those things that they can produce well. For example, Egypt specializes in making cotton products, such as towels or clothing. Chile produces many kinds of fruit. Nations rich in petroleum produce petroleum products. These countries then trade for other items they want or need.

Currency and the Exchange Rate

Today, most people use currency, or money, for trade. Different countries have their own currencies. The United States uses the dollar. Nigeria uses the naira, Iraq the dinar, and Japan the yen.

To do business, people must have a way of knowing the exchange rate—the price of one country's currency shown in another currency. Foreign exchange markets determine how many naira, dinars, or yen equal a U.S. dollar. This allows businesses in different countries to receive and make payments.

Trade Barriers

Competition happens between countries, too. Sometimes, however, countries try to protect their industries from competition by setting up trade barriers. There are three barriers that are common:

Reading **HELP**DESK (CCSS)

tariff a tax on imports

Reading Strategy: *Summarizing*

When you summarize a passage or list, you find the main idea and summarize it in your own words. Summarize the lists presented in this section.

1. A **tariff** is a tax on imports. Tariffs raise the price of imports so domestic industries can sell at lower prices.
2. An import quota restricts the number of units of a product that can be brought into the country.
3. An embargo bans the import or export of a good.

In recent years, however, many countries have agreed to free trade, or getting rid of trade barriers.

✔ PROGRESS CHECK

Identifying What types of goods is Egypt known for? Chile?

Economic Literacy

GUIDING QUESTION *What influences how you make your economic decisions?*

You and everyone around you are consumers who play an important role in the economic system. It is important that you know how to spend—or not spend—your money wisely.

Decision Making as a Consumer

The first decision a consumer must make is whether or not to buy an item. Surprisingly, people often buy on impulse. Before making a decision to buy something, answer these questions:

- Do I really need this item? Why? Real needs are few. Most items are wants. It is important to know which is which.
- Is this good or service worth the time I spent earning the income to pay for it?
- Is there any better use for my income now? Should I save instead for future needs?

Many nations around the world have their own currency.

Robert Clare/Taxi/Getty Images

Deciding on the Right Purchase

After you have made up your mind to buy a certain good or service, you are faced with more questions:

- Do I want high, medium, or low quality? Quality refers to appearance, materials used, and how long a product will last. Higher quality often means a higher price.
- If I am buying an appliance, car, or computer, how much will it cost to operate and service each year?
- Should I wait until there is a sale on the item I want?
- If I am looking for an expensive item, should I buy it new or used? How can I protect myself if I buy a used item?
- Should I buy a product with a brand name even though it may cost more than a product without a brand name?
- What do consumer magazines or friends say about the product?
- Does the warranty promise to fix or replace an item that is defective? How does it compare to other warranties?
- What are the terms of the return, or exchange, policy of the store where I am thinking of buying this product?

Why Save Money?

Saving is setting aside income so that it can be used later. You may already be saving some of your **income.** Generally, people save money by putting it in a bank where it will be safe from loss and earns interest. Interest is received when people lend money or allow a bank to use their money. A person receives interest on a savings account while funds are in the account.

Banks offer safety but a low rate of interest. If people wish to **maximize** their returns, they can invest their money in others ways, such as in stocks and bonds. Stocks and bonds offer investors the chance of greater returns, but with more risk of losing money.

Set Savings Goals

Goals can help people save money. A goal may be short-term—something you expect to achieve soon. Goals may also be long-term. It is good to have both short- and long-term goals.

What Is Credit?

Credit involves borrowing money to buy goods and services today with the promise to pay back the money in the future. The amount owed—the debt—is equal to the principal plus interest.

Spending money is easy. Making wise purchasing decisions, however, takes thought and planning.

(l) JUPITERIMAGES/ Brand X / Alamy, (b) Comstock Images

Reading **HELP**DESK (CCSS)

Academic Vocabulary

income money received
maximize make as large as possible

Visual Vocabulary

A **credit card** is a piece of plastic that is used to make a credit purchase. Stores that accept the card get payment for the good or service from the credit card company. The company then collects payment from the cardholder.

The principal is the amount originally borrowed. The interest is the amount the borrower must pay for the use of someone else's money. That "someone else" may be a bank, a credit card company, or a store. A bank, for instance, may loan money at a set interest rate—for example, 8 percent a year. So, the interest on $100 would be $8 for one year.

Using credit and taking out a loan work the same way. In both cases, you must pay interest for the use of someone else's money.

Why People Use Credit

Most Americans borrow and buy on credit sometimes. For expensive items, such as a car or a house, they consider borrowing necessary.

Some people suggest that you are better off saving to buy a large purchase such as a pickup truck. During the years you are saving, however, you don't get the benefit of driving it. Many people would rather buy on credit and enjoy the use of an item now rather than later.

Maintain Good Credit

Using credit can be a very useful tool. At the same time, it can lead you to spend more money than you can afford. If you charge more than your credit card balance or are unable to make payments, it can lead to serious financial problems. Later purchases such as a car or a home are affected by how you use credit today.

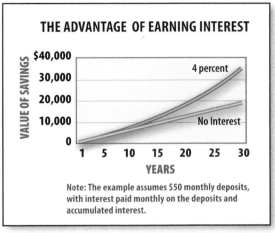

THE ADVANTAGE OF EARNING INTEREST

Note: The example assumes $50 monthly deposits, with interest paid monthly on the deposits and accumulated interest.

Compare the lines of this graph to see the difference between saving $50 a month at no interest compared to saving $50 a month at just 4 percent interest.

▶ **CRITICAL THINKING**
Calculating How much more would you save over 30 years at 4 percent interest compared to no interest?

✓ **PROGRESS CHECK**

Expressing What are some questions you should ask yourself before you make a purchase?

LESSON 3 REVIEW (CCSS)

Review Vocabulary

1. Use the words *entrepreneur* and *capital* in a sentence that demonstrates your understanding of these terms.

2. Explain the significance of the following terms:
   a. opportunity cost   **b.** market economy
   c. free enterprise system   **d.** tariff

Answer the Guiding Questions

3. *Describing* In the United States, what is the role of the government in the economy?

4. *Making Connections* What might happen to the price of apples in a market system if bad weather wipes out the apple crop?

5. *Explaining* Why is trade important to every nation?

6. **INFORMATIVE/EXPLANATORY** Entrepreneurs and inventors play an important role in the United States economy. Write a paragraph that explains how people who take risks and bring new products to market help the economy.

Lesson 4
Civics and Government

ESSENTIAL QUESTION *What makes a responsible citizen?*

IT MATTERS BECAUSE
Understanding how government works helps us understand what has been and still is important to the people of the United States.

Rights of U.S. Citizens

GUIDING QUESTION *What are the rights of citizens?*

Civics is the study of the rights and duties of citizens. The concept of citizenship dates back more than 2,500 years to ancient Greece and Rome. In those days, only a few people could be citizens.

Today, every country has rules about how citizens gain citizenship. The U.S. Constitution established two ways to become a citizen. One way is by birth: Anyone born in the U.S. is a U.S. citizen. The second way is for foreign-born people to choose to become citizens through a legal process called **naturalization.**

All American citizens have certain basic rights. These are outlined and **guaranteed** in the Constitution. Citizens also have specific responsibilities. Living in a democracy means that every citizen is partly responsible for how society is governed and the actions the government takes.

Due Process

The Fifth Amendment to the Constitution states that no person shall "be deprived of life, liberty, or property, without due process of law." **Due process** means that the government must treat all people by certain procedures established by law and the Constitution.

(l) Photodisc, (cl) Ocean/Corbis, (cr) Royalty-Free/CORBIS, (r) Richard Ellis/Getty Images News/Getty Images

Reading **HELP**DESK (CCSS)

Taking Notes: *Outlining*

As you read, use a graphic organizer like this one to outline the types of government systems and forms of government.

I. Types of Government Systems
    A.
    B.
    C.
II. Forms of Government
    A.
    B.
    C.
      1.
      2.

Content Vocabulary
• **naturalization**
• **due process**
• **federal system**

Equal Protection

The Fourteenth Amendment requires every state to give citizens "equal protection of the laws." Americans of all races, religions, and beliefs must be treated the same.

Basic Freedoms

The basic freedoms of citizens include those outlined in the First Amendment—freedom of speech, religion, and the press, plus the right to assembly and to petition the government. In a democracy, citizens must be able to exchange ideas freely.

Limits on Rights

The government can limit rights to protect the health, safety, security, and moral standards of a community. Rights can also be limited so that one person's rights do not interfere with the rights of others. The restrictions of rights by the government must be reasonable and apply to everyone equally.

✔ PROGRESS CHECK

Identifying In what part of the Constitution are many basic freedoms stated?

The Bill of Rights, made up of the first 10 amendments to the Constitution, protects everyone's rights.

Government: Structure and Functions

GUIDING QUESTION *What are the structure and functions of government?*

It is the job of government to make and carry out laws for a nation, society, or community. Different governments approach this job in different ways.

Different Systems of Government

Each country in the world has a government. All of these governments fall into one of three categories: unitary, confederation, or federal.

In a unitary government, all decision making rests in the hands of a single national government. This means that the national government controls the nation's cities, towns, and states. In a confederation, the states hold the power, and the power of the national government is limited. Finally, in the **federal system,** the power is split between a central, national government and state and local governments.

Photodisc

---

naturalization the legal process of becoming a citizen
due process procedures the government must follow that are established by law

federal system type of government in which power flows between state and local governments and the national government

Academic Vocabulary

guarantee to promise that something will take place

The United States has a federal system of government. In this system, the Constitution divides authority between the federal (national) government and state governments.

All levels of government—federal, state, and local—also have the power to pass laws. While the federal government's laws are supreme, it cannot overrule state and local laws unless they conflict with federal laws.

Our nation's Constitution does not mention local governments. States have full authority in establishing local governments and defining their powers and responsibilities.

Division of Powers in the United States

The Constitution describes what the national and state governments can do. Certain powers are given to the national government, others to state governments. Some other powers are shared. In the country's early years, the powers of the national government were a common source of debate.

Forms of Government

One of the ways of classifying governments is by asking: Who governs? In an autocracy, a single person holds unlimited power. An oligarchy gives power to a small, elite group. In a democracy, the people rule. The role of the citizen in government differs depending on the form of government.

There are two forms of democracy. One is direct democracy. Here, all the citizens take a direct role in the government. The city-state of ancient Athens had a direct democracy. All citizens met to debate government matters and vote on laws.

Ocean/Corbis

DIAGRAM SKILL

This diagram explains the division of powers in the U.S. federal system.

1 LISTING Give an example of a power held only by the national government, only by the state governments, and by both governments.

2 CRITICAL THINKING
Identifying Central Issues Do you think the division of powers makes the national government more or less powerful? Explain.

DIVISION OF POWERS

National Government

Maintain the military

Declare war

Coin money

Regulate trade between states and with foreign nations

Make all laws necessary for carrying out delegated powers

Both

Enforce laws (state governments enforce different laws than the federal government)

Establish courts

Borrow money

Protect the health and safety of the people

Build roads

Collect taxes

State Governments

Conduct elections

Establish schools

Regulate businesses within state

Establish local government

Issue marriage licenses

Assume other powers not given to the national government

Visual Vocabulary

A **jury** is a group of citizens who listen to testimony and make a decision at a trial.

In the federal system of the U.S. government, the national, state, and local levels of government have different powers and roles.

Many countries today, including the United States, have a representative democracy, or republic. Citizens elect representatives to make laws and govern on their behalf.

✔ PROGRESS CHECK

Categorizing What kind of government does the United States have?

Citizens in Action

GUIDING QUESTION *What are the duties and responsibilities of citizens?*

From colonial times, Americans have recognized that citizens have duties and responsibilities. Duties are things the law requires us to do. Responsibilities are things we should do to help our community. We need to meet both our duties and responsibilities to support a good government and our rights.

Duties

Americans have four basic duties:

- **Obey the law** Laws help keep order. They protect the health, safety, and property of citizens. They also make it possible for people to live together peacefully. Citizens working with elected representatives can change laws.
- **Pay taxes** The government uses tax money for a variety of purposes, such as defending the nation, providing services to the needy, and building roads and bridges.
- **Serve on juries** Americans are guaranteed the right to a trial by a **jury** of their peers (equals). This duty is necessary to guarantee everyone a fair and speedy trial.

Thinking Like a
HISTORIAN

Making Comparisons

Imagine a government today that practiced direct democracy. What would be the advantages of such a system? What might some of the challenges of such a system be? Create a diagram that compares direct democracy with the representative democracy practiced in the United States today. Consider the benefits and drawbacks of each. Write a statement in which you explain why you think our nation's founders chose a representative democracy. For more about making comparisons, review Lesson 1 "Thinking Like a Historian."

Over the course of United States history, voting rights for citizens have steadily expanded. In addition to many laws, constitutional amendments have extended the right to vote to African American men (the Fifteenth Amendment) and then all women (the Nineteenth Amendment). The Twenty-fourth Amendment outlawed poll taxes used to block voting rights, and the Twenty-sixth Amendment lowered the voting age to 18.

- **Defend the nation** All males aged 18 and older must register with the government in case they are needed for military service. Men and women can also volunteer to serve.

Responsibilities

Responsibilities are not as clear-cut as duties. Because responsibilities are **voluntary,** people are not arrested or punished if they do not fulfill responsibilities. Yet the quality of our lives is reduced if people neglect their responsibilities.

Perhaps your most important responsibility as a citizen will be to vote when you reach the age of 18. Voting allows you to take part in government and guide its direction. If you disapprove of the job your representatives are doing, you can express your views to them or help elect other people in the next election.

Shared Beliefs

The United States is a diverse country. Many different racial, ethnic, and religious groups live together peacefully. People with such varied backgrounds can succeed as a nation only when they share core values and respect the rights and beliefs of others.

What core beliefs do Americans share? Although people would disagree on some shared beliefs, all lists would include:

- **Respect** for the rights of each individual to equal treatment under the law, as described in the Constitution.
- **Appreciation** of the cultural contributions of all peoples.
- **Belief** in democracy as the best form of government.
- **Awareness** that it is each citizen's responsibility to participate thoughtfully in civic life.

Americans share basic values and beliefs, regardless of their racial, ethnic, and religious backgrounds.

Richard Ellis/Getty Image News/Getty Images

Academic Vocabulary
voluntary done by choice

Service Learning

Service learning involves performing tasks that meet community needs. Examples of service projects include cleaning and fixing parks, teaching younger children to read, and sharing time with older people. Service learning requires using your time and your talents. You and your service team play an active role in planning a project and deciding how to use your skills and talents to complete your tasks.

Why Should I Participate?

You can make a difference. Sharing your time, knowledge, and skills helps others in your school and community. As you take part in service learning, you will also gain new knowledge and skills. You help set goals for the project, decide what you will do and how you will do it, and share your thoughts about the experience with others.

How Do I Get Involved?

Many students are already taking part in service learning. National organizations such as AmeriCorps and Learn and Serve America are always looking for volunteers. Forty-eight state education agencies operate service-learning programs, and chances are good your school already has service-learning opportunities available. In addition, by exploring the needs of your community, you can plan and organize your own service-learning project.

PRIMARY SOURCE

❝ The end of all education should surely be service to others. ❞

—César E. Chávez

✔ **PROGRESS CHECK**

Contrasting What is the difference between duties and responsibilities?

Florida Learn & Serve

LESSON 4 REVIEW

Review Vocabulary

1. Identify the significance of the following terms.

   a. naturalization   **b.** due process
   c. federal system

Answer the Guiding Questions

2. *Identifying* What documents present and guarantee the basic rights of American citizens?

3. *Contrasting* What is the difference between direct democracy and representative democracy?

4. *Explaining* Why is it important to fulfill both our duties and our responsibilities as citizens?

5. **ARGUMENT** Write an essay that explains the importance of civic responsibility and that urges young people to take part in public service.

Write your answers on a separate piece of paper.

1 Exploring the Essential Questions

INFORMATIVE/EXPLANATORY Why would your history textbook include a chapter about geography, economics, and civics? Write an essay about how these different subjects can help a student gain an understanding of history and historical events.

2 21st Century Skills

USING INTERVIEW SKILLS Interview someone from your community to learn more about its history and features. For your interview, identify an adult subject who has lived in the community for at least 10 years—longer, if possible. Ask the person questions about the community that will help you learn about its geography, history, and economy. Use the five themes of geography to organize your questions and answers. If necessary, supplement your interview with research on the Internet to create a report on the past and present of your community.

3 Thinking Like a Historian

ANALYZING AND INTERPRETING INFORMATION Create a diagram like the one to the right to describe the key features of your state.

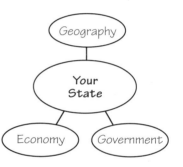

4 Visual Literacy

ANALYZING PAINTINGS Study this painting. What can you tell about the time in which it was painted? What part of the world do you think the figures come from, and how can you tell? How would you describe the attitude or mood of the figures? Write a paragraph about this picture that includes answers to these questions.

REVIEW THE GUIDING QUESTIONS

Choose the best answer for each question.

1 Throughout history, people have kept track of time by making
  A. secondary sources.
  B. calendars.
  C. labels.
  D. sacred texts.

2 Primary sources are
  F. first-person accounts of events.
  G. secondhand accounts of events.
  H. textbooks and library books.
  I. video games and board games.

3 Human-environment interaction refers to
  A. a type of movement in geography.
  B. a specific place in the United States.
  C. the relationship between people and their environments.
  D. encounters between animals and humans.

4 In economics, the idea of scarcity explains why all people
  F. make choices.
  G. steal to make ends meet.
  H. provide money to charitable causes.
  I. buy the most expensive item.

5 The Fourteenth Amendment requires every state to grant its citizens
  A. equal opportunity for jobs.
  B. the right to bear arms.
  C. freedom of speech and religion.
  D. equal protection of the laws.

6 In the federal system of government, government power is distributed
  F. from state governments to local governments.
  G. from the state governments to the federal government.
  H. from local governments to the federal government.
  I. from city governments to town governments.

DBQ ANALYZING DOCUMENTS

7 **Categorizing** Study the map at the right. This map is an example of a

A. political map.

B. physical map.

C. population density map.

D. special purpose map.

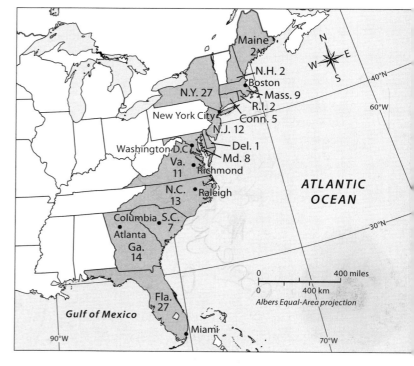

8 **Locating** According to this map, the relative location of Maine is

F. in New England.

G. east of New Hampshire.

H. impossible to determine.

I. south of Delaware.

SHORT RESPONSE

In 1492 Christopher Columbus wrote this description of the native people whom he met in the Americas.

Saturday, October 13th

"At dawn many of these men came down to the shore. All are, as already said, youths of good size and very handsome. ... They came to the ship in canoes, made out of trunks of trees, all in one piece, like a long boat, and wonderfully built according to the locality, ... in some of them forty or forty-five men came; others were smaller, and in some but a single man came."

9 What is an example of a fact a historian might be able to get from this primary source excerpt?

10 What are some of the opinions that Columbus shares in this primary source excerpt?

EXTENDED RESPONSE

11 **Informative/Explanatory** Write a one-page paper in which you describe what credit is, identify the reasons that people use credit, and explain how a person might consider the benefits and drawbacks of using credit in making a decision to buy a car.

Need Extra Help?

If You've Missed Question	1	2	3	4	5	6	7	8	9	10	11
Review Lesson	1	1	2	3	4	4	2	2	1	1	3

The Reconstruction Era

1865–1896

netw⚬rks

There's More Online about events of the Reconstruction era.

CHAPTER 2

The Story Matters . . .

Frederick Douglass has done as much as any American in winning freedom for African Americans. Formerly enslaved, Douglass became a powerful voice for the abolitionist cause. During the Civil War, he shared his advice with President Lincoln himself. Now, he is looking forward to the rebuilding of the nation—Reconstruction. He says, "Whether the tremendous war so heroically fought and so victoriously ended shall pass into history a miserable failure . . . must be determined one way or another by the present session of Congress." In this chapter, you will read about Congress's response to Douglass's challenge.

◄ *In the years leading up to the Civil War and after, Frederick Douglass was a leading voice for African American rights.*

39

Place and Time: United States 1865 to 1896

After the Civil War, the federal government faced the task of putting the nation back together. At the same time, the nation continued to grow and confront a variety of challenges all across the continent.

Step Into the Place

MAP FOCUS The federal government admitted Southern states back into the Union, and the nation sought to establish control of the West.

1 PLACE Which former Confederate state was the first to rejoin the Union?

2 HUMAN-ENVIRONMENT INTERACTION Which states and territories are likely to be impacted by completion of the transcontinental railroad? Explain your answer.

3 CRITICAL THINKING
Making Inferences Why do you think different states reentered the Union at different times?

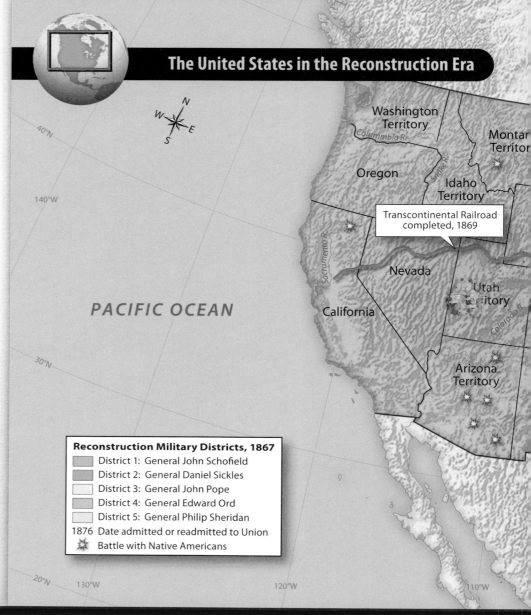

The United States in the Reconstruction Era

Washington Territory
Columbia R.
Montar Territor
Oregon
Idaho Territory
Transcontinental Railroad completed, 1869
Sacramento R.
Nevada
Utah Territory
California
Colorado R.
PACIFIC OCEAN
Arizona Territory

40°N
140°W
30°N
20°N
130°W
120°W
110°W

Reconstruction Military Districts, 1867
District 1: General John Schofield
District 2: General Daniel Sickles
District 3: General John Pope
District 4: General Edward Ord
District 5: General Philip Sheridan
1876 Date admitted or readmitted to Union
Battle with Native Americans

Step Into the Time

TIME LINE Look at the time line. When was the First Reconstruction Act passed? How much longer did Reconstruction last?

Abraham Lincoln 1861–1865
A. Johnson 1865–1869
U. S. Grant 1869–1877

U.S. PRESIDENTS
U.S. EVENTS
WORLD EVENTS

1860
1870

1870 Fifteenth Amendment ratified

1861 Southern states form Confederacy

1865 Civil War ends

1867 Russia sells Alaska to United States

1868 Fourteenth Amendment ratified

1871 Bismarck *unifies Germany*

1867 First Reconstruction Act passed

White House Historical Association

networks

There's More Online!

☑ **MAP** Explore the interactive version of this map on NETWORKS.

☑ **TIME LINE** Explore the interactive version of this time line on NETWORKS.

CANADA

New Hampshire
Vermont
Maine

Massachusetts

Rhode Island
Connecticut

New Jersey

Delaware
Maryland

L. Superior

Minnesota

Dakota
Territory

Missouri R.

Wisconsin

L. Huron

L. Michigan

Michigan

L. Ontario

New York

L. Erie

Pennsylvania

Wyo.
Terr.

Nebraska
1867

Iowa

Mississippi R.

Great Chicago Fire,
1871

Platte R.

Illinois

Ind.

Ohio

W.
Va.

Virginia
1870

Colorado
1876

Exodusters, 1879

10th Cavalry,
Buffalo Soldiers

Ohio R.

Kentucky

North
Carolina
1868

Kansas

Missouri

New
Mex.
Terr.

Indian
Territory

Arkansas R.

Arkansas
1868

Tennessee
1866

Tennessee R.

South
Carolina
1868

ATLANTIC OCEAN

9th Cavalry,
Buffalo Soldiers

Mississippi R.

Miss.
1870

Alabama
1868

Georgia
1870

Texas
1870

La.
1868

Rio Grande

Florida
1868

Gulf of Mexico

MEXICO

```
0        300 miles
0        300 km
```
Lambert Azimuthal Equal-Area projection

60°W
40°N
30°N
90°W   80°W   70°W

R. B. Hayes 1877–1881	James Garfield 1881	Chester Arthur 1881–1885	Grover Cleveland 1885–1889	Benjamin Harrison 1889–1893	Grover Cleveland 1893–1897

1880   **1890**   **1900**

1877 Reconstruction ends

1882 Egypt comes under British control

1891 Famine spreads across Russia

1896 Ethiopia defeats invading Italians

1879–1880 Edison perfects the electric incandescent lightbulb

1889 Hull House opens in Chicago

networks

There's More Online!

☑ **GRAPHIC ORGANIZER**
Reconstruction Plans

☑ **SLIDE SHOW**
• Reconstruction in the South
• Lincoln's Funeral Procession

Lesson 1
Planning Reconstruction

ESSENTIAL QUESTION *How do new ideas change the way people live?*

IT MATTERS BECAUSE
Plans for Reconstruction after the Civil War proved difficult and divisive.

The Reconstruction Debate

GUIDING QUESTION *Why did leaders disagree about the South rejoining the Union?*

The Confederate states tried and failed to break away from the United States. Now, they had to rejoin that Union. In addition, the war left the South's economy and society in ruins. It would take much effort to restore the states that had experienced so much destruction during the war.

The task of rebuilding the former Confederate states and readmitting them to the Union was called **Reconstruction** (ree•kuhn•STRUHK•shuhn). The president and members of Congress had different ideas about how to achieve these goals. The debate over Reconstruction led to bitter conflict in the years following the Civil War.

Lincoln's Ten Percent Plan

President Lincoln offered the first plan for bringing Southern states back into the Union. In December 1863, while the Civil War still raged, Lincoln presented his ideas. Lincoln's plan required voters in each Southern state to take an oath of loyalty to the Union. When 10 percent of the voters in a state had taken the oath, the state could form a new state government. The state would also be required to adopt a new constitution that banned

(l) Library of Congress [LC-DIG-cwpb-03370], (c & r) Library of Congress LC-USZC4-1155

Reading **HELP**DESK **CCSS**

Taking Notes: *Summarizing*

Using a graphic organizer like the one shown here, write short summaries of the Reconstruction plans proposed by Abraham Lincoln, the Radical Republicans, and Andrew Johnson.

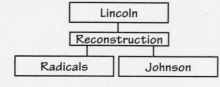

Content Vocabulary
• **Reconstruction**
• **amnesty**

slavery. Once a state had met these conditions, it could send representatives to Congress. Lincoln's proposal was known as the Ten Percent Plan.

Lincoln did not want to punish the South after the war ended. He believed that punishment would accomplish little and would slow the nation's healing from the war. Lincoln wanted to see white Southerners who supported the Union take charge of their state governments. He offered **amnesty** (AM·nuh·stee)— forgiveness for any crimes committed—to those who would swear loyalty to the Union. Only Confederate leaders would not be offered amnesty.

In 1864, three states—Louisiana, Arkansas, and Tennessee— set up new governments under Lincoln's plan. Congress, however, was not willing to accept the new states. It refused to seat their senators and representatives.

The Radical Republicans

Some members of Congress thought Lincoln's plan went too easy on the South. A group of Republican representatives favored a more **radical** approach to Reconstruction. This group was known as the Radical Republicans, or the Radicals. Radical leader Thaddeus Stevens said that Southern institutions "must be broken up and relaid, or all our blood and treasure have been spent in vain." The Radicals were powerful. The Republican Party controlled Congress, and the Radicals had much influence in the party. Congress could—and did—vote to deny seats to any state that sought to reenter the Union under Lincoln's plan.

The city of Richmond, Virginia, shown here, was the capital of the Confederacy and an industrial center.

▶ **CRITICAL THINKING**
Determining Cause and Effect What challenges do you think this type of destruction presented to the economy of Virginia?

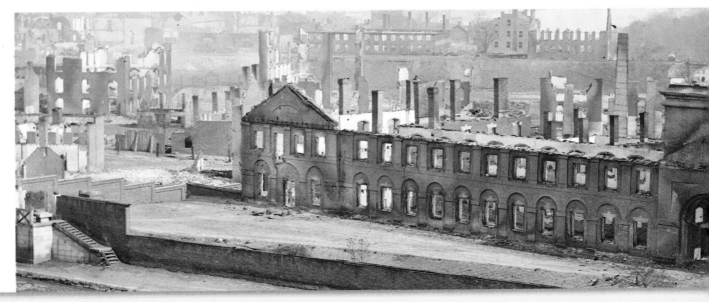

Library of Congress [LC-DIG-cwpb-03370]

Reconstruction the period of rebuilding the South and readmitting Southern states into the Union
amnesty the granting of a pardon to a large number of persons

Academic Vocabulary
radical extreme

Acting on his sympathies for the Confederacy, John Wilkes Booth assassinated President Lincoln on April 14, 1865. Lincoln had had less than a week to celebrate the Union victory.

▶ **CRITICAL THINKING**

Analyzing Images How does the artist use actions of the people in this picture to create a mood? Explain your answer.

In July 1864, Congress passed its plan for Reconstruction. The Wade-Davis Bill stated that to rejoin the Union, a state must meet three requirements. First, a majority of the state's white male adults had to pledge loyalty to the Union. Second, only white males who swore they had not fought against the Union could vote for delegates to a state constitutional convention. Third, all new state constitutions had to ban slavery. The bill also barred former Confederates from holding public office.

Lincoln objected to the harshness of this plan. Lincoln wanted new state governments to be quickly established and the rebuilding of the South to get underway. Because Congress was about to end its session, he was able to "pocket veto" the bill: He refused to sign it, and the bill died after Congress adjourned. Still, the Wade-Davis Bill made President Lincoln realize that he would have to compromise with the Radicals.

Founding the Freedmen's Bureau

In March 1865, Lincoln and Congress together created the Freedmen's Bureau. Its main purpose was to help African Americans **adjust** to life after slavery. The Freedmen's Bureau provided food, clothing, and medical care to poor Southerners, especially those freed from slavery. It set up schools, some staffed with teachers from the North. The bureau helped some people get their own land to farm or find work for fair pay.

☑ **PROGRESS CHECK**

Listing What were the three requirements for rejoining the Union stated in the Wade-Davis Bill?

Library of Congress/3b52661

Reading **HELP**DESK **CCSS**

Academic Vocabulary

adjust to become more suited to new conditions

Johnson's Reconstruction Plan

GUIDING QUESTION *How did Lincoln's assassination change the plans for the South rejoining the Union?*

Events took a dramatic turn on the night of April 14, 1865. As the president enjoyed a play at Ford's Theater in Washington, D.C., actor and Confederate sympathizer John Wilkes Booth shot Lincoln in the head. Hours later, Lincoln died.

News of the president's assassination swept across the nation. African Americans mourned the death of the man who helped bring an end to slavery. White Northerners grieved for the president who had restored the Union.

Vice President Andrew Johnson became president. Although he was a Southerner, Johnson had supported the Union during the Civil War. Johnson had his own ideas about rebuilding the South. His Reconstruction plan gave amnesty to most Southerners who swore loyalty to the Union. However, high-ranking Confederates could receive pardons only by appealing to the president. This part of his plan was meant to humiliate Confederate leaders. He believed that they had tricked other Southerners into secession. Johnson also opposed equal rights for African Americans. "White men alone must manage the South," he stated.

President Johnson's plan did require that Southern states outlaw slavery before they could rejoin the Union. They also had to ratify the Thirteenth Amendment to the Constitution. Passed by Congress in January 1865, the Thirteenth Amendment abolished slavery in the United States. By the end of 1865, all former Confederate states except Texas had set up new governments under Johnson's plan. These newly reformed states were now ready to rejoin the Union.

☑ PROGRESS CHECK

Specifying What did the Thirteenth Amendment accomplish?

Thinking Like a HISTORIAN

Analyzing Primary Sources

In his Second Inaugural Address, President Lincoln said: "With malice toward none, with charity for all, with firmness in the right as God gives us to see the right, let us strive on to finish the work we are in, to bind up the nation's wounds." Lincoln wanted the South to be treated with compassion. Explain how Reconstruction might have been different if Lincoln had not been assassinated. For more about analyzing primary sources, review *Thinking Like a Historian.*

LESSON 1 REVIEW

Review Vocabulary

1. Explain the meaning of the term *Reconstruction*.

2. Use the word *amnesty* in a sentence.

Answer the Guiding Questions

3. *Explaining* What was the nature of the disagreement about the terms under which former Confederate states might rejoin the Union after the Civil War?

4. *Speculating* How would Lincoln's assassination affect the debate over Reconstruction?

5. **INFORMATIVE/EXPLANATORY** You have been hired by the newly formed Freedmen's Bureau to promote the new organization. Write a brief description of the bureau, its work, and why it is important to the future of the nation.

netw⊙rks
There's More Online!

- ☑ **CHART/GRAPH**
  Radical Republicans

- ☑ **GRAPHIC ORGANIZER**
  The Fourteenth and
  Fifteenth Amendments

- ☑ **MAP** Reconstruction
  Military Districts

- ☑ **SLIDE SHOW** Violence in
  the South

- ☑ **VIDEO**

Lesson 2
The Radicals Take Control

ESSENTIAL QUESTION *How do new ideas change the way people live?*

IT MATTERS BECAUSE
Reconstruction under the Radical Republicans advocated rights for African Americans and harsh treatment of former Confederates.

Protecting African Americans' Rights

GUIDING QUESTION *How did the North attempt to assist African Americans in the South?*

In 1865 former Confederate states began creating new governments based on President Johnson's plan. These states elected leaders to again represent them in the Congress. When the new senators and representatives arrived in Washington, D.C., Congress would not seat them. The Radical Republicans were not willing to readmit the Southern states on Johnson's easy terms. Radicals were determined to make the former Confederacy's return to the Union difficult for the white South.

Black Codes and Civil Rights

Events in the South strengthened the Radicals' determination. By early 1866, legislatures in the Southern states had passed laws called **black codes.** These laws were designed to help control the newly freed African Americans. Some black codes made it illegal for African Americans to own or rent farms. The laws also made it easy for white employers to take advantage of African American workers. Some black codes allowed officials to fine or

---

Reading **HELP**DESK

Taking Notes: *Determining Cause and Effect*

As you read, take notes on the impact of the Fourteenth and Fifteenth Amendments on African Americans. Use a diagram like the one shown here to organize your notes.

Fourteenth Amendment ⇨ [ ]

Fifteenth Amendment ⇨ [ ]

Content Vocabulary
- **black codes**
- **override**
- **impeach**

even arrest African Americans who did not have jobs. To freed men and women and their supporters, life under the black codes was little better than slavery.

At the same time, Congress tried to protect the rights of the South's African Americans. In 1866 it passed a bill that gave the Freedmen's Bureau new powers. The Bureau could now set up special courts to try persons charged with violating African Americans' rights. African Americans could sit on the juries in these courts and judge accused white Southerners.

To combat the black codes, Radical Republicans pushed the Civil Rights Act of 1866 through Congress. This law gave the federal government power to get involved in state affairs to protect African Americans' rights. It also granted citizenship to African Americans. This act was meant to counter the Supreme Court decision in the 1857 case *Dred Scott v. Sandford*. The Supreme Court had ruled that African Americans were not citizens.

President Johnson vetoed both bills. He claimed that the federal government was exceeding its authority. Johnson also argued that both bills were unconstitutional. He reasoned that they had been passed by a Congress that did not include representatives from all the states. By raising this issue, he was warning that he would veto any law passed by a Congress in which the South was not represented.

Republicans in Congress were able to **override,** or defeat, both vetoes, and the bills became law. Radical Republicans began to see that Congress and Johnson would not be able to work together on Reconstruction. They gave up hope of compromising with the president and began to create their own plan for dealing with the South.

The Fourteenth Amendment

Congress did worry that the courts might overturn the Civil Rights Act. It proposed another amendment to the Constitution, which the states ratified in 1868. The Thirteenth Amendment had ended slavery. The Fourteenth Amendment took the next step by stating that:

PRIMARY SOURCE

66 All persons born or naturalized in the United States, and subject to the jurisdiction thereof, are citizens of the United States and of the State wherein they reside. 99

—the Fourteenth Amendment

Radical Republicans such as Charles Sumner of Massachusetts were determined not only to rebuild the South but also to remake Southern society.

black codes laws passed in the South just after the Civil War aimed at controlling freed men and women, and allowing plantation owners to take advantage of African American workers
override to reject or defeat something that has already been decided

This language protected the citizenship extended to African Americans by the Civil Rights Act of 1866. It guaranteed that citizenship could not later be taken away by passing another law. The amendment made it clear that if a state barred any adult male citizen from voting, that state could lose some representation in Congress.

Another part of the Fourteenth Amendment said that no state could take a person's life, liberty, or property "without due process of law." It stated that every person was entitled to "equal protection of the laws." It also **excluded** former Confederate leaders from holding any national or state office unless Congress had pardoned them.

Some people considered amending the Constitution to protect African Americans to be an extreme measure. Increasing violence toward African Americans across the South convinced moderate Republicans that an amendment was necessary. Congress required that the Southern states ratify the Fourteenth Amendment as another condition of rejoining the Union. Because most refused to do so at first, this delayed the amendment's ratification until 1868.

☑ **PROGRESS CHECK**

Defining Identify two key features of the Civil Rights Act of 1866.

North Wind Picture Archives

White mobs killed nearly 50 African Americans and burned their homes, churches, and schools in Memphis, Tennessee, in May 1866. Reactions to such violence helped Republicans win an overwhelming victory in the 1866 elections.

▶ **CRITICAL THINKING**
Making Connections Why would such violent acts have helped Republicans win elections?

Reading **HELP**DESK CCSS

Academic Vocabulary

exclude to prevent from being involved in something

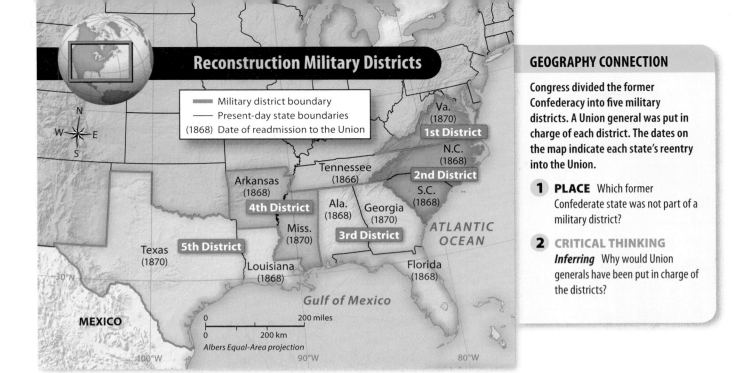

Reconstruction Military Districts

Legend:
- Military district boundary
- Present-day state boundaries
- (1868) Date of readmission to the Union

Va. (1870) — 1st District
N.C. (1868) — 2nd District
S.C. (1868)
Tennessee (1866)
Arkansas (1868) — 4th District
Ala. (1868)
Georgia (1870) — 3rd District
Miss. (1870)
Texas (1870) — 5th District
Louisiana (1868)
Florida (1868)

ATLANTIC OCEAN

Gulf of Mexico

MEXICO

0 — 200 miles
0 — 200 km
Albers Equal-Area projection

N W E S
30°N
100°W 90°W 80°W

GEOGRAPHY CONNECTION

Congress divided the former Confederacy into five military districts. A Union general was put in charge of each district. The dates on the map indicate each state's reentry into the Union.

1 **PLACE** Which former Confederate state was not part of a military district?

2 **CRITICAL THINKING** *Inferring* Why would Union generals have been put in charge of the districts?

Radical Republicans in Charge

GUIDING QUESTION *What elements were included in the Radical Republican idea of Reconstruction?*

President Johnson campaigned against the Radical Republicans in the congressional elections of 1866. He attacked the Fourteenth Amendment and made it a major issue in the campaign. Many Northerners disliked Johnson's tone. Some feared the clashes between whites and African Americans that were taking place in the South. Voters rejected Johnson's views, and the Republicans won an overwhelming majority in Congress. This meant that Johnson could no longer prevent them from overriding his vetoes. A period known as Radical Reconstruction began.

The Reconstruction Acts

By 1867, 10 of the former Confederate states had not ratified the Fourteenth Amendment. In response, Congress passed the First Reconstruction Act. This law required that those states form new governments. Only Tennessee, which had ratified the amendment, kept its government and rejoined the Union.

The act divided the 10 defiant states into five military districts. Each district would be governed by an army general until new state governments were formed. Former Confederate leaders were banned from serving in these new governments. Each state also had to submit a new state constitution to Congress for approval. Finally, the act guaranteed African American men the right to vote in state elections. A Second Reconstruction Act empowered the army to register voters in each district and to help organize state constitutional conventions.

Many white Southerners refused to take part in the elections for constitutional conventions and new state governments. Thousands of newly registered African Americans did cast ballots. These developments favored the Republicans, who took control of Southern state governments. By 1868, Alabama, Arkansas, Florida, Georgia, Louisiana, North Carolina, and South Carolina had set up new governments, ratified the Fourteenth Amendment, and rejoined the Union. By 1870, the remaining three states—Mississippi, Virginia, and Texas—had also been readmitted.

Impeaching the President

The Constitution makes the president the commander in chief of the military. This gave President Johnson control over the military governors created by the First Reconstruction Act.

This ticket entitled the holder to attend the impeachment trial of President Johnson.

▶ **CRITICAL THINKING**
Speculating Why might Johnson's conviction and removal have weakened the office of president?

Because Johnson strongly opposed the Reconstruction Acts, Congress passed a series of laws to limit his power. One of these laws was the Tenure of Office Act. This law stated that the president could not remove government officials, including members of his own cabinet, without the Senate's approval. Congress wanted to protect Secretary of War Edwin Stanton. Stanton was the cabinet official in charge of the military and a supporter of Radical Reconstruction.

Tensions between Johnson and the Radical Republicans continued to grow. In August 1867, while Congress was not in session, Johnson **suspended** Stanton—temporarily stopped him from working—without the Senate's approval. When the Senate met again, it refused to approve the suspension. Johnson then fired Stanton. This action deliberately violated the Tenure of Office Act. Johnson also appointed people the Radical Republicans opposed to command some of the military districts in the South.

The House of Representatives voted to **impeach** (ihm· PEECH) President Johnson—that is, formally charge him with wrongdoing. In 1868 the case went to the Senate for a trial. The trial lasted almost three months. Johnson's defenders claimed that the president had exercised his right to challenge laws he considered unconstitutional. They argued that the House had impeached Johnson for political reasons. Johnson's critics said that Congress had supreme power to make the laws and that Johnson's use of the veto interfered with that power.

North Wind Picture Archives

Reading **HELP**DESK CCSS

impeach to formally charge a public official with misconduct in office

Academic Vocabulary
suspend to stop temporarily

The Senate did not get the two-thirds majority it needed to convict President Johnson. Some moderate Republicans supported the president, arguing that he should not be removed from office for political reasons. As a result, Johnson remained president until Lincoln's second term ended in 1869. During that time, President Johnson did little to interfere with Congress's Reconstruction plans.

The Fifteenth Amendment

Most Southern states had rejoined the Union by the time the presidential election of 1868 drew near. Most Americans hoped that the turbulent period of Reconstruction was over. The Republican Party rejected Johnson and instead nominated Civil War hero Ulysses S. Grant. The Democrats chose New York governor Horatio Seymour as their candidate. Most African American voters supported Grant, and he won the presidency. The election results also showed that voters continued to support Radical Reconstruction.

Congress took one more major step in Reconstruction in 1869 when it proposed the Fifteenth Amendment. This amendment guaranteed that state and federal governments could not deny the right to vote to any male citizen because of "race, color, or previous condition of servitude."

When the states ratified the Fifteenth Amendment in 1870, Republicans thought their job was largely done. They believed that they had succeeded in giving African American men the right to vote. They also thought the power of the vote would allow African Americans to better protect themselves against unfair treatment by white people. Both beliefs would prove to be too optimistic.

☑ **PROGRESS CHECK**

Describing How did Congress organize the South during Reconstruction?

LESSON 2 REVIEW (CCSS)

Review Vocabulary

1. Define each of the following terms, then use each term in a sentence.

   a. suspend   **b.** impeach   **c.** override

Answer the Guiding Questions

2. *Describing* What threats did African Americans continue to face in the South, and what measures did Congress take to deal with these threats?

3. *Analyzing* What measures did the Radical Republicans take to make Reconstruction harder for the white South?

4. **ARGUMENT** Assume the role of President Andrew Johnson. Write a short speech to give at your trial, explaining why senators should not convict you of wrongdoing.

netw⊙rks

There's More Online!

☑ **CHART/GRAPH**
  • Illiteracy Rates
  • African Americans in Congress

☑ **GRAPHIC ORGANIZER**
  Improvements in Education

Lesson 3
The South During Reconstruction

(l) Library of Congress/3b49620,
(c & r) The Granger Collection, NYC

ESSENTIAL QUESTION *How do new ideas change the way people live?*

IT MATTERS BECAUSE
Reconstruction brought significant—but not necessarily lasting—change to the South.

Republicans in Charge

GUIDING QUESTION *How were African Americans discouraged from participating in civic life in the South?*

Republicans controlled Southern politics during the Reconstruction period. Groups in charge of state governments supported the Republican Party. These groups included African Americans, some white Southerners, and white newcomers from the North.

African Americans in Government

Though they had fewer rights than white Southerners, African Americans greatly influenced Southern politics. During Reconstruction, African Americans played important roles as voters and as elected officials. In some states their votes helped produce victories for Republican candidates—including African American candidates. For a short time, African Americans held the majority in the lower house of the South Carolina legislature. Overall, the number of African Americans holding top positions in most Southern states during Reconstruction was small. African Americans did not control any state government. At the national level, 16 African Americans served in the House of Representatives and 2 served in the Senate between 1869 and 1880.

Reading **HELP**DESK (CCSS)

Taking Notes: *Classifying*

As you read, use a diagram like the one shown here to describe improvements in the education of African Americans in the South during Reconstruction.

Improvements in Education

Content Vocabulary
• **scalawag**   • **sharecropping**
• **corruption**
• **integrate**

At the center of this picture of leading Reconstruction politicians is Frederick Douglass. Beside him are Hiram Revels (right), who in 1870 became the first African American elected to the United States Senate, and Blanche K. Bruce, who became the first African American to serve a full term in the Senate.

▶ CRITICAL THINKING
Making Inferences Why do you think Douglass appears at the center of this picture?

Carpetbaggers and Scalawags

Some Southern whites supported the Republican Party. These were often pro-Union business leaders and farmers who had not owned enslaved people. Former Confederates who held resentment against those who had been pro-Union called these people **scalawags** (SKA•lih•wagz), a term meaning "scoundrel" or "worthless rascal."

Republicans also had the support of many Northern whites who moved to the South after the war. White Southerners called these Northerners carpetbaggers. The term referred to cheap suitcases made of carpet fabric—what white Southerners might have thought untrustworthy newcomers might carry. White Southerners were suspicious of the Northerners' intentions. Some carpetbaggers were dishonest people looking to take advantage of the South's difficulties, but most were not. Many sincerely wanted to help rebuild the South.

White Southerners accused Reconstruction governments of **corruption** (kuh•RUHP•shuhn)—dishonest or illegal actions. Some officials did make money illegally. Yet there is no evidence that corruption in the South was greater than in the North.

Library of Congress/3b49620

scalawag name given by former Confederates to Southern whites who supported Republican Reconstruction of the South
corruption dishonest or illegal actions

Build Vocabulary: *Word Origins*

Today the term *carpetbagger* is used to criticize candidates who run for office in a place where they have not lived for long.

This picture shows a school for African American children in Charleston, South Carolina.

Resistance to Reconstruction

Life during Reconstruction was difficult for African Americans. Most Southern whites did not want African Americans to have more rights. White landowners often refused to rent land to freed people. Store owners refused them **credit.** Many employers would not hire them. Many of the jobs available to African Americans were those that whites were unwilling to do.

A more serious danger to the freed people in the South was secret societies such as the Ku Klux Klan. These groups used fear and violence to deny rights to freed men and women. Disguising themselves in white sheets and hoods, Klan members threatened, beat, and killed thousands of African Americans and the whites who supported them. Klan members burned African American homes, schools, and churches. Many Democrats, planters, and other white Southerners supported the Klan. Some saw violence as a way to oppose Republican rule.

In 1870 and 1871, Congress passed several laws to try to stop the growing Klan violence. These laws were not always effective. White Southerners often refused to testify against those in their own communities who attacked African Americans and their white supporters.

✔ PROGRESS CHECK

Explaining Why did many Southerners resent scalawags and carpetbaggers?

The Granger Collection, NYC

Reading **HELP**DESK **CCSS**

integrate to unite, or to blend into a united whole
sharecropping system of farming in which a farmer works land for an owner who provides equipment and seeds and receives a share of the crop

Academic Vocabulary

credit a loan, or the ability to pay for a good or service at a future time rather than at the time of purchase
academy a school or college for special training

Education and Farming

GUIDING QUESTION *What were some improvements and some limitations for African Americans?*

During the early days of Reconstruction, African Americans built their own schools. Many Northerners came south to teach. In the 1870s, Reconstruction governments created public schools for both races. Soon about 50 percent of white children and 40 percent of African American children attended school in the South.

African Americans also made gains in higher education. Northerners set up **academies** in the South. These academies grew into a network of colleges and universities for African Americans.

African American and white students usually went to different schools. Few states had laws requiring schools to be **integrated** (IHN•tuh•grayt•uhd). Schools that are integrated have both white and African American students. Often, integration laws were not enforced.

In addition to education, freed people wanted farmland. Having their own land would enable them to support their families. Some African Americans bought land with the help of the Freedmen's Bank. Many freed people, however, had no choice but to farm on land owned by whites.

In the **sharecropping** (SHEHR•krah•peeng) system, landowners rented land to sharecroppers, or farmers. Sharecroppers gave a percentage of their crops to the landowner. Landowners often demanded an unfairly large percentage that left sharecroppers with almost nothing to support themselves. For many, sharecropping was little better than slavery.

✓ **PROGRESS CHECK**

Describing How did sharecroppers get land to farm?

LESSON 3 REVIEW

Review Vocabulary

1. Use the following terms in sentences that illustrate the meaning of these terms.

   a. integrate   **b.** sharecropping

2. How are the terms *corruption* and *scalawag* connected?

Answer the Guiding Questions

3. ***Explaining*** In what ways was life during Reconstruction difficult for African Americans?

4. ***Describing*** How did education improve in the South during Reconstruction?

5. **INFORMATIVE/EXPLANATORY** Charlotte Forten was an African American who moved from the North to teach freed children in South Carolina. Of her students, she wrote, "The long, dark night of the Past, with all its sorrows and its fears, was forgotten; and for the Future—the eyes of these freed children see no clouds in it." Write an explanation of what you think Forten meant.

netw⊙rks

There's More Online!

☑ **GRAPHIC ORGANIZER**
The New South

☑ **MAP** Election of 1876

☑ **PRIMARY SOURCE**
Sharecropper Contract

☑ **SLIDE SHOW**
Southern Textile Industry

Lesson 4
The Post-Reconstruction Era

ESSENTIAL QUESTION *How do new ideas change the way people live?*

IT MATTERS BECAUSE

After Reconstruction, a "New South" emerged, but African Americans steadily lost freedoms.

Reconstruction Ends

GUIDING QUESTION *How did Democrats regain control of Southern governments?*

As a general, Ulysses S. Grant had led the North to victory in the Civil War. His reputation as a war hero carried him into the White House in the election of 1868 and to reelection in 1872. Unfortunately, Grant had little experience in politics.

Scandal and corruption plagued Grant's presidency. In addition, a severe economic depression began during his second term. A crisis arose when a powerful banking firm declared bankruptcy. This triggered a wave of fear known as the Panic of 1873. It set off a depression that lasted much of the decade.

The depression and the scandals in the Grant administration hurt the Republican Party. In the 1874 congressional elections, the Democrats won back control of the House of Representatives. Democrats also made gains in the Senate. These changes cost the Radical Republicans much of their power.

Meanwhile, Southern Democrats worked hard to regain control of their state governments. They got help from groups such as the Ku Klux Klan, which terrorized African Americans and other Republican voters. The Democrats who came to power in the South called themselves "redeemers." They claimed to have redeemed, or saved, their states from "black Republican" rule.

(c & r) The Granger Collection, NYC

Reading **HELP**DESK ⓒⒸⓈⓈ

Taking Notes: *Summarizing*

As you read, use a diagram like this one to summarize the main ideas about the New South.

```
        The New South
       /            \
  Goal for        Goal for
  Industry:       Agriculture:
```

Content Vocabulary

- **poll tax**
- **literacy test**
- **grandfather clause**
- **segregation**
- **lynching**

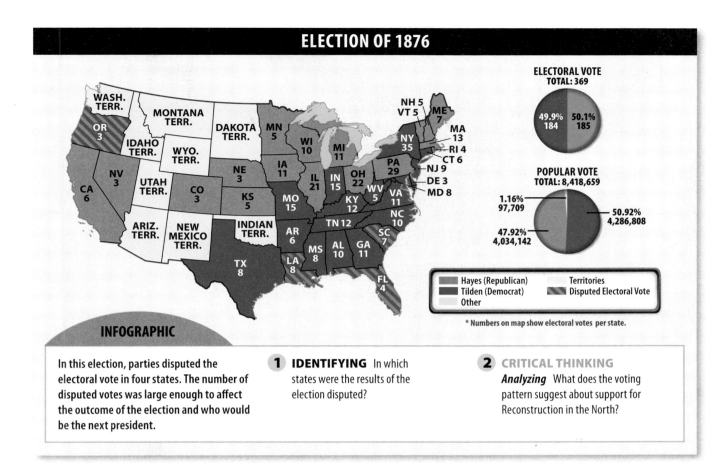

ELECTION OF 1876

ELECTORAL VOTE
TOTAL: 369

49.9% 184 | 50.1% 185

POPULAR VOTE
TOTAL: 8,418,659

1.16% 97,709
50.92% 4,286,808
47.92% 4,034,142

Hayes (Republican)
Tilden (Democrat)
Other
Territories
Disputed Electoral Vote

* Numbers on map show electoral votes per state.

INFOGRAPHIC

In this election, parties disputed the electoral vote in four states. The number of disputed votes was large enough to affect the outcome of the election and who would be the next president.

1 IDENTIFYING In which states were the results of the election disputed?

2 CRITICAL THINKING
Analyzing What does the voting pattern suggest about support for Reconstruction in the North?

The Election of 1876

Republicans attempted to keep control of the White House by choosing Ohio Governor Rutherford B. Hayes as their candidate for president in 1876. Hayes held moderate views on Reconstruction. Republicans hoped he would appeal to voters in both the North and the South.

Hayes ran against Democrat Samuel Tilden, the governor of New York, in a very close election. Neither got a majority of the electoral votes, mainly because of confusing election returns from three Southern states. These states—Florida, South Carolina, and Louisiana—were still under Republican rule. Republicans insisted that many voters in these states favored Hayes, but their votes had not been counted. Congress named a **commission** to decide which candidate should receive the disputed electoral votes. The commission recommended giving them all to Hayes. Doing this would make Hayes president by one electoral vote.

Connections to
TODAY

The Election of 2000

A voting dispute in Florida also affected the 2000 presidential election. An extremely close vote count led to a bitter dispute between Republican George W. Bush and Democrat Al Gore over whether and how to recount the ballots. The dispute kept either party from gaining enough electoral votes to win the election. This time, a U.S. Supreme Court ruling helped make Bush the winner and president.

Academic Vocabulary

commission a group of officials chosen for a specific responsibility

INDUSTRY IN THE NEW SOUTH

Before the Civil War, the backbone of the Southern economy was agriculture. It remained so through the rest of the nineteenth century, though industry in the region made dramatic gains.

1 CALCULATING About how many more manufacturing establishments did Florida have in 1900 than in 1860?

2 CRITICAL THINKING
Analyzing Which two Southern states experienced the greatest growth in manufacturing between 1860 and 1900? Explain.

MANUFACTURING IN THE SOUTHERN STATES 1860–1900*			
State	**1860**	**1880**	**1900**
Alabama	1,459	2,070	5,602
Arkansas	518	1,202	4,794
Florida	185	426	2,056
Georgia	1,890	3,593	7,504
Louisiana	1,744	1,553	4,350
Mississippi	976	1,479	4,772
North Carolina	3,689	3,802	7,226
South Carolina	1,230	2,078	3,762
Tennessee	2,572	4,326	8,016
Texas	983	2,996	12,289
TOTAL	**15,246**	**23,525**	**60,371**

*Number of manufacturing establishments

To ensure that Congress accepted this **outcome,** Republicans made many promises to the Democrats. One of these was a pledge to withdraw the troops who had been stationed in the South since the end of the Civil War. Shortly after Hayes took office in 1877, the last troops left the South.

Rise of the "New South"

By the 1880s, forward-looking Southerners were convinced that their region must develop an industrial economy. They argued that the South had lost the Civil War because its industry did not match the North's. Atlanta newspaper editor Henry Grady headed a group that urged Southerners to "out-Yankee the Yankees" and build a "New South." This "New South" would have industries based on the region's coal, iron, tobacco, cotton, and lumber resources. Southerners would create this new economy by embracing a spirit of hard work and regional pride.

Southern industry made great gains in the 1880s. Textile mills sprang up across the region. The American Tobacco Company, developed largely by James Duke of North Carolina, came to control nearly all of the tobacco manufacturing in the country. By 1890, the South produced nearly 20 percent of the nation's

Reading HELPDESK CCSS

poll tax a tax a person must pay in order to vote

Academic Vocabulary

outcome the effect or result of an action or event

iron and steel. Much of the industry was in Alabama, near deposits of iron ore. In Florida, port cities Jacksonville and Pensacola prospered because of strong demand for lumber and other products.

The South possessed a cheap and reliable supply of labor. A railroad-building boom also helped development. By 1870, the railroad system, destroyed by the war, was nearly rebuilt. Between 1880 and 1890, track mileage more than doubled.

The New South's Rural Economy

In spite of these gains, the South did not develop an industrial economy as strong as the North's. Agriculture remained the South's main economic activity.

Supporters of the New South hoped to promote small, profitable farms that grew a variety of crops instead of relying on cotton. A different economy emerged, however. Many landowners held on to their large estates. When estates were divided, much of the land went to sharecropping and tenant farming. Neither of these activities was profitable.

Debt also caused problems. Poor farmers used credit to buy supplies. Merchants who provided credit also charged high prices, and farmers' debts rose. To repay debts, farmers turned to cash crops. As in the past, the main cash crop was cotton. Higher cotton production drove cotton prices down. Lower prices led farmers to plant even more cotton. The growth of sharecropping and the heavy reliance on a single cash crop helped prevent improvements in the conditions of Southern farmers.

By 1880, a third of the South's farmers were sharecroppers or tenant farmers, systems that helped keep African Americans in a condition not much better than slavery.

 PROGRESS CHECK

Describing Why did Southern industry grow in the late 1800s?

A Divided Society

GUIDING QUESTION *Why did freedom for African Americans become a distant dream after Reconstruction ended?*

As Reconstruction ended, African Americans' dreams for justice faded. Laws passed by the redeemer governments denied Southern African Americans many of their newly won rights.

Voting Restrictions

The Fifteenth Amendment barred a state from denying someone the right to vote because of race. White Southern leaders found ways to get around the amendment. One way was by requiring a **poll tax,** a fee required for voting. Many African Americans could not afford to pay the tax, so they could not vote.

After Reconstruction, white Southern leaders used a variety of means to deny African Americans their right to vote.

Another means of denying voting rights was the **literacy test** (LIH•tuh•ruh•see TEHST). This approach required potential voters to read and explain difficult parts of state constitutions or the federal Constitution. Because most Southern African Americans had little education, literacy tests prevented many from voting.

Both poll taxes and literacy tests also kept some whites from voting. To prevent this, some states passed **grandfather clauses** (GRAND•fah•thuhr KLAHZ•ihz). These laws allowed people to vote if their fathers or grandfathers had voted before Reconstruction. Because African Americans could not vote until 1867, they were excluded. Such laws and the constant threat of violence caused African American voting to decline sharply.

Jim Crow Laws

By the late 1800s, segregation had also become common across the South. **Segregation** (seh•grih•GAY•shuhn) is separation of the races. Southern states passed so-called Jim Crow laws that required African Americans and whites to be separated in almost every public place. In 1896 the Supreme Court upheld segregation laws in *Plessy* v. *Ferguson*. The case involved a Louisiana law that required separate sections on trains for African Americans and whites. The Court ruled that segregation was legal as long as African Americans had access to public places equal to those of whites.

In practice, the separate facilities for African Americans were far from equal. Southern states spent much more money on schools and other facilities for whites than on those for African Americans. Still, this "separate but equal" doctrine gave legal support to segregation for more than 50 years.

Violence against African Americans also rose. One form of violence was **lynching** (LIHN•cheeng), in which angry mobs killed people by hanging them. Some African Americans were lynched because they were suspected of crimes—others because they did not act as whites thought they should.

The Granger Collection, NYC

Reading **HELP**DESK

literacy test a method used to prevent African Americans from voting by requiring prospective voters to read and write at a specified level

grandfather clause a device that allowed persons to vote if their fathers or grandfathers had voted before Reconstruction began

segregation the separation or isolation of a race, class, or group
lynching putting to death by the illegal action of a mob

Exodusters and Buffalo Soldiers

Formerly enslaved people began to leave the South during Reconstruction. They called themselves "Exodusters." This name came from the biblical book of Exodus, which describes the Israelites' escape from slavery in Egypt.

During the exodus of the 1870s, more than 20,000 African Americans migrated to Kansas. They hoped their journey would take them far from the poverty that they experienced in the South. Other African Americans escaped the South by becoming soldiers. They served in segregated army units and fought in the western Indian Wars from 1867 until 1896. According to legend, the men were called "buffalo soldiers" by the Apache and Cheyenne. The soldiers adopted the name as a sign of honor and respect. Units of Buffalo Soldiers answered the nation's call to arms not only in the West, but also in Cuba, the Philippines, Hawaii, and Mexico.

Reconstruction's Impact

Reconstruction was a success in some ways and a failure in others. It helped the South rebuild its economy. Yet much of the South remained agricultural and economically poor. African Americans gained greater equality and shared power in government, but their advances did not last. In the words of the great African American writer and civil rights leader W.E.B. Du Bois, "The slave went free; stood a brief moment in the sun; then moved back again toward slavery." Yet the seeds of freedom and equality had been planted. For a long time, African Americans struggled to gain their full rights.

✔ PROGRESS CHECK

Explaining What were Jim Crow laws?

LESSON 4 REVIEW

Review Vocabulary

1. Explain the meaning of the terms by using them in a sentence.

   a. literacy test   b. poll tax

2. What was the purpose of grandfather clauses?

Answer the Guiding Questions

3. *Describing* In what ways was the economy of the New South different from—and similar to—the economy of the past?

4. *Summarizing* How did Democrats regain control of Southern governments from the Republican Party?

5. *Explaining* Why did freedom for African Americans become a distant dream after Reconstruction ended?

6. **INFORMATIVE/EXPLANATORY** How did the South after Reconstruction compare to the South before the Civil War? Write a paragraph that answers this question.

Write your answers on a separate piece of paper.

1 Exploring the Essential Question

INFORMATIVE/EXPLANATORY Would Reconstruction have taken a different course if Lincoln had not been assassinated? Write an essay to explain your answer.

2 21st Century Skills

INFORMATION LITERACY Review this chapter and draw a time line of key events during Reconstruction. Identify the event that you think had the most impact and write a short essay justifying your choice.

3 Thinking Like a Historian

MAKING COMPARISONS How were poll taxes and literacy tests similar? How were they different?

4 Visual Literacy

ANALYZING PHOTOGRAPHS Look at the image of workers processing tobacco. Write a caption for the image that explains what is happening and how it reflects the new realities of the post-Civil War South.

CORBIS

REVIEW THE GUIDING QUESTIONS

Choose the best answer for each question.

1 Which was a reason that Northern leaders disagreed over the South rejoining the Union?
A. Some leaders wanted the South to pay for damage done during the Civil War.
B. Some leaders wanted harsher treatment of the South for leaving the Union.
C. Some leaders wanted to keep slavery legal in the South.
D. Some leaders felt that allowing Southern states back into the Union would delay westward expansion.

2 Which of the following protected the rights of African Americans in the South?
F. the Civil Rights Act of 1866
G. black codes
H. Jim Crow laws
I. sharecropping and tenant farming

3 Which of the following was a method used by state governments to prevent African Americans from voting?
A. the Ten Percent Plan
B. the Wade-Davis bill
C. the Freedmen's Bureau
D. literacy tests

4 Which of the following brought major improvement to the lives of African Americans in the South?
F. sharecropping
G. the Fourteenth Amendment
H. segregation laws
I. redeemer governments

5 How did the scandals surrounding the Grant administration and the Panic of 1873 affect politics in the United States?
A. Democrats regained control of Southern governments.
B. Republicans retained control of Southern governments.
C. President Grant was impeached.
D. Jim Crow laws were enforced.

6 For many African Americans in the South, sharecropping was
F. forbidden to them.
G. highly profitable.
H. more desirable that factory work.
I. not much better than slavery.

DBQ ANALYZING DOCUMENTS

The following are examples of Jim Crow laws in the South.

"The schools for white children and the schools for negro children shall be conducted separately." (Florida)

"Books shall not be interchangeable between the white and colored schools, but shall continue to be used by the race first using them." (North Carolina)

—Martin Luther King, Jr., National Historic Site

7 **Specifying** Which statement best represents the purpose of these laws?

A. The laws forced separation of the races.

B. The laws denied African Americans any access to schools.

C. The laws required inferior facilities for African Americans.

D. The laws made it difficult for African Americans to get an education.

8 **Analyzing** Which of the following was an effect of the North Carolina law?

F. African American schools were not permitted to have textbooks.

G. White schools could not give textbooks to African American schools.

H. Only white schools received new textbooks.

I. No money was set aside to buy textbooks for African American schools.

SHORT RESPONSE

"I have confidence … in the endurance, capacity and destiny of my people [African Americans]. We will … seek our places, sometimes in the field of letters, arts, science and the professions. More frequently mechanical pursuits will attract and elicit our efforts; more still of my people will find employment … as the cultivators of the soil. The bulk of this people—by surroundings, habits, adaptation, and choice will continue to find their homes in the South. … Whatever our ultimate position in the … republic … we will not forget our instincts for freedom nor our love for country."

—Senator Blanche K. Bruce, from a speech in 1876

9 How did Bruce expect most African Americans to earn a living?

10 According to Bruce, how did African Americans feel about their country?

EXTENDED RESPONSE

11 **Informative/Explanatory** What do you think was Reconstruction's greatest success? What was its greatest failure? Explain your answer.

Need Extra Help?

If You've Missed Question	1	2	3	4	5	6	7	8	9	10	11
Review Lesson	1	2	4	2	4	3	4	4	3	3	1-4

Opening the West

1858–1896

ESSENTIAL QUESTIONS • *Why do people make economic choices?*
• *How does geography influence the way people live?* • *Why does conflict develop?*
• *How do governments change?*

The Story Matters . . .

His eyes look out at the land of his parents and his parents' parents. This place has been good to his people. It has provided good hunting and all the things they need to live.

Now strangers have come. They act as though the land is theirs. At first, he hoped the strangers would leave without a fight. Then he saw them building farms, ranches, and towns on the land where the buffalo had run free. He knows now that these strangers have come to the West to stay—and that his people's future is uncertain.

In the years to come, Native Americans will face many challenges, as settlers, mining, ranching, and railroads change the West forever.

◄ *Chief Geronimo led the Apache people.*

PoodlesRock/Corbis

Place and Time: American West 1858 to 1896

In the last half of the 1800s, American settlement continued its spread into the western United States. Settlers moved onto the Great Plains and beyond. Much like earlier groups of American migrants, they came into conflict with Native Americans who called these lands their home.

Step Into the Place

MAP FOCUS The map shows the extent of territory occupied by Native American groups of the West in the late 1800s.

1 REGION Which part of the West was already largely without Native American settlement in 1860?

2 PLACE In which territory or state is the largest amount of Native American land in 1890?

3 CRITICAL THINKING
Describing How would you describe what happens to the territory occupied by Native American groups over this time period?

Red Cloud and other Sioux chiefs met with American officials in 1868 at Fort Laramie, Wyoming. They signed a treaty granting Native Americans land exclusively for their use—an agreement that was later broken.

Buffalo were the main source of food, clothing, and building materials for the Native Americans of the Great Plains. Railroad companies hired hunters to kill the animals to feed the crews building the tracks. The railroads even offered hunting trips to shoot the buffalo for sport.

Step Into the Time

TIME LINE Look at the time line. Which event do you think had the greatest impact on the settlement of the West? Explain your answer.

James Buchanan 1857–1861
Abraham Lincoln 1861–1865
A. Johnson 1865–1869
U. S. Grant 1869–1877

U.S. PRESIDENTS
U.S. EVENTS
WORLD EVENTS

1860
1870

1869 First transcontinental railroad completed

1861 Italians establish a united kingdom

1869 Suez Canal opens

1871 Great Chicago Fire destroys most of city

(l and c)The Granger Collection, New York / The Granger Collection, (b) White House Historical Association

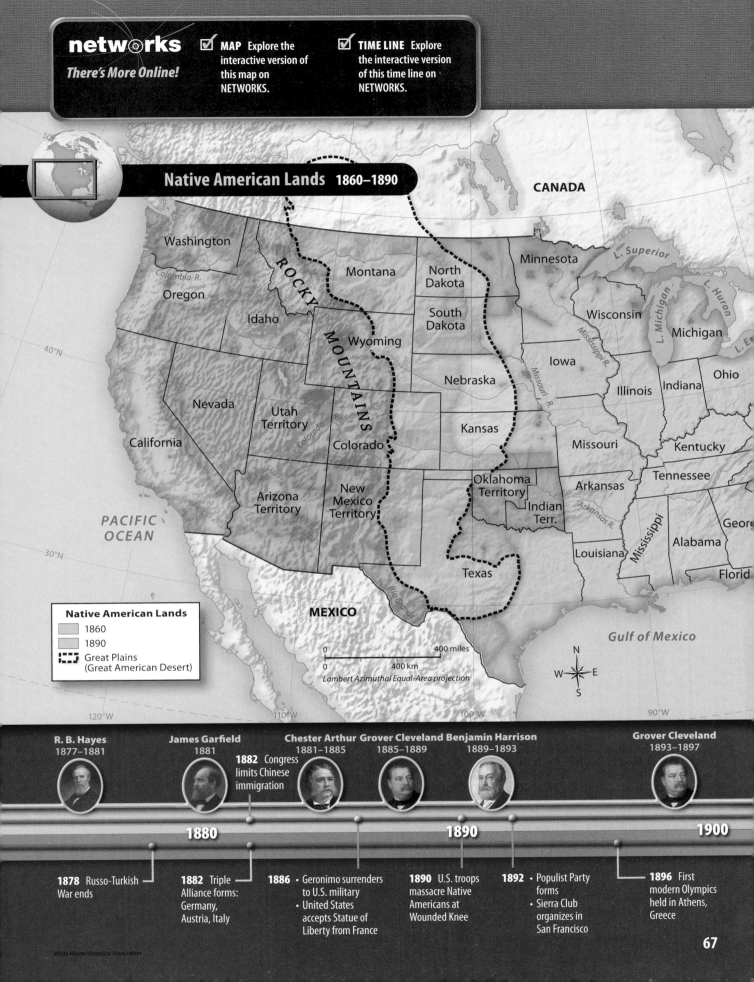

networks
There's More Online!

☑ **MAP** Explore the interactive version of this map on NETWORKS.

☑ **TIME LINE** Explore the interactive version of this time line on NETWORKS.

Native American Lands 1860–1890

CANADA

Washington

Columbia R.

Oregon

ROCKY MOUNTAINS

Montana

North Dakota

South Dakota

Minnesota

L. Superior

Idaho

Wyoming

Wisconsin

L. Michigan

L. Huron

Michigan

40°N

Nevada

Utah Territory

Colorado R.

Colorado

Nebraska

Iowa

Mississippi R.

Missouri R.

Illinois

Indiana

Ohio

California

Kansas

Missouri

Kentucky

PACIFIC OCEAN

30°N

Arizona Territory

New Mexico Territory

Oklahoma Territory

Indian Terr.

Arkansas

Arkansas R.

Tennessee

Mississippi

Louisiana

Alabama

Georg

Florid

Texas

Rio Grande

MEXICO

Gulf of Mexico

0 | 400 miles
0 | 400 km

Lambert Azimuthal Equal-Area projection

N W E S

Native American Lands
- 1860
- 1890
- ▪▪▪ Great Plains (Great American Desert)

120°W   110°W   100°W   90°W

R. B. Hayes 1877–1881

James Garfield 1881

1882 Congress limits Chinese immigration

Chester Arthur 1881–1885

Grover Cleveland 1885–1889

Benjamin Harrison 1889–1893

Grover Cleveland 1893–1897

1880

1890

1900

1878 Russo-Turkish War ends

1882 Triple Alliance forms: Germany, Austria, Italy

1886 • Geronimo surrenders to U.S. military
• United States accepts Statue of Liberty from France

1890 U.S. troops massacre Native Americans at Wounded Knee

1892 • Populist Party forms
• Sierra Club organizes in San Francisco

1896 First modern Olympics held in Athens, Greece

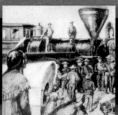

Lesson 1
Mining and Railroads in the West

ESSENTIAL QUESTION *Why do people make economic choices?*

IT MATTERS BECAUSE
Discoveries of gold and silver sent miners flocking to the American West.

Gold, Silver, and Boomtowns

GUIDING QUESTION *How did mining lead to the creation of new states?*

The California Gold Rush was over by the mid-1850s. Yet "gold fever" raged on. Still hoping to strike it rich, disappointed miners began searching other parts of the West for treasure.

In 1858 prospectors—people who seek valuable minerals—found gold at Pikes Peak in the Colorado Rockies. According to newspaper reports, miners there were making $20 a day panning for gold. That was a large **sum** of money at a time when many workers earned less than $1 a day.

By the spring of 1859, about 50,000 prospectors had flocked to the Colorado goldfields. People panned gold dust from streams or scratched gold particles from the ground.

Most of the gold, however, was in the form of ore found deep underground. Ore is a mineral in which the gold or other valuable material is mixed with less-valuable substances. Mining the ore and then **extracting** the gold from it required machinery, workers, and an organized business. A company had a better chance of getting rich from mining gold than an individual did.

Boom and Bust

In 1859 prospectors made an amazing discovery along the Carson River in what is now Nevada. They found one of the world's richest deposits of silver-bearing ore. People called the

Reading **HELP**DESK **CCSS**

Taking Notes: *Determining Cause and Effect*

As you read, use a diagram like this one to identify the effects of the mining booms.

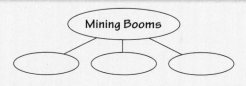

Mining Booms

Content Vocabulary
• **subsidy**
• **transcontinental**
• **time zone**

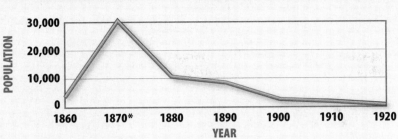

VIRGINIA CITY, NEVADA: BOOMTOWN

POPULATION (y-axis): 0, 10,000, 20,000, 30,000

YEAR (x-axis): 1860, 1870*, 1880, 1890, 1900, 1910, 1920

*Estimate according to various Nevada historical sources   **Source**: Nevada State Library and Archives, 2007.

GRAPH SKILL

After miners discovered gold in the region, Virginia City, Nevada, became one of the largest cities in the West.

1 **SUMMARIZING** How did the population of Virginia City change from 1860 to 1920?

2 **CRITICAL THINKING** *Determining Cause and Effect* What kinds of challenges do you think those population changes might bring for town residents?

discovery the Comstock Lode after Henry Comstock, one of the owners of the claim. A lode is a rich vein of ore. Thousands of mines opened near the Comstock Lode, but only a few were profitable. Several miners and entrepreneurs made fortunes.

Gold and silver strikes created boomtowns—towns that seemed to pop up almost overnight near mining sites. Virginia City, Nevada, was the Comstock boomtown.

Boomtowns were lively, often lawless places. Miners made money quickly, and many spent or gambled it away just as fast. Violence was common because many people carried guns and a lot of cash. Few boomtowns had police or jails, so citizens took the law into their own hands. Vigilantes captured and punished suspected wrongdoers without holding trials or following legal processes.

The population in a boomtown was mostly men. Some women also opened businesses or worked as cooks or entertainers. More often, women founded schools and churches. Despite the promise of prosperity, however, many mining "booms" became "busts." When the ore was gone, people left, and boomtowns became ghost towns.

In 1866 the streets of Virginia City were bustling with activity. Within a few years, much of this crowd would be gone.

(l) Bettmann/CORBIS

Academic Vocabulary

sum total amount
extract to remove or take out with force

Lesson 1   **69**

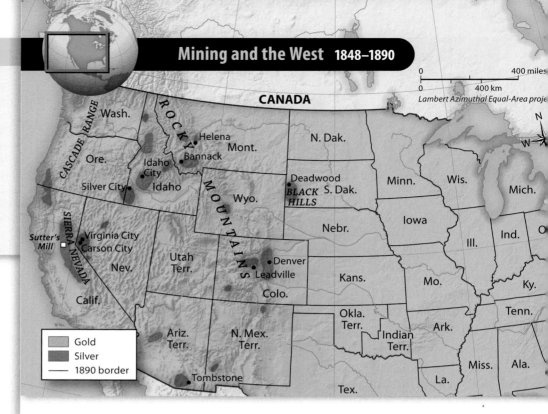

Mining and the West 1848–1890

Mining in the West led to growth in population and the addition of new states and territories.

1 LOCATION Which mineral did people find in the Black Hills? In the area around Tombstone?

2 CRITICAL THINKING
Making Inferences Why do you think Denver became the capital of Colorado?

0 — 400 miles
0 — 400 km
Lambert Azimuthal Equal-Area proje

Gold
Silver
1890 border

Westward Growth

As the gold and silver disappeared, mining for other metals such as copper, lead, and zinc increased. Areas around the mines became more populated. At the same time, thousands of settlers also headed west. They farmed the fertile valleys and started ranches. Others opened businesses in towns to serve the growing populations. By 1890 Colorado, North Dakota, South Dakota, Washington, Montana, Wyoming, and Idaho had become states.

☑ **PROGRESS CHECK**

Explaining Why did many boomtowns turn into ghost towns?

Railroads Connect East and West

GUIDING QUESTION *How did the railroads help the mining industry grow in the West?*

Transportation was vital to the survival of mining communities. Gold, silver, and other metals had little value unless they reached factories, ports, and markets. Similarly, people in western boomtowns needed shipments of supplies. Yet the industrial centers of the East and Midwest were hundreds of miles away.

Reading **HELP**DESK (CCSS)

subsidy money or goods given by a person or government to support a project that benefits the public

transcontinental going across a continent

Wagons and stagecoaches could not move people and goods fast enough, but railroads could. The nation's railroad network grew rapidly between 1865 and 1890. During that time, track length in the United States soared from about 35,000 miles (56,327 km) to more than 150,000 miles (241,402 km).

The Government Helps

To help with high construction costs, the government gave railroad companies large **subsidies** (SUHB·suh·deez)—financial aid and land grants. Leaders knew a rail network connecting East and West would bring important benefits to the entire nation. The federal government granted more than 130 million acres (52,609,180 ha) of land to railroad companies. The government got much of that land by buying it from or making treaties with Native Americans.

Government land grants included land for the tracks plus strips of land, 20 to 80 miles (32 to 129 km) wide, alongside the tracks. Railroad companies sold this land to raise money to pay for construction.

States and local communities also offered subsidies. They did this because their communities might not survive without railroads. Los Angeles, for example, gave the Southern Pacific Railroad money and paid for a passenger terminal to ensure that the company would build its railroad near the town.

Spanning the Continent

In the 1850s, railroad companies began to search for a route for a **transcontinental** rail line—one that would connect the Atlantic and Pacific coasts. Southerners wanted the route to run through the South; Northerners wanted it to go through the North. During the Civil War, the Union government chose a northerly route.

The government offered land grants to companies that were willing to build the transcontinental line. The challenge was enormous—to lay more than 1,700 miles (2,736 km) of track across hot plains, over rivers, and through mountain ranges.

Two companies accepted the challenge. The Central Pacific Company worked eastward from Sacramento, California. The Union Pacific Company laid track westward. It began work in Omaha, Nebraska, at the western edge of the existing American rail network.

Because companies got subsidies for each mile of track built, they each raced to cover as much land as possible. Both companies hired thousands of workers. In general, they received low wages to labor in choking summer heat and icy winter winds.

Most workers for the Central Pacific Railroad were Chinese. They had come a long way across the Pacific in hopes of finding gold. Instead they found dangerous work, a harsh climate, and discrimination.

North Wind Picture Archives

It took nearly six and a half years for the Union Pacific and Central Pacific railroads to connect here at Promontory Summit in Utah Territory.

Four special gold and silver spikes were used for the Promontory Summit ceremony.

They cleared forests, blasted tunnels through mountains, and built tracks across the country. The Union Pacific relied on Irish immigrants and African American workers. Most Central Pacific workers were Chinese immigrants. Central Pacific workers, who covered more difficult terrain, laid 742 miles (1,194 km) of track. Union Pacific workers laid 1,038 miles (1,670 km) of track.

On May 10, 1869, workers completed construction of the transcontinental railroad. A Chinese crew laid the final 10 miles (16 km) of track. The two sets of track met at Promontory Summit in Utah Territory. Leland Stanford, governor of California, drove a final golden spike that joined the tracks. With the final hammer blow, telegraph lines flashed the news across the country: "The last rail is laid! The last spike driven! The Pacific Railroad is completed!"

Effects of the Railroads

By 1883 railroad companies built two more transcontinental lines and dozens of shorter lines. The tracks connected cities in the West with the rest of the nation.

The economic impact was enormous. Trains brought thousands of workers west. Freight cars carried metals and produce east and manufactured goods west. As people laid more train tracks, the need for steel increased. This demand boosted the nation's steel industry. Coal producers, railroad car manufacturers, and construction companies also benefited.

Reading **HELP**DESK (CCSS)

time zone a geographic region in which the same standard time is used

Build Vocabulary: *Word Origins*

The word *promontory* (PRAH • muhn • tawr • ee) means "a high point of land" or "a prominent mass of land overlooking or projecting into a lowland." The word comes from the Latin *promunturium*, meaning "mountain ridge, headland."

Numerous towns sprang up along the rail lines. Some towns, like Denver, Colorado, eventually grew into large cities. Railroads also brought the next wave of settlers to the West—ranchers and farmers.

Railroads even changed how people measured time. Before the 1880s, each community kept its own time based on the sun's position at noon. Clocks in Boston, for example, were 11 minutes ahead of clocks in New York City. These differences in timekeeping could cause scheduling errors and even collisions when two trains traveled on the same track.

To make rail service safer and more reliable, the American Railway Association—a group that included the nation's railroad companies—divided the country into four **time zones** in 1883. All communities within a time zone would have the same time. Each zone was exactly one hour later than the zone to its west. Congress made the time zones official in 1918.

Meanwhile, new technology enabled trains to pull longer and heavier loads. Railroad systems became so efficient that the average cost of shipping one ton (0.91 t) of freight one mile (1.6 km) dropped from two cents in 1860 to three-quarters of a cent in 1900.

The nationwide rail network also helped unite Americans in different regions. Nebraska's *Omaha Daily Republican* newspaper wrote in 1883 that railroads had "made the people of the country homogeneous [alike], breaking through the peculiarities and provincialisms [local ways] which marked separate and unmingling sections." This was a bit of an exaggeration, but it recognized that railroads were changing American society.

THEN

Trains of the past used steam power, but modern trains use fuel-burning engines or electricity for power. Modern trains still run on metal rails, though, not unlike the past.

NOW

▶ **CRITICAL THINKING**
Making Connections How have trains changed over time?

✓ **PROGRESS CHECK**

Determining Cause and Effect How did railroads affect the American economy in the middle to late 1800s?

LESSON 1 REVIEW **CCSS**

Review Vocabulary

1. Write a sentence explaining why the government gave railroads subsidies in the late 1800s.

2. Use the terms *transcontinental* and *time zones* in a short paragraph about railroads.

Answer the Guiding Questions

3. *Describing* What was life like in a boomtown?

4. *Explaining* How did mining in the West help lead to the construction of railroads?

5. *Making Inferences* Why do you think the government chose a northern route for the transcontinental railroad?

6. **NARRATIVE** You are a miner in a boomtown. Write a letter to a friend in Boston describing your new life. Explain why you moved west and whether you think it would be a good idea for your friend to move west to join you.

(t) imagebroker.net/SuperStock, (b) Sankei via Getty Images

netw☉rks

There's More Online!

☑ **GAME**

☑ **GRAPHIC ORGANIZER**
Settlement of the
Great Plains

☑ **MAP** Railroads and Cattle Trails

☑ **PRIMARY SOURCE**
• African American Cowhands
• The Exodusters

☑ **SLIDE SHOW** Land Rushes

Lesson 2

Ranchers and Farmers

ESSENTIAL QUESTION *How does geography influence the way people live?*

IT MATTERS BECAUSE

Americans eager to own land and build homes migrated to the Great Plains, transforming their lives as well as the region.

Cattle on the Plains

GUIDING QUESTION *How did ranchers get their cattle to markets in the North and East?*

When the Spanish first came to Texas in the 1500s, they brought cattle for food. Some of the cattle escaped and survived in the wild. In time, these wild cattle developed into a new, tough breed called longhorns.

By the 1800s, thousands of wild longhorns roamed the Texas plains. At that time, much of Texas was still open range. The land was not fenced or divided into lots. Seeing a good business opportunity, settlers in Texas rounded up the wild longhorns and started ranches.

The Cattle Business

Texas ranchers had plenty of cattle, but their profits were low. Because the supply was high, longhorns sold for only $3 or $4 each in Texas. Yet, in the cities of the North and East, demand for beef was high. Cattle sold there for $40 per head. If Texans could get their cattle to those markets, their profits would be huge.

Trains were the best shipping method, but Texas had no railroads linking it to eastern cities. Then, in the early 1860s, the Missouri Pacific Railroad reached Sedalia, Missouri. Texas ranchers began driving their herds—that is, forcing them to walk—north to Missouri.

(l) Bettmann/CORBIS, (cl) J.N. Templeman/CORBIS, (c) Library of Congress/LC-USZC4-12003, (cr and r) Bettmann/CORBIS

Reading **HELP**DESK **CCSS**

Taking Notes: *Listing*

As you read, use a diagram like this one to list the reasons people settled on the Great Plains.

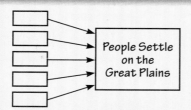
People Settle on the Great Plains

Content Vocabulary
• **long drive**
• **vaquero**
• **homestead**
• **sodbuster**
• **dry farming**

The Long Drives

To reach the railroads **located** in Missouri, and later in Kansas, Nebraska, Colorado, and Wyoming, Texas ranchers had to drive their cattle hundreds of miles. Ranchers called these journeys **long drives.** Most long drives started in spring, when enough grass was growing along the way to feed the cattle. Ranchers followed several trails, such as the Chisholm Trail from central Texas to Abilene, Kansas.

Abilene and other railroad towns that sprouted at the end of cattle trails became known as "cow towns." There, ranchers sold their cattle. Then workers loaded the animals onto trains for shipment east to Chicago and other cities.

Cowhands

Cattle-driving was hard work. An average long drive took two or three months. Cowhands rode all day in all kinds of weather. They faced many dangers, including violent storms and "rustlers" who tried to steal cattle. Another danger was stampedes. These occurred when something frightened the cattle, causing the animals to panic and run. Cowhands had to ride among thousands of pounding hooves to chase down the sprinting cattle and bring the herd under control.

Many cowhands were Civil War veterans or African Americans who moved west in search of a better life. Some were Native Americans. Western cowhands of Hispanic background were known as **vaqueros** (vah·KEHR·ohs). The vaqueros represented a long tradition of ranching in the Spanish Southwest. They introduced many of the riding, roping, and branding skills cowhands used. Vaqueros also brought much of the language of ranching. For example, the word *ranch* comes from the Mexican-Spanish word *rancho.*

The Cattle Kingdom Ends

From the late 1860s to the mid-1880s, more than 5 million Texas cattle moved north on long drives. Many ranchers and traders became rich as cattle prices boomed. The "Cattle Kingdom," however, collapsed even faster than it rose.

The collapse occurred for several reasons. Hoping for more profits, ranchers expanded their herds. The result was overgrazed land and falling prices. Ranchers also lost much of their free grazing land as people began fencing their property.

Born into slavery in Tennessee, Nat Love was one of the many African Americans who made their way West in the years after the Civil War.

Bettmann/CORBIS

---

long drive a trip of several hundred miles on which ranchers led their cattle to railroads and distant markets

vaquero a cowhand of Hispanic origin

Academic Vocabulary

locate to settle at a place; to exist at a place

The cattle industry survived but was changed forever. Meanwhile, another type of economic activity was rising on the Great Plains—farming.

✓ PROGRESS CHECK

Describing How did railroads help the cattle industry grow?

Farmers Settle the Plains

GUIDING QUESTION *What brought more settlers to the Great Plains?*

Early pioneers who reached the Great Plains did not believe the dry, treeless area was good for farming. In fact, most maps labeled the region the "Great American Desert." Still, farmers began settling there in the late 1860s.

Several **factors** brought settlers to the Great Plains. Railroads made the journey west easier and less expensive. New laws offered free land. Finally, new technology and above-average rainfall in the 1870s convinced settlers that they would be able to farm in the region.

The Homestead Act

In 1862 Congress passed the Homestead Act to encourage settlement on the Great Plains. This law gave up to 160 acres (65 ha) of land to any head of a family who paid a $10 filing fee and lived on the land for five years. Later laws increased the amount of land available. The policy brought farmers to the Plains to homestead—earn ownership of land by settling on it.

Lured by land, settlers by the thousands were willing to move west. Some of those settlers were women. Married women could not claim land, but single women and widows could acquire property through the Homestead Act. In Colorado and Wyoming, for example, 12 percent of all those who filed homestead claims were women.

Some homesteaders were African Americans. They, too, were attracted by free land and opportunities for better lives. Many also hoped to escape the segregation and violence that followed Reconstruction. By 1881 more than 40,000 African Americans had migrated to Kansas.

This family was just one of thousands who left the East to homestead on the Great Plains.

▶ CRITICAL THINKING
Speculating What do you think it would be like to live in a house like this one?

J.N. Templeman/Corbis

homestead to earn ownership of land by living on it

Academic Vocabulary

factor a contributing cause

Build Vocabulary: *Word Origins*

Ranch is not the only word we use that comes from Mexican Spanish. For example, the word *stampede* comes from *estampida,* and *lasso* is from *lazo.* How many more English words can you think of that come from Spanish?

Railroads and Cattle Trails 1870s–1880s

Legend:
- Goodnight-Loving Trail
- Western Trail
- Chisholm Trail
- Sedalia Trail
- +++ Railroad

0 200 miles
0 200 km
Lambert Azimuthal Equal-Area projection

GEOGRAPHY CONNECTION

The rise of the cattle industry accompanied the building of railroads across the United States.

1 LOCATION Which trail went through Dodge City?

2 CRITICAL THINKING
Analyzing What advantage might ranchers have had by following the Sedalia Trail?

Legal immigrants could also file homestead claims, and thousands did. Many came from Scandinavia, a region of Northern Europe. Their influence remains strong in the Dakotas today.

Cheap Land

Not all settlers on the Great Plains were homesteaders. Some people bought their land. Railroad companies charged low prices for land. For them, more settlers meant more business.

The railroads promoted the Great Plains as a great place to live with advertisements in the East and in Europe. So did steamship companies, land speculators, and western states and territories. Lured by promises of cheap land, independence, and easy profits, thousands of settlers headed for the Great Plains.

Living on the Great Plains

Life on the Great Plains was not easy for new settlers. The first challenge was building a house. With few trees, not much lumber was available to build homes. There was, however, acre after acre of grass. Many settlers built "soddies." These were houses made of sod—densely packed soil held together by grass roots.

The extreme climate of the Great Plains presented settlers with their greatest challenge. Some years, excessive rainfall caused flooding. Other years brought drought, or less-than-normal amounts of rain. Brushfires swept rapidly, destroying crops, livestock, and homes. Summer might bring clouds of grasshoppers, which could quickly destroy a field of crops.

On April 22, 1889, the Oklahoma land rush officially began. On horseback, in wagons, in buggies, and on foot, thousands of people raced forward to claim land.

Winter was worse. Winds howled, and deep snow could bury animals and trap families in their homes. Farm families had to plan ahead and store food for the winter.

Farming on the Great Plains was a family affair. Men labored in the fields. Women often did the same work, but they also cared for the children, made clothing and candles, and cooked and preserved food. As soon as they were able, children worked on the family farm. This often kept children from attending school.

New Farming Methods

Farmers on the Great Plains had to adapt to the environment and unusual conditions on the plains. Known as **sodbusters,** these farmers developed new farming methods and tools.

Most of the region had little rainfall and few streams for irrigation. To adapt, sodbusters practiced **dry farming.** In this method, farmers took steps to trap the limited moisture in the soil, such as plowing their land after each rainfall. Farmers also dug deep wells and used windmills to pump water from them.

Sodbusters adapted in other ways. To cut through the tough layers of sod, they relied on a new invention—the steel plow. Farmers planted winter wheat, which grows well in dry, harsh climates. Instead of using wood, they used newly invented barbed wire to build fences.

Bettmann/CORBIS

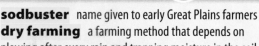

Reading **HELP**DESK **CCSS**

sodbuster name given to early Great Plains farmers
dry farming a farming method that depends on plowing after every rain and trapping moisture in the soil in dry, non-irrigated land

Reading Strategies: *Questioning*

When you read, you might find it helpful to change a heading into a question to find the main idea. Make the heading above a question: *What were the new farming methods?* Now read to find the answer, which is the main idea of the passage.

Even with all these efforts, few family farms produced large crops. The 160-acre (65 ha) grants were too small to support many families. Most farmers needed at least 300 acres (121 ha) and advanced machinery to make a profit. Many farmers went into debt in an effort to keep their farms. Others lost ownership of their farms and had to rent the land.

The Oklahoma Land Rush

By the 1880s, only one large region of the Great Plains remained closed to settlers—Indian Territory in present-day Oklahoma. By law, only Native Americans were allowed to live there. However, one part of Indian Territory was not assigned to any Native American group. After years of pressure from land dealers and settlers, the federal government agreed to open these "unassigned lands" to homesteaders.

On the morning of April 22, 1889, more than 10,000 people lined up on the edges of the unassigned lands. When the signal was given, homesteaders charged across the borders to stake their claims. The eager settlers soon discovered that some people had slipped into the area ahead of time. These "sooners" had already claimed most of the best land. Many legal fights resulted.

Settling the Oklahoma Territory was the last chapter in a great westward push. By 1890 the census showed that there was no longer a region where Americans had not settled. Americans now occupied much of the land between the coasts. Settlement had changed life on the Great Plains, especially for Native Americans.

During the Oklahoma Land Rush, settlers scrambled eagerly to claim lots.

☑ **PROGRESS CHECK**

Identifying What new farming methods and tools did farmers use on the Great Plains?

LESSON 2 REVIEW (CCSS)

Review Vocabulary

1. Use the term *vaquero* in a sentence about a long drive.

2. Explain the meaning of *dry farming* as it relates to sodbusters.

Answer the Guiding Questions

3. ***Describing*** Describe how the era of long drives developed on the Great Plains.

4. ***Determining Cause and Effect*** Why did many early settlers on the Great Plains build sod houses?

5. ***Speculating*** How do you think the Oklahoma land rush of 1889 affected Native Americans?

6. ***Explaining*** Why did many African Americans move to the Great Plains?

7. **ARGUMENT** Design a brochure about the Great Plains in the 1870s that could have persuaded people in other countries to move to the American West.

netw⊙rks
There's More Online!

☑ **BIOGRAPHY**
• Sitting Bull
• Geronimo

☑ **GAME**

☑ **GRAPHIC ORGANIZER**
Government Actions Toward Native Americans

☑ **MAP** Native American Battles and Reservations

☑ **VIDEO**

Lesson 3

Native American Struggles

ESSENTIAL QUESTION *Why does conflict develop?*

IT MATTERS BECAUSE

The increase in white settlers in the West led to conflict with Native American groups living there.

First People of the Plains

GUIDING QUESTION *How did settlement on the Great Plains threaten Native Americans?*

In the mid-1800s, miners, ranchers, and farmers began to settle on the Great Plains. In many places, they competed for land and resources with the Native Americans who already lived there. Conflict with settlers and the government grew as Native Americans tried to preserve their ways of life.

Native American groups had lived on the Great Plains for centuries. Some, like the Omaha and the Osage, lived in communities as farmers and hunters. Most, including the Sioux, the Comanche, and the Blackfoot, were **nomadic.** They moved often and traveled long distances, following huge herds of buffalo—their main source of food, clothing, shelter, and tools.

Despite their differences, the Plains people were similar in many ways. Their nations, sometimes numbering several thousand people, were divided into bands. Each band had a governing council, but most members took part in making decisions. Women raised the children, cooked, and prepared hides. Men hunted, traded, and protected their band. Most Plains people believed in the spiritual power of the natural world.

For most of their history, Native Americans of the Great Plains had millions of buffalo to meet their needs. As American settlers pressed onto the Great Plains, however, the buffalo

Reading HELPDESK (CCSS)

Taking Notes: *Listing*

As you read, record the actions of the U.S. government toward Native Americans in a graphic organizer like this one.

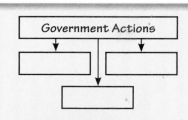

Content Vocabulary
• **nomadic** • **reservation**

population declined steeply. American hunters targeted buffalo to sell the hides in the East. Railroad companies also hired hunters to kill the buffalo to feed the railroad crews and to prevent giant herds from blocking the trains. By the end of the 1800s, only a few hundred buffalo survived.

☑ **PROGRESS CHECK**

Comparing and Contrasting How were the lifestyles of different Plains people similar? How were they different?

Conflict on the Plains

GUIDING QUESTION *Why did conflict start between the Native Americans and whites?*

In 1867 the federal government set up the Indian Peace Commission. Its job was to develop a policy for relations with Native Americans living within U.S. borders. The commission recommended moving all Native Americans to a few large **reservations**—areas of land set aside for them. Moving Native Americans to reservations was not a new policy, but the government now increased its efforts. It gave the army authority to deal forcefully with any groups that refused to move.

BUILDING A TEPEE

Three or four poles were tied together near the top and raised upright. Up to 12 additional poles were leaned against these and also tied at the top.

Where the sides of the tepee cover met, wooden pins acted as a seam. The door flap was also attached with a pin.

Part of the Plains people's nomadic life was the tepee, a tent-like home that could be moved easily. Two women, who were typically responsible for taking care of tepees, could usually raise one in less than an hour. It was made of tanned buffalo skins.

A completed tepee was about 15 feet in diameter.

INFOGRAPHIC

1 **DESCRIBING** What materials did Native Americans use to build their tepees?

2 **CRITICAL THINKING** *Making Connections* How did the construction of their homes reflect the Plains culture?

nomadic moving from place to place in a fixed pattern
reservation an area of land set aside for use by a group

THE DECLINE OF THE BUFFALO

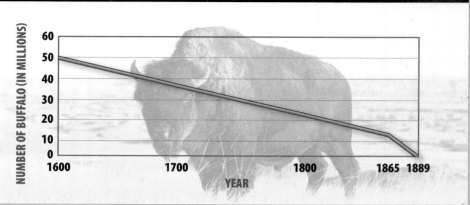

Many Plains groups hunted buffalo for food, clothing, fuel, and shelter.

1 **CALCULATING** According to the graph, how did the buffalo population change between 1800 and 1865?

2 **CRITICAL THINKING**
Predicting How do you think the loss of so many buffalo affected Native Americans?

Life on a Reservation

Congress created the largest reservations on the Great Plains. Indian Territory in present-day Oklahoma was reserved for Native Americans who were relocated from the Southeast in the 1830s. The Sioux, originally from the Great Lakes region, had a large reservation in the Dakota Territory.

The federal Bureau of Indian Affairs managed the reservations. Its agents often used trickery to persuade Native American nations to move to reservations. Native American leaders wanted to **ensure** that their people would be able to farm and hunt. Many reservations, however, were on land that was unfit for farming or hunting. In addition, the government often failed to deliver promised food and supplies. Goods they did deliver were often of poor quality.

At first, many Native Americans agreed to move to reservations. After experiencing the harsh conditions, many wanted to leave their reservations, and some did. Others refused to go at all. To protect their lands and ways of life, many Native Americans believed they needed to fight. The stage was set for conflict.

Conflict Begins

Violent clashes soon broke out between Native Americans and whites. One took place in Minnesota in the summer of 1862. Angry at what they felt were broken promises from the government, Sioux warriors burned and looted the homes of white settlers. Hundreds of people died before U.S. Army troops put down the uprising. The government forced most Sioux to move to reservations in the Dakota Territory.

Eastcott Momatiuk/Getty Images

Reading **HELP**DESK (CCSS)

Academic Vocabulary

ensure to make certain

Reading in the Content Area: *Reading a Diagram*

Diagrams show how something is constructed or how it works. Labels explain what the parts are or what they do. Diagrams provide information to help you better understand the main text. What does the tepee diagram on the previous page show?

Meanwhile, tensions were increasing in Colorado Territory. The miners rushing there in search of gold and silver displaced and angered Native Americans who already lived there. Bands of Cheyenne and Arapaho raided wagon trains and stole cattle and horses from ranches. About 200 settlers were killed. U.S. troops responded with attacks on Native American villages in the territory.

Colorado's territorial governor ordered the Native Americans to surrender at Fort Lyon. He told them they would have food and protection there. In November 1864, Chief Black Kettle and several hundred Cheyenne went to the fort to negotiate a peace treaty. They camped nearby at Sand Creek. Colonel John Chivington and his troops, on their way to the fort, attacked the unsuspecting Cheyenne. Fourteen U.S. soldiers and hundreds of Cheyenne died in what became known as the Sand Creek Massacre.

Cheyenne retaliation was swift and widespread. Finally, in October 1865, some of the Cheyenne and Arapaho leaders agreed to stop the fighting.

Other Native American groups, however, continued to fight. Having already been forced from Minnesota, the Sioux were alarmed when the U.S. Army began building forts along the Bozeman Trail. This trail to Montana's gold mines went through Sioux country. Led by Red Cloud, the Sioux launched a series of attacks on the forts. One of the bloodiest occurred on December 21, 1866. The Sioux trapped and killed 80 U.S. soldiers in what became known as Fetterman's Massacre.

Little Bighorn

An 1868 treaty was supposed to bring peace with the Sioux. Yet more conflict erupted, this time over white settlement of the Black Hills in the Dakotas. The U.S. government had promised the Sioux that "no white person or persons shall be permitted" to settle in the Black Hills. Then, rumors that the hills held gold brought many white miners into the area.

The Sioux protested. Instead of protecting the Sioux's rights, the U.S. government tried to buy the hills. Sitting Bull, a leader of the Lakota Sioux, refused. "I do not want to sell any land. ... Not even as much as this," he said, holding a pinch of dust.

In June 1876, Sitting Bull gathered Sioux and Cheyenne warriors along the Little Bighorn River in Montana Territory. They were joined by Crazy Horse, another Sioux chief, and his forces. With only about 250 soldiers, Lieutenant Colonel George Custer of the U.S. Army faced thousands of warriors. Still, he attacked. In the battle, Custer and almost all of his men were killed.

Custer's defeat at Little Bighorn shocked the nation and prompted the U.S. government to send large armies west.

▶ **CRITICAL THINKING**
Interpreting Why did Sitting Bull choose not to negotiate with the U.S. government?

BIOGRAPHY

Sitting Bull (c. 1831–1890)

Sitting Bull was a member of the Teton Dakota, one of several Sioux groups of the Great Plains. Early in life, he built a reputation as a great and fearless warrior. Sitting Bull also grew to distrust the U.S. government and resisted its attempts to control the Sioux. One journalist reported that Sitting Bull said, "I never taught my people to trust Americans. I have told them the truth—that the Americans are great liars. I never dealt with the Americans." Under his leadership, the Sioux united to resist control by the U.S. government.

Geronimo (1829–1909)

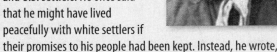

Born in Mexico, Geronimo led his people against the colonization of Apache lands by both Mexican and U.S. settlers. He once said that he might have lived peacefully with white settlers if their promises to his people had been kept. Instead, he wrote,

"We were reckless of our lives, because we felt that every man's hand was against us. If we returned to the reservation we would be put in prison and killed; if we stayed in Mexico they would continue to send soldiers to fight us."

▶ **CRITICAL THINKING**
Identifying Points of View Who did Sitting Bull and Geronimo blame for the conflict between their people and the U.S. government? Why?

News of the U.S. Army's defeat at Little Bighorn shocked the nation. Yet the army soon crushed the Native American uprising, sending most of the Native Americans to reservations. Sitting Bull and his followers fled north to Canada. By 1881, starving and exhausted, the Lakota and Cheyenne agreed to live on a reservation.

The Long March of the Nez Perce

The Nez Perce (NEHZ PUHRS) were a large and powerful group of the Pacific Northwest. Their relations with white settlers were friendly and peaceful until the 1860s, when gold was discovered on Nez Perce land in Oregon.

In 1877 the U.S. government ordered the Nez Perce to leave their land and move to a reservation in Idaho or be forcibly removed. Their leader, Chief Joseph, decided to leave. Before he could act, a small group of Nez Perce attacked and killed several settlers. Knowing that his small band had no chance of defeating the U.S. Army, Joseph decided to retreat to Canada. With only about 200 warriors and nearly 600 women and children, he started north.

After traveling more than 1,000 miles (1,609 km), the group stopped to rest just 40 miles (64.4 km) from the Canadian border. It was a costly error. Army troops surrounded the Nez Perce and **initiated** a five-day siege. They blocked Joseph's people from getting out to find food and water. Finally, Chief Joseph surrendered, vowing, "From where the sun now stands, I will fight no more forever."

Reading **HELP**DESK CCSS

Academic Vocabulary

initiate to begin

Reading Strategy: *Visualizing*

When you visualize, you create pictures in your mind of what you are reading. Good readers "see" the author's words, making it easier to remember details. As you read the page above, what do you visualize?

The army took Chief Joseph and his people to a reservation in what is now Oklahoma. Later, in 1885, he and many of his people moved to a reservation in Washington. Joseph spent the rest of his life trying to get better treatment for Native Americans.

The Apache Wars

Trouble also broke out in the Southwest between Native Americans and government troops. In the 1870s, the government forced the Chiricahua (chihr•uh•KAH•wuh) Apache to move to a reservation in Arizona. The Apache leader, Geronimo, then fled to Mexico.

During the 1880s, Geronimo led raids in Arizona. Thousands of U.S. Army troops pursued the Apache leader and his warriors. In 1886 Geronimo finally gave up the fight—the last Native American to surrender. The conflicts, however, were not over.

A Changing Culture

Many factors changed Native American life—white people moving onto their lands, the killing of the buffalo, U.S. Army attacks, and the reservation policy. Change also came from reformers who wanted Native Americans to fit into white culture.

In 1887 Congress passed the Dawes Act. With this law, Congress hoped to change what white people saw as weaknesses in Native American cultures: the lack of private property and nomadic habits. The Dawes Act called for breaking up reservations and ending Native Americans' identification with a tribal group.

GEOGRAPHY CONNECTION

White settlers and the U.S. military fought with many Native American groups. After the Civil War, the U.S. government put in place a stronger reservation policy. Some Native Americans moved to reservations. Others resisted.

1 **LOCATION** In which state or future state did the flight of the Nez Perce end?

2 **CRITICAL THINKING**
Drawing Conclusions Based on the map, why do you think Native American groups might have resisted being confined to reservations?

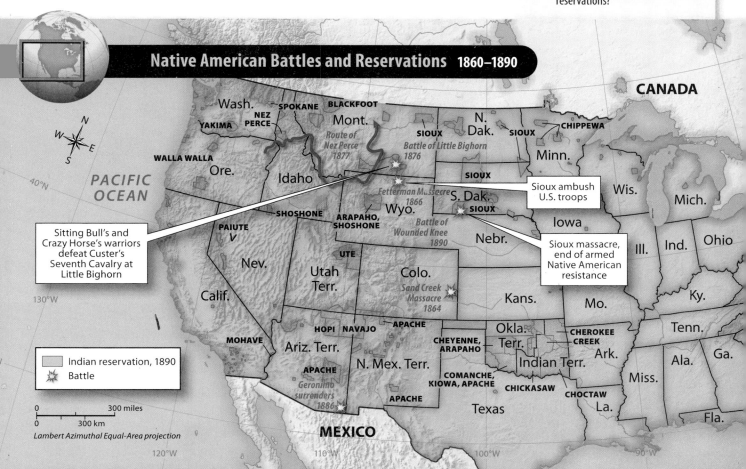

Native American Battles and Reservations 1860–1890

CANADA

Wash. SPOKANE BLACKFOOT
NEZ
YAKIMA PERCE Mont. N. Dak. SIOUX CHIPPEWA
Route of SIOUX
Nez Perce Battle of Little Bighorn Minn.
WALLA WALLA 1877 1876
PACIFIC Ore. SIOUX Wis. Mich.
OCEAN Idaho
40°N Fetterman Massacre S. Dak.
1866 SIOUX Iowa
SHOSHONE Wyo. Ill. Ind. Ohio
PAIUTE ARAPAHO, Battle of
Sitting Bull's and SHOSHONE Wounded Knee Nebr.
Crazy Horse's warriors 1890
defeat Custer's Nev. UTE
Seventh Cavalry at Utah Colo. Kans. Mo. Ky.
Little Bighorn Terr. Sand Creek
130°W Calif. Massacre Tenn.
1864 Okla.
HOPI NAVAJO APACHE Terr. CHEROKEE
MOHAVE CHEYENNE, CREEK Ark. Ala. Ga.
Ariz. Terr. ARAPAHO Indian Terr. Miss.
APACHE N. Mex. Terr. COMANCHE, CHICKASAW
Geronimo KIOWA, APACHE CHOCTAW La.
surrenders APACHE
1886 Texas Fla.

MEXICO

Sioux ambush U.S. troops

Sioux massacre, end of armed Native American resistance

Indian reservation, 1890
Battle

0 300 miles
0 300 km
Lambert Azimuthal Equal-Area projection

120°W 110°W 100°W 90°W

According to the plan, every Native American would receive a plot of reservation land. Reformers hoped that the native peoples would become farmers and, in time, adopt the way of life practiced by most American citizens.

Some Native Americans became successful farmers or ranchers, but many had little training or eagerness for the jobs. Like homesteaders, Native Americans often found the plots of land they received too small to be profitable, so they sold them.

Wounded Knee

In 1889 many western Native Americans began to perform a ceremony called the Ghost Dance. This dance celebrated a hoped-for day when the settlers would disappear, the buffalo would return, and Native Americans could go back to traditional ways of life. As tensions between Native Americans and white settlers increased, the popularity of the Ghost Dance spread.

U.S. government officials became alarmed and banned the dance. The officials believed that Sitting Bull was responsible for the Ghost Dance movement, so they tried to arrest him. During a scuffle, police shot and killed him.

After Sitting Bull's death, several hundred Lakota Sioux gathered at Wounded Knee, a creek in southwestern South Dakota. They were armed. In December 1890, the U.S. Army sent troops to Wounded Knee. Their mission was to collect the Sioux weapons. As they did this, one of the guns discharged—fired a shot. The army, in turn, opened fire. When the shooting ended, more than 200 Sioux and 25 soldiers lay dead. Wounded Knee marked the end of armed conflict between the U.S. government and Native Americans.

The year after Wounded Knee, a young girl from the Oglala band of the Lakota Sioux sits in front of a tepee on the Pine Ridge Reservation in South Dakota.

✔ **PROGRESS CHECK**

Evaluating How effective was the Dawes Act?

LESSON 3 REVIEW (CCSS)

Review Vocabulary

1. Use the terms *nomadic* and *reservation* in a sentence about the Dawes Act.

Answer the Guiding Questions

2. ***Specifying*** Why did American railroad workers hunt buffalo?

3. ***Describing*** What was the stated purpose of the Dawes Act, and what was its actual effect?

4. ***Predicting*** What do you think happened to the Native American population of the United States after Wounded Knee?

5. ***Comparing and Contrasting*** List the similarities and differences between nomadic life and reservation life.

6. **INFORMATIVE/EXPLANATORY** You are a newspaper reporter and have just witnessed a Ghost Dance. Write an article describing the Ghost Dance, its importance to Native Americans, and why it might be of concern to American government officials.

networks

There's More Online!

☑ **GAME**

☑ **GRAPHIC ORGANIZER**
Successes and Failures of Farm Groups

☑ **MAP** Election of 1896

☑ **PRIMARY SOURCE**
Pro-Bryan Sheet Music

Lesson 4
Farmers—A New Political Force

ESSENTIAL QUESTION *How do governments change?*

IT MATTERS BECAUSE

Growing economic problems plaguing farmers led to the rise of a new political movement.

Farmers Unite

GUIDING QUESTION *How did the National Grange and the Farmers' Alliances try to help farmers?*

In the late 1800s, American farmers experienced great economic hardships. The expansion of farming on the Great Plains was a major cause. The supply of crops kept increasing, but the demand did not. Without enough buyers, farmers had to lower their prices to attract more. In 1866 a bushel of wheat sold for $1.45. By the mid-1880s, the price was 80 cents, and by the mid-1890s, it was 49 cents. At the same time, farmers' expenses—for seed, equipment, and transporting their goods to market—remained high.

Farmers had other financial problems. Railroad companies charged them high rates to ship their crops. Bankers charged them high interest rates on loans for seed or farm equipment. Senator William A. Peffer of Kansas summarized farmers' problems, saying that the railroad companies "took possession of the land" and the bankers "took possession of the farmer."

The National Grange

Farmers began to organize in order to solve their problems. They believed they would have more power if they banded together. Before long, they had created a political movement.

Reading HELPDESK (CCSS)

Taking Notes: *Identifying*

As you read, use a chart like this one to identify the successes and failures of the National Grange, the Farmers' Alliances, and the Populist Party.

	Successes	Failures
National Grange		
Farmers' Alliances		
Populist Party		

Content Vocabulary
• **National Grange**
• **cooperative**
• **populism**

In the 1880s, it was expensive for farmers to buy the equipment they needed, like this wheat thresher and the horses to pull it.

The first large farmers' organization was a network of local groups that became the **National Grange.** At first, its main purpose was social. For lonely farm families, the Grange held social gatherings. For new farmers, the Grange library provided books on planting crops and raising livestock.

When the national economy suffered in the 1870s, the Grange focused on encouraging economic independence. It set up "cash-only" **cooperatives,** stores owned by and operated for the benefit of farmers. Cooperatives charged lower prices than regular stores and provided an outlet for farmers' crops. The cash-only policy kept farmers from buying on credit and going into debt.

The Grange also became politically active. It asked state legislatures to limit railroad-shipping rates. Many Midwestern states passed such laws. By 1878, however, under pressure from the railroads, the states repealed the laws. Also, farmers were always short of cash and had to borrow money until they sold their next crop. As a result, the cash-only cooperatives failed. By the late 1880s, the Grange had declined.

New Organizations

Meanwhile, a new network of organizations called Farmers' Alliances appeared in the West and the South. By 1890 the Southern Alliance had more than 3 million members. The Colored Farmers' National Alliance, a separate group of African American farmers, had 1 million members.

Like the Grange, the Farmers' Alliances supported cooperative buying and selling. They also proposed that the federal government build warehouses where farmers could store crops while waiting for prices to rise. While waiting, the farmers could use government loans to survive. They would pay back those loans when they sold their crops. With this plan, the Alliances hoped to reduce the power that railroads and banks had over farmers and gain some federal protection.

The Farmers' Alliances could have been a powerful force. As you will read, regional differences got in the way of the movement's success.

☑ PROGRESS CHECK

Determining Cause and Effect Why did farmers create organizations like the Grange and the Farmers' Alliances?

Bettmann/CORBIS

Reading **HELP**DESK CCSS

National Grange a network of local farmers' groups
cooperative enterprise owned by and operated for the benefit of a certain group

populism an appeal to the common people

Academic Vocabulary
currency money

A Party of the People

GUIDING QUESTION *What were the ideas of the Populist Party?*

The Farmers' Alliances became active in politics during the 1890 elections at the state and national levels. Their candidates won 6 governorships, 3 seats in the U.S. Senate, and 50 seats in the House of Representatives.

As a result of their success, Farmers' Alliance leaders decided to turn the movement into a national political party. In February 1890, Alliance members formed the People's Party of the U.S.A., also known as the Populist Party. The party's goals were rooted in **populism,** or an appeal to the common people.

The Populist View

The Populist Party believed government—not private companies— should own railroads and telegraph lines. Populists also wanted to replace the nation's gold-based **currency.** In general, the gold standard tended to drive prices down. This favored lenders, because it meant borrowers repaid loans with money that could buy more than the money they had borrowed.

Populists proposed a system of "free silver"—the unlimited production of silver coins. By putting more silver coins into the economy, Populists believed farmers would see prices and income rise. This would make it easier for them to pay their debts.

The Populists also supported several political and labor reforms. They wanted to limit the president and vice president to a single term, elect senators directly, and introduce the use of secret ballots. They called for shorter hours for workers and the creation of a national income tax that would tax people who had higher earnings more heavily.

Connections to
TODAY

Farmers' Organizations

The Grange is still active in 2,700 local communities in 40 states. Its 200,000 members work on a variety of issues— including economic development, education, and legislation—to help assure a strong rural America.

INFOGRAPHIC

The donkey is a symbol of the Democratic Party. Supporters of the free-silver movement: **A** Senator Ben Tillman of South Carolina; **B** William Jennings Bryan; **C** Governor John P. Altgeld of Illinois

▶ CRITICAL THINKING

Interpreting According to the cartoon, what is happening to the free-silver movement?

FREE SILVER IN THE PRESS

The Granger Collection, New York

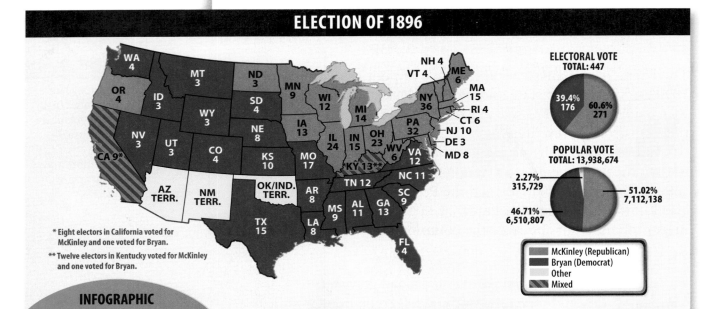

ELECTION OF 1896

WA 4
OR 4
MT 3
ID 3
WY 3
NV 3
UT 3
CA 9*
AZ TERR.
NM TERR.
ND 3
SD 4
NE 8
CO 4
KS 10
OK/IND. TERR.
TX 15
MN 9
IA 13
MO 17
AR 8
LA 8
WI 12
IL 24
MS 9
MI 14
IN 15
KY 13**
TN 12
AL 11
GA 13
FL 4
OH 23
WV 6
VA 12
NC 11
SC 9
NH 4
VT 4
ME 6
MA 15
NY 36
RI 4
CT 6
PA 32
NJ 10
DE 3
MD 8

ELECTORAL VOTE
TOTAL: 447
39.4% 176
60.6% 271

POPULAR VOTE
TOTAL: 13,938,674
2.27% 315,729
51.02% 7,112,138
46.71% 6,510,807

McKinley (Republican)
Bryan (Democrat)
Other
Mixed

* Eight electors in California voted for McKinley and one voted for Bryan.

** Twelve electors in Kentucky voted for McKinley and one voted for Bryan.

INFOGRAPHIC

In 1896 the Democratic presidential nominee William Jennings Bryan ran on a free-silver platform. Republican candidate William McKinley favored business, the gold standard, and a high tariff.

1 MAKING CONNECTIONS Besides revealing a divide between industrial and rural areas, what other sectional divide does this map show?

2 CRITICAL THINKING *Speculating* If Arizona, New Mexico, and Oklahoma had been states instead of territories, how do you think their citizens might have voted? Explain.

In the local elections of 1894, the Populists did well. They had hopes of building even more support in the presidential election of 1896. Despite choosing energetic candidates, however, the Populists lacked money and organization.

The Movement Grows

As if these problems were not enough, hostility between the North and the South after the Civil War divided the Populist Party. In spite of their **mutual** interests, many white Southerners would not join their forces with African American Populists. In addition, Democrat-controlled Southern state legislatures in the 1890s limited the voting rights of African Americans—many of whom might have supported the Populists.

Still, support for free silver grew. Silver-mining companies in the West also supported the cause. If the government coined large quantities of silver, the mining companies would have a ready-made buyer for their metal.

The wide appeal of free silver did not go unnoticed. As 1896 approached, some Democrats took up the issue as their own.

The 1896 Election

At the Democratic National Convention in 1896, a young Congressman from Nebraska made an electrifying speech in support of free silver. He concluded with this stirring call:

Reading HELPDESK CCSS

Academic Vocabulary

mutual shared in common

Reading in the Content Area: *Literary Allusions*

Writing often contains references to well-known lines or images in other literature. When you read a passage such as the excerpt of the Bryan speech, look for phrases or images that are unfamiliar but seem meaningful, such as *cross of gold* or *crown of thorns*. It is likely that such images refer to other literature.

" If they dare to come out in the open field and defend the gold standard as a good thing, we shall fight them to the uttermost. . . . Having behind us . . . the commercial interests and the laboring interests and all the toiling masses, we shall answer their demands for a gold standard by saying to them, you shall not press down upon the brow of labor this crown of thorns. You shall not crucify mankind upon a cross of gold. "

William Jennings Bryan, in a speech to the Democratic National Convention, July 9, 1896

The final lines refer to the Christian Bible account of the last hours of Jesus, who was given a crown of thorns and then put to death on a cross.

Following his speech, William Jennings Bryan became known as the "Great Commoner" because of his appeal to average Americans. Bryan passionately believed in farmers' causes. He supported free silver and other Populist goals. For these reasons, the Populists also endorsed Bryan as their candidate.

The Republican candidate was William McKinley of Ohio, who opposed free silver. McKinley had served in Congress for 14 years and as governor of Ohio for four.

Bryan traveled the country giving dynamic speeches, while McKinley allowed supporters to come to him in Ohio. By election time, the economic depression was ending. Bryan's message no longer seemed urgent. McKinley won in a landslide.

Populist ideas still made an impact, however. In the early 1900s, the United States adopted an eight-hour workday, an income tax, the secret ballot, and the direct election of senators. In 1933 the nation abandoned the gold standard.

The Democrat ticket of William Jennings Bryan and Arthur Sewall campaigned on the belief that free silver would help farmers and the working class.

✓ **PROGRESS CHECK**

Summarizing Why did people support the Populist Party?

CORBIS

LESSON 4 REVIEW CCSS

Review Vocabulary

1. Use the terms *National Grange, cooperative,* and *populism* in a paragraph about American farmers in the late 1800s.

Answer the Guiding Questions

2. *Explaining* How did cooperatives help farmers in the late 1800s? Why did those cooperatives fail?

3. *Analyzing* Why did the Populists believe free silver would help farmers and debtors?

4. *Evaluating* Was the Populist Party successful? Explain your answer.

5. *Determining Cause and Effect* Why did economic reform movements develop in the late 1800s?

6. ARGUMENT You are a magazine writer assigned to find out how people feel about the Populist Party. Write your article describing the support for and opposition to the party.

Write your answers on a separate piece of paper.

1 Exploring the Essential Questions

INFORMATIVE/EXPLANATORY Write an essay addressing how different ethnic groups contributed to the history of the American West in the mid- to late 1800s. Consider the contributions of miners, ranchers, homesteaders, Native Americans, and immigrant railroad workers.

2 21st Century Skills

COMMUNICATION Think about the ideas, people, and places in this chapter. Then write a song or a poem about something you read. When you finish, perform your work for the class. Here is an example to get you thinking:

They came to the west, the best of the best,
To find freedom and space to grow.
They mined it, they farmed it, they traveled its trails,
And then, on the way, they laid down some rails,
In a wonderful quest to join East and West.
Through mountains and valleys below.

3 Thinking Like a Historian

ANALYZING AND INTERPRETING INFORMATION The price of gold varies, just like the prices of other goods. If a good is scarce, the price goes up. People are willing to pay more to have it. If the supply of something is greater than the demand for it, the price goes down. When they hammered in the transcontinental railroad's golden spike, gold was $18.93 an ounce. In 1996 gold was $369 an ounce. The next year it was $287 an ounce. In recent years the price has soared much higher, to around $1500 an ounce in early 2011. Use the Internet or a newspaper to check the price of gold today and over the past month. How has the price changed? Report on your findings.

4 Visual Literacy

ANALYZING POLITICAL CARTOONS This 1891 cartoon is about the Populist Party. The cartoon's title is "A Party of Patches." How do you think the artist feels about the way the party is organized? Explain your answer.

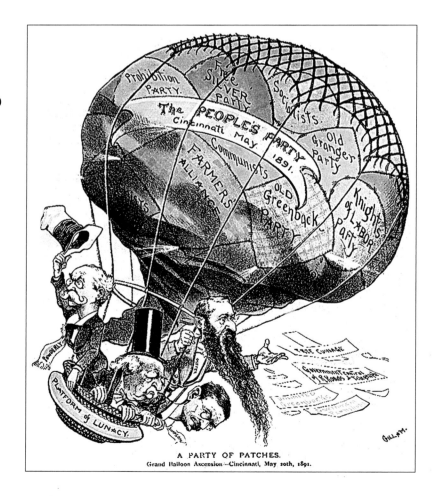

A PARTY OF PATCHES.
Grand Balloon Ascension--Cincinnati, May 20th, 1891.

AP Images

REVIEW THE GUIDING QUESTIONS

Choose the best answer for each question.

1 Discovered in 1859, Nevada's Comstock Lode contained
  A. scattered deposits of gold and iron ore.
  B. large concentrations of coal.
  C. the biggest seam of copper ever found.
  D. a rich lode of silver-bearing ore.

2 What event occurred in 1868 along the Little Bighorn River?
  F. Hundreds of Cheyenne negotiated a peace deal with the U.S. government.
  G. The Sioux and Cheyenne defeated a U.S. force led by George Custer.
  H. Apache leader Geronimo formally surrendered to the United States.
  I. Thousands of Lakota Sioux performed a Ghost Dance.

3 Which of the following developed the proposal to break up the reservations and encourage Native Americans to become farmers?
  A. Bureau of Indian Affairs
  B. Freedmen's Bureau
  C. Dawes Act
  D. Native American Act

4 The network of farmers' self-help organizations eventually came to be called the
  F. Comstock Lode.
  G. National Grange.
  H. Long Drive.
  I. Pikes Peak.

5 Cattle became big business in the West because of the spread of
  A. railroads.
  B. Native Americans.
  C. mining boomtowns.
  D. the National Grange.

6 One of the goals of the Populist Party was
  F. returning to the gold currency standard.
  G. government ownership of railroads.
  H. extending the term of the president.
  I. passage of the Fifteenth Amendment.

DBQ ANALYZING DOCUMENTS

Explaining Sioux warrior Kicking Bear spoke these words in a speech to a Sioux council in the 1890s:

"My brothers, I bring to you the promise of a day in which there will be no white man to lay his hand on the bridle of the Indian's horse; when the red men of the prairie will rule the world and not be turned from the hunting-grounds by any man. I bring you word from your fathers the ghosts, that they are now marching to join you. … I have seen the wonders of the spirit-land, and have talked with the ghosts."

7 According to the document, Kicking Bear promised the council that
   A. there would soon be fewer Native Americans on the prairie.
   B. the spirit-land was preferable to the real world.
   C. the ghosts were coming to drive them away.
   D. one day there would be no more white men on the prairie.

8 **Identifying** Who gave Kicking Bear this message?
   F. the Great Spirit   H. the ghosts of Sioux warriors
   G. Chief Sitting Bull   I. Geronimo

SHORT RESPONSE

J. Ross Browne recorded these impressions of Virginia City, Nevada, in 1865:

"The business part of the town has been built up with astonishing rapidity. In the spring of 1860, there was nothing of it save a few frame shanties and canvas tents, and one or two rough stone cabins. It now presents some of the distinguishing features of a metropolitan city."

—from *Harper's New Monthly Magazine*

9 According to Browne, how had Virginia City changed?

10 What might Browne think of as distinguishing features of a metropolitan city in 1865?

EXTENDED RESPONSE

11 **Narrative** You live in Utah near the new Transcontinental Railroad. Write a letter to a friend in the East about the project. Explain what it means now that people can travel back East or go farther west by train. Be sure to include negative as well as positive effects resulting from the new technology.

Need Extra Help?

If You've Missed Question	1	2	3	4	5	6	7	8	9	10	11
Review Lesson	1	3	3	4	2	4	3	3	1	1	1–4

The Industrial Age

1865–1914

ESSENTIAL QUESTION *How does technology change the way people live and work?*

◄ *Young boys helped mine the coal that powered the Industrial Age.*

The Granger Collection, NYC

netw⊚rks

There's More Online about the industrialization of the United States.

CHAPTER 4

The Story Matters . . .

It's noon and time for a short rest. These boys are halfway through their long workday. They are breaker boys, and their job is to pick out the bits of rock that are mixed in with the coal that the older miners have dug from the mine. The work is hard on the hands—and on the lungs. The air is full of coal dust, which covers their faces and clothes. These boys, however, are earning money to help support their families. They are also looking forward to the day when they can enter the mine and earn a few more cents for their day's work.

Now, however, it's time for lunch—and then back to work! There's a lot more coal to be cleaned before they can go home for the day.

Place and Time: The United States 1865 to 1914

The late 1800s was a time of invention and advances in technology. These breakthroughs combined with railroad expansion and new business practices to launch an age of industry. Government policies encouraged growth, and large corporations became an important part of the economy. Meanwhile, poor pay and working conditions led workers to form unions in an attempt to improve their lives.

Step Into the Place

MAP FOCUS Most industry that developed by 1900 was located east of the Mississippi River.

1 PLACE What industries were most important in New York?

2 LOCATION What cities became centers of the steel industry?

3 CRITICAL THINKING
Making Connections How might the development of a nationwide railroad system help cities on this map?

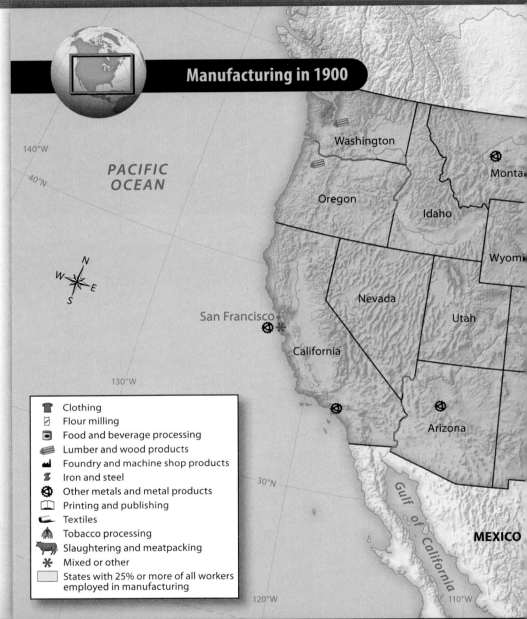

Manufacturing in 1900

PACIFIC OCEAN

140°W
40°N
130°W
30°N
120°W
110°W

Washington
Oregon
Idaho
Montana
Wyoming
Nevada
Utah
California
San Francisco
Arizona
Gulf of California
MEXICO

Legend:
- Clothing
- Flour milling
- Food and beverage processing
- Lumber and wood products
- Foundry and machine shop products
- Iron and steel
- Other metals and metal products
- Printing and publishing
- Textiles
- Tobacco processing
- Slaughtering and meatpacking
- * Mixed or other
- States with 25% or more of all workers employed in manufacturing

Step Into the Time

TIME LINE Look at the time line. Which events in Europe do you think will have the greatest impact on the United States?

U.S. PRESIDENTS

Andrew Johnson 1865–1869
Ulysses S. Grant 1869–1877
Rutherford B. Hayes 1877–1881

U.S. EVENTS
WORLD EVENTS

1860
1870

1867 Diamonds discovered in Cape Colony in South Africa

1869 First transcontinental railroad completed

1870 Rockefeller organizes Standard Oil Company

1876 Bell patents the telephone

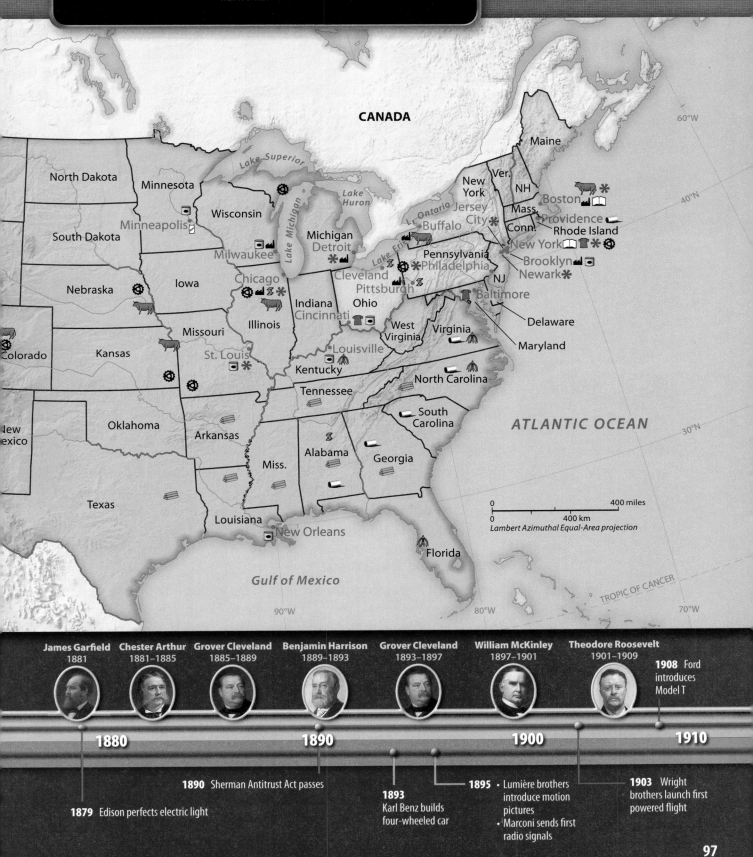

networks
There's More Online!

☑ **MAP** Explore the interactive version of this map on NETWORKS.

☑ **TIME LINE** Explore the interactive version of this time line on NETWORKS.

CANADA

Maine

North Dakota

Minnesota

Lake Superior

Wisconsin

Lake Michigan

Lake Huron

Michigan

Detroit

Lake Erie

New York

Ver.

NH

Boston

Mass.

Providence

Conn.

Rhode Island

New York

Brooklyn

Newark

Lake Ontario

Buffalo

Jersey City

South Dakota

Minneapolis

Milwaukee

Chicago

Pennsylvania

Philadelphia

NJ

Cleveland

Pittsburgh

Baltimore

Delaware

Maryland

Nebraska

Iowa

Illinois

Indiana

Cincinnati

Ohio

West Virginia

Virginia

Colorado

Kansas

Missouri

St. Louis

Louisville

Kentucky

North Carolina

New Mexico

Oklahoma

Arkansas

Tennessee

South Carolina

ATLANTIC OCEAN

Texas

Miss.

Alabama

Georgia

Louisiana

New Orleans

Florida

Gulf of Mexico

60°W

40°N

30°N

TROPIC OF CANCER

90°W

80°W

70°W

0 ——— 400 miles
0 ——— 400 km
Lambert Azimuthal Equal-Area projection

James Garfield 1881

Chester Arthur 1881–1885

Grover Cleveland 1885–1889

Benjamin Harrison 1889–1893

Grover Cleveland 1893–1897

William McKinley 1897–1901

Theodore Roosevelt 1901–1909

1908 Ford introduces Model T

1880

1890

1900

1910

1890 Sherman Antitrust Act passes

1893 Karl Benz builds four-wheeled car

1895 • Lumière brothers introduce motion pictures
• Marconi sends first radio signals

1903 Wright brothers launch first powered flight

1879 Edison perfects electric light

There's More Online!

☑ **GRAPHIC ORGANIZER**
Effects of Railroad Expansion

☑ **MAP** Railroads and Time Zones

☑ **VIDEO**

Lesson 1
Railroads Lead the Way

ESSENTIAL QUESTION *How does technology change the way people live and work?*

IT MATTERS BECAUSE
Railroads transformed the economy and the geography of the United States in the late 1800s.

The Growth of Railroads

GUIDING QUESTION *How did railroads pave the way for growth and expansion?*

Railroad building grew tremendously in the last half of the 1800s. This expansion powered a growing economy. In 1860 the United States already had about 30,000 miles (48,280 km) of railroad track—almost as much as the rest of the world combined. By 1900 that total had grown to nearly 193,000 miles (310,603 km) of track. Between 1870 and 1916, workers laid an average of 11 miles (18 km) of track every day. Work songs such as "John Henry" and "I've Been Working on the Railroad" became popular among the immigrants and other Americans who **labored** to build those miles of track.

Combining Railroads

Along with expansion of railroads came **consolidation** (kuhn•sah•luh•DAY•shun)—the practice of combining separate companies. Large railroad companies bought smaller companies or drove them out of business. Consolidation made the large companies more efficient, or able to do more work with fewer resources. For example, the companies could set standard prices and processes. Consolidation also sometimes allowed a few large companies to control an entire industry.

(l) Library of Congress, (r) Private Collection, Peter Newark American Pictures/Bridgeman Art Library

Reading HELPDESK **CCSS**

Taking Notes: *Determining Cause and Effect*
As you read, create a diagram like this one to record the effects of railroad expansion in the United States. Title your diagram "Effects of Railroad Expansion."

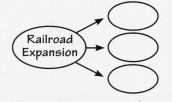

Content Vocabulary
• **consolidation**   • **rebate**
• **railroad baron**   • **pool**
• **standard gauge**

The Railroad Barons

After consolidation, a few powerful **individuals** known as **railroad barons** (BEHR•uhnz) controlled the nation's rail traffic. Cornelius Vanderbilt was one of the first railroad barons. His railroad empire stretched from New York City to the Great Lakes.

Another baron was James J. Hill. He built the Great Northern line between Minnesota and the state of Washington. Other barons, including Collis P. Huntington and Leland Stanford, founded the Central Pacific. This line connected California and Utah and formed part of the first transcontinental, or cross-continent, railroad. The barons were very competitive. They worked in an age when few laws limited their business practices.

☑ **PROGRESS CHECK**

Analyzing What are the possible advantages and disadvantages of consolidation?

Railroads Aid Economic Growth

GUIDING QUESTION *What industries benefited from the expansion of the railroad system?*

Railroads carried raw materials such as iron ore, coal, and timber to factories. They moved manufactured goods from factories to markets. They also shipped crops from farming areas to the cities.

At first, demand for iron tracks and locomotives helped the iron industry grow. Around 1880, railroads began using tracks of steel. Steel is stronger than iron. This shift helped the steel industry grow. Railroads also helped the lumber industry, which supplied wood for railway ties, and the coal industry, which provided fuel. In addition, railroad companies provided thousands of jobs.

Making a National Rail System

The first railroads covered only a small area. Different railroads used tracks of different gauges, or distances between the rails. Trains of one railroad could not use another line's tracks.

Thinking Like a HISTORIAN

Analyzing Primary Sources

Cornelius Vanderbilt once said, "What do I care about law. Ain't I got the power?" What does this quote and the cartoon below tell you about Vanderbilt? For more about analyzing primary sources, review *Thinking Like a Historian*.

NOW THEN JIM... NO JOCKEYING YOU KNOW!

LET EM RIP COMMODORE — BUT DON'T STOP TO WATER OR YOU'LL BE BEAT

HUDSON RIVER R.R.

N.Y. CENTRAL R.R.

ERIE R.R.

THE GREAT RACE FOR THE WESTERN STAKES 1870

Cornelius Vanderbilt was a railroad baron known for his tight grip on his railroad empire.

---

consolidation the practice of combining different companies into one

railroad baron powerful business leader who controlled a major railroad

Academic Vocabulary

labor to work or try hard
individual a single person

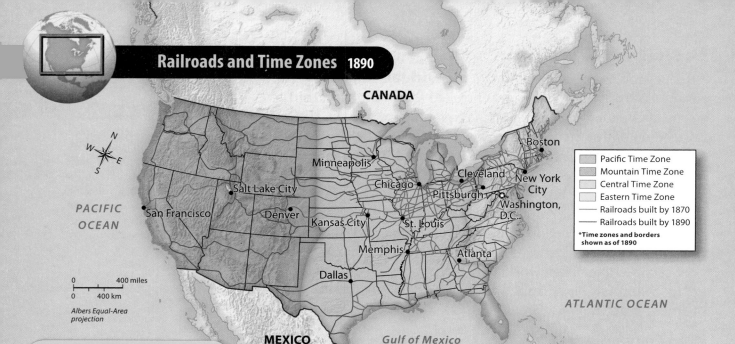

Railroads and Time Zones 1890

CANADA

Boston
Minneapolis
Cleveland
Chicago
New York
City
Pittsburgh
Salt Lake City
Washington,
D.C.
San Francisco
Denver
Kansas City
St. Louis
PACIFIC
OCEAN
Memphis
Atlanta
Dallas
ATLANTIC OCEAN

MEXICO
Gulf of Mexico

Legend:
Pacific Time Zone
Mountain Time Zone
Central Time Zone
Eastern Time Zone
Railroads built by 1870
Railroads built by 1890
*Time zones and borders
shown as of 1890

0   400 miles
0   400 km
Albers Equal-Area
projection

GEOGRAPHY CONNECTION

Before railroads existed, each community set its own time. In order to create sensible schedules, the country needed a shared system for setting times. This system divided the country into four different time zones. Each zone was exactly one hour apart from its neighboring zone.

1 REGION Which time zone had the most miles of railroad track?

2 CRITICAL THINKING
Speculating How might the lack of standard time zones have complicated travel?

If a manufacturer wanted to ship goods over more than one railroad line, workers had to unload goods from one train and move them to another. This slowed rail travel and also made it more expensive.

As railroad companies consolidated, they began using a **standard gauge** (GAYJ) of 4 feet, 8.5 inches (1 m, 41.6 cm). The use of a standard gauge drove down shipping times and costs.

New Technology Improves Railroads

New technology also improved railway transportation. Four developments were especially important. Inventor George Westinghouse created air brakes that improved the system for stopping trains, making them safer. Janney car couplers, named after inventor Eli H. Janney, made it easier for railroad workers to link cars. Gustavus Swift developed refrigerated railroad cars, allowing railroads to ship meat and crops over long distances without spoiling. Finally, George Pullman developed the Pullman sleeping car. This was a luxury railway car with seats that changed into beds for overnight journeys.

Railroads Compete for Customers

Railroad companies competed fiercely to keep old customers and win new ones. Large railroads offered discounts called **rebates** (REE•bayts) to their biggest customers. Smaller

Reading HELP DESK CCSS

standard gauge 4 feet, 8.5 inches, the distance between rails agreed upon by all railroad companies
rebate a discount or return of part of a payment

pool a group sharing in some activity, for example, among railroad barons who made secret agreements and set rates among themselves

railroads that could not match these prices were often forced out of business. Giving discounts to big customers, however, meant higher rates for farmers and other customers who shipped small loads.

The railroad barons also made secret agreements with one another to form **pools.** The companies in a pool divided up business among themselves and set identical rates. This eliminated competition that might drive rates down. Higher rates meant higher profits. There were some laws to regulate the railroads, but they did little to stop the barons.

Railroads Change America

The growing railroad network helped American industry expand into the West. For example, the manufacturing center for farm equipment moved from New York State to Illinois and Wisconsin. Railroads also changed where people lived. Trains brought homesteaders, merchants, and mine workers onto the Great Plains and into the West. They moved people from rural areas to cities as well.

More powerful locomotives and steel rails allowed railroads to haul bigger loads.

☑ **PROGRESS CHECK**

Describing What were some new technologies that improved railroad travel in the late 1800s?

Private Collection, Peter Newark American Pictures/Bridgeman Art Library

---

LESSON 1 REVIEW

Review Vocabulary

1. Examine the two terms below. Then write a sentence explaining what the terms have in common.

   a. consolidation **b.** railroad baron

2. Write a sentence about railroads that uses the following terms.

   a. pool **b.** rebate

Answer the Guiding Questions

3. *Analyzing* In what ways did railroads help the nation's economy grow?

4. *Explaining* How did railroads affect where people settled in the United States?

5. **NARRATIVE** Write a description of a long train trip in the late 1800s that illustrates how the change to standard-gauge track has improved travel in that era.

networks

There's More Online!

☑ **GAME**

☑ **GRAPHIC ORGANIZER**
Effects of Major Inventions

☑ **SLIDE SHOW**
Accomplishments in Aviation

☑ **VIDEO**

Lesson 2
Inventions Change Society

ESSENTIAL QUESTION *How does technology change the way people live and work?*

IT MATTERS BECAUSE
New technologies began a transformation of society that has helped shape the world we live in today.

Technology Changes Communications

GUIDING QUESTION *How did innovations in communications change society?*

By 1910 Americans in cities drove cars through streets lit with electric lights. They went to department stores where they could buy everything from shoes to kitchen sinks. Americans also could do their shopping by mail—or pick up the telephone and order groceries from the local store.

Inventors built the first automobile and telephone in the late 1800s. Within a few decades, these inventions had become part of everyday life. They helped people and ideas move quickly over long distances. In the process, they also helped unify the country and promote economic growth.

Morse's Telegraph and Code

During the 1830s, Samuel Morse developed the telegraph. He got help from Congress to build the nation's first telegraph line. In 1844 Morse sent the first telegram—from Baltimore to Washington, D.C. By 1860 the United States had thousands of miles of telegraph lines. Western Union Telegraph Company's trained operators **transmitted** messages in Morse code.

Reading **HELP**DESK **CCSS**

Taking Notes: *Identifying*

As you read, create a chart like this one to identify the effects of major inventions.

Invention	Effects
Telegraph	
Telephone	
Electric lightbulb	

Content Vocabulary
• **Model T**
• **assembly line**
• **mass production**

Telegrams—messages sent by telegraph—offered almost instant communication over long distances. This was a huge improvement over written communications delivered by hand. Even with trains, a letter could take days to travel from one part of the country to the other.

Telegrams served many purposes. Shopkeepers relied on them to order goods. Reporters used them to send stories to their newspapers. Ordinary people also used telegrams to send personal messages to friends and family.

The telegraph soon linked the United States and Europe. Before the telegraph, news crossed the ocean by ship. This process could take weeks. Cyrus Field wanted to speed it up. After several unsuccessful attempts, Field managed to lay a telegraph cable across the Atlantic Ocean in 1866. The new transatlantic telegraph transmitted messages in a matter of seconds.

Bell and the Telephone

Alexander Graham Bell invented a device that had an even greater impact on communications. Born and educated in Scotland, Bell moved to the United States as a young man. Here he studied methods for teaching people with hearing impairments how to speak. He also experimented with sending the sound of a voice over electrical wires.

By 1876 Bell made great advances in developing a device for transmitting speech—the telephone. While preparing to test the device, he accidentally spilled battery acid on his clothes. Panicked, Bell called out to his assistant, Thomas Watson, who was in another room: "Mr. Watson—come here—I want to see you!" Watson heard Bell's voice through the telephone. The invention worked.

Bell formed the Bell Telephone Company in 1877. By the 1890s, he had sold hundreds of thousands of phones. Businesses were the first customers to use the new technology. Before long, though, people began to bring this new communication device into their homes.

Telegraph operators used machines like this to send messages. They tapped out the coded messages using the circular pad on the right.

✔ **PROGRESS CHECK**

Contrasting Describe the difference between a telegraph and a telephone.

Comstock Images/Alamy

Academic Vocabulary

transmit to send a message by electronic signal; to pass from one person or place to another

The Genius of Invention

GUIDING QUESTION *How did new inventions improve people's lives?*

The late 1800s saw a burst of inventiveness in the United States. Between 1860 and 1890, the government granted more than 400,000 patents for new inventions. A patent is a license issued by the government that gives someone the right to make, use, and sell an invention without others copying it.

Many of the inventions were designed to help businesses operate more efficiently. Among these were Christopher Sholes's typewriter (1868) and William Burroughs's adding machine (1888).

Other inventions affected everyday life. In 1888 George Eastman invented a small box camera—the Kodak—that made it easier and less costly to take photographs. John Thurman developed a vacuum cleaner in 1899 that simplified housework.

The Wizard of Menlo Park

In his childhood, Thomas Edison was called "dull" by his teachers. Because of his poor hearing, he had trouble in school and often did not attend. His mother finally removed him from school and taught him at home. Edison loved anything related to science, and his mother allowed him to set up a chemistry lab in the family's basement.

While still in his 20s, Edison decided to go into the "invention business." In 1876 he set up a workshop in Menlo Park, New Jersey. In the following years, his famous laboratory produced the **phonograph,** the motion picture projector, and the storage battery. Edison's most important invention by far, though, was the lightbulb.

Edison developed the first workable lightbulb in 1879. He then designed power plants that could produce electric power and send it over a wide area. In 1880 Edison used 40 bulbs to light up Menlo Park. Visitors flocked to see the "light of the future." Then, in 1882, Edison built the first central electric power plant in New York City. It provided electric light to 85 buildings.

Inventor George Westinghouse took Edison's work with electricity even further. In 1885 Westinghouse developed and built transformers, which could send electric power more

In the late 1800s, companies such as Montgomery Ward and Sears sold a wide range of goods—from shoes to farm equipment—through mail-order catalogs.

▶ **CRITICAL THINKING**

Analyzing Visuals What does this catalog cover suggest about the appeal of shopping by mail?

(t) Getty Images, (b) Science & Society, Picture Library/Contributor/Getty Images

---

Reading **HELP**DESK CCSS

Build Vocabulary: *Word Origins*

The word *phonograph* comes from the Greek words *phono-*, which means "sound" and *graphos*, which means "writing."

Visual Vocabulary

phonograph a device for reproducing sounds by means of using a needle that follows grooves made on cylinders, such as the ones here, or on a disc

cheaply over longer distances. Electricity became the power source for factories, trolleys, streetlights, and lamps throughout the United States. Westinghouse also created a method for safely transporting natural gas and invented many other safety devices.

African American Inventors

A number of African Americans contributed to the era of invention. Engineer Lewis Howard Latimer developed an improved wire for use in the lightbulb. He joined Thomas Edison's company. Granville Woods was an electrical and mechanical engineer from Ohio. He patented dozens of inventions. Among them were an electric incubator and an improved brake for railroads. Elijah McCoy invented a **mechanism** for oiling machinery. Jan E. Matzeliger developed a shoe-making machine. It performed many steps that had been done by hand and revolutionized the shoe industry.

Lewis Latimer invented many useful devices, including an improved version of the lightbulb that lasted much longer than Edison's original.

✔ PROGRESS CHECK

Evaluating Which of Edison's inventions do you think is the most valuable to our world today?

A Changing Society

GUIDING QUESTION *How did the inventions of the late 1800s change society?*

In the 1900s, improvements produced a whole new era of transportation. At the heart of this revolution was the automobile, which became a practical machine for moving people and goods from place to place.

Henry Ford's Vision

Henry Ford worked as an engineer in Detroit, Michigan, in the 1890s. He had an interest in automobiles—and a vision. Other people were building cars, but few people could afford them. Ford wanted to build an inexpensive car that would last a lifetime. He experimented with an engine powered by gasoline. In 1903 he started his own auto-making company in Detroit.

In 1906 Ford told Charles Sorenson, one of his workers, "We're going to get a car now that we can make in great volume and get the prices way down." For the next year, Ford and Sorenson worked on the **Model T,** building the car and testing it on rough roads.

Westinghouse appliances in homes today are made by a company that George Westinghouse founded in 1886 to develop and produce devices powered by electricity. His biggest competitor was General Electric, the company founded in 1890 by his rival, Thomas Edison.

▶ CRITICAL THINKING
Assessing How is the work of Edison and Westinghouse still affecting us today?

Model T early Ford car

Academic Vocabulary

mechanism a set of moving or working parts in a machine or other device

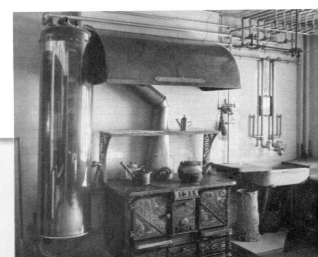

This assembly line at a Ford factory lowered the cost of manufacturing automobiles.

▶ **CRITICAL THINKING**

Speculating How do you think the development of the assembly line affected workers?

In 1908 Ford introduced the Model T to the public. Sorenson described the sturdy black vehicle as "a car which anyone could afford to buy, which anyone could drive anywhere, and which almost anyone could keep in repair." These qualities made the Model T very popular. During the next 18 years, Ford's company sold more than 15 million Model Ts in the United States. It also sold more than a million cars overseas. Model T sales accounted for about half of the automobiles on the road in the world during that time.

Henry Ford also pioneered a new, less expensive way to manufacture cars—the **assembly line.** On the assembly line, each worker performed an assigned task again and again. This method proved more efficient than having one person do several different tasks while building an automobile. The assembly line revolutionized other industries as well. It enabled manufacturers of many different items to produce large quantities of goods more quickly. This **mass production** (pruh•DUHK•shuhn) of goods decreased manufacturing costs, so products could be sold more cheaply.

The First Airplane

Inventors began experimenting with powered flight in the early 1890s. In 1896 American astronomer Samuel Langley built a model airplane that was powered by a steam engine. Langley's model flew almost a mile before it ran out of fuel and crashed.

Reading **HELP**DESK CCSS

assembly line factory method in which work moves past stationary workers who perform a single task

mass production factory production of goods in large quantities

Owners of a bicycle shop, Wilbur and Orville Wright used their skills as mechanics to pioneer human flight. Between 1900 and 1902, they built and tested a series of non-powered gliders. They then designed a plane powered by a gasoline engine. In September 1903, the brothers began testing this new plane at Kitty Hawk, North Carolina. Seven weeks of trial and error at last produced success. On December 17, 1903, the brothers each piloted their plane. Of the four flights that day, the last was most successful. Although Wilbur stayed in the air for just under a minute, longer flights were soon to come. The airplane was born—though it would take some years for this invention to have its full effect on the American way of life.

✔ **PROGRESS CHECK**

Identifying What was Henry Ford's vision?

The longest of the Wright Brothers' first flights covered 852 feet (260 m) and lasted 59 seconds.

LESSON 2 REVIEW (CCSS)

Review Vocabulary

1. Examine the terms below. Then write a sentence explaining what they have in common.

   a. mass production
   b. assembly line
   c. Model T

Answer the Guiding Questions

2. *Explaining* How did the invention of the telegraph and telephone affect communication?

3. *Determining Cause and Effect* How did new inventions change people's daily lives?

4. *Making Generalizations* How did the inventions of the late 1800s change the nation?

5. **ARGUMENT** Which of the inventions discussed in this lesson do you think has had the greatest effect on our way of life today? Write a paragraph defending your choice.

There's More Online!

☑ **CHART/GRAPH**
  • Factors of Production
  • Ford Stock Prices

☑ **GRAPHIC ORGANIZER**
  The Oil and Steel
  Industries

Lesson 3
An Age of Big Business

ESSENTIAL QUESTION *How does technology change the way people live and work?*

IT MATTERS BECAUSE
Industrial expansion was made possible in part by the development of new business practices and organizations—though there were costs to the new way of doing business.

The Growth of Big Business

GUIDING QUESTION *What is the role of the factors of production in making goods and services?*

In western Pennsylvania, people had long noticed a sticky black oil—petroleum—that seeped from the ground. Some people actually used the oil as a kind of medicine. Then, in the 1850s, researchers found they could burn petroleum to make heat and smoke-free light. It also was good for lubricating machinery. Suddenly, oil was valuable.

Edwin L. Drake believed that he could find large amounts of petroleum by digging a well. Many people thought Drake was wrong. At that time, few people knew that pools of oil did indeed exist underground. They did not imagine that oil wells could lead to great fortune.

In 1859 Drake drilled a well in Titusville, Pennsylvania. He struck oil. This led to the creation of a multimillion-dollar petroleum industry.

The Factors of Production

During the late 1800s, new technology, transportation, and business methods allowed business leaders in the country to tap its rich supply of natural resources. This continued the

(l) Bettmann/CORBIS, (cl) Bettmann/CORBIS(cr) The Print Collector/Age FotoStock America (r) Bettmann/CORBIS

Reading **HELP**DESK ⓒⓒⓢⓢ

Taking Notes: *Organizing*

As you read, create two diagrams like this one to organize information about the oil and steel industries.

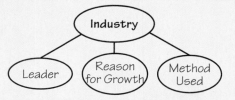

Content Vocabulary

• **factors of production**
• **entrepreneur**
• **corporation**
• **stock**
• **shareholder**
• **dividend**
• **trust**
• **monopoly**
• **merger**

shift in the United States from an economy based on farming to one based on industry. The change was possible because the United States had the resources needed for a growing economy. Among these resources were what economists call the **factors of production**—land, labor, and capital.

As a factor of production, land refers not just to the land itself but also to all natural resources in it. Petroleum is an example. The United States held many natural resources.

The second factor of production is labor. It takes large numbers of workers to turn raw materials into goods. Between 1860 and 1900, the population of the country more than doubled.

The third factor of production is capital. These are the things people use to make other goods and services. The machines, buildings, and tools used to make automobiles, for example, are capital goods. Money is another type of capital.

Finding Capital for Expansion

With the economy growing after the Civil War, many businesses looked for ways to expand. To do so, **entrepreneurs** (ahn•truh•pruh•NURZ)—people who start businesses—had to raise capital in the form of money. They needed this capital to buy raw materials and equipment, pay workers, and cover other costs.

One way a company can raise capital is by becoming a **corporation** (kawr•puh•RAY•shuhn). This is a type of business organization that can have many owners and grow very large. A corporation often sells shares—part-ownership of the corporation—called **stock.** It then uses the money raised to build the business. The people who buy the stock are the corporation's **shareholders** (SHEHR•hohl•duhrz).

When a corporation does well, shareholders earn **dividends** (DIH•vuh•dehndz). These are cash payments from the corporation's profits.

The rise of corporations helped fuel industry in the late 1800s. Railroads were the first to form corporations. Manufacturing firms, banks, and other businesses followed.

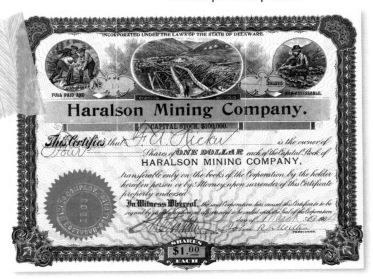

Buyers of stock receive certificates that represent their partial ownership in the corporation.

✔ **PROGRESS CHECK**

Explaining Why is capital important for economic growth?

---

factors of production land, labor, and capital used to make goods and services
entrepreneur a person who starts a business

corporation legally defined organization of people and resources with the purpose of doing business
stock shares of ownership a company sells in its business

shareholder a person who invests in a company by buying stock
dividend a stockholder's share of a company's profits, usually as a cash payment

The Growth of Oil and Steel

GUIDING QUESTION *How did John D. Rockefeller and Andrew Carnegie build fortunes in the oil and steel industries?*

As news of Edwin L. Drake and his oil strike of 1859 spread, prospectors and investors hurried to western Pennsylvania. "Oil rush" towns with names such as Oil City and Petroleum Center sprang up overnight. The oil boom expanded as prospectors struck oil in Ohio and West Virginia.

John D. Rockefeller was the most famous figure of the oil industry. When he was just 26, he and four **partners** built an oil refinery—a plant to process oil—in Cleveland, Ohio. In 1870 Rockefeller organized the Standard Oil Company of Ohio. He then set out to dominate the oil industry.

Rockefeller and the Standard Oil Trust

One method Rockefeller used was horizontal integration. This means combining competing companies of the same type into one corporation. Standard Oil grew powerful and wealthy.

Rockefeller lowered prices to drive competitors out of business. He pressured customers not to deal with rival companies, and he got the railroads to give him low rates. In 1882 Rockefeller formed a **trust,** a group of companies managed by a single board of trustees. Shareholders of these companies traded their stock for Standard Oil stock, which paid higher dividends. In this way, Standard Oil gained partial ownership and control

Newspapers and magazines often portrayed corporations as "monopoly monsters" that were too powerful to be controlled.

▶ **CRITICAL THINKING**
Summarizing Describe what is taking place in this cartoon.

Bettmann/CORBIS

of the other companies. Rockefeller had created a **monopoly**—total control of an industry by a single producer.

Carnegie and the Steel Industry

Steel became a big business during this era, too. This strong metal was ideal for making railroad tracks, bridges, and many other products.

Two new methods of making steel—the Bessemer process, developed by English inventor Henry Bessemer, and the open-hearth process—changed the industry. With these new methods, mills were able to make large amounts of affordable steel. In the 1870s, companies built large steel mills in western Pennsylvania and eastern Ohio. Pittsburgh, Pennsylvania, became the steel capital of the nation. Cleveland, Chicago, Detroit, and Birmingham, Alabama, also became important hubs for steel production.

The leading figure in steelmaking was Andrew Carnegie, the son of a Scottish immigrant. Starting as a messenger and telegraph operator, he worked his way up to become manager of the Pennsylvania Railroad. Carnegie soon realized that there was a huge market for steel. After learning about the Bessemer process, he built a steel plant near Pittsburgh.

By 1890 Carnegie dominated the steel industry. He did this through vertical integration: He acquired companies at all stages of the steel-making process. Carnegie bought iron and coal mines—the raw materials of steel. He bought warehouses, ore ships, and railroads for storing and moving raw materials. In this way, Carnegie gained control of all steps of his business. This allowed Carnegie to reduce the cost of making steel and the prices he charged for it. Many other steel companies could not compete. By 1900 the Carnegie Steel Company was making a third of the nation's steel.

Before the Bessemer converter, shown here, making steel was a slow, costly process. This device made possible the mass production of steel.

monopoly total control of a type of industry by one person or one company

Millionaires and Philanthropists

Carnegie, Rockefeller, and other industrial millionaires of the era grew interested in philanthropy—the use of money to benefit the community. They used their fortunes to found schools, universities, libraries, and more. Carnegie donated $350 million to various organizations. He built Carnegie Hall—one of the world's most famous concert halls—in New York City. He also funded the building of more than 2,000 libraries worldwide. Rockefeller used his fortune to establish the University of Chicago in 1890 and to found New York's Rockefeller Institute for Medical Research.

Corporations Grow Larger

In 1889 New Jersey encouraged the **trend** toward monopolies by allowing formation of holding companies. A holding company could gain power over multiple other companies by buying their stock instead of buying the companies outright. Other states also made **mergers**—the combining of companies—easier.

Some people admired large businesses. Others felt they hurt consumers. With little competition, corporations were under no pressure to improve their products or services. In 1890 Congress passed the Sherman Antitrust Act, which made trusts and monopolies illegal. At first, however, it did little to curb the power of big business.

✔ **PROGRESS CHECK**

Describing How did Standard Oil become a monopoly?

merger the combining of two or more businesses into one

Academic Vocabulary

trend a general direction of events

Andrew Carnegie was a leading industrialist of the late 1800s.

Bettmann/CORBIS

LESSON 3 REVIEW **CCSS**

Review Vocabulary

1. Use the following words in a sentence that illustrates what the terms have in common.

   a. corporation   **b.** stock

2. Examine the terms below. Then write a sentence explaining what the terms have in common.

   a. merger   **b.** monopoly

Answer the Guiding Questions

3. ***Summarizing*** What are factors of production, and what role do they play in producing goods and services?

4. ***Explaining*** How did horizontal and vertical integration help Rockefeller and Carnegie gain control of the oil and steel industries?

5. **INFORMATIVE/EXPLANATORY** Why do you think wealthy industrialists such as Rockefeller and Carnegie became philanthropists? Write a paragraph that answers this question.

netw*rks*

There's More Online!

☑ **BIOGRAPHY**
 • Samuel Gompers
 • Mary Harris Jones

☑ **CHART/GRAPH** The Fair
 Labor Standards Act

☑ **GRAPHIC ORGANIZER**
 Strike Causes and Effects

☑ **MAP** Labor Action 1877–1914

☑ **PRIMARY SOURCE** Jones and
 Gompers on Labor

☑ **VIDEO** The Struggle for Rights

Lesson 4
Workers in the Industrial Age

ESSENTIAL QUESTION *How does technology change the way people live and work?*

IT MATTERS BECAUSE

Industrialization created a large group of workers and also difficult working conditions. The result was the beginnings of the labor movement.

The Industrial Workforce

GUIDING QUESTION *How did working conditions change during the Industrial Age?*

Industrial growth created jobs. Yet factory workers paid a price for economic progress. They generally worked for 10 or 12 hours a day, six days a week. They could be fired at any time for any reason. Many lost their jobs during business downturns. Immigrants willing to take lower pay drove down wages.

People often worked in unsafe and unhealthful conditions. Steelworkers suffered terrible burns. Coal miners died in cave-ins. Garment workers toiled in crowded and dangerous urban factories known as **sweatshops** (SWEHT·shahps).

By 1900 more than 1 million women had joined the industrial workforce. Women generally earned about half of what men did for the same work. Hundreds of thousands of children under 16 also worked in industry. Many states passed child-labor laws that said children working in factories had to be at least 12 years old and should not work more than 10 hours a day. Employers, however, widely ignored child-labor laws.

☑ **PROGRESS CHECK**

Calculating How many hours a week did industrial laborers typically work?

Reading HELPDESK (CCSS)

Taking Notes: *Determining Cause and Effect*

As you read, use a chart like this one to record the reasons events occurred and what happened as a result.

Event	Reason	Outcome
Haymarket Riot		
Homestead Strike		
Pullman Strike		

Content Vocabulary

• **sweatshop**
• **labor union**
• **collective bargaining**
• **strikebreaker**
• **injunction**

Industrial workers in the early 1900s found that it was not easy to earn enough money to meet expenses.

Average Hourly Wages*	Average Expenses*
Bricklayers: 50¢	Rent: $4–10 per month
Plasterers: 50¢	Butter: 22¢ per pound
Newspaper compositors: 36¢	Milk: 6¢ per quart
Machine woodworkers: 25¢	Bread: 5¢ per loaf
Construction workers: 17¢	Rib roast: 13¢ per pound
Metalworkers: 16¢	Postage: 2¢ per ounce

(*in **Chicago** 1903) (*in **Chicago** 1903)

CHART SKILL

1 CALCULATING How many hours would a machine woodworker have to work in order to pay rent of $8 in Chicago in 1903?

2 CRITICAL THINKING *Speculating* What other expenses, besides food and housing, would a typical worker have?

The Growth of Labor Unions

GUIDING QUESTION *Why did workers form labor unions?*

Dissatisfied workers organized into groups—**labor unions**—to demand better pay and working conditions. Earlier in the 1800s, skilled workers in certain trades or crafts had formed unions. These trade unions represented only one trade, however, and had too few members to have a wide impact. By the mid-1800s, as working conditions worsened, labor leaders looked to include larger numbers of workers in their unions.

In 1869 garment cutters in Philadelphia founded a trade union known as the Noble and Holy Order of the Knights of Labor. At the time, employers could fire workers who joined labor organizations. For this reason, the Knights met secretly and used special handshakes to **identify** one another.

Under the leadership of Terence V. Powderly, the Knights of Labor became a national labor organization in the 1880s. Unlike most unions, the Knights recruited people who were usually not allowed to join trade unions. For example, they encouraged women, African Americans, immigrants, and unskilled laborers to join their union.

The Knights of Labor grew to more than 700,000 members by 1886. Its links to several violent acts turned public opinion against it, however. The Knights lost power in the 1890s.

CORBIS

Reading **HELP**DESK (CCSS)

sweatshop a shop or factory where workers work long hours at low wages under unhealthy conditions

labor union organization of workers who seek better pay and working conditions

Academic Vocabulary

identify to show or prove who someone is; to recognize someone or something

BIOGRAPHY

Samuel Gompers (1850–1924)

Born in London, England, Samuel Gompers went to work making cigars at the age of 10. After moving to the United States with his family, he became involved in the labor movement. He helped organize and lead the American Federation of Labor from its founding in 1886. He believed strongly in collective bargaining. "The individual workman is as weak against the combination of wealth as would be a straw in a cyclone."

Mary Harris Jones (c.1837–1930)

Mary Harris "Mother" Jones was born in Ireland and trained to be a teacher. She married a union organizer, and after her husband and four children died in a yellow fever epidemic, she got involved in the movement herself. Mother Jones traveled the country to organize workers and to support strikes. "There are no limits," she insisted, "to which powers of privilege will not go to keep the workers in slavery."

The American Federation of Labor

In 1886 a group of national trade unions joined together to form the American Federation of Labor (AFL). The AFL represented skilled workers in a large number of trades and crafts.

Jewish immigrant, Samuel Gompers, the practical-minded president of the Cigar Makers' Union, led the AFL. The organization pressed for higher wages, shorter hours, and better working conditions. It also sought the right to **collective bargaining** (kuh·LEHK·tihv BAHR·guh·ning)—when unions represent a group of workers in talks with management over wages and other matters.

Union involvement in violence turned public feeling against workers and unions in the late 1880s. Yet the AFL survived. By 1904, it claimed more than 1.6 million members and remained a significant force in industry.

The Rights of Working Women

Many unions would not admit women. That did not keep women from playing a role in the labor movement. Mary Harris "Mother" Jones spent 50 years fighting for workers' rights. She was especially active in the drive to organize mine workers—virtually all of whom were men.

Women also formed their own unions. In 1911 fire broke out at the Triangle Shirtwaist Company, a New York sweatshop located on the top three floors of a 10-story building. Workers, mostly young immigrant women, were trapped. Survivors reported that some of the doors leading out were locked.

▶ **CRITICAL THINKING**

Comparing What is one feature both Gompers and Jones share in common besides their involvement in labor organizing?

Analyzing How did Gompers and Jones view the employers of the workers they hoped to organize?

collective bargaining discussion between an employer and union representatives of workers over wages, hours, and working conditions for the union membership as a whole

Labor Action 1877–1914

CANADA

Coeur d'Alene 5

Idaho

2 Chicago 4 7 Scranton
Pa.
6 Pullman Homestead
Colo. Ill. W. 1
8 Ludlow Va. Martinsburg

La.

New Orleans 3

MEXICO

90°W

0   400 miles
0   400 km
Albers Equal-Area projection

1 1877 **Great Railway Strike**
Workers protest pay cuts

2 1886 **Haymarket Affair**
Labor rally ends in violence

3 1892 **New Orleans**
Workers from 42 unions
demand shorter hours and
better pay

4 1892 **Homestead Strike**
Steelworkers protest
wage cut

5 1892 **Silver Mine Unrest**
State jails hundreds of
striking workers

6 1894 **Pullman Strike**
Federal troops end riots

7 1902 **Anthracite Coal Strike**
Miners strike to win union
recognition

8 1914 **Ludlow Massacre**
State militia burns striking
miners' tent colony

GEOGRAPHY CONNECTION

Workers organized many strikes
and protests, some of which led
to violence.

1 **REGION** Based on this map,
what industrial operations
existed in the far West?

2 **CRITICAL THINKING**
Analyzing Visuals Based on
this map, which industries
were especially troubled by
serious strikes?

Nearly 150 workers died, many after jumping from the windows.
The disaster led the International Ladies' Garment Workers
Union (ILGWU) to push for a safer working **environment.**

The Unions Take Action

Economic depressions in the 1870s and the 1890s hit working
people hard. After a financial panic in 1873, for example, many
companies cut costs by forcing workers to take pay cuts. In some
cases, they fired workers. Unions responded with large strikes
that sometimes sparked violence.

In July 1877, angry railroad strikers in several locations
burned rail yards, ripped up track, and destroyed property.
Railroad companies hired **strikebreakers** (STRYK•bray•kuhrs)
to replace the striking workers. Federal troops restored order.

Another bloody clash occurred between police and strikers
in Chicago's Haymarket Square in May 1886. Workers from the
McCormick Harvester Company had been striking in favor of
an eight-hour workday. Several were injured when the police
broke up a labor rally. The next day, a crowd gathered in protest.
As police ordered the crowd to break up, an unidentified person
threw a bomb. The blast touched off a riot. When it was over,
seven police officers and several civilians were dead, and 60
people were injured. Afterward, many Americans linked the
labor movement with violence and disorder.

Reading HELPDESK CCSS

strikebreaker person hired to
replace a striking worker in order to break
up a strike

injunction a court order to
stop something from happening

Academic Vocabulary

environment a person's
surroundings

In 1892 workers went on strike at Andrew Carnegie's steel plant in Homestead, Pennsylvania. In an attempt to weaken the union, plant managers had cut workers' wages. In response, the union called a strike.

Homestead managers hired nonunion workers and brought in 300 armed guards to protect them. A fierce battle followed in which at least 10 people died.

Pennsylvania's governor Robert E. Pattison sent the state's militia to restore order. The plant reopened with nonunion workers. After the failure of the Homestead Strike, membership in the steelworkers' union dwindled.

In 1894 when the company cut their wages, employees of the Pullman railway-car plant went on strike. Pullman responded by closing the plant. Workers in the American Railway Union then refused to handle trains that included Pullman cars. The union's action paralyzed rail traffic across the nation.

Pullman and the railroad owners persuaded U.S. Attorney General Richard Olney to obtain an **injunction** (ihn·JUHNK·shuhn), or court order, against the union for "obstructing the railways and holding up the mails." When union leader Eugene V. Debs refused to end the strike, he was sent to jail.

President Grover Cleveland sent in federal troops and the strike ended. The failure of the Pullman Strike dealt another blow to the union movement. Despite these setbacks, workers continued to organize to campaign for better wages and working conditions.

On May 4, 1886, a crowd gathered in Chicago's Haymarket Square to protest police violence. As the meeting was breaking up, someone threw a bomb. The exchange of gunfire that followed left several police officers and civilians dead.

▶ CRITICAL THINKING
Analyzing What effect did the Haymarket affair have on the labor movement?

Bettmann/CORBIS

✔ PROGRESS CHECK

Explaining Why were there growing anti-labor feelings in the late 1800s?

LESSON 4 REVIEW CCSS

Review Vocabulary

1. Use the terms below in a sentence that illustrates how the terms are connected.

   a. labor union   b. collective bargaining

2. Examine the two terms below. Then write a sentence explaining what the terms have in common.

   a. strikebreaker   b. injunction

Answer the Guiding Questions

3. *Describing* What were working conditions like for many workers in the Industrial Age?

4. *Explaining* How did workers hope that labor unions would help to improve their lives?

5. **INFORMATIVE/EXPLANATORY** Explain why so many women and children worked in the industrial labor force, and describe the treatment they received.

Write your answers on a separate piece of paper.

1 **Exploring the Essential Question**

INFORMATIVE/EXPLANATORY Consider the ways that technology changed how people lived and worked in the late 1800s and the early 1900s. Write an essay in which you use examples from the chapter to explore the benefits—and the drawbacks—of these changes. How was life overall improved by the changes in ways of living and working? What were some of the challenges introduced?

2 **21st Century Skills**

COMMUNICATION Imagine you are living in the late 1800s or early 1900s. Create a magazine ad or radio commercial for one of the inventions you have learned about in this chapter. Your creation should try to convince consumers to purchase this product, about which they will have no knowledge. Decide who your customers are, then craft an ad to convince them why they need or should want this product.

3 **Thinking Like a Historian**

UNDERSTANDING CAUSE AND EFFECT Investigate one of the changes in business operations, manufacturing processes, or technology that you have learned about in this chapter. Assess the effect of that change on life today. For example, you might trace the change from Edison's phonograph to today's MP3 players. Prepare a poster or a slide show presentation to report your findings to the class.

4 **Visual Literacy**

INTERPRETING POLITICAL CARTOONS This political cartoon is about the power of giant corporations that arose in the late 1800s. What point of view does the cartoonist have about the growth of "big business"— in particular, the Standard Oil monopoly—during this period? What details in the cartoon give you clues about the opinions the cartoonist holds?

Bettmann/CORBIS

CHAPTER 4 Assessment

REVIEWING THE GUIDING QUESTIONS

Choose the best answer for each question.

1 Which industry probably benefited least from the expansion of the railroad system in the late 1800s?
   A. coal mining
   B. steel
   C. automobile
   D iron mining

2 The first major improvement in communications was introduced by
   F. Alexander Graham Bell.
   G. Thomas Edison.
   H. Samuel Morse.
   I. George Westinghouse.

3 The iron ore that Andrew Carnegie used to manufacture steel is an example of what factor of production?
   A. land
   B. capital
   C. labor
   D. an entrepreneur

4 The trust that John D. Rockefeller formed to gain control of the oil industry is an example of
   F vertical integration.
   G. mass production.
   H. horizontal integration.
   I. a factor of production.

5 The typical industrial worker in the late 1800s
   A. was a woman or a child.
   B. worked 60 to 72 hours a week.
   C. belonged to a craft union.
   D. worked in a sweatshop.

6 In general, how did the public react to the labor actions of the late 1800s?
   F. It supported the goals of the unions.
   G. It held business owners responsible for violent clashes.
   H. It held unions responsible for violent clashes.
   I. It was sharply critical of strikebreakers.

DBQ **ANALYZING DOCUMENTS**

These words are from the workers' song "Drill, Ye Tarriers, Drill." "Tarrier" was the name given to Irish drillers who dug tunnels for the railroads.

"The new foreman is Dan McCann, / I'll tell you sure he's a blame mean man, / Last week a premature blast went off, / And a mile in the air went big Jim Goff.

* * *

When pay day next it came around, / Poor Jim's pay a dollar short he found, / "What for?" says he, then came this reply, / "You were docked for the time you were up in the sky."

Source: Norm Cohen, *Long Steel Rail: The Railroad in American Folksong*

7 **Analyzing Primary Sources** Goff's pay was a dollar short because

A. the union had taken some of his pay.

B. his boss was kind.

C. he had damaged company property.

D. his accident kept him from working.

8 **Drawing Conclusions** Based on this song, you would expect that people who worked on the railroad

F. felt they were paid fairly.

G. believed their employers treated them unfairly sometimes.

H. had no desire to join a union.

I. were especially concerned about safety.

SHORT RESPONSE

"God gave me my money. … Having been endowed with the gift I possess, I believe it is my duty to make money and still more money and to use the money I make for the good of my fellow man according to the dictates of my conscience."

—*John D. Rockefeller*

Source: Suzy Platt, *Respectfully Quoted*

9 What did Rockefeller mean when he said, "God gave me my money"?

10 Why did Rockefeller think it was his duty to earn as much as he could?

EXTENDED RESPONSE

11 **Informative/Explanatory** Using the information from these documents and the knowledge gained from the chapter, write an essay that evaluates the industrialists' approach to improving society.

Need Extra Help?

If You've Missed Question	1	2	3	4	5	6	7	8	9	10	11
Review Lesson	1	2	3	3	4	4	4	4	3	3	3, 4

An Urban Society

1865–1914

networks

There's More Online about how the rise of cities changed American life.

CHAPTER 5

ESSENTIAL QUESTIONS • *Why do people move?*
• *How do new ideas change the way people live?*

The Story Matters . . .

The grand and massive structure has taken 14 years to build. Its design is pure genius. Its construction has been the product of sweat and blood. During the project, tragic deaths occurred at the worksite. Charges of corruption troubled the project since its beginning.

In the end, however, triumph prevails. In 1883 the Brooklyn Bridge opens. As people and carriages make their way over the river, it seems as if there is nothing the American people cannot do—and no limits to the heights to which the American city can soar.

◄ *The Brooklyn Bridge in New York City was a brilliant symbol of the booming American cities of the late 1800s and early 1900s.*

The Granger Collection, NYC

121

Place and Time: United States 1865 to 1914

From the beginning, the United States had been a rural farming country. In the late 1800s, however, industry flourished. Along with the growth of industry came the growth of large cities.

Step Into the Place

MAP FOCUS From the Atlantic Coast to the Mississippi River, America was becoming a more crowded place. Industries were centered in these regions, too, especially in the Northeast.

1 PLACE Which color in the map key shows the most population density, or crowding?

2 PLACE Which part of the West Coast has the greatest population density?

3 CRITICAL THINKING
Drawing Conclusions Why do you think the eastern United States is more densely populated than the western part at this time in history?

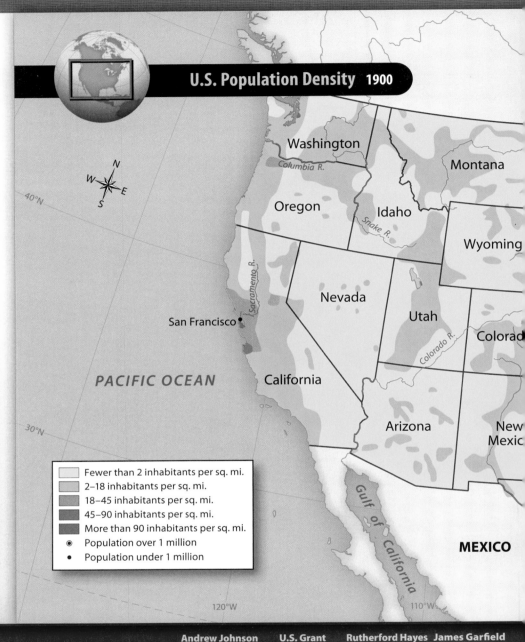

U.S. Population Density 1900

Washington
Columbia R.
Montana
Oregon
Idaho
Snake R.
Wyoming
Nevada
Utah
Colorad
Sacramento R.
San Francisco
Colorado R.
California
PACIFIC OCEAN
Arizona
New Mexic

Fewer than 2 inhabitants per sq. mi.
2–18 inhabitants per sq. mi.
18–45 inhabitants per sq. mi.
45–90 inhabitants per sq. mi.
More than 90 inhabitants per sq. mi.
⊙ Population over 1 million
• Population under 1 million

Gulf of California

MEXICO

120°W   110°W

Step Into the Time

TIME LINE Look at the time line. The era begins with a major breakthrough: the transatlantic telegraph line. If you were a telegraph operator, which three events on this time line would you want to broadcast? Why?

Andrew Johnson
1865–1869

U.S. Grant
1869–1877

Rutherford Hayes
1877–1881

James Garfield
1881

U.S. PRESIDENTS

U.S. EVENTS   1865   1875

WORLD EVENTS

1866 Transatlantic telegraph line successfully completed

1869 Transcontinental railroad completed

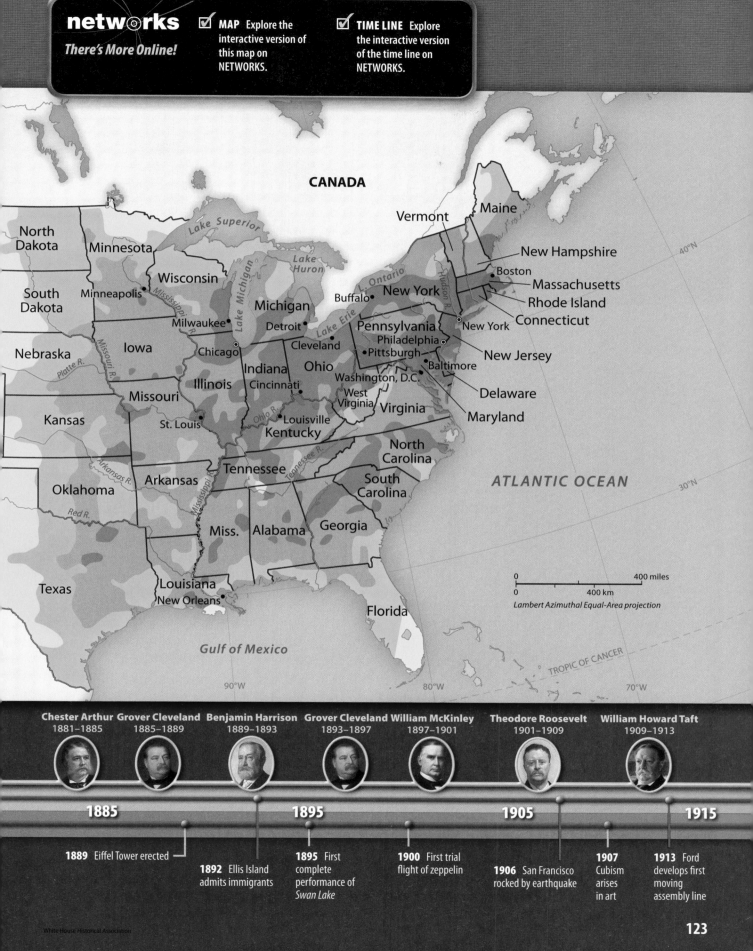

networks

There's More Online!

☑ **MAP** Explore the interactive version of this map on NETWORKS.

☑ **TIME LINE** Explore the interactive version of the time line on NETWORKS.

CANADA

North Dakota

Minnesota

South Dakota

Wisconsin

Lake Superior

Minneapolis

Milwaukee

Mississippi R.

Lake Michigan

Lake Huron

Michigan

Detroit

Lake Erie

Lake Ontario

Vermont

Maine

New Hampshire

Boston

Massachusetts

Rhode Island

Connecticut

New York

Buffalo

Hudson R.

Nebraska

Iowa

Chicago

Illinois

Indiana

Cincinnati

Ohio

Cleveland

Pennsylvania

Philadelphia

Pittsburgh

New York

New Jersey

Missouri R.

Platte R.

Missouri

St. Louis

Louisville

Kentucky

West Virginia

Washington, D.C.

Baltimore

Delaware

Maryland

Kansas

Virginia

Ohio R.

North Carolina

Arkansas

Tennessee

Arkansas R.

Tennessee R.

South Carolina

ATLANTIC OCEAN

Oklahoma

Red R.

Miss.

Alabama

Georgia

Mississippi R.

Louisiana

New Orleans

Texas

Florida

Gulf of Mexico

0 — 400 miles
0 — 400 km
Lambert Azimuthal Equal-Area projection

TROPIC OF CANCER

40°N
30°N

90°W   80°W   70°W

Chester Arthur
1881–1885

Grover Cleveland
1885–1889

Benjamin Harrison
1889–1893

Grover Cleveland
1893–1897

William McKinley
1897–1901

Theodore Roosevelt
1901–1909

William Howard Taft
1909–1913

1885

1895

1905

1915

1889 Eiffel Tower erected

1892 Ellis Island admits immigrants

1895 First complete performance of *Swan Lake*

1900 First trial flight of zeppelin

1906 San Francisco rocked by earthquake

1907 Cubism arises in art

1913 Ford develops first moving assembly line

Lesson 1
The New Immigrants

ESSENTIAL QUESTION *Why do people move?*

IT MATTERS BECAUSE
Immigrants to the United States brought with them the cultural heritage of their homelands.

A Flood of Immigrants

GUIDING QUESTION *Why did many people immigrate to the United States during this period?*

Immigration to the United States shifted in the late 1800s. Before 1865, most immigrants other than enslaved Africans had came from northern and western Europe. After the Civil War, immigrants from other countries began making the journey to the United States.

Coming to a New Land

In the mid-1880s, large groups of "new" immigrants began arriving from eastern and southern Europe. Greeks, Russians, Hungarians, Italians, Turks, and Poles were among the newcomers. Meanwhile, the number of "old" immigrants from northern and western Europe went down. By 1907 southern and eastern Europe supplied 80 percent of all immigrants.

Many of these newcomers were Catholics or Jews. Few of them spoke English. To some Americans, they did not seem to blend into society as easily as earlier immigrants had. Often, they lived in neighborhoods together with others of the same nationality. There, they could speak their own languages, practice their own religions, and celebrate their own cultural festivals.

(l) Visions of America/Joe Sohm/Photodisc/Getty Images, (cl) The Granger Collection, NYC, (c) The Granger Collection, NYC,

Reading **HELP**DESK (CCSS)

Taking Notes: *Sequencing*

As you read, place immigration laws and agreements on a time line like this one, taking notes on the purpose of each.

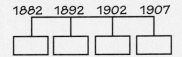

Content Vocabulary
• **emigrate**   • **recruit**
• **ethnic group** • **assimilate**
• **steerage**   • **nativist**

In addition to growing immigration from eastern and southern Europe, many people came to the United States from China and Japan after the Civil War. They, too, brought unfamiliar languages and religious beliefs. And they, too, had difficulty blending into American society. After 1900, immigration from Mexico also increased.

"Push" Factors: Leaving Troubles Behind

Why did so many people leave their homelands for the United States in the late 1800s and early 1900s? Many people **emigrated** (EH•muh•gray•ted), or left their homelands, because of economic hardship. In Italy and Hungary, people faced overcrowding and poverty. It was hard to find jobs. Farmers in places such as Croatia and Serbia could not own enough land to support their families. Farmers in Sweden suffered major crop failures. Elsewhere, new machines put craftworkers out of work.

People sometimes had to flee from their homelands. Some countries made unfair laws against certain **ethnic groups**—people who share a common culture or heritage. More than 2.5 million Jews fled such treatment between 1880 and 1924. They came mostly from Russia and Poland, in eastern Europe. Most came to the United States.

GEOGRAPHY CONNECTION

People came to the United States from many countries during this era.

1 **MOVEMENT** What country accounted for the largest number of immigrants?

2 **CRITICAL THINKING**
Comparing Write a statement comparing immigration from Asia with immigration from Europe.

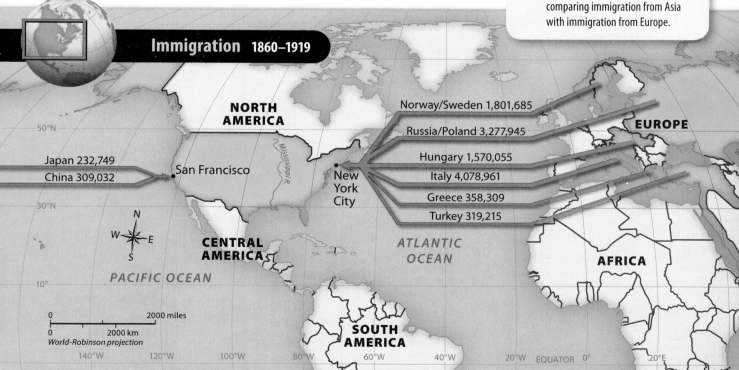

Immigration 1860–1919

Norway/Sweden 1,801,685
Russia/Poland 3,277,945
Hungary 1,570,055
Italy 4,078,961
Greece 358,309
Turkey 319,215

Japan 232,749
China 309,032

San Francisco

New York City

NORTH AMERICA
EUROPE
CENTRAL AMERICA
ATLANTIC OCEAN
AFRICA
PACIFIC OCEAN
SOUTH AMERICA

0 2000 miles
0 2000 km
World-Robinson projection

emigrate to leave one's homeland to live somewhere else

ethnic group people who share a common culture or heritage

Build Vocabulary: *Word Parts*

The words *immigrant* and *emigrant* are related. The prefix *im-* means "to come in," and the prefix *e-* means "to go out." Someone *emigrates* from a country, but *immigrants* arrive on a new country's shores.

The torch is a symbol of liberty. The crown's rays stand for the seven seas and seven continents of the world.

Liberty holds a tablet that represents the book of law. In Roman numerals it reads "July 4, 1776."

At Liberty's feet lies a broken chain, which stands for freedom from tyranny.

INFOGRAPHIC

1 MAKING CONNECTIONS
How does the date on the tablet relate to the broken chain?

2 CRITICAL THINKING
Finding the Main Idea What American values are represented in the statue's symbols?

"Pull" Factors: Opportunity

Immigrants viewed the United States as a place of jobs, land, and hope. They found what they were looking for: Some immigrants returned to their homelands after a few years, but most stayed.

The journey to the United States was often difficult. Immigrants first had to travel to a port city, which might be hundreds of miles from home. Then came the long ocean voyage. It took 12 days to sail from Europe and several weeks from Asia. Immigrants often could afford only the cheapest tickets. They traveled in cramped quarters on the lower decks of the ships. This section was known as **steerage** (STEER·ij).

Entering the United States

Most immigrants from Europe landed at New York City. For those who arrived after 1886, the magnificent sight of the Statue of Liberty greeted them as they sailed into New York Harbor. The statue, a gift from the nation of France, seemed to promise hope for a better life. On its base, the stirring words of poet Emma Lazarus welcomed the newcomers:

Reading **HELP**DESK **CCSS**

steerage inexpensive quarters for passengers below the deck of a ship

" Give me your tired, your poor, Your huddled masses yearning to breathe free, The wretched refuse of your teeming shore. Send these, the homeless, tempest-tossed to me, I lift my lamp beside the golden door! "

—from the poem "The New Colossus," by Emma Lazarus

Before the new arrivals could pass through the "golden door," however, they had to pass through government reception centers. In the East, immigrants stopped first at Castle Garden on Manhattan Island. Castle Garden was once a fort. Starting in 1892, immigrants came through Ellis Island in New York Harbor. Most Asian immigrants sailed to California. They went through the processing center on Angel Island in San Francisco Bay.

Examiners at the centers recorded the immigrants' names. Sometimes they shortened a name they found too long or difficult to write. The examiners asked the immigrants where they came from, their occupation, and whether they had relatives in the United States. New immigrants also were given health exams. Those with contagious illnesses could be stopped from entering the United States.

Many immigrant workers did piecework in their cramped apartments, making clothing for the garment industry.

✔ PROGRESS CHECK

Summarizing What was the overall "pull" that drew people to America? What was the "push" that caused them to leave their native countries?

The Immigrant Experience

GUIDING QUESTION *How did immigrants adjust to their new life in the United States?*

Those immigrants who made it through the reception center faced questions. Where would they go? How would they live? Some had relatives or friends to stay with and to help them find jobs. Others knew no one and had to strike out completely on their own.

Finding a Job

An immigrant's greatest challenge was finding work. Sometimes organizations in his or her homeland **recruited** (ree•KROO• ted), or tried to sign up, workers for jobs in the United States. These recruiters supplied American employers with unskilled workers to unload cargo, dig ditches, or do similar work.

The country's fastest-growing industries hired immigrants. In the steel mills of Pittsburgh, for example, most laborers in the early 1900s were immigrant men. They often worked 12 hours a day, 7 days a week. Many other immigrants, including women and children, worked in sweatshops making clothing.

New Ways of Life

Immigrants tried to preserve their cultures. Yet most also wanted to **assimilate** (uh•SIH•muh•layt), or become part of the larger American culture. These two wishes sometimes clashed.

Many immigrant parents continued to speak their native languages. Their children spoke English at school and with friends. Often, their grandchildren spoke only English.

Furthermore, in the United States, women generally had more freedom than women in European and Asian countries. New lifestyles sometimes conflicted with traditional ways.

Setting Up Neighborhoods

Most new immigrants came from rural areas. However, they were too poor to buy farmland in the United States. They often settled in cities instead. With little or no education, they usually worked in unskilled jobs.

Ethnic groups often formed their own communities. Neighborhoods of Jewish, Italian, Chinese, and other groups developed in many cities.

Immigrants tried to re-create some aspects of their former lives. Most important were churches and synagogues. There, immigrants held services and celebrated holidays as they had "back home." Religious leaders also served as community leaders.

Many Chinese came to America to escape poverty and civil war.

The Granger Collection, NYC

Immigrants published newspapers in their native languages. They opened stores and theaters, and organized social clubs. Ethnic communities helped immigrants preserve their rich cultural heritage.

Assimilation was slowed by the **attitudes** of many native-born Americans, who resented the new wave of immigrants. They feared immigrants would take away jobs or drive down wages by working for lower pay. These Americans argued that the new immigrants would not fit into U.S. society. Some blamed immigrants for crime, unemployment, and other problems. The **nativist** (NAY•tih•vihst) movement, which had opposed immigration since the 1830s, grew in the late 1800s. Calls for restrictions on immigration increased.

Government leaders responded quickly to anti-immigrant feeling. In 1882 Congress passed the Chinese Exclusion Act, which prohibited Chinese workers from entering the United States for 10 years. Congress extended this law in 1892 and again in 1902. Similarly, in 1907 the United States and Japan agreed to limit the number of Japanese immigrants.

Other legislation **affected** immigrants from all nations. In 1897 Congress passed a bill that required immigrants to be able to read and write in some language. Although the president vetoed the bill, Congress later passed a similar law.

Yet, Americans generally supported immigration. They recognized that immigrants supplied the country's industries with a steady supply of workers. Today, we appreciate that immigrants also enrich the country with the culture of their homelands.

✅ **PROGRESS CHECK**

Classifying What were the main reasons some people opposed immigration?

LESSON 1 REVIEW

Review Vocabulary

1. Examine the three terms below. Then write a sentence explaining what the terms have in common.

   a. emigrated   **b.** steerage   **c.** recruit

2. Examine the terms below. Then write a short paragraph about new immigrants in the United States using all three terms.

   a. assimilate   **b.** ethnic groups   **c.** nativist

Answer the Guiding Questions

3. ***Determining Cause and Effect*** What is meant by the term "push" factor and "pull" factor with regard to immigration?

4. ***Synthesizing*** How did immigrants adjust to their new lives in the United States?

5. **ARGUMENT** What do you think was the greatest challenge facing new immigrants? Write a paragraph describing that challenge.

What Do You Think? CCSS

Should Immigration Be Limited?

In Israel Zangwill's 1908 play about immigrants, *The Melting Pot*, the writer claimed that the United States gave everyone a fresh start. He felt that in the United States, the old hatreds that caused so much trouble in the rest of the world could not survive. Zangwill believed the American melting pot "burned away" old impurities, resulting in a new creature, the American. Senator Ellison DuRant Smith used a similar argument but for a different purpose. He wanted to prevent further immigration so that those who were already here would become "pure" Americans.

No

PRIMARY SOURCE

ISRAEL ZANGWILL

❝ America is God's **Crucible,** the great Melting-Pot where all the races of Europe are melting and reforming … Germans and Frenchmen, Irishmen and Englishmen, Jews and Russians— into the Crucible with you all! God is making the American. ❞

—Israel Zangwill from his play, *The Melting Pot*, 1908–1909

These immigrants from Hungary arrived at Ellis Island in 1907.

Bob Krist/CORBIS

THE HIGH TIDE OF IMMIGRATION—A NATIONAL MENACE.

Immigration statistics for the past year show that the influx of foreigners was the greatest in our history, and also that the hard-working peasants are now being supplanted by the criminals and outlaws of all Europe.

A political cartoon from this era shows immigration as a "national menace."

Yes

PRIMARY SOURCE

ELLISON DuRANT SMITH

66 Without offense, but with regard to the salvation of our own, let us shut the door and assimilate what we have, and let us breed pure American citizens and develop our own American resources. . . . If we may not have that, then I am in favor of putting the **quota** down to the lowest possible point, with every selective element in it that may be.

66 We do not want to tangle the **skein** of America's progress by those who imperfectly understand the genius of our Government and the opportunities that lie about us. Let us keep what we have, protect what we have, make what we have the realization of the dream of those who wrote the Constitution. 99

—South Carolina Senator Ellison DuRant Smith, address to the Senate, April 9, 1924

Vocabulary

crucible
vessel used to melt things

quota
number or share assigned to a group

skein
yarn or thread loosely wound around a spool

What Do You Think? DBQ

1 *Identifying* What is happening to immigrants in Zangwill's play?

2 *Comparing* What does Senator Smith's viewpoint have in common with Zangwill's viewpoint?

3 *Speculating* What do you think Senator Smith thought of the melting-pot idea?

Andy Moursund

networks
There's More Online!

- ☑ **BIOGRAPHY**
  Clara Barton
- ☑ **CHART/GRAPH**
  Suspension Bridges
- ☑ **GRAPHIC ORGANIZER**
  Growth of Cities
- ☑ **PRIMARY SOURCE**
  Tenement Buildings
- ☑ **VIDEO**

Lesson 2
Moving to the City

ESSENTIAL QUESTION *Why do people move?*

IT MATTERS BECAUSE
Immigrants and rural Americans migrated to the rapidly growing cities for jobs and opportunity.

The Rise of Cities

GUIDING QUESTION *What factors led to the growth of cities?*

In 1870 one of four Americans lived in a community of 2,500 or more people. By 1910 nearly half lived in an **urban** area—a thickly populated city or town. The nation was changing.

Immigrants played a big part in the growth of cities. In **major** urban centers such as New York, Detroit, and Chicago, immigrants and their children made up 80 percent or more of the population in 1890. Native-born Americans also contributed to urban growth. One reason was new farm machinery. Fewer people were needed to produce crops, so former farmworkers moved to cities in huge numbers to look for jobs.

After the Civil War, many African Americans began to move to Southern cities. They, too, were looking for work. Beginning in 1914, large numbers of African Americans moved to Northern cities, hoping to find better economic opportunities.

Transportation and Resources Help Cities Grow

A growing network of railroads fed city growth. Railroads helped move people and raw materials for industry. For example, Chicago and Kansas City developed into meatpacking centers because trains could easily bring cattle there.

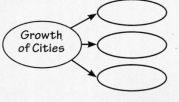

Reading **HELP**DESK (CCSS)

Taking Notes: *Describing*

As you read, use a diagram like this one to describe the effects of the growth of cities.

Growth of Cities

Content Vocabulary
- **urban**
- **tenement**
- **slum**
- **middle class**
- **suburb**
- **settlement house**
- **skyscraper**

132 *An Urban Society*

Some cities had access to key resources. Nearby iron ore and coalfields helped make Pittsburgh a center for iron and steel manufacturing. Seaports such as New York and San Francisco grew as trade with the rest of the world increased.

Life in a Tenement

In the most crowded cities, the poorest people—including most immigrants—lived in **tenements** (TE·nuh·muhnts). Originally, a tenement was simply a building in which several families rented rooms. By the late 1800s, the word had come to mean an apartment building in the **slums**—poor, run-down urban neighborhoods.

Tenements were usually crowded, with several families sharing a cold-water tap and a toilet. In 1896 an inspector wrote of the "filthy and rotten tenements" of the Chicago slums. He described how children filled "every nook, eating and sleeping in every windowsill, pouring in and out of every door."

Few families in the working class could hope to own a home. Most spent their lives in crowded tenements.

The Growth of the Middle Class

The cities also had a growing **middle class,** made up of people who enjoyed a comfortable life but not great wealth. Among the middle class were the families of doctors, lawyers, and ministers, as well as teachers, managers, office clerks, and others.

A growing network of streetcars allowed some middle-class people to move to the **suburbs,** residential areas that sprang up outside city centers. There they lived in houses with hot water, indoor toilets, and—by 1900—electricity. Middle-class families might have servants and the time to enjoy music, art, and literature.

"The Breakers" was the summer home of the Vanderbilt family. Cornelius Vanderbilt made millions by developing shipping and railroad networks.

The Very Rich

At the top of the economic and social ladder were the very rich. They built mansions in the cities and huge estates in the country. Their wealth—and the poverty that lay beneath it—is one reason why this era became known as the Gilded Age. The word *gilded* refers to something covered with a thin layer of gold.

☑ **PROGRESS CHECK**

Analyzing What kinds of resources help a city grow?

(t) The Granger Collection, NYC,
(b) Travel Ink/Getty Images

urban of or like a city
tenement a type of residence that is often run-down and crowded
slum highly populated, poor, run-down, urban area

middle class social class occupied by comfortable but not wealthy people
suburb residential area outside a city center

Academic Vocabulary

major important, significant

Clara Barton (1821–1912)

Clara Barton spent a lifetime helping others. During the Civil War, she cared for wounded Union soldiers. At the end of the war, she set up an office to find information on thousands of soldiers who were missing in action. In 1881 Barton organized the American Red Cross. Under her leadership, this group raised money to aid victims of flood, fire, disease, and other disasters. Between 1881 and 1904, Barton helped respond to many disasters, including a forest fire in Michigan in 1881 and the Johnstown, Pennsylvania, flood in 1889.

▶ **CRITICAL THINKING**
Making Generalizations What common goal did Barton seek in all of her jobs and projects?

Troubles in the Cities

GUIDING QUESTION *What problems faced the people who lived in urban areas?*

The rapid growth of cities led to some serious problems. Garbage and horse manure piled up in city streets. Sewers could not handle the flow of human waste. All the filth acted as a breeding ground for quickly spreading diseases. In one Chicago neighborhood in 1900, large numbers of babies died of such ailments as whooping cough, diphtheria, or measles. One section of New York City was called the "lung block" because so many of its residents had tuberculosis, a lung disease.

In an effort to control the spread of disease, New York City began to take action. Officials screened schoolchildren for contagious diseases, sent visiting nurses to mothers with young children, and set up public health clinics.

Disease was not the only threat to city life. Poverty in the cities led to crime. Orphaned and homeless children sometimes resorted to committing **minor,** or less serious, crimes. Gangs roamed the poor neighborhoods.

The problems of the cities did not go unnoticed. Many dedicated people worked to improve urban life and help the poor. Some of this help came from religious groups that ran orphanages, prisons, hospitals, and recreation centers. Establishments called **settlement houses** offered many types of assistance to the urban poor. One of the most famous was Chicago's Hull House, founded by Jane Addams in 1889.

☑ **PROGRESS CHECK**

Explaining In what ways were cities unhealthy places to live?

The Changing City

GUIDING QUESTION *What actions addressed the problems of cities?*

As American cities grew, their look and feel changed. Skyscrapers, new kinds of public transportation, new bridges, and public parks began to appear.

Building to the Sky

Because of the limited space in cities, imaginative architects, such as Louis Sullivan, began to build upward rather than outward. In the 1860s, architects started to use iron frames to

Royalty-Free/CORBIS

Reading **HELP**DESK (CCSS)

settlement house place in large cities where people get assistance with social problems and challenges related to urban life

Academic Vocabulary

minor of lesser importance

strengthen building walls. Iron supports—together with the safety elevator that Elisha Otis invented in 1852—made taller buildings possible.

In 1884 William LeBaron Jenney put up a 10-story office building in Chicago. It was the world's first **skyscraper** (SKY•skray•puhr). Others followed. New York's Woolworth Building, completed in 1913, soared an incredible 55 stories— 792 feet (241 m) high. People sometimes called the building the "Cathedral of Commerce."

Finding Beauty in City Life

Some people looked to reshape the urban landscape. A group known as the "City Beautiful" movement believed city dwellers should be able to enjoy the beauties of nature.

Frederick Law Olmsted was a leader of this movement. Olmsted designed New York's Central Park, several parks in Boston, and campuses and public spaces from Palo Alto, California, to Washington, D.C. He also designed the grounds for the World's Fair held in Chicago in 1892 and 1893. The fair showed that American architecture was dynamic and original.

Modern Forms of Transportation

Growing cities needed new ways to move people. Streetcars, which horses pulled on tracks, provided public transportation at the time. In 1873 San Francisco began to construct cable-car lines. A large underground cable powered by a motor at one end of the rail line moved passengers along. In 1888 the city of Richmond, Virginia, pioneered the use of the trolley car. A trolley is a small train powered by overhead electric cables. In 1897 Boston opened the nation's first subway, or underground railway. In 1904 New York City opened the first section of what was to become the largest subway system in the world.

The towers and detailed carvings of the Woolworth Building show how people felt about the importance and novelty of skyscrapers.

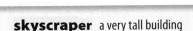
skyscraper a very tall building

THE GREAT BRIDGE

Workers finish a cable on the Brooklyn Bridge during construction.

The Brooklyn Bridge was the first suspension bridge to use woven steel cable wire, a technology developed by John Roebling, chief engineer. Four suspension cables support the bridge. Each cable contains 5,434 wires.

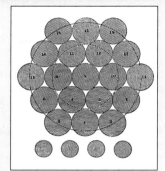

INFOGRAPHIC

To accommodate a growing population, New York City officials built the Brooklyn Bridge over the East River, between Manhattan and Brooklyn. Its long, high span was designed to allow for the passage of ships beneath. The bridge took 14 years to build. When completed in 1883, it was the longest suspension bridge in the world.

1 **EXPLAINING** Why do you think it was important to allow ships to sail beneath the bridge?

2 **CRITICAL THINKING** *Understanding Cause and Effect* How do you think the bridge helped the city grow and expand economically?

Bridges and Transportation

Bridge construction also improved transportation in cities. Architects and engineers designed huge steel bridges. These bridges linked sections of cities that were divided by rivers. The Eads Bridge in St. Louis spanned the Mississippi River. It opened in 1874 with a span of 520 feet (158 m). Nine years later, New York's majestic Brooklyn Bridge, with a main span 1,600 feet (488 m) long, connected Manhattan and Brooklyn. Both bridges are still in use today.

New forms of transportation not only helped people travel within cities. They also helped cities grow. Suburbs developed along train or trolley lines that stretched away from the city's center. People who moved out of the central city could still travel there easily to work, shop, or seek entertainment.

✓ **PROGRESS CHECK**

Making Inferences How did iron and steel change the way cities looked and worked?

(tl and tr) The Granger Collection, New York

LESSON 2 REVIEW (CCSS)

Review Vocabulary

1. Write a brief paragraph using the terms below to discuss the living conditions of poor people in cities.

   a. urban **b.** tenement **c.** slum
   d. settlement house

2. Write a sentence explaining what the terms below have in common.

   a. suburban **b.** middle class

Answer the Guiding Questions

3. *Determining Cause and Effect* Explain how immigration affected cities in the late 1800s.

4. *Describing* How did the rapid growth of cities lead to problems in the cities?

5. *Identifying* What were some of the efforts made to improve city life in the late 1800s and early 1900s?

6. **INFORMATIVE/EXPLANATORY** Write a paragraph that discusses one positive effect and one negative effect of the growth of large cities.

Lesson 3

A Changing Culture

ESSENTIAL QUESTION *How do new ideas change the way people live?*

IT MATTERS BECAUSE
The culture of a society changes over time and reflects the beliefs and values of that society.

Expanding Education

GUIDING QUESTION *What changes expanded opportunities for education?*

Americans in 1865 went to school for an average of just four years. However, in an industrialized, urbanized nation, education was increasingly the key to success. Many believed that young people needed more education. As a result, legislatures across the country began to pass new laws. By 1914 most states required children to have at least some schooling. More than 80 percent of all children between the ages of 5 and 17 were enrolled in school.

Changes in Public Schools

The growth of public education was greatest at the high school level. The number of public high schools increased from 100 in 1860 to 12,000 in 1914. Despite this increase, many teenagers did not attend high school. Boys often went to work. The majority of high school students were girls.

Also, not everyone shared equally in the benefits of a public school education. In the South, many African Americans received little or no education. In many parts of the country, African Americans had to attend poor-quality schools that were segregated—separate from schools for white students.

Reading HELPDESK ⓒⒸⓈⓈ

Taking Notes: *Describing*

As you read, use a table like this to describe the achievements of the people discussed.

Individual	Achievement
Booker T. Washington	
Edith Wharton	
Paul Laurence Dunbar	

Content Vocabulary
• **land-grant college**
• **yellow journalism**
• **spectator sport**
• **vaudeville**
• **jazz**
• **ragtime**

"If one thing more than another has taught me to have confidence in the masses of my own people it has been their willingness (and even eagerness) to learn and their disposition to help themselves."
—Booker T. Washington, *My Larger Education,* 1911

Tuskegee students construct a building. Such efforts show Tuskegee's emphasis on self-reliance and education in the trades.

Progressive Education

Around 1900, schools began practicing a new educational **philosophy** (fuh•LAH•suh•fee), or set of ideas and beliefs. The movement was called "progressive education." John Dewey, a leader of the movement, believed that children should "learn by doing," not by memorizing facts. With progressive education, students worked together on projects requiring hands-on learning. They learned skills for solving problems and for working together as members of society.

Colleges and Universities

Colleges and universities changed as well. The 1862 Morrill Act gave states land they could sell to raise money. States used these funds to start schools called **land-grant colleges.**

In 1865 few American colleges admitted women. The new land-grant schools did. So did new women's colleges, such as Vassar, Smith, Wellesley, and Bryn Mawr (BRIN MAR). By 1910 almost 40 percent of all American college students were women.

African Americans also saw new opportunities. Colleges such as Hampton Institute and Howard University provided higher education for African Americans.

One Hampton Institute student, Booker T. Washington, became an educator. In 1881 he founded the Tuskegee Institute in Alabama. In 1896 scientist George Washington Carver joined the

(t) Bettmann/CORBIS, (inset) CORBIS

Reading **HELP**DESK **CCSS**

land-grant college college funded by the Morrill Acts of 1862 and 1890

Academic Vocabulary

philosophy a set of ideas or beliefs

Tuskegee staff. His research changed agriculture in the South. Carver developed hundreds of products, including plastics and paper, from one crop—the peanut.

Reservation schools and boarding schools opened to educate and train Native Americans. Although these schools provided useful training, they also **isolated,** or cut off, Native Americans from their cultural traditions.

✅ **PROGRESS CHECK**

Explaining Who benefited most from the growing educational opportunities?

A Nation of Readers

GUIDING QUESTION *How did the literature of this time period reflect the values of American society?*

With education came increased interest in reading. Publishers put out new books, magazines, and newspapers. In 1881 Andrew Carnegie, the steel industrialist, made a pledge. He said he would build a public library in any city that would pay to run it. With gifts from Carnegie and others, and the efforts of state and local governments, every state established free public libraries.

Literature Reflects American Life

Many writers of the era explored new themes and subjects. One new approach to literature was *realism*. Realism is based on the lives of ordinary people. Another new approach was regionalism. *Regionalism* focuses on a particular region of the country. Realism and regionalism are related.

Mark Twain was a realist and a regionalist. Many of his books, including *The Adventures of Huckleberry Finn* and *The Adventures of Tom Sawyer*, are set along the Mississippi River, where Twain grew up. Stephen Crane wrote about city slums in *Maggie: A Girl of the Streets* and about the Civil War in *The Red Badge of Courage*. In books such as *The Call of the Wild* and *The Sea Wolf*, Jack London presented a picture of the lives of miners and hunters in the far Northwest. Edith Wharton described upper-class Easterners in *The House of Mirth* and *The Age of Innocence*.

Paul Laurence Dunbar was the son of former enslaved African Americans. Dunbar wrote books that used the dialects and folktales of Southern African Americans. Dunbar was one of the first African American writers to achieve wide fame.

Poet and novelist Paul Laurence Dunbar was one of the first African American writers to gain international recognition.

In her long writing career, Edith Wharton wrote more than 40 books. Her work included novels, short stories, poetry, and nonfiction.

Academic Vocabulary

isolate to set apart or cut off

Low-priced paperback books appeared for the first time in the late 1800s. Horatio Alger wrote a series of books for young adults, such as *Work and Win* and *Luck and Pluck*. Based on themes of success through hard work and honesty, Alger's books sold millions of copies.

Extra! Extra!

New inventions related to printing, papermaking, and communications made it possible to publish daily newspapers for large numbers of readers. The growing cities provided a seemingly endless supply of readers. By 1900 more than twice as many newspapers were published in the United States as in 1880.

In 1883 Joseph Pulitzer bought the New York *World* newspaper. He created a new kind of news reporting. The paper grabbed the reader's attention with illustrations, cartoons, and sensational stories that seemed larger than life. Even the headlines were huge. Under Pulitzer's management, the *World* had more than 1 million readers every day.

Joseph Pulitzer's *The World* was a groundbreaking newspaper of the late 1800s.

Other newspapers soon copied Pulitzer's style. The New York *Morning Journal*, purchased by William Randolph Hearst in 1895, became even more successful than the *World*. Hearst had his reporters exaggerate the dramatic or shocking aspects of stories. This writing style became known as **yellow journalism** (JUR•nuh•lih•zum). The name came from the ink used for a popular newspaper comic strip character, the Yellow Kid.

Ethnic and minority newspapers also did well. By 1900 New York City had seven daily Yiddish-language newspapers. Yiddish is a language spoken by some Jewish people. German-language newspapers were also published in New York and other major cities. African Americans, too, started hundreds of newspapers during this era. The most influential of these was the *Chicago Defender*, a weekly newspaper that first appeared in 1905.

More magazines made use of improvements in printing and transportation to reach a national market. Between 1865 and 1900, the number of magazines in the United States rose from about 700 to 5,000. Some magazines of that era—*Atlantic Monthly*, *Harper's Magazine*, and *Ladies' Home Journal*—are still published today.

☑ **PROGRESS CHECK**

Discussing Why were so many newspapers and magazines published?

Bettmann/CORBIS

Reading **HELP**DESK **CCSS**

yellow journalism a type of journalism based on sensational stories

Leisure and the Arts

GUIDING QUESTION *Why did new forms of recreation develop?*

During this era, Americans enjoyed increasing amounts of leisure time. Industrial work was demanding and often involved longer hours than similar jobs today. Yet unlike round-the-clock farmwork, factory jobs often left people with hours and even days of free time. To fill this time, Americans developed new ways to have fun. These included sports, art, music, and other forms of popular entertainment.

Sports Grow in Popularity

Spectator (SPEK·tay·tuhr) **sports**—games watched for enjoyment in one's free time—grew in popularity. Baseball was the most popular. By the early 1900s, two main leagues had formed—the National and American Leagues. Each league had teams from major cities. Games drew large crowds of enthusiastic fans. The first World Series between the top teams in each league took place in 1903.

Another popular spectator sport was football, which developed from the English game of rugby. The first college football game was played in 1869 between two colleges, Rutgers and Princeton. By the 1890s, college football games were drawing huge crowds.

Basketball, invented by Dr. James Naismith of Springfield, Massachusetts, also became popular. Naismith developed the game in the 1890s as an indoor winter sport for students to play in gym class.

Americans not only watched but also played sports. Wealthy people played tennis and golf in private clubs. Bicycling grew in popularity after the "safety" bicycle was developed. Older bicycles had a large wheel in front and a small one in back, but the new ones had two air-filled rubber tires that were the same size. These improvements helped bicycle-riding take the country by storm. One romantic song was based on bicycle riding: "It won't be a stylish marriage / I can't afford a carriage / but you'll look sweet upon the seat / of a bicycle built for two."

In the first basketball games, developed by James Naismith, pictured below, the players shot a ball into peach baskets. This is how the sport got its name.

spectator sport a sport played for the entertainment of spectators

Bettmann/CORBIS

Vaudeville and Movies

Americans became eager fans of shows and movies. Large cities had many theaters offering a wide range of options. The theaters staged performances ranging from Shakespeare tragedies and comedies to **vaudeville** (VAWD•vil) shows, which featured dancing, singing, comedy, and magic acts.

With inexpensive tickets, vaudeville was the most popular show in town in the early 1900s. The circus was another popular attraction that brought large crowds. In 1910 the United States had about 80 circuses that traveled from town to town giving performances.

The well-known inventor Thomas Edison introduced "moving pictures" in the 1880s. The "movies" soon became wildly popular in the United States.

The first movie theaters were called nickelodeons. The name came from the fact that it cost a nickel to see a short silent film. The nickelodeons marked the beginning of today's film industry.

American Artists and Musicians

For most of the 1800s, most American art and music reflected the influence and styles of Europe. After the Civil War, artists and musicians in the United States began to develop their own styles that were purely American.

Some American painters had realist themes in their works. Frederic Remington portrayed life in the American West. His work focused on uniquely Western subjects such as cowhands and Native Americans. Winslow Homer painted Southern farmers, Adirondack campers, and stormy sea scenes. The Impressionist Childe Hassam painted scenes of life in New York City and

Winslow Homer, whose 1874 painting *The Sick Chicken* is shown here, was a noted American painter. Homer's art focused on distinctly American themes.

Winslow Homer/National Gallery of Art, Washington DC

Reading **HELP**DESK **CCSS**

vaudeville a type of theatrical show, with dancing, singing, comedy, and magic acts
jazz an American music style combining work songs, gospel music, spirituals, and African rhythms

ragtime a type of music characterized by syncopation in the melody

Build Vocabulary: *Word Origins*

Ragged time refers to syncopation, a special type of rhythm. This term was shortened to *ragtime*.

landscapes of the New York and New England countrysides. James Whistler's *Arrangement in Grey and Black,* commonly known as "Whistler's Mother," is one of the best-known American paintings.

Distinctively American kinds of music were also becoming popular. Bandleader John Philip Sousa composed many stirring marches, including "The Washington Post" and "The Stars and Stripes Forever."

African American musicians in New Orleans developed an entirely new kind of music—jazz. **Jazz** combined elements of work songs, gospel music, spirituals, and African rhythms in a new and exciting mix. The first important jazz composer was Jelly Roll Morton.

Although New Orleans is considered the birthplace of jazz, the vibrant new music became popular across the country. In fact, the first recording of jazz music was made in New York City in 1917.

Related to jazz was **ragtime** music. Like jazz, one of ragtime's major features was syncopation (sin•ko•PAY•shun), a shifting of the usual musical accent. The pianist Scott Joplin was the leading ragtime composer.

Americans also proved skilled at playing the world's great music. The symphony orchestras of New York, Boston, and Philadelphia, all founded before 1900, were among the world's finest orchestras. Great singers and conductors from all over the world came to New York's Metropolitan Opera House to perform.

The Marx Brothers were a vaudeville performing team that later worked in film.

Pictorial Press Ltd/Alamy

 PROGRESS CHECK

Summarizing What styles of American music developed during this era?

LESSON 3 REVIEW (CCSS)

Review Vocabulary

1. Examine the two terms below. Then write a sentence explaining what the terms have in common.

   a. spectator sport   **b.** vaudeville

2. Examine the two terms below. Then use them in a sentence that describes the music of this period.

   a. jazz   **b.** ragtime

Answer the Guiding Questions

3. *Describing* How did education change in the late 1800s and early 1900s in the United States?

4. *Analyzing* How did the literature of this time period reflect the values of American society?

5. **NARRATIVE** Taking the perspective of a young person living in this era, write a letter to a friend in another country explaining the new forms of popular entertainment that have appeared in recent years. Be sure to talk about several different forms of entertainment.

CHAPTER 5 Activities

Write your answers on a separate piece of paper.

❶ Exploring the Essential Questions

INFORMATIVE/EXPLANATORY Explore the new situations immigrants faced as they adjusted to American culture in the early 1900s. You may discuss school, work, or neighborhood. List and explain two ways the new situations affected immigrants and how they might have adjusted.

❷ 21st Century Skills

COLLABORATION Working with a small group, read "The New Colossus," by Emma Lazarus. You can obtain the poem online or from a printed source. Practice reading it aloud, and use a dictionary to help you define hard words. Then, rewrite the poem together in your own words.

❸ Thinking Like a Historian

ANALYZING AND INTERPRETING INFORMATION People who came to the United States for political freedom might have been inspired by American documents such as the Constitution. With a classmate, read the Preamble to the Constitution. It begins with the words "We the People." Imagine you are a recent immigrant to the United States in 1900. Write a paragraph explaining how the preamble gives you hope for a better life.

❹ Visual Literacy

ANALYZING PHOTOGRAPHS This photo of three homeless boys sleeping in an alley appeared in Jacob Riis's *How the Other Half Lives: Studies Among the Tenements of New York,* 1890.

Who do you think is the "other half" referred to in the title of Riis's book? What do you think Riis hoped to accomplish by publishing pictures such as this?

REVIEW THE GUIDING QUESTIONS

Choose the best answer for each question.

1 Which answer characterizes immigration to the United States in the late 1800s?

A. People came mainly from northern and western Europe.

B. Many enslaved Africans arrived.

C. People came mainly from southern and eastern Europe.

D. All immigration was blocked by law.

2 By the 1900s, where were middle-class Americans most likely to live?

F. in a mansion

G. in the suburbs

H. in tenements

I. in settlement houses

3 Why were skyscrapers built?

A. They replaced the tenements.

B. They allowed the city to grow, but upward.

C. City leaders understood that the cities had to have a better image.

D. The land set aside for parks had to be made up for.

4 Which answer best describes "progressive education"?

F. Most children were required by law to go to school.

G. School was possible only for the middle class and wealthy.

H. Teachers stressed memorization of facts.

I. Teachers sought to encourage "learning by doing."

5 What change in people's lives caused them to have increased leisure time?

A. Incomes increased sharply.

B. Immigrants took most of the jobs.

C. Farms became smaller because of a shortage of land.

D. Industrial jobs did not require round-the-clock work as farms did.

6 Which style of music was related to jazz?

F. ragtime

G. symphony orchestra

H. rousing marches

I. opera

DBQ ANALYZING DOCUMENTS

7 **Drawing Conclusions** The message of this cartoon is that
A. rich Americans should remember their roots.
B. the new immigrant will get rich.
C. immigration should be halted.
D. all immigrants are poor.

8 **Recognizing Bias** What does the artist think about rich Americans?
F. They are right to stop new immigrants.
G. They should go back to their homelands.
H. They have forgotten their past.
I. The artist prefers new immigrants to rich Americans.

SHORT RESPONSE

The immigrant of the former time came almost exclusively from western and northern Europe. ... Immigrants from southern Italy, Hungary, Austria, and Russia ... made up hardly more than one per cent of our immigration. To-day the proportion has risen to something like forty per cent. ... These people ... are beaten men from beaten races; representing the worst failures in the struggle for existence. ... They have none of the ideas and [abilities] which fit men to take up readily and easily the problem of self-care and self-government.

Source: F. A. Walker, "Restriction of Immigration," 1907

9 Why did Walker oppose immigration from southern and eastern Europe?

10 Would Walker have blocked "the immigrant of the former time"? Defend your answer.

EXTENDED RESPONSE

11 **Informative/Explanatory** Explain why some Americans grew more concerned about new immigrants' ability or willingness to assimilate in the late 1800s and early 1900s.

Need Extra Help?

If You've Missed Question	**1**	**2**	**3**	**4**	**5**	**6**	**7**	**8**	**9**	**10**	**11**
Review Lesson	1	2	2	3	3	3	1, 2	1, 2	1	1	1, 2

The Progressive Era

1877–1920

ESSENTIAL QUESTIONS • *Why do societies change?*
• *What are the causes and consequences of prejudice and injustice?*

The Story Matters...

In the early 1900s, John D. Rockefeller, Sr., and his Standard Oil Company dominate the oil industry. Rockefeller has destroyed his competition, but in journalist Ida Tarbell he finds an opponent he cannot overcome. Tarbell investigates Standard Oil and reports on the questionable business practices Rockefeller has used to create his oil monopoly. Tarbell's work leads to the breakup of Standard Oil. It also inspires a new type of journalism known as muckraking.

During the Progressive Era, other journalists followed in Tarbell's footsteps. With each new muckraking report, people called for reforms to improve society.

◄ *Ida Tarbell helped expose Rockefeller's business practices.*

CORBIS

The struggle for woman suffrage was decades old in 1919. The movement was among the most bitterly fought battles of the Progressive Era.

Step Into the Place

MAP FOCUS By 1919, many states had spoken on the question of woman suffrage.

1 REGION In what regions of the country had the majority of states granted women full or partial suffrage?

2 REGION In which regions of the country had states not granted women suffrage?

3 CRITICAL THINKING
Making Generalizations How would you describe the attitude toward woman suffrage nationwide in 1919?

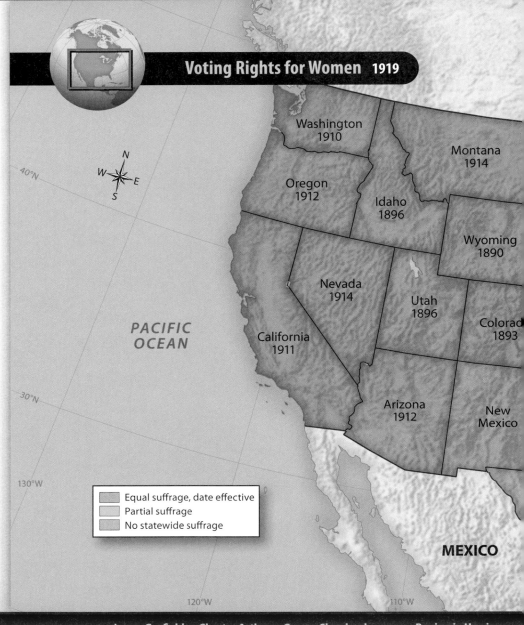

Voting Rights for Women 1919

Washington 1910
Montana 1914
Oregon 1912
Idaho 1896
Wyoming 1890
Nevada 1914
Utah 1896
Colorado 1893
California 1911
Arizona 1912
New Mexico

PACIFIC OCEAN

40°N
30°N
130°W
120°W
110°W

N W E S

MEXICO

- Equal suffrage, date effective
- Partial suffrage
- No statewide suffrage

Step Into the Time

TIME LINE Look at the time line. What event shows that rights for women were improving in other countries?

U.S. PRESIDENTS

James Garfield 1881
Chester Arthur 1881–1885
Grover Cleveland 1885–1889
Benjamin Harrison 1889–1893

1890 Congress passes Sherman Antitrust Act

U.S. EVENTS 1880 — 1890
WORLD EVENTS

1889 Brazil becomes a republic

1890 First general election in Japan

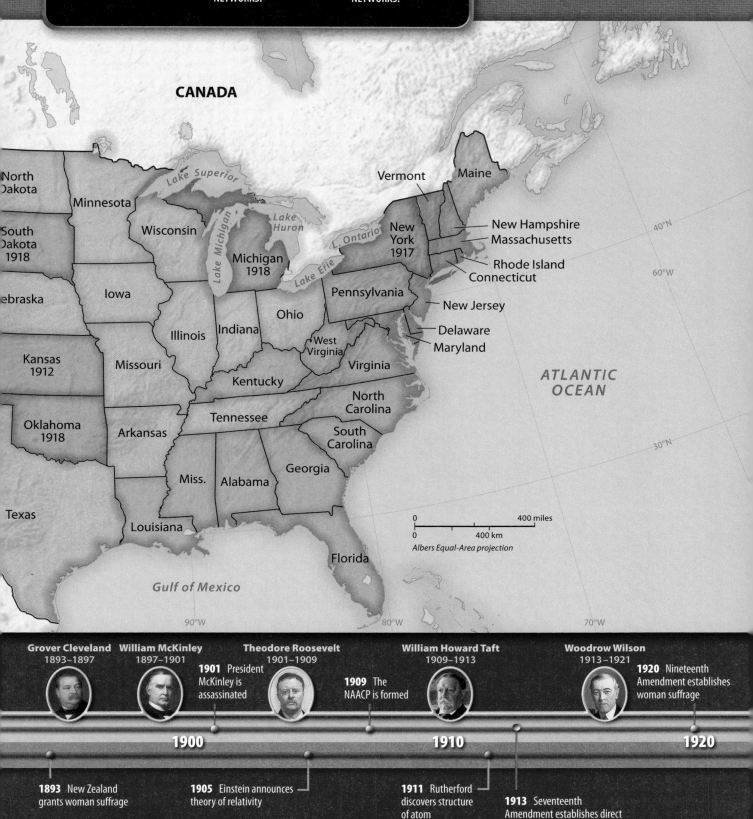

networks
There's More Online!

☑ **MAP** Explore the interactive version of this map on NETWORKS.

☑ **TIME LINE** Explore the interactive version of this time line on NETWORKS.

CANADA

North Dakota

Minnesota

South Dakota 1918

Wisconsin

ebraska

Iowa

Lake Superior

Lake Michigan

Lake Huron

Michigan 1918

Lake Erie

L. Ontario

Vermont

Maine

New Hampshire

Massachusetts

New York 1917

Rhode Island

Connecticut

Pennsylvania

New Jersey

Kansas 1912

Missouri

Illinois

Indiana

Ohio

West Virginia

Kentucky

Virginia

Delaware

Maryland

ATLANTIC OCEAN

Oklahoma 1918

Arkansas

Tennessee

North Carolina

South Carolina

40°N

60°W

30°N

Texas

Miss.

Alabama

Georgia

Louisiana

Florida

0   400 miles
0   400 km
Albers Equal-Area projection

Gulf of Mexico

90°W   80°W   70°W

Grover Cleveland
1893–1897

William McKinley
1897–1901

1901 President McKinley is assassinated

Theodore Roosevelt
1901–1909

1909 The NAACP is formed

William Howard Taft
1909–1913

Woodrow Wilson
1913–1921

1920 Nineteenth Amendment establishes woman suffrage

1900

1910

1920

1893 New Zealand grants woman suffrage

1905 Einstein announces theory of relativity

1911 Rutherford discovers structure of atom

1913 Seventeenth Amendment establishes direct election of U.S. senators

netw⦿rks

There's More Online!

☑ **GAME**

☑ **GRAPHIC ORGANIZER**
Describing the Impact of the Seventeenth Amendment

☑ **SLIDE SHOW** William M. Tweed

Lesson 1
The Movement Begins

ESSENTIAL QUESTION *Why do societies change?*

IT MATTERS BECAUSE
Individuals and groups worked to remedy what they believed were unjust and unfair conditions and policies.

Taking on Corruption

GUIDING QUESTION *Which reforms addressed political and economic problems?*

In the late 1800s, calls for reform—the correction of abuses or errors in society—grew louder in the United States. The reformers were called progressives, and they had several goals for fixing urban problems, improving government, and regulating business. They claimed that government and big business were taking advantage of the American people rather than serving them.

Fighting the Political Machines

Political machines were powerful groups linked to political parties. These machines controlled local government in many cities. In each political district in a city, a member of a political machine controlled jobs and services. This person was the political boss. A boss was often a citizen's closest link to local government, but bosses were often dishonest.

Corrupt politicians found ways to make money illegally. They took bribes from landlords to overlook violations of city housing codes. They took campaign money from companies that hoped to do business with the city. They also took kickbacks, or

Reading **HELP**DESK ⓒⒸⓈⓈ

Taking Notes: *Describing*

As you read, use a diagram like this one to show how the Seventeenth Amendment reformed the political process.

Before → Seventeenth Amendment → After

Content Vocabulary
- **oligopoly**
- **muckraker**
- **initiative**
- **referendum**
- **recall**

(l) The Granger Collection, NYC, (cl) CORBIS (c) APIC/Contributor/Hulton Archive/Getty Images, (cr) Bettmann/CORBIS (c) CORBIS

illegal payments. For example, a builder would add extra fees to the amount of the bill for city work. The builder then "kicked back" some of that money to the boss.

One corrupt city boss was William M. Tweed. Known as Boss Tweed, he controlled New York City's Democratic political machine in the 1860s and 1870s. Boss Tweed led a group of city officials called the Tweed ring.

The Tweed ring controlled the city's police, the courts, and even some newspapers. They collected millions of dollars in illegal payments from companies doing business with the city. Thomas Nast exposed the Tweed ring in his political cartoons for *Harper's Weekly*. Tweed was sent to prison.

Reformers wanted to stop the power of political bosses. They founded organizations such as the National Municipal League to make city governments more honest and efficient. For example, Galveston, Texas, changed to a government run by five people called commissioners. After the city was devastated by a hurricane in 1900, the task of rebuilding overwhelmed the mayor and city council. The new commission seemed to handle massive rebuilding efforts well. Soon, many other cities adopted this new form of government. By 1917 commissioners governed nearly 400 cities.

This cartoon shows Boss Tweed as a

...you think
...r so large in

Tackling the Spoils System

Since the presidency of Andrew Jackson, the spoils system had been common practice. Under this system, elected leaders gav[e] government jobs and other favors to their political supporters. These rewards are also called patronage. The spoils system existed at all levels of government. Many people who receive[d] government jobs were not qualified, and some were dishonest.

PAYMENT FOR WORK COMPLETED ON NEW COURTHOUSE		
To	**For**	**Amount**
Andrew Garvey	Plastering, Repairs, Decorating	$1,958,910.27
Keyser & Co.	Plumbing	$800,686.56
Ingersoll & Co. (1870)	Furniture, Cabinets, Repairs, etc.	$1,026,678.93
Archibald Hall, Jr.	Painting	$186,907.93
Total expended on courthouse 1869–part of 1871		$8,223,979.89

Source: "How New York Is Governed: Frauds of the Tammany Democrats," *New York Times Edition*, 1871

CHART SKILLS

Some money paid to these workers and companies wound up in the pockets of corrupt politicians.

1 CALCULATING Which was the most costly job shown?

2 CRITICAL THINKING
Analyzing Why do you think the public would be concerned about such overpayments?

Reading Strategy: *Reading in the Content Area*

When reading tables, understand that information on the far left side of each row represents the subject for all the other content in that row. So, for example, Andrew Garvey did plastering and repairs and received $1,958,910.27.

The hurricane that struck Galveston in September 1900 killed thousands and nearly destroyed the city. City leaders decided that a commission government was the best way to handle such emergencies—and to run a city.

In the late 1870s, President Rutherford B. Hayes tried and failed to change the spoils system. James Garfield then took office in 1881 and also tried to reform the system. His presidency was cut short when an unsuccessful job seeker assassinated him.

Chester Arthur became president. Shocked by Garfield's murder, Arthur pushed Congress to end the spoils system. In 1883 Congress passed the Pendleton Act, which set up the Civil Service Commission to give tests for federal jobs. Job seekers had to demonstrate their skills before being hired. By 1900 the commission controlled the hiring of many federal workers.

Controlling Business

Most Americans believed that trusts, or powerful groups of companies, had too much control over the economy and the government. This concern led to new laws regulating big business. In 1890 Congress passed the Sherman Antitrust Act, the first federal law to control trusts. The law was meant to protect against actions or groups that "restrained," or held back, normal commerce and trade.

During the 1890s, however, the government almost never used the Sherman Antitrust Act to limit business. Instead, it used the act against labor unions. The government claimed that labor strikes hurt trade. It was not until the early 1900s that the government used the Sherman Act to win cases against trusts.

CORBIS

Build Vocabulary: *Multiple Meaning Words*

Commission can mean a group charged with a specific task, as on this page. It can also mean the act of committing something or a fee paid for doing a service.

Reining in the Railroads

In the late 1800s, railroads were vital to the way people lived and worked. The railroads formed an **oligopoly** (ol·ih·GAH·puh·lee). In an oligopoly, a group of businesses agree to limit competition and raise their prices to make larger profits. Reformers called for rules to control the prices railroads charged. In 1887 Congress passed the Interstate Commerce Act, requiring railroads to charge and publish "reasonable and just" rates. The act set up the Interstate Commerce Commission (ICC) to oversee the railroad and, later, trucking industries.

Lowering Tariffs

Tariffs are taxes charged on imported goods. The Tariff Bill of 1890, sponsored by Republican Representative William McKinley of Ohio, raised tariffs sharply. Supporters of the tariff argued that high tariffs helped the country's struggling industries. Tariffs make imported goods more costly—and so less attractive than those made at home. While many business owners supported the high tariffs, consumers generally opposed them because they raised prices. Voters opposing high tariffs sent many Democrats to Congress. Grover Cleveland, who became president in 1893, also favored lower tariffs.

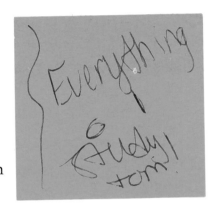

{ Everything o study tom!

✓ PROGRESS CHECK

Explaining How did the Pendleton Act help end the spoils system?

The New Reformers

GUIDING QUESTION *Why did reformers emerge during this era?*

In the early 1900s, reformers in America had new ideas for ending injustice and solving social problems. These ideas included socialism and progressivism.

Socialists believed government should own resources and operate major industries on **behalf** of all the people. Eugene V. Debs was a labor leader who helped found the American Socialist Party in 1898. With Debs as its leader, the party gained some support in the early 1900s. Debs ran for president five times, but he never received more than 6 percent of the popular vote.

At the same time, progressives brought new energy to the reform movement. Like the socialists, progressives were alarmed that a small number of people held most of the nation's wealth and power.

Eugene V. Debs led the American Socialist Party in the late 1800s and early 1900s.

APIC/ Contributor/Hulton Archive/Getty Images

oligopoly a few large companies that control prices for an entire industry

Academic Vocabulary
behalf in the interest of

Unlike the socialists, progressives wanted government to regulate industry rather than own it. They also wanted government to be more efficient and less influenced by powerful businesses. Society, progressives believed, had a duty to protect and help all of its members. Many progressive reforms aimed to help people who did not have wealth or power.

The Rise of the Muckrakers

Reporters helped the reformers. They wrote newspaper and magazine stories that told people about problems. Called **muckrakers,** these reporters "raked"—or exposed—the "muck"— dirt and corruption—in business. One of the most effective muckrakers was Lincoln Steffens. Working for *McClure's Magazine,* Steffens exposed corrupt machine politics in New York and other cities. Ida Tarbell, also with *McClure's,* described the oil trust's unfair practices. Her articles increased the public call for government to take charge of big business.

In his book *The Jungle* (1906), Upton Sinclair described the horrors of the Chicago meatpacking industry. He had hoped to expose the mistreatment of workers. Instead, his vivid writing about the filthy conditions in meatpacking plants shocked Americans. In response,

Bettmann/CORBIS

This political cartoon shows President Roosevelt working with a muckrake.

▶ **CRITICAL THINKING**
Analyzing What does the cartoon suggest about the effect of muckraking on people?

A NAUSEATING JOB, BUT IT MUST BE DONE
(President Roosevelt takes hold of the investigating muck-rake himself in the packing-house scand
From the *Saturday Globe* (Utica)

muckrakers investigative reporters who exposed corruption
initiative the right of voters to place an issue on the ballot in a state election

referendum the right of voters to accept or reject laws
recall the right of voters to remove incompetent elected officials from office

Academic Vocabulary
accurate correct, precise

Congress passed the Meat Inspection Act and the Pure Food and Drug Act in 1906. Now food and medicine had to be **accurately** labeled, and food that might cause harm could not be sold.

Progressives backed many reforms that increased citizens' role in government. Robert La Follette reformed Wisconsin's electoral system. He introduced the "Wisconsin idea," a direct primary election in which voters chose candidates to appear on the ballot. Previously, party bosses and state conventions chose candidates.

The Oregon System

Oregon also introduced important reforms. The **initiative** (ih·NIH·shuh·tiv) allowed citizens to place an issue on the ballot in a state election. The **referendum** (REF·uh·REN·dum) gave voters the opportunity to accept or reject laws. The **recall** allowed voters to remove incompetent elected officials. These reforms, called the Oregon System, were adopted by other states, especially in the West.

The Seventeenth Amendment

Progressives also wanted to change the way U.S. senators were elected. The Constitution gave state legislatures the responsibility of choosing senators. Party bosses and business interests often controlled these legislatures. Progressives believed people should be able to vote for their senators directly.

After much criticism of the Senate in newspapers and magazines, Congress passed the Seventeenth Amendment to the Constitution in 1912. This amendment provided for the direct election of senators by voters. Ratified in 1913, the amendment gave the people a greater voice in their government.

☑ **PROGRESS CHECK**

Comparing What was a key difference between socialists and progressives?

LESSON 1 REVIEW (CCSS)

Review Vocabulary

1. Explain the significance of

   a. oligopoly **b.** muckraker

2. Use the following words in a sentence about the political reform movement of this era.

   a. initiative **b.** referendum **c.** recall

Answer the Guiding Questions

3. *Describing* What problem did the Sherman Antitrust Act help resolve?

4. *Discussing* Why did reformers want regulation of the railroads, and what was the government's response?

5. *Explaining* How did the muckrakers contribute to the Progressive movement?

6. **ARGUMENT** You are a muckraker. Choose something you think is unfair in business, society, or government, and write a two- or three-paragraph article about it. Try to move your readers to improve the situation.

Counting on Grace

by Elizabeth Winthrop

Elizabeth Winthrop (1948–) was inspired to write *Counting on Grace* after seeing a photograph of a 12-year-old girl named Addie at work in a textile mill in Vermont. The photograph, taken by child labor photographer Lewis Hine in 1910, has been reprinted hundreds of times and has even appeared on a U.S. postage stamp.

In *Counting on Grace*, the main character is a 12-year-old girl who leaves school to work at the thread mill in a Vermont town in 1910. She joins her mother, Mamère, her father, her sister Delia, and several childhood friends who work at the mill.

> **❝** *You're not supposed to work in the mill until you're fourteen, but visiting is fine.* **❞**
>
> — from *Counting on Grace*

This photograph of mill worker Addie Card inspired Elizabeth Winthrop to write the novel *Counting on Grace*.

❝ I've been in the mill lots of times.

Summers ever since I was nine, I've been cooking the hot meal for Mamère and Papa and Delia and taking in the dinner pails in the middle of the day. Delia let me push her bobbin dolly. I played **mumblety-peg** or roll the bobbin with Dougie and Bridget and Felix when he was a summer sweeper boy in the spinning room. . . .

But now I'm here to work, not play.

The air in the mill is stuffy and linty and sweaty at the same time 'cause all day long water sprays down on the frames from little hoses on the ceiling. Wet keeps the threads from breaking. The windows are shut tight even in the summer. You don't breathe too deep for fear of what you might be sucking down your throat. . . .

You're not supposed to work in the mill until you're fourteen, but visiting is fine. French Johnny likes us kids going in and out all the time. He says, that way we get used to the work.

The only people you worry about are the state inspectors. When French Johnny blows the whistle, all the kids in the mill, even the ones just visiting, know to run as fast as we can so he can hide us in the elevator that carries the cotton between the floors.\ The inspector always stops in at the front office and **dawdles** around there for a while so us kids have time to hide. Seems to me he don't really want to find us. We skitter across the room like those big cockroaches that come up through the floorboards in the summertime. Our mothers make a wall out of themselves to hide us.

It gets hot in that old elevator and the inspector can take hours to look through the mill, top to bottom. A couple kids fainted last August and French Johnny had to throw cold water on them when he slid open the metal doors.

I didn't feel so good myself, but I didn't say a word.

"You look kind of green," Pierre Gagnon said to me when we filed out.

"Green Grace, green Grace," Felix shouted, and everybody called me that for a while. When nobody was looking I smacked Felix hard on the top of his head. By the time he turned around I was gone. I've got fast feet, fast hands and fast fingers.

Now I'm really going to need them. ❞

Vocabulary

mumblety-peg game in which players throw or flip a jackknife in various ways so that the knife sticks in the ground
dawdle waste time

Literary Element

A **symbol** is an object or event in a story that stands for something else. Authors often use symbols to stress key points or themes. As you read, look for symbols—for example, the elevator in the passage here. Think about what the symbols might mean.

Analyzing Literature   DBQ

❶ *Analyzing* Describe the relationship between Grace and the other young workers.

❷ *Interpreting* What clues does Grace use to determine that the state inspectors are making a half-hearted effort to find underage workers?

❸ *Predicting* In your opinion, will Grace have a positive experience at work? Will she turn out to be a good employee? Explain.

Lesson 2
Women and Progressives

ESSENTIAL QUESTION *Why do societies change?*

IT MATTERS BECAUSE
Women joined together to work for their social, political, and economic rights.

New Roles for Women

GUIDING QUESTION *How did opportunities for women change during this era?*

The lives of middle-class women changed during the late 1800s. As people moved from farms to cities, fewer children were needed to help a family survive. As a result, families became smaller. More children spent the day at school, and men worked away from home. Women also gained free time as technology made housework easier.

With more free time, more middle-class women began to seek higher education. About 40 percent of college students in 1910 were women. Educated women were starting new careers. Many **professional** (pruh•FESH•nuhl) women were teachers, but some worked in nursing and other fields. Between 1890 and 1910, the female workforce almost doubled.

The "New Woman"

These changes created the "new woman." This term referred to educated, modern women who pursued interests outside their homes. A leading example of the "new woman" was Jane Addams. She set up Hull House, a Chicago settlement house at which the urban poor could get help with a variety of issues. She became a pioneer in the new field of social work.

(l) Library of Congress (LC-USZ62-120667), (cl) Fotosearch/Stringer/Archive Photos /Getty Images, (r) Private Collection, Peter Newark American Pictures/Bridgeman Art Library, (cr) Library of Congress, Prints and Photographs Division (LC-USZ62-75334), (r) Private Collection, Peter Newark American Pictures/Bridgeman Art Library

Taking Notes: *Describing*

As you read, use a diagram like this one to describe the Eighteenth and Nineteenth Amendments.

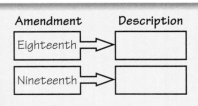

Amendment		Description
Eighteenth	→	
Nineteenth	→	

Content Vocabulary
• **suffragist**
• **prohibition**

Mary Church Terrell established kindergarten classes for African American children as well as a nursery for children of working mothers.

Working with disadvantaged people gave Addams an outlet for her energy and **intelligence** (in•TEH•luh•juhnts). Inspired by Addams and others, many more women got involved in public life.

Women Join Forces

Women found another way to use their talents and energy in women's clubs. The number of women's clubs grew rapidly. At first they focused on things such as music and painting. Many clubs, however, became more concerned about social problems.

Some clubs started by white women refused to admit African Americans. In response, African American women created their own organizations. Clubs such as the Phyllis Wheatley Club of New Orleans provided classes, recreational activities, and social services. Women from these clubs formed the National Association of Colored Women. Mary Church Terrell, its founder and first president, was an active leader for women's rights. The association founded homes for orphans, established hospitals, and worked for woman suffrage. It fulfilled its motto "Lifting As We Climb."

✓ **PROGRESS CHECK**

Identifying What were the characteristics of the "new woman" of the 1800s?

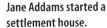

Jane Addams started a settlement house.

Academic Vocabulary

professional showing a high degree of specialized skill
intelligence the ability to learn facts and skills and apply them

Suffragists organized marches to gain support for woman suffrage.

Women and Voting Rights

GUIDING QUESTION *What was the goal of the suffrage movement?*

In 1848 Elizabeth Cady Stanton helped organize a women's rights convention in Seneca Falls, New York. This meeting helped launch what became the American women's rights movement. A key part of this movement was the demand for woman suffrage—voting rights for women.

Stanton was joined in her quest by Susan B. Anthony. Together these women led the women's rights movement for 50 years. Stanton and Anthony were also joined after the Civil War by former abolitionists. Many of these reformers became **suffragists** (SUHF•rih•jists), active supporters of a woman's right to vote.

Stanton helped found the National Woman Suffrage Association in 1869 and was named its president. This group joined together with another suffrage organization in 1890 to form the National American Woman Suffrage Association (NAWSA). Stanton was elected president. When she resigned

Bettmann/CORBIS

Reading **HELP**DESK (CCSS)

suffragist person who fought for woman suffrage, or women's right to vote

in 1892 Anthony became president. Anna Howard Shaw, a minister and doctor, and Carrie Chapman Catt, an educator and newspaper editor, were also leaders of this group. In a speech in 1902, Catt spoke about women's rights:

PRIMARY SOURCE

❝ The whole aim of the movement has been to destroy the idea that obedience is necessary to woman . . . and to train men to such comprehension of equity [fairness] they would not exact [demand] it. ❞

—quoted in *The American Reader*

Many working-class women also wanted the vote. They hoped to elect leaders who would pass labor laws protecting women. The movement also gained strength when people such as Jane Addams spoke out in support of woman suffrage.

As the movement grew, women began putting pressure on lawmakers. They organized marches and made speeches on street corners. On March 3, 1913, the day before President Woodrow Wilson's inauguration, suffragists marched on Washington, D.C.

The Struggle Continues

Suffragists won victories in some states. At the same time, they kept up their struggle to win the vote everywhere. Alice Paul founded the National Woman's Party in 1916. She was seeking greater equality, as well as suffrage, for women. In 1917 Paul met with President Wilson. Though he would later change his mind, Wilson at this time refused to support woman suffrage. In response, Paul led protesters in front of the White House. They were arrested for blocking the sidewalk. After their arrest, the women started a hunger strike. Alva Belmont, one of the protesters, proudly said that all the women had done was stand there "quietly, peacefully, lawfully, and gloriously."

The Nineteenth Amendment

By 1917 the tide was turning in favor of woman suffrage. NAWSA had more than 2 million members. President Wilson changed his position and began supporting woman suffrage.

Connections to TODAY

Voter Turnout for Women

In the 1920 election, the first after the granting of suffrage, women did not turn out to vote in large numbers. Today, however, women generally vote in greater numbers than men.

Starting in 1920, women throughout the United States got to enjoy the experience of casting a ballot.

Reading Strategies: *Sequencing*

To understand the sequence of events in something such as the suffrage movement, make a time line. Then, write down events and the dates on which they occurred along the time line.

Soon New York and, a year later, South Dakota and Oklahoma, joined a number of other states in granting woman suffrage. Congress turned its attention toward debating the issue.

In 1918 the House of Representatives passed a woman suffrage amendment. The next year, the Senate also passed the amendment. After three-fourths of the states had ratified it, the Nineteenth Amendment went into effect in 1920. The amendment came in time for women to vote in that year's presidential election.

☑ **PROGRESS CHECK**

Describing What were some of the reasons suffragists wanted the vote for women?

Women and Social Reform

GUIDING QUESTION *What methods did women use to bring about social reform?*

During the Progressive Era, women became involved in many reform movements in addition to woman suffrage. Many middle-class women worked to improve the lives of others. They helped working-class people, immigrants, and society as a whole.

Women supported and staffed libraries, schools, and settlement houses. They raised money for charities. They sponsored laws to regulate the labor of both women and children and to require the regular inspection of workplaces by the government. Their pressure on Congress helped create the Children's Bureau in the Labor Department.

Some women demonstrated at saloons as part of their campaign against the use of alcohol.

Private Collection, Peter Newark American Pictures/Bridgeman Art Library

Reading **HELP**DESK (CCSS)

prohibition laws that banned making or selling alcohol

Women also worked for reforms in the food and medicine industries. They put pressure on state legislatures to provide more support for widows and for abandoned mothers with children.

Working women were also active. In 1903 they formed the Women's Trade Union League (WTUL) to help improve employment conditions for women. The WTUL urged working women to form labor unions. It also supported laws to protect the rights of women factory workers.

Temperance

Women led the crusade against the use of alcohol. The Woman's Christian Temperance Union (WCTU) formed in 1874, and the Anti-Saloon League was created in 1893. Both organizations were at the forefront of the fight against alcohol. Members called for temperance, urging people to stop drinking. They also supported **prohibition**—laws that would ban the making or selling of alcohol in the United States. Through state WCTU chapters, women combined their roles as guardians of the home with social activism.

Some Americans wanted to ban alcohol because they thought drinking was immoral. Other reformers cited the social impact of alcohol abuse—crime, the breakup of families, and poverty. In response to all these forces, Congress in 1917 passed a constitutional amendment declaring it illegal to make, transport, or sell alcohol in the United States. The states ratified the Eighteenth Amendment, known as the Prohibition Law, in 1919. The states later reversed this amendment with the 1933 ratification of the Twenty-first Amendment. Still, prohibition was a big victory for women of the Progressive Era.

✓ PROGRESS CHECK

Explaining What was the goal of the temperance movement?

LESSON 2 REVIEW (CCSS)

Review Vocabulary

1. Explain the meaning of the following terms by using each in a sentence.

   a. suffragist   **b.** prohibition

Answer the Guiding Questions

2. *Summarizing* In what ways did middle-class women's roles change near the end of the 1880s?

3. *Sequencing* What events occurred starting in 1917 that led to suffrage for women?

4. *Identifying* In what ways did reformers try to improve the lives of working women?

5. **ARGUMENT** Which individual did the most for reform during this era and why?
   • Jane Addams
   • Mary Church Terrell
   • Elizabeth Cady Stanton

netw⦿rks

There's More Online!

☑ **GRAPHIC ORGANIZER**
Comparing and Contrasting
Roosevelt and Taft

☑ **MAP** The Election of 1912

☑ **SLIDE SHOW** The National
Park System

☑ **TIME LINE** The Federal
Income Tax

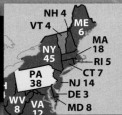

Lesson 3
Presidents of the Progressive Era

ESSENTIAL QUESTION *Why do societies change?*

IT MATTERS BECAUSE

Beginning in the Progressive Era, presidents made efforts to regulate business and protect the environment.

Theodore Roosevelt

GUIDING QUESTION *How successful was Roosevelt in implementing his policies?*

Theodore Roosevelt was the Republican choice for vice president in 1900. Mark Hanna, a Republican leader, distrusted Roosevelt. He called him a "cowboy" and warned that if Roosevelt was elected, only one life would stand between Roosevelt and the White House. When the Republicans did win, Hanna told President McKinley, "Now it is up to you to live." Less than a year later, McKinley was assassinated. Suddenly 42-year-old Theodore Roosevelt became president. He was the youngest president in the nation's history. When Roosevelt took office in 1901, he brought progressive ideas with him.

Roosevelt the "Trustbuster"

President McKinley favored big business. President Roosevelt, in contrast, supported regulation of business and other progressive reforms. During his term, Roosevelt ordered the Justice Department to take legal action against certain trusts that violated the Sherman Antitrust Act.

His first target was the Northern Securities Company. This railroad monopoly fought the charges of illegal activity all the way to the Supreme Court. In 1904 the Supreme Court decided

(l) Bettmann/Corbis
(cl) Popperfoto/Getty Images
(cr) The Granger Collection, NYC

Reading **HELP**DESK ⦿ⒸⒸⓈⓈ

Taking Notes: *Comparing and Contrasting*

As you read, use a diagram like this one to identify how the beliefs of Theodore Roosevelt were similar to and different from those of William Howard Taft.

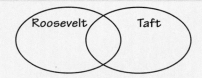

Roosevelt   Taft

Content Vocabulary
• **trustbuster**   • **conservation**
• **arbitration**
• **Square Deal**

that Northern Securities had illegally limited trade. The Court ordered that the trust be taken apart. The Court's decision encouraged the government to take action against other trusts.

During Roosevelt's presidency, he brought legal charges against trusts in the beef, oil, and tobacco industries. Although called a **trustbuster,** Roosevelt did not want to break up all trusts. He wanted to regulate trusts, not destroy them. He viewed some trusts as "good" and others as "bad." Good trusts, he believed, were concerned with public welfare, but bad trusts were not.

Trouble with Labor

In 1902 the nation faced a major labor crisis. More than 100,000 members of the United Mine Workers went on strike. They wanted better pay and an eight-hour workday. They also wanted recognition of the union's right to represent members in talks with mine owners.

The mine owners refused to negotiate with the workers. The coal strike dragged on for months. Winter approached—along with the need for coal. The American people called for action. President Roosevelt stepped in and asked the union and the owners to accept **arbitration** (ahr·buh·TRAY·shun), in which both sides agree to accept a settlement offered by a neutral party. The union agreed, but the owners refused the plan. Roosevelt was angry and threatened to send federal troops to work in the mines. The owners finally agreed to arbitration. Mine workers won a pay increase and a reduction in hours. They did not, however, gain recognition for their union.

Roosevelt's action marked a change in relations between business and labor. Earlier presidents used troops against strikers. Roosevelt made company owners negotiate with them. In other cases, however, Roosevelt supported employers in disputes with workers.

Square Deal

Roosevelt ran for president in 1904. He promised the people a **Square Deal**—fair and equal treatment for all. He easily won, with more than 57 percent of the popular vote.

President Roosevelt's Square Deal called for government regulation of business. This approach differed from that of some earlier American presidents.

In this cartoon, trustbusting President Roosevelt "tames" a group of lions—trusts.

▶ CRITICAL THINKING
Analyzing Visuals Does this cartoon portray Roosevelt in a positive or negative way? Explain your answer.

THE LION-TAMER

Bettmann/Corbis

trustbuster a government official who investigates and combats business alliances formed to control competition and prices

arbitration the process of resolving disputes between people or groups by agreeing to accept the decision of a neutral party

Square Deal Theodore Roosevelt's promised program of fair and equal treatment for all

These leaders had favored a policy of *laissez-faire* (LEH•say FEHR). This French term means "let the people do as they choose." In economics, it means having little government involvement in business affairs.

President Roosevelt also defended the public interest on consumer issues. He supported the Meat Inspection Act and the Pure Food and Drug Act. These gave the government power to visit businesses and **inspect** products.

Conserving the Wilderness

Roosevelt had a lifelong interest in the great outdoors. He believed in the need for **conservation** (KAHN•suhr•VAY•shun), the protection and preservation of natural resources.

As president, Roosevelt took steps to conserve forests, mineral deposits, and water resources. In 1905 he proposed creation of the U.S. Forest Service. He pushed Congress to set aside millions of acres for the nation's first wildlife preserves. He formed the National Conservation Commission, which produced the first survey of the country's natural resources.

Roosevelt has been called the first environmental president. He made conservation a leading public issue. Roosevelt also saw the need to use resources for economic growth and development. He tried to balance business interests with conservation.

☑ **PROGRESS CHECK**

Describing What was President Roosevelt's approach to relations between business and labor?

Theodore Roosevelt enjoyed the outdoors. He said "The farther one gets into the wilderness, the greater is the attraction of its lonely freedom."

▶ **CRITICAL THINKING**
Paraphrasing Based on this quote, what does Roosevelt seem to appreciate most about the wilderness?

Popperfoto/Getty Images

Reading **HELP**DESK (CCSS)

conservation protection and preservation of natural resources

Academic Vocabulary

inspect examine carefully in order to judge quality

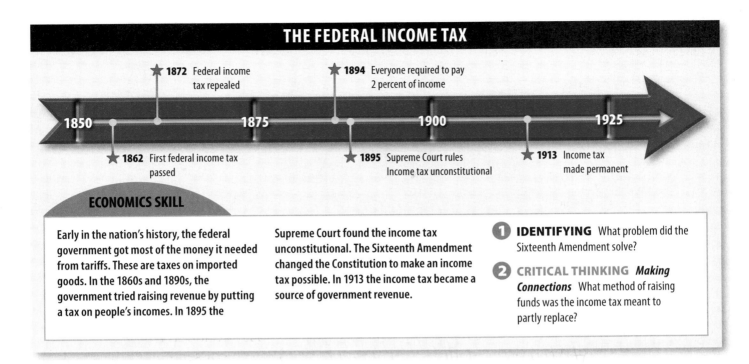

THE FEDERAL INCOME TAX

1872 Federal income tax repealed

1894 Everyone required to pay 2 percent of income

1850   1875   1900   1925

1862 First federal income tax passed

1895 Supreme Court rules Income tax unconstitutional

1913 Income tax made permanent

ECONOMICS SKILL

Early in the nation's history, the federal government got most of the money it needed from tariffs. These are taxes on imported goods. In the 1860s and 1890s, the government tried raising revenue by putting a tax on people's incomes. In the 1895 the Supreme Court found the income tax unconstitutional. The Sixteenth Amendment changed the Constitution to make an income tax possible. In 1913 the income tax became a source of government revenue.

1 IDENTIFYING What problem did the Sixteenth Amendment solve?

2 CRITICAL THINKING *Making Connections* What method of raising funds was the income tax meant to partly replace?

President Taft in Office

GUIDING QUESTION *What were the similarities and differences between the policies of Roosevelt and Taft?*

No U.S. president had ever served more than two terms. In keeping with that tradition, Roosevelt decided not to run for reelection in 1908. Instead Roosevelt called for his friend and fellow Republican William Howard Taft to run for president. Roosevelt thought that Taft would carry on the progressive Republican agenda. Taft easily gained the Republican nomination and defeated Democrat William Jennings Bryan.

Taft lacked Roosevelt's flair. Still, he carried out—and went beyond—many of Roosevelt's policies. The Taft administration won more antitrust cases in four years than Roosevelt won in seven. Taft also favored safety standards for mines and railroads.

President Taft supported the Sixteenth Amendment. It allowed Congress to tax people's incomes to collect money for the federal government. Progressives believed income taxes were more fair than other taxes. They hoped a new tax would allow government to lower tariffs, leading to lower prices—and relief for the poor. The states ratified the Sixteenth Amendment in 1913. Congress then passed laws so that higher incomes were taxed at a higher rate than lower incomes.

Taking Notes: *Comparing and Contrasting*

The Guiding Question asks you to compare and contrast the policies of Presidents Roosevelt and Taft. You can use a Venn diagram such as the one you started at the beginning of this lesson to make comparisons and contrasts.

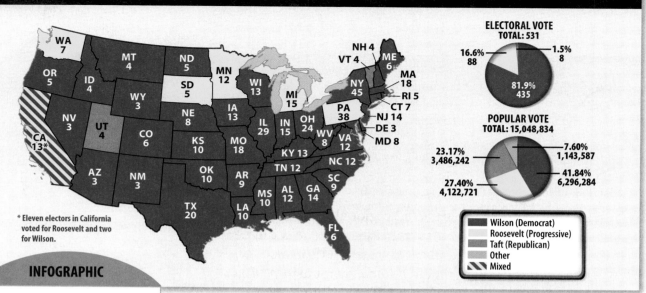

THE ELECTION OF 1912

ELECTORAL VOTE
TOTAL: 531

16.6% 88 — 1.5% 8
81.9% 435

POPULAR VOTE
TOTAL: 15,048,834

23.17% 3,486,242 — 7.60% 1,143,587
27.40% 4,122,721 — 41.84% 6,296,284

WA 7
OR 5
MT 4
ND 5
MN 12
WI 13
MI 15
NH 4
VT 4
ME 6
NY 45
MA 18
RI 5
CT 7
NJ 14
DE 3
MD 8
ID 4
WY 3
SD 5
IA 13
IL 29
IN 15
OH 24
PA 38
WV 8
VA 12
NV 3
UT 4
CO 6
NE 8
KS 10
MO 18
KY 13
NC 12
CA 13*
AZ 3
NM 3
OK 10
AR 9
TN 12
SC 9
TX 20
LA 10
MS 10
AL 12
GA 14
FL 6

*Eleven electors in California voted for Roosevelt and two for Wilson.

Wilson (Democrat)
Roosevelt (Progressive)
Taft (Republican)
Other
Mixed

INFOGRAPHIC

Though Wilson won only 42 percent of the popular vote, he carried most of the states.

1 IDENTIFYING Who won more states, Roosevelt or Taft?

2 CRITICAL THINKING
Analyzing How was Wilson able to win so many states even though he got only 42 percent of the votes?

Despite President Taft's reforms, he disappointed progressives such as Theodore Roosevelt. They were upset that Taft failed to fight for a lower tariff and that he changed some conservation policies to favor businesses.

Roosevelt Challenges Taft

By 1912, Roosevelt was unhappy with President Taft. Claiming that Taft "completely twisted around" his own policies, Roosevelt decided to seek the Republican presidential nomination himself. The showdown came at the Republican convention in Chicago. Roosevelt had won every **primary** (PRY•mehr•ee)—elections parties hold to help them choose candidates. President Taft, however, had the backing of party leaders and business interests. He won the nomination.

Instead of accepting defeat, Roosevelt and his supporters formed a new political party, the Progressive Party. In August the Progressives held their own convention in Chicago. They nominated Roosevelt for president. Declaring himself ready to battle, Roosevelt said, "I feel as fit as a bull moose!" From then on, the Progressive Party was known as the Bull Moose Party.

The Election of 1912

The split in the Republican Party hurt both Taft and Roosevelt. While the Republican and Bull Moose parties battled each other, Democrat Woodrow Wilson, a progressive reformer and former governor of New Jersey, won the election. Wilson won the presidency by the largest electoral majority up to that time. He swept 435 of the 531 electoral votes.

Wilson's Progressive Presidency

Woodrow Wilson had criticized big government and big business during his campaign. He called his program the "New Freedom." In 1913 Wilson reached a long-held progressive goal. He got the Democrat-controlled Congress to adopt a lower tariff. Wilson believed that foreign competition would force American manufacturers to improve their products and lower their prices.

That same year Congress passed the Federal Reserve Act to regulate banking. The act created 12 regional banks supervised by a central board. Many banks were required to join the Federal Reserve System and follow its rules. Wilson also worked to strengthen government control over business. In 1914 Congress established the Federal Trade Commission (FTC). The FTC's job was to investigate corporations for unfair trade practices. Wilson also supported the Clayton Antitrust Act of 1914. This act was one of the government's chief weapons for fighting trusts. The government also tried to regulate child labor. The Keating-Owen Act of 1916 banned goods produced by child labor from being sold in interstate commerce. This law, however, was struck down as unconstitutional two years later.

Despite Wilson's achievements, the public was losing interest in progressive ideas. Increasingly Americans turned their attention to world affairs—especially the war that began in Europe in 1914.

Woodrow Wilson appears in formal dress on the day of his inauguration.

The Granger Collection, NYC

✓ PROGRESS CHECK

Analyzing How did Roosevelt's run for the presidency affect the election of 1912?

LESSON 3 REVIEW (CCSS)

Review Vocabulary

1. Explain these terms as they relate to Theodore Roosevelt.

   a. trustbuster   **b.** Square Deal

2. Explain the significance of the following terms in connection with Roosevelt's presidency.

   a. arbitration   **b.** conservation

Answer the Guiding Questions

3. *Identifying* What policies regarding big business was Roosevelt able to implement?

4. *Making Inferences* Why has Roosevelt been called the country's first environmental president?

5. *Contrasting* How did Taft differ from Roosevelt in his conservation policies?

6. **ARGUMENT** Write a paragraph explaining which of the following was more important for progressive reform and why.

   • Theodore Roosevelt
   • William Howard Taft

netw⊙rks
There's More Online!

☑ **BIOGRAPHY**
• Booker T. Washington
• W.E.B. Du Bois

☑ **GRAPHIC ORGANIZER**
Comparing and Contrasting
Washington and Du Bois

☑ **SLIDE SHOW**
Tuskegee Institute

Lesson 4
Excluded From Reform

ESSENTIAL QUESTION *What are the causes and consequences of prejudice and injustice?*

IT MATTERS BECAUSE
Groups and organizations formed during the Progressive Era to meet the needs of minority groups.

Prejudice and Discrimination

GUIDING QUESTION *What problems did members of ethnic and religious groups face?*

During the 1800s, the majority of Americans were white Protestants who were born in the United States. Many believed that the United States should remain a white, Protestant nation. Nonwhite, non-Protestant, and non-native residents often faced **discrimination** (dihs•KRIH•muh•NAY•shun)—unequal treatment because of their race, religion, ethnic background, or place of birth. The government did little to fight discrimination in this era.

Discrimination against Catholics

Some Americans faced discrimination because of their religion. America's largely Protestant population feared that the rise in the number of Catholic immigrants threatened the "American" way of life. Anti-Catholic people formed the American Protective Association (APA) in 1887. Its members vowed not to hire or to vote for Catholics.

By the mid-1890s, the APA claimed to have 2 million members across the nation. Among other activities, the APA spread false rumors that Catholics were making plans to take over the country.

Reading **HELP**DESK

Taking Notes: *Comparing and Contrasting*

As you read, use a diagram like this one to show how Booker T. Washington and W.E.B. Du Bois differed in their beliefs for achieving equality.

	Beliefs
Booker T. Washington	
W.E.B. Du Bois	

Content Vocabulary
• **discrimination**   • **barrio**
• **segregation**
• **mutualista**

Anti-Semitism

Many Jewish immigrants came to the United States to escape discrimination in their homelands. Some found anti-Semitic, or anti-Jewish, attitudes in the United States as well.

Some property owners, employers, and even schools discriminated against Jews. Those from eastern Europe faced even more discrimination. Some Americans viewed eastern Europeans as more "foreign" than western Europeans who had come to the United States in the past. The newcomers' languages and customs were quite different from those of earlier immigrants.

Anti-Asian Policies

In California and other Western states, Asians faced prejudice and resentment. White Americans claimed that Chinese immigrants accepted lower wages and took jobs from them. Congress passed the Chinese Exclusion Act in 1882 to prevent Chinese immigrants from coming to the United States.

America's westward expansion created opportunities for thousands of Japanese immigrants. They came to the United States to find work. Like the Chinese, Japanese immigrants met with prejudice. California passed laws against Asians. One law made it illegal for Asians to buy land. Other Western states passed similar laws.

President Theodore Roosevelt gave in to this rise in anti-Japanese feeling. He negotiated a so-called Gentlemen's Agreement with Japan in 1907. The Gentleman's Agreement helped cut Japanese immigration to the United States. It also damaged Japanese-American relations while doing little to dampen anti-Japanese feeling in the United States.

Prejudice against Catholics is shown in this cartoon, which shows a Catholic leader trying to force children to attend Catholic school rather than public school.

▶ CRITICAL THINKING
Analyzing Visuals How do the mother and children appear to be reacting to the order to attend Catholic school?

discrimination unfair treatment, usually based on prejudice toward a certain race, ethnic group, religion, age group, or gender

The Granger Collection, NYC

Discrimination Against African Americans

African Americans faced discrimination in the North, South, and West. Free from slavery, African Americans were still **denied** basic rights.

In the post-Civil War years, most African Americans lived in the South. They worked as sharecroppers or in low-paying jobs in the cities. African Americans were cut off from white society. They had separate neighborhoods, schools, parks, restaurants, theaters, and even cemeteries. In 1896 the Supreme Court legalized this **segregation** (SEH•grih•GAY•shun), or separation of groups, in the case of *Plessy* v. *Ferguson*. This case allowed "separate but equal" facilities for blacks and whites. In fact, most facilities were not equal at all.

The Ku Klux Klan was a terror group that targeted African Americans after the Civil War. It was reborn in Georgia in 1915. The new Klan wanted a white, Protestant America. The Klan lashed out against minorities including Catholics, Jews, and immigrants, as well as African Americans. Calling for "100 percent Americanism," the number of Klan supporters grew and spread beyond the South. Many Klan members were from northern as well as southern cities and towns.

Racial Violence

The nation went through sharp economic downturns in 1893 and 1907. Many people lost their jobs. Frustrated white people sometimes lashed out against African Americans and other minorities. More than 2,600 African Americans were lynched—murdered by mobs—between 1886 and 1916. Lynching also was used to terrorize Chinese immigrants in the West.

✔ **PROGRESS CHECK**

Identifying Which Supreme Court decision legalized segregation?

Bettmann/CORBIS

The new Ku Klux Klan showed its strength with this 1925 march in Washington, D.C.

Reading **HELP**DESK (CCSS)

segregation separation of one group from another

Academic Vocabulary

deny to refuse

Booker T. Washington (1856–1915)

Booker T. Washington was willing to accept segregation in return for basic economic opportunity. "In all things that are purely social," he said of relations between black and white, "we can be as separate as the fingers, yet one as the hand in all things essential to mutual progress."

W.E.B. Du Bois (1868–1963)

W.E.B. Du Bois at times criticized Washington for accepting inequality. Du Bois insisted on voting rights and social equality for African Americans. "Any attempt to deny this equality by law or custom," he wrote, "is a blow at Humanity, Religion and Democracy."

These two men led the way toward African American equality—from very different directions.

▶ **CRITICAL THINKING**
Comparing How did Washington and Du Bois differ in their views on racial equality?

Seeking Equal Opportunity

GUIDING QUESTION *How did minority groups react to discrimination?*

In the late 1800s and the early 1900s, many Americans held **biased,** or prejudiced, views. This included progressive reformers. Reformers often came from the middle and upper classes. They did not question their right to make decisions for all society. In fact, they saw themselves as moral leaders who worked to improve the lives of the less fortunate. The reforms they supported, though, often discriminated against one group as they tried to help another. For example, trade unions often did not allow African Americans, women, or immigrants to join. The unions argued that skilled laborers could obtain better working conditions if they did not demand improved conditions for all workers.

Minorities were banned from joining many progressive organizations. They had to battle for justice and opportunity on their own. African Americans, Native Americans, Mexican Americans, and Jewish Americans formed organizations that would work to improve their lives.

CORBIS

Academic Vocabulary

bias prejudice, an unfair dislike of someone or something

Journalist Ida B. Wells urged African Americans to speak out for their rights.

Struggle for Equality

African Americans rose to the challenge. Born into slavery, Booker T. Washington taught himself to read. In 1881 he founded the Tuskegee Institute in Alabama. The school taught African Americans farming and industrial skills. Washington believed African Americans needed more economic power. With it, they would be able to win social equality and civil rights. Washington founded the National Negro Business League in 1900 to promote business development among African Americans.

W.E.B. Du Bois also worked for civil rights. He was the first African American to receive a doctoral degree from Harvard University. Du Bois argued that the right to vote was key to ending racial inequality and lynching, and to gaining better schools. "The power of the ballot we need in sheer self-defense," he said, "else what shall save us from a second slavery?"

Du Bois helped start the Niagara Movement in 1905. This movement demanded equal economic and educational opportunity for African Americans. It also insisted on an end to legalized segregation and discrimination. Although it never gained wide support, the Niagara Movement led to the creation of the National Association for the Advancement of Colored People in 1909. This organization would become a leader in the fight for African American civil rights.

☑ PROGRESS CHECK

Comparing What goals did Booker T. Washington and W.E.B. Du Bois have in common?

African American Women Take Action

African American women also formed groups to end discrimination. The National Association of Colored Women formed in 1896 to fight violence against African Americans. Ida B. Wells started a national effort to stop lynching. In 1895 Wells published a book, *A Red Record*. She showed that lynching was used mainly against African Americans who became prosperous or who had competed with white businesses. "Can you remain silent and inactive when such things are done in your own community and country?" she asked.

Congress failed to pass an anti-lynching bill. However, the number of lynchings declined significantly due in great part to the efforts of Wells and other activists.

Library of Congress/LC-USZ62-107756

Reading **HELP**DESK (CCSS)

mutualista Mexican American aid group
barrio Mexican neighborhood

Rise to World Power

1865–1917

ESSENTIAL QUESTION *Why does conflict develop?*

The Story Matters . . .

As a boy, Theodore "Teddy" Roosevelt suffers from poor health. His eyesight is weak, and asthma keeps him from engaging in rough, outdoor play. Yet he refuses to give in to his weaknesses, and he works to build his strength through exercise. In fact, Roosevelt grows to be a powerful man. He loves camping and hunting, and he participates in many sports, including boxing. Roosevelt believes in living "the strenuous life," which involves forceful physical activity and strong ideas and actions.

Roosevelt's can-do attitude matched that of his country in the late 1800s and early 1900s. During this time, the nation built up its strength and power—and did not back down from the opportunity to use it.

◄ *Theodore Roosevelt led the United States as it gained strength around the world.*

The Granger Collection, NYC

Place and Time: The World 1865 to 1915

The United States in the late 1800s was expanding its involvement and its territory to include Latin America, Asia, Alaska, and many Pacific islands.

Step Into the Place

MAP FOCUS Use the map to answer the following questions.

1 PLACE Which of the possessions shown on the map were acquired in 1857?

2 PLACE Which were acquired in 1899?

3 LOCATION Which possession was the closest to the U.S.? Which was farthest from the U.S.?

4 CRITICAL THINKING
Drawing Conclusions Which do you think was the most important possession and why?

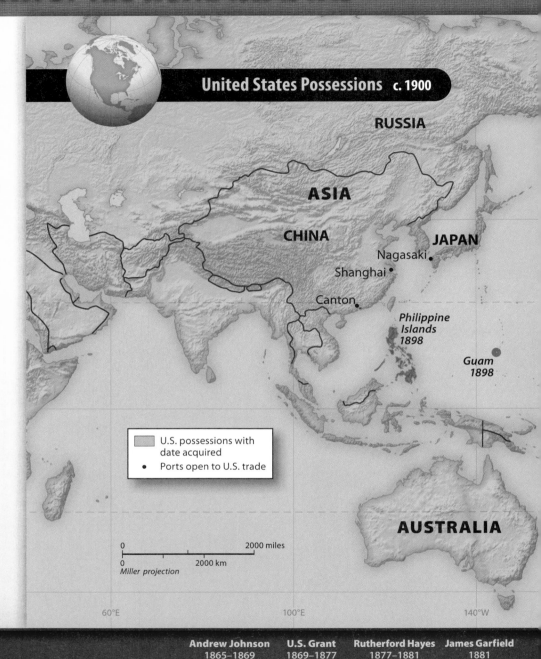

United States Possessions c. 1900

RUSSIA

ASIA

CHINA

JAPAN

Nagasaki

Shanghai

Canton

Philippine Islands 1898

Guam 1898

AUSTRALIA

U.S. possessions with date acquired

• Ports open to U.S. trade

0   2000 miles
0   2000 km
Miller projection

60°E   100°E   140°W

Step Into the Time

TIME LINE Identify which U.S. president was in office when the following events occurred:

• The U.S. purchases Alaska

• The U.S. bans Chinese Immigration

• Martí leads revolt in Cuba

Andrew Johnson 1865–1869
U.S. Grant 1869–1877
Rutherford Hayes 1877–1881
James Garfield 1881

1867 United States purchases Alaska

U.S. PRESIDENTS

U.S. EVENTS

WORLD EVENTS

1865   1875

1869 Suez Canal opens

1871 German Empire proclaimed

1882 United States enacts ban on Chinese immigration

White House Historical Association

networks

There's More Online!

☑ **MAP** Explore the interactive version of this map on NETWORKS.

☑ **TIME LINE** Explore the Interactive version of this time line on NETWORKS.

Alaska
1867

Aleutian Islands 1867

CANADA

**NORTH
AMERICA**

N
W   E
S

40°N

PACIFIC OCEAN

UNITED STATES

ATLANTIC
OCEAN

Midway
Islands
1867

Hawaiian
Islands
1898

TROPIC OF CANCER

MEXICO

Puerto
Rico
1898

Wake Island
1899

Johnston Island
1858

Howland
Island
1857

Kingman Reef 1858

Palmyra Island 1898

EQUATOR

0°

**SOUTH
AMERICA**

Baker Island
1857

Jarvis Island 1857

American
Samoa
1899

TROPIC OF CAPRICORN

40°S

180°   140°W   100°W   60°W

Chester Arthur	Grover Cleveland	Benjamin Harrison	Grover Cleveland	William McKinley	Theodore Roosevelt	William Howard Taft
1881–1885	1885–1889	1889–1893	1893–1897	1897–1901	1901–1909	1909–1913

1885   **1895**   **1905**   **1915**

1883 Vietnam becomes French protectorate

1895 José Martí leads revolt in Cuba

1900 Boxer Rebellion occurs in China

1912 Alaska becomes a U.S. territory

1890 Alred Thayer Mahan publishes *The Influence of Sea Power Upon History*

1898 Spanish-American War erupts

1904 Roosevelt Corollary to the Monroe Doctrine issued

1916 National Park Service established

networks
There's More Online!

☑ **CHART**
Parts of a Ship

☑ **GRAPHIC ORGANIZER**
Expanding U.S. Influence

☑ **MAP**
The Alaska Purchase

Lesson 1
Seeking New Frontiers

ESSENTIAL QUESTION *Why does conflict develop?*

IT MATTERS BECAUSE

During the late 1800s, the U.S. built the foundation for its role as a world economic and political leader.

Changing Foreign Policy

GUIDING QUESTION *What did the United States do to open trade with Japan?*

In his Farewell Address, George Washington warned Americans to "steer clear of permanent alliances with any portion of the foreign world." His words helped guide American foreign policy for about 100 years. There was, however, disagreement about just what Washington meant. Some said he had argued for **isolationism** (EYE•suh•LAY•shuh•nih•zuhm), or noninvolvement in world affairs. Others believed Washington supported trade with other countries, not isolation from them.

After Washington left office, Americans expanded their territory by moving west and south. This **expansionism** (ihk•SPAN•shuh•nih•zuhm) was a driving force in American history. Most of the land between the Atlantic Coast and the Pacific Coast was settled. Americans then looked beyond the nation's borders to new frontiers overseas. American merchants already traded with China. They also wanted to trade with Japan, which had long been isolated from the West.

In 1853 Commodore Matthew Perry traveled to Japan. He steamed into Tokyo Bay with four powerful warships and a letter from President Millard Fillmore. President Fillmore's letter firmly asked the Japanese to open their ports to U.S.

(r) MIKA/age fotostock

Reading **HELP**DESK (CCSS)

Taking Notes: *Describing*

As you read, use a diagram like this one to describe how the United States was able to expand its influence during the age of imperialism.

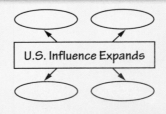

U.S. Influence Expands

Content Vocabulary
• **isolationism**
• **expansionism**
• **imperialism**

trade. Perry told the Japanese he would come back in several months for their answer. When Perry returned in 1854, it was again with a fleet of warships. On this visit, Japanese leaders agreed to the Treaty of Kanagawa. Under its terms, Japan opened two ports to American trading ships. Perry's mission marked the start of a greater United States involvement in Asia.

☑ PROGRESS CHECK

Making Inferences How do you think Perry's warships affected Japan's decision to trade with the United States?

An Age of Imperialism

GUIDING QUESTION   *How did Alaska become a territory of the United States?*

Many more nations also expanded their trade in Asia and other parts of the world. The late 1800s and the early 1900s were called an age of **imperialism** (ihm•PIHR•ee•uh•lih•zuhm). Powerful European nations built large empires by gaining economic and political control over weaker nations.

The search for materials and markets drove imperialism. The nations of Europe needed raw materials for making new products. They also needed new markets to sell the goods they made. This led to competition among European powers for influence in Asia and Africa. This competition had effects that lasted throughout the twentieth century. For example, it helped lead to World War I, which you will read about later.

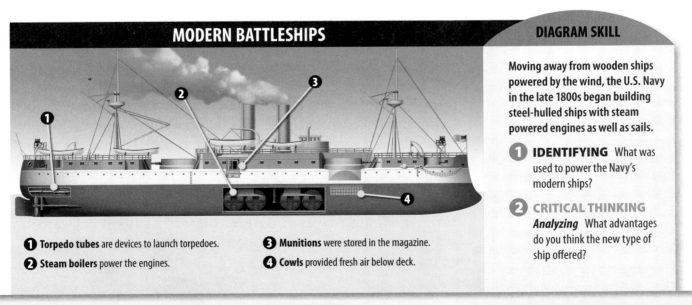

MODERN BATTLESHIPS

DIAGRAM SKILL

Moving away from wooden ships powered by the wind, the U.S. Navy in the late 1800s began building steel-hulled ships with steam powered engines as well as sails.

❶ **IDENTIFYING** What was used to power the Navy's modern ships?

❷ **CRITICAL THINKING**
Analyzing What advantages do you think the new type of ship offered?

❶ **Torpedo tubes** are devices to launch torpedoes.
❷ **Steam boilers** power the engines.
❸ **Munitions** were stored in the magazine.
❹ **Cowls** provided fresh air below deck.

isolationism the belief that a nation should stay out of the affairs of other nations
expansionism the practice of spreading a nation's territorial or economic control beyond its borders

imperialism the policy of extending a nation's rule over other territories and countries

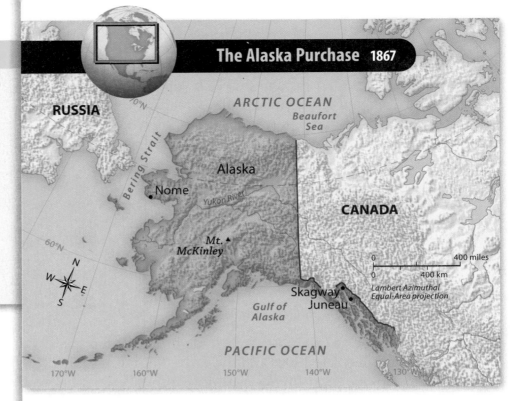

GEOGRAPHY CONNECTION

In 1867 the United States agreed to buy Alaska from Russia for $7.2 million. Congress approved because it removed the Russian presence from North America.

1 **LOCATION** What nation does Alaska border?

2 **CRITICAL THINKING**
Speculating The U.S. purchased Alaska for the low price of two cents an acre. Why do you think the land was so inexpensive?

Visions of American Empire

After the Civil War, some Americans wanted their nation to build an empire. By adding new lands, they argued, the United States would join the ranks of the world's great powers.

Secretary of State William H. Seward supported this view. Seward pictured an American empire dominating the Caribbean, Central America, and the Pacific. New transportation and **communication** networks would link the many parts of this empire. For example, Seward imagined a canal across Central America. The canal would link the Atlantic and Pacific Oceans and help connect far-reaching rail and telegraph systems.

The Purchase of Alaska

In 1867 Seward moved closer to making his **vision** a reality: He arranged for the United States to buy Alaska from Russia for $7.2 million. It was a great bargain for a territory twice the size of Texas.

Many people thought of Alaska only as an icy, barren place. They mocked it as "Seward's **icebox**" and a "polar bear garden." However, after gold was discovered there in the 1890s, Seward's "folly" seemed more like a wise purchase. In 1912 Alaska became a U.S. territory.

Reading **HELP**DESK (CCSS)

Academic Vocabulary

communication the exchange of messages or information
vision an imagined plan of action

Visual Vocabulary

icebox This object was used by people in the 1860s to keep ice. It was called an icebox.

"Lifting Up" the World

Some Americans had another reason for favoring imperialism. They believed they could "lift up" the world's "uncivilized" people by sharing Christianity and Western civilization. Josiah Strong, a Congregational minister, proposed an "imperialism of righteousness." He thought Americans should bring their religion and culture to Africa, Asia, and Latin America.

American Interest in Latin America

In the late 1800s, the United States had a strong trading relationship with Latin America. American merchants, however, wanted more. In 1884 James G. Blaine, then the Republican nominee for president, declared that the United States should "improve and expand its trade with the nations of America."

As secretary of state in 1889, Blaine invited Latin American leaders to attend a conference in Washington, D.C. The conference led to the Pan-American Union, which promoted cooperation among member nations.

A Stronger Navy

As the United States expanded its influence overseas, Captain Alfred Thayer Mahan, president of the Naval War College, wanted to improve the navy. "Sea power," Mahan said, "is essential to the greatness of every splendid people." The United States would be able to use its colonies as bases to refuel its ships.

During the 1880s, the U.S. Navy shifted from sails to steam power and from wooden to steel hulls. By the early 1900s, the United States had the naval power it needed for an expanded role in foreign affairs. At the same time, use of these powerful ships required a wide-ranging network of ports.

✅ **PROGRESS CHECK**

Explaining What factors led to imperialism?

LESSON 1 REVIEW (CCSS)

Review Vocabulary

1. What did people mean when they said that George Washington supported a policy of isolationism?

2. Explain the relationship between expansionism and imperialism.

Answer the Guiding Questions

3. *Explaining* How did Commodore Perry's actions in Japan represent a change in U.S. foreign policy?

4. *Summarizing* What vision did the 1867 purchase of Alaska help fulfill?

5. **INFORMATIVE/EXPLANATORY** "Alaska is nothing but Seward's Icebox." Explain in your own words what this statement means. Then explain whether this statement holds true today.

netw⊙rks

There's More Online!

☑ **CHART**
Gross Domestic Product

☑ **GRAPHIC ORGANIZER**
Relations with Japan

☑ **VIDEO**
Theodore Roosevelt's Presidency

Lesson 2

Imperialism in the Pacific

ESSENTIAL QUESTION *Why does conflict develop?*

IT MATTERS BECAUSE

By spreading its influence to Asia and the Pacific, the United States solidified its position as a world leader.

Hawaii and the United States

GUIDING QUESTION *Why did the Hawaiians resist American influence in their country?*

Since the mid-1800s, many Americans had wanted to build a trading empire in the Pacific. In 1867 Secretary of State William H. Seward arranged to acquire the Pacific islands of Midway. These islands lie more than 3,000 miles (4,828 km) west of California. They provided a stopping place for ships traveling to China. Midway, however, was not enough to establish a foothold in the Pacific.

A Growing American Presence

The Hawaiian Islands sit about 2,000 miles (3,219 km) west of California. In the 1790s, Americans and Hawaiians began to trade with each other. A few decades later, Christian missionaries came to Hawaii to spread their religion. American merchants in the whaling trade also came to settle in the Hawaiian Islands.

An American firm planted sugarcane in Hawaii in the 1830s. This valuable crop grew well in the warm, wet climate. American missionaries and traders began buying land and setting up sugar plantations. These planters earned huge profits. Over time the Americans took control of most of the land and businesses.

(l) The Granger Collection, New York (c) Bloomberg/Contributor

Reading **HELP**DESK (CCSS)

Taking Notes: *Explaining*

As you read, use a diagram like this one to explain why these events strained relations between Japan and the United States.

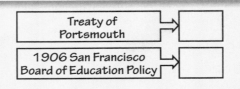

Content Vocabulary
• **provisional government**
• **sphere of influence**

186 *Rise to World Power*

American Planters' Revolt

In 1891, Queen Liliuokalani (lih•LEE•uh•woh•kuh•LAH•nee), became Hawaii's ruler. She wanted native Hawaiians to regain control of their islands. In response, American planters forced Liliuokalani from power. They set up their own **provisional government,** or temporary government, in 1893.

The United States Annexes Hawaii

The leaders of the provisional government asked the United States to annex, or add, Hawaii to the United States. Most Hawaiians were against annexation. Liliuokalani, herself, visited the United States and called on members of the U.S. Congress to reject such a step. In spite of her efforts, President Benjamin Harrison signed an annexation treaty. The Senate, however, failed to ratify the treaty before Harrison finished his term. Without that Senate ratification, the treaty could not go into effect.

The new president was Grover Cleveland. After careful study, Cleveland withdrew the treaty from the Senate. He called American actions in Hawaii "disgraceful" and the use of U.S. Marines to help in the planters' revolt a violation of "national honesty." Hawaii's provisional government decided to wait until Cleveland left office. After William McKinley became president, Congress approved annexation of Hawaii. In 1900 it became a territory of the United States.

Samoa

About 3,000 miles (4,828 km) south of Hawaii are the Samoan Islands. Samoa allowed the Americans to build a naval station at Pago Pago. Samoa also granted special trading rights to the United States. Great Britain and Germany also got trading rights in the islands. As a result, tensions among the three powers grew.

In 1899 the United States, Great Britain, and Germany met in Berlin. Without **consulting** the Samoans, the United States and Germany divided Samoa between them. The United States quickly annexed its portion. Great Britain withdrew from the area in return for rights to other Pacific islands.

✔ **PROGRESS CHECK**

Explaining Why did the planters want Hawaii as a U.S. territory?

When Queen Liliuokalani took away the powers of U.S. planters, they staged a military revolt and declared a provisional government.

▶ **CRITICAL THINKING**
Identifying Which group did Queen Liliuokalani want to control the economy of Hawaii?

The Granger Collection, New York

provisional government
temporary government

Academic Vocabulary
consult to seek an opinion

An Open Door to China

GUIDING QUESTION *How did the United States expand its trading interests in China?*

Pacific island territories were stepping-stones to a larger prize—China. Weakened by war, China also lacked industry. It could not resist the efforts of foreign powers that wanted to **exploit,** or make use of, its vast resources and markets.

Rivalries in China

By the late 1890s, Japan and several European powers had carved out **spheres of influence** in China. These were sections of the country in which each of the foreign nations enjoyed special rights and powers. Japan, Germany, Great Britain, France, and Russia all acquired spheres of influence in China. This struggle for economic power among the European nations caused a rise in tensions between the countries. Within a few decades, these escalating tensions would contribute to the outbreak of global war.

Hay's "Open Door"

The competition for economic influence in China also caused worry in the United States. U.S. government and business leaders feared being left out of the China trade. To protect American interests, Secretary of State John Hay proposed an Open Door policy. It gave each nation rights to trade freely in each other's sphere of influence. At first, the other powers did not accept the policy. Then, dramatic events in China led to a change of heart.

The Boxer Rebellion

In 1899 a secret Chinese society known as the Boxers rose up against "foreign devils" in China. The Boxers were angry at European attempts to carve up the country. Many foreigners died in violent clashes. The next year, foreign troops finally put down the Boxer Rebellion.

The Boxer Rebellion led to a second Open Door proposal. This version stressed the importance of China's independence and respect for its borders. Alarmed by the revolt, the other foreign powers accepted Hay's new policy.

☑ PROGRESS CHECK

Analyzing Explain the purpose of the Open Door policy.

Bloomberg/Contributor

Reading HELPDESK CCSS

sphere of influence
section of a country in which a foreign nation enjoys special rights and powers

Academic Vocabulary

exploit make use of

Relations with Japan

GUIDING QUESTION *How did the United States help settle the Russo-Japanese War?*

Japan was eager to expand its power in Asia and ignored the Open Door. In the early 1900s, Japan and Russia clashed over Manchuria, a Chinese province rich in natural resources. On February 8, 1904, this conflict erupted into the Russo-Japanese War.

Treaty of Portsmouth

President Roosevelt met with Russian and Japanese leaders in Portsmouth, New Hampshire, to help resolve the conflict. Russia and China reached an agreement and signed the Treaty of Portsmouth in September 1905. Unfortunately, tensions in Asia continued. Japan soon built up its naval power and challenged the United States in the region.

Strained Relations

Meanwhile, relations between the U.S. and Japan suffered additional strains. Many Japanese now lived in the United States, where they faced discrimination. In 1906, officials in San Francisco ordered the city's Asian students to attend separate schools from white students. President Roosevelt persuaded city officials to change this policy of segregation. In return, Japan agreed to a "gentlemen's agreement," promising to limit the flow of immigrants. Japan, however, resented the deal and relations between the countries worsened.

Some Americans wanted war. Although Roosevelt had no plan for war, he sent a "Great White Fleet" of 16 battleships on a cruise around the world. The ships impressed the Japanese. By 1909, the two countries resolved many of their differences.

Wikimedia/Henry Reuterdahl

✓ PROGRESS CHECK

Describing What role did the U.S. play in the end of the Russo-Japanese War?

LESSON 2 REVIEW

Review Vocabulary

1. Explain the significance of the following terms to the content of this lesson:

   a. provisional government

   b. sphere of influence

Answer the Guiding Questions

2. ***Explaining*** What did Queen Liliuokalani do to try to help the Hawaiian people? Was she successful?

3. ***Interpreting*** How did other nations feel at first about Hay's idea of an Open Door policy? Why did they change their minds?

4. ***Describing*** How did President Roosevelt help settle the conflict between Japan and Russia?

5. **ARGUMENT** Write a speech that Theodore Roosevelt might have given to San Francisco officials to convince them to reverse their policy of separating Asian students from white students.

networks

There's More Online!

☑ **GRAPHIC ORGANIZER**
Land Acquired

☑ **MAP**
Spanish-American War

☑ **SLIDE SHOW**
Spanish-American War

☑ **VIDEO**

Lesson 3
War with Spain

ESSENTIAL QUESTION *Why does conflict develop?*

IT MATTERS BECAUSE
The United States emerged from the Spanish-American War as a world power with colonies in the Caribbean and Pacific.

"A Splendid Little War"

GUIDING QUESTION *Why did the United States go to war with Spain?*

After centuries of Spanish rule, the people of Cuba rebelled in the late 1800s. Rebels destroyed property in hopes of forcing the Spanish to leave. The Spanish responded with harsh measures. As a result, thousands of Cubans died of starvation and disease.

Yellow Journalism

The Cuban people's struggle caused great concern in the United States. Business leaders worried about the loss of property and trade in Cuba. Government leaders worried about a rebellion taking place so close to the United States. Many Americans were horrified by Spain's treatment of the Cuban people.

The American press reported the tragedy in Cuba in detail. Newspapers, including Joseph Pulitzer's *World* and William Randolph Hearst's *Journal*, tried to outdo one another. In an effort to whip up public opinion—and sell more newspapers—they printed shocking reports about the revolution. The publishers were such strong supporters of U.S. military involvement in Cuba that observers suspected the newspapers exaggerated or even invented events to upset the public and pressure the U.S. government.

(c) The Granger Collection, New York
(r) Library of Congress, Prints and Photographs Division

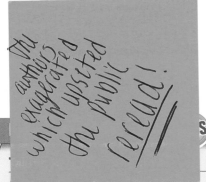

the authors exagerated which upsted the public *reread!*

As you read, use a diagram like this one to identify the lands that the United States acquired after the Spanish-American War.

Land Acquired

Content Vocabulary
• **armistice**
• **protectorate**
• **territory**

This type of sensational, biased, and often false reporting got the nickname "yellow journalism." The term came from the yellow ink used in a popular cartoon strip that appeared in the newspapers. Yellow journalism played a major role in shaping pro-war opinion in the United States.

"Remember the *Maine*"

Responding to pressure from the public, President McKinley sent the battleship USS *Maine* to Havana. The goal was to protect American citizens and property. Then, on the night of February 15, 1898, a huge explosion shattered the USS *Maine*, killing 260. American newspapers blamed the Spanish, who denied responsibility. Much later, evidence indicated that the explosion might have been accidental. At the time, though, Americans wanted war with Spain. The slogan "Remember the *Maine*" became a rallying cry for revenge.

President McKinley took a firm stand with Spain. He demanded a truce and an end to brutality against the Cubans. The Spanish agreed to some demands. McKinley and Congress, however, were not satisfied. On April 25, 1898, Congress declared war on Spain.

Fighting in the Philippines

Events in Cuba **triggered** the Spanish-American War. The first battles, however, occurred thousands of miles away in the Philippines. This is a group of islands off the coast of China. At the time, the Philippines was a Spanish colony and home to part of the Spanish fleet. On May 1, 1898, Commodore George Dewey launched a surprise attack at Manila Bay and destroyed most of the Spanish ships there.

American troops arrived in July. Filipino rebels, led by Emilio Aguinaldo (ah•gee•NAHL•doh), joined the Americans. After helping capture the city of Manila and the main island of Luzon, the rebels declared independence for the Philippines. They expected American support. They were disappointed when the United States instead began to debate what to do with the islands.

The War in Cuba

Meanwhile, American ships trapped the main Spanish fleet in the harbor of Santiago, Cuba. About 17,000 American troops—nearly a quarter of them African American—came ashore to fight alongside the Cuban forces. Heavy fighting followed.

Thinking Like a HISTORIAN

Distinguishing Fact From Opinion

Many newspapers today make an effort to separate news from opinion by restricting opinions to the editorial pages. Many others, however, regularly use splashy headlines and dramatic photos to arouse readers' emotions. Today, cable television, radio, and the Internet provide many more outlets for yellow journalism than Hearst and Pulitzer could ever have imagined. For more about distinguishing fact from opinion, review *Thinking Like a Historian.*

During the Spanish-American War, patriotic Americans wore buttons like this to help them "Remember the Maine."

Academic Vocabulary

trigger something that causes another event to happen

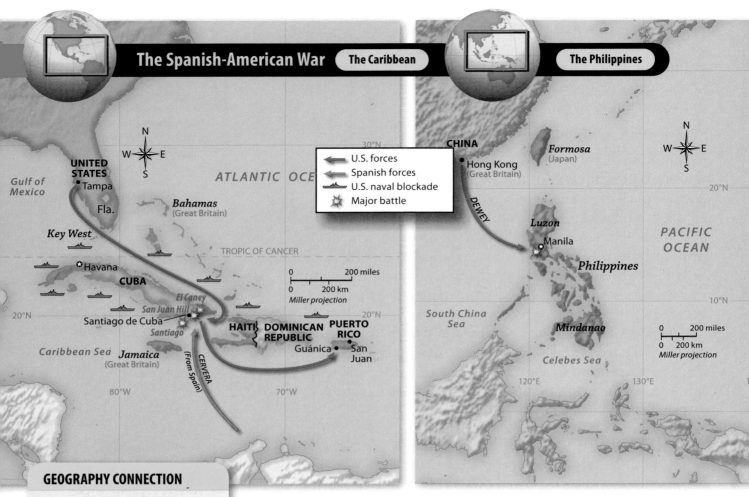

U.S. forces
Spanish forces
U.S. naval blockade
Major battle

GEOGRAPHY CONNECTION

The Spanish-American War took place in two locations—in the Caribbean, off the Florida coast, and in the Philippines, a group of islands near the coast of China.

1 LOCATION On what two Caribbean islands did U.S. forces land?

2 CRITICAL THINKING
Analyzing How do you think fighting in two places affected the war effort for the United States?

At the start of the war, Theodore Roosevelt was serving in a post with the navy. He left this job to join the fighting in Cuba. He formed a regiment of volunteers, mainly former cowhands and college students. This regiment was popularly known as the Rough Riders. On July 1, the Rough Riders, along with African American soldiers from other regiments, joined the Battle of San Juan Hill.

The U.S. forces captured the hill after heavy fighting. Two days later, the Spanish fleet tried to break out of Santiago Harbor. U.S. ships destroyed the Spanish fleet. Spanish resistance in Cuba came to an end.

The United States next turned to the Spanish colony of Puerto Rico. American troops landed in late July and quickly took control of the island. On August 12, the Spanish signed an **armistice** (AHR•muhs•tuhs), or truce. The Spanish-American War was over.

Reading **HELP**DESK CCSS

armistice an agreement to end fighting

Reading Strategy: *Reading in the Content Area*

Side-by-side maps such as the ones on this page show a single event as it affects two areas. Read the maps in terms of the single, overriding theme.

Impact of the War

Secretary of State John Hay called the Spanish-American War "a splendid little war." In less than four months of battle, about 400 Americans died from battle wounds. More than 2,000 died of yellow fever, malaria, and other tropical diseases. The African Americans who served suffered from discrimination even as they fought alongside American and Cuban troops.

The war also marked a change in America's international role. The United States was now recognized as a major military power with interests in foreign affairs and overseas possessions. This new role would have a big impact on the nation's future.

✓ PROGRESS CHECK

Identifying Who were the Rough Riders?

Acquiring New Lands

GUIDING QUESTION *How were Cuba, Puerto Rico, and the Philippines ruled after the Spanish-American War?*

The United States and Spain signed the Treaty of Paris on December 10, 1898. The treaty broke up most of the Spanish Empire.

Cuba became a U.S. **protectorate** (pruh·TEK·tuh·ruht). A protectorate is an independent country, but it is under the control of another country. Puerto Rico and Guam became territories of the United States. A **territory** (TEHR·uh·TAWR·ee) is an area that is completely controlled by another country. Spain also surrendered the Philippines to the United States in exchange for $20 million. The American empire had become a reality—though not everyone liked the idea.

Cuban Protectorate

After much debate, the United States granted Cuba independence in 1901. Yet Congress also adopted the Platt Amendment. This prohibited Cuba from making treaties and gave the United States a base on the island at Guantanamo Bay. (The United States still has this base.) The amendment also allowed the United States to take action if Cuba's independence was threatened. In short, the Platt Amendment ensured that the United States would remain deeply involved in Cuban affairs.

This cartoon shows President McKinley, at right, and Uncle Sam. The menu includes "Cuba Steak," "Porto Rico Pig," "The Philippine Floating Islands," and "The Sandwich Islands."

▶ CRITICAL THINKING
Interpreting What does the menu represent?

WELL, I HARDLY KNOW WHICH TO TAKE FIRST!

protectorate a country under the control of a different country
territory area completely controlled by a country

Academic Vocabulary

eventual at some later time

The Granger Collection, New York

New Government for Puerto Rico

In 1900 the United States set up a new government for Puerto Rico. Later, in 1917, the Jones Act made Puerto Rico a territory. It granted all Puerto Ricans American citizenship, though many still wanted independence for Puerto Rico.

Debate over the Philippines

The U. S. role in the Philippines caused fierce debate. Anti-imperialists argued that rule of the Philippines went against democratic principles. Others opposed the troops needed to control the islands and also competition from Filipino laborers. Leading Americans—including business giant Andrew Carnegie and author Mark Twain—joined the anti-imperialist campaign.

Imperialists argued that the Philippines would give the United States another Pacific naval base, a stopover on the way to China, and a large market for American goods. Others felt that the Americans had a duty to help "less civilized" peoples.

The imperialists won the debate. On February 6, 1899, the Treaty of Paris made the Philippines a United States territory.

Filipinos Rebel

Americans soon found that controlling an empire was costly. In February 1899, Emilio Aguinaldo's forces began a fight for independence. More than 4,000 U.S. soldiers died in the fighting. About 220,000 Filipinos died, most from disease and hunger.

After Aguinaldo was captured in March 1901, some Filipinos refused to surrender. William Howard Taft led a new government that tried to prepare the islands for **eventual** self-rule. The Philippines gained independence in 1946.

Anti-imperialists such as Mark Twain (above) and Andrew Carnegie argued against making the Philippines a United States territory.

Library of Congress, Prints and Photographs Division

✔ PROGRESS CHECK

Contrasting What is the difference between a protectorate and a territory?

LESSON 3 REVIEW

Review Vocabulary

1. Explain the meaning of the term *armistice* by using it in a sentence.

2. Use the terms *protectorate* and *territory* in a sentence.

Answer the Guiding Questions

3. *Describing* How did newspapers contribute to the U.S. declaring war against Spain?

4. *Describing* Describe the different approaches taken by the United States toward its new possessions after the war.

5. *Analyzing* How do you think the conquest and rule of territories such as the Philippines challenged American ideas of democracy?

6. **NARRATIVE** Write an account of the Battle of San Juan Hill from the point of view of a soldier taking part in the fight.

networks
There's More Online!

☑ **BIOGRAPHY** John Hay

☑ **GRAPHIC ORGANIZER**
Policies and Principles of
U.S. Foreign Policy

☑ **MAP** Panama Canal

☑ **SLIDE SHOW** John Hay

☑ **VIDEO**

Lesson 4
Latin American Policies

ESSENTIAL QUESTION *Why does conflict develop?*

IT MATTERS BECAUSE
The complex relationship between the United States and its neighbors to the south was largely forged in the early years of the twentieth century.

The United States in Panama

GUIDING QUESTION *What steps did the United States take to build the Panama Canal?*

Americans and Europeans had long wanted to build a canal across Central America. Such a canal would connect the Caribbean and the Pacific Oceans—and **eliminate** the need for the long voyage around South America.

In the 1880s, a French company tried to build a canal across Panama. Panama is an **isthmus** (ihs•muhs)—a narrow strip of land connecting two larger bodies of land—about 50 miles (80 km) wide. The French effort ended in failure.

Around this time, the United States was in the process of acquiring territory in both oceans. U.S. desire for a canal grew.

Revolution in Panama

In 1903 Panama was part of Colombia, a South American country. Secretary of State John Hay negotiated a treaty with Colombia. The treaty gave the United States control of a piece of land across the isthmus for 99 years. For this the United States would pay $10 million, plus an **annual** rent of $250,000.

The plans of the United States hit a snag when the Colombian Senate rejected the treaty. President Roosevelt was not discouraged.

(l) Getty Images, (cr) CDC
(r) Library of Congress, Prints & Photographs Division, LC-DIG-ggbain-29882

Reading **HELP**DESK ⓒⓒⓢⓢ

Taking Notes: *Comparing*

As you read, use a diagram like this one to compare the basic principles of each American foreign policy.

Policy		Principle
Roosevelt Corollary	➤	
Dollar Diplomacy	➤	
Moral Diplomacy	➤	

Content Vocabulary
• isthmus
• anarchy
• dollar diplomacy

John Hay (1838–1905)

John Milton Hay enjoyed a long career as a writer and public servant. As a lawyer in Springfield, Illinois, he befriended Abraham Lincoln and later became his personal secretary. Hay then served as a diplomat in Europe and as an editor for the *New York Tribune*. He became secretary of state under President McKinley in 1897. In that role, Hay helped bring an end to the Spanish-American War, put in place the Open Door policy in China, and negotiated the treaty that made the Panama Canal possible.

▶ **CRITICAL THINKING**
Analyzing In your opinion, what was John Hay's greatest accomplishment? Why?

He began looking for other ways to get control of the land. He wrote that he would "be delighted if Panama were an independent state." The people of the area had staged unsuccessful revolts against Colombia in the past. Now, they had reason to hope the United States would support such a revolt.

On November 2, 1903, the American warship *Nashville* steamed into the port of Colón. Encouraged by this show of support, Panamanians declared independence. Colombia sent forces to stop the revolt, but the United States turned them back.

The Panama Canal

The United States recognized Panama's independence immediately. Hay quickly signed a treaty with the new nation giving the United States rights to a 10-mile (16-km) strip across the isthmus. The U.S. paid Panama the same amount it had offered earlier to Colombia.

Roosevelt's actions angered many Latin Americans, some members of Congress, and other Americans. The president, however, took great pride in his accomplishment. He later said: "I took the canal zone and let Congress debate, and while the debate goes on, the canal does also."

Building the canal, however, would not be easy. An English writer described Panama as "a damp, tropical jungle, intensely hot, swarming with mosquitoes." The insects carried deadly diseases—yellow fever and malaria. These would kill thousands of workers before a U.S. Army doctor, Colonel William Gorgas, developed effective mosquito control measures.

Opening the Canal

The Panama Canal opened on August 15, 1914. A cargo ship named the *Ancon* made the first voyage through the new waterway. From the start, the canal was a great success. Before it opened, ships sailing from New York to San Francisco traveled 12,600 miles (20,277 km) around the tip of South America. After the canal opened, the trip was only 4,900 miles (7,886 km). This greatly reduced shipping time and costs.

The Panama Canal also helped extend American naval power. The U.S. naval fleet could now move freely between the Atlantic and Pacific Oceans. The canal was a valuable property that the United States would protect. This meant that the U.S. would involve itself in Latin America.

Hutton Archive/Getty Images

Reading **HELP**DESK

isthmus a narrow strip of land connecting two larger bodies of land
anarchy disorder and lawlessness caused by lack of effective government

Academic Vocabulary
eliminate get rid of
annual yearly

Some Latin Americans remained bitter over how the United States got the land for the canal. This feeling soured relations between the United States and Latin America for years. The United States eventually turned the canal over to Panama at the end of 1999.

☑ PROGRESS CHECK

Identifying What problem faced workers on the canal?

Policing the Western Hemisphere

GUIDING QUESTION *What was the United States's foreign policy in Latin America?*

President Roosevelt often quoted an African proverb, "Speak softly and carry a big stick." He believed the United States should respond to foreign crises not with threats but with action. Roosevelt also believed that America must exercise "an international police power." He felt that this was necessary to preserve order and to prevent **anarchy** (A•nuhr•kee)—disorder and lawlessness.

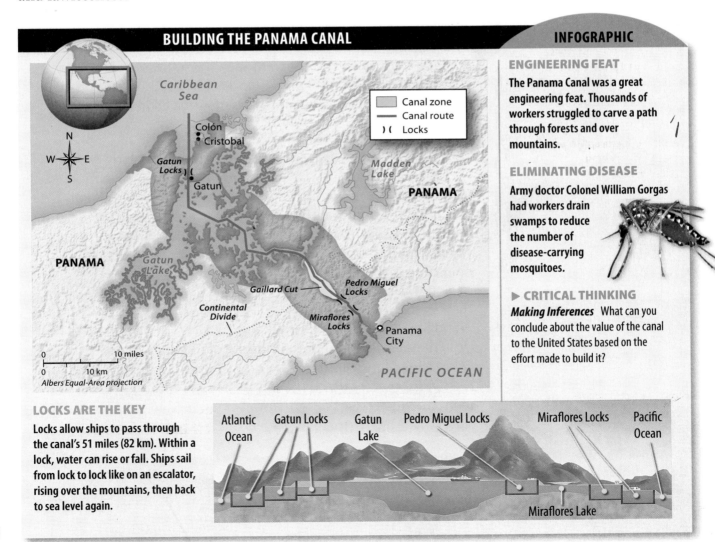

BUILDING THE PANAMA CANAL

INFOGRAPHIC

Caribbean Sea

Colón
Cristobal

Gatun Locks)(
Gatun

Canal zone
Canal route
)(Locks

Madden Lake

PANAMA

PANAMA

Gatun Lake

Gaillard Cut

Pedro Miguel Locks

Continental Divide

Miraflores Locks

Panama City

0   10 miles
0   10 km
Albers Equal-Area projection

PACIFIC OCEAN

ENGINEERING FEAT

The Panama Canal was a great engineering feat. Thousands of workers struggled to carve a path through forests and over mountains.

ELIMINATING DISEASE

Army doctor Colonel William Gorgas had workers drain swamps to reduce the number of disease-carrying mosquitoes.

▶ **CRITICAL THINKING**

Making Inferences What can you conclude about the value of the canal to the United States based on the effort made to build it?

LOCKS ARE THE KEY

Locks allow ships to pass through the canal's 51 miles (82 km). Within a lock, water can rise or fall. Ships sail from lock to lock like on an escalator, rising over the mountains, then back to sea level again.

Atlantic Ocean   Gatun Locks   Gatun Lake   Pedro Miguel Locks   Miraflores Locks   Pacific Ocean

Miraflores Lake

Roosevelt Corollary

U.S. presidents had long followed the Monroe Doctrine. This policy aimed to keep European powers from getting involved in Latin America. In 1904, President Roosevelt added to the Monroe Doctrine with the Roosevelt Corollary. This corollary—a statement that follows naturally from an earlier one—held that the United States had the right to get involved in the affairs of Latin American nations whenever they seemed unstable. The United States would act as a "police power" in Latin America.

The United States first applied the Roosevelt Corollary in 1905. It took control of the Dominican Republic's finances following a revolution that had toppled the country's government. Then in 1906, the United States used the policy again when troops were sent to Cuba to stop a revolution there.

Dollar Diplomacy

Roosevelt's successor, William Howard Taft, hoped to change American policy by "substituting dollars for bullets." Taft's policy was known as **dollar diplomacy** (DAH·luhr duh·PLOH·muh·see). It meant using economic power—for example, making loans—to gain influence and protect U.S. interests. This policy had good and bad effects. Investments by the United States in Latin America grew. Money from the United States helped build roads and harbors and increase trade and profits. However, the approach also increased anti-U.S. feelings.

Relations With Mexico

In the early 1900s, Mexico was a poor country. A tiny group of rich landholders and U.S. investors controlled the nation. In 1911 a reformer named Francisco Madero (muh·DEHR·oh) led a successful revolution. Just two years later, General Victoriano Huerta (WEHR·tuh) killed Madero. Huerta favored the wealthy and foreign interests. The new president, Woodrow Wilson, refused to recognize Huerta's "government of butchers."

Wilson's "Moral Diplomacy"

Woodrow Wilson hoped to avoid further imperialism by the United States. He sought to promote democracy in other nations as a means of preventing war and revolution. Like Roosevelt and Taft, Wilson recognized the importance of military power and economic interests. Wilson, however, wanted to base his foreign policy on moral principles—ideas of right and wrong.

Francisco Madero tried to reform the Mexican economy and society, but he was killed just two years after taking power.

dollar diplomacy the policy of using economic investment to protect U.S. interests abroad

Wilson's "moral diplomacy" faced a challenge in Mexico. After Huerta took power, civil war broke out. Wilson hoped Huerta's government would fall. It did not. Wilson authorized arms sales to Huerta's rival, Venustiano Carranza (kuh·RAN·zuh).

Problems came to a head in April 1914. Wilson ordered U.S. troops to seize the port of Veracruz after the arrest of some U.S. sailors. This show of force strengthened Carranza, and Carranza took power.

Francisco "Pancho" Villa

Huerta's fall did not end the civil war. Rebel leader Francisco "Pancho" Villa rose up against Carranza. In January 1916, Villa shot 16 U.S. workers in Mexico because of U.S. support for Carranza. Villa hoped to damage Mexican-U.S. relations, but the United States did not respond. Then Villa's rebels burned a town in New Mexico and killed 18 there.

Villa's actions outraged the leaders and people of the United States. President Wilson sent a force under General John J. Pershing into Mexico. They chased Villa for almost a year without success. After the United States turned its attention to the war in Europe in 1917, Pershing's troops left Mexico.

The nations had come close to war, and U.S. actions led to great resentment in Mexico. As in the Caribbean, however, the United States had shown other nations that it would use its power when its interests were threatened.

✔ **PROGRESS CHECK**

Contrasting How did Taft's views about diplomacy differ from Roosevelt'

Bold, smart, and loved by the Mexican people, Pancho Villa (front row, second from the left) commanded a strong rebel force in northern Mexico.

Library of Congress, Prints & Photographs Division, LC-DIG-ggbain-29882

[handwritten note: last part Reread table notes]

LESSON 4 REVIEW (CCSS)

Review Vocabulary

1. Explain the meaning of each of the following terms by using each in a sentence about this lesson.

   a. isthmus **b.** anarchy **c.** dollar diplomacy

Answer the Guiding Questions

2. *Identifying* How did the United States benefit from the construction of the Panama Canal?

3. *Analyzing* How did the effort to acquire the land for the canal and build the canal affect U.S. relations with other nations?

4. *Discussing* How did the beliefs of U.S. presidents shape Latin American foreign policies?

5. **ARGUMENT** If you were president, would you adopt the policy of dollar diplomacy in Latin America? Why or why not?

① Exploring the Essential Question

INFORMATIVE/EXPLANATORY Review the military conflicts that involved the United States during this period. Select one of these conflicts and write an essay that describes the changes that resulted from it.

② 21st Century Skills

CRITICAL THINKING AND PROBLEM SOLVING Working with a small group, create a three-column chart that compares the approaches to foreign policy suggested by the Roosevelt Corollary, dollar diplomacy, and moral diplomacy. Then imagine an armed rebellion in a South American nation, and discuss the probable reactions of the U.S. using each of the three approaches. When your group has come to a general agreement, add these actions to the third column on the chart.

③ Thinking Like a Historian

UNDERSTANDING CAUSE AND EFFECT Economic issues played a major role in the events in Hawaii during this period. Create a diagram like the one below that details the dates and chain of events that led to the planters' revolt and the eventual annexation of Hawaii. Begin with the U.S. missionaries' arrival in Hawaii and end with the annexation of Hawaii. Focus on the economic reasons behind events.

④ Visual Literacy

ANALYZING PHOTOGRAPHS

President Theodore Roosevelt visits the site of the Panama Canal. What does this picture tell you about Roosevelt's attitudes toward the project?

Underwood & Underwood/CORBIS

REVIEW THE GUIDING QUESTIONS

Directions: Choose the best answer for each question.

1 Commodore Perry used warships to help open ports in

A. Latin America.

B. Alaska.

C. Japan.

D. Europe.

2 The "Open Door" referred to efforts to

F. trade with China.

G. trade with Samoa.

H. prevent Japan from trading with Korea.

I. annex Hawaii.

3 The Spanish-American War began after

A. Dewey destroyed the Spanish fleet in Manila.

B. the USS *Maine* exploded in Havana Harbor.

C. Theodore Roosevelt organized the Rough Riders.

D. Aguinaldo's troops revolted in the Philippines.

4 Aguinaldo's troops fought against the U.S. in the Philippines because they

F. wanted control of the sugarcane trade.

G. wanted independence.

H. were loyal to the Spanish.

I. hoped to become a Spanish protectorate.

5 The revolt that resulted in Panama's independence succeeded because

A. Colombia sided with the rebels.

B. the French withdrew support for Colombia.

C. yellow fever and malaria weakened the government's army.

D. U.S. military forces backed it.

6 Pancho Villa's actions

F. helped Mexico gain independence.

G. caused President Roosevelt to use military force.

H. brought Mexico and the U.S. close to war.

I. prevented President Taft from using dollar diplomacy.

DBQ ANALYZING DOCUMENTS

7 **Analyzing** This cartoon shows Roosevelt "taking" Panama. How does the cartoon portray Panama?

A. as small and weak in comparison to U.S. power

B. as an independent country capable of defending itself

C. as a dangerous place because of tropical diseases

D. as a country that several nations would like to take over

8 **Drawing Conclusions** How does the cartoon portray Roosevelt?

F. as understanding of Panama's economic problems

G. as a respected war hero

H. as arrogant in his support of rebellion in Panama

I. as a president willing to negotiate with Panama

THE COUP d'ETAT.

SHORT RESPONSE

The following is taken from a letter from Hawaiian queen Liliuokalani to the U.S. government about the proposed annexation of Hawaii.

"[M]y people, about forty thousand in number, have in no way been consulted by those ... who claim the right to destroy the independence of Hawaii. ...

"[The] treaty ignores, not only the civic rights of my people, but, further, the hereditary property of their chiefs. ...

"[The] treaty ignores ... all treaties made by ... sovereigns with other friendly powers, and it is thereby a violation of international law."

9 What is Queen Liliuokalani's basic position on the treaty?

10 What reasons does she give for her position?

EXTENDED RESPONSE

11 **Argument** Take the side of either the imperialists or anti-imperialists in the debate about acquiring the Philippines. Write a one-page paper that persuades others of your viewpoint.

Need Extra Help?

If You've Missed Question	❶	❷	❸	❹	❺	❻	❼	❽	❾	❿	⓫
Review Lesson	1	2	3	3	4	4	4	4	2	2	3

The Granger Collection, NYC

World War I

1914–1919

ESSENTIAL QUESTION *Why does conflict develop?*

◄ *American flying ace Eddie Rickenbacker stands by his plane in 1918.*

The Granger Collection, NYC

The Story Matters . . .

By 1917 the people of the United States already know and admire Eddie Rickenbacker as a daring race car driver. Now he is ready for a bigger challenge. When his country enters World War I, Rickenbacker learns to fly airplanes. As part of the army's new Air Service, Rickenbacker fights and wins some of the first air battles in the history of warfare. He becomes the nation's top flying "ace," destroying 26 enemy aircraft. Along the way, Rickenbacker helps the United States win the war—and changes the way nations do battle.

Place and Time: The World 1914 to 1919

In 1914 World War I broke out in Europe. Many nations around the globe took sides in the conflict. Included were colonies of the war's main participants. One side, which included Germany and Austria-Hungary, became known as the Central Powers. The other side, including Great Britain, France, and eventually the United States, was known as the Allies.

Step Into the Place

MAP FOCUS World War I started in Europe but affected many countries and continents.

1 PLACE What European nations were allies with the United States during World War I?

2 LOCATION On what continent did the Central Powers have most of their colonies?

3 CRITICAL THINKING
Analyzing What is one difficulty you think the United States faced in helping its allies?

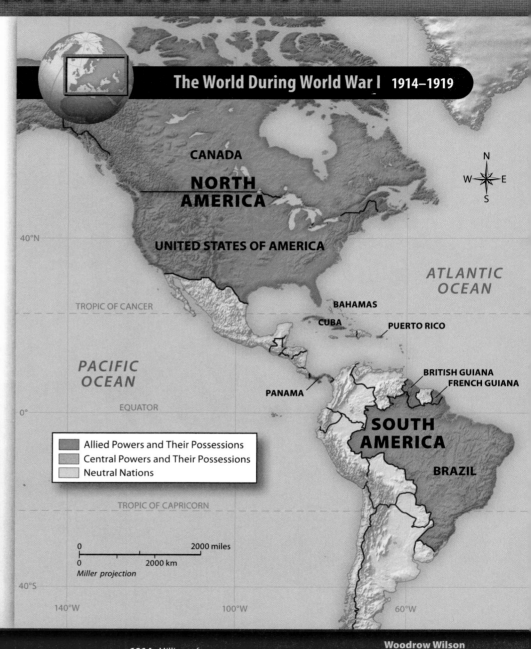

The World During World War I 1914–1919

CANADA
NORTH AMERICA
UNITED STATES OF AMERICA
40°N
TROPIC OF CANCER
PACIFIC OCEAN
EQUATOR
0°
BAHAMAS
CUBA
PUERTO RICO
PANAMA
ATLANTIC OCEAN
BRITISH GUIANA
FRENCH GUIANA
SOUTH AMERICA
BRAZIL
TROPIC OF CAPRICORN
40°S
140°W   100°W   60°W

Allied Powers and Their Possessions
Central Powers and Their Possessions
Neutral Nations

0   2000 miles
0   2000 km
Miller projection

Step Into the Time

TIME LINE Look at the time line. Write a sentence speculating on which events may have led the United States into the war.

Woodrow Wilson 1913–1921

U.S. PRESIDENTS
U.S. EVENTS
WORLD EVENTS

1914 Millions of immigrants from southern and eastern Europe enter U.S.

1915 German U-boat sinks the *Lusitania*

1914

1916

1914 • Franz Ferdinand assassinated
• World War I begins

1915 International Congress of Women held at The Hague in the Netherlands

ARCTIC OCEAN

RUSSIAN EMPIRE

ASIA

UNITED KINGDOM

GERMANY

EUROPE

BELG.

FRANCE

AUST.-HUNG.

ITALY

SERB.

ROMANIA

BULGARIA

MONTENEGRO

GREECE

OTTOMAN EMPIRE

PORTUGAL

CHINA

JAPAN

ALGERIA

TRIPOLI

EGYPT

INDIA

AFRICA

FRENCH WEST AFRICA

ANGLO-EGYPTIAN SUDAN

ADEN

ERITREA

SIAM

FRENCH INDO-CHINA

PHILIPPINES

NIGERIA

KAMERUN

ITALIAN SOMALILAND

SIERRA LEONE

GOLD COAST

TOGO

BRITISH EAST AFRICA

BISMARCK ARCHIPELAGO

LIBERIA

FRENCH EQUITORIAL AFRICA

BELGIAN CONGO

GERMAN EAST AFRICA

INDIAN OCEAN

NEW GUINEA

ANGOLA

PORTUGUESE EAST AFRICA

MADAGASCAR

GERMAN SOUTHWEST AFRICA

UNION OF SOUTH AFRICA

AUSTRALIA

20°E   60°E   100°E   140°E

1917 • Zimmermann telegram angers U. S.
• United States enters World War I
• Selective Service Act passed

1918 National War Labor Board established

1919 President Woodrow Wilson wins Nobel Peace Prize

1920 Senate rejects League of Nations

1918

1920

1917 Lenin leads Bolshevik Revolution in Russia

1918 • World War I ends
• Flu epidemic kills more than 20 million people

1919 Treaty of Versailles signed

1920 • The Hague chosen as seat of International Court of Justice
• League of Nations headquarters moves to Geneva, Switzerland

Lesson 1
War in Europe

ESSENTIAL QUESTION *Why does conflict develop?*

IT MATTERS BECAUSE
World War I was a catastrophe that was many years in the making.

Troubles in Europe

GUIDING QUESTION *What factors led to the outbreak of war in Europe?*

It was June 28, 1914, and the people of Sarajevo, Bosnia, crowded the city streets. Archduke Franz Ferdinand, next in line to the throne of the Austro-Hungarian Empire, was in town for a visit. As he and his wife rolled along in their open car, a gunman attacked. Both the archduke and his wife were killed.

The assassination did more than take the lives of the royal couple. It upset a delicate balance among the powers of Europe. Within weeks, these powers were at war.

Though the fighting spread quickly, the tensions that led to what we now call World War I, went back years. They grew as nations formed empires, built up armies, and made alliances.

A Rise in Nationalism

Much of the tension in Europe in 1914 came from a rise in **nationalism** (NASH•nuh•lih•zuhm), a feeling of intense loyalty to a country or group. Nationalism encouraged newly united nations such as Italy and Germany to show their power. Their actions threatened older nations, Great Britain and France.

Nationalism also inspired some ethnic groups to break away from nations or empires of which they were a part. Some of these ethnic groups demanded nations of their own.

(l) Austrian Archives/CORBIS/ (cl) ullstein bild/The Granger Collection, NYC, (c) CORBIS, (cr) Art Archive/Dagli Orti, (r) Hutton Archive/Getty Images

---

Reading **HELP**DESK (CCSS)

Taking Notes: *Identifying*

As you read, use a diagram like this one to list causes of tensions that led to World War I.

Causes of tensions
that led to World War I

Content Vocabulary

• **nationalism**   • **balance of power**
• **militarism**   • **stalemate**
• **alliance system** • **U-boat**

Competing for Empires

European tensions also grew as powerful countries built great empires in the late 1800s and early 1900s. European countries competed for colonies in Africa, Asia, and other parts of the world. These colonies not only provided new markets and raw materials, they also boosted a nation's status.

Great Britain and France had built large overseas empires, but both wanted to expand them even more. Germany, Italy, and Russia wanted to increase their colonial holdings as well. Each nation's attempt to expand its overseas empire brought it into conflict with another.

Military Buildup

To aid in their quest for empire, European powers strengthened their armies and navies. When one nation increased its military strength, its rivals felt threatened and built up as well. This growing **militarism** (MIH•luh•tuh•rih•zuhm) pushed Germany, France, and Russia to develop huge armies in the early 1900s. Great Britain and Germany built large navies.

A Network of Alliances

The military buildup made countries nervous. In response, they created an **alliance system** (uh•LY•uhnts SIHS•tuhm) in which different nations promised to help one another if any one of them came under attack. By 1914 two major alliances divided Europe. Germany, Austria-Hungary, and Italy formed the Triple Alliance. Great Britain, France, and Russia formed the Triple Entente (en•TAHNT). An *entente* is an understanding among nations.

Alliances were supposed to help keep peace by creating a **balance of power.** When such a balance exists, no one country can gain power over the others. However, the alliance system posed a great danger. With it, a small dispute between two countries could quickly entangle many others and trigger a larger war.

Competition and alliances caused some to view Europe in 1914 as a keg of gunpowder. One American diplomat noted that it would take "only a spark to set the whole thing off." That spark would come from the region known as the Balkans.

European nations made alliances to help defend one another. Countries sometimes broke alliances and formed new ones. This 1915 poster criticizes Italy for changing sides. Italy allied with Germany and Austria-Hungary at first, then formed an alliance with France, Russia, and Great Britain.

▶ **CRITICAL THINKING**
Making Inferences What made Italy's action so troublesome?

nationalism a feeling of intense loyalty to a country or group
militarism celebration of military ideals, and a rapid buildup of military power
alliance system a system in which countries agree to defend each other
balance of power an equality of power among different countries that discourages any group from acting aggressively

The assassination of Archduke Franz Ferdinand provided the incident that ignited war in Europe.

In the early 1900s, the Balkan Peninsula was seething with nationalist and ethnic feeling. Several nations argued over territory. Slavic nationalists hoped to unite all Slavic peoples in the region. One conflict was especially bitter. The Slavic people in Austria-Hungary wanted independence. The small country of Serbia supported this effort.

Assassination and War

Gavrilo Princip was a member of a Serbian nationalist group. Princip and his group plotted the murder of Franz Ferdinand. They hoped to bring down the Austro-Hungarian Empire and unite the Slavs. It was Princip who fired the shots that killed the archduke and his wife.

Austria-Hungary blamed Serbia for the assassination. With Germany's support, it gave Serbia a list of demands, which Serbia refused. Austria-Hungary declared war on Serbia on July 28, 1914.

Europe's alliance system caused the conflict to spread quickly. Russia, which was Serbia's protector, prepared for war. Germany then came to the side of Austria-Hungary. Germany declared war on Russia on August 1, 1914, and then declared war on France, Russia's ally, on August 3. A day later, Germany invaded Belgium. Great Britain, honoring a pledge to protect Belgium, declared war on Germany.

✓ PROGRESS CHECK

Explaining How did nationalism help lead to war in Europe?

A World War Begins

GUIDING QUESTION *What changes made World War I become a long and deadly war?*

The "Great War" had begun. On one side were the Allied Powers, or the Allies. They included Great Britain, France, and Russia. On the other side, Germany, Austria-Hungary, and the Ottoman (Turkish) Empire made up the Central Powers.

Japan was a rival of Germany in Asia. It joined the Allies in August 1914. Italy refused to honor its alliance with Germany and Austria-Hungary. Instead, it joined the Allies in 1915.

ullstein bild/The Granger Collection, NYC

Reading **HELP**DESK (CCSS)

stalemate a situation in a conflict in which neither side can make progress against the other

The Western Front

Germany had invaded Belgium in order to reach France. The Germans hoped to defeat the French quickly and then move east against Russia. The Belgians, however, held out for nearly three weeks. This gave France and Britain time to react.

When the Germans at last overcame the Belgians, they marched into France to within 15 miles (24 km) of the capital, Paris. The British and French met the Germans at the Marne River. The Battle of the Marne, fought in September 1914, stopped the German advance.

The battle also made it clear that neither side could win the war quickly or easily. The war in Western Europe became a **stalemate,** in which neither side could make progress against the other. For the next three years, opposing forces faced off from a network of trenches, which both armies dug in along the front lines. These trenches sheltered soldiers from bullets and artillery shells. In between was a "no man's land" of shell craters and barbed wire, which neither side controlled.

To break the standstill, both sides launched major offensives in 1916. The Germans launched the Battle of Verdun in northeastern France in February. Verdun was one of the longest and bloodiest battles of the war. At its end in December 1916, more than 750,000 French and German soldiers were dead. Many more were wounded.

GEOGRAPHY CONNECTION

The assassination in Sarajevo set in motion events that quickly led to the outbreak of war.

1 REGIONS What nations made up the Central Powers in 1914?

2 CRITICAL THINKING
Determining Cause and Effect
Explain how alliances created conditions that led to world war.

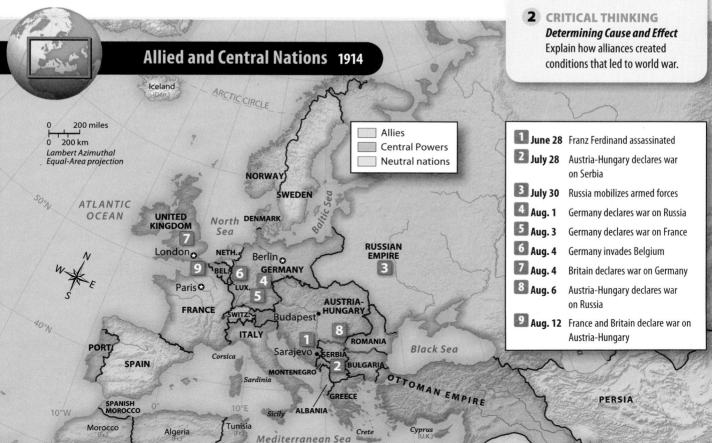

Allied and Central Nations 1914

Allies
Central Powers
Neutral nations

0   200 miles
0   200 km
Lambert Azimuthal
Equal-Area projection

1 June 28 Franz Ferdinand assassinated

2 July 28 Austria-Hungary declares war on Serbia

3 July 30 Russia mobilizes armed forces

4 Aug. 1 Germany declares war on Russia

5 Aug. 3 Germany declares war on France

6 Aug. 4 Germany invades Belgium

7 Aug. 4 Britain declares war on Germany

8 Aug. 6 Austria-Hungary declares war on Russia

9 Aug. 12 France and Britain declare war on Austria-Hungary

THE DEADLY TECHNOLOGY OF WORLD WAR I

German soldiers fire a machine gun.

Both sides used aircraft for observation, ground support, and bombing missions.

The British introduced the tank in 1916.

Armies on both sides used poison gas. Soldiers without gas masks faced death or lung damage.

INFOGRAPHIC

Warring nations used several new or improved weapons during World War I. Machine guns, modern artillery, poison gas, tanks, aircraft, and submarines produced horrific casualty rates.

▶ CRITICAL THINKING

Explaining How did new technology make combat more deadly?

While the Battle of Verdun raged, the Allies launched their own offensive in July—the Battle of the Somme. This battle also produced horrifying casualties, and the Allies gained only 7 miles (11.2 km).

New Weapons on the Battlefield

New deadly weapons introduced during the war caused large numbers of injuries and deaths. Improved artillery fired larger shells at great distances. Better rifles enabled soldiers to hit targets with greater accuracy. Yet as the number of dead and wounded grew, each side fought on—and each side looked for a way to gain an advantage over the other.

The Germans first used poison gas against Allied troops in April 1915. The gas could kill or seriously injure anyone who breathed it. A British officer described the effects of a gas attack:

PRIMARY SOURCE

❝ They fought with their terror, running blindly in the gas cloud, and dropping in agony. ❞

—quoted in *Avoiding Armageddon*

After the Germans had introduced gas to the battlefield, the Allies began to use poison gas as well. To protect themselves, soldiers began carrying gas masks.

(l) CORBIS, (cl) Art Archive/Dagli Orti, (cr) The Granger Collection, New York, (r) Art Archive/Imperial War Museum

Reading HELPDESK CCSS

U-boat a German submarine

Academic Vocabulary

dimension the level on which something exists or takes place
equip to outfit

Build Vocabulary: *Origins of Sayings*

The term *no-man's land* was used in trench warfare but dates back to the 1300s. People may refer to any unclaimed or murky area between opposing sides—whether on land or in the world of ideas—as a no-man's land.

The Allies also sought a decisive advantage on the battlefield. For example, they introduced the armored tank to battle in January 1916. Tanks were designed to break the stalemate of trench warfare. They could cross no-man's land and fire on the enemy at close range. By crushing barbed wire, tanks also made an easier route for advancing troops. After seeing the effectiveness of tanks, the Germans began making them, too.

The most dramatic new weapon was the airplane. Planes took warfare to a new **dimension** (duh·MEHN·shuhn). Both sides used planes to watch troop movements and bomb targets.

Daring pilots waged duels in the skies called "dogfights." The first fighter planes were **equipped** (ih·KWIHPT) only with machine guns fastened to the top wing. The Germans used the zeppelin, or blimp, to bomb Allied cities.

On the Seas

With their land armies deadlocked in Western Europe, both sides turned to the sea. Great Britain blockaded all ports under German control. Over time, this produced serious shortages. Many Germans went without food and other supplies.

Germany had an effective naval weapon of its own: the submarine. Known as **U-boats** (YOO·BOHTS)—from the German word *Unterseeboot*—these submarines sank ships carrying supplies to Britain. U-boat attacks on ships at sea eventually brought the United States into the war.

✔ **PROGRESS CHECK**

Summarizing What new or greatly improved technologies and techniques were used in World War I?

Thinking Like a HISTORIAN

Drawing Inferences and Conclusions

The "Red Baron" was a nickname for the Baron von Richthofen (below), a famous German pilot in World War I.

What are some possible reasons why he may have been given this nickname?

To learn more about drawing inferences and conclusions, review *Thinking Like a Historian.*

LESSON 1 REVIEW (CCSS)

Review Vocabulary

1. Examine the two terms below. Then write a sentence about the early 1900s that explains the connection between them.

    a. alliance system   b. balance of power

2. Write a sentence about German U-boats and their impact on World War I.

Answer the Guiding Questions

3. *Determining Cause and Effect* What were two effects of a rise in nationalism in Europe?

4. *Summarizing* How did military buildup help lead to World War I?

5. *Drawing Conclusions* Why did the use of trenches prolong World War I?

6. *Analyzing* Why was the airplane an important weapon during World War I?

7. **INFORMATIVE/EXPLANATORY** Write a short essay explaining the factors that made World War I different from earlier wars.

networks

There's More Online!

☑ **BIOGRAPHY**
Jeannette Rankin

☑ **CHART/GRAPH**
• Size of Armies
• Parts of a Submarine

☑ **GRAPHIC ORGANIZER** Events
Causing U.S. Entry Into War

☑ **VIDEO**

Lesson 2

America's Road to War

ESSENTIAL QUESTION *Why does conflict develop?*

IT MATTERS BECAUSE

The United States found it was unable to pursue its goal of neutrality, and the country eventually entered World War I.

American Neutrality

GUIDING QUESTION *Why did the United States try to remain neutral during the war?*

President Wilson had long said that the United States should be neutral in the war in Europe. Most Americans supported this view. They did not think that the war concerned them. This view expressed in an editorial in a New York newspaper spoke for many:

PRIMARY SOURCE

❝ There is nothing reasonable in such a war . . . and it would be [foolish] for this country to sacrifice itself to . . . a clash of ancient hatreds which is urging the Old World to destruction. ❞

—from the *New York Sun*

Plenty of Americans, however, did take sides. More than a third of the nation's 92 million people were either foreign-born or children of immigrants. Many favored the countries their families had come from. Some of the 8 million Americans of German or Austrian background favored the Central Powers. So did many of the 4.5 million Irish Americans, who resented the British because of their rule of Ireland.

(l) ullstein bild/The Granger Collection, New York, (c) MPI/Archive Photos/Getty Images, (cr and r) CORBIS

Reading **HELP**DESK **CCSS**

Taking Notes: *Identifying*

As you read, use a diagram like this one to show events that caused the United States to enter World War I.

U.S. enters
World War I

Content Vocabulary
• **propaganda**
• **autocracy**

Even more Americans favored the Allies. Ties of language, customs, and traditions linked the United States to Great Britain. Among these people was President Wilson. He told the British ambassador, "Everything I love most in the world is at stake." A German victory, Wilson said, "would be fatal to our form of government and American ideals."

Propaganda and Public Opinion

Both sides in the war used **propaganda** (PRAH·puh·GAN·duh)—information designed to influence opinion. Allied propaganda **stressed** the German invasion of neutral Belgium. Posters told horror stories of German cruelty. They referred to the Germans as "barbarians."

Propaganda from the Central Powers was also fierce. Because of sympathy for the British, however, Allied propaganda was more effective in influencing Americans.

The United States and the War

As a neutral nation, the United States sought trade with both sides in the war. Both sides needed goods of all kinds, and American businesses were happy to provide them. However, Britain's blockade made trade with Germany difficult.

The British navy stopped and searched American ships headed for German ports. Often, they not only searched the ships, but seized the goods they carried. The United States complained its ships should be free to pass without interference. The British responded that they were fighting for their survival.

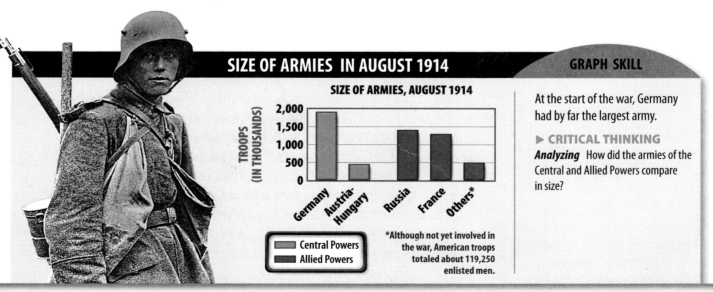

SIZE OF ARMIES IN AUGUST 1914

SIZE OF ARMIES, AUGUST 1914

TROOPS (IN THOUSANDS): 2,000 / 1,500 / 1,000 / 500 / 0

Germany, Austria-Hungary, Russia, France, Others*

Central Powers
Allied Powers

*Although not yet involved in the war, American troops totaled about 119,250 enlisted men.

GRAPH SKILL

At the start of the war, Germany had by far the largest army.

▶ CRITICAL THINKING

Analyzing How did the armies of the Central and Allied Powers compare in size?

propaganda information used to influence opinion

Academic Vocabulary

stress to call attention to

Reading in the Content Area: *Bar Graph*

To read bar graphs, use a ruler or pencil to help you determine the amount represented by each bar.

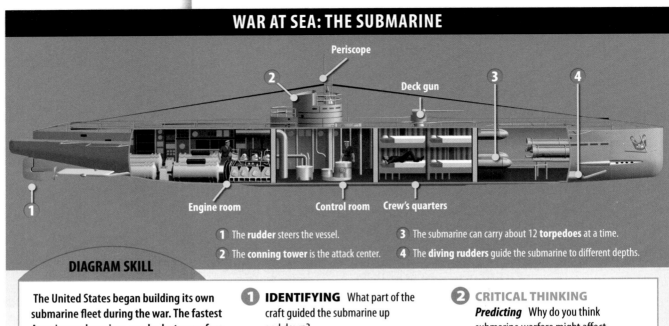

WAR AT SEA: THE SUBMARINE

Periscope

2

Deck gun

3

4

Engine room   Control room   Crew's quarters

1

1 The **rudder** steers the vessel.

2 The **conning tower** is the attack center.

3 The submarine can carry about 12 **torpedoes** at a time.

4 The **diving rudders** guide the submarine to different depths.

DIAGRAM SKILL

The United States began building its own submarine fleet during the war. The fastest American submarines reached a top surface speed of 14 knots (a little more than 16 miles, or 25.7 km, per hour).

1 **IDENTIFYING** What part of the craft guided the submarine up and down?

2 **CRITICAL THINKING**
Predicting Why do you think submarine warfare might affect the countries of Europe and the United States?

"If the American shipper grumbles," wrote a London newspaper, "our reply is that this war is not being conducted for his pleasure or profit."

While blocked from trade with Germany, the United States continued trading with Britain. In fact, American trade with the Allies soared. In addition, Great Britain and France borrowed billions of dollars from American banks to help pay for their war efforts. All this business caused an economic boom in the United States. It also upset the Germans, who watched the supposedly neutral United States helping the Allies.

Submarines Take Their Toll

The Germans could not match the British blockade. They did, however, have the U-boat. To stop American aid to Britain, Germany said in February 1915 that it would sink any vessels that entered or left British ports. President Wilson warned that the United States would hold Germany responsible for any American lives lost in submarine attacks. The Germans ignored Wilson's threat. On May 7, 1915, a German U-boat torpedoed the British passenger liner called the *Lusitania* near the coast of Ireland. The captain reported what happened:

Reading **HELP**DESK (CCSS)

Build Vocabulary: *Word Parts*

The word *submarine* is made up of two parts: The prefix *sub* means "under." The root *marine* comes from the Latin word *mare,* which means "the sea." How do the word parts describe the vessel's action?

❝ I saw a torpedo speeding toward us, and immediately I tried to change our course, but was unable to [maneuver] out of the way. There was a terrible impact as the torpedo struck the starboard side of the vessel, and a second torpedo followed almost immediately. ❞

—from W. T. Turner, captain of the *Lusitania*

More than 1,000 people died when the *Lusitania* sank. Among the dead were 128 American citizens.

The sinking of the *Lusitania* angered the American public. President Wilson criticized the attack. Later it was learned that the ship had carried war materials.

A few months later, a German U-boat attacked the unarmed French passenger ship *Sussex*. Several Americans suffered injuries. Germany began to fear that the angry Americans might enter the war. To help soothe this anger, Germany offered money to those injured on the *Sussex*. Germany also promised to warn neutral ships and passenger vessels before attacking. The Sussex Pledge seemed to resolve the conflict over submarine warfare.

☑ **PROGRESS CHECK**

Explaining Why did the United States have such a difficult time remaining neutral during the war?

The End of Neutrality

GUIDING QUESTION *What made the United States decide to enter the war?*

In spite of the Sussex Pledge, Congress was alarmed. In the summer of 1916, it doubled the size of the army and provided funding for the construction of new warships.

President Wilson still hoped to stay out of the war. Antiwar sentiment remained strong. Some Americans saw the nation's military buildup as a step toward entering the war. The phrase "He [Wilson] Kept Us Out of War" became the Democrats' campaign slogan in 1916. Wilson, however, only narrowly defeated the Republican candidate, Charles Evans Hughes.

Americans read about the sinking of the *Lusitania* in newspapers.

▶ **CRITICAL THINKING**
Drawing Conclusions Do you think newspaper headlines like this one changed Americans' opinions about neutrality? Explain.

The New York Times.

LUSITANIA SUNK BY A SUBMARINE, PROBABLY 1,000 DEAD; TWICE TORPEDOED OFF IRISH COAST; SINKS IN 15 MINUTES; AMERICANS ABOARD INCLUDED VANDERBILT AND FROHMAN; WASHINGTON BELIEVES THAT A GRAVE CRISIS IS AT HAND

Build Vocabulary: *Word Origins*

The word *U-boat* comes from the German word *U-Boot*, or *Unterseeboot*. *Untersee* means "undersea," and *boot* means "boat."

Jeannette Rankin (1880–1973)

Fifty-six members of the House and Senate voted against war with Germany. One of those was Jeannette Rankin of Montana. As a young woman, Rankin worked as a social worker and fought for woman suffrage. In 1916 she became the first woman elected as a representative to Congress. She took her seat in March 1917 in the midst of the debate over American entry into World War I. During the vote on the declaration of war, she said, "I want to stand by my country—but I cannot vote for war." Her pacifism probably cost her the Republican Senate nomination in 1918. She was reelected to Congress in 1940 on an antiwar platform and voted against World War II as well.

▶ **CRITICAL THINKING**

Analyzing Why do you think Rankin made the statement "I want to stand by my country" at the time she voted against a declaration of war?

The United States at the Brink of War

In January 1917, Germany again changed course in its use of submarine warfare. It announced it would sink on sight all merchant vessels sailing to Allied ports—regardless of whether or not they were armed.

The Germans knew that introducing unrestricted submarine warfare risked drawing the United States into the war against them. The Germans believed, however, that they would be able to defeat the Allies before the United States could mount a serious war effort and have an impact on the battlefield.

A few weeks later, British agents intercepted a secret telegram sent by the German foreign minister, Arthur Zimmermann. The telegram was bound for Mexico. It offered a German alliance with Mexico against the United States in the event the Americans entered the war. The Zimmermann Note angered Americans and set off a new wave of anti-German feeling in the United States.

Dramatic events continued to push the United States into the war. First, in March 1917, a **revolution** took place in Russia. The Russian people overthrew their monarchy, which was headed by the czar. In place of the monarchy, the Russians set up a temporary government promising free elections. The new Russian government also vowed to continue the fight to defeat the Germans.

This change in Russia from an **autocracy** (aw•TAH•kruh•see), in which one person with unlimited powers rules, to a more democratic government raised Allies' hopes. Wilson could now argue that the Allies were fighting a war for democracy, making public support for war more likely.

Other critical events took place at sea. In March 1917, the Germans attacked and sank four American merchant ships. Thirty-six people died in these attacks.

CORBIS

Reading **HELP**DESK **CCSS**

autocracy a government in which one person with unlimited power rules

Academic Vocabulary

revolution a war to overthrow a government

The United States Enters the War

President Wilson decided the United States could no longer remain neutral. On the cold, rainy evening of April 2, 1917, he asked Congress for a declaration of war against Germany. After some debate, Congress decided that the nation had to defend its rights if it wished to remain a world power. Congress passed a declaration of war, and Wilson signed it on April 6.

The United States had to raise an army quickly. On May 18, Congress passed the Selective Service Act, setting up a military draft. Men aged 21 to 30 registered by the millions. By war's end, some 24 million men had registered. Of them, about 3 million were called to serve. Another 2 million joined voluntarily. In addition, for the first time, women enlisted in the armed forces. They served in noncombat roles, such as radio operators, clerks, and nurses.

More than 300,000 African Americans joined the armed forces. They suffered unfair treatment and racism. Most held low-level jobs at military bases. Among the 140,000 African American soldiers sent to Europe, 40,000 saw combat. Many served with honor, including a regiment that received medals for bravery from France. One member, Henry Johnson, became the first American to receive France's Cross of War, a medal for bravery.

World War I gave African Americans the opportunity to show their loyalty and patriotism. In 1917 the War Department created two divisions of primarily African American combat units.

✔ PROGRESS CHECK

Identifying What events triggered American entry into the war?

CORBIS

LESSON 2 REVIEW (CCSS)

Review Vocabulary

1. Write a sentence describing the meaning of the word *propaganda* and its role in World War I.

2. Use the term *autocracy* to describe the importance of the revolution in Russia in 1917.

Answer the Guiding Questions

3. ***Explaining*** Why were the Germans upset by the United States trading with the Allies?

4. ***Identifying*** What was the Sussex Pledge?

5. ***Summarizing*** How did the Zimmermann Note help push the United States into entering World War I?

6. ***Discussing*** Why did most members of Congress agree to pass a declaration of war?

7. **ARGUMENT** Write a letter to President Wilson to persuade him either to keep the United States out of the war or that the United States should enter the war.

netw☺rks
There's More Online!

☑ **GRAPHIC ORGANIZER** Causes of the Armistice

☑ **MAP** Europe During World War I

☑ **PRIMARY SOURCE** Armistice in World War I

☑ **TIME LINE** Rise of the Bolsheviks

☑ **VIDEO** U.S. in World War I

Lesson 3
Americans Join the Allies

ESSENTIAL QUESTION *Why does conflict develop?*

IT MATTERS BECAUSE
The United States helped bring an end to the terrible destruction of World War I.

Supplying the Allies

GUIDING QUESTION *How did American troops help to turn the tide of the war toward the Allies?*

By 1917 the years of trench warfare had exhausted the Allied armies. The signs of strain among the military were clear. After one failed offensive, some French troops refused to continue fighting. The British were running low on war supplies as well as on food. German submarines were taking a deadly toll on Allied shipping. They sank one of every four ships that left British ports.

The American entry into the war had an immediate impact. To ensure that needed supplies reached Great Britain, the U.S. Navy helped the British destroy and protect against German submarines. The Allies used **convoys** (KAHN·VOYS), in which teams of navy ships sailed side-by-side with merchant ships across the Atlantic Ocean. If a U-boat wanted to attack a merchant ship, it had to face the risk of coming under attack by the armed ships escorting it.

The convoy system worked well. In one year, Allied shipping losses dropped from 900,000 tons per month to 300,000 tons per month. Not one American soldier bound for Europe was lost to a submarine attack.

(l) Bettmann/CORBIS, (cl) CORBIS, (cr) Photograph courtesy of the Pocumtuck Valley Memorial Association, Memorial Hall Museum, Deerfield, Massachusetts,

Reading **HELP**DESK (CCSS)

Taking Notes: *Determining Cause and Effect*

As you read, use a diagram like this one to show what events lead to the signing of the armistice.

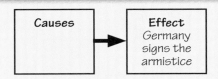

Causes		Effect Germany signs the armistice

Content Vocabulary
• **convoy**
• **kaiser**

These Russian recruits, shown training in Petrograd in 1917, were among 6,000 women who fought on the Russian side in World War I.

The Russians Quit the War

The arrival of American troops also helped offset the loss of Russia from the Allied cause. In March 1917, Nicholas II had given up his throne as czar, or ruler, in Russia's first revolution. The government that replaced the czar supported the war. It was not, however, able to solve Russia's many serious problems, such as food shortages.

In November 1917, riots broke out over the new Russian government's handling of the war and the scarcity of food and fuel. A group called the Bolsheviks overthrew this government. Led by Vladimir Lenin, the Bolsheviks wanted to pull out of the war so they could focus on setting up a new Communist state.

In March 1918, Lenin signed the Treaty of Brest-Litovsk with Germany. Peace had come to the Eastern Front—the line of battle separating Russia and the Central Powers. In the treaty, Russia lost a large amount of territory to the Germans. Russia's withdrawal allowed the Germans to move thousands of troops from the Eastern Front to the Western Front, the line separating the warring armies near the French-German border.

convoy a group of ships that escort and protect other ships

Vladimir Lenin signed the Treaty of Brest-Litovsk with Germany.

▶ **CRITICAL THINKING**
Determining Cause and Effect
How do you think the treaty affected Russia's relationship with the Allies?

French citizens welcome the arrival of American troops.

General John J. Pershing led American forces in Europe and received a hero's welcome.

Germany Makes a Final Push

In March 1918, German forces launched a massive attack along the Western Front. German leaders hoped to break the Allied lines. They wanted to capture the city of Amiens before **proceeding** (proh·SEE·dihng) to Paris.

At first, the plan seemed to work. For weeks, the Germans hammered at Allied lines. They pushed the Allies back to within 40 miles (64 km) of Paris. After years of stalemate along the Western Front, it looked as if Germany might win the war.

The Americans Join the Battle

While revolution shook Russia and Germany went on the attack, the Americans were preparing to join the fight. In May 1917, General John J. Pershing became supreme commander of what was called the American Expeditionary Force (AEF), the American army in Europe. His arrival in France cheered that war-weary nation. Reporter Floyd Gibbons described the welcome that Pershing received:

PRIMARY SOURCE

❝ The sooty girders of the Gare du Nord [railroad station] shook with cheers when the special train pulled in. . . . A minute later, there was a terrific roar from beyond the walls of the station. The crowds outside had heard the cheering within. . . . Pershing took Paris by storm. ❞

—from *And They Thought We Wouldn't Fight*

Pershing had the AEF ready for battle by the spring of 1918. The French and British wanted to use the American soldiers to build up their own troops. However, General Pershing refused. He preferred to keep the AEF a separate force.

Doughboys in Battle

American soldiers were nicknamed "doughboys" because the buttons on their uniforms resembled boiled dough dumplings, a popular food. They saw their first serious fighting in June 1918, when the AEF helped turn back German forces at Château-Thierry (SHAH·TOH-TYEH·REE) on the Marne River east of Paris. The

(t) CORBIS, (b) Bettmann/CORBIS

Reading **HELP**DESK (CCSS)

American troops then advanced to Belleau Wood. For the next three weeks, doughboys battled around the clock through the forest against a solid wall of German machine-gun fire.

The American and French forces fought back German attacks along the Marne and the Somme Rivers. By mid-July they had stopped the great German offensive that had come close to ending the war. General Pershing wrote that the battles "turned the tide of war."

Fighting in the Argonne Forest

The Allies now began an attack of their own. In mid-September, a half million American soldiers defeated the Germans at Saint-Mihiel (san-mee•YEHL). Later that month, more than 1 million American troops joined the Allies in the Battle of the Argonne Forest. It became the biggest attack in American history.

The Battle of the Argonne Forest raged for nearly seven weeks. Soldiers struggled over the rugged, heavily-forested ground. Rain, mud, barbed wire, and German machine-gun fire hindered the Allies' advance. Many soldiers died. Yet by early November, the Allies had won the battle. They had pushed back the Germans and broken through their lines. The Germans now faced an invasion of their own country.

GEOGRAPHY CONNECTION

The Western Front was the scene of many fierce battles.

1 **LOCATION** In what country was the Battle of the Somme fought?

2 **CRITICAL THINKING**
Analyzing Visuals Based on this map, which nation's civilians likely suffered the most during the war? Explain your answer.

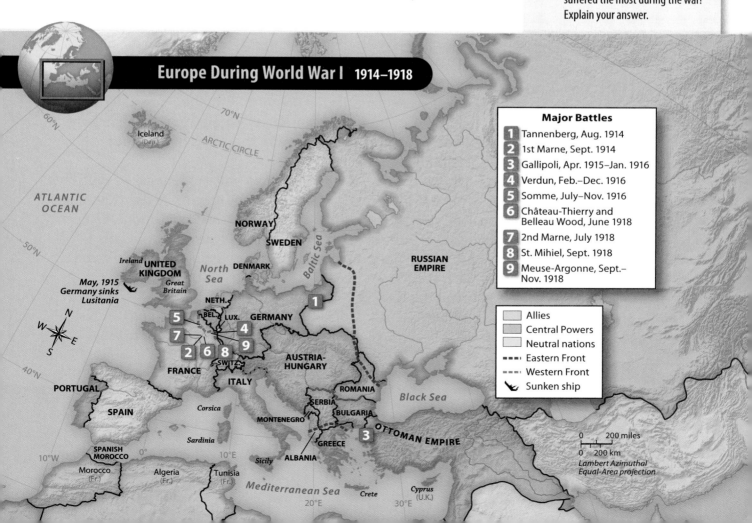

Europe During World War I 1914–1918

Major Battles

1 Tannenberg, Aug. 1914
2 1st Marne, Sept. 1914
3 Gallipoli, Apr. 1915–Jan. 1916
4 Verdun, Feb.–Dec. 1916
5 Somme, July–Nov. 1916
6 Château-Thierry and Belleau Wood, June 1918
7 2nd Marne, July 1918
8 St. Mihiel, Sept. 1918
9 Meuse-Argonne, Sept.–Nov. 1918

Allies
Central Powers
Neutral nations
Eastern Front
Western Front
Sunken ship

Iceland (Den.)
ARCTIC CIRCLE
ATLANTIC OCEAN
NORWAY
SWEDEN
Baltic Sea
DENMARK
North Sea
Ireland UNITED KINGDOM
Great Britain
May, 1915 Germany sinks Lusitania
NETH.
BEL. LUX. GERMANY
RUSSIAN EMPIRE
FRANCE
SWITZ.
AUSTRIA-HUNGARY
ITALY
PORTUGAL
SPAIN
Corsica
ROMANIA
Black Sea
SERBIA
MONTENEGRO
BULGARIA
OTTOMAN EMPIRE
Sardinia
GREECE
SPANISH MOROCCO
Morocco (Fr.)
Algeria (Fr.)
Tunisia (Fr.)
Sicily
ALBANIA
Mediterranean Sea
Crete
Cyprus (U.K.)

0   200 miles
0   200 km
Lambert Azimuthal Equal-Area projection

The Allied victory featured some brilliant individual acts of heroism. For example, Eddie Rickenbacker was a captain in the 94th Aero Squadron. He fought 134 air battles and shot down 26 enemy aircraft. During the fighting at Argonne Forest, Corporal Alvin York killed several German soldiers, captured machine guns, and took 132 prisoners. Both Rickenbacker and York received the Medal of Honor for their actions.

☑ PROGRESS CHECK

Identifying What were the key battles in which United States forces played a part in World War I?

The End of the War

GUIDING QUESTION *What events occurred that led to the armistice being signed?*

While Germany struggled on the Western Front, its allies faced defeat elsewhere. In late 1918, the Ottoman Empire was on the brink of collapse. Austria-Hungary broke apart, as protests in major cities helped bring down that centuries-old empire. For example, in October 1918, Poland, Hungary, and Czechoslovakia declared independence. By early November, the governments of Austria-Hungary and the Ottoman Empire had surrendered to the Allied Powers.

Germany Seeks an Armistice

Meanwhile, German leaders realized their hopes of winning the war were gone. American troops and supplies had strengthened the Allied war effort. In addition, Germans on the home front were suffering greatly from severe shortages of food and other supplies.

On October 4, 1918, the German government asked President Wilson for an armistice, an agreement to end the fighting. Wilson **consented,** but only under certain conditions. Germany had to accept his plan for peace and promise not to renew fighting. All German troops had to leave Belgium and France. Finally, Wilson said he would deal only with nonmilitary government leaders.

While German leaders considered Wilson's demands, unrest erupted in their country. On November 3, sailors revolted in Kiel, the main base of the German fleet. Within days, groups of

Before World War I, the U.S. military often had a difficult time identifying dead soldiers after a battle. By 1917 each American soldier was required to wear an identification badge around the neck. Soldiers named them "dog tags."

▶ CRITICAL THINKING
Making Inferences Why do you think identifying fallen soldiers was an important issue for the military?

Photograph courtesy of the Pocumtuck Valley Memorial Association, Memorial Hall Museum, Deerfield, Massachusetts

Reading **HELP**DESK (CCSS)

kaiser German emperor

Academic Vocabulary

consent to agree

workers and soldiers seized control of other German towns. As the revolution spread, the German **kaiser** (KY•zuhr), or emperor, decided to step down. On November 9, Germany became a republic. The leaders of Germany's new government agreed to President Wilson's terms for an armistice.

Peace Returns

The armistice began on November 11, 1918—at the 11th hour on the 11th day of the 11th month. Under its terms, Germany agreed to withdraw all land forces west of the Rhine River, to withdraw its fleet to the Baltic Sea, and to surrender huge amounts of equipment. The guns fell silent and the fighting stopped.

What had been called the Great War—the most destructive conflict in human history to that time—was over at last. President Wilson declared:

Parades, such as this one in Paris, celebrated the signing of the armistice.

PRIMARY SOURCE

❝ Everything for which America fought has been accomplished. It will now be our fortunate duty to assist by example, by sober friendly counsel and by material aid in the establishment of a just democracy throughout the world. ❞

—from "Proclamation of the Armistice with Germany"

PROGRESS CHECK

Describing What happened to the German government in the final days of the war?

LESSON 3 REVIEW (CCSS)

Review Vocabulary

1. Write a sentence that uses the term *convoy* and explains its significance in World War I.

2. Then write a sentence about the end of World War I that uses the term *kaiser*.

Answer the Guiding Questions

3. *Summarizing* What role did the United States play in winning the Battle of the Argonne Forest?

4. *Explaining* What was the significance of the Battle of the Argonne Forest?

5. *Describing* Why did Austria-Hungary surrender to the Allies?

6. *Summarizing* What problems in Germany helped lead the German government to appeal for an armistice?

7. **NARRATIVE** Think about what it was like to be a soldier on the front line in World War I. Write a letter home describing battle conditions.

networks
There's More Online!

☑ **GRAPHIC ORGANIZER**
 Controlling Public Opinion

☑ **SLIDE SHOW**
 World War I Posters

☑ **VIDEO**

Lesson 4
The War at Home

ESSENTIAL QUESTION *Why does conflict develop?*

⟳ IT MATTERS BECAUSE
The war effort demonstrated the American people's ability to work hard and make sacrifices.

Mobilizing the Nation

GUIDING QUESTION *How did the United States prepare to fight the war?*

After the United States declared war on Germany in 1917, Americans began to focus on getting ready to fight the war. **Mobilization** (moh•buh•luh•ZAY•shuhn), or the gathering of resources and the preparation for war, affected almost every part of American life.

The military needed a steady supply of vital war materials. To ensure this, the government created the National War Labor Board in April 1918. Preventing work stoppages was one goal. The board pressured businesses to grant workers some key demands. As a result, employees won an eight-hour work day. They also received overtime pay, equal pay for women, and the right to form unions. In return, workers agreed not to go on strike.

Meeting the Need for Workers

To pay for the war, the United States government raised taxes and borrowed money by selling war bonds. Industries expanded their production to make war materials. At the same time, industries faced a labor shortage. Millions of men had left their jobs to serve in the armed forces. Also, immigration slowed sharply during the war. Fewer immigrants were arriving to take on the jobs.

(l) CORBIS, (cl) The Granger Collection, NYC, (c) David Pollack/CORBIS, (cr) CORBIS, (r) Swim Ink 2, LLC/CORBIS

Reading **HELP**DESK **CCSS**

Taking Notes: *Describing*

As you read, use a chart like this one to describe how these three acts helped control public opinion.

	Description
Espionage Act	
Sabotage Act	
Sedition Act	

Content Vocabulary
- **mobilization**
- **ration**
- **socialist**
- **pacifist**
- **dissent**

The labor shortage provided new job opportunities for women. Many women joined the workforce for the first time, taking on jobs that had been held by men.

Jobs also lured hundreds of thousands of African Americans to Northern cities from the rural South. From 1914 to 1920, between 300,000 and 500,000 African Americans made the move. This huge population movement was known as the Great Migration. In addition, thousands of Mexicans migrated to the United States in search of jobs.

Supplying the War Effort

Now at war, the country had to produce food not only for its own needs but also for the Allies. President Wilson chose Herbert Hoover to head a new Food Administration. The agency encouraged farmers to raise more and the public to eat less.

The Food Administration also encouraged voluntary **rationing** (RA·shuhn·ihng), or the limitation of use. These efforts were successful. Americans **consumed** less and produced and exported more of many key goods.

The War Industries Board supervised industry. It helped factories shift to producing war-related goods and set prices for key consumer products. Finally, the Fuel Administration managed the nation's coal and oil. To save fuel, the agency introduced daylight saving time and called for "Heatless Mondays."

Building Public Support

Antiwar feeling remained strong even after the United States entered the war. To mobilize public support, the president named journalist George Creel to head the Committee on Public Information.

The committee worked to promote the war as a battle for democracy and freedom. It sent out millions of pamphlets, posters, articles, and books with a pro-war message. It fed government accounts of the war to newspapers. The committee hired speakers, writers, artists, and actors to build support for the war.

✓ PROGRESS CHECK

Summarizing What were three key mobilization challenges facing the United States?

Women wrap missiles in this New York factory.

mobilization the gathering of resources and troops in preparation for war
ration a limited use

Academic Vocabulary
consume to use

WARTIME POSTERS

James Montgomery Flagg's depiction of Uncle Sam for the U.S. Army is the most famous American wartime poster.

The Food Administration urged people to observe "Wheatless Mondays," "Meatless Tuesdays," and "Porkless Thursdays," and to plant "victory gardens."

With millions of men serving in the military, women were needed to take their places in the labor force.

The government sold war bonds to help pay for the cost of the war.

INFOGRAPHIC

During the war, posters were a common means of influencing public opinion.

1 DRAWING CONCLUSIONS Why do you think so many posters targeted women?

2 CRITICAL THINKING
Synthesizing What common message can you find in all four of these posters?

Public Opinion and the War

GUIDING QUESTION *Why did the U.S. government approve legislation to control public opinion?*

World War I proved a boost to the American economy. Yet the war also placed great strains on American society. In an effort to unite the country behind the war effort, the government tried to silence opposition. Some Americans became intolerant of those they saw as different.

Who opposed the involvement of the United States in World War I? There were several main groups. Some German Americans and Irish Americans felt sympathy with the Central Powers. Many **socialists** (SOH•shuh•lihsts)—people who believe the public should own key industries—opposed the war. They thought it would help rich business owners and hurt working people. **Pacifists** (PA•suh•fihsts)—people who oppose the use of violence—were also against the war.

The Committee on Public Information took strong steps to silence **dissent** (dih•SEHNT). Dissent is disagreement or opposition. For example, the committee questioned the patriotism of anyone who was against the war. To many, it became un-American to criticize government actions or decisions.

(tl) The Granger Collection, NYC, (tcl) David Pollack/CORBIS, (tcr) CORBIS, (tr) Swim Ink 2/ LLC/CORBIS

Reading **HELP**DESK (CCSS)

socialist a person who believes industries should be publicly owned
pacifist a person who is opposed to the use of violence
dissent disagreement or opposition

Academic Vocabulary

perceive to view; to become aware of by observing

Congress passed the Espionage Act of 1917, which provided stiff penalties for espionage, or spying. People who aided the enemy or interfered with army recruiting also faced penalties.

Congress passed even harsher measures in 1918. The Sabotage Act penalized anyone who damaged or destroyed war supplies, property, or transport. The Sedition Act made it a crime to say, print, or write any criticism **perceived** (puhr·SEEVD) as negative about the government:

66 Whoever, when the United States is at war, . . . shall willfully utter, print, write, or publish any disloyal . . . or abusive language about the form of government of the United States . . . shall be punished by a fine of not more than $10,000 or imprisonment for not more than twenty years, or both. 99

—from the Sedition Act of 1918

Thousands of people were convicted under these laws.

Some people spoke out against the laws and the growing intolerance. At least two of the convictions were challenged and were heard in the Supreme Court. The question was whether the Sedition Act was in line with the Constitution, or whether it violated a person's right to free speech. The Supreme Court upheld the law. Overall, most Americans believed that in wartime, no measure could be too drastic toward traitors and disloyal Americans.

☑ PROGRESS CHECK

Describing What were the purposes of the Espionage Act, the Sabotage Act, and the Sedition Act?

This cartoon shows the Sedition Act threatening "Honest Opinion," "Free Speech," and "Free Press."

▶ CRITICAL THINKING
Analyzing Visuals Do you think the cartoonist supported the Sedition Act? Explain.

AS GAG-RULERS WOULD HAVE IT.
—Satterfield in the Jersey City *Journal.*

LESSON 4 REVIEW (CCSS)

Review Vocabulary

1. Examine the two terms below. Then write a brief paragraph about the effects of the war at home that explains the connection between the terms.

    a. mobilization   **b.** ration

2. Write a one- or two-sentence statement that describes the views of American socialists and pacifists in the World War I era.

Answer the Guiding Questions

3. ***Explaining*** Why did the United States face a labor shortage during the early days of World War I?

4. ***Summarizing*** How did the War Industries Board help prepare the United States for war?

5. ***Explaining*** Why did the Committee on Public Information portray people who were against the war as unpatriotic?

6. **ARGUMENT** Was government action to suppress public opposition to the war justified? Formulate your own opinion, and use facts to defend it.

networks

There's More Online!

☑ **GRAPHIC ORGANIZER**
Conditions of the Treaty
of Versailles

☑ **MAP** Europe After
World War I

☑ **SLIDE SHOW** President Wilson's
Fourteen Points

☑ **VIDEO**

Lesson 5
Searching for Peace

ESSENTIAL QUESTION *Why does conflict develop?*

IT MATTERS BECAUSE
The end of World War I touched off a vigorous debate about the proper role of the United States in the world.

Making a Peace

GUIDING QUESTION *Why did the Allies oppose Wilson's plan for peace?*

Leaders from 27 nations gathered in Paris, France, in January 1919. They met for the peace conference following World War I. President Woodrow Wilson arrived to cheering crowds. Europeans looked to Wilson to help build a better postwar world. They did not see the huge challenges that lay ahead.

The landscape, farms, and towns of Europe lay in ruins. The bloody fighting had cost France, Russia, Germany, and Austria-Hungary each between 1 million and 2 million lives. Millions more suffered injuries. Civil war raged in Russia. Poles, Czechs, and other peoples struggled to form their own nations. Adding to the misery, a worldwide influenza epidemic was taking millions of lives.

The Fourteen Points

In spite of these difficulties, Woodrow Wilson was optimistic. He had a vision of a just and lasting peace. He outlined his plan in what was called the Fourteen Points. Some of his points dealt with adjusting boundaries in Europe and creating new nations. These points reflected Wilson's belief in **national self-determination** (sehlf-dih·TUHR·muh·NAY·shuhn)—the right of people to decide how they should be governed. Wilson also suggested rules for carrying out relations between countries. He supported

(c and r) Bettmann/CORBIS

Reading **HELP**DESK (CCSS)

Taking Notes: *Listing*

As you read, use a diagram like the one here to list the conditions that Germany agreed to under the Treaty of Versailles.

Conditions of the
Treaty of Versailles

Content Vocabulary
• **national self-determination**
• **reparation**

free trade and freedom of the seas and an end to secret treaties or agreements among nations. He called for limits on arms and peaceful settlement of disputes over colonies.

Wilson Proposes a League of Nations

Wilson's **final** point was the creation of a League of Nations. League members would preserve peace and prevent future wars. They would respect and protect one another's independence.

Europeans welcomed Wilson's ideas at first. Trouble appeared, though, when nations put their own interests first. Also, some of Wilson's points lacked clarity on some difficult questions. For example, Wilson was not clear how to **achieve** self-determination in regions in which different cultural groups lived close together.

Allies Offer Little Support

The Allies did not invite Germany or Russia to the peace talks. A group called the Big Four dominated the meeting. The Big Four were President Wilson; Prime Minister David Lloyd George of Great Britain; France's premier, Georges Clemenceau; and Italian prime minister Vittorio Orlando.

Wilson won little support for the Fourteen Points. There were also clashes over treatment of the defeated nations. Everyone but Wilson wanted revenge. Clemenceau wanted Germany broken up into smaller countries. He and Lloyd George also demanded that Germany make large **reparations** (REH•puh•RAY•shuhns), or payments, for the great damage suffered during the war.

GEOGRAPHY CONNECTION

World War I changed the map of Europe. The victors divided up the lands of the Central Powers, leading to the establishment of several new nations.

1 LOCATION Which new nations bordered Germany?

2 CRITICAL THINKING
Speculating How do you think conquered nations, such as Germany, felt about the outcome of the treaty?

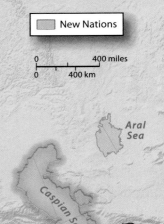

Europe After World War I

New Nations

0   400 miles
0   400 km

Wilson struggled to uphold the principles of his Fourteen Points. He was forced, however, to give in to the other Allies in many cases.

The Treaty of Versailles

The Allies and Germany signed the Treaty of Versailles (vuhr•SY) on June 28, 1919. Under its harsh terms, Germany had to accept full responsibility for the conflict. It had to pay the Allies billions of dollars. It had to disarm completely and give up its overseas colonies and some territory in Europe.

The treaty also carved up the Austro-Hungarian and Russian Empires. It created some new nations and restored old ones. Border disputes, however, would lead to future conflicts.

President Woodrow Wilson leads the procession after the signing of the Treaty of Versailles.

Wilson was able to get his League of Nations included in the treaty. He believed that the League would correct any mistakes in the rest of the treaty.

✓ PROGRESS CHECK

Comparing How did Wilson's views differ from the other Big Four?

Opposition at Home

GUIDING QUESTION *Why did the U.S. Senate reject the Treaty of Versailles and the League of Nations?*

In the United States, the Senate must agree to, or ratify, all treaties. Wilson presented the Treaty of Versailles to the Senate in July 1919. "Dare we reject it and break the heart of the world?" he asked. In spite of Wilson's plea, many Americans had doubts about the treaty. Some thought it dealt too harshly with Germany. Others worried that the League of Nations would commit the United States to a permanent role in world affairs.

Bettmann/CORBIS

Reading **HELP**DESK (CCSS)

national self-determination the right of people to decide how they should be governed
reparation payment for damages caused during a war

Academic Vocabulary
final last
achieve to accomplish

Republicans, who controlled the Senate, saw a chance to embarrass Wilson. Some hoped to weaken the Democrats before the 1920 elections. Others had sincere concerns about the League of Nations. A few opposed signing any treaty.

Lodge Opposes Wilson

Wilson's greatest challenge came from longtime foe Henry Cabot Lodge of Massachusetts. Lodge headed the Senate Foreign Relations Committee. Lodge argued that with the League,

PRIMARY SOURCE

NOT ROOM FOR BOTH

66 American troops and American ships may be ordered to any part of the world by nations other than the United States, and that is a proposition to which I, for one, can never assent. 99

—from *Vital Forces in Current Events*, 1920

Lodge delayed a vote on the treaty so opponents could present their cases. He then proposed a number of reservations that would limit United States obligations under the treaty.

Wilson toured the nation in September to rally support for the treaty and the League of Nations. The effort exhausted the weary president. His health collapsed, and he suffered a stroke.

The Senate Rejects the Treaty

In the months after Wilson's stroke, opposition to the treaty grew. In March 1920, the Senate voted on the treaty with Lodge's changes. It rejected the Treaty of Versailles.

Wilson hoped the 1920 election would be a "great and solemn referendum" on the League. He even considered running for a third term. In the end, however, Wilson did not run. In 1921 the United States signed a separate peace treaty with each of the Central Powers. The United States never joined the League of Nations.

Under the Covenant, or constitution, of the League of Nations, members pledged to defend any member nation attacked by any other nation. Many Americans believed this would enable other nations to commit American troops to conflicts overseas.

▶ CRITICAL THINKING
Identifying Points of View Does the cartoon express a view for or against joining the League of Nations? How do you know?

Bettmann/CORBIS

✔ **PROGRESS CHECK**

Summarizing Why did many Americans object to the League of Nations?

LESSON 5 REVIEW (CCSS)

Review Vocabulary

1. Use the term *national self-determination* in a sentence about Wilson's Fourteen Points.

2. Why did the leaders of Great Britain and France demand that Germany make large reparations? Define the term in your answer.

Answer the Guiding Questions

3. *Identifying* What principles for international relations did Wilson's peace plan include?

4. *Describing* What were the major disagreements the Allies had with Wilson's peace plan?

5. *Determining Cause and Effect* What role did Henry Cabot Lodge play in the Senate's rejection of the Treaty of Versailles?

6. ARGUMENT If the League of Nations had existed before 1914, do you think World War I could have been avoided? Explain.

Write your answers on a separate piece of paper.

1 **Exploring the Essential Question**

INFORMATIVE/EXPLANATORY Think about the events that led up to World War I and the tensions that eventually led to the outbreak of war. What conflicts caused World War I, and how did the war change the world? Write an essay that addresses these questions.

2 **21st Century Skills**

COLLABORATING Working with a small group, consider the issues and events that lead to international conflict. Write a list of points, similar to the Fourteen Points, that outlines your ideas for how to achieve a just and lasting world peace. Then compare your group's list with those of other groups in the class. How do the points differ from group to group?

3 **Thinking Like a Historian**

DRAWING CONCLUSIONS The Sedition Act made it a crime to say, print, or write anything perceived as negative about the government. Consider whether or not the act violated free speech and freedom of the press. Prepare a short speech on this question and present it to the class.

4 **Visual Literacy**

ANALYZING PHOTOGRAPHS This photo shows the living quarters of some soldiers who were engaged in trench warfare. What does this picture suggest about the challenges facing soldiers during World War I?

REVIEW THE GUIDING QUESTIONS

Choose the best answer for each question.

1 As a result of trench warfare, fighting in World War I often resulted in
  A. few injuries.
  B. stalemate.
  C. German victory.
  D. long periods of inactivity.

2 Ties of language, customs, and traditions most strongly linked the United States to
  F. Germany.
  G. Austria-Hungary.
  H. Belgium.
  I. Great Britain.

3 In 1917 Germany offered Mexico an alliance against the United States in the
  A. Treaty of Brest-Litovsk.
  B. Selective Service Act.
  C. Zimmermann Note.
  D. Triple Entente.

4 The Battle of the Argonne Forest
  F. became the most massive attack in American history.
  G. triggered U.S. entry into World War I.
  H. led to revolution in Austria-Hungary.
  I. convinced the German kaiser to remain in power.

5 The Committee on Public Information
  A. supervised the nation's industrial production.
  B. encouraged American farmers to produce more food.
  C. promoted U.S. involvement in the war.
  D. pressured businesses to grant worker demands.

6 President Wilson's vision of a just and lasting peace was called the
  F. Fourteen Points.
  G. Treaty of Versailles.
  H. Lodge Amendments.
  I. Sedition Act.

DBQ ANALYZING DOCUMENTS

7 **Analyzing** This American poster is from 1917. What does the statue in the poster symbolize?

A. war

B. peace

C. militarism

D. nationalism

8 **Identifying** Toward which group of people was this poster directed?

F. immigrants

G. socialists

H. pacifists

I. soldiers

SHORT RESPONSE

The table below shows the number of military deaths by country in World War I.

Country	Number of Deaths
Austria-Hungary	1,200,000
France	1,375,800
Germany	1,773,700
Great Britain	908,371
Italy	650,000
Russia	1,700,000
United States	126,000

9 Which two countries had the most deaths?

10 Why do you think that U.S. deaths were low in comparison?

EXTENDED RESPONSE

11 **Informative/Explanatory** Woodrow Wilson's Fourteen Points were based on his ideas about how peoples and nations should govern themselves and get along. Write a one-page summary of Wilson's ideas and the ideals they represented.

Need Extra Help?

If You've Missed Question	**1**	**2**	**3**	**4**	**5**	**6**	**7**	**8**	**9**	**10**	**11**
Review Lesson	1	2	2	3	4	5	4	4	1–3	1–3	5

The Jazz Age

1920–1929

ESSENTIAL QUESTIONS • *How do new ideas change the way people live?*
• *How does technology change the way people live?*

The Story Matters . . .

While working as a busboy in the Wardman Park Hotel in Washington, D.C., Langston Hughes has a chance meeting. A well-known poet, Vachel Lindsay, is dining in the hotel's restaurant. Hughes musters up his courage and places three of his poems on the table beside Lindsay's dinner plate.

The next morning begins like any other for Hughes. He buys the morning paper as usual—but to his surprise finds himself in one of the articles! He reads that Lindsay has discovered an African American busboy poet. Later, when Hughes arrives at the hotel for work, he is greeted by reporters hoping to interview him about his poetry. His days working in hotels are over. Soon he is a leading figure of the Jazz Age.

◄ *Langston Hughes was a celebrated poet of the Harlem Renaissance.*

Place and Time: United States 1920 to 1929

The 1920s was a time of many changes. Among these changes was the ongoing shift in African American population—the Great Migration. Thousands of mostly rural African Americans made their way north during this time.

For many Americans, the 1920s were a time of prosperity and confidence. The young women in this photograph show off the newest fashions and hair styles.

Step Into the Place

MAP FOCUS The map shows some of the main routes taken by African Americans as they migrated from the South.

1 **MOVEMENT** To which cities in the North did African Americans migrate?

2 **MOVEMENT** Based on the map, to which cities did most African Americans from Georgia migrate?

3 **CRITICAL THINKING**
Speculating Why do you think many African Americans moved to urban areas in the North?

Sacco and Vanzetti were immigrants and radicals who were convicted of robbery and murder. Some observers argued that the two men did not receive a fair trial.

Step Into the Time

TIME LINE Look at the time line. The 1920s brought many changes to the United States. How long did it take after women won full voting rights for women to be elected to high office?

U.S. PRESIDENTS

Warren G. Harding
1921–1923

U.S. EVENTS

WORLD EVENTS

1918

1921

1920 • Prohibition begins
• Nineteenth Amendment grants woman suffrage

1918 Flu pandemic kills millions worldwide

1921 • Ireland becomes an independent country
• Albert Einstein wins Nobel Prize for Physics

(t) H. Armstrong Roberts/CORBIS, (c) Burstein Collection/CORBIS, (b) White House Historical Association

networks
There's More Online!

☑ **MAP** Explore the interactive version of this map on NETWORKS.

☑ **TIME LINE** Explore the interactive version of this time line on NETWORKS.

The Great Migration

Southern states
Primary migration routes
CANADA
MEXICO
Lake Superior
Lake Michigan
Lake Huron
L. Ontario
Lake Erie
Gulf of Mexico
ATLANTIC OCEAN
Mont.
Wyo.
North Dakota
South Dakota
Nebraska
Colorado
Kansas
N.M.
Oklahoma
Texas
Minnesota
Iowa
Missouri
Arkansas
Louisiana
Wisconsin
Illinois
Michigan
Indiana
Ohio
Ky.
Tennessee
Miss.
Alabama
Georgia
Florida
South Carolina
North Carolina
Virginia
W. Va.
Pennsylvania
New York
New Jersey
Md.
Del.
Maine
Ver.
N.H.
Mass.
Conn.
R.I.
Chicago
Detroit
Cleveland
Pittsburgh
Indianapolis
Cincinnati
New York City
Philadelphia
N
E
S
W
40°N
70°W
30°N
100°W
90°W
80°W
0
400 miles
0
400 km
Albers Equal-Area projection

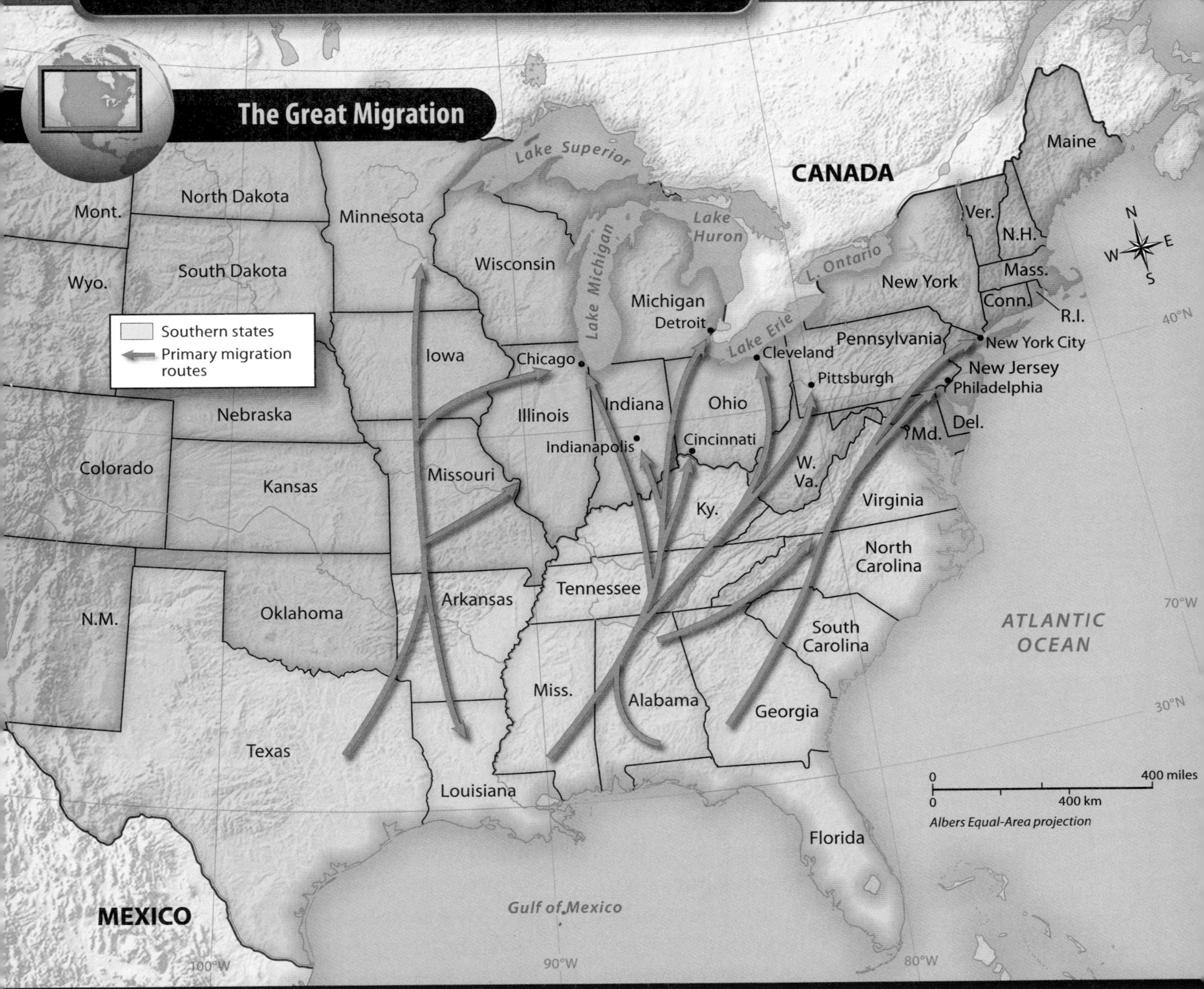

Calvin Coolidge
1923–1929

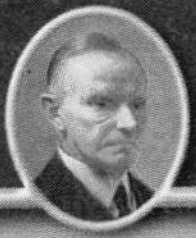

1922 Teapot Dome Scandal

1924 Wyoming and Texas elect female governors

1924 First Winter Olympics staged in Chamonix, France

1927 • Charles Lindbergh flies across the Atlantic • Babe Ruth hits 60 home runs

1928 Kellogg-Briand Pact aims to outlaw war

1924 | 1927 | 1930

Lesson 1
Time of Turmoil

ESSENTIAL QUESTION *How do new ideas change the way people live?*

IT MATTERS BECAUSE

Postwar adjustments in American society produced tensions and conflict.

Fear of Radicalism

GUIDING QUESTION *How did Americans respond to people who had new ideas about social change?*

The years after World War I were an uncertain time in the United States. Tired of war and world responsibilities, the American people longed for a return to a way of life they viewed as **normal.** As a result, many people grew more suspicious of foreigners and those holding views different from their own.

The Russian Revolution fueled some of these suspicions. In 1917 the Bolsheviks had gained control in Russia. The Bolsheviks were Communists who believed that all people should share ownership of property. They urged workers around the world to overthrow **capitalism** (KA•puh•tuh• lihz•uhm), the economic system based on private property and free enterprise. Many Americans feared that "Bolshevism" threatened society.

Fanning the fears were the actions of **anarchists** (A•nuhr• kihsts)—people who believe there should be no government. A series of anarchist bombings in 1919 in New York City, Seattle, and other cities frightened Americans.

(l) Hulton-Deutsch Collection/CORBIS,
(c) MPI/Getty Images,
(r) NY Daily News via Getty Images

Reading **HELP**DESK **CCSS**

Taking Notes: *Determining Cause and Effect*

As you read, use a diagram like this one to identify reasons union membership dropped in the 1920s.

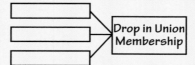

Drop in Union Membership

Content Vocabulary

- capitalism
- anarchist
- deport
- integration

Fear of the "Reds"

Reds was a popular term for Communists, and the term *Red Scare* refers to this time of heightened public fear. During the Red Scare, the government went after Communists and others with radical views. In late 1919 and early 1920, Attorney General A. Mitchell Palmer and his deputy, J. Edgar Hoover, arrested more than 10,000 suspected Communists and anarchists. Palmer and Hoover also led raids on the headquarters of "suspicious" groups. They never found the large supplies of weapons they claimed they were seeking. The government **deported**—expelled from the United States—a few hundred of the aliens it arrested. It quickly released many others for lack of evidence.

Sacco and Vanzetti

The case of Nicola Sacco and Bartolomeo Vanzetti highlighted the fears and suspicions of this time. The two men were Italian immigrants and admitted anarchists. They were also accused of killing two men during a robbery. Though they claimed innocence, Sacco and Vanzetti were convicted of this crime in July 1921 in Massachusetts. They were then sentenced to death.

Some people felt Sacco and Vanzetti did not get a fair trial. It was clear that their beliefs and nationality had played some part in their conviction. Others, however, demanded their execution. In 1927 a special advisory committee upheld the verdict. Sacco and Vanzetti were put to death.

✔ PROGRESS CHECK

Analyzing What events of the 1920s might be used as examples of prejudice against immigrants?

Thinking Like a
HISTORIAN

Analyzing Primary Sources

The Alien Act, which Congress passed in October 1918, stated that the United States could expel from the country any alien who was a member of any anarchist organization. Journalist and critic H. L. Mencken responded angrily to this law. He said, "Government, today, is growing too strong to be safe. There are no longer any citizens in the world; there are only subjects." For more about analyzing and interpreting information, review *Thinking Like a Historian.*

▶ CRITICAL THINKING

Analyzing Primary Sources Explain what you think Mencken meant when he said "There are no longer any citizens in the world. There are only subjects."

Boston police in this 1920s photo are shown collecting radical literature. Raids on the headquarters of "suspicious groups" did not turn up large supplies of weapons.

capitalism an economic system based on private property and free enterprise

anarchist someone who believes there should be no government

deport to expel from a country

Academic Vocabulary

normal like what people are used to

Hulton-Deutsch Collection/CORBIS

Labor and Racial Strife

GUIDING QUESTION *Why did social change lead to labor unrest and racial tension?*

After World War I, industrial workers used strikes to get wage increases that would keep up with rapidly rising prices. Many Americans believed that Bolsheviks and radicals were causing this labor unrest. At the same time, racial tensions increased. In the North, many whites resented African American competition for factory jobs.

Workers Go on Strike

During World War I, the Russian Revolution put Communists in control in Russia. A series of strikes in the United States after World War I created fears that Communists were trying to start a revolution in the United States, too. Attorney General A. Mitchell Palmer viewed these strikes as a threat to the American values of religion, private property, and democracy. He declared, "The blaze of revolution [is] eating its way into the homes of the American workman."

In September 1919, about 350,000 steelworkers went on strike. They demanded an increase in wages and an eight-hour workday. The steel companies accused the strikers of being "Red agitators." The strikers lost public support and were forced to end the strike—but not before 18 strikers died in a riot in Gary, Indiana.

That same month, Boston police officers went on strike. They wanted the right to form a union. Many Americans did not think public safety employees, such as police officers and firefighters, should be allowed to strike. They applauded when Massachusetts governor Calvin Coolidge called out the National Guard. When the strike collapsed, the entire police force was fired.

Many workers linked labor unions to the idea of radicalism and refused to join them. Such distrust of unions, as well as pressure from employers and government, led to a sharp drop in union membership in the 1920s.

Despite the unions' decline, a **dynamic** leader named A. Philip Randolph started the Brotherhood of Sleeping Car Porters. This union of African American railroad workers gained additional members in the 1930s, when the government began giving greater support to unions.

A. Philip Randolph organized a labor union of African American railroad workers and then went on to become a key civil rights activist.

Reading **HELP**DESK (CCSS)

integration whites and African Americans living side-by-side

Academic Vocabulary

dynamic energetic, forceful

Build Vocabulary: *Origin of Names*

Communists came to be called "Reds" because they had chosen solid red for the color of their flags.

Racial Tensions and a Response

In 1919 rising racial tensions led to violence. In the South, more than 70 African Americans were lynched. In the North, conflict followed the Great Migration. Hundreds of thousands of African Americans had moved north during and after World War I. Some whites lashed out at the new racial landscape.

In Chicago, for example, violence raged out after a group of whites threw stones at an African American youth swimming in Lake Michigan. The youth drowned, and the incident set off rioting. For two weeks African American and white gangs roamed city streets. The riot left 15 whites and 23 African Americans dead and more than 500 people injured.

Many African Americans turned to Marcus Garvey for answers to the growing racial tensions. Garvey, a powerful leader with a magnetic personality, was born to a poor family in Jamaica. He did not support **integration** (ihn·tuh·GRAY·shuhn)—African Americans and whites living side-by-side. Instead he offered a message of racial pride. Garvey supported a "back-to-Africa" movement, urging African Americans to establish their own country in Africa. Garvey founded the Universal Negro Improvement Association (UNIA) in 1914 to promote African American achievement and pride. With offices in New York City's Harlem neighborhood, the association promoted economic strength for African Americans. Garvey gained a large following in New York and other cities.

A dynamic black leader from Jamaica, Marcus Garvey, led the "back-to-Africa" movement.

☑ PROGRESS CHECK

Explaining Did Marcus Garvey support or oppose integration? Explain.

LESSON 1 REVIEW (CCSS)

Review Vocabulary

1. Use each of these terms in a sentence that explains the term's meaning.

   a. anarchist   **b.** deport   **c.** integration

2. Explain the Bolshevik view of capitalism.

Answer the Guiding Questions

3. ***Explaining*** What was the outcome of the Boston police strike of 1919?

4. ***Summarizing*** What was the Red Scare, and how did it relate to the fear of radicalism in this era?

5. ***Describing*** What was the purpose of the UNIA?

6. **NARRATIVE** Write a newspaper article about the arrest and trial of Sacco and Vanzetti that highlights the tensions of the time.

netw⊙rks

There's More Online!

☑ **GRAPHIC ORGANIZER**
The Harding and Coolidge Presidencies

☑ **PRIMARY SOURCE**
Coolidge as President

☑ **VIDEO**

Lesson 2
Desire for Normalcy

ESSENTIAL QUESTION *How do new ideas change the way people live?*

IT MATTERS BECAUSE
Searching for "normalcy," the American people turned to pro-business and isolationist leadership.

Harding and Coolidge

GUIDING QUESTION *How did Harding and Coolidge try to return America to quieter ways?*

In the 1920 campaign, Warren G. Harding promised a return to "normalcy." What Harding meant by "normalcy" was not really clear. However, the word sounded reassuring to Americans. Many people longed for a simpler time, free of war and other frightening problems. Harding understood that longing.

Harding's running mate was Massachusetts governor Calvin Coolidge. The Republican team won a landslide victory in November 1920—the first presidential election in which women could vote. They easily defeated the Democratic candidate, Governor James Cox of Ohio, and his young running mate, Franklin Delano Roosevelt of New York.

Harding named several talented people to his cabinet, or team of advisors. For example, he included Charles Evans Hughes, a former Supreme Court justice, as secretary of state. Andrew Mellon, a Pittsburgh banker, headed the Treasury Department. Herbert Hoover, a skilled organizer, became secretary of commerce.

Political Scandals

Though President Harding named some talented people to his cabinet, he also gave top jobs to political supporters—the so-called Ohio Gang. Many of these people were unqualified.

Reading **HELP**DESK (CCSS)

Taking Notes: *Comparing and Contrasting*

As you read, use a diagram like this one to compare and contrast the presidencies of Harding and Coolidge.

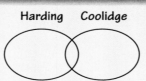

Harding   Coolidge

Content Vocabulary
• **lease**
• **laissez-faire**

Some turned out to be dishonest. One example was Albert Fall, Harding's secretary of the interior. In 1922 Fall secretly **leased,** or rented, government oil reserves to two oil companies. In return, Fall received more than $400,000. A court found Fall guilty of bribery. He became the first cabinet official ever to go to prison. Newspapers called the scandal "Teapot Dome," after the location of one of the oil reserves. The affair became a symbol of widespread dishonesty in the Harding government.

Harding himself was not involved in any scandals. As the rumors spread, however, he grew troubled. In the summer of 1923, Harding took a trip west to escape his political problems. During the trip, he suffered a heart attack and died.

Harding's easygoing nature reassured the American people and won the support of voters.

Coolidge as President

Vice President Calvin Coolidge learned of Harding's death while he was vacationing in Vermont. Coolidge's father, a justice of the peace, administered the presidential oath of office to his son.

Calvin Coolidge was the opposite of Harding in many ways. Harding loved to talk and meet people. Coolidge earned the nickname "Silent Cal." The new president also had a reputation for honesty. Coolidge supported investigations into the Harding scandals, and he quickly replaced dishonest members of the Ohio Gang.

Like Harding, Coolidge believed in **laissez-faire** (leh•say•FEHR)—the idea that government should be involved as little as possible in the lives of citizens and businesses. He said, "If the federal government should go out of existence, the common run of the people would not **detect** the difference for a considerable length of time."

People use political buttons and posters to show support for a candidate.

▶ **CRITICAL THINKING**
Comparing and Contrasting
How are these campaign items similar to and different from one another?

---

lease to rent
laissez-faire a belief that government should have as little involvement in private life as possible

Academic Vocabulary

detect to notice

Build Vocabulary: *Origins of Sayings*

Observers use the metaphor of a landslide to describe an overwhelming election win. One of histories largest "landslide victories" occurred in 1984, when incumbent president Ronald Reagan captured 525 electoral votes. His opponent, Walter Mondale, received only 13.

WHAT A FRIEND WE HAVE IN COOLIDGE!

THE CASH REGISTER CHORUS.

Daniel R. Fitzpatrick, editorial cartoonist for the *St. Louis Post-Dispatch*, drew this cartoon in 1924. It shows business leaders gathered around a cash register singing about their friend, President Calvin Coolidge.

▶ **CRITICAL THINKING**
Analyzing Visuals What does the cash register represent?

Support for Business

President Coolidge and the Republican-controlled Congress believed government could aid prosperity by supporting business. Under their leadership, the government cut spending, lowered income tax rates on wealthy Americans and corporations, and raised tariffs. Their government also overturned laws regulating child labor and women's wages. All of these steps helped make it easier for American businesses to earn greater profits.

The 1924 Election

The public loved Coolidge. The Republicans eagerly nominated him to run in 1924. The Democrats nominated John W. Davis of West Virginia as their candidate. Wisconsin senator Robert La Follette was the choice of a third party, the Progressives. Coolidge swept the opposition away, however, winning 54 percent of the popular vote.

Also in 1924, two American women made election history. For the first time, women won governors' races—Nellie Tayloe Ross in Wyoming and Miriam Ferguson in Texas.

☑ **PROGRESS CHECK**

Describing Why was Harding's focus on "normalcy" an effective campaign strategy?

Foreign Policy

GUIDING QUESTION *How did the United States try to avoid involvement in international disputes?*

Many Americans supported limited American involvement with other nations, a policy known as isolationism. Both Harding and Coolidge also favored a limited role for the nation in world affairs. They desired world peace but did not want the nation to enter the League of Nations or join foreign alliances. Harding had promised the American people that he would not lead them into the League "by the side door, back door, or cellar door."

The Granger Collection, NYC

Seeking Peace

After World War I ended, the United States, Britain, and Japan began a naval arms race. The Harding administration, however, made serious efforts for peace. In 1921 Secretary of State Charles Evans Hughes met with officials from Japan and Britain to discuss the arms race. In February 1922, the three nations, along with France and Italy, signed the Five-Power Treaty to limit the size of the nations' navies. The treaty marked the first time in modern history that world powers agreed to disarm.

In addition, in August 1928 the United States joined 14 other nations in signing the Kellogg-Briand Pact. This agreement called for outlawing war. Within a few years, 48 other nations signed the pact. The pact, however, lacked any way to force countries to live up to their agreement.

A More Peaceful Neighbor

To support American businesses, the United States **intervened** in Latin America several times in the early 1900s. By 1920 American troops were stationed in the Dominican Republic and Nicaragua, and relations with Mexico were tense.

During the 1920s, the United States took a more peaceful stance. American troops withdrew from the Dominican Republic and Nicaragua after those countries held elections. American investors asked President Coolidge to send troops into Mexico when its government threatened to take over foreign-owned companies. Instead, President Coolidge chose to negotiate and reached a peaceful settlement with Mexico.

☑ **PROGRESS CHECK**

Explaining Why would the Kellogg-Briand Pact prove to be ineffective?

Connections to
TODAY

Third Parties

Throughout its history, the United States has usually had only two main political parties. However, third parties, such as the Progressive Party, have appeared from time to time. In the 2008 presidential election, third party candidates won a combined total of more than 1 million popular votes.

LESSON 2 REVIEW (CCSS)

Review Vocabulary

1. Use each of these terms in a sentence that explains the term's meaning.

   a. lease **b.** laissez-faire

Answer the Guiding Questions

2. *Analyzing* Why did President Harding give important government jobs to unqualified people?

3. *Drawing Conclusions* Why did Harding and Coolidge attempt to return the nation to "normalcy"?

4. *Summarizing* What was the U.S. approach to foreign policy during the Harding and Coolidge years?

5. **ARGUMENT** Neither Harding nor Coolidge wanted the United States to join the League of Nations. Do you agree with their position? Write a paragraph that explains and argues for your point of view.

There's More Online!

☑ **GRAPH**
The Model T

☑ **GRAPHIC ORGANIZER**
Business Practices

☑ **PRIMARY SOURCE**
1920s Advertisement

☑ **SLIDE SHOW**
Five Largest Cities, 1930

Lesson 3

A Booming Economy

ESSENTIAL QUESTION *How does technology change the way people live?*

IT MATTERS BECAUSE
New ways of making products helped change the way people lived their lives.

Growth in the 1920s

GUIDING QUESTION *How did electricity improve the lives of people in the 1920s?*

After World War I, the United States went through a **recession** (ree•SEH•shuhn), or economic downturn. Then, in the early 1920s, the economy began to grow. It continued growing for most of the decade. In 1922 the nation's **gross national product** (GNP)—the total value of all goods and services produced—was $70 billion. By 1929 GNP had risen to $100 billion.

Technology helped spur rapid industrial growth. Electricity provided the power. Before World War I, 30 percent of U.S. factories ran on electricity. By 1929 electricity powered 70 percent of all factories. Because electricity was cheaper than steam power, the cost of making factory products dropped. Businesses spent less money to make their products. This meant they could charge less for them—and increase profits at the same time.

New Ways of Managing

Businesses also changed the way they operated. Many employers hired **experts** with advanced knowledge to create scientific management methods. These methods enabled workers to do more with less effort. Scientific management lowered costs and increased **productivity**—the amount of work each worker could do. This also helped the economy grow.

(l) Image courtesy of The Toaster Museum Foundation, www.toaster.org

Reading **HELP**DESK

Taking Notes: *Listing*

As you read, use a chart like this one to record new American business management changes and what they were intended to achieve.

Business Practice	Goal

Content Vocabulary
• **recession**
• **gross national product**
• **productivity**
• **installment buying**

246 *The Jazz Age*

Larger businesses began using mass-production **techniques.** Henry Ford used the assembly line in his automobile factories. Assembly lines increased productivity and cut production costs.

Businesses also tried to build better relations with workers. They set up safety programs that lowered the risk of death or injury on the job. Some provided health and accident insurance. Others encouraged workers to buy stock in the company. These efforts, known as welfare capitalism, aimed to link workers more closely to the company they worked for. One goal of these efforts was to keep workers happier and less likely to join labor unions.

The Economy and the Consumer

Electricity helped create an economy driven by consumer buying. By the 1920s, more than 60 percent of American households had electricity. Availability was uneven. It would be some years before power lines reached many farming communities. Still, availability of electric power was growing. As more households got electricity, companies made new electric devices—refrigerators, stoves, vacuum cleaners, and radios. Using electric appliances made many household chores easier. It gave people more leisure time and a better standard of living.

To sell their new products, businesses spent more money on advertising. Newspapers and magazines were filled with ads. The spread of radio helped create a new advertising form—the commercial announcement.

Encouraged by ads, consumers found a new way to make purchases. With **installment buying,** consumers bought goods by making small, regular payments over a period of time.

Rising use of electricity as a power source spurred the use of electric appliances such as the toaster.

☑ PROGRESS CHECK

Explaining Why did the price of some consumer goods decrease?

ECONOMIC CHANGE IN THE 1920s			

Industry (Percentage Increase, 1922–28)		Workers (Percentage Increase, 1922–28)	
Industrial production	70%	Workers' incomes	11%
Gross national product	40%	Average workweek	-4%
Corporate profits	62%		

Source: Jules Tygiel, "The 1920s Economy: A Statistical Portrait"

ECONOMICS SKILL

During the 1920s, the United States saw strong economic growth. New industries emerged, and workers became more productive.

▶ CRITICAL THINKING

Drawing Conclusions Who benefited more economically from increased production—workers or corporations?

recession an economic downturn
gross national product the total value of all goods and services produced by a nation

productivity worker output, per given amount of time and resources
installment buying purchasing products by making small payments over a period of time

Academic Vocabulary

expert a person with advanced knowledge
technique a method for accomplishing a task

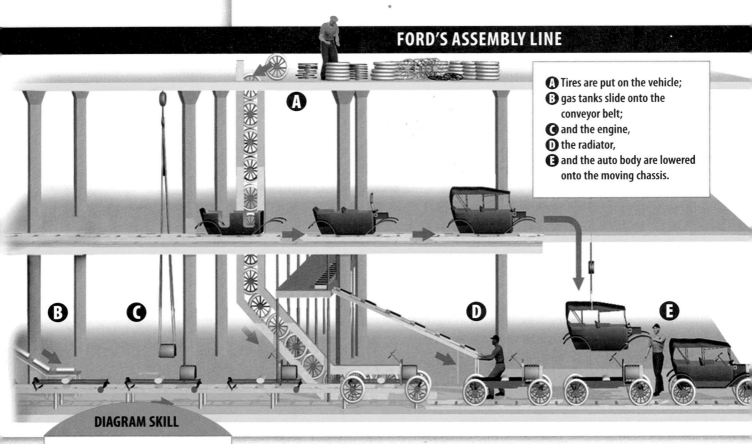

FORD'S ASSEMBLY LINE

A Tires are put on the vehicle;
B gas tanks slide onto the conveyor belt;
C and the engine,
D the radiator,
E and the auto body are lowered onto the moving chassis.

DIAGRAM SKILL

Ford's assembly line greatly improved the speed and efficiency of car manufacturing. Many other industries soon copied Ford's assembly line idea and became more efficient as well.

1 DESCRIBING What is the job of the worker at step E of this assembly line?

2 CRITICAL THINKING
Explaining How did the use of conveyor belts make the manufacturing process more efficient?

The Automobile Age

GUIDING QUESTION *How did the automobile change America during the 1920s?*

The car became a major part of American life and the American economy in the 1920s. Nearly 4 million Americans worked in the automobile industry or in related jobs. Detroit, Michigan, became the auto-making center of the world.

Henry Ford was the industry's great pioneer. He built his Model T using assembly-line methods. The car was sturdy, reliable, and inexpensive. In 1914 Ford began paying workers the high wage of five dollars a day. Many workers bought their own Model T's.

Soon, General Motors and others cut into Ford's sales. All carmakers made improvements and the industry grew rapidly.

Cars and Prosperity

The demand for cars led to greater prosperity. Governments built new highways to satisfy Americans' love of driving. Thousands got jobs on these projects. Thousands of gas stations and restaurants made money from drivers traveling around the country.

Reading **HELP**DESK (CCSS)

Reading in the Content Area: *Diagrams*

In the assembly line diagram, each lettered description matches the part of the illustration labeled with the same letter.

Industries that made products used in cars also did well. The steel, rubber, and glass industries grew. Cars also helped suburbs grow. Because people could drive to work, they could live farther from their jobs in the city.

Uneven Prosperity

Not all Americans shared in the boom times of the 1920s. Farmers, in particular, had difficulties. During the war, the government had bought wheat, corn, and other products. Prices were high, and farmers prospered. After the war, American farmers saw a decrease in demand for their crops. European farmers began to grow food again. As a result, European countries needed to import less food from the United States. This competition meant that American farmers had to accept lower prices. Farm incomes dropped. Many farmers had trouble paying their debts and lost their farms.

Farmers were not alone. New technology created difficult times for railroad workers and coal miners as well. Carmakers now produced trucks that companies could use to carry their products. Trucks began to take business from railroads, and electricity replaced coal as a power source.

Textile workers also suffered. Americans were buying less cotton clothing and more clothes made of synthetic fibers. Cotton prices plunged and many textile factories shut down. By 1929 nearly three-fourths of all families had incomes below $2,500, the amount considered necessary for a comfortable life.

☑ **PROGRESS CHECK**

Explaining Which groups did not share in the nation's prosperity?

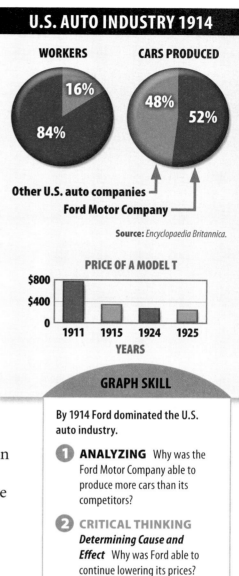

U.S. AUTO INDUSTRY 1914

WORKERS — 16% / 84%

CARS PRODUCED — 48% / 52%

Other U.S. auto companies — Ford Motor Company

Source: *Encyclopaedia Britannica.*

PRICE OF A MODEL T

$800 / $400 / 0

1911 1915 1924 1925

YEARS

GRAPH SKILL

By 1914 Ford dominated the U.S. auto industry.

1 **ANALYZING** Why was the Ford Motor Company able to produce more cars than its competitors?

2 **CRITICAL THINKING** *Determining Cause and Effect* Why was Ford able to continue lowering its prices?

LESSON 3 REVIEW (CCSS)

Review Vocabulary

1. Use each of these terms in a sentence that explains the term's meaning.

   a. gross national product

   b. productivity

   c. recession

2. What does it mean when someone says he or she wants to use installment buying to purchase a new vacuum cleaner?

Answer the Guiding Questions

3. ***Explaining*** What was the role of electric power in the booming economy of the 1920s?

4. ***Describing*** How did businesses try to build better relations with workers?

5. ***Identifying*** Identify two key Ford innovations.

6. ***Summarizing*** Why was the automobile so important to the American economy?

7. **NARRATIVE** Write a short story about a family that buys its first automobile. Explain how the car changes this family's life.

networks
There's More Online!

☑ **BIOGRAPHY**
Charles Lindbergh

☑ **GAME**

☑ **GRAPHIC ORGANIZER**
Themes in the Arts

☑ **MAP** The Election of 1928

☑ **PRIMARY SOURCE**
Langston Hughes Poem

☑ **SLIDE SHOW**
The Lost Generation

Lesson 4
The Roaring Twenties

ESSENTIAL QUESTION *How do new ideas change the way people live?*

IT MATTERS BECAUSE

The 1920s was a period of many social and cultural changes but it was also a period of conflict between traditional and modern values.

Social and Cultural Change

GUIDING QUESTION *Why did American art and society change during the 1920s?*

While the economy was booming, American culture was also undergoing rapid change. New styles, habits, and entertainment challenged old ways of thinking.

New Opportunities for Women

Women were perhaps most affected by the cultural change. One important development was the ratification of the Nineteenth Amendment in 1920. The amendment guaranteed women in all states the right to vote. Women soon ran for political offices.

Most married women continued to work at home as mothers and homemakers. The number of women working outside the home, however, grew steadily. Most working women became nurses, teachers, or office workers. A few college-educated women began professional careers. The symbol of the new "liberated" woman of the 1920s was the **flapper**—a carefree young woman with short "bobbed" hair, heavy makeup, and a short skirt.

New Forms of Communication

The growth of **mass media**—forms of communication that reach a wide audience—helped spread cultural changes. Mass media such as newspapers and radio grew, reaching millions.

(l) Bettmann/CORBIS, (cl) MPI/ Stringer/Archive Photos/Getty Images, (cr) Hulton Archive/Archive Photos/Getty Images

Reading **HELP**DESK (CCSS)

Taking Notes: *Listing*

As you read, use a chart like this one to list the major themes that appeared in the arts during the 1920s.

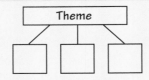

Content Vocabulary
- flapper
- mass media
- expatriate
- Prohibition
- nativism
- quota system
- evolution

Movies were also a form of communication that grew in the 1920s, and the motion picture industry became a big business. The radio was another **device** that changed American life. In the 1920s, radio networks broadcast news, concerts, sporting events, and comedies to growing audiences. Businesses realized that the radio offered an **enormous** audience for messages about their products. They began to sponsor radio programs. Radio stations also sold advertising time to companies.

Popular Events and Activities

Radio allowed listeners to listen to sporting events live, making sports like baseball and football more popular. Sports stars such as baseball player Babe Ruth became national heroes.

Americans also took up new activities with enthusiasm. Board games and crossword puzzles became widely popular. Contests such as flagpole sitting and dance marathons made headlines.

Jazz and the Harlem Renaissance

Jazz was not new in the 1920s. However, the exciting, upbeat music captured the spirit of the era so well that the 1920s are often called the Jazz Age.

Jazz was rooted in African American culture, and many top performers were African Americans. They include trumpeter Louis Armstrong, composer Duke Ellington, and singer Bessie Smith. W.C. Handy, who won fame for pioneering a type of jazz known as the blues, was also making music at this time.

The rhythm and themes of jazz helped inspire a blossoming of culture in Harlem, an African American neighborhood of New York City. During this "Harlem Renaissance," writers such as Langston Hughes, James Weldon Johnson, and Zora Neale Hurston shared the African American experience in novels, poems, and stories.

The Lost Generation

Beyond Harlem, some writers were questioning American ideals in the aftermath of World War I. Some became **expatriates** (ek•SPAY•tree•uhts)—people who choose to live in another country. Writer Gertrude Stein called these Americans "the lost generation." Among them were F. Scott Fitzgerald and Ernest Hemingway. Fitzgerald, for example, wrote of a deep unhappiness beneath the high spirits of the times.

BIOGRAPHY

Charles Lindbergh (1902–1974)

Airplanes were a new and exciting part of American life in 1927. In that year, a daring young pilot attempted something no person had ever done. He flew all alone across the Atlantic Ocean. Charles Lindbergh had good training. By his mid-20s, he had spent hundreds of hours in the air. He also experienced his share of close calls. Four times he had to parachute from a plane. This lack of fear helped encourage him to attempt his greatest feat. Tempted by a prize of $25,000 for the first person to fly from New York to Paris, France, Lindbergh made his daring attempt. His success made him a hero in the United States—and around the world. His flight represented the high hopes and forward vision of the United States in the 1920s.

▶ **CRITICAL THINKING**
Analyzing What personal qualities did Lindbergh bring to his quest to be the first to fly across the Atlantic?

Bettmann/CORBIS

flapper a carefree young woman of the 1920s
mass media forms of communication that can reach millions of people
expatriate someone who chooses to live in another country

Academic Vocabulary

device equipment
enormous huge

Other writers remained at home and wrote about life in America. Novelist Sinclair Lewis presented a critical view of American culture. In *Winesburg, Ohio,* Sherwood Anderson explored small-town life in the Midwest.

✅ PROGRESS CHECK

Explaining What leisure activities were popular during the 1920s?

A Clash of Cultures

GUIDING QUESTION *Why did various groups clash over important issues?*

Many Americans did not identify with the new, urban America of the 1920s. They believed that known and valued traditions were under attack. Disagreements arose between those who defended traditional beliefs and those who welcomed the new.

Prohibition

One issue that divided Americans was the use of alcohol. The temperance movement, the campaign against alcohol use, was rooted in a belief that society would benefit if people could not drink.

With ratification of the Eighteenth Amendment to the Constitution in 1919, the movement reached its goal. This amendment established **Prohibition** (proh•uh•BIH•shuhn)—a ban on the manufacture, sale, and transportation of liquor. In the rural South and Midwest, Prohibition had some success. Elsewhere, continuing demand for alcohol led many people to break the law. Illegal bars and clubs, known as speakeasies, sprang up in cities.

The ban on alcohol contributed to organized crime. Powerful gangsters, such as Chicago's Al Capone, made millions of dollars from bootlegging—producing and selling illegal alcohol. They used their profits to influence businesses, labor unions, and governments.

The nation came to realize that Prohibition had failed. In 1933, the Twenty-First Amendment repealed Prohibition. It is the only amendment that overturned an earlier amendment.

An Upsurge in Nativism

The rapid changes in society were frightening to many Americans. Their concerns led to a rise in **nativism** (NAY•tih•vih•zuhm)—the belief that native-born Americans are superior to foreigners.

A public safety official from Philadelphia destroys kegs of beer that were produced illegally during Prohibition.

The Granger Collection, New York

Reading **HELP**DESK (CCSS)

Prohibition a total ban on the manufacture, sale, and transportation of liquor throughout the United States, achieved through the Eighteenth Amendment

nativism belief that native-born Americans are superior to foreigners

quota system an arrangement setting the number of immigrants allowed from each country

evolution scientific theory that humans and other species changed and developed over long periods of time

252 *The Jazz Age*

Along with this renewed nativism came a revival of the Ku Klux Klan. The new Klan, set up in 1915, still preyed on African Americans. It also targeted Catholics, Jews, immigrants, and other groups it believed to represent "un-American" values. In the 1920s, the Klan spread from the South to other areas of the country.

Nativism also arose because some Americans believed foreigners would take their jobs. Southern and eastern Europeans and Asians were the main targets of this prejudice.

In 1921 Congress responded to these fears by passing the Emergency Quota Act. This law set up a **quota system,** a fixed number of immigrants allowed from each country each year. The act limited annual immigration from a country to 3 percent of that country's American population in 1910. The policy favored immigration from northern and western Europe.

Three years later, Congress went even further. The Immigration Act of 1924 cut the country quota from 3 percent to 2 percent. It also set a total immigration limit of 150,000 to go into effect in 1927. The 1924 act based the 2 percent quota on the census of 1890, when few southern or eastern Europeans lived in the United States. The law also excluded Japanese immigrants completely. The Chinese were already excluded under an 1890 law.

Quotas did not apply to Western Hemisphere countries. As a result, immigration from Canada and Mexico increased. By 1930 more than 1 million Mexicans had come to live in the United States.

During this era, the United States took steps to sharply reduce the number of immigrants coming to the country.

▶ CRITICAL THINKING
Analyzing Visuals Describe what is happening in this cartoon. What action is Uncle Sam taking, and what is its impact?

The Scopes Trial

The role of religion in society became an issue in the 1920s. The conflict gained national attention in 1925 in one of the most famous trials of the era.

In 1925 Tennessee passed a law making it illegal to teach **evolution** (eh•vuh•LOO•shuhn)—the scientific theory that humans and other species developed over vast periods of time. Christian fundamentalists—people who believe in strictly following the Bible—supported the law. They believed in the Biblical story of creation, and they saw evolution as a challenge to their beliefs.

John Scopes, a young high school teacher, wanted to challenge the Tennessee law. He deliberately broke it and was arrested. His trial took place during the summer of 1925. The nation followed it with great interest.

Lawyers Clarence Darrow (left) and William Jennings Bryan (right) played leading roles in the Scopes trial, in which Scopes was found guilty.

Two famous lawyers took opposing sides in the Scopes trial. William Jennings Bryan, Democratic candidate for president in 1896, 1900, and 1908 and a strong opponent of evolution, led the prosecution. Clarence Darrow, who had defended many radicals and labor union members, represented Scopes.

Scopes was found guilty of breaking the law and fined $100. The fundamentalists, however, lost the larger battle. Darrow's defense made it appear that Bryan wanted to force his religious beliefs on the entire nation. Later, the Tennessee Supreme Court overturned Scopes's conviction.

Although the Scopes case may have dealt a blow to fundamentalism, the movement continued to thrive. Rural people, especially in the South and Midwest, remained faithful to their religious beliefs. When large numbers of farmers migrated to cities during the 1920s, they took fundamentalism with them.

✓ PROGRESS CHECK

Analyzing How did new laws limit immigration?

The Election of 1928

GUIDING QUESTION *Who were the presidential candidates of 1928, and what were the major issues of the campaign?*

In 1927 President Coolidge was expected to run for another term. When he announced that he would not, Herbert Hoover declared his candidacy for the Republican nomination.

Hoover had won respect for his efforts to organize food relief for Europe during World War I. He showed such a gift in this role that "to Hooverize" came to mean "to economize, to save and share." Later, as secretary of commerce, he became known as a supporter of business. He easily won the nomination.

Because he favored a ban on sales of alcohol, Hoover was considered the "dry" candidate. The Democrats nominated a far different kind of candidate—Alfred E. Smith, governor of New York. The son of immigrants and a man of the city, Smith opposed Prohibition. He championed the rights of the poor and the working class.

Getty Images

Reading **HELP**DESK

Build Vocabulary: *Word Origins*

The fundamentalist movement takes its name from a 1910 series of books called *The Fundamentals,* which attacked more modern interpretations of the Bible.

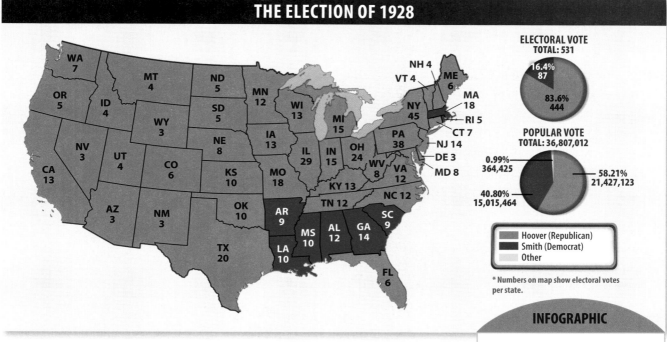

THE ELECTION OF 1928

ELECTORAL VOTE
TOTAL: 531

16.4% 87
83.6% 444

POPULAR VOTE
TOTAL: 36,807,012

0.99% 364,425
58.21% 21,427,123
40.80% 15,015,464

Hoover (Republican)
Smith (Democrat)
Other

* Numbers on map show electoral votes per state.

INFOGRAPHIC

Hoover easily won the election of 1928.

1 **REGION** Based on the map, in which region of the country did Smith win the most states?

2 **CRITICAL THINKING**
Analyzing Why do you think this area supported Smith?

As the first Roman Catholic nominee for president, Smith was the target of anti-Catholic prejudice. Hoover spoke out against these attacks. Still, the charges hurt Smith's candidacy.

Smith's bigger problem, however, was the prosperity of the 1920s. Republicans took credit for the economic growth, and voters elected Hoover in a landslide. The contest reflected many of the social, cultural, and political tensions present in the United States at that time.

☑ **PROGRESS CHECK**

Summarizing Why was Hoover elected by a landslide in 1928?

LESSON 4 REVIEW

Review Vocabulary

1. Explain the meaning of:

  a. expatriate **b.** mass media **c.** nativism

2. Examine the two terms below. Then write a sentence explaining what the terms have in common in the context of this chapter.

  a. Prohibition **b.** quota system

Answer the Guiding Questions

3. *Summarizing* How did the arts in the United States reflect changes in society in the 1920s?

4. *Describing* What were the key cultural conflicts of the 1920s?

5. *Contrasting* How did the election of 1928 reflect the tensions of the times?

6. **ARGUMENT** You are running for governor of your state in 1928. Write a campaign speech that will persuade your audience to vote for you. Address major cultural and social issues of this era.

CHAPTER 9 Activities CCSS

Write your answers on a separate piece of paper.

1 Exploring the Essential Questions

INFORMATIVE/EXPLANATORY How did new ideas and technology change the way people lived during the 1920s? Write a short essay that answers this question. Be sure to include some examples of how new ideas and technology improved life but also created tensions. Use examples from the chapter to help you organize your essay.

2 21st Century Skills

COLLABORATION Working with a small group, create a political advertisement for a presidential candidate in the 1920s. Define the candidate's opinions about three major areas: labor issues, immigration, and discrimination.

3 Thinking Like a Historian

ANALYZING PRIMARY SOURCES The United States still has rules for who can and cannot immigrate to this country. Use the Internet to find out what the steps are for a person wishing to come to the United States to live. Make a list of the major steps a would-be immigrant must complete. Keep a record of the sources from which you got your information. Share your information with the class.

4 Visual Literacy

ANALYZING PHOTOGRAPHS Charles Lindbergh completed a solo, nonstop transatlantic flight in the *Spirit of St. Louis.* What three adjectives might you use to describe Lindbergh as shown in this photograph?

Bettmann/CORBIS

REVIEW THE GUIDING QUESTIONS

Choose the best answer for each question.

1 What contributed to the sharp drop in labor union membership in the 1920s?

A. rising prices

B. racial tensions

C. rising wages

D. government and employer pressure

2 Many Americans feared Bolsheviks because the Bolsheviks wanted to

F. allow integration.

G. increase immigration to the United States.

H. overthrow capitalism.

I. enact strict Prohibition laws.

3 Why did President Harding give important government jobs to people who were unqualified for their positions?

A. He was rewarding them for their political support.

B. He hoped to hurt his political rivals.

C. He knew he could pay them a lower salary.

D. He wanted to change the way government was run.

4 Why did businesses hire scientific management experts in the 1920s?

F. to determine more efficient work methods

G. to create advertisements for new products

H. to stop workers from forming unions

I. to help recruit workers from the suburbs

5 Ford increased the sales of his automobiles by

A. building new highways.

B. establishing labor unions in his factories.

C. shutting down the assembly line.

D. steadily dropping the price of the Model T.

6 Why did nativism arise in the 1920s?

F. Women wanted government support for entering the workforce.

G. Citizens were angered by Prohibition laws.

H. Some Americans thought foreigners would take their jobs.

I. Workers wanted to be able to move to the suburbs but work in the city.

DBQ **ANALYZING DOCUMENTS**

Base your answer to the questions on this excerpt from *A Farewell to Arms*, which describes the Italian front during World War I.

"At the start of the winter came the permanent rain and with the rain came the cholera [a deadly disease]. But it was checked and in the end only seven thousand died of it in the army."

Source: Ernest Hemingway, *A Farewell to Arms*

7 **Analyzing** What is the narrator's tone in Hemingway's story?

A. uncertain

B. angry

C. weary

D. horrified

8 **Drawing Conclusions** What is the purpose of Hemingway's use of the word *only*?

F. He is using sarcasm to underscore the terribly brutality of the war.

G. He is hoping to shield readers from the reality of the situation.

H. He is embellishing facts to exaggerate the effects cholera had on society.

I. He is attempting to prove that cholera was easily contained.

SHORT RESPONSE

The following is an excerpt from a 1920 memoir by Evalyn McLean, who talks about the kinds of friendships Warren G. Harding developed during his presidency.

"Unhappily, for many persons [Harding] had become something other than a friend; he was to all of these no less a thing than Opportunity."

Source: Henry Steele Commager, *Witness to America*

9 Why would people consider Harding an "Opportunity?"

10 Explain why you think Harding's administration ended in scandal.

EXTENDED RESPONSE

11 **Argument** Using the information from the text and your knowledge of social studies, write an essay in which you summarize the needs and goals of most Americans after World War I. Convince readers that Harding, Coolidge, or Hoover represented or did not represent most Americans.

Need Extra Help?

If You've Missed Question	1	2	3	4	5	6	7	8	9	10	11
Review Lesson	1	1	2	3	3	4	4	4	2	2	1–4

The Depression and the New Deal

1929–1939

ESSENTIAL QUESTIONS · *Why do people make economic choices?*
· *How do governments change?* · *How do new ideas change the way people live?*

The Story Matters . . .

What do you do when you have lost everything? Many Americans face this question in the 1930s. The out of work and out of luck face a future of uncertainty. The unemployed wonder how they will feed themselves and their hungry children. The homeless worry where they will be in a week or a month or a year. Everyone has questions, and nobody, it seems, has answers.

The 1930s were a time of crisis unlike any the nation had ever endured. Millions lived with doubt, hunger, and fear. The government responded with steps that continue to impact the nation today.

◄ *A 32-year-old mother of seven anxiously faces an uncertain future as she and her family seek work in the farm fields of California.*

Library of Congress/LC-USF34- 009058-C

Nowhere was the economic suffering of the 1930s more severe than on the Great Plains. Bad weather and poor farming methods created a disaster known as the Dust Bowl. Many of the people living in the region were left with no choice but to move elsewhere.

Step Into the Place

MAP FOCUS For several years, severe drought and winds scoured the farmland of the Great Plains.

1 REGION Which states were most affected by the Dust Bowl conditions?

2 MOVEMENT What does the map suggest about how the Dust Bowl affected the populations of these states?

3 CRITICAL THINKING
Drawing Conclusions Use the information from the map to explain why farming in the Dust Bowl would have been difficult.

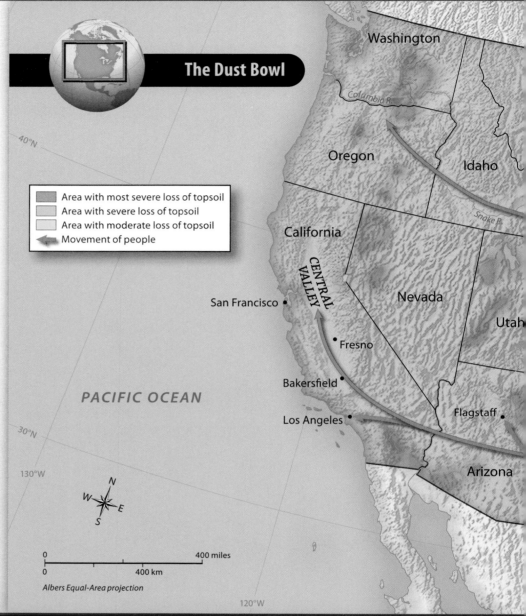

The Dust Bowl

- Area with most severe loss of topsoil
- Area with severe loss of topsoil
- Area with moderate loss of topsoil
- → Movement of people

Washington

Columbia R.

Oregon

Idaho

Snake R.

California

CENTRAL VALLEY

Nevada

Utah

San Francisco

Fresno

Bakersfield

Flagstaff

Los Angeles

PACIFIC OCEAN

Arizona

40°N

30°N

130°W

120°W

```
0                    400 miles
0          400 km
```
Albers Equal-Area projection

Step Into the Time

TIME LINE Look at the time line. What evidence do you see that the economic events that affected the United States may also have led to unrest and tensions in other parts of the world?

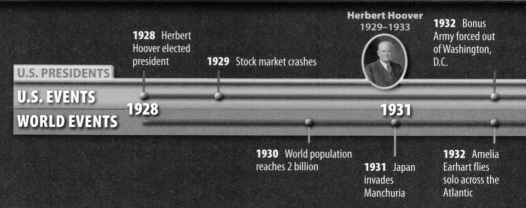

Herbert Hoover
1929–1933

1928 Herbert Hoover elected president

1929 Stock market crashes

1932 Bonus Army forced out of Washington, D.C.

U.S. PRESIDENTS

U.S. EVENTS

WORLD EVENTS

1928

1931

1930 World population reaches 2 billion

1931 Japan invades Manchuria

1932 Amelia Earhart flies solo across the Atlantic

White House Historical Association

networks

There's More Online!

☑ **MAP** Explore the interactive version of this map on NETWORKS.

☑ **TIME LINE** Explore the interactive version of this time line on NETWORKS.

CANADA

Lake Superior

Missouri R.

Montana

North Dakota

Minnesota
Fargo

Lake Huron

L. Ontario

New York

Wisconsin

Lake Michigan

Michigan
Detroit

L. Erie

Cleveland

Pennsylvania

Wyoming

South Dakota
Minneapolis

Iowa

Chicago

Indiana

Ohio

West Virginia

Md.
Washington D.C.

Nebraska
Omaha

Missouri R.

Illinois

St. Louis

Ohio R.

Louisville

Kentucky

Virginia

Grand Junction

Denver

Kansas
Kansas City

Missouri

Cumberland R.

North Carolina

Colorado

Arkansas R.

Santa Fe

Tulsa

Oklahoma City

Oklahoma

Arkansas

Tennessee

Tennessee R.

Atlanta

South Carolina

Albuquerque

New Mexico

Dallas

Mississippi R.

Miss.

Alabama

Georgia

Texas

Louisiana

Mobile

Florida

30°N

MEXICO

Rio Grande

Houston

New Orleans

Gulf of Mexico

30°N

Franklin D. Roosevelt
1933–1945

1933 Franklin D. Roosevelt becomes president

1935 Social Security Act passes

1936 President Roosevelt wins reelection

1937 Court-packing bill defeated

1938 Fair Labor Standards Act passes

1934

1937

1940

1933 Hitler comes to power in Germany

1936 American Jesse Owens wins four gold medals at Berlin Olympic Games

1939 World War II begins in Europe as Germany invades Poland

netwⓞrks

There's More Online!

☑ **GAME**

☑ **GRAPH**
U.S. Unemployment Rates

☑ **GRAPHIC ORGANIZER**
Stock Market Crash Time Line

☑ **VIDEO**

Lesson 1
The Great Depression

ESSENTIAL QUESTION *Why do people make economic choices?*

IT MATTERS BECAUSE
The Great Depression caused widespread suffering, and it changed the way people thought about themselves and their government.

The Stock Market Mania

GUIDING QUESTION *Why did the stock market crash?*

For much of the 1920s, the United States economy was a great success story. Leaders declared that the nation had entered a new era. Everyone would prosper, they said. The head of General Motors told people to buy stocks. Buying stock is a way of **investing**—using money in hopes of making more money. Many followed his advice. "Grocers, motormen, plumbers, seamstresses, and … waiters were in the market," reported writer Frederick Lewis Allen. The "market had become a national mania." Everyone, it seemed, was trying to get rich quickly. Few people worried about the risks of investing—that they might lose money.

Then, in October 1929, everything changed. The value of stocks plunged. Millionaires lost fortunes. Thousands of others lost their savings. The stock market had crashed. The nation stood on the brink of a crisis.

The Market Boom

A **stock exchange** is a system for buying and selling stock—shares of corporations. In the late 1920s, the value of stocks went up and up. A person might buy a share of stock for $5. In a few

Reading **HELP**DESK **CCSS**

Taking Notes: *Sequencing*
Create a time line like this one to record the events that happened in September and October of 1929 and led to the stock market crash.

Content Vocabulary
• **invest**   • **relief**
• **stock exchange** • **public works**
• **default**

months, it might be worth $7.50. Often, it kept climbing. If the person sold the stock at a stock exchange, he or she would make money. The steep rise in stock prices in the 1920s led many to invest heavily in the market. By 1929, one in ten households had invested in stock.

Many investors bought stocks "on margin." This means they borrowed money to buy the stock. Here is how buying on margin worked: Say a stock cost $10 a share. An investor might pay $2 in cash and borrow the rest. When stock prices went up, buying on margin worked well. If the investor could sell the share for $15, he or she could pay off the $8 loan—with $7 left over. If the stock price dropped to $5, however, the investor would still owe $8. If the investor sold at $5 a share, he or she would have to come up with another $3 to pay off the loan. The investor would lose the $2 paid for the stock, plus $3 more.

The Market Crash

In September 1929, some investors began to worry that stock prices were set to fall. They began to sell their stocks. Those who lent money to investors got nervous. They began demanding that borrowers repay their loans. To do this, more people sold more stock. The more stock people sold, the lower stock prices fell.

The **decline** in prices continued through the first three weeks of October. Still, many experts thought there was no need to worry. Investors did not listen. Stock prices plunged as investors sold millions of shares each day. On October 24, panicked traders sold almost 13 million shares. That day became known as "Black Thursday."

Following a few days of calm, the crisis worsened. On Tuesday, October 29, stock prices plummeted. The New York Stock Exchange closed for a few days to prevent more panic selling.

The stock market crash brought economic hardship to many people who had once been well off.

☑ **PROGRESS CHECK**

Defining What does buying stock "on margin" mean?

---

invest to commit money in the hopes of making more money in the future

stock exchange a place where shares in corporations are bought and sold through an organized system

Academic Vocabulary

decline to drop or go down steadily

Build Vocabulary: *Multiple Meaning Words*

As a verb, *exchange* means to give one thing in return for another. As a noun, *exchange* means a trade or a place where things of value are traded.

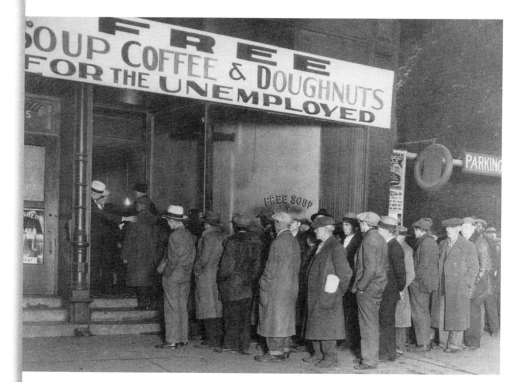

During the Great Depression, local governments and charities distributed food at soup kitchens like this one.

The Great Depression Begins

GUIDING QUESTION *How did the Great Depression bring hardship?*

Over the next two years, the nation slid into a severe economic crisis—the Great Depression. Business activity slowed sharply. In 1929 the United States produced goods and services worth $104 billion. In 1932 output dropped to $58 billion.

What caused the **collapse?** The market crash was one factor. It was not, however, the only cause of the Depression. Other factors also helped send the economy into a tailspin.

Economic Weaknesses

Some experts saw problems in the economy in the early 1920s. Farm income, for example, shrank throughout the decade.

Later in the decade, factories found they were turning out more goods than people could buy. In the months before the crash, the auto and construction industries especially suffered. Struggling companies cut wages and laid off workers. These workers began buying fewer goods. This hurt even more companies.

Another warning sign was the growing gap between rich people and everyone else. In 1929 less than 1 percent of the population owned nearly 33 percent of the country's wealth. Meanwhile, many American families lived in poverty or close to it.

Bettmann/CORBIS

Reading **HELP**DESK (CCSS)

default to fail to meet an obligation, especially a financial one

Academic Vocabulary

collapse a sudden fall or failure of something, such as a structure or the value of money

A Banking and Credit Crisis

Borrowed money fueled much of the 1920s economy. Farmers bought land, equipment, and supplies by borrowing money. Consumers borrowed to buy cars. Investors borrowed to buy stocks. Small banks suffered when farmers **defaulted,** or failed to meet loan payments. Large banks, which owned stocks, suffered huge losses in the crash. Thousands of banks closed between 1930 and 1933. When banks collapsed, millions of people lost money. The savings they had put in these banks were gone.

Other Nations Affected

In 1930 Congress passed the Hawley-Smoot Tariff. A tariff is a tax on imported goods. The Hawley-Smoot Tariff raised the price of goods purchased from other countries. As a result, Americans bought fewer of these goods. This hurt foreign countries.

Foreign countries responded by raising their own tariffs on American products. As a result, foreign countries purchased fewer American goods. This hurt American business.

Joblessness Spreads

By 1932 about 25 percent of American workers were out of work. The unemployment rate remained near 20 percent throughout the 1930s. Many workers who managed to keep their jobs worked only part-time or had their hourly wages cut.

The unemployed lost more than their jobs. New Yorker Sidney Lens wrote about his "feeling of worthlessness—and loneliness; I began to think of myself as a freak and misfit." Some tried to earn a few cents by shining shoes or selling apples on street corners.

People waited for hours to get a slice of bread, a cup of coffee, or a bowl of soup from soup kitchens. Long lines of hungry people snaked through the streets of the nation's cities. Peggy Terry, a young girl in Oklahoma City, told how each day after school her mother sent her to the soup kitchen.

ECONOMICS SKILL

Unemployment hurts people. It also hurts the economy. When people are not working, they are not using their skills to benefit others. The unemployed earn less and spend less. This lowers the amount of taxes government can collect. At the same time, government may have to spend more to provide help to the unemployed. Business income goes down, as do the taxes businesses pay. Struggling businesses also pay workers less—and the cycle continues.

1 CALCULATING When did unemployment hit its peak?

2 CRITICAL THINKING
Explaining Explain how a high unemployment rate can be harmful to an economy.

UNEMPLOYMENT IN THE GREAT DEPRESSION

NUMBER OF WORKERS* (IN THOUSANDS)

55,000
50,000
45,000
40,000
35,000
30,000

1929   1930   1931   1932   1933

YEARS

— Total available to work
— Total employed

*14 years and older

Source: Statistical Abstract of the United States

Many who lost their homes had to find some form of shelter or build it out of whatever materials they could find.

PRIMARY SOURCE

❝ If you happened to be one of the first ones in line, you didn't get anything but water that was on top. So we'd ask the guy that was ladling out soup into the buckets—everybody had to bring their own bucket to get the soup—he'd dip the greasy, watery stuff off the top. So we'd ask him to please dip down to get some meat and potatoes from the bottom of the kettle. But he wouldn't do it. ❞

—from *Hard Times*, by Studs Terkel

Homeless people gathered to live in makeshift villages known as Hoovervilles. This name was a sarcastic reference to President Hoover. Across the country Americans wondered why the president did not act to end the suffering.

☑ **PROGRESS CHECK**

Explaining Why did the Hawley-Smoot Tariff make the Depression more severe?

Hoover Reacts to the Depression

GUIDING QUESTION *How did Hoover start to involve the government in the economic crisis?*

President Hoover thought the economic crisis was temporary. He believed that prosperity was "just around the corner." He also believed that the "depression cannot be cured by legislative action or executive pronouncement." Instead, Hoover called on business leaders not to cut wages or factory output. He asked charities to do their best to help the needy. Voluntary action by citizens and local governments, Hoover thought, would pull the nation through the crisis.

Charities, churches, and volunteers worked hard to provide **relief.** State and local governments did as well. The number of people who needed help, however, was overwhelming.

Hoover Tries to Help

Hoover at last saw that the federal government had to take action. Pressed by Congress, he agreed in 1931 to federal spending on **public works**—projects such as highways, parks, and libraries meant for the public to use. Public works projects, the thinking went, would create new jobs. Unfortunately, state and local governments were already out of money. Even with the federal spending, overall government spending went down.

Seattle Post-Intelligencer Collection; Museum of History and Industry/CORBIS

Reading **HELP**DESK (CCSS)

relief aid for the needy; welfare

public works projects such as the building of highways, parks, and libraries built with public funds for public use

In January 1932, Hoover asked Congress to create the Reconstruction Finance Corporation (RFC). The RFC lent money to businesses. It also provided funds for state and local programs. However, the RFC's leaders were unwilling to make risky loans. The RFC did not use much of its available funds. It did little to reduce suffering and unemployment.

The Bonus Army

By 1932 Americans were growing more and more restless. Then, a march on Washington by World War I veterans turned public opinion firmly against President Hoover.

In 1924 Congress had agreed to give each veteran of World War I a bonus—a cash award. Congress had promised to hand out this bonus in 1945. When the Depression hit, jobless veterans asked to receive their bonuses right away. In the summer of 1932, they formed what they called the "Bonus Army." They marched to Washington, D.C., to demand the money.

Congress voted against meeting the Bonus Army's demands. After the vote, many veterans left the city. About 2,000, however, vowed to remain. When the police tried to break up the veterans' camp, conflict broke out. Two people died in the fighting.

Hoover responded by calling in U.S. Army troops. Veterans and their families fled as the troops burned their camp. Americans were horrified that the government had attacked war veterans. Hoover seemed out of touch with ordinary people.

Police attempts to break up the Bonus Army's camp in Washington, D.C., led to violence.

✓ **PROGRESS CHECK**

Explaining What was the response of the public to the way Hoover got the Bonus Army out of Washington, D.C.?

LESSON 1 REVIEW (CCSS)

Review Vocabulary

1. Write a sentence about the stock market collapse that uses the following terms.

   a. stock exchange   **b.** default

2. Examine the two terms below. Then write a sentence that explains what the terms have in common.

   a. relief   **b.** public works

Answer the Guiding Questions

3. *Specifying* What factors caused the stock market crash?

4. *Explaining* What factors contributed to the start of the Great Depression?

5. *Describing* What was President Hoover's approach to the economic crisis?

6. **NARRATIVE** Study the photo on page 263. Write a paragraph that expresses the thoughts the man might be having.

networks

There's More Online!

- ☑ **BIOGRAPHY** Eleanor Roosevelt
- ☑ **GAME**
- ☑ **GRAPHIC ORGANIZER** Roosevelt's New Deal
- ☑ **MAP**
  - The Election of 1932
  - The Tennessee Valley Authority

Lesson 2
The New Deal

ESSENTIAL QUESTION *How do governments change?*

IT MATTERS BECAUSE

The New Deal involved government in social and economic concerns and changed the way government relates to its citizens.

Roosevelt in the White House

GUIDING QUESTION *What did Roosevelt do to improve the American economy?*

In 1932 the nation's economy seemed to be falling apart. President Hoover hoped for reelection in that year's presidential election. With the country's economy worsening, though, his chances were slim. He knew that many voters had turned against him.

Democrats, on the other hand, were hopeful about the election. They chose New York Governor Franklin D. Roosevelt as their candidate. Roosevelt—or FDR, as he was called—told the Democrats and the nation, "I pledge you, I pledge myself, to a new deal for the American people."

FDR's Early Career

Franklin D. Roosevelt was a distant cousin of former president Theodore Roosevelt. He came from a wealthy New York family. Ambitious and charming, FDR decided as a young man on a career in politics. In 1905 he married Theodore Roosevelt's niece, Eleanor Roosevelt. She became a tireless partner in his life.

Young FDR enjoyed great early success. In 1910 he won election to the New York Senate. There he became known as a leader with the ability to get others to support his views. In 1913 Roosevelt became assistant secretary of the navy. In 1920

(l) Library of Congress/LC-USZ62-54474, (cl) Library of Congress, Prints & Photographs Division, LC-USZ62-17300 (cr) Arthur Rothstein/CORBIS, (r) Library of Congress/LC-DIG-fwac-1a34185

Reading **HELP**DESK (CCSS)

Taking Notes: *Identifying*

As you read, create a diagram like this one to note what areas of American life and business were affected by Roosevelt's New Deal.

Banks

New Deal

Content Vocabulary
- **work relief**
- **subsidy**

268 *The Depression and the New Deal*

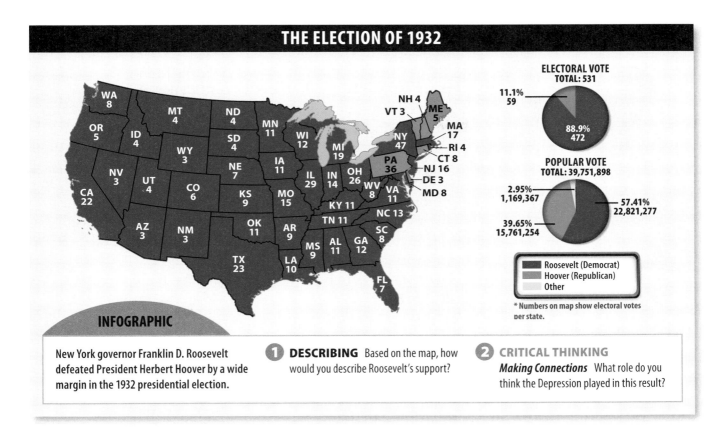

THE ELECTION OF 1932

WA 8
OR 5
MT 4
ND 4
MN 11
WI 12
MI 19
NH 4
VT 3
ME 5
MA 17
NY 47
RI 4
CT 8
NJ 16
DE 3
MD 8
ID 4
WY 3
SD 4
IA 11
NE 7
IL 29
IN 14
OH 26
PA 36
WV 8
VA 11
NV 3
UT 4
CO 6
KS 9
MO 15
KY 11
NC 13
CA 22
AZ 3
NM 3
OK 11
AR 9
TN 11
SC 8
MS 9
AL 11
GA 12
TX 23
LA 10
FL 7

ELECTORAL VOTE
TOTAL: 531
11.1% 59
88.9% 472

POPULAR VOTE
TOTAL: 39,751,898
2.95% 1,169,367
57.41% 22,821,277
39.65% 15,761,254

■ Roosevelt (Democrat)
■ Hoover (Republican)
□ Other

* Numbers on map show electoral votes per state.

INFOGRAPHIC

New York governor Franklin D. Roosevelt defeated President Herbert Hoover by a wide margin in the 1932 presidential election.

1 DESCRIBING Based on the map, how would you describe Roosevelt's support?

2 CRITICAL THINKING
Making Connections What role do you think the Depression played in this result?

---

the Democrats chose him as their candidate for vice president. The Democrats lost the election to Warren G. Harding. Franklin Roosevelt's future, however, seemed bright.

Then in 1921 polio struck Roosevelt. The illness left him paralyzed in both legs. In spite of this disability, his will remained strong. He refused to give in. "Once I spent two years lying in bed trying to move my big toe," he said later. "After that, anything else looked easy."

The Return to Politics

After a few years, Franklin D. Roosevelt decided to return to politics. He never discussed his illness in public. He asked reporters not to photograph his leg braces or wheelchair.

Roosevelt won election as governor of New York in 1928. He was then reelected in 1930. In this time, Roosevelt earned a national reputation as a reformer.

During the 1932 campaign, Roosevelt relied heavily on advice from a group of advisers known as the "Brain Trust." These advisers helped their candidate develop new ideas for overcoming the nation's severe economic problems.

Roosevelt was stricken with polio in 1921, which left him wheelchair-bound. He worked hard to prove that his disability did not affect his ability to lead.

Build Vocabulary: *Word Parts*

The word *disability* is made up of the word *ability* and a prefix. The prefix *dis-* means "the opposite of." *Disability,* therefore, means "the opposite of an ability," or the inability to do something.

**Eleanor Roosevelt
(1884–1962)**

Eleanor Roosevelt came from a family of leaders. She was the niece of Theodore Roosevelt, who was president in the early 1900s. She was also a distant relative of the man she married, Franklin Roosevelt.

Before Eleanor Roosevelt became First Lady, president's wives generally did not take active roles in public life. Eleanor Roosevelt changed that. She wrote a popular newspaper column and took part in many causes. She became well known—and well loved. After Franklin Roosevelt died, Eleanor Roosevelt continued to enjoy an active public career. In one of her roles, she served as the only woman among the U.S. delegates to the newly created United Nations.

▶ **CRITICAL THINKING**
Summarizing In what way did Eleanor Roosevelt help redefine the role of First Lady?

FDR declared that "the country needs and … demands bold, persistent experimentation." He also spoke of trying to help "the forgotten man at the bottom of the economic pyramid."

Voters were drawn to Roosevelt's confidence and energy. They elected him in a landslide. Democrats also won important victories in Congress. People clearly wanted a change.

Rebuilding the Nation's Confidence

In the four months between Roosevelt's election and inauguration, the economy worsened. People became increasingly afraid. On Inauguration Day, as Roosevelt took office, he calmed the rising fears. He told the American people, "The only thing we have to fear is fear itself."

A first step was to help the nation's banks. Banks are key to a healthy economy. People use them to keep their money safe. Banks also lend money to businesses and people. During the Depression, many borrowers could not repay their loans. A surge in bank failures caused panic. When a bank failed, people with savings there lost their money. People began to take money out of even healthy banks. This caused even more bank failures.

In response to the crisis, Roosevelt ordered all banks closed for four days. Congress passed the Emergency Banking Relief Act to help banks reorganize. Those that passed government inspection could then reopen. The goal was to assure people they could trust their bank. After a week in office, Roosevelt was able to tell Americans in a radio broadcast that "it is safer to keep your money in a … bank than under the mattress."

The president's radio talk was the first of many "fireside chats." The talks got this name because the president sat next to a fireplace in the White House as he spoke. These fireside chats helped FDR gain the public's trust.

The Hundred Days

Roosevelt was just getting started. More ideas for combatting the Depression followed. During his first months in office—a period that came to be called the "Hundred Days"—Congress approved many FDR proposals. Optimism swept through the capital. Journalist Thomas Stokes recalled, "The gloom … of the closing months of the Hoover administration had vanished."

☑ **PROGRESS CHECK**
Explaining Why did Roosevelt broadcast his fireside chats?

TEXT: Franklin D. Roosevelt, The Forgotten Man, April 7, 1932, Democratic Party, National Committee Papers, The Franklin D. Roosevelt Presidential Library and Museum; Franklin D. Roosevelt, Address at Oglethorpe University, May 22, 1932, The Franklin D. Roosevelt Presidential Library and Museum. PHOTO: Library of Congress

Reading **HELP**DESK CCSS

work relief programs that give needy people jobs
subsidy a grant of money, often from the government, to a person or a company for an action intended to benefit the public

The New Deal Takes Shape

GUIDING QUESTION *How did the New Deal affect areas of American life?*

The FDR proposals that Congress passed came to be called the "New Deal." This sweeping set of laws and regulations affected banking, the stock market, industry, agriculture, public works, relief for the poor, and conservation of resources. In fact, the New Deal changed the face of the United States dramatically.

Help for the Jobless and Poor

Roosevelt worked hard to put the jobless to work through **work relief** programs. During his first month in office, Roosevelt asked Congress to create the Civilian Conservation Corps (CCC). Over the next 10 years, the CCC employed about 3 million young people. CCC workers toiled on projects that helped the public, including planting trees to reforest areas, building levees for flood control, and improving national parks.

The president also called for direct aid to people in need. Congress passed the Federal Emergency Relief Act (FERA) in May 1933. This agency gave money to the states to provide food and assistance to the needy. Roosevelt named Harry Hopkins to lead the FERA. Hopkins became one of Roosevelt's closest advisers. He was also involved in several other New Deal programs.

Roosevelt did not forget farmers. On May 12, 1933, he signed the Agricultural Adjustment Act (AAA). The act aimed to raise farm prices quickly. It also sought to control production so that farm prices would stay up over the long term.

In the AAA's first year, farmers grew more food than they could sell. The excess of crops drove prices down, hurting farmers. The AAA paid farmers to destroy crops, milk, and livestock.

It shocked many Americans to encourage the throwing away of good food when millions of people were going hungry. However, New Dealers claimed the action was necessary to bring up prices.

To control production and farm prices, the AAA paid farmers not to use some of their land. If market prices of key farm products fell below a certain level, the AAA would pay farmers **subsidies** (SUHB•suh•deez), or payments, to make up the difference. In the first three years of the New Deal, farmers' incomes rose by about 50 percent. In 1936, however, the Supreme Court ruled that the AAA was unconstitutional. The case that produced this ruling was *United States* v. *Butler*.

Thinking Like a
HISTORIAN

Analyzing Political Cartoons

This cartoon from the 1930s shows Franklin D. Roosevelt playing Ring Around the Rosie, a popular children's game of the times. The letters on the clothing of the children represent New Deal programs.

For more about analyzing political cartoons, review *Thinking Like a Historian*.

▶ **CRITICAL THINKING**
Analyzing What do you think this cartoon is saying about Roosevelt's attitude toward the various New Deal programs he helped create?

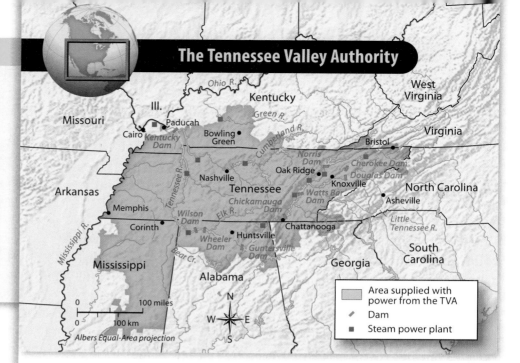

GEOGRAPHY CONNECTION

The Tennessee Valley Authority was intended to boost economic conditions in the Tennessee River valley region.

1 HUMAN-ENVIRONMENT INTERACTION According to the map, in which states did Americans benefit from the power provided by the TVA?

2 CRITICAL THINKING
Speculating How might the greater availability of electricity help the region?

Rebuilding a Region

One of the boldest Hundred Days programs was the Tennessee Valley Authority (TVA). The TVA aimed to **promote** the economic well-being of the Tennessee Valley region. The TVA built dams along the Tennessee and other rivers. These dams helped control the terrible floods so common to the region. The dams also used the power of flowing water to **generate** electricity. As a result, thousands of farms and homes got electricity for the first time.

Some critics charged that funds for the TVA should be used to support nationwide programs rather than a regional one. Power companies also attacked the program as unfair and socialistic. When the spring rains came in 1937, however, the system worked. Dams helped stop flooding. In the end, most observers agreed that the TVA was a great success.

Helping Business and Labor

On the last day of the Hundred Days—June 16, 1933—Congress passed the National Industrial Recovery Act (NIRA). Roosevelt called this "the most important and far-reaching legislation" ever passed in the United States. The goal of the NIRA was to boost the economy by helping business regulate itself.

The NIRA created the National Recovery Administration (NRA). This body pushed businesses to set a minimum wage and abolish child labor. The NRA also tried to set up codes

Reading **HELP**DESK 🅒🅒🅢🅢

Academic Vocabulary

promote to help the progress of something
generate to produce or make something exist

governing pricing and other practices for every industry. Businesses taking part in the NRA displayed the blue eagle symbol and slogan—"We Do Our Part."

The NIRA also established the Public Works Administration (PWA). The PWA's goal was to boost the economy through huge public works projects. The PWA led to the hiring of people to build roads, shipyards, hospitals, and schools. Many PWA projects—such as New York City's Lincoln Tunnel and Kentucky's Fort Knox—are still in use. The PWA spent its funds slowly, though. As a result, the impact on unemployment was not immediate.

To avoid future banking crises, Roosevelt called for reform of the banking system. Near the end of the Hundred Days, Congress created the Federal Deposit Insurance Corporation (FDIC). The FDIC guaranteed that up to $2,500 placed in an insured bank would not be lost if the bank failed. Congress also passed a law regulating stocks and bonds. Then, in 1934, Congress formed the Securities and Exchange Commission, or SEC. The SEC had power to punish dishonest dealers of stocks. It helped rebuild confidence in the stock market.

Impact of the Early New Deal

The New Deal did not cure all the nation's ills. Hardships did not cease, and farmers continued to lose their land. Unemployment remained at high levels. Yet the panic of 1932 and 1933 had faded. The flurry of activity from the nation's capital had restored some measure of confidence.

✓ **PROGRESS CHECK**

Identify What was the goal of the TVA?

Workers employed as part of the Tennessee Valley Authority operate jackhammers to break away rock and soil.

Arthur Rothstein/CORBIS

LESSON 2 REVIEW (CCSS)

Review Vocabulary

1. Examine the terms below. Then use these terms in a sentence about the New Deal.

   a. work relief **b.** subsidies

Answer the Guiding Questions

2. *Identifying* What actions did Roosevelt take during the Hundred Days to try to help the nation's collapsing economy?

3. *Analyzing* What do you think President Roosevelt meant when he said "The only thing we have to fear is fear itself"?

4. ARGUMENT Private power companies harshly criticized the TVA for using government funds to make electricity available at low rates. Do you think this criticism was fair? Write a paragraph to answer this question and explain your point of view.

What Do You Think? ⬤CCSS

Was the New Deal an Abuse of Government Power?

Roosevelt's New Deal program tried to regulate the American economy to ease the Great Depression. This differed from a long tradition of government taking a hands-off approach to the economy.

During his presidency, Herbert Hoover had refused to interfere in the economy. Later, he opposed the New Deal. Many Americans supported it, however, partly because government work relief programs reduced the hardships of unemployment.

No

PRIMARY SOURCE

66 I could furnish instance after instance of old people who have worked hard all their lives, only to face desperate need in their old age; of middle-aged workers cast adrift not through their own incapability, but of those who employed them; of young people who have just completed their education and find that the working world has no place for them. . . . I heartily applaud the work that the government has done in this direction, and . . . I feel that it must continue as long as the necessity exists. . . . There is a social need which private business cannot or will not meet, it must be met by the American people as a whole, as a worthwhile investment in its own citizens. 99

— Rabbi Simon Cohen, letter to President Roosevelt, October 27, 1935

Public works projects, such as construction of California's Shasta Dam, shown here, provided jobs during the Great Depression.

Yes

Library of Congress/LC-DIG-fsac-1a34185

PRIMARY SOURCE

❝ You cannot extend the mastery of government over the daily life of a people without somewhere making it master of people's souls and thoughts . . . . Every step in that direction poisons . . . political equality, free speech, free press, and equality of opportunity. It is the road not to more liberty but to less liberty. True liberalism is found not in striving to spread **bureaucracy,** but in striving to set bounds to it. . . .

Through four years of experience this New Deal attack upon free institutions has emerged as the **transcendent** issue in America . . . .

Surely the NRA and the AAA alone, should prove what the New Deal philosophy of government means . . . .

But their illegal invasions of the Constitution are but the minor **artillery** with which this New Deal philosophy of government is being forced upon us. They are now . . . taking vast sums of the people's money and then manipulating its spending to build up personal power. ❞

—Herbert Hoover, speech given October 30, 1936

In St. Johns, Arizona, people line up to get surplus supplies from a charitable group. Herbert Hoover favored voluntary action and charity—not government programs—as the best response to the Great Depression.

Vocabulary

bureaucracy
a system of government marked by lots of rules and regulation

transcendent
most important

artillery
large guns

What Do You Think?   **DBQ**

❶ *Analyzing* Why does Cohen think the government work programs should continue?

❷ *Inferring* How do you think Hoover would feel about the programs that Cohen describes?

❸ *Evaluating* With which position do you agree more? Explain your answer.

Lesson 3
Living Through the Depression

ESSENTIAL QUESTION *Why do people make economic choices?*

IT MATTERS BECAUSE

The Great Depression affected the lives of millions of people, especially on the Great Plains, where terrible drought added to the misery.

Hard Times in America

GUIDING QUESTION *Why was the Depression difficult for Americans?*

The Depression was a terrible time for millions of Americans. Thousands of letters arrived at the White House addressed to First Lady Eleanor Roosevelt. They came from desperate Americans begging for help. "I am writing to you for some of your old soiled dresses," wrote one seventh-grade girl. "I have to stay out of school because I have no books or clothes to ware [wear]."

It was not just children who went without. Young and old alike faced hard times. People could not afford food and medical care. Many lost their homes. Families broke apart as the jobless took to the road in search of work. Children were sent away to fend for themselves.

Women Take Jobs

Desperation drove women into the workforce. Many people felt that women should not hold jobs as long as so many men were unemployed. In addition, women usually earned less than men. Yet the earnings of a woman helped many families survive.

(l) Getty Images, (cl) The Granger Collection, NYC, (c) Time & Life Pictures/Getty Images (cr) The Granger Collection, NYC, (r) CORBIS

Reading **HELP**DESK (CCSS)

Taking Notes: *Categorizing*

Create a chart like this one to record information about the various groups that were affected during the Depression.

Group	How It Was Affected
Women	

Content Vocabulary
• **migrant worker**
• **fascism**

The Depression also increased demands on women at home. To save money, they sewed more clothing, baked more bread, and canned more vegetables. To make money, some women started home businesses, such as laundries or boardinghouses.

The New Deal era opened doors for women in public life. President Roosevelt named the first woman ever to serve in the cabinet when he chose Frances Perkins to be secretary of labor. He also named more than 100 other women to federal posts. Among them was Ellen Sullivan Woodward. She started a program to provide jobs for women.

Eleanor Roosevelt played a major role in her husband's presidency. The president's disability made travel difficult. Eleanor Roosevelt acted as his "eyes and ears." She made many fact-finding trips in his place. Mrs. Roosevelt also was a powerful voice for women and families in need.

First Lady Eleanor Roosevelt forever changed the position of First Lady. Her work on behalf of children and the poor earned her respect around the world.

The Dust Bowl

During the 1930s, the southern Great Plains suffered an environmental disaster. The region came to be known as the Dust Bowl. Humans and nature both played roles in the catastrophe. Farmers had been using new technology, such as tractors and disc plows, to clear millions of acres of sod. They did not realize that grass held soil in place. When drought struck in 1931, crops died. Soil dried up and then blew away in the strong prairie windstorms.

The drought and the storms—"black blizzards"—continued for years. Each storm stripped away more precious soil. Huge dust clouds blocked out the sun. In some areas, dust piled in drifts as high as 6 feet (1.8 m). Dust buried roads and vehicles.

This North Texas farm shows the damage done by dust storms.

▶ CRITICAL THINKING
Drawing Conclusions What does this picture suggest about how dust harmed farms in the Dust Bowl?

Thousands of Dust Bowl farmers went bankrupt and had to give up their farms. About 400,000 **migrated** to California. They became **migrant workers,** moving from place to place to harvest crops. Local people called the migrants "Okies," after the state of Oklahoma from which many had come.

✔ PROGRESS CHECK

Identifying What was the "Dust Bowl"?

Minorities in the Depression

GUIDING QUESTION *How did minority groups adapt to hard times?*

Before the Great Depression, African Americans, Native Americans, and Mexican Americans were already on the lower rungs of the economic ladder. Hard times hit them especially hard.

African Americans

More than half of all African Americans in the South had no jobs. Many of those who had work found their jobs taken by white people who had lost theirs. The collapse of farm prices crushed African American farmers.

About 400,000 African American men, women, and children migrated to northern cities in the 1930s. These migrants did not fare much better in the North, however. The jobless rate for African Americans remained high.

African Americans did make some gains during the Depression. The National Association for the Advancement of Colored People (NAACP) worked to fight discrimination in the labor movement. As a result, more than 500,000 African Americans were able to join labor unions.

African Americans also won a greater voice in government. President Roosevelt named a number of African Americans to federal posts. He sought the advice of a group known as the "Black Cabinet." Among this group were Robert Weaver, a college professor, and Ralph Bunche, who later became a civil rights leader. Mary McLeod Bethune, who founded Bethune-Cookman College in Florida, was another trusted presidential adviser.

Eleanor Roosevelt used her influence to help African Americans. In 1939 the private Constitution Hall refused to host a performance by singer Marian Anderson because she was African American. The First Lady helped arrange for Anderson to give a historic concert at the Lincoln Memorial.

Ralph Bunche (above) and Mary McLeod Bethune (below) helped advise President Roosevelt.

▶ CRITICAL THINKING
Drawing Conclusions Why do you think President Roosevelt included African Americans in his administration?

Getty Images

Reading **HELP**DESK CCSS

migrant worker a person who moves from place to place to find work

Academic Vocabulary

migrate to move from one place to another to live or work

Native Americans

While Native Americans as a group suffered widespread poverty, they did make gains in the 1930s. The head of the Bureau of Indian Affairs, John Collier, introduced reforms known as the "Indian New Deal." These changes helped restore Native American cultures damaged by past government actions.

Collier halted the sale of reservation land and got jobs for 77,000 Native Americans in the Civilian Conservation Corps. He also got Public Works Administration funds to build new reservation schools. Most importantly, Collier pushed Congress to pass the Indian Reorganization Act of 1934. This law restored traditional tribal government and provided money to enlarge some reservations.

Latinos

At the start of the Great Depression, some 2 million Latinos lived in the United States. Most lived in California and the Southwest. Many had come from Mexico. Some worked as farmers on small pieces of land. Others were factory or migrant workers.

As unemployment spread, Mexican Americans became targets of resentment. Many lost their jobs. Politicians and labor unions demanded that Mexican Americans be forced to leave the United States.

The government encouraged Mexican immigrants to return to Mexico. Authorities gave them one-way train tickets to Mexico or simply rounded them up and shipped them across the border. More than 500,000 Mexican Americans left the United States during the early years of the Great Depression. Many left the country against their will.

These Mexican migrant workers found work picking carrots on an Edinburg, Texas, farm in 1939.

The Granger Collection, NYC

Those Mexican Americans who stayed in the United States faced discrimination. They faced roadblocks getting relief money or they received less relief than whites. Many hospitals and schools also turned away Mexican Americans. To resist job discrimination, some migrant workers tried to form labor unions. Local food producers and officials cracked down on these organizations.

The Spread of Radical Ideas

Hard times helped fuel the growth of radical groups. These groups **advocated** extreme and immediate change. Socialists and Communists viewed the Depression as the death of a failed economic system. They called for sweeping changes.

Communism won some support with promises to end economic and racial injustice. Although both socialism and communism had significant influence, neither became a political force in the United States.

The 1930s also saw the rise of fascists in Europe. **Fascism** (FA•shih•zuhm) is a set of ideas that stresses the glory of the nation above individual needs and that favors dictatorship. Germany and Italy were two countries ruled by fascists. In Spain, a fascist-supported group won a bloody civil war.

Although fascism attracted few Americans, it drew enough attention to be dangerous. During the Depression, fascists blamed Jews, Communists, and liberals for the nation's troubles.

✅ **PROGRESS CHECK**

Analyzing How did the National Association for the Advancement of Colored People help African Americans?

Depression-Era Entertainment

GUIDING QUESTION *How did the 1930s become a golden age in entertainment and the arts?*

The Depression produced two trends in entertainment and the arts. One was escapism—light or romantic entertainment that helped people forget about their problems. The other was social criticism—portraits of the injustice and suffering of Depression-era America.

Radio and the Movies

Radio became enormously popular during the 1930s. "Soap operas" were daytime dramas. Their name came from the fact that many of the shows featured ads for laundry

During the Depression, the radio was a source of entertainment and news. One big story of the day was Amelia Earhart's 1937 quest to fly around the world—and her tragic disappearance as she neared her goal.

Time & Life Pictures/Getty Images

Reading **HELP**DESK **CCSS**

fascism a political philosophy that stresses the glory of the state over the individual and that favors dictatorship

Academic Vocabulary

advocate to publicly support something

detergents. Adventure programs such as Dick Tracy and Superman had millions of listeners. So did shows featuring comedians George Burns and Gracie Allen and Jack Benny.

By 1930 about 80 million people per week were going to movie theaters. Movies offered an escape from worries. Walt Disney made the successful animated film *Snow White and the Seven Dwarfs* in 1937. Two years later, audiences flocked to see *The Wizard of Oz,* a colorful and uplifting musical.

Some movies explored serious topics. For example, *The Grapes of Wrath* (1940) was based on John Steinbeck's novel about Dust Bowl migrants. The 1939 film of Margaret Mitchell's novel *Gone With the Wind* also showed people coping with hard times. It was set during the Civil War.

Painters, Photographers, and Writers

Many writers and painters portrayed the grim realities of Depression life. Richard Wright's novel *Native Son* told the story of an African American man growing up in Chicago. Writer James Agee and photographer Walker Evans depicted poor Southern farm families in *Let Us Now Praise Famous Men.*

Photographer Margaret Bourke-White also recorded the plight of American farmers, and Dorothea Lange took gripping photographs of migrant workers. Painters such as Grant Wood and Thomas Hart Benton showed ordinary people facing the hardships of Depression life.

During the Depression, audiences flocked to theaters to watch movies such as *The Wizard of Oz.*

▶ **CRITICAL THINKING**
Drawing Conclusions Why do you think movies such as the one pictured here appealed to Depression audiences?

✓ **PROGRESS CHECK**

Analyzing Why were movies and radio so popular during the Depression?

Getty Images

LESSON 3 REVIEW (CCSS)

Review Vocabulary

1. Write a sentence about the Depression that uses the term *migrant worker.*

2. Explain the meaning of the term *fascism* by using it in a sentence.

Answer the Guiding Questions

3. ***Explaining*** In what ways did the Depression impact the lives of ordinary Americans?

4. ***Describing*** Why was the Depression especially hard on African Americans and Latinos?

5. ***Explaining*** How did the entertainment industry help people cope with the Great Depression?

6. **NARRATIVE** Imagine you are a young person living on a farm in the Dust Bowl. Write a letter to a relative living in some other part of the country. Try to explain the effects of the storms on your farm and the region.

The Grapes of Wrath

by John Steinbeck

John Steinbeck (1902–1968) was born in Salinas, California. He attended Stanford University but did not earn a degree. In 1925 he moved to New York, where he worked as a newspaper reporter and a bricklayer. Steinbeck published his first novel in 1929 and eventually returned to California. In 1939 Steinbeck published *The Grapes of Wrath*, a story about a migrant farm family's experiences in California during the Depression. He received the Pulitzer Prize for this book. In 1962 Steinbeck was awarded the Nobel Prize for Literature.

In the story, the Joad family has been forced off their farm in Oklahoma. They pile all their belongings in a pickup truck and head west to find work. The road is crowded with migrants—many of them fleeing ruined farms for a better life. They find, however, that life in California is not what they had hoped.

John Steinbeck's novel *The Grapes of Wrath* is set during the Great Depression.

Traveling to find work was tough for migrants during the Great Depression.

66 The moving, **questing** people were migrants now. Those families which had lived on a little piece of land, who had lived and died on forty acres, had eaten or starved on the produce of forty acres, had now the whole West to rove in. And they scampered about, looking for work; and the highways were streams of people, and the ditch banks were lines of people. Behind them more were coming. The great highways streamed with moving people. There in the Middle and Southwest had lived a simple **agrarian** folk who had not changed with industry, who had not farmed with machines or known the power and danger of machines in private hands. They had not grown up in the paradoxes of industry. Their senses were still sharp to the ridiculousness of the industrial life.

And then suddenly the machines pushed them out and they swarmed on the highways. The movement changed them; the highways, the camps along the road, the fear of hunger and the hunger itself, changed them. The children without dinner changed them, the endless moving changed them. They were migrants. And the hostility changed them, welded them, united them—hostility that made the little towns group and arm as though to repel an invader, squads with pick handles, clerks and storekeepers with shotguns, guarding the world against their own people.

In the West there was panic when the migrants multiplied on the highways. Men of property were terrified for their property. Men who had never been hungry saw the eyes of the hungry. Men who had never wanted anything very much saw the flare of want in the eyes of the migrants. And the men of the towns and of the soft suburban country gathered to defend themselves; and they reassured themselves that they were good and the invaders bad, as a man must do before he fights. 99

TEXT: Chapter 21, from THE GRAPES OF WRATH by John Steinbeck, copyright 1939, renewed ©1967 by John Steinbeck. Used by permission of Viking Penguin, a division of Penguin Group (USA) Inc. The Grapes of Wrath, by John Steinbeck, copyright © 1939 by Viking Press

Vocabulary

questing
seeking, on a quest

agrarian
having to do with farming

Literary Element

Mood is the atmosphere of a story. The choice of details, images, and words all contribute toward creating a specific mood. As you read, think about the mood of the story.

Analyzing Literature DBQ

❶ *Analyzing* How would you describe the mood of these passages?

❷ *Interpreting* Several times the author refers to the migrants as "streaming" to California. Why do you think the author chose this word?

❸ *Predicting* What do you think will happen to the migrants who arrive in California?

networks
There's More Online!

☑ **GRAPHIC ORGANIZER**
New Deal Complaints
and Suggestions

☑ **PRIMARY SOURCE**
• Roosevelt and Ruin
• General Motors Strike

☑ **SLIDE SHOW** Works Progress
Administration

Lesson 4
Effects of the New Deal

ESSENTIAL QUESTION *How do new ideas change the way people live?*

IT MATTERS BECAUSE
*People still debate the impact of the New Deal on the Depression
and on the nation overall.*

The New Deal Draws Fire

GUIDING QUESTION *Why did Roosevelt's New Deal programs face growing opposition?*

At first, Franklin D. Roosevelt counted on big business
to support his economic plans. Yet increasingly, business
opposed the New Deal. Business leaders accused Roosevelt
of spending too much money. Many also felt the New Deal
gave government too much power over business and over the
economy itself.

Roosevelt also drew fire from critics who felt government
had not done enough to cure the nation's ills. Three men won
wide support with **schemes** to go beyond the New Deal in
offering help to the average American.

Father Charles Coughlin, a Detroit priest, reached millions
of listeners through his weekly radio show. Coughlin called
for high taxes on the wealthy. He called on government to
take over the nation's banks. Coughlin attacked bankers, Jews,
Communists, and labor unions, as well as the New Deal. Over
time, Coughlin lost support because of his extreme views.

Francis Townsend was a California doctor. He called for a
monthly **pension** (PEHN•shuhn), or payment for retired people.
Townsend's plan won little support in Congress. It did, however,
get Americans thinking about the needs of the elderly poor.

(l) Fotosearch/Archive Photos/Getty Images; (r) Sheldon Dick/Hulton Archive/Getty Images

Reading **HELP**DESK (CCSS)

Taking Notes: *Organizing*

As you read, create a chart like this to record the
major complaint or suggestion of each of the
reformers who criticized Roosevelt's New Deal.

Reformer	Complaint/Suggestion
Charles Coughlin	
Francis Townsend	
Huey Long	

Content Vocabulary
• pension
• unemployment
  insurance

The biggest threat to Roosevelt was Huey Long. As governor of Louisiana, Long used public works projects to build his popularity. He won election to the Senate in 1930—and later set his sights on national office.

Long's "Share Our Wealth Plan" called for taxing the rich heavily. Long wanted to use that money to give every American a home and $2,500 a year. Long's plans appealed to the poor. Polls showed that in 1936 he might receive as many as 4 million votes on a third-party ticket. In 1935, however, an assassin killed Long.

☑ **PROGRESS CHECK**

Identifying What group was Townsend's pension plan designed to help?

Roosevelt's Second New Deal

GUIDING QUESTION *What did the Second New Deal introduce to America?*

The economy showed signs of improvement by the mid-1930s, but the Depression was far from over. To bring in more government funds, Roosevelt pushed Congress to pass the Revenue Act of 1935. The act raised taxes on wealthy people and corporations. Critics accused him of "soaking the rich." Many other people cheered.

In 1935 Roosevelt launched a new set of reforms. These are often called the Second New Deal. The laws passed at this time changed American life even more than those passed in the Hundred Days at the start of Roosevelt's presidency.

Father Coughlin drew large audiences with his sharp criticism of the New Deal.

Creating More Jobs

One of every five workers remained unemployed in 1935. To help address this problem, Congress created the Works Progress Administration (WPA). The WPA provided paying work to 2 million people between 1935 and 1941. WPA workers helped the country by building airports, public buildings, bridges, and roads.

The WPA also helped unemployed writers, artists, and musicians. WPA painters created murals in public buildings. The WPA produced books that recorded folktales and songs, African American narratives, and Native American traditions.

Fotosearch/Archive Photos/Getty Images

pension a sum paid regularly to a person, usually after retirement

Academic Vocabulary

scheme a plan or arrangement for doing or organizing something

WPA Projects	
Total	**Projects**
651,087	Miles of highways, roads built
124,031	Bridges repaired
125,110	Public buildings erected
8,192	Public parks created
853	Airports built or improved
2,565	Murals painted

Source: The Depression and New Deal

CHART SKILL

WPA workers completed a variety of public works projects.

1 MAKING CONNECTIONS
How did the WPA benefit the unemployed and the employed?

2 CRITICAL THINKING
Explaining Why was the WPA popular with many Americans?

More Help for the Needy

In August 1935, Congress passed the Social Security Act. The act placed a tax on workers and employers. Money from the tax paid for monthly pensions for retired people.

The Social Security Act also placed a tax on employers to help fund **unemployment insurance**—payments to those who lose their jobs. Social Security also helped people with disabilities, the elderly poor, and children of poor families.

With the Social Security Act, the federal government took responsibility for the **welfare** of all citizens. The act launched what would become a larger American welfare system.

The Labor Movement Grows

In late 1936, workers at the General Motors plant in Flint, Michigan, began using a new technique—the sit-down strike. Strikers continuously occupied the plant and refused to work. After 44 days, management accepted the workers' right to be represented by the union of their choice—the United Auto Workers.

Unions in the American Federation of Labor (AFL) represented mostly skilled workers organized by craft. John L. Lewis of the United Mine Workers helped form a new labor group, the Congress of Industrial Organizations (CIO). The CIO aimed to organize entire industries, not just workers of a certain craft. By 1938, the CIO had 4 million members, including many women and African Americans.

In 1935 Congress passed the National Labor Relations Act, known as the Wagner Act. It guaranteed workers the right to form unions to bargain collectively with employers. In

Andy Sotiriou/Getty Images

unemployment insurance payments by the government for a limited period of time to people who have lost their jobs

Academic Vocabulary

welfare the good health, happiness, and comfort of a person or group; care for the health and safety of a group

1938 Congress passed the Fair Labor Standards Act (FLSA). This banned child labor and set a minimum wage of 40 cents per hour.

☑ **PROGRESS CHECK**

Explaining How did the labor movement change during the Depression?

Roosevelt and the Supreme Court

GUIDING QUESTION *Why was the Second New Deal challenged by the Supreme Court?*

In 1935 the Supreme Court began declaring some parts of the New Deal unconstitutional. The 1936 presidential campaign focused on one issue: Did Americans support Roosevelt and the New Deal? On election day, he won 61 percent of the popular vote.

After his victory, Roosevelt asked Congress to increase the number of seats on the Court from 9 to 15. He planned to fill these seats with justices who would support the New Deal. To many, FDR appeared to be trying to "pack" the Court and upset the system of checks and balances. Even his supporters were troubled.

When the Court ruled in favor of the Wagner Act and the Social Security Act, Roosevelt dropped his Court-packing plan. Still, the whole episode cost him much support.

Roosevelt also ran into trouble with the economy. In 1937 economic recovery seemed to be in full swing. Then, a new economic downturn took hold and lasted into 1938.

It was clear the economy had not fully recovered. Increasingly, however, events overseas caused Americans to focus on foreign affairs.

Strikers at the General Motors plant in Flint, Michigan, refused to work or to leave the factory. Their sit-down strike resulted in a victory in 1937.

☑ **PROGRESS CHECK**

Explaining Why did people criticize Roosevelt's Supreme Court plan?

LESSON 4 REVIEW

Review Vocabulary

1. Examine the terms below. Then write a sentence explaining what the terms have in common.

   a. pension   **b.** unemployment insurance

Answer the Guiding Questions

2. *Analyzing* Why did many business leaders oppose the New Deal?

3. *Explaining* How did Social Security launch the nation's welfare system?

4. *Describing* How did the Supreme Court view Roosevelt's New Deal?

5. **ARGUMENT** If you had lived during the Great Depression, would you have supported or opposed the New Deal? Write a paragraph that gives reasons for your position.

Write your answers on a separate piece of paper.

① Exploring the Essential Questions

INFORMATIVE/EXPLANATORY The Great Depression affected millions of Americans. Write an essay to explain how and why this is true. Think about how this era challenged people's ideas about political leadership, government, and the economy. Use examples from the chapter to help you organize your essay.

② 21st Century Skills

COMMUNICATION Place yourself in the role of an adviser to President Roosevelt during the Great Depression. He has told you about his plan to get six more justices on the Supreme Court so that the majority of the justices will decide in favor of New Deal policies. Evaluate his plan, analyzing the pros and the cons. Prepare a summary of how you see the situation, and offer your advice.

③ Thinking Like a Historian

READING A TIME LINE Create a time line of the major events of the New Deal and the Great Depression.

1932 1933 1934 1935 1936 1937 1938 1939 1940

④ Visual Literacy

ANALYZING POLITICAL CARTOONS
This political cartoon is about President Roosevelt's policy of spending more and more money to solve the nation's economic problems. What is the cartoonist's point of view about Roosevelt's policies? How does the cartoonist present those views?

CHAPTER 10 Assessment CCSS

REVIEW THE GUIDING QUESTIONS

Choose the best answer for each question.

1. Which was a cause of the stock market crash in 1929?
   A. Brokers repaid their bank loans.
   B. People bought everything factories produced.
   C. Investors panicked when stock prices fell.
   D. Stock prices went up in value after a steep drop.

2. What program was created to produce electricity for a region?
   F. Civilian Conservation Corps
   G. the Tennessee Valley Authority
   H. the Works Projects Administration
   I. the National Industrial Recovery Act

3. The environmental disaster in the Great Plains was called the
   A. Dust Bowl.
   B. Great Plains Disaster.
   C. Great Drought.
   D. Great Migration.

4. John Collier worked on behalf of this group during the Depression:
   F. African Americans.
   G. Native Americans.
   H. Mexican Americans.
   I. Italian Americans.

5. Which person was a known critic of the New Deal?
   A. Harry Hopkins
   B. John Lewis
   C. Huey Long
   D. Robert Wagner

6. The Social Security Act provided which of the following?
   F. jobs
   G. the right to join a union
   H. a minimum wage
   I. a pension

DBQ **ANALYZING DOCUMENTS**

"Now, a lot of people remember [the WPA] as boondoggles and raking leaves…Maybe in some places it was. Maybe in the big city machines or something. But I can take you to our town and show you things, like a river front that I used to hike through once that was a swamp and is now a beautiful park-like place built by WPA."

—Ronald Reagan

7 **Describing** What was Ronald Reagan's opinion of the WPA?

A. Most of the work did not have a lasting effect.

B. The WPA did more in big cities.

C. Swampy areas should not have been altered.

D. The WPA had a lasting and positive impact in some areas.

8 **Making Inferences** Based on this quote, what does Ronald Reagan imply about other opinions of the WPA?

F. Some people believed that small towns were left out of the WPA's improvements.

G. Some people viewed the work of the WPA as cleaning and maintenance, and without lasting impact.

H. Some people viewed the WPA as abusing its power.

I. Some people did not think the WPA would be successful.

SHORT RESPONSE

"Bread Line," a poem by Florence Converse, was first published in 1932.

"What if we should be destroyed
By our patient unemployed?"

Source: David A. Shannon, *The Great Depression*

9 What concern is the poet expressing?

10 Which New Deal programs would this poet have supported and why?

EXTENDED RESPONSE

11 **Informative/Explanatory** In the 1920s, many Americans thought they could get rich. Instead, the Depression left millions in poverty. Write an essay that evaluates how people were able to hold onto hope in the face of this dramatic change in fortune.

Need Extra Help?

If You've Missed Question	1	2	3	4	5	6	7	8	9	10	11
Review Lesson	1	2	3	3	4	4	2	2	1, 3	2, 4	1–4

America and World War II

1939–1945

ESSENTIAL QUESTION *Why does conflict develop?*

◄ *Welder Petrina Moore worked in a New Jersey shipyard during World War II.*

The Granger Collection, New York

netw☉rks
There's More Online about the people and events of World War II.

CHAPTER 11

The Story Matters . . .

Women play major roles in the success of World War II. As men volunteer or are drafted to serve in the armed forces, women take their places in the workforce. Women are the ones who make many of the weapons and equipment the men need to fight. It is women who fill the shipyards and assembly lines, making planes, tanks, and ammunition. Their contributions make possible the efforts of those on the front lines. In fact, the war helps everyone see that a woman can do a job just as well as a man.

Place and Time: The World 1939–1945

For the Allies—the United States, Great Britain, the Soviet Union, and France—the military situation in 1942 looks grim. The Axis Powers of Germany, Italy, and Japan control huge parts of Europe, Africa, and Asia. The Allies know it will take years of bloody fighting before they can achieve victory.

Step Into the Place

MAP FOCUS The map shows the extent of the area in which World War II was fought.

1 LOCATION Which battle was fought at the easternmost point that Germany reached in the Soviet Union?

2 REGION Which countries of the Japanese Empire are on the main landmass of the Asian continent?

3 CRITICAL THINKING
Contrasting How do you think the task of defeating the Japanese Empire will differ from the task of defeating the Germans?

Rescue boats approach the burning USS *West Virginia* and USS *Tennessee* following the Japanese surprise attack of December 7, 1941, at Pearl Harbor, Hawaii.

World War II Battles, 1941–1942

1	Siege of Leningrad	September 1941–January 1944
2	Fall of Manila	January 2, 1942
3	Fall of Singapore	February 15, 1942
4	Battle of the Coral Sea	May 4–8, 1942
5	Battle of Midway	June 4–6, 1942
6	Guadalcanal	August 1942–February 1943
7	Battle of Stalingrad	September 1942–February 1943
8	Battle of El Alamein	October–November 1942

Step Into the Time

TIME LINE Look at the time line. How many years passed between the first battles of World War II and the entry of the United States into the war?

Franklin D. Roosevelt
1933–1945

U.S. PRESIDENTS

U.S. EVENTS

WORLD EVENTS

1937 Congress passes latest "Neutrality Act" limiting trade with warring nations

1939 Congress revises Neutrality Acts to allow sale of U.S. goods to warring nations

1937

1939

1939 Germany invades Poland, starting World War II

(t) Bettmann/CORBIS, (b) White House Historical Association

networks

There's More Online!

☑ **MAP** Explore the interactive version of this map on NETWORKS.

☑ **TIME LINE** Explore the interactive version of this time line on NETWORKS.

Countries Under Axis Control 1942

N
W E
S

NORWAY

GREAT BRITAIN

GERMANY

SOVIET UNION 1

SOVIET UNION 7

FRANCE

SPAIN

TUNISIA
ALGERIA
LIBYA

EGYPT 8

SOMALIA

INDIAN OCEAN

BRITISH INDIA

BURMA

THAILAND

MANCHURIA

CHINA

KOREA

JAPAN

PACIFIC OCEAN

Wake Is.

5

PHILIPPINES 2

3

DUTCH EAST INDIES

6

4

50°N
40°N
30°N
20°N
10°N
0°
10°S
20°S
30°S

0   2,000 miles
0   2,000 km
Miller projection

☐ Countries under German/Italian control
▨ Japanese Empire

0°W 0° 10°E 20°E 30°E 40°E 50°E 60°E 70°E 80°E 90°E 100°E 110°E 120°E 130°E 140°E 150°E 160°E

1940 Congress passes Selective Training and Service Act

1941
• Lend-Lease Act passes
• United States enters World War II

1942 U.S. ramps up mobilization effort on home front

1944 Supreme Court upholds internment of Japanese American civilians

Harry S. Truman
1945–1953

1941

1943

1945

1940
• German troops occupy Paris
• Hitler orders bombing of Great Britain

1941
• Germany attacks the Soviet Union
• Japan bombs Pearl Harbor, Hawaii

1942 Allies invade North Africa

1944 D-Day: Allies invade France

1945 U.S. drops atomic bombs on Hiroshima and Nagasaki, Japan

networks

There's More Online!

☑ **GRAPHIC ORGANIZER**
Dictatorships of the 1920s and 1930s

☑ **PRIMARY SOURCE**
• Hitler's Speech on the Nuremberg Laws
• Hitler Political Cartoon

Lesson 1
War Clouds Gather

ESSENTIAL QUESTION *Why does conflict develop?*

IT MATTERS BECAUSE

In the 1930s, the hostile actions of aggressive world leaders helped lead the whole world into war.

The Rise of Dictators

GUIDING QUESTION *What events led to the rise of dictators in Europe?*

In his book *Mein Kampf* ("My Struggle"), Adolf Hitler wrote: "He who wants to live must fight, and he who does not want to fight in this world where eternal struggle is the law of life has no right to exist." When Hitler became Germany's leader, he put those words into action.

Hitler was one of several ruthless leaders who came into power in the 1920s and 1930s. These leaders took advantage of public anger and distress. Many Europeans were unhappy with the Treaty of Versailles, which ended World War I. Then, in the 1930s, economic depression hit. Fear added to anger to create an explosive mixture. Leaders such as Hitler promised prosperity and a return to national greatness. They persuaded frightened, angry citizens to support them. Once in control, these leaders became **dictators** who claimed absolute power and ruled their people by force.

Mussolini in Italy

The first dictator to rise in postwar Europe was Italy's Benito Mussolini. He appealed to Italians who wanted order in an unsettled time. Mussolini also spoke to Italians angry that their country had won little in the Versailles treaty. Mussolini made

(l) Hugo Jaeger/Time Life Pictures/Getty Images, (c) Michael Nicholson/Corbis, (r) Bettmann/CORBIS

Reading **HELP**DESK (CCSS)

Taking Notes: *Identifying*

As you read, use a diagram like this one to list the dictator and country where each political party originated.

	Nazi Party	Fascist Party	Communist Party
Dictator			
Country			

Content Vocabulary
• **dictator**
• **anti-Semitism**
• **totalitarian**
• **appeasement**

Crowds at a rally in Nuremberg, Germany, salute their leader, Adolf Hitler.

fascism—dictatorial government that stresses the greatness of a race or nation—popular. By 1922 his Fascist Party forced Italy's king to name Mussolini the head of government.

Italians called Mussolini *Il Duce* (DOO•chay)—the leader. He quickly outlawed rival political parties and ended democratic rule in Italy. Civil liberties and a free press ceased to exist. Meanwhile, Mussolini built up Italy's military. In 1935 his army conquered the African nation of Ethiopia. The League of Nations made a mild protest. Italy left the League and continued its expansion. In 1939 Mussolini's forces invaded Italy's neighbor, Albania.

Germany

Just as Mussolini had done in Italy, Hitler played on people's emotions. The Great Depression hit Germany hard. Businesses failed, and millions lost their jobs. Hitler took advantage of people's fears to gain support. He also used people's bitterness over the Versailles Treaty to his advantage. Many Germans resented that their country had to take all the blame for World War I. They also disliked losing lands they felt belonged to them.

Hitler led the National Socialist Party, or Nazi Party. The Nazis believed the German people were superior to others. Hitler blamed the Jews, including German Jews, for Germany's problems. His **anti-Semitism** (an•tee SEH•muh•tih•zuhm)—hatred of the Jews—would lead to unspeakable horrors.

After gaining power in 1933, Hitler ended democracy in Germany. He set up totalitarian rule. In a **totalitarian** (toh•ta•luh•TAR•ee•uhn) state, leaders crush all opposition and totally control all aspects of society.

In addition to dominating Germany, Hitler sought to dominate other nations. He claimed that Germany had a right to expand. Germany's neighbors watched uneasily as he broke the Versailles treaty and rebuilt Germany's military. Hitler also formed an alliance with Italy in 1936.

Mussolini and Hitler were totalitarian leaders who shared a similar set of beliefs.

▶ **CRITICAL THINKING**
Drawing Conclusions What does this picture suggest about the similarities between Hitler (right) and Mussolini?

(t) Hugo Jaeger/Time Life Pictures/Getty Images, (b) Michael Nicholson/Corbis

---

dictator leader who has absolute power and rules a nation by force

anti-Semitism dislike of or discrimination against Jews as a religious, ethnic, or racial group

totalitarian seeking to control all aspects of life through dictatorial control

Ⓐ The Soviet Union's Stalin
Ⓑ Germany's Hitler
Ⓒ Turkey's Inönü

NEXT!

INFOGRAPHIC

Economic problems brought dictators to power in several countries in the years after World War I. This June 1941 cartoon comments on Hitler's strong influence.

❶ ANALYZING VISUALS
Why is Hitler cutting the hair of Inönü (en•ON•u) and Stalin? How are they reacting?

❷ CRITICAL THINKING
Identifying Points of View
What commentary do you think the cartoonist is making about Hitler?

The Soviet Union and Japan

The Soviet Union and Japan also tilted toward dictatorship during this era. In the late 1920s, Joseph Stalin rose to power as the Communist leader of the Soviet Union. He used force to **obtain** obedience from his people. Stalin killed rivals and sent millions of people he thought were disloyal to labor camps.

Japan suffered from a lack of jobs and food shortages during the depression of the 1930s. Japan's leader was Emperor Hirohito. In fact, Japan's military held great power and played a key role in setting an aggressive course for Japan. Military leaders believed Japan needed more land and resources. In September 1931, Japan's army invaded Manchuria, China's mineral-rich northeastern region. One of the generals who led the invasion was Hideki Tōjō. He later became Japan's prime minister.

The League of Nations criticized Japan's invasion but took no action. In 1937 the Japanese army invaded China. Three years later, Japan joined Germany and Italy in the "Axis" alliance.

The United States Tries to Stay Neutral

Most Americans wanted to stay out of the storms brewing in other lands. Between 1935 and 1937, Congress passed Neutrality Acts. *Neutral* (NOO•truhl) means not siding with either party in a disagreement. The Neutrality Acts banned selling weapons and making loans to nations at war. One reason for this was that European nations still had not paid back their World War I loans.

☑ PROGRESS CHECK

Comparing What plans did Mussolini and Hitler share?

Reading **HELP**DESK (CCSS)

appeasement the policy of giving in to the demands of others in an effort to keep peace

Academic Vocabulary

obtain to gain
unify to join together

(l) Art Archive/Culver Pictures, (r) Bettmann/CORBIS

Germany Pushes the Limits

GUIDING QUESTION *Why did other nations allow Germany to expand its territory?*

In March 1936, Adolf Hitler ordered troops into Germany's Rhineland. Even though the Versailles treaty forbade Germany from having troops in this area, there was little complaint.

Next, Hitler insisted German-speaking Austria be **unified** with Germany. Again, there was only mild protest. Then he turned his attention to the Sudetenland (soo•DAY•tuhn•land), a part of Czechoslovakia (CHECK•oh•slo•VAH•kee•uh) where many German-speaking people lived. Hitler claimed they were being mistreated and declared Germany's right to the territory.

Czechoslovakia was ready to fight, but Britain and France sought a peaceful solution. They thought they could avoid the outbreak of war by giving in to Germany's demands—a policy known as **appeasement** (uh•PEEZ•mihnt). In September 1938, European leaders met at the Munich Conference in Germany. They told Czechoslovakia to give up the Sudetenland or fight Germany on its own. In return, Hitler pledged not to seek further expansion of German territory. British leader Neville Chamberlain declared the deal would bring "peace in our time."

Hitler soon broke his promise. In March 1939, German troops took the rest of Czechoslovakia. Hitler also planned to invade Poland, which bordered the Soviet Union. However, he worried that such a move would threaten Stalin. Hitler and Stalin signed the Soviet-German Nonaggression Pact in August 1939. This left Hitler free to attack Poland without fear of a Soviet response.

☑ **PROGRESS CHECK**

Explaining Why was Germany able to invade Poland?

Connections to
TODAY

A Modern Dictatorship

Dictators still control some countries. For example, North Korea has been a Communist dictatorship under three generations of the Kim family. Kim Jong Un, the present ruler, came to power in 2011. He succeeded his father, Kim Jong Il, who had begun his rule in 1994. Kim Jong Un's grandfather was Kim Il Sung, who held control from North Korea's founding in 1948 to his death in 1994. Research and share information about the Kim family's rule of North Korea.

LESSON 1 REVIEW (CCSS)

Review Vocabulary

1. Explain the meaning of *dictator* by using the word in a sentence.

2. Explain the meaning of *appeasement* by using the word in a sentence.

Answer the Guiding Questions

3. ***Explaining*** What were some of the problems that led to the rise of dictators in Germany and Italy?

4. ***Defending*** Why did people in the United States think the country needed the Neutrality Acts?

5. ***Explaining*** How did the policy of appeasement work in Hitler's favor?

6. ***Analyzing*** What argument did Hitler use to justify his invasion of Austria?

7. **NARRATIVE** Write a dialogue between two Americans expressing their views on the neutrality of the United States in the 1930s. Have one person defend the policy, and have the other person oppose it.

networks

There's More Online!

 CHART/GRAPH
- U.S. Military Personnel on Active Duty
- U.S. Military Aircraft Production
- Pearl Harbor Casualties

 GRAPHIC ORGANIZER The Allies and the Axis Powers

☑ **VIDEO**

Lesson 2
World War II Begins

ESSENTIAL QUESTION *Why does conflict develop?*

IT MATTERS BECAUSE

War began in Europe, and the United States found itself drawn in—despite the widespread desire for neutrality.

War in Europe

GUIDING QUESTION *How did World War II begin?*

In 1937 President Roosevelt spoke out against the growing "epidemic of world lawlessness." He knew the American people favored isolationism. "We are determined to keep out of war," Roosevelt promised. At the same time, he saw the danger posed by Japan, Germany, and Italy. "We cannot insure ourselves against the disastrous effects of war and the dangers of involvement," he warned. These words proved true.

On September 1, 1939, Hitler sent his armies into Poland. Two days later, Great Britain and France declared war on Germany. World War II had begun.

The German attack on Poland was swift and fierce. The Germans called the offensive a **blitzkrieg** (BLIHTS·kreeg), or "lightning war." While German planes hit their **targets,** German tanks punched through Polish defenses. Thousands of German soldiers poured into the country.

The German blitzkrieg was so effective that Britain and France could do nothing to help Poland. The country fell within weeks. By late September 1939, Hitler and Stalin were dividing Poland between them, as planned in their prewar agreement.

(l) CORBIS, (c to r) Bettmann/Corbis

Reading **HELP**DESK ⓒⓒⓢⓢ

Taking Notes: *Categorizing*

As you read, use a diagram like this one to list the nations that were part of the Allied Powers and the nations that were part of the Axis Powers.

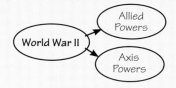

Content Vocabulary
- **blitzkrieg**
- **disarmament**

298 *America in World War II*

Stalin also forced Latvia, Lithuania, and Estonia to allow Soviet military bases on their soil. When he tried to do the same to Finland, war broke out between the two nations. The Finns held out heroically until March 1940 before surrendering.

The Spread of War

The British and French—the Allies— believed Germany would turn west after defeating Poland and attack France. Allied forces settled in on the Maginot (mah•zhuh•NOH) Line, a string of steel-and-concrete bunkers along the French-German border. Through the winter of 1939–1940, these troops waited for an attack that did not come.

April finally brought a German attack—but not in France. German forces attacked Denmark and Norway to the north. In May the Germans at last turned west to invade the Netherlands and Belgium. After German bombing raids, the Netherlands surrendered. The Belgians fought courageously. Yet in spite of help from Allied troops, the Germans overwhelmed them.

After Belgium collapsed, Allied troops retreated to the northern French port of Dunkirk. These troops found themselves trapped between the Germans and the French coast of the English Channel. In a daring move, more than 800 British ships—warships, ferries, and fishing boats—crossed the channel again and again. These ships rescued more than 300,000 French and British soldiers from the shore and carried them to safety.

German tanks roll through Poland. It would take Hitler's forces only a month to crush the Poles and conquer their country.

Bettmann/CORBIS

MOBILIZING FOR WAR

INFOGRAPHIC

U.S. MILITARY AIRCRAFT PRODUCTION

NUMBER OF AIRCRAFT (UNITS)

100,000
80,000
60,000
40,000
20,000
0

1939 1940 1941 1942 1943 1944 1945

YEAR

Source: John Ellis, *World War II: A Statistical Survey*

U.S. Military Personnel on Active Duty	
1939	334,473
1940	458,365
1941	1,801,101
1942	3,858,791
1943	9,044,745
1944	11,541,719
1945	12,123,455

Source: Bureau of the Census, *Historical Statistics of the United States*

After Germany's invasion of Poland, the United States began to expand its armed forces and defense plants.

1 CALCULATING Between which years did the United States military personnel see its greatest numerical increase? Its greatest percentage increase?

2 CRITICAL THINKING
Making Inferences Why do you think increases in the armed forces and military production rose greatly after 1941?

There was no rescuing France, however. In June, the Germans crossed the Somme River and swept into France. Italy joined the war on the side of Germany and attacked France from the southeast. Germany and Italy—and later Japan—formed the Axis Powers. On June 14, 1940, German troops marched into Paris. The French surrendered one week later.

Britain Battles for Survival

In the summer of 1940, all that stood between Hitler and control of Western Europe was Great Britain. The island nation prepared for invasion. First, though, came terror from the sky. In August 1940, German warplanes began bombing British air bases, shipyards, and factories. The planes also bombed cities, destroying parts of London and killing many people.

Hitler believed the bombing raids would destroy the British air force and break British morale. The British people, however, did not give up. One reason was the leadership of the new prime minister, Winston Churchill. When Hitler called for Britain to surrender, Churchill refused:

When Prime Minister Neville Chamberlain resigned in May 1940, Winston Churchill (right) succeeded him.

▶ CRITICAL THINKING
Analyzing Visuals What does this picture suggest about Churchill's personality?

PRIMARY SOURCE

66 We shall defend our island, whatever the cost may be. We shall fight on the beaches, we shall fight on the landing grounds, we shall fight in the fields and in the streets, we shall fight in the hills; we shall never surrender. 99

—from a speech to the British House of Commons

The Battle of Britain continued in the skies until October. The British Royal Air Force mounted a heroic defense. The Germans suffered heavy losses, and Hitler gave up his invasion plans.

Germany Turns on Stalin

Germany's defeat in Britain shook Hitler. He decided Germany needed the Soviet Union's resources and its land as "living space." In June 1941, he broke his agreement with Stalin and attacked the Soviet Union.

TEXT: Reproduced with permission of Curtis Brown Ltd, London on behalf of the Estate of Sir Winston Churchill Copyright © Winston S. Churchill
PHOTO: Bettmann/CORBIS

Reading HELPDESK (CCSS)

blitzkrieg fast, sudden attack by massed forces

Academic Vocabulary

target object of an attack

Reading In the Content Area: *Analyzing Primary Sources*

Read the quotation from Winston Churchill on this page. Explain the inspirational qualities of Churchill's words and how they might have affected the people of Great Britain during the Battle of Britain.

In the early phase of Hitler's invasion, German troops destroyed Soviet planes and tanks and captured half a million Soviet soldiers. Stalin ordered a scorched-earth policy: The Soviets burned their cities, destroyed crops, and blew up dams that provided electric power. This made it harder for the Germans to supply their troops and to keep advancing.

☑ PROGRESS CHECK

Examining Why did Hitler end plans to invade Britain?

The United States and the War

GUIDING QUESTION *Why did the United States gradually become involved on the side of the Allies?*

Most Americans sided with the Allies, but they did not want war. Isolationists formed the America First Committee. It promoted the idea that the United States should stay out of Europe's problems.

Roosevelt vowed to remain neutral. At the same time, he prepared for the possibility of war. In 1938 Congress voted to increase the size of the navy. Then, in 1939, it revised the Neutrality Acts to allow warring nations to buy U.S. goods if they paid cash and moved the goods in their own ships. In 1940 Roosevelt made a deal with the British to give them 50 destroyers from the existing U.S. fleet in exchange for leases on eight British military bases. That same year, Roosevelt also signed the Selective Training and Service Act. This was the first U.S. peacetime draft. It called up men aged 21–35 to serve in the military.

The 1940 Election

With the world in crisis, President Roosevelt chose to run for a third term. He became the first president to break George Washington's two-term tradition. Roosevelt promised, "Your boys are not going to be sent into any foreign wars." Republican candidate Wendell L. Willkie agreed with most Roosevelt policies, but Americans preferred to keep a president they knew.

President Roosevelt won a third term in 1940. Many Americans were reluctant to change presidents with the world at war.

Bettmann/CORBIS

Build Vocabulary: *Multiple Meaning Words*

You can use the word *target* as a verb, meaning "to aim at."

Although the United States did not officially enter the war until December 8, 1941, hostile fire killed a number of Americans before that date. Among them were the crew of the USS *Reuben James*, an American destroyer that was escorting a convoy headed for Great Britain with war supplies. A German submarine torpedoed the *Reuben James* early on October 31, 1941, sinking the ship and killing 115 of the 160 crew. It was the first U.S. Navy ship lost in the months leading up to the entry of the United States into the war. How do you think the United States responded to the sinking of the *Reuben James*? For more about predicting consequences, review *Thinking Like a Historian*.

The United States' Involvement Grows

In March 1941, Congress passed the Lend-Lease Act. It allowed the United States to sell, lend, or lease weapons to any country "vital to the defense of the United States." Isolationists opposed the law. They believed that it would bring the United States closer to war.

Roosevelt also instructed the navy to protect British ships when they were close to American shores. After Germans fired on U.S. ships, Roosevelt ordered Americans to shoot German and Italian ships on sight in certain areas.

The Atlantic Charter

President Roosevelt also worked with Prime Minister Churchill to draw up what was called the Atlantic Charter. The document was not a military alliance, but it did set goals for the world after "the final destruction of the Nazi tyranny." In the Atlantic Charter, the two nations urged **disarmament** (dihs•ARM•uh•mihnt)—giving up weapons. They also called for creation of a "permanent system" for preserving peace.

☑ **PROGRESS CHECK**

Explaining Why did isolationists oppose the Lend-Lease Act?

The Japanese Threat

GUIDING QUESTION *What happened as the result of the attack on Pearl Harbor?*

While the war went on in Europe, Japan continued its expansion in the Far East. After the fall of France, Japan seized French Indochina. Japan also planned to take the Dutch East Indies, British Malaya, and the American territory of the Philippines.

The United States Responds

Trying to halt Japan's expansion, the United States applied economic pressure. Roosevelt froze all Japanese **funds,** or money, in U.S. banks. He also stopped the sale of gasoline and other resources that Japan needed. This angered the Japanese.

The Japanese prime minister, Fumimaro Konoye (FOO•mee•ma•roh koh•no•YEH), wanted to hold talks with the United States. He did not believe Japan could defeat the United States in a war. General Tōjō did not agree, and Konoye

disarmament giving up military weapons

Academic Vocabulary
funds money

resigned. On November 20, talks went forward in Washington. Meanwhile, Tōjō planned a surprise attack on the United States.

Attack on Pearl Harbor

At 7:55 A.M. on Sunday, December 7, 1941, Japanese warplanes attacked the United States military base at Pearl Harbor, Hawaii. Ships, anchored in a neat row, and airplanes, grouped together on the airfield, made easy targets. The people at Pearl Harbor were taken completely by surprise.

The attack destroyed many ships and airplanes. More than 2,300 soldiers, sailors, and civilians were killed. In addition, more than 1,000 individuals were injured. Lieutenant Commander Charles Coe recalled the scene:

PRIMARY SOURCE

66 The capsizing of the *Oklahoma* was . . . the most awful thing I had ever seen. To watch this big battleship capsize and to see only her bottom sticking up out of the water like the back of a turtle and to realize that U.S. officers and men were still in there—well, I just couldn't believe it. It made me realize that war had come to Hawaii. 99

—from *December 7, 1941*

Calling December 7 a "date which will live in infamy," Roosevelt asked Congress to declare war on Japan. On December 11, Germany and Italy—Japan's allies—declared war on the United States. Congress then declared war on them. The United States had joined the Allies in the fight against the Axis.

 PROGRESS CHECK

Explaining Why did Japan attack Pearl Harbor?

U.S. LOSSES AT PEARL HARBOR

Casualties	Killed	Wounded
Navy	1,998	710
Marine Corps	109	69
Army	233	364
Civilian	48	35

Ships		Aircraft	
Sunk or beached	12	Destroyed	164
Damaged	9	Damaged	159

INFOGRAPHIC

1 MAKING INFERENCES Why do you think so many naval personnel were killed or injured at Pearl Harbor?

2 CRITICAL THINKING *Speculating* If the Japanese attack on Pearl Harbor had not done such damage to U.S. citizens and property, do you think the United States would have entered the war? Explain.

LESSON 2 REVIEW CCSS

Review Vocabulary

1. Describe the significance of the following terms to the early years of World War II:

   a. blitzkrieg   **b.** disarmament

Answer the Guiding Questions

2. *Identifying* What was the outcome of the presidential election in 1940?

3. *Listing* What were the main goals of the Atlantic Charter?

4. *Identifying* Explain why the United States entered World War II.

5. **INFORMATIVE/EXPLANATORY** President Roosevelt called December 7 "a date which will live in infamy." Write a paragraph explaining what you think he meant by this statement.

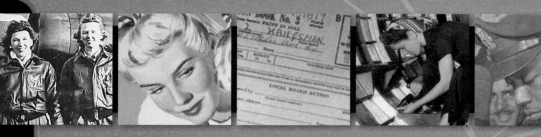

netw⊙rks

There's More Online!

☑ **GRAPHIC ORGANIZER**
New Roles for Men and Women

☑ **SLIDE SHOW**
Minority Forces of World War II

☑ **VIDEO**

Lesson 3
On the Home Front

ESSENTIAL QUESTION *Why does conflict develop?*

IT MATTERS BECAUSE
Getting ready for and fighting World War II brought out the best in the people of the United States.

The United States Prepares

GUIDING QUESTION *How did the United States change its economy to provide supplies for the war effort?*

The Japanese attack on Pearl Harbor united Americans. With great speed, the nation and its people prepared to fight.

Building the Military

Even before Pearl Harbor, the United States had been building up its military with the Selective Service Act. Now that the country was at war, more than 15 million more Americans entered the armed services as volunteers or draftees.

Recruits had to pass a physical exam to enter military service. Then they got uniforms and equipment. Clothing was labeled "G.I." for "Government Issue." In this way, U.S. soldiers came to be called "GIs."

New GIs went through basic training for eight weeks. They learned to handle weapons, read maps, set up tents, and dig trenches. They also learned to work as a team.

For the first time, large numbers of women served in the military. About 250,000 served in the WAC (Women's Army Corps), the WAVES (Women Appointed for Volunteer Emergency Service in the navy), and women's units in the Marines, Coast Guard, and Army Air Corps. Women did not fight in combat, but

(l) US Air Force Museum, (c) Superstock, (c) Wikimedia, (c)(l) Library of Congress

Taking Notes: *Describing*

As you read, use a diagram like this one to describe the new roles adopted by American men and women during World War II.

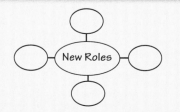

New Roles

Content Vocabulary
• **ration**
• **civil defense**
• **internment camp**

their work was vital to the war effort. Most worked in military offices or as nurses. Some served as Women's Air Force Service Pilots (WASPs). WASPs flew airplanes to and from bases for repair. They also served as co-pilots on night searchlight missions, flew weather planes, and performed many other tasks.

A Changing Economy

Equipping the troops required changes to the nation's economy. The government set up new agencies to speed the preparations for war. For example, the National War Labor Board helped settle labor disputes that could slow down war production. The War Production Board supervised the change from peacetime industries to war production. It helped automakers **shift** from making cars to building trucks, jeeps, tanks, and planes. By the summer of 1942, almost all major industries and some 200,000 companies had changed over to war production.

Women rushed to join the work force, laboring on assembly lines that turned out tanks and airplanes. Eventually, 2.5 million women worked in shipyards, aircraft factories, and other manufacturing plants. Although most women left the factories after the war, their efforts changed American attitudes about women in the workplace.

Funding the War

The United States spent more than $320 billion on the war effort—10 times the spending in World War I. To raise money, the government relied on taxes. The Revenue Act of 1942 raised business taxes and required most Americans to pay income tax. Congress approved withholding taxes from workers' paychecks—a practice still in effect today.

The government also borrowed money from ordinary Americans by selling war bonds. A bond is a certificate promising to pay the buyer a set amount at a future date. So, a citizen might pay $75 for a bond that could be cashed in for $100 at a future date. The government gets to use the $75 for a time, and the buyer earns a little money. Movie stars and other celebrities urged people to buy bonds to support the war effort.

About 2,000 women were accepted into the Women's Air Force Service Pilots. Thirty-eight WASPs lost their lives serving the country.

✓ PROGRESS CHECK

Explaining What was the purpose of the War Production Board?

US Air Force Museum

Academic Vocabulary

shift to move

GUIDING QUESTION *How did Americans help the war effort?*

Americans who remained at home provided food and shelter for those in uniform. Civilians—people not in the military—also provided training, equipment, transportation, and medical care.

Making Sacrifices for Victory

The war required sacrifices from most Americans. For example, people had to deal with shortages of products needed for the war effort. Government **rationed** these products, meaning consumers could buy only limited numbers or amounts of them. People got government-issued ration stamps, which allowed them to buy their limited share of gas, tires, shoes, sugar, coffee, meat, and other goods.

Many Americans had to face a much more serious sacrifice— separation from a family member serving **overseas.** Those at home lived in dread of getting the news that a loved one had been wounded, captured, or killed.

Helping in Many Ways

Despite the hardships, people found creative ways to help the war effort. Many planted "victory gardens" to grow vegetables and ease food shortages. Children collected scrap metal for industry.

Many people took part in **civil defense**—protective measures taken in case of attack. Volunteer spotters scanned the skies for possible enemy aircraft. Coastal cities enforced blackouts at night so that lights could not serve as beacons for enemy pilots. Meanwhile, the Office of War Information promoted patriotism to unite Americans behind the war effort.

Women at Work

Even for women who did not join the military, life changed. As you have read, millions stepped in to fill the jobs of men who went to war. An ad campaign featuring "Rosie the Riveter" encouraged women to

The government issued books of ration stamps, which people used to buy their share of food, gasoline, and other necessities.

▶ **CRITICAL THINKING**
Making Connections What do you think the poster below says about the role of children in World War II?

"Even a little can help a lot -*NOW*"

Buy U.S. WAR STAMPS *and* BONDS

ILLUSTRATION COURTESY OF LADIES' HOME JOURNAL

(t) Hulton Archive/Getty Images, (b) Superstock

Reading HELPDESK CCSS

ration to make scarce items available to people on a limited basis
civil defense protective measures taken by civilians in case of attack

Academic Vocabulary

overseas across the ocean

take these jobs. Many had never worked outside their homes. Sybil Lewis, a riveter for Lockheed Aircraft in Los Angeles, gave this description of her wartime job:

66 The women worked in pairs. I was the riveter and this big, strong, white girl from a cotton farm in Arkansas worked as the bucker. The riveter used a gun to shoot rivets through the metal and fasten it together. The bucker used a bucking bar on the other side of the metal to smooth out the rivets. Bucking was harder than shooting rivets; it required more muscle. Riveting required more skill. 99

—from "Rosie the Riveter"

African Americans

The war also changed attitudes about minority groups. About 1 million African Americans served in World War II. At first, most received low-level assignments and served only in segregated units. In 1942, however, the army began training whites and African Americans together. African Americans began to fill combat assignments in 1944.

African Americans made key contributions in combat. For example, pilots trained at the Tuskegee Army Air Field—the Tuskegee Airmen—destroyed more than 250 enemy planes. One unit's commander, Benjamin Davis, Jr., later became the first African American general in the Air Force. His father, Benjamin Davis, Sr., was the first African American general in the army.

During the war, women worked at jobs traditionally held by men. These women are working on a section of a B-17F bomber aircraft—a "Flying Fortress."

Though forced to serve in segregated units, African Americans served courageously. These members of the famed Tuskegee Airmen served in Italy.

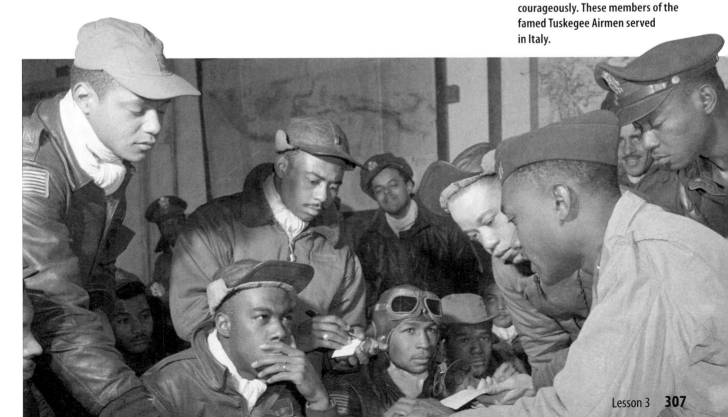

Outside of the military, African Americans also sought change. In 1941, labor leader A. Philip Randolph demanded that the government outlaw job discrimination in American defense industries. In response, President Roosevelt signed an executive order creating the Fair Employment Practices Committee. The order states, "There shall be no discrimination in the employment of workers in defense industries or government because of race, creed, color, or national origin."

Native Americans

Thousands of Native Americans worked in defense industries or served in the armed forces. Ira Hayes of the Pima tribe became a hero in the battle for Iwo Jima in the Pacific. A special group of Navajo formed a unit called the "code talkers." They used a code based on the Navajo language to send vital military messages about troop movement and battle plans. The Japanese never broke this code.

Latinos

Hundreds of thousands of Latinos served in the United States military. In fact, 13 Mexican Americans won the Medal of Honor, the nation's highest military medal. Mercedes Cubría of Cuba became the first Latina woman officer in the Women's Army Corps. Horacio Rivero of Puerto Rico became the first Latino four-star admiral to serve in the United States Navy since Civil War hero David Farragut.

Latinos also contributed at home. Prompted by the wartime need for labor, U.S. labor agents recruited thousands of farm and railroad workers from Mexico. This effort, called the *Bracero*

Starting in World War II, the Mexican government helped provide the United States with a temporary supply of workers—*braceros*. Under the *Bracero* Program (1942–1964), millions of Mexican workers were contracted to work in the United States.

Bettmann/CORBIS

Reading **HELP**DESK **CCSS**

internment camp camp where Japanese Americans were kept during World War II

(brah•SEHR•oh) Program, encouraged emigration from Mexico. Like African Americans, Mexican Americans suffered from discrimination. In spite of their contributions, they were not welcomed in some cities.

Japanese Americans

As the war progressed, second-generation Japanese Americans served in the 100th Infantry Battalion and the 442nd Regimental Combat team. Together, these units became the most decorated in the history of the U.S. military.

U.S. Internment Camps

Japanese Americans won glory on the battlefield, but they faced trouble at home. Some military and political leaders worried what Japanese Americans would do if Japan invaded the United States. As a result, President Roosevelt ordered the relocation of more than 100,000 Japanese Americans living on the West Coast. The army forced them to move to **internment** (ihn•TUHRN•muhnt) **camps,** which were crowded and uncomfortable.

Most Japanese Americans were forced to stay in the camps for three years. Some lost businesses and homes.

Some Americans disagreed with the internment. The Supreme Court, however, upheld the order in a 1944 case, *Korematsu* v. *United States*. Only in 1988 did the United States acknowledged the injustice. Congress issued an apology and gave each survivor $20,000 as a token of the nation's regret.

✔ **PROGRESS CHECK**

Explaining What was the purpose of the *Bracero* Program?

LESSON 3 REVIEW

Review Vocabulary

1. Write a sentence that uses the following terms to describe the home front during the war.

  a. ration **b.** civil defense

2. Use the term *internment camp* in a sentence that explains the term's meaning.

Answer the Guiding Questions

3. *Identifying* What kinds of sacrifices did American civilians make during wartime?

4. *Analyzing* Explain why some consumer goods were in short supply during the war.

5. *Summarizing* Besides living with rationing of goods, in what ways did American men, women, and children support the war effort at home?

6. **ARGUMENT** Decide how you feel about the detention of Japanese Americans during the war. Then write a persuasive paragraph to convince a reader to agree with your point of view on this issue.

networks

There's More Online!

☑ **BIOGRAPHY**
  • Audie Murphy
  • Ruby Bradley

☑ **GRAPHIC ORGANIZER**
  Events in North Africa

☑ **MAP**
  • D-Day
  • Major Battles, European Theater

☑ **PRIMARY SOURCE**
  Kristallnacht

☑ **SLIDE SHOW** The Holocaust

☑ **VIDEO**

Lesson 4
The European Theater of War

ESSENTIAL QUESTION *Why does conflict develop?*

IT MATTERS BECAUSE

With a determined effort, the Allies stopped the Axis Powers in Europe—but not before the Nazis murdered millions in the Holocaust.

Focusing on the Nazi Threat

GUIDING QUESTION *What strategies allowed for a successful campaign against the Axis Powers in North Africa?*

After Pearl Harbor, the United States joined Great Britain, the Soviet Union, and 23 other nations in the war against the Axis Powers. Although Japan was taking territories in the Pacific, the Allies decided to **concentrate** on defeating Hitler first. The situation in the "European Theater" was at a critical point. Axis armies occupied most of Europe and much of North Africa. They were also threatening the Soviet Union. If Hitler's armies won there, Germany might be unstoppable.

Setting a Strategy

Stalin wanted the Allies to cross the English Channel and attack Hitler's forces in Europe. This move would force Hitler to pull back forces that were pounding the Soviet Union. Churchill argued that the United States and Britain were not ready for such a fight. He wanted to attack the edges of Germany's empire, and Roosevelt agreed. As a result, the Allies made plans to invade North Africa. This invasion would give U.S. troops combat experience while helping take pressure off British forces already in Egypt.

(l and r) Time & Life Pictures/Getty Images, (cl) AFP/Getty Images, (c) ilian/Alamy Images, (cr) NY Daily News via Getty Images

---

Reading **HELP**DESK (CCSS)

Taking Notes: *Determining Cause and Effect*

Fill in a pyramid like the one shown with events that led to the Allied victory in North Africa.

Allied Victory

Content Vocabulary
• siege
• genocide
• Holocaust
• concentration camp

Academic Vocabulary
concentrate to focus

Allied Success in North Africa

German Field Marshal Erwin Rommel led the Axis forces in North Africa. His success in desert warfare had already earned him the nickname "Desert Fox." In November 1942, however, the British beat Rommel at the battle of El Alamein (ehl ah•luh•MAYN) in Egypt.

The victory gave a boost to Allied morale. It also stopped the Germans from taking the Suez Canal, a key supply route. Still, Rommel's forces remained a threat in North Africa.

Medics used blood plasma to help keep the wounded alive until they could be removed from the battlefield and taken to a hospital. Here a medic treats a soldier hit by shrapnel in Italy.

Soon after El Alamein, U.S. and British forces under the command of U.S. General Dwight D. Eisenhower landed in Morocco and Algeria, in the western part of North Africa. This force moved east while British forces moved west from Egypt. They closed in on Rommel and, in May 1943, drove the Germans out of North Africa.

The Allies Attack Italy

After victory in North Africa, the Allies moved into southern Europe. They took the island of Sicily and landed on Italy's mainland in September 1943. Once more, Eisenhower organized and directed the invasion. U.S. General George Patton and British General Bernard Montgomery led the troops.

As the Allies advanced, the Italians forced dictator Benito Mussolini from power. Italy's new government then surrendered to the Allies. However, German forces in Italy fought on. Finally, in June 1944, the Allies took Rome, Italy's capital.

Meanwhile, the Allies launched air attacks on Germany. Day and night, bombs battered factories and cities and killed thousands. Still Germany fought on.

✔ PROGRESS CHECK

Explaining Why did the Allies invade North Africa first instead of Europe?

Build Vocabulary: *Multiple Meaning Words*

Tense as an adjective means "anxious" or "on edge." As a term in grammar, *tense* refers to a verb inflection, such as present, past, or future.

**Audie Murphy
(1924–1971)**

Audie Murphy, the orphaned son of Texas sharecroppers, joined the army only after the Marines would not accept him because of his small size. By the end of the war, he was the most decorated combat soldier of World War II. His motto was: "You lead from the front."

**Ruby Bradley
(1907–2002)**

About 440 U.S. women serving in the military died during World War II. Eighty-eight were taken as prisoners of war. Colonel Ruby Bradley is the nation's most decorated military woman. During World War II, she was a prisoner of war for 37 months.

▶ **CRITICAL THINKING**
Drawing Conclusions What qualities do you think Murphy and Bradley shared in common?

The Allies Take Control in Europe

GUIDING QUESTION *How did the two-front war fought by the Allies lead to the defeat of the Axis Powers?*

While British and U.S. forces fought German troops in North Africa and Italy, Soviets and Germans battled on Soviet soil. For months, the Soviets bore the brunt of Germany's war machine.

The Soviets Defend the Eastern Front

After invading the Soviet Union in June 1941, German troops advanced on Leningrad. This major city was a military center and a symbol of the Soviet state. The citizens of Leningrad joined Red Army troops in defending the city. The Germans then began a **siege** (SEEJ), or military blockade, of Leningrad. The siege lasted nearly 900 days. As food ran out, hundreds of thousands of people died. Still the Soviets refused to surrender. In early 1944, Soviet troops finally broke the siege.

German forces also attacked other Soviet cities. In 1941 they approached the capital city, Moscow. Heavy losses and wintry weather slowed the Germans. They finally reached Moscow before a Soviet counterattack forced them to retreat.

Then, in 1942, the Germans targeted the industrial city of Stalingrad. After the Germans had taken most of the city, the Soviets struck back. They surrounded the city and cut off German supply lines. Cold and starving, the few surviving Germans finally surrendered in February 1943.

The German defeat at Stalingrad was devastating. It marked a major turning point in the war. From that point on, the Soviets were on the attack. German forces were in full retreat.

D-Day

After Stalingrad, the Soviets were pushing toward Germany from the east. Meanwhile, Allied forces under General Eisenhower prepared for Operation Overlord, the invasion of occupied Europe. Eisenhower later wrote of the **tense** days of preparation: "All southern England was one vast military camp, crowded with soldiers awaiting final word to go."

June 6, 1944, was D-Day. Ships carried troops and equipment across the English Channel to the French region of Normandy. Planes dropped paratroopers into areas around the beaches.

At dawn, guns on Allied warships opened fire. Thousands of shells rained down on the beaches, which were code-named

(t) Bettmann/CORBIS, (b) AP Images

Reading **HELP**DESK (CCSS)

siege military blockade

Academic Vocabulary
tense anxious

Build Vocabulary: *Multiple Meaning Words*
Tense as an adjective means "anxious" or "on edge." As a term in grammar, *tense* refers to a verb inflection, such as present, past, or future.

D-Day June 6, 1944

UNITED KINGDOM

Southampton
Portsmouth
Shoreham–by–Sea
Dover
Calais
Boulogne
Strait of Dover
Portland
Dartmouth
Utah
Omaha
Gold
Juno
Sword
Channel
English
Cherbourg
Dieppe
FRANCE
Le Havre
Rouen
Saint-Lô
Caen
Normandy
Seine River

2°E
50°N
0°
4°W
2°W

Allied territory
Axis territory
British troops
Canadian troops
U.S. troops
Airborne and glider landing zones force
Major German fortification

0 — 250 miles
0 — 250 km
Lambert Azimuthal Equal-Area projection

N
W   E
S

"Utah," "Omaha," "Gold," "Sword," and "Juno." After the barrage, troops waded ashore from landing craft. They faced land mines and fierce fire from the Germans. Resistance was especially fierce at Omaha beach.

The bloodshed was horrifying. More than 9,000 Allied troops were killed or wounded on that first day. Most troops made it through, however. Nearly 35,000 U.S. soldiers came ashore at Omaha and another 23,000 at Utah. More than 75,000 British and Canadian soldiers landed at Gold, Juno, and Sword and began moving inland as well. At great cost, the invasion had succeeded.

Within a few weeks, the Allies landed 1 million troops. These soldiers pushed across France, driving the Germans back. On August 25, French and American soldiers marched through joyful crowds to free the city of Paris from the German army.

Victory in Europe

In the fall of 1944, Germany fought for survival. Soviet forces pushed from the east, and U.S. and British forces came from the west. The advance was so fast that many believed the war would soon end. In December of that year, however, the Germans attacked along a 50-mile (80 km) front in Belgium. As their troops advanced, they pushed back the Allies, creating a bulge in their lines. The attack became known as the Battle of the Bulge. It took weeks of hard fighting, but the Allies eventually pushed back the Germans. Then they headed into Germany.

The Germans were also losing ground in the East. The Soviets drove them from Russia, into Poland, and then into Germany. By February 1945, Soviet troops stood just outside Berlin. Hitler realized his fight was hopeless. On April 30 he committed suicide.

GEOGRAPHY CONNECTION

D-Day required tens of thousands of Allied troops and thousands of ships and planes.

1 MOVEMENT What did Allied troops cross to reach Normandy?

2 CRITICAL THINKING
Explaining Why was planning so critical to the success of the invasion?

British Prime Minister Winston Churchill popularized the "V for Victory" sign during World War II.

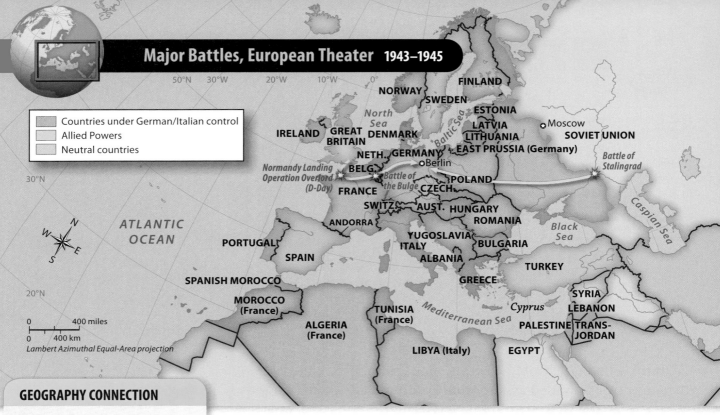

Major Battles, European Theater 1943–1945

Countries under German/Italian control
Allied Powers
Neutral countries

NORWAY SWEDEN FINLAND
ESTONIA
North Sea LATVIA Moscow
IRELAND GREAT BRITAIN DENMARK LITHUANIA SOVIET UNION
NETH. GERMANY EAST PRUSSIA (Germany) Battle of Stalingrad
Normandy Landing Operation Overlord (D-Day) BELG. Berlin Battle of the Bulge POLAND
FRANCE CZECH.
SWITZ. AUST. HUNGARY
ANDORRA ROMANIA Black Sea
PORTUGAL YUGOSLAVIA BULGARIA
SPAIN ITALY ALBANIA Caspian Sea
SPANISH MOROCCO GREECE TURKEY
MOROCCO (France) TUNISIA (France) Mediterranean Sea SYRIA LEBANON
ALGERIA (France) Cyprus PALESTINE TRANS-JORDAN
LIBYA (Italy) EGYPT

ATLANTIC OCEAN

400 miles
400 km
Lambert Azimuthal Equal-Area projection

GEOGRAPHY CONNECTION

Fighting in Europe took place along two main fronts.

1 LOCATION What was the target of the Allied forces coming from the east and west?

2 CRITICAL THINKING
Explaining Why were the Battle of the Bulge and the Battle of Stalingrad decisive losses for Germany?

Germany signed an unconditional surrender on May 7. This ended the war in Europe. The Allies declared May 8 V-E Day for "Victory in Europe."

President Roosevelt did not live to share the joy of victory. While on vacation in Warm Springs, Georgia, he died unexpectedly on April 12, 1945. The death of the man who had led the United States for 12 difficult years saddened the American people. Vice President Harry S. Truman became president.

✔ **PROGRESS CHECK**

Explaining Why was the Battle of the Bulge an important Allied victory?

The Holocaust

GUIDING QUESTION *What is the Holocaust, and how did it begin?*

As the Allies freed German-held areas, they discovered the full extent of Nazi cruelty. During the war, the Nazis had developed what they called the "final solution." This "solution" was **genocide** (JEH•nuh•syd)—wiping out an entire group of people. About two-thirds of Europe's Jews—6 million people— were murdered in the **Holocaust** (HAH•luh•kawst). Millions of

Reading **HELP**DESK CCSS

genocide attempt to kill an entire population, such as an ethnic group

Holocaust the name given to the mass slaughter of Jews by the Nazis during World War II

others—Slavs, Roma (Gypsies), communists, homosexuals, and people with handicaps—were also killed, though Jews were the only group singled out for total extermination.

Persecution of Germany's Jews

Ever since Hitler gained power in 1933, the Nazis had persecuted the Jews of Germany. They first quickly deprived Jews of many rights that all Germans had long taken for granted. In September 1935, the Nuremberg laws removed citizenship from Jewish Germans and banned marriage between Jews and other Germans. Other laws kept Jews from voting, holding public office, and employing non-Jewish Germans. Later, Jews were banned from owning businesses and practicing law and medicine. With no source of income, life became difficult for Jews in Germany.

By the end of the decade, Nazi actions against the Jews became more violent. On the night of November 9, 1938, the Nazis burned Jewish places of worship, destroyed Jewish shops, and killed many Jews. About 30,000 Jewish men were sent to **concentration** (kahn·suhn·TRAY·shuhn) **camps,** large prison camps used to hold people for political reasons.

The Persecution Spreads

During World War II, the Nazis terrorized and abused Jews in each of the lands they conquered. They forced Jews to identify themselves by wearing a yellow, six-pointed star on their clothing. The mass killing of Jews began when the German army invaded the Soviet Union in 1941. Special Nazi forces carried out these murders. They rounded up thousands of Jews, shooting them and throwing them into mass graves. Josef Perl, who survived a massacre of Czech Jews, wrote of the act:

PRIMARY SOURCE

" We marched into a forest where a huge long ditch was already dug. . . . I could hear . . . a machine gun going. . . . All of a sudden, . . . I saw my mother and four sisters lined up and before I had a chance to say, 'Mother!' they were already dead. Somehow time stands still. . . . But what woke me was the sight of my five nieces and nephews being marched, and the murderers had the audacity to ask them to hold hands. . . . I would have been almost the next one but all of a sudden the bombers came over, we were ordered to lay face downwards, but everyone started running. . . . and I . . . ran deep into the forest."

—from *Remembering: Voices of the Holocaust*

concentration camp large prison camp used to hold people for political reasons

The events of November 9, 1938, came to be known as *Kristallnacht*—the night of shattered glass—because of the Jewish shop windows broken by Nazi mobs.

TEXT: Excerpt from Josef Perl in Remembering Voices of the Holocaust by Lyn Smith. Copyright © 2005 Carroll &Graf Publishers, New York. PHOTO: Getty Images

Nazi troops crammed thousands more into railroad cars like cattle, depositing them in concentration camps, such as Buchenwald (BOO•kuhn•vahlt) in Germany. Guards took the prisoners' belongings, shaved their heads, and tattooed camp numbers on their arms. Prisoners often had only a crust of bread or watery soup to eat. Hundreds of thousands became sick and died.

The Final Solution

In January 1942, the Nazis agreed on what they called the "final solution" to destroy the Jews. They built death camps, such as those at Auschwitz (OWSH•vihtz) and Treblinka in Poland. At these camps, many people died in poison gas chambers. Others died of starvation. Still others were victims of cruel experiments carried out by Nazi doctors. Of the estimated 1.6 million people who died at Auschwitz, about 1.3 million were Jews.

Upon arrival at a death camp, healthy prisoners were chosen for slave labor. The elderly, disabled, sick, and mothers and children were sent to poison gas chambers, after which their bodies were burned in giant furnaces.

The Allies discovered German concentration camps, where Jews and others were murdered.

AFP/Getty Images

Reading **HELP**DESK (CCSS)

Build Vocabulary: *Word Origins*

The word *holocaust* comes from ancient Greek words *holos*, which means "whole," and *kaustos*, which means "burnt." It once referred to sacrifices burned as part of religious services. It came to mean widespread destruction.

Although information about the unfolding Holocaust had reached western leaders well before 1945, Allied forces moving through Germany and Poland after V-E Day saw the unspeakable horrors of the camps firsthand. British soldier Peter Coombs described the survivors in a camp:

PRIMARY SOURCE

" One has to see their emaciated faces, their slow staggering gait and feeble movements. . . . they are dying and nothing can save them. Their end is inescapable. They are too far gone to live. "

—from *Crime Through Time*

People around the world were stunned by this terrible result of Nazi tyranny. Allied governments, however, had evidence of the death camps as early as 1942. Historians today debate why and how an event as horrifying as the Holocaust could have occurred. They also discuss why so relatively little was done to stop it.

In Remembrance

The United States Holocaust Memorial Museum is located near the National Mall in Washington, D.C. This memorial provides a national mark of respect for all victims of Nazi persecution.

In 2004 the National World War II Memorial opened on a site on the National Mall. This memorial is dedicated to the 16 million who served in the military, the more than 400,000 who died, and the men and women who supported the war effort on the home front.

☑ **PROGRESS CHECK**

Identifying What groups did the Nazi government victimize?

Thinking Like a
HISTORIAN

Drawing Inferences and Conclusions

The Nazis forced Jews to wear badges such as this on their clothing. The word *Jude* is German for "Jew." Why do you think the Nazis would make Jews identify themselves in this way? For more about drawing inferences and conclusions, review *Thinking Like a Historian.*

ilian / Alamy

LESSON 4 REVIEW (CCSS)

Review Vocabulary

1. Use the following terms in a paragraph to explain their meanings.

   a. genocide **b.** concentration camp

   c. Holocaust

2. Use the term *siege* in a sentence about the Battle of Stalingrad.

Answer the Guiding Questions

3. *Explaining* When the United States joined the Allies, why did the Allies concentrate first on defeating Hitler?

4. *Identifying* What was the significance of Operation Overlord?

5. *Describing* What was the Nazis' "final solution"?

6. *Summarizing* What strategies did the Allies pursue in Europe and Africa to defeat the Axis Powers in World War II?

7. **NARRATIVE** Write about D-Day from the point of view of a reporter covering his or her first battle. Use sensory words. What do you see, hear, smell, and feel?

Night

by Elie Wiesel

Elie Wiesel (1928–) was fifteen years old when he and his family were sent to Auschwitz by the Nazis. His mother and younger sister died there. The Germans later transported Elie and his father to Buchenwald, where his father died shortly before the camp was liberated in April 1945.

Elie Wiesel is a survivor of the Holocaust. He was imprisoned in Birkenau, Auschwitz, Buna, Gleiwitz, and finally liberated from Buchenwald. In *Night,* Wiesel shares his experiences so that people may better understand what life was like during the Holocaust. In the excerpt on the next page, Wiesel tells about one frightening experience in a concentration camp.

Elie Wiesel (above) appears in the second row of bunks, seventh from the left, next to the vertical beam.

> 66 *The searchlights came on. Hundreds of SS [Nazi guards] appeared out of the darkness, accompanied by police dogs. The snow continued to fall.* 99

—from *Night*

" Two o'clock in the afternoon. The snow continued to fall heavily.

Now the hours were passing quickly. Dusk had fallen. Daylight disappeared into a gray mist.

Suddenly the *Blockältests* remembered that we had forgotten to clean the **block**. He commanded four prisoners to mop the floor. . .One hour before leaving camp! Why? For whom?

"For the liberating army," he told us. "Let them know that here lived men and not pigs."

So we were men after all? The block was cleaned from top to bottom.

At six o'clock the bell rang. The death **knell** (NEHL). The funeral. The procession was beginning its march.

"Fall in! Quickly!"

In a few moments, we stood in ranks. Block by block. Night had fallen. Everything was happening according to plan.

The searchlights came on. Hundreds of SS [Nazi guards] appeared out of the darkness, accompanied by police dogs. The snow continued to fall.

The gates of the camp opened. It seemed as though an even darker night was waiting for us on the other side.

The first blocks began to march. We waited. We had to await the exodus of the fifty-six blocks that preceded us. It was very cold. In my pocket, I had two pieces of bread. How I would have liked to eat them! But I know I must not. Not yet.

Our turn was coming: Block 53 . . . Block 55 . . .

"Block 57, forward! March!"

It snowed on and on. "

Literary Element: *Imagery*

Imagery is the use of words that appeal to the senses (sight, hearing, touch, smell, and taste) to help readers form a mental picture of the scene. As you read, look for words that describe specific details—a color, a sound, an action, a feeling—anything that stirs your senses. Think about the mental pictures that form when you read the words.

Vocabulary

block a large building used to house prisoners

knell sound of a bell rung slowly as an indication of the end of something

Analyzing Literature DBQ

1 *Explaining* Why did the head of the block order four prisoners to wash the wooden floor?

2 *Analyzing* How does the author use imagery? Use examples from the text to support your answer.

3 *Interpreting* Although this excerpt covers only part of one night in the life of Elie Wiesel, what does it reveal about his and the other men's lives?

netw⦿rks

There's More Online!

☑ **BIOGRAPHY** Ira Hayes

☑ **GRAPHIC ORGANIZER**
Events on the Pacific Front

☑ **MAP** War in the Pacific

☑ **PRIMARY SOURCE**
The Atomic Bomb

Lesson 5
The War in the Pacific

ESSENTIAL QUESTION *Why does conflict develop?*

IT MATTERS BECAUSE

Allied victories forced the Japanese to surrender unconditionally, ending World War II.

The Pacific Front

GUIDING QUESTION *What events occurred on the Pacific front?*

As Japanese were attacking Pearl Harbor, they were bombing U.S. airfields in the Philippines as well. Japanese bombers also hit the islands of Wake and Guam—key U.S. bases in the Pacific.

In the days that followed, Japanese troops invaded Thailand and Malaya. They captured Guam, Wake Island, and Hong Kong.

In mid-December, Japanese troops landed in the Philippines. They quickly captured the capital of Manila and forced General Douglas MacArthur's American and Filipino troops to retreat. MacArthur's troops moved to the Bataan Peninsula, west of Manila, and to the small island of Corregidor.

The Japanese Take the Philippines

For months battles raged on Bataan. On April 9, 1942, the exhausted Allied troops finally surrendered. The forces defending Corregidor held out for another month.

The Japanese forced the prisoners of Bataan—many sick and near starvation—to march to a prison camp more than 60 miles (97 km) away. About 76,000 prisoners began what became known as the Bataan Death March. Only about 54,000 prisoners reached the camp. As survivor Marion Lawton recalled:

(l) Bettmann/CORBIS, (cl) AP Images, (c) CORBIS, (cr and r) Getty Images

Reading **HELP**DESK (CCSS)

Taking Notes: *Sequencing*

On a time line like this one, track the important events on the Pacific front in 1945.

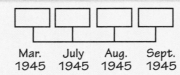

Mar. July Aug. Sept.
1945 1945 1945 1945

Content Vocabulary

• **island hopping**
• **kamikaze**

“ We'd march all day, a continuous plodding along, just trying to keep up. I always tried to stay in the middle of the column rather than on the flanks. That way I was further away . . . and might avoid a . . . beating. I don't know how to explain a typical day except that it was brutal, exhausting, hot, and your feet and legs just ached. ”

—from *Death March: The Survivors of Bataan*

Several weeks before American and Filipino troops surrendered, President Roosevelt ordered MacArthur to leave the Philippines and go to Australia. MacArthur told the Filipinos, "I shall return."

The Island Hopping Strategy

With every Japanese victory in the Pacific, American morale sank. Then, in April 1942, U.S. airplanes from an aircraft carrier in the Pacific bombed Tokyo. The daring raid, led by Lieutenant Colonel James "Jimmy" Doolittle, did little real damage to Japan. It did, however, lift Americans' spirits.

More meaningful victories would soon follow. In May 1942, U.S. battleships defeated a Japanese fleet in the Battle of the Coral Sea. The following month, the United States scored an even greater victory. In the Battle of Midway, northwest of Hawaii, the navy destroyed four Japanese aircraft carriers and hundreds of airplanes. In a war fought mainly among scattered islands in a wide ocean, Japan's losses at Midway were crippling.

Filipino and American prisoners of war make the Death March from Bataan.

Now the United States prepared to go on the offensive against Japan. The U.S. commanders—General MacArthur and Admiral Chester Nimitz—chose a strategy known as **island hopping.** It meant that they would attack and capture key islands. These islands would become bases from which to attack others. In this way, the Allies would move ever closer to the Philippines—and to Japan.

Between August 1942 and February 1943, U.S. forces fought for control of Guadalcanal, one of the Solomon Islands. The Japanese put up stiff resistance. After intense fighting, U.S. forces were able to **secure** the island.

In June 1944, U.S. forces captured Guam and other nearby islands. Guam gave U.S. bombers a base from which they could reach targets in Japan. In October, U.S. ships destroyed most of the Japanese fleet at the Battle of Leyte Gulf in the Philippines.

On Toward Japan

U.S. forces were closing in on Japan. In March 1945, they seized the island of Iwo Jima and in June the island of Okinawa. These victories brought the Allies within easy reach of Japan itself. The battles were very costly, however. Thousands of Americans died in the fighting. Many thousands more were wounded.

By this point, the Allies had destroyed most of Japan's air force and navy. U.S. bombers pounded Tokyo and other Japanese cities. In desperation, the Japanese unleashed suicide pilots— **kamikazes** (kah·mih·KAH·zee). These pilots crashed their planes into U.S. ships and sank several destroyers during the battle for Okinawa.

☑ **PROGRESS CHECK**

Explaining What is significant about the Battle of Midway?

The Atomic Bomb Ends the War

GUIDING QUESTION *How did the United States's use of the atomic bomb bring about Japan's surrender?*

Iwo Jima and Okinawa showed that even in the face of sure defeat, the Japanese would fight on. Because they refused to surrender, the United States decided to use a powerful new weapon: the atomic bomb.

AP Images

Reading **HELP**DESK

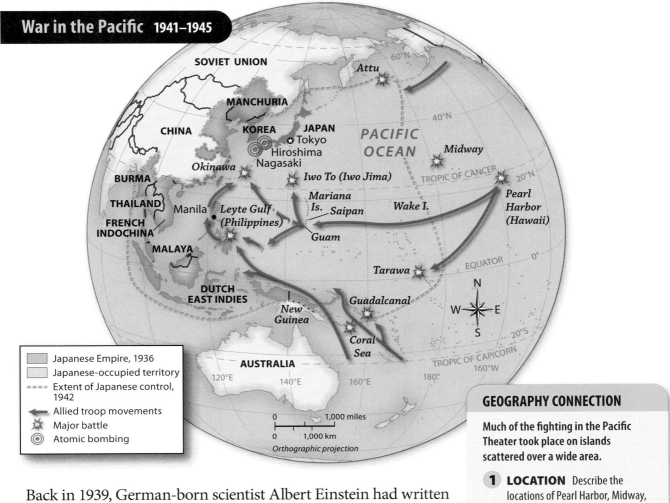

War in the Pacific 1941–1945

Japanese Empire, 1936
Japanese-occupied territory
Extent of Japanese control, 1942
Allied troop movements
Major battle
Atomic bombing

0   1,000 miles
0   1,000 km
Orthographic projection

GEOGRAPHY CONNECTION

Much of the fighting in the Pacific Theater took place on islands scattered over a wide area.

1 **LOCATION** Describe the locations of Pearl Harbor, Midway, and Okinawa.

2 **CRITICAL THINKING**
Drawing Conclusions Why do you think defending Iwo Jima and Okinawa was of vital importance to the Japanese?

Back in 1939, German-born scientist Albert Einstein had written to President Roosevelt. Einstein warned that the Nazis might try to use the energy of the atom to build "extremely powerful bombs." In response, Roosevelt gathered a group of scientists to study the technology. In 1941 this group met with British scientists who were working on the kind of bomb Einstein had described. The British research impressed the American scientists. They urged Roosevelt to start an American atomic bomb program.

President Roosevelt created the top-secret Manhattan Project. In 1942 scientists at the University of Chicago built the world's first nuclear reactor. A nuclear reactor is a device that splits apart atoms, releasing large amounts of energy. The scientists believed that such energy could create a powerful bomb.

They were right. After years of work at a secret laboratory in Los Alamos, New Mexico, another team of scientists and engineers built an atomic bomb. On July 16, 1945, they tested the bomb in the New Mexico desert near a place called Alamogordo.

Build Vocabulary: *Word Origins*

The word *nuclear* is an adjective based on the noun *nucleus*, which means "the center." In this case, "the center" is the center part of an atom. It is the splitting of an atom's nucleus that releases energy and creates an atomic bomb blast.

Connections to — TODAY

Suicide Bombers

Kamikazes were suicide bombers who used planes to blow up ships during World War II. Suicide bombers used planes to blow up buildings in the September 11, 2001, attacks on the United States. In addition, suicide bombers today often use cars and even their own bodies in attacks around the world.

Deciding to Use the A-Bomb

Even as they were testing the atomic bomb, U.S. officials debated how—or whether—to use it. The final decision rested with President Harry S. Truman. He had taken office after President Roosevelt died in April 1945. Truman did not even know the bomb existed until a few weeks before he had to decide whether to use it.

President Truman later wrote that he "regarded the bomb as a military weapon and never had any doubts that it should be used." Truman's advisers warned that if U.S. soldiers had to invade Japan, casualties would be high. Truman believed it was his duty to use every weapon available to save American lives.

Before using the bomb, the Allies warned the Japanese. The Potsdam Declaration promised that if Japan did not surrender, it faced "prompt and utter destruction." Japan ignored the warning, so Truman ordered the use of the atomic bomb.

Japan Surrenders

On August 6, 1945, an American B-29 bomber, the *Enola Gay*, dropped an atomic bomb on the Japanese city of Hiroshima. Three days later, the United States dropped a second atomic bomb on Nagasaki, Japan.

With news of Japan's surrender, Americans everywhere celebrated V-J—Victory over Japan—Day.

Reading **HELP**DESK CCSS

Academic Vocabulary

conflict a war; prolonged struggle

The atomic bombs caused terrible destruction. The first bomb leveled Hiroshima and killed between 80,000 and 120,000 people. The Nagasaki bomb killed between 35,000 and 74,000. Thousands more suffered burns and illness caused by atomic energy.

Faced with this destruction, Japanese Emperor Hirohito said that "the unendurable must be endured." He ordered his government to surrender. August 15, 1945, became V-J Day. Americans expressed happiness and relief that the fighting was over, and sorrow that so many had died. Japan signed the formal surrender on September 2 aboard the battleship *Missouri*. World War II had finally ended.

After the war, Allied authorities put the top Nazi and Japanese leaders on trial for war crimes and crimes against humanity. The Allies held the trials in Nuremberg, Germany, and in Tokyo, Japan.

The Costs of War

World War II was the most destructive **conflict** in history. More than 55 million people died. More than half of the dead were civilians. They perished in bombings or from starvation, disease, torture, and murder. American casualties—about 322,000 dead and 800,000 wounded—were high. However, the losses were light compared with those of other nations. In the Soviet Union alone, at least 18 million people died—perhaps millions more.

The war's survivors faced great challenges. Rebuilding shattered bodies and shattered nations would take time. Reestablishing order in the world would lead to new hopes for peace—and new tensions.

☑ **PROGRESS CHECK**

Describing What was the goal of the Manhattan Project?

THEN

During the war, an atomic bomb turned Nagasaki into a pile of rubble. Today the Japanese people have rebuilt the city.

NOW

▶ CRITICAL THINKING
Speculating Do you think the rebuilding of Nagasaki will alter or affect people's memory of what happened in 1945? Explain.

LESSON 5 REVIEW (CCSS)

Review Vocabulary

1. Use the term *kamikaze* in a sentence to explain its meaning.

Answer the Guiding Questions

2. ***Explaining*** What was the strategy of island hopping, and what was its purpose?

3. ***Describing*** What was the Manhattan Project?

4. ***Analyzing*** Why were the battles on the islands of Iwo Jima and Okinawa significant to the Americans?

5. **NARRATIVE** You are a reporter interviewing General MacArthur about the battle in the Philippines. Write an article about how he felt during the fight and especially how he felt when he had to leave the people behind. Be sure to include his famous quotation in some way.

Write your answers on a separate piece of paper.

1 **Exploring the Essential Question**

INFORMATIVE/EXPLANATORY What strategies allowed the Allies to defeat the Axis Powers in Europe and in the Pacific? Write an essay to answer the question. Use your answers to the Guiding Questions in the lesson reviews to help you organize your ideas.

2 **21st Century Skills**

COMMUNICATING Research recent conflicts in which many people believe genocide is taking or has taken place. Write a research report about what has taken place and who is involved in this conflict. Be sure to discuss some of the lessons learned from the experience of the Holocaust.

3 **Thinking Like a Historian**

ANALYZING AND INTERPRETING INFORMATION How are communities funded in time of need? During World War II, the government sold special bonds to raise money for the war effort. Municipal bonds are sold by states, cities, and counties to raise money, usually for special projects such as building schools, bridges, and roads. Research how bonds are sold and used in your community. How much money will a person make by buying one of the bonds? Present your findings to the class in the form of a poster.

4 **Visual Literacy**

ANALYZING PICTURES This image of five Marines and one sailor raising the American flag on Mount Suribachi on Iwo Jima is one of the most famous photographs in history. Why do you think this photograph had such an impact? Can you think of any other pictures that are as famous and easily identifiable?

CORBIS

REVIEW THE GUIDING QUESTIONS

Choose the best answer for each question.

1 One of the factors that contributed to the rise of European dictators was
   A. American aggression.
   B. the failure of any nation to adopt the League of Nations.
   C. the economic boom of the 1920s.
   D. joblessness and resentment.

2 Great Britain and France declared war on Germany two days after Hitler's army invaded
   F. Lithuania.
   G. Poland.
   H. Belgium.
   I. England.

3 How did the U.S. economy change when the United States entered World War II?
   A. Many women lost their jobs.
   B. African American workers faced discrimination.
   C. Factories shifted to producing materials needed to fight the war.
   D. The military began drafting factory workers.

4 After the Japanese bombed Pearl Harbor, many Japanese Americans were
   F. held prisoner in internment camps.
   G. shipped off to Japan.
   H. forced to work in airplane factories.
   I. welcomed into the White House by President Roosevelt.

5 Who was the German leader in command of Axis forces in North Africa?
   A. Dwight D. Eisenhower
   B. George Patton
   C. Erwin Rommel
   D. Douglas MacArthur

6 The war with Japan ended when the United States
   F. unleashed suicide pilots.
   G. imposed an economic blockade.
   H. offered concessions for surrender.
   I. dropped atomic bombs on Japanese cities.

DBQ ANALYZING DOCUMENTS

In his Annual Message to Congress, January 6, 1941, Roosevelt stated:

"... [W]e are committed to all-inclusive national defense. ... [W]e are committed to full support of all those resolute people everywhere who are resisting aggression. ... By this support we express our determination that the democratic cause shall prevail. ... We ... will never ... acquiesce in [agree to] a peace dictated by aggressors. ... We know that enduring peace cannot be bought at the cost of other people's freedom."

❼ Making Inferences Which statement implies that the United States might give financial aid to countries in war-torn Europe?

A. "We are committed to all-inclusive national defense."

B. "We are committed to full support of all...who are resisting aggression."

C. "We express our determination that the democratic cause shall prevail."

D. "We will never acquiesce in a peace dictated by aggressors."

❽ Drawing Conclusions What does the speech tell you about Roosevelt's view of peacekeeping?

F. We should agree to a peace dictated by aggressors.

G. We should help make every country democratic.

H. The U.S. should not get involved in another country's problems.

I. The U.S. should not settle for a peace dictated by aggressors.

SHORT RESPONSE

In her book *War: The Lethal Custom*, journalist Gwynne Dyer described the week-long bombing of Hamburg, Germany, by the Allies in 1943:

"Practically all the apartment blocks in the firestorm area had underground shelters, but nobody who stayed in them survived; those who were not cremated died of carbon monoxide poisoning. But to venture into the streets was to risk being swept by the wind into the very heart of the firestorm."

❾ Based on this excerpt, who are the victims of this bombing campaign?

❿ How might such a campaign help achieve victory in a war?

EXTENDED RESPONSE

⓫ Informative/Explanatory What role did Harry S. Truman play in ending World War II? Write a one-page newspaper feature about Truman's role.

Need Extra Help?

If You've Missed Question	❶	❷	❸	❹	❺	❻	❼	❽	❾	❿	⓫
Review Lesson	1	2	3	3	4	5	2	2	4	4	4,5

The Cold War Era

1945–1960

ESSENTIAL QUESTIONS • What are the consequences when cultures interact?
• Why do people make economic choices? • Why does conflict develop?
• How do new ideas change the way people live?

◄ Dwight D. Eisenhower went from World War II hero to president of the United States in the 1950s.

CORBIS

netw⚬rks

There's More Online about the Cold War era that followed World War II.

CHAPTER 12

The Story Matters . . .

For American voters in the 1950s, the man who led troops to victory in Europe during World War II is the perfect person to lead the nation in a challenging time of uncertainty and hope. Dwight D. "Ike" Eisenhower inspires trust and calm in a changing world of new opportunities and new dangers.

Twice Eisenhower easily wins election to the presidency. His steady hand helps lead the nation in the early years of the Cold War. You will read more about this era in this chapter.

Place and Time: Europe 1945 to 1960

In the years following World War II, Europe was divided into two parts—one made up of democratic nations friendly to the United States, one under the firm Communist grip of the Soviet Union. This division helped shape American life in the postwar years.

Step Into the Place

MAP FOCUS The line dividing East and West zigged and zagged right through the heart of Europe.

1 PLACE Which country was divided by the line between East and West?

2 REGION Which European countries lay between the Soviet Union and the countries of the West?

3 CRITICAL THINKING *Identifying Central Issues* Why do you think the United States might have been worried about the division of Europe into opposing sides?

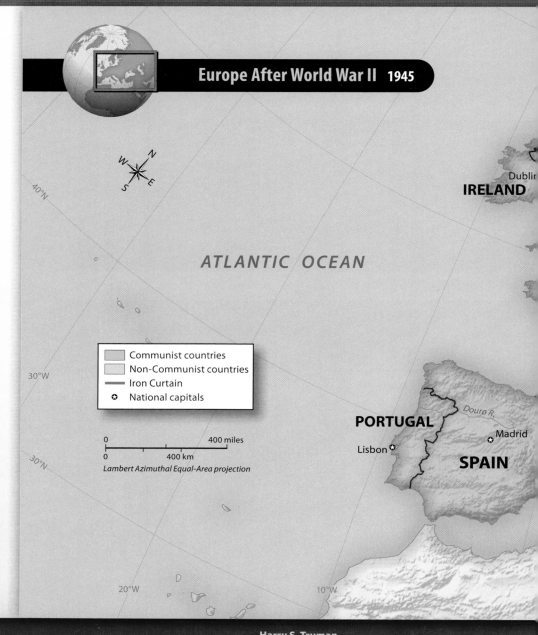

Europe After World War II 1945

ATLANTIC OCEAN

IRELAND
Dublin

Communist countries
Non-Communist countries
Iron Curtain
National capitals

0   400 miles
0   400 km
Lambert Azimuthal Equal-Area projection

PORTUGAL
Lisbon
Douro R.
Madrid
SPAIN

Step Into the Time

TIME LINE Look at the time line. Which event shows that the end of World War II did not lead to lasting world peace?

Harry S. Truman
1945–1953

U.S. PRESIDENTS

U.S. EVENTS

WORLD EVENTS

1945 Franklin Roosevelt dies

1948 Marshall Plan enacted

1944

1948

1945 Yalta Conference sets plans for postwar world

1948 • Soviets blockade West Berlin
• State of Israel is created

networks
There's More Online!

☑ **MAP** Explore the interactive version of this map on NETWORKS.

☑ **TIME LINE** Explore the interactive version of this time line on NETWORKS.

NORWAY
Oslo
SWEDEN
FINLAND
Helsinki
Stockholm
North Sea
UNITED KINGDOM
DENMARK
Copenhagen
Baltic Sea
Moscow
NETHERLANDS
The Hague
ndon
Elbe R.
Berlin
EAST GERMANY
Vistula R.
Warsaw
POLAND
SOVIET UNION
Volga R.
Brussels
Bonn
Oder R.
BELGIUM
Rhine R.
Prague
Don R.
Paris
Seine R.
WEST GERMANY
CZECHOSLOVAKIA
LUXEMBOURG
Dnieper R.
FRANCE
Bern
Vienna
Budapest
WITZERLAND
AUSTRIA
HUNGARY
Rhone R.
Po R.
ROMANIA
Bucharest
Black Sea
Belgrade
Danube R.
Corsica
ITALY
YUGOSLAVIA
Rome
BULGARIA
Sofia
Sardinia
Tiranë
Ankara
ALBANIA
TURKEY
GREECE
Sicily
Athens
20°E
30°E
Mediterranean Sea
Crete
Cyprus

1955 · Polio vaccine becomes available
· Minimum wage increases to $1 an hour

Dwight D. Eisenhower
1953–1961

1956 Federal Highway Act enacted

1954 Senator Joseph McCarthy censured

1952

1956

1960

1950 Korean War begins

1953 Edmund Hillary and Tenzing Norgay climb Mt. Everest

1954 Roger Bannister is first to run one mile in under four minutes

1957 Soviet Union launches *Sputnik*

1959 Fidel Castro comes to power in Cuba

netw⊙rks

There's More Online!

☑ **GRAPHIC ORGANIZER**
Postwar Organizations

☑ **MAP** Berlin Airlift

☑ **SLIDE SHOW**
McCarthy Telegram

☑ **VIDEO**

Lesson 1

Roots of the Cold War

ESSENTIAL QUESTION *What are the consequences when cultures interact?*

IT MATTERS BECAUSE
The tensions that emerged after World War II led to a conflict that dominated U.S. foreign policy for decades.

Wartime Relationships

GUIDING QUESTION *What plans were created for the organization of the postwar world?*

In February 1945, the "Big Three" Allied leaders met at Yalta, a city in the Soviet Union. Franklin D. Roosevelt, Winston Churchill, and Joseph Stalin came to talk about Europe's future after the war.

Roosevelt and Churchill feared the spread of Soviet control in Eastern Europe. Stalin wanted this area as a shield to protect the Soviet Union from the West. Germany's future was another challenging question.

The Allies finally agreed to divide Germany into four zones, each run by an Allied power: the United States, Great Britain, the Soviet Union, and France. Stalin agreed to free elections in Eastern Europe. He also offered help in planning a new international organization. Roosevelt and Churchill felt hopeful about a peaceful postwar world. These hopes were not met.

Founding of the United Nations

On April 12, 1945, President Roosevelt died suddenly. Vice President Harry S. Truman took office. Facing huge challenges, Truman told reporters, "When they told me [of Roosevelt's death], I felt like the moon, the stars, and all the planets had fallen on me."

(l)Bettmann/CORBIS, (c)Hulton-Deutsch Collection/CORBIS, (cr) AFP/Getty Images, (r) The Granger Collection, NYC

Reading **HELP**DESK ⒸⒸⓈⓈ

Taking Notes: *Listing*

As you read, use a diagram like this one to list organizations created after World War II.

New Organizations

Content Vocabulary

• **iron curtain**   • **cold war**   • **perjury**
• **containment**   • **subversion**   • **censure**
• **airlift**   • **espionage**

Truman continued the plans for the international organization discussed at Yalta. On June 26 in San Francisco, California, 50 nations held the first meeting of the United Nations (UN). They all hoped the UN could settle disputes between countries and prevent wars.

Soviet Expansion

The UN could not, however, prevent trouble between the West and the Soviets. It became clear that Stalin would not live up to his Yalta pledge. He set up Communist governments and kept Soviet forces in Eastern Europe. There were no free elections.

Winston Churchill feared Stalin's actions were permanent. In 1946 Churchill said that an **iron curtain** had come down on Europe. The iron curtain cut off much of Eastern Europe from the West. What's more, Churchill thought the Soviets would try to gain control of other parts of the world.

As the war in Europe wound down, Allied leaders met in Yalta to discuss challenging questions about the postwar world. The Soviets would break many of the agreements reached at Yalta.

Bettmann/CORBIS

iron curtain symbolic division between East and West in Europe during the Cold War

To address this threat, Truman turned to U.S. diplomat George F. Kennan. Kennan was an expert on the Soviet Union. He believed the two countries could not **cooperate,** or work together. The United States had to be firm with its new enemy. Kennan called for a policy of **containment** (kuhn•TAYN• muhnt), meaning the United States had to "contain," or hold back, the Soviets. Doing this might require military and nonmilitary actions.

U.S. Responses

The policy of containment soon went into effect. Civil war raged in Greece, as Communists attempted to overthrow the country's pro-Western government. At the same time, the Soviets pressured Turkey to give them naval bases that offered access to the Mediterranean Sea.

In March 1947, Truman asked Congress for money to help aid Greece and Turkey. In his request, Truman promised that the U.S. would help any free nation resisting Communist aggression. This promise came to be called the Truman Doctrine.

A few months later, U.S. Secretary of State George Marshall came up with a plan to aid Western Europe. Many areas were still struggling to recover from World War II. Many people were hungry and unable to work. Unrest was growing. From 1948 to 1951, the Marshall Plan pumped $13 billion worth of supplies, machinery, and food into Western Europe. The aid helped speed recovery and weaken the appeal of communism.

The plight of war refugees, such as this homeless German girl, was a major challenge facing the conquerors of Europe.

 PROGRESS CHECK

Explaining What did the Truman Doctrine and the Marshall Plan work toward?

Crisis in Berlin

GUIDING QUESTION *How did Western Allies respond to Soviet attempts to halt their plans for West Germany?*

After the war, Germany was divided into four zones. The Soviet Union controlled the eastern part of the country. The United States, Britain, and France held zones in the western part. The German capital of Berlin also was divided among the four

Bettmann/CORBIS

Berlin Airlift 1948–1949

American Zone
Soviet Zone
British Zone
Berlin

0   250 miles
0   250 km
Lambert Azimuthal Equal-Area projection

EAST GERMANY

50°N   50°N

WEST GERMANY

American Zone
French Zone

N
W   E
S

◄┼► Air corridor

0°   5°E   20°E
55°N

GEOGRAPHY CONNECTION

Stalin's blockade cut off West Berlin. To reach the city, all planes in the airlift traveled along one of three corridors.

1 MOVEMENT From where did all planes fly into West Berlin during the Berlin Airlift?

2 CRITICAL THINKING
Speculating What might have happened to West Berlin if the Allies had not conducted the airlift?

nations. This city, however, lay deep inside the Soviet zone.

President Truman argued that Germany should be united. Stalin feared that a strong Germany would once again **pose** a threat to the Soviet Union. He wanted to keep Soviet influence in a divided Germany. This disagreement led to a crisis in 1948.

The Berlin Blockade and Airlift

On June 7, 1948, the United States, Britain, and France announced a plan. They would unite their zones to form a new West German nation. It would include the parts of Berlin under Western control, and it would have full Western support.

Threatened by this action, Stalin reacted quickly. On June 24, 1948, Soviet troops lined the edge of West Berlin. They stopped traffic on all land routes into West Berlin. As a result, West Berlin's citizens were cut off from needed supplies. The Soviets hoped the blockade would force the West out of Berlin.

President Truman was clear: "We stay in Berlin, period." Yet the president did not want to risk war by using military force to break the blockade. Instead, the United States and Great Britain organized an **airlift** to save the city. American and British planes began flying food, fuel, and other supplies into West Berlin.

A Divided Germany

The airlift worked. In May 1949, Stalin finally gave in and ended the blockade. By the end of the year, there were two German states. The Federal Republic of Germany (West Germany) was allied with the United States. The German Democratic Republic (East Germany) was a Communist state tied to the Soviet Union. Berlin remained a divided city within East Germany.

☑ **PROGRESS CHECK**

Analyzing Why did the Soviet Union oppose reuniting Germany?

ECONOMICS SKILL

THE BERLIN AIRLIFT

How much food, fuel, clothing, and medicine do 2 million people need? The Berlin blockade prevented all land shipments to West Berlin. It cut off all the businesses in the city. There was no way for the people to buy or sell needed goods. Meeting the needs of the city's people through the air was a gigantic effort. In just over 10 months, the Allies made an incredible 278,000 flights. These flights carried 2 million tons (1.8 million t) of cargo.

1 EXPLAINING Why was the Berlin Airlift necessary?

2 CRITICAL THINKING
Identifying Central Issues
Why was the blocking of road, rail, and water routes into the western part of Berlin such a threat to the city's survival?

The Cold War Deepens

GUIDING QUESTION *How did the United States and the Soviet Union become rivals and influence the world?*

The Berlin crisis was an early battle in a brewing **cold war**—a war without actual combat. Rather than meet on a battlefield, the two sides built up their armed forces and tried to frighten each other.

The Western democracies agreed that military cooperation was the best way to contain the Soviets. In 1949 the United States, Canada, and 10 Western European nations formed the North Atlantic Treaty Organization (NATO). Member states agreed to aid any member that was attacked. Six years later, West Germany was allowed to form an army and join NATO. In 1955 the Soviets responded by setting up the Warsaw Pact, a military alliance of the Communist governments of Eastern Europe.

Independence Movements

The Cold War was just one development on the world scene. At the same time, the old colonial era was coming to a close. Many nations were winning their independence. The Philippines achieved independence from the United States in 1946. In the late 1940s, India, Pakistan, and Burma won freedom from British rule. During the following two decades, more than 25 African nations gained independence. The path to freedom was sometimes bloody. New nations faced the difficult task of building modern societies.

Hulton-Deutsch Collection/CORBIS

Reading **HELP**DESK CCSS

cold war a war in which two enemies do not fight in combat but instead compete and conflict in other ways

subversion attempts to overthrow or undermine a government by working secretly within that government

espionage spying
perjury the crime of lying under oath

The Jewish State of Israel Established

In the Middle East, Jews and Arabs both claimed Palestine, an area the British had controlled. In 1947 the United Nations decided to divide Palestine into independent Jewish and Arab states. The Jews accepted the plan, but the Arabs did not. After declaring independence in 1948, the Jewish state of Israel came under attack by the armies of neighboring Arab countries in the first of six major wars between the Arabs and Israelis.

Communism in China

China was another country undergoing big changes. In 1949 Communist forces under Mao Zedong (MOW DZUH•DUNG) defeated armies led by China's leader Chiang Kai-shek (jee•AYNG KY•SHEHK). Mao Zedong formed a new Communist state, the People's Republic of China. Chiang Kai-shek retreated to the island of Taiwan. The United States treated the government in Taiwan as the true government of all China.

The Soviet Union now had a powerful ally in Asia. It looked as if all of Asia could fall to communism.

Mao Zedong led Communist forces and successfully created the People's Republic of China.

✓ PROGRESS CHECK

Analyzing How did the spread of communism in China affect the Soviet Union?

A New Red Scare

GUIDING QUESTION *How did the Cold War heighten American fears of communism?*

The Cold War increased Americans' fears of Communist **subversion** (suhb•VUHR•zhuhn), or secret attempts to overthrow the government from within. Many Americans worried that Communists—"Reds"—were sneaking into the government. U.S. leaders began probing for evidence of Communist influence in the government.

Spies Revealed

Stories of **espionage** (EHS•pee•uh•nahzh), or spying, gripped the country. In 1948 Whittaker Chambers, a magazine editor, claimed that he had been a Soviet spy. He accused Alger Hiss, a former state department official, of giving him secret U.S. documents. Chambers showed copies of secret information that he said came from Hiss. Hiss was found guilty of **perjury** (PUHR•juh•ree), or lying under oath, and sent to prison.

AFP/Getty Images

This cartoon from 1954 criticizes Senator Joe McCarthy by comparing him to a vandal who recklessly damages property.

The most dramatic spy case involved the atomic bomb. Julius and Ethel Rosenberg, a New York couple, were members of the Communist Party. They were accused of passing secrets about the atomic bomb to the Soviet Union. The Rosenbergs denied the charges but were found guilty and given death sentences. Many believed the Rosenbergs were victims of a Red Scare. Public calls for mercy failed. The Rosenbergs were executed in 1953.

McCarthyism

In 1950 Republican Senator Joseph McCarthy of Wisconsin led the hunt for Communists. McCarthy said a Communist network existed inside the U.S. government. He called government employees to defend themselves against his charges. Many charges were based on little evidence. The word "McCarthyism" came to describe a reckless use of unproven charges.

Still, millions of Americans believed McCarthy. In 1954 McCarthy claimed that Communists had infiltrated the U.S. Army. In a series of hearings, McCarthy hurled charges at respected army officials. Toward the end of the hearings, Joseph Welch, an attorney for the army, challenged McCarthy: "Until this moment, Senator, I think I never really gauged your cruelty or your recklessness. ... Have you left no sense of decency?"

censure to formally criticize

Many Americans came to view McCarthy as a bully with little basis for his accusations. Congress also turned against him. In December 1954, the Senate voted to **censure** (SEN•shuhr), or formally criticize, McCarthy for "conduct unbecoming a senator."

✔ **PROGRESS CHECK**

Analyzing What claims did McCarthy make against U.S. government employees?

The Granger Collection, NYC

LESSON 1 REVIEW CCSS

Review Vocabulary

1. Use the terms *iron curtain, containment,* and *cold war* in a short paragraph that demonstrates your understanding of each term.

2. Use the terms *espionage* and *perjury* in a sentence that demonstrates their meaning.

Answer the Guiding Questions

3. *Identifying* What was the result of the Yalta discussions of creating a postwar international organization?

4. *Summarizing* How did the Western Allies resist the Soviet blockade of West Berlin?

5. *Contrasting* How did the goals of the Soviet Union and the United States differ after World War II?

6. *Evaluating* Why did people criticize Senator Joseph McCarthy's campaign to find Communists in the United States government?

7. **ARGUMENT** Write an essay that might have appeared in a U.S. newspaper during the Cold War arguing in favor of the Marshall Plan.

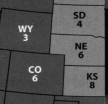

networks

There's More Online!

☑ **BIOGRAPHY**
Margaret Chase Smith

☑ **CHART** Noted Recipients
of the GI Bill

☑ **GRAPHIC ORGANIZER**
Postwar Changes

☑ **MAP**
Election of 1948

☑ **PRIMARY SOURCE**
Margaret Chase Smith Speech

Lesson 2
Early Cold War Politics

ESSENTIAL QUESTION *Why do people make economic choices?*

IT MATTERS BECAUSE
Government efforts to address the economic, political, and social problems of the Cold War era changed the nation.

The Peacetime Economy

GUIDING QUESTION *Why did the United States face rising prices and labor unrest during the late 1940s?*

With the end of World War II, the United States faced another challenge—adjusting to a peacetime economy. Industries had to go from making war goods to making things for consumers. Defense workers had to be retrained to do these new jobs. Returning soldiers also needed jobs and training.

During the war, the government had set limits on prices. This kept the cost of consumer goods **stable,** or unchanging. When the government lifted these controls, prices began to climb. This rise in prices, or **inflation** (ihn•FLAY•shuhn), came from a huge increase in consumer spending. During the war, people could not get many consumer goods. Now they were eager to buy things. When people spend a lot of money, prices tend to go up. This happened after the war.

Inflation caused prices to rise faster than wages. This meant the same paycheck paid for fewer goods. During the war, workers had accepted government limits on wages. They agreed not to strike. After the war, though, things were different. When employers refused to raise wages, labor strikes broke out. In 1946 a miners' strike raised fears about coal supplies. Meanwhile, a strike by railroad workers led to a shutdown of the nation's railroads.

Reading **HELP**DESK

Taking Notes: *Describing*

As you read, use a diagram like this one to describe social and economic changes in the postwar United States.

Postwar
Changes

Content Vocabulary

• **inflation**   • **desegregate**
• **Fair Deal**
• **closed shop**

Lesson 2   **339**

(l) Gamma-Keystone via Getty Images, (c) Mark Kauffman/Time Life Pictures/Getty Images, (r) Time & Life Pictures/Getty Images

Rent ($25 mo.)	$300
Utilities	120
Food ($10 wk)	520
Bank loan	264
Furniture payment	150
Clothes	60
Baby doctor	40
Recreation	50
Life insurance	67
One-Year Total	$1,571

ECONOMICS SKILL

In 1944 Congress took steps to give an economic boost to returning members of the armed forces—GIs. It passed the "GI Bill of Rights," a law that gave billions of dollars to help GIs go to college or get special job training. Money also went to help them start businesses or buy homes. The bill also helped provide money and health care for GIs as they looked for jobs.

1 EXPLAINING How did the GI Bill help war veterans?

2 CRITICAL THINKING
Evaluating How do you think it helped the United States to give a boost to all the returning members of the armed services?

THE GI BILL

President Truman pressured striking miners and railroad workers to go back to their jobs. In May 1946, he threatened to draft them into the army. He said he had to take such steps to keep industries going. President Truman finally forced the miners back to work by having the government take over the mines. He also got mine owners to grant many of the workers' demands.

☑ PROGRESS CHECK

Analyzing What happened as the government lifted the controls on prices of consumer goods after the war?

Truman Faces Republican Opposition

GUIDING QUESTION *Why did Truman and the Republicans disagree about how to solve the nation's economic problems?*

In September 1945, President Truman presented a plan of **domestic** reforms. Truman's plan was aimed at solving some of the postwar problems in the economy. For example, he wanted to increase government spending to create jobs, build housing, and create a health insurance system. Truman later called this program the **Fair Deal.** However, the measures did not pass in Congress.

Gamma-Keystone via Getty Images

Reading **HELP**DESK (CCSS)

inflation increase in prices
Fair Deal a program aimed at solving some of the nation's economic problems after World War II

Academic Vocabulary

stable unchanging
domestic having to do with the home or the home country

A Republican Congress

Many Americans blamed Truman and the Democrats for the nation's problems. They called for change. The Republicans took advantage of this feeling in the congressional elections of 1946. The slogan "Had Enough?" helped the Republican Party win control of both houses of Congress.

The new Republican Congress had different plans for fixing the economy. They wanted to limit government spending and reverse New Deal policies. Conservative Republicans especially favored big business and wanted to limit the power of labor unions.

In the spring of 1947, Republicans introduced a measure that became known as the Taft-Hartley Act. This measure limited the actions workers could take against their employers. It outlawed the **closed shop,** an agreement under which a business owner hires only union members.

Taft-Hartley also gave the government power to halt temporarily any strike that endangered public health or safety. This part of the act was meant to stop strikes such as the strikes of miners or railroad workers.

Labor unions sharply attacked the Taft-Hartley Act. They said that the law erased many of the gains that labor had made since 1933. Truman, realizing that the Democrats needed the support of labor, vetoed the act. This means he refused to sign it into law. The Republican-controlled Congress, however, overrode Truman's veto. The Taft-Hartley Act became law.

Government Reorganization

Although Truman and Congress disagreed about economic policies, they did agree on ways to improve how the federal government worked. Government had become much larger since the New Deal and the war. It needed to be more efficient.

In 1947 Congress passed the National Security Act. It combined the armed services under the Department of Defense. A National Security Council would advise the president on foreign and military matters. The National Security Act also set up the Central Intelligence Agency (CIA). The job of the CIA would be to collect information about other countries. The CIA would then study the information and pass it on to the president. Many Americans feared that the CIA would be used to spy on American citizens. Truman, however, promised that the new agency would operate only in foreign lands. It would not bring "police state methods" into the country.

Mark Kauffman/Time Life Pictures/Getty Images

BIOGRAPHY

Margaret Chase Smith (1897–1995)

One of the Republicans doing battle with President Truman in the post-World War II years was Margaret Chase Smith. She had come to Congress in 1940 to take the place of her husband, who had died in office. In 1948 Smith won election to the Senate. A sharp critic of Truman, she once wrote "America is rapidly losing its position as leader of the world simply because the Democratic administration has pitifully failed to provide effective leadership." However, Smith was also among the first to take a stand against her fellow Republican, Joseph McCarthy.

▶ **CRITICAL THINKING**
Speculating Why do you think Smith decided to take a stand against Joseph McCarthy?

---

closed shop practice of businesses hiring only union members

Build Vocabulary: *Acronyms*

Acronyms are words or abbreviations formed from the first letters of other words. CIA is an example of an acronym. GI (formed from the words *government issue*) is another.

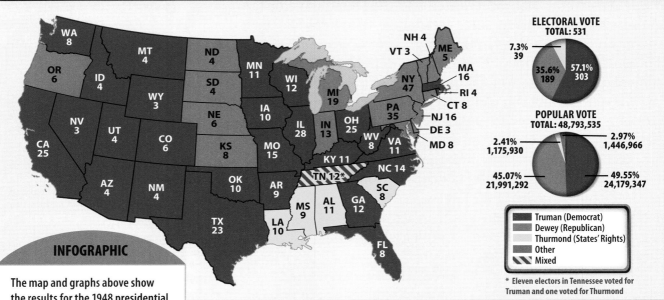

ELECTION OF 1948

ELECTORAL VOTE
TOTAL: 531

7.3%
39

35.6%
189

57.1%
303

POPULAR VOTE
TOTAL: 48,793,535

2.41%
1,175,930

2.97%
1,446,966

45.07%
21,991,292

49.55%
24,179,347

Truman (Democrat)
Dewey (Republican)
Thurmond (States' Rights)
Other
Mixed

* Eleven electors in Tennessee voted for Truman and one voted for Thurmond

The Election of 1948

The year 1948 was a presidential election year. Economic problems made Truman unpopular with many voters. Truman's failure to get Congress to pass many of his plans made him look weak and ineffective.

Democratic Party problems also helped the Republicans. Truman supported civil rights for African Americans. Some conservative Southern Democrats did not like this. They formed the States' Rights Democratic Party, known as the Dixiecrats. They nominated South Carolina Governor Strom Thurmond for president. Meanwhile, more liberal Democrats formed the Progressive Party. They named Henry Wallace as their nominee for president. Wallace opposed Truman's foreign policy. He called for closer American-Soviet ties.

Dewey Leads Polls

It looked as though Republican Governor Thomas Dewey of New York would be unbeatable in the election. Truman, however, was determined. He ran an energetic campaign—traveling more than 21,000 miles (33,796 km) by train through the country. In town after town, he attacked Congress for rejecting his Fair Deal.

Reading **HELP**DESK **CCSS**

desegregate to end the system of separating races

Truman Pulls an Upset

The *Chicago Daily Tribune* newspaper was so sure of a Republican victory that on the evening of the election, it issued a special edition proclaiming: "Dewey Defeats Truman." Yet when the votes were counted, Truman beat Dewey by more than 2 million votes. Democrats also won control of both houses of Congress.

✓ **PROGRESS CHECK**

Describing What made Truman's 1948 victory so surprising?

Truman's Fair Deal

GUIDING QUESTION *What civil rights reform did the Truman administration push for?*

Truman quickly returned his Fair Deal plan to Congress. Laws were passed raising the minimum wage and expanding Social Security. Congress also agreed to fund low-income housing.

In 1948 Truman asked Congress to end discrimination based on race, religion, or ethnic origins. He tried to get Congress to protect voting rights of African Americans and make lynching a federal crime. Although these efforts failed, the president took steps to advance civil rights. He ordered federal agencies to end job discrimination against African Americans. He ordered the armed forces to **desegregate** (dee•SEH•grih•gayt)—to end the separation of races. The president also instructed the Justice Department to enforce existing civil rights laws.

In 1949 Truman asked Congress for government-backed medical insurance, higher minimum wages, and more money for public schools. Many of his requests were defeated, but Truman had made a start in improving the lives of millions of people.

✓ **PROGRESS CHECK**

Explaining What civil rights reforms did President Truman achieve?

In 1948 President Truman issued an executive order that desegregated the armed services of the United States.

LESSON 2 REVIEW

Review Vocabulary

1. Write a paragraph about the Truman presidency in which you use the following terms:

   a. Fair Deal   **b.** closed shop   **c.** desegregate

Answer the Guiding Questions

2. ***Explaining*** Why were many American workers dissatisfied with the economy in the late 1940s?

3. ***Contrasting*** What were key areas of disagreement between President Truman and the Republicans over the economy?

4. ***Explaining*** How did President Truman demonstrate his support for civil rights?

5. **ARGUMENT** After the war, many workers felt that they had a right to strike for higher wages. Do you agree with them? Express your opinion in a brief essay.

netw⊚rks

There's More Online!

 GRAPHIC ORGANIZER
Nations Involved in the Korean War

 MAP Korean War

☑ **PRIMARY SOURCE**
General MacArthur Speech

NORTH KOREA
P'yŏngyang
P'anmunjŏm
Seoul

Lesson 3
The Korean War

ESSENTIAL QUESTION *Why does conflict develop?*

IT MATTERS BECAUSE
The Korean War tested how far the United States was willing to go to stop the spread of communism around the world.

Conflict in Korea

GUIDING QUESTION *Why did the U.S. under the United Nations' flag fight the Korean War in the 1950s?*

At the end of World War II, the East Asian country of Korea came under control of the United States and the Soviet Union. The two powers divided Korea at the 38th parallel of latitude. A Communist government took control in North Korea. A U.S.-backed government took over South Korea. Relations between the two Koreas were tense.

Hoping to unite Korea, North Korean troops invaded South Korea on June 25, 1950. By September, the Communists had control over most of the peninsula. The South Korean army held only a small area in the southeast around the port city of Pusan.

The United States Responds

North Korea's invasion alarmed President Truman. He believed the Soviet Union supported the attack. Acting quickly and without a declaration of war, Truman ordered American forces into action. "Korea is the Greece of the Far East," he said. "If we are tough enough now, if we stand up to them like we did in Greece three years ago, they won't take any next steps."

(c)Pfc. James Cox/CORBIS, (r) CORBIS

Reading **HELP**DESK **CCSS**

Taking Notes: *Describing*

As you read, use a table like this one to keep track of how key nations were involved in the Korean War.

Country	Role
Soviet Union	
United States	
North Korea	
South Korea	
China	

Content Vocabulary
• **demilitarized zone**

Truman also asked the United Nations to take action. The UN called on North Korea to remove its forces from South Korea. When North Korea ignored this demand, the UN agreed to send troops.

Most of the UN forces came under the command of U.S. general and World War II hero Douglas MacArthur. That September, General MacArthur led the UN forces in a daring landing. They came ashore near the port of Inch'ŏn, well behind enemy lines. MacArthur's forces took that key city. From there they were able to enter the South Korean capital city, Seoul, on September 25. Pushing on from there, they forced the North Koreans back across the 38th parallel. South Korea came under the control of UN forces.

MacArthur Presses the Attack

General MacArthur was encouraged by this success. He urged President Truman to order the invasion of North Korea. General MacArthur **assured** Truman that neither China nor the Soviet Union would enter the war. He also promised to have troops "home by Christmas."

Truman sought UN approval for an invasion of the North. The goal was to unify Korea. In October, the UN approved the advance into North Korea.

With his orders, MacArthur moved north of the 38th parallel. Fighting well, his troops advanced toward the Chinese border. The Chinese Communists saw the advancing troops as a threat.

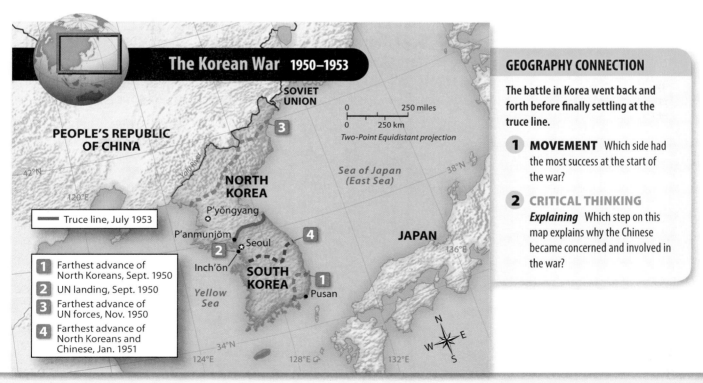

The Korean War 1950–1953

PEOPLE'S REPUBLIC OF CHINA

SOVIET UNION

NORTH KOREA

P'yŏngyang

P'anmunjŏm

Seoul

Inch'ŏn

SOUTH KOREA

Yellow Sea

Pusan

Sea of Japan (East Sea)

JAPAN

0   250 miles
0   250 km
Two-Point Equidistant projection

—— Truce line, July 1953

1 Farthest advance of North Koreans, Sept. 1950
2 UN landing, Sept. 1950
3 Farthest advance of UN forces, Nov. 1950
4 Farthest advance of North Koreans and Chinese, Jan. 1951

GEOGRAPHY CONNECTION

The battle in Korea went back and forth before finally settling at the truce line.

1 **MOVEMENT** Which side had the most success at the start of the war?

2 **CRITICAL THINKING**
Explaining Which step on this map explains why the Chinese became concerned and involved in the war?

Academic Vocabulary

assure to promise or to make sure

They replied with force. Hundreds of thousands of Chinese troops crossed into Korea. They drove the UN forces back to South Korea. By January 1951, the Communists had captured Seoul, South Korea's capital. The capital city would change hands several times during this conflict.

✔ **PROGRESS CHECK**

Explaining Why did President Truman and the UN send troops to Korea?

American Leadership Splits

GUIDING QUESTION *Why did Truman and MacArthur disagree over how to fight the Korean War?*

By spring of 1951, UN forces had recovered. Once again, they pushed the Communists across the 38th parallel. At this point, the war became a stalemate, in which neither side was able to gain much ground. The stalemate lasted for almost two years. There was much bitter fighting along the 38th parallel.

Truman and MacArthur

The stalemate dragged. Truman wanted to negotiate an end to the fighting. MacArthur argued that dropping atomic bombs on Chinese bases and supply lines would bring a quick victory. Truman opposed MacArthur's plan. He feared it could lead to a larger war.

MacArthur criticized the president. In a letter to a member of Congress, MacArthur said he was being kept from doing his job. "We must win," he wrote. "There is no substitute for victory." In April 1951, the president removed MacArthur.

Pfc. James Cox/CORBIS

A U.S. machine gun crew prepares for combat, November 1950.

demilitarized zone region where military forces are not allowed

Academic Vocabulary

conclude to figure out or decide

Truman **concluded** that it was the only action he could take and "still be president of the United States." Truman wrote: "If I allowed him to defy the civil authorities in this manner, I myself would be violating my oath to uphold and defend the Constitution."

The United States erupted in protest over MacArthur's firing. The general was popular. Polls showed that most Americans supported him against the president. Also, MacArthur did not go quietly. He returned home to a hero's welcome and made a dramatic farewell speech before Congress. "Old soldiers never die," he said; "they just fade away."

The Fighting Ends

Talks to end the Korean War began in July 1951. Negotiators finally reached a cease-fire agreement in July 1953. This was during the presidency of Dwight D. Eisenhower. The agreement set up a **demilitarized zone** (dee•MIH•luh•tuh•ryzd ZOHN)—a region in which no military forces are allowed. The zone lay between the two Koreas. It stretched along the border near the 38th parallel.

Neither side could claim victory in the Korean War. When it was over, hardly any territory had changed hands. More than 36,000 Americans were dead, and another 103,000 had been wounded. Nearly 2 million Koreans and Chinese were killed.

The United States had shown the Soviets that it was willing to use force to block the spread of communism. At the same time, the lack of a clear victory led to uncertainty at home about the nation's foreign policy.

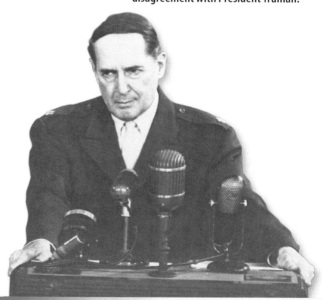

General Douglas MacArthur was relieved of his duties after his disagreement with President Truman.

CORBIS

☑ PROGRESS CHECK

Summarizing Why did President Truman remove General MacArthur?

LESSON 3 REVIEW (CCSS)

Review Vocabulary

1. Use the term *demilitarized zone* to write a sentence about the end of the Korean War.

Answer the Guiding Questions

2. *Describing* Describe the conflict that triggered the Korean War.

3. *Summarizing* How was MacArthur's approach to fighting in Korea different from the approach of President Truman?

4. *Describing* Why were many Americans upset over President Truman's decision to relieve MacArthur of his command?

5. **INFORMATIVE/EXPLANATORY** Truman believed he had no choice but to remove MacArthur from his post. Explain Truman's view in a brief essay.

networks

There's More Online!

☑ **BIOGRAPHY**
Hank Williams

☑ **GRAPH** Per Capita
Income in Appalachia

☑ **GRAPHIC ORGANIZER**
Changes to American Society

☑ **PRIMARY SOURCE** "I Like Ike"
Television Ad

☑ **SLIDE SHOW** Hank Williams

☑ **TIME LINE** Race to the Moon

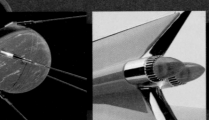

Lesson 4
Life in the 1950s

ESSENTIAL QUESTION *How do new ideas change the way people live?*

IT MATTERS BECAUSE
While Cold War tensions lingered in the background, the United States built a new kind of society after the war.

Eisenhower in the White House

GUIDING QUESTION *What policies did Eisenhower promote for prosperity at home and to compete against the Soviets?*

American voters elected Dwight D. Eisenhower to the presidency in November 1952. Eisenhower defeated his Democratic opponent, Illinois governor Adlai E. Stevenson. The Republicans also won control of Congress.

Eisenhower was born in Texas and raised in rural Kansas. He rose steadily through the U.S. Army to become supreme commander of the Allied forces in Europe during World War II. People called him "Ike," and voters trusted him. He won wide support with his pledge to bring the Korean War to an "early and honorable end."

Eisenhower Domestic Policy

Eisenhower followed a middle-of-the-road domestic policy. He did not seek far-reaching new government programs. At the same time, he resisted the pressure to end popular older ones. Sometimes he even expanded them.

President Eisenhower wanted government to be "smaller rather than bigger." He backed free enterprise. That is, he favored letting businesses and people make economic decisions

(l)Michael Ochs Archives/Getty Images, (cl)Picture Press / Alamy, (cr)Transtock/Corbis, (r)H. Armstrong Roberts/ClassicStock/The Image Works

Reading **HELP**DESK (CCSS)

Taking Notes: *Listing*

As you read, use a diagram like this one to list changes to American society in the 1950s.

Changes to
American society

Content Vocabulary

• **surplus**   • **standard of living**
• **arms race**   • **affluence**
• **summit**   • **materialism**

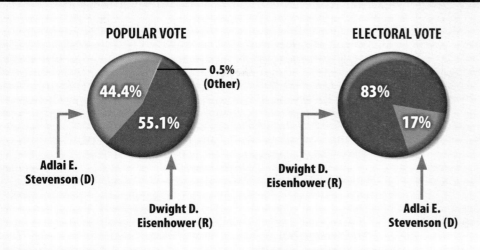

POPULAR VOTE

44.4%

55.1%

0.5% (Other)

Adlai E. Stevenson (D)

Dwight D. Eisenhower (R)

ELECTORAL VOTE

83%

17%

Dwight D. Eisenhower (R)

Adlai E. Stevenson (D)

GRAPH SKILL

Eisenhower won a clear victory over his opponent, Adlai Stevenson. Republican candidates for Congress also had success.

1 CALCULATING Was Eisenhower's margin of victory over Stevenson larger in the popular vote or in the electoral vote?

2 CRITICAL THINKING *Drawing Conclusions* What does the size of the electoral vote victory suggest about Eisenhower's popularity?

with as little government interference as possible. He cut federal spending. When Eisenhower completed his second term, the federal budget had a surplus of $300 million. A budget **surplus** is an amount left over after meeting all expenses.

One big government program from the Eisenhower years was the Federal Highway Act of 1956. This act funded the building of more than 40,000 miles (64,374 km) of highways. The new roads tied the nation together. They linked people to areas that had been remote and hard to reach. They were called interstate highways. The program helped the **economy** grow, especially the automobile and oil industries. It also improved the military's ability to move its forces in case of an attack.

Rivalry With the Soviet Union

During the 1950s, the United States and the Soviet Union engaged in an **arms race,** a competition for military supremacy. Both sides built more and more **nuclear** weapons, which used energy stored in atoms. These enormously powerful weapons gave each side the power to destroy the other side many times over. With the threat so great, the United States and the Soviet Union had to act carefully.

By the mid-1950s, the superpowers wanted to ease Cold War tensions. In July 1955, Eisenhower, NATO leaders, and Soviets held a meeting—a **summit**—in Geneva, Switzerland. Yet in spite of the good feeling, tensions remained. In 1956 the superpowers faced two new crises that threatened the fragile peace.

The growing threat of nuclear weapons, such as the one being tested in this photograph, added a layer of tension to the Cold War.

surplus an amount left over
arms race competition between countries for stronger military power
summit meeting of heads of government

Academic Vocabulary

economy the overall system by which goods are made, distributed, and used
nuclear relating to the energy contained in the nucleus of an atom

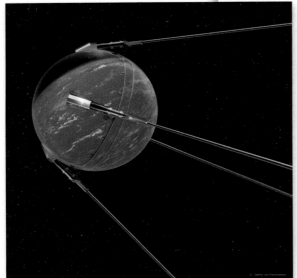

The Soviet Union took an early lead in the space race when it successfully launched *Sputnik* in October 1957. This was the first artificial satellite, or object that circles the Earth.

▶ **CRITICAL THINKING**

Analyzing How do you think the rivalry between the Soviet Union and the United States influenced scientific developments in the "space race"? How would scientific and engineering advances have progressed without this competition?

First, trouble arose when Egypt's president Gamal Abdel Nasser seized the Suez Canal from its European owners. Nasser then blockaded Israeli shipping. In October, Britain, France, and Israel invaded Egypt. Britain and France hoped to get rid of Nasser. Israel wanted to end Egypt's military threat. The Soviet Union then threatened to crush the invaders, raising American concerns. The crisis ended when the invading forces pulled out of Egypt.

Hungary was the scene of the second 1956 crisis. This Eastern European country lived under Soviet domination. A new government there called for Soviet troops to leave the country.

In November 1956, Soviet leader Nikita Khrushchev (kroosh•CHAWF) ordered Soviet forces to stop the revolt. President Eisenhower criticized the crackdown but took no further action.

The United States and Soviet Union competed for influence around the globe—and beyond. Soon the superpowers were engaged in a "space race." In October 1957, the Soviets sent the world's first artificial satellite into outer space. The device was called *Sputnik*. The United States set up a space program headed by the National Aeronautics and Space Administration (NASA).

✅ **PROGRESS CHECK**

Describing How did the interstate highway system help the economy in the United States?

Prosperity and Change

GUIDING QUESTION *How did a booming economy change the social and cultural life in America in the 1950s?*

The U.S. economy grew rapidly during the 1950s. Americans were earning higher wages than ever before. They bought more consumer goods. As a result, factory production soared. A "baby boom," or increased birth rate, promised even more economic growth in the future.

Women in large numbers left the workforce to stay home and raise children. The demand for baby products and services grew. School enrollment soared as the "baby boomers" reached school age. This put a strain on the educational system.

Picture Press / Alamy

COMPARING THE COST OF LIVING

1950	Comparing by Cost	2010
$0.88	Milk, per gallon	$3.15
$0.67	Eggs, per dozen	$1.41
$0.15	Loaf of bread	$1.61
$0.13	Bananas, per pound	$0.40
$0.44	Chicken, per pound	$3.44
$0.03	Cost of first-class postage stamp	$0.44
$0.49	Movie ticket	$7.95
$250	Television set	$375
$1,510	Average cost of a new car	$28,400
$3,300	Median income for a family of four	$74,000

Source: From various sources

Median means "in the middle." A median family income is one in which there is the same number of people earning more as there is people earning less.

1 CALCULATING What share of a median family income did a new car represent in 1950? What did it represent in 2010?

2 CRITICAL THINKING *Drawing Conclusions* Would you rather be a family with a median income in 2010 or in 1950? Why?

The Consumer Society

Overall, Americans of the 1950s enjoyed a higher **standard of living,** or economic comfort, than in previous decades. Spurred by several factors, the nation went on a buying spree. One of these factors was **affluence** (A•floo•uhns), or greater wealth. Another was the growing number and types of products available. Increased advertising also played a role. Buying goods became easier, too. Americans used credit cards, charge accounts, and easy payment plans to purchase goods. With these tools, a person could buy a product today and pay for it later, a little bit at a time.

Consumers were eager to buy the latest products—dishwashers, washing machines, television sets, stereos, and clothes made from new fabrics. The market for cars was growing. Automakers tried to outdo one another by making bigger, faster, and flashier cars. New models added stylish features, such as chrome-plated bumpers and soaring tail fins.

Television ads, along with radio and magazines, helped create fads. These quickly swept the nation. In the late 1950s, Americans bought millions of hula hoops—large plastic rings they twirled around their waists. Other popular fads included crew cuts for boys, poodle skirts for girls, and a new snack—pizza. Fashion dolls such as Barbie™ were another fad introduced in this decade.

TV and American Culture

More than 900,000 U.S. households had television sets by 1949. The sets had small screens that showed grainy black-and-white pictures. Still, people loved them.

This car was an example of the kind popular in the late 1950s.

► **CRITICAL THINKING**
Analyzing Visuals How do you think this car reflects the ongoing space race between the United States and Soviet Union?

Transtock/Corbis

Beginning in the 1950s, television became the primary source of entertainment in many households.

During the 1950s, factories made an average of 6.5 million sets each year. By the end of the decade, most American families had one.

Television changed American life. It became the main form of entertainment. It was also an important source of news and information. Millions of Americans gathered to watch weekly episodes of programs such as *I Love Lucy* and *Father Knows Best*. The images shown in many programs—of happy families in neat homes—helped shape people's goals for their own lives.

Teenagers took up rock 'n' roll in the 1950s. This new form of music grew from the rhythm-and-blues music African American musicians had been making for years. Rock also borrowed from country music. In rock 'n' roll, the tempo was fast. It used electrically amplified guitars and other instruments. One of the first rock hits was Bill Haley and the Comets' *Rock Around the Clock*. It topped the charts in 1955. Borrowing styles from African American performers such as Chuck Berry and Little Richard, Elvis Presley burst on the scene in 1956. Presley quickly became an idol to millions of young Americans. Many young men copied his haircut and swaggering style.

Sharing music helped teens forge a common identity. The differing attitudes of the older and younger generation toward music and other forms of popular culture would widen in the years ahead.

Vaccines prevented numerous childhood diseases and improved the lives of many.

(t)H. Armstrong Roberts/ClassicStock/The Image Works, (b)Bettmann/CORBIS

Reading HELPDESK (CCSS)

Reading Strategy: *Summarizing*

When you summarize a reading, you find the main idea of the passage and restate it in your own words. Read the paragraph headed "Medical Advances" on the next page. Summarize the reading in one or two sentences.

Medical Advances

By the 1950s, medical science had made great strides in fighting disease. Antibiotics and vaccines helped control diseases such as diphtheria, influenza, and typhoid fever. A vaccine for polio continued to escape the medical profession. Polio left many of its victims paralyzed for life. It became the era's most dreaded disease.

Dr. Jonas Salk developed the first safe and effective vaccine against polio. School children began receiving the vaccine in large numbers beginning in 1955. The vaccine almost completely eliminated polio. The nation hailed Salk as a hero.

Expanding Suburbs

After World War II, the nation faced a severe housing shortage. During the war, building of new homes had slowed to a standstill. Then hundreds of thousands of GIs came home. Many of them got married and began looking for homes.

Affordable open land for building was scarce in the cities. The solution was to create new planned communities in the suburbs—the land on the outskirts of the cities. Suburbs had existed since the late 1800s, but they grew rapidly after World War II.

One early planned community was started in 1946 about 30 miles (48 km) from New York City. Called Levittown, it had row upon row of single-family homes. It also had parks, playgrounds, and shopping centers. Each home was exactly the same and sold for the same price: $7,990.

Suburban housing appealed to many Americans. The homes were affordable. They offered privacy and escape from urban problems. They had space for cars. The suburbs, however, were not an option for everyone. Builders of the nation's postwar suburbs often refused to sell homes to minorities.

New Technologies

Technological advances helped the economy grow. Business, industry, and agriculture adopted new technology and new production methods. The result was greater productivity. This means workers were able to produce more goods with the same amount of labor.

The computer represented one of the 1950s important technological advances. Unlike today's small personal computers, early computers were huge, weighing tons and filling whole rooms. Used only by the military and the government at first, computers soon appeared in large corporations.

✓ PROGRESS CHECK

Explaining The United States in the 1950s was called a consumer society. What does this mean?

BIOGRAPHY

Hank Williams (1923–1953)

Hank Williams was a musical superstar of the era. Born in the small town of Mount Olive, Alabama, Williams made many popular country music and gospel recordings. His death at the age of 29 added to his legend. Artists from the fields of popular music and jazz as well as country music have recorded his songs.

▶ **CRITICAL THINKING**
Drawing Conclusions Why do you think Williams's early death added to his legend?

Michael Ochs Archives/Getty Images

Problems in a Time of Plenty

GUIDING QUESTION *Why did many Americans not share in the prosperity of the 1950s?*

Not everyone prospered in the 1950s. In fact, more than one in five Americans lived in poverty. Millions more struggled to survive on incomes just above the poverty level. Such poverty marred the landscape of the so-called affluent society.

Many farmers did not share in the success of the 1950s. Businesses created large farms. These used new technology to grow huge amounts of food. Small farms could not compete. Many small-farm families sold their land and migrated to urban areas. Small farmers who continued to farm struggled to make a living.

Appalachia—a rural region stretching along the Appalachian Mountains—went through a decline in the coal industry. This plunged thousands of people into poverty. During the 1950s, about 1.5 million people left Appalachia to seek a better life in the nation's cities.

The Urban Poor

A growing number of Americans moved to the suburbs in the 1950s. They left the poor behind. Some inner cities became islands of poverty.

Still, people came to cities looking for work. African Americans continued their migration from rural areas of the South. More than 3 million of them moved to cities in the North and the Midwest between 1940 and 1960. For many, however, life proved to be little better in Northern cities. Many poor Latinos— Puerto Ricans in the East and Mexicans in the Southwest and West—also moved to U.S. cities.

The shift of poor African Americans and Latinos to Northern cities helped push many whites to the suburbs. This "white flight" turned some areas of cities into ghettos. These are neighborhoods filled with poor people from a minority group.

There were few good jobs for the urban poor. Many factories and businesses also moved to suburban areas. In addition, many factories began using machines to do numerous factory jobs.

By 1950, when this photo was taken, the neighborhood of Spanish Harlem in New York City was home to a large Latino community. Many Spanish Harlem residents trace their roots to Puerto Rico.

Roy Stevens/Time & Life Pictures/Getty Images

Reading **HELP**DESK (CCSS)

materialism focus on collecting money and possessions

This meant less work in the industries that remained. It became more and more difficult for the urban poor to rise from poverty and improve their lives.

The urban poor struggled not only with poverty. They also faced discrimination in employment, housing, and education. Crime and violence often grew out of inner-city poverty, especially among young people who saw no hope for escape from life in the ghetto.

Social Critics of the 1950s

Americans living in poverty had good reason to wonder about the nation in the 1950s. They were not the only ones who were concerned. Some people took a critical look at the values of the era. In the workplace and in suburban life, they saw millions of people living, acting, and even thinking in the same way. This sameness caused some to regret a loss of independent thinking. Others criticized American **materialism** (muh· TIHR·ee·uh·lih·zuhm)—a focus on collecting money and possessions. Materialism, critics said, caused people to ignore many more important things, including the plight of the nation's poor. A group of writers known as the "Beats" had a sharper view of the situation. Renowned Beat writer Jack Kerouac (KEHR·oo·wahk) expressed it as "weariness with all forms of the modern industrial state."

The changes in U.S. society were dramatic and ongoing. Soon groups such as women and African Americans would begin asking difficult questions about what was taking place in the United States.

✓ PROGRESS CHECK

Identifying What groups did not benefit from the prosperity of the 1950s?

— Connections to —
TODAY

Dawn of the Computer Age

The ENIAC machine shown here could perform about 5,000 calculations per second. It took up an entire room, and it took days for a team to program the machine to do a single job. Today's computers can fit in a backpack and do many millions of calculations per second.

This 1946 photograph shows the size and scale of the earliest computers.

LESSON 4 REVIEW (CCSS)

Review Vocabulary

1. Use the terms *arms race* and *summit* in a sentence about the 1950s.

2. Write a sentence explaining what the terms *affluence* and *materialism* have in common.

Answer the Guiding Questions

3. *Discussing* How did the U.S. space program extend American competition with the Soviet Union?

4. *Listing* What are four new products or cultural changes that Americans were introduced to in the 1950s?

5. *Explaining* How did life in the inner city differ from life in the suburbs in the 1950s?

6. **INFORMATIVE/EXPLANATORY** Write a short essay that answers these questions: How did the interstate highway system change U.S. society? How did it change urban areas and the suburbs?

CHAPTER 12 Activities CCSS

1 Exploring the Essential Questions

INFORMATIVE/EXPLANATORY Describe the political changes the United States experienced during the Cold War. Explain how Americans responded to the challenges of this era.

2 21st Century Skills

INFORMATION LITERACY Conduct research on the Internet about the interstate highway system and its development in the 1950s. Explain how this system made traveling easier for people in the United States.

3 Thinking Like a Historian

UNDERSTANDING CAUSE AND EFFECT Senator Joseph McCarthy was accused of making charges of wrongdoing with little evidence to support his claims. Write an essay about the importance of the principle of "innocent until proven guilty." Explain what can happen if people are not given the chance to prove their innocence.

4 Visual Literacy

ANALYZING PHOTOGRAPHS Examine the picture here. What does the paper say? What actually happened in this election? What does this photo say about the need for accurate information in reporting?

Bettmann/CORBIS

356 *The Cold War Era*

REVIEW THE GUIDING QUESTIONS

Choose the best answer for each question.

1 Allied leaders Franklin Roosevelt, Winston Churchill, and Joseph Stalin met in February 1945 to discuss issues of the post-World War II world in

  A. Yalta.

  B. Geneva.

  C. San Francisco.

  D. Germany.

2 The Truman Doctrine

  F. set up an international organization to promote peace.

  G. sent economic aid to Eastern Europe.

  H. pledged that the U.S. would help countries resist communism.

  I. called for the reunification of Germany.

3 The legislation that allowed the government to temporarily stop any strike that endangered public health or safety was the

  A. Fair Deal.

  B. New Deal.

  C. Marshall Plan.

  D. Taft-Hartley Act.

4 An end to the separation of races is called

  F. domestic.

  G. desegregation.

  H. segregation.

  I. unionization.

5 For the United States and the United Nations, the Korean War became more complicated with the involvement of troops from

  A. China.

  B. Japan.

  C. Germany.

  D. Thailand.

6 Urban poverty became an issue in the 1950s as more and more people moved to the

  F. cities.

  G. suburbs.

  H. rural areas.

  I. country.

DBQ **ANALYZING DOCUMENTS**

Julius and Ethel Rosenberg were on trial for espionage. The Rosenbergs' lawyer, Emanuel Bloch, made the following plea.

"Through you [Judge Kaufman] the rest of the world will either believe that we are a compassionate nation, a nation built upon the ideals of humanity and justice, or a nation that has been gripped in panic and fear and is embarked upon mad acts."

Source: Emanuel Bloch, NCRRC Letters

7 **Making Inferences** Which of the following might be one of the "mad acts" Bloch was referring to?

A. selling secrets to the Soviets

B. producing nuclear weapons

C. releasing the Rosenbergs

D. executing the Rosenbergs

8 **Making Connections** Bloch was referring to a fear of which of the following in his plea?

F. hunger

G. poverty

H. the affluent society

I. communism

SHORT RESPONSE

President Truman explained why he was relieving General Douglas MacArthur of his command in South Korea.

"The free nations have united their strength in an effort to prevent a third world war. That war can come if the Communist rulers want it to come. This Nation and its allies will not be responsible for its coming."

Source: Department of State Bulletin, April 16, 1951

9 What concern did President Truman have about General MacArthur?

10 According to Truman, who would be responsible if a third world war occurred?

EXTENDED RESPONSE

11 **Informative/Explanatory** Describe the social and economic changes that occurred in American society during the Cold War. Describe the challenges Americans faced and how they responded to these challenges.

Need Extra Help?

If You've Missed Question	**1**	**2**	**3**	**4**	**5**	**6**	**7**	**8**	**9**	**10**	**11**
Review Lesson	1	1	2	2	3	4	1	1	3	3	1–4

The Civil Rights Era

1954–1974

ESSENTIAL QUESTIONS • *Why does conflict develop?*
• *How do new ideas change the way people live?*

◄ *Dr. Martin Luther King, Jr., was a religious and civil rights leader.*

netw⊙rks

There's More Online about the civil rights movement.

CHAPTER 13

The Story Matters . . .

At the age of six, Martin Luther King, Jr., learns a painful lesson—one that helps shape the rest of his life. That year, he begins going to a different school than the one his white friends attend. A white playmate tells King that his parents will no longer allow the two boys to play together.

Years later, on a visit to Connecticut, King sees a world where African Americans and whites mix more freely. "Negroes and whites go [to] the same church," he writes to his parents in surprise.

King would grow to become a leader in the struggle for civil rights. You will read about this struggle, as well as the movement to expand the rights of other groups in the United States.

TEXT: The Papers of Martin Luther King, Jr., Volume 6, By Martin Luther King (Jr.). Writings of Martin Luther King, Jr. copyright © 1992 by the Estate of Martin Luther King, Jr. PHOTO: The Granger Collection, NYC

359

Place and Time: The United States 1954–1968

Until the mid-1950s, formal laws and informal customs enforced strict segregation between African Americans and whites in many parts of the country. The struggle to change these practices resulted in conflict, especially in the South.

1963 Police in Birmingham, Alabama, use a high-pressure water cannon against civil rights marchers.

Step Into the Place

MAP FOCUS Events related to the struggle for civil rights occurred in many states. Several of these events are noted on the map.

1 **LOCATION** Look at the map. Which city and event that is shown on the map is located farthest north?

2 **PLACE** In which two states are the most events illustrated?

3 **CRITICAL THINKING** *Drawing Conclusions* Why do you think so many of the events shown occurred in Southern states?

1954 Civil rights lawyer Thurgood Marshall sits with students on the steps of the Supreme Court. Marshall argued the case *Brown* v. *Board of Education* before the Court.

Step Into the Time

TIME LINE Look at the time line. What event in South Africa indicates that the country might have been experiencing conflicts similar to the ones in the United States? Explain your answer.

1954 *Brown* v. *Board of Education* ruling

1955 Montgomery bus boycott begins

Dwight Eisenhower
1953–1961

U.S. PRESIDENTS

U.S. EVENTS

WORLD EVENTS

1954

1959

1959 Fidel Castro seizes power in Cuba

(c)Wally McNamee/CORBIS, (c)Bettmann/CORBIS, (b)White House Historical Association

The Civil Rights Movement

CANADA

Maine
Ver.
New Hampshire
Massachusetts
Rhode Island
Connecticut
New Jersey
New York
Pennsylvania
Delaware
Maryland

North Dakota
Minnesota
South Dakota
Wisconsin
Michigan
Nebraska
Iowa
Illinois
Indiana
Ohio
West Virginia
Virginia
Kentucky
Missouri
Kansas
Topeka
Col.
Oklahoma
Tennessee
North Carolina
Greensboro
South Carolina
Memphis
Oxford
Little Rock
Arkansas
Birmingham
Jackson
Alabama
Selma
Montgomery
Georgia
Miss.
Louisiana
Texas
Florida
Washington D.C.
MEXICO
Gulf of Mexico
ATLANTIC OCEAN

40°N
30°N
70°W
80°W
90°W
TROPIC OF CANCER

1954
Brown v. *Board of Education* orders desegregation of schools

1963
March on Washington, "I Have a Dream" speech by Dr. Martin Luther King, Jr.

1960
First lunch counter sit-in protests segregation in restaurants

1962
The University of Mississippi is desegregated with the help of federal troops

1968
Dr. Martin Luther King, Jr., assassinated

1957
Desegregation of Central High School using federal troops

1963
Dr. Martin Luther King, Jr., arrested and jailed in desegregation protest

1963
NAACP leader Medgar Evers murdered

1965
Protesters marching in support of equal voting rights are attacked by police

1955–1956
Bus boycott protests segregation in city transportation

0 ____ 400 miles
0 ____ 400 km
Lambert Azimuthal Equal-Area projection

John F. Kennedy 1961–1963
Lyndon B. Johnson 1963–1969
Richard Nixon 1969–1974
Gerald Ford 1974–1977

1964 Civil Rights Act passes

1968 • Dr. Martin Luther King, Jr., assassinated • Indian Civil Rights Act passes

1970 Grape workers gain better pay and working conditions

1964 • **1969** • **1974**

1964 Civil rights activist Nelson Mandela receives life sentence in South Africa

1967 First heart transplant performed in South Africa

1972 • Britain imposes direct rule on Northern Ireland • Terrorists kill Olympic athletes

White House Historical Association

Lesson 1
The Civil Rights Movement

ESSENTIAL QUESTION *Why does conflict develop?*

IT MATTERS BECAUSE
A movement to end decades of mistreatment of African Americans took hold during this era.

Ending Inequality in Education

GUIDING QUESTION *How did supporters of civil rights challenge discrimination in public schools?*

After suffering **discrimination** and unfair treatment for centuries, African Americans in the mid-1900s began to make real progress in winning an equal place in American life. They fought for equal rights in jobs, housing, and education. They also fought against segregation, the separation of people of different races. At that time, many African Americans lived with segregation in schools, housing, and many public places.

The World War II Years: The Movement Begins

World War II had been one turning point. African Americans' demands for more rights helped end discrimination in factories that did work for the government. African Americans also won better job opportunities in the military.

James Farmer and George Houser founded the Congress of Racial Equality (CORE) in Chicago in 1942. A year later, CORE led a protest targeting public places that refused to serve African Americans. CORE protesters helped end segregation in many restaurants, theaters, and other public places in Chicago, Detroit, Denver, and Syracuse, a city in New York.

(l) Carl Iwasaki/Time & Life Pictures/Getty Images, (cl) Francis Miller/Time Life Pictures/Getty Images, (c) Gene Herrick/AP Images, (cr)Flip Schulke/CORBIS, (r) Library of Congress/LC-USF33-011490-M5

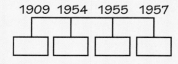

After the war, African American soldiers returned home. They hoped their wartime sacrifices would earn them greater respect and freedom. In many cases, they were disappointed. Change was slow, and the strong desire to end unfairness soon led to protest. This became the **civil** rights movement. The word *civil* means "having to do with citizens and their government."

Brown v. Board of Education

At the head of this growing movement was the National Association for the Advancement of Colored People (NAACP). The NAACP had worked since its founding in 1909 to improve African Americans' rights. One method they used was to work to change segregation of public education. In the 1950s, NAACP lawyers made a stunning breakthrough.

The U.S. Supreme Court had upheld segregation in the past. In 1896 in *Plessy* v. *Ferguson*, the Court ruled that it was legal to have "separate but equal" facilities for African Americans. In reality, separate facilities were often not equal at all.

Thurgood Marshall was the chief lawyer for the NAACP. He decided to challenge the idea of "separate but equal" schools. To do it, he used the case of seven-year-old Linda Brown. The African American girl was not allowed to attend an all-white school just blocks from her house. She had to go to an all-African American school across town. Her family asked a court to let her go to the nearby school. They lost. Marshall and the NAACP took her case all the way to the Supreme Court.

The case of *Brown* v. *Board of Education of Topeka, Kansas* reached the Supreme Court in December 1952. Marshall argued that, under segregation, schools provided for African American students were not—and could not be—equal to white schools.

On May 17, 1954, the Court gave its ruling. The Court ruled 9–0 that separating schoolchildren by race went against the Constitution.

In *Brown* v. *Board of Education,* the Supreme Court found that segregated classrooms denied children like Linda Brown (first row, far right, with hands folded) an equal education. The decision said: "In these days, it is doubtful that any child may reasonably be expected to succeed in life if he is denied the opportunity of an education. Such an opportunity . . . must be made available to all on equal terms."

Carl Iwasaki/Time & Life Pictures/Getty Images

Segregation was widespread in the United States.

1 **REGION** Which category had the largest number of states in it—those segregated by law or those where segregation was not allowed?

2 **CRITICAL THINKING**
Speculating Why do you think segregation was widespread in the South and prohibited in the North?

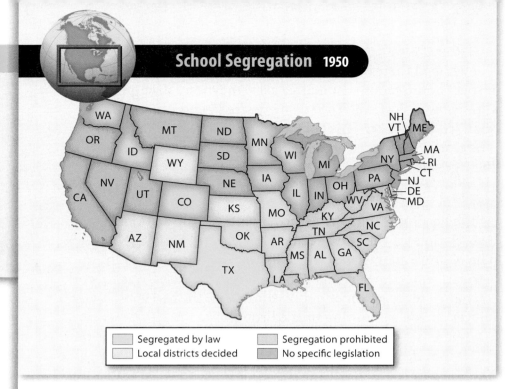

School Segregation 1950

Legend:
- Segregated by law
- Local districts decided
- Segregation prohibited
- No specific legislation

The *Brown* decision reversed the *Plessy* v. *Ferguson* ruling. Chief Justice Earl Warren summarized the Court's new ruling. He wrote:

PRIMARY SOURCE

❝ In the field of public education, the doctrine of 'separate but equal' has no place. Separate educational facilities are ... unequal.❞

—from *Brown* v. *Board of Education of Topeka, Kansas*

The Challenge of Integration

The Court's decision in *Brown* applied only to public schools. Its impact, however, went far deeper. The ruling threatened the whole system of segregation. It helped many people see that it was time to oppose other forms of discrimination. The decision also angered many white Southerners, who became more determined to defend segregation.

In 1955 the Supreme Court followed up its decision in *Brown* v. *Board of Education* with another ruling. This ruling called on public schools to make plans for **integrating** their classrooms. The Court did not set a deadline for the schools. Instead, it instructed schools to act "with all deliberate speed." This unclear language would lead to trouble.

Reading **HELP**DESK CCSS

Academic Vocabulary

integrate to bring races together

Some school systems followed the order quickly. However, in parts of the South, local leaders vowed to keep African American children out of white schools. A clash between the federal government and these states seemed likely.

The Little Rock Showdown

In 1957 a judge ordered an all-white school, Central High School in Little Rock, Arkansas, to admit African Americans. Arkansas governor Orval Faubus was against integration. In September, he called out the state's National Guard to stop African Americans from entering the high school.

When classes began for the year, Guard members blocked the school's entrance. They turned away nine African American students. One of them, 15-year-old Elizabeth Eckford, tried to squeeze past a soldier. "He raised his bayonet," she remembered, "and then the other guards moved in and raised their bayonets."

For the first time since the Civil War, a Southern state had defied the federal government. President Eisenhower had doubts about the *Brown* decision. Still, he believed he had to enforce the law. The president warned Faubus that if the students were not let in, the federal government would act.

When a federal judge ruled that the governor had broken the law, Faubus removed the National Guard. Eisenhower sent hundreds of federal troops to Little Rock to protect the African American students, and they entered the school.

✓ PROGRESS CHECK

Analyzing How had the *Plessy* ruling contributed to segregation?

Francis Miller/Time Life Pictures/Getty Images

Elizabeth Eckford tries to enter Central High School on her first day of classes.

Rosa Parks (1913–2005)

Rosa Parks was a civil rights activist as early as the 1940s. It was her role in the Montgomery bus boycott, however, that began an era of real change for African Americans. Late in life, she said: "I do the very best I can to look upon life with optimism and hope and looking forward to a better day. . . . [Yet] it pains me that there is still a lot of . . . racism." In 1999 Parks was awarded the Congressional Gold Medal.

▶ **CRITICAL THINKING**
Analyzing Primary Sources What did Parks find to be a challenge to her optimism?

Moving Beyond the Schoolhouse

GUIDING QUESTION *How did nonviolent protests help African Americans secure their rights?*

Public education was only one front in the growing civil rights movement. African Americans were also working to gain fair treatment outside of the schools. In 1955 events in Montgomery, Alabama, sparked a mass movement that would change the nation forever.

A Bus Boycott in Montgomery

Rosa Parks was an African American who lived and worked in Montgomery, Alabama. She also served as secretary of the local chapter of the NAACP. On December 1, 1955, she boarded a city bus and found a seat in the "whites only" seating area.

The driver ordered Parks to move, but Parks refused. At the next stop, police arrested her and fined her $10.

The arrest led African Americans in the city to **boycott**— refuse to use—city buses. The boycotters had strength in numbers. About 75 percent of bus riders in Montgomery were African American.

At a boycott meeting, a young minister, Dr. Martin Luther King, Jr., stood to speak. Not yet widely known, Dr. King was already a powerful orator. He inspired the crowd, saying: "[T]here comes a time when people get tired of being trampled over by the iron feet of oppression."

The boycott upset many people's daily lives. Yet African Americans of Montgomery stayed strong. Students got rides to school. Workers walked or rode bikes to their jobs. Community leaders set up car pools to shuttle people from place to place. They all found ways to exist without using the buses.

The bus boycott lasted more than a year. During that time, Dr. King's house was fire-bombed. City officials arrested Dr. King and other leaders under an old law that prohibited boycotts. The bus company lost money in fares. Businesses in Montgomery lost customers. Finally, the Supreme Court settled the matter. It ruled that the bus segregation law was unconstitutional. In December 1956, the boycott ended.

The Practice of Nonviolence

The victory in Montgomery helped make Dr. King a leader of the civil rights movement. Short in stature and gentle in manner, King was at the time just 27 years old. Yet he had

TEXT: Quote by Rosa Parks, Raymond and Rosa Parks Institute., From Dr. Martin Luther King, Jr., at the start of the Montgomery Bus Boycott, Dec. 6, 1955. Reprinted by arrangement with The Heirs to the Estate of Martin Luther King Jr., c/o Writers House as agent for the proprietor

Reading **HELP**DESK **CCSS**

boycott to refuse to use
civil disobedience the refusal to obey laws that are considered unjust

Build Vocabulary: *Word Origins*

The word *boycott* comes from a British official, Charles Boycott, whose actions in Ireland led to the first protest of the type that now bears his name.

been well prepared to take on the challenge of leadership that awaited him. His father, Martin Luther King, Sr., was the pastor of the Ebenezer Baptist Church in Atlanta, Georgia, and an advocate of civil rights. His mother, Alberta Williams King, was the daughter of a popular minister and leader in the African American community.

King was also strongly influenced by two leaders from outside his family who had protested against injustice: A. Philip Randolph, the nation's most prominent African American labor leader, and Mohandas Gandhi, who used nonviolent protest to help India gain independence from Britain. Gandhi had used protest methods based on **civil disobedience,** or the refusal to obey laws that were considered unjust.

Like Gandhi, Dr. King encouraged his followers to disobey unjust laws without using violence. He was certain that using such a method of protest would one day lead the government to end segregation.

Dr. Martin Luther King, Jr., was not the only important minister in the bus boycott. Many of the other leaders were African American ministers. The success of the boycott was greatly influenced by the support of the African American churches in the city.

In January 1957, Dr. King and 60 other ministers started a new organization called the Southern Christian Leadership Conference (SCLC). SCLC leaders prepared African Americans for the struggle for equal rights. They showed civil rights workers how to protect themselves from violent attacks, how to choose issues to protest, and how to organize people for support.

TEXT: Martin Luther King, Jr., Acceptance Address at Nobel Peace Prize Ceremony, Oslo, Norway, December 10, 1964. Reprinted by arrangement with The Heirs to the Estate of Martin Luther King Jr., c/o Writers House as agent for the proprietor New York, NY. Copyright 1963 Dr. Martin Luther King Jr; copyright renewed 1991 Coretta Scott King; PHOTO: Flip Schulke/CORBIS

✓ **PROGRESS CHECK**

Explaining What was the final resolution of the bus boycott in Montgomery, Alabama?

BIOGRAPHY

Dr. Martin Luther King, Jr. (1929–1968)

In the 1950s, Dr. Martin Luther King, Jr., became a leader of the civil rights movement. A minister and a stirring speaker, Dr. King organized marches, boycotts, and demonstrations that opened many people's eyes to the need for change. In 1964 he won the Nobel Peace Prize. He said, "I have the audacity [boldness] to believe that peoples everywhere can have three meals a day for their bodies, education and culture for their minds, and dignity, equality, and freedom for their spirits." Dr. King was assassinated in 1968 in Memphis, Tennessee.

▶ **CRITICAL THINKING**

Making Inferences How would you describe Dr. King's tone when he stated that his beliefs required "audacity"?

LESSON 1 REVIEW

Review Vocabulary

1. Write a sentence to explain how a boycott might be seen as an example of civil disobedience.

Answer the Guiding Questions

2. ***Explaining*** How did *Brown* v. *Board of Education* challenge discrimination in schools?

3. ***Summarizing*** What were the public responses to court-ordered desegregation?

4. ***Describing*** What impact did the Montgomery bus boycott have on securing equal rights for African Americans?

5. **ARGUMENT** In a short essay, explain which of the following events you think was more important for the civil rights movement:
• the *Brown* ruling
• integration at Little Rock's high school
• the Montgomery bus boycott

Roll of Thunder, Hear My Cry

by Mildred D. Taylor

TEXT: From ROLL OF THUNDER, HEAR MY CRY by Mildred Taylor. © 1976 by Mildred D. Taylor. Used by permission of Dial Books for Young Readers, A Division of Penguin Young Readers Group, A Member of Penguin Group (USA) Inc., 345 Hudson Street, New York, NY 10014. All rights reserved PHOTO: Library of Congress/LC-USF33-011490-M5

Mildred D. Taylor (1943–) was born in Jackson, Mississippi, but grew up in Ohio. Taylor and her family made frequent trips back to Mississippi, where she learned about the people and stories that make up her books.

In this story, we meet young Cassie. She and her family live in the Deep South during the Depression. Cassie has been protected from much of the ugly racism surrounding them. In this scene, during a visit to town with her grandmother, Cassie comes face to face with what it means to be African American in a segregated South. She has just angered the white storekeeper, Mr. Barnett, by complaining about his service. Then, she runs into two white acquaintances, Lillian Jean and Jeremy Simms.

PRIMARY SOURCE

❝ I had a good mind to go back in and find out what had made Mr. Barnett so mad. I actually turned once and headed toward the store, then remembering what Mr. Barnett had said about my returning, I swung back around, kicking at the sidewalk, my head bowed.

It was then that I bumped into Lillian Jean Simms.

"Why don't you look where you're going?" she asked huffily. Jeremy and her two younger brothers were with her. "Hey, Cassie," said Jeremy.

"Hey, Jeremy," I said solemnly, keeping my eyes on Lillian Jean.

"Well, apologize," she ordered.

"What?"

"You bumped into me. Now you apologize."

Life was difficult for African Americans in the South in the 1930s.

I did not feel like messing with Lillian Jean. I had other things on my mind. "Okay," I said, starting past, "I'm sorry."

Lillian Jean sidestepped in front of me. "That ain't enough. Get down in the road."

I looked up at her. "You crazy?"

"You can't watch where you're going, get in the road. Maybe that way you won't be bumping into decent white folks with your little nasty self."

. . . "I ain't nasty," I said, properly holding my temper in check, . . . "Ah, let her pass, Lillian Jean," said Jeremy. "She ain't done nothin' to you."

"She done something to me just standing in front of me." With that, she reached for my arm and attempted to push me off the sidewalk. I braced myself and swept my arm backward, . . . But someone caught it from behind, painfully twisting it, and shoved me off the sidewalk into the road. . . . Mr. Simms glared down at me. "When my gal Lillian Jean says for you to get yo'self off the sidewalk, you get, you hear?"

. . . "You hear me talkin' to you, gal? You 'pologize to Miz Lillian Jean this minute."

I stared up at Mr. Simms, frightened. Jeremy appeared frightened too. "I—I apologized already."

Jeremy seemed relieved that I had spoken. "She d-did, Pa. R-right now, 'fore y'all come, she did—"

Mr. Simms turned an angry gaze upon his son and Jeremy faltered, looked at me, and hung his head.

Then Mr. Simms jumped into the street. I moved away from him, trying to get up. . . . I scrambled up and ran blindly for the wagon. Someone grabbed me and I fought wildly, . . . "Stop, Cassie!" Big Ma said. "Stop, it's me. We're going home now."

"Not 'fore she 'pologizes to my gal, y'all ain't," said Mr. Simms.

. . . "Tell her, Aunty—"

Big Ma looked at me again, her voice cracking as she spoke. "Go on, child . . . apologize."

. . . "I'm sorry," I mumbled.

"I'm sorry, *Miz* Lillian Jean," demanded Mr. Simms.

. . . A painful tear slid down my cheek and my lips trembled. "I'm sorry . . . M-Miz . . . Lillian Jean."

. . . I turned and fled crying into the back of the wagon. No day in all my life had ever been as cruel as this one. **99**

Literary Element

The **antagonist** in a story is a character who stands in opposition to the main character, or the **protagonist.** If Cassie is the protagonist here, who do you think is the antagonist?

Analyzing Literature DBQ

1 *Analyzing* What descriptions in the scene suggest that Cassie has been protected from the racism around her?

2 *Interpreting* What do you think Lillian Jean's purpose is in confronting Cassie?

3 *Describing* How would you describe what Jeremy is feeling in this scene?

4 *Analyzing* Why do you think Cassie considers this the most cruel day of her life?

networks

There's More Online!

☑ **CHART/GRAPH**
35th and 36th Presidents

☑ **GRAPHIC ORGANIZER**
New Frontier and
Great Society

☑ **MAP** Election of 1960

☑ **VIDEO**

Lesson 2
Kennedy and Johnson

ESSENTIAL QUESTION *How do new ideas change the way people live?*

IT MATTERS BECAUSE

Kennedy's New Frontier and Johnson's Great Society made sweeping changes to American society.

Kennedy and the New Frontier

GUIDING QUESTION *Why did John F. Kennedy's presidency appeal to many Americans?*

The year 1960 was a presidential election year. The Republicans named Vice President Richard M. Nixon to be their candidate. He pledged to continue the policies of President Eisenhower. The Democratic candidate, John F. Kennedy, promised new programs to "get the country moving again."

Polls showed Nixon leading Kennedy through much of the campaign. One issue that seemed to hurt Kennedy was his Roman Catholic religion. No Catholic had ever served as president before, and many Americans feared Kennedy might show more loyalty to his church than to his country. To calm these worries, Kennedy stressed his belief in the separation of church and state. He assured voters that his religious beliefs would not determine his actions.

A Hero in World War II

Other parts of Kennedy's background worked strongly in his favor. For example, he came from one of the country's wealthiest and most powerful families. His father, Joseph P. Kennedy, was a successful business leader and the American ambassador to Britain at the start of World War II.

(c)Steve Schapiro/CORBIS, (r)Wikimedia/LBJ Museum & Library

Reading **HELP**DESK **CCSS**

Taking Notes: *Identifying*

As you read, use a chart like this one to identify the major aspects of each of these plans.

New Frontier	Great Society

Content Vocabulary
• **poverty line**
• **Medicare**
• **Medicaid**

Kennedy also boasted a fine military record. During World War II, he joined the United States Navy. He was **assigned** to active duty in the Pacific. When the Japanese sank the patrol torpedo (PT) boat he commanded, Kennedy saved the life of an injured crew member by swimming to shore with him on his back. His actions won him praise as a hero.

Kennedy's political career began in 1946 when he won a seat in Congress from Massachusetts. Six years later, he was elected to the United States Senate. After easily winning reelection to the Senate in 1958, Kennedy ran for the presidency in 1960.

A Debate, and the Power of TV

A key moment in the 1960 election was the first-ever televised presidential debate. Because Nixon was recovering from an illness, he looked tired and sick. Kennedy appeared handsome and youthful. People who listened to the debate on radio thought Nixon had won. The huge TV audience, however, saw it differently. They thought Kennedy was the clear winner.

In November, nearly 70 million voters turned out to vote. The results were very close. In the popular vote, Kennedy won 49.7 percent, while Nixon received 49.5 percent. In the electoral vote, Kennedy gained a greater margin over Nixon—303 to 219 votes.

INFOGRAPHIC

John Kennedy won the 1960 election by a thin margin.

1 IDENTIFYING In what regions of the country did Kennedy receive the strongest support? In what regions was support for Nixon the strongest?

2 CRITICAL THINKING *Speculating* Which candidate do you think Byrd's candidacy likely hurt more? Explain your answer.

ELECTION OF 1960

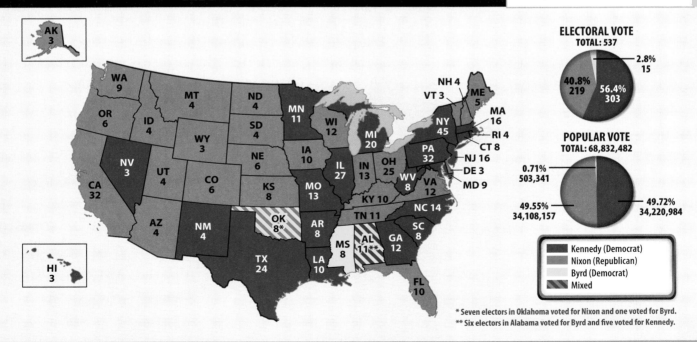

* Seven electors in Oklahoma voted for Nixon and one voted for Byrd.
** Six electors in Alabama voted for Byrd and five voted for Kennedy.

Academic Vocabulary

assign to appoint; to give the job of

Presidential Firsts

John Kennedy was the nation's first Catholic president. In 2009 Barack Obama became the nation's first African American president. To gain the Democratic nomination, he defeated Hillary Clinton, who had hoped to become the nation's first woman president.

Kennedy was sworn in as the 35th president of the United States on January 20, 1961. The young president promised to face the nation's challenges with determination. He also roused the American people to action:

PRIMARY SOURCE

66 And so, my fellow Americans: ask not what your country can do for you—ask what you can do for your country. 99

—From John F. Kennedy's Inaugural Address

Kennedy's Ideas for Change

As president, Kennedy pushed forward a program that came to be called the "New Frontier." He backed federal aid for education and for the poor. Congress, however, did not want to fund expensive programs.

President Kennedy also supported civil rights. He also feared that moving too quickly would anger white Southern Democrats, whose support he needed. In 1963 Kennedy's civil rights bill passed in the House but stalled in the Senate.

The Assassination of a President

On November 22, 1963, Kennedy visited Dallas with his wife, Jacqueline. As the president's car drove through the city, an assassin struck. Kennedy was shot and killed. Vice President Lyndon B. Johnson became president.

The assassination stunned the nation. Then, Lee Harvey Oswald, who was charged with the killing, was murdered as he was moved from one jail to another. Some Americans believed the Kennedy assassination was a conspiracy—an act planned by more

Bettmann/CORBIS

John and Jacqueline Kennedy greet cheering crowds as their open limousine drives through the streets of Dallas shortly before the president was assassinated.

Reading HELPDESK (CCSS)

poverty line income level deemed necessary to acquire the necessities of life.

Medicare federal health insurance program mainly for older people
Medicaid federal-state health insurance program for low-income people

Academic Vocabulary

consist to be made up of; to include

than one person. A commission headed by Supreme Court Chief Justice Earl Warren later investigated the assassination and stated that Oswald had acted alone.

☑ **PROGRESS CHECK**

Describing What was the turning point in the 1960 election?

Johnson's Great Society

GUIDING QUESTION *How did the Johnson administration expand Kennedy's domestic plans?*

President Johnson outlined a set of programs known as the "Great Society." His War on Poverty **consisted** of programs that helped people living below the **poverty line**—the income level required to obtain life's necessities. Two examples are the Head Start program, which provided preschool education, and the Job Corps, which trained young people seeking work.

In 1965 Congress passed **Medicare** and **Medicaid.** Medicare established a health insurance program for elderly people. Medicaid provided health care to low-income families.

In 1966 Congress created the Department of Housing and Urban Development (HUD), which funded public housing. Another program, Model Cities, helped rebuild cities. The Elementary and Secondary Education Act of 1965 helped schools.

As president, Johnson supported civil rights. He helped Congress pass the nation's most far-reaching civil rights act. The Civil Rights Act of 1964 outlawed discrimination in public places, employment, and voter registration. It banned discrimination by race, gender, religion, and national origin.

Lyndon Johnson was a master at persuading others to support his plans. His method, known as "the Johnson Treatment," was highly effective.

☑ **PROGRESS CHECK**

Explaining What was the purpose of the Job Corps?

LESSON 2 REVIEW CCSS

Review Vocabulary

1. Write a sentence explaining how *Medicaid* and the *poverty line* might be connected.

2. Explain the significance of the word *Medicare* to Johnson's presidency.

Answer the Guiding Questions

3. *Analyzing* What factors contributed to John F. Kennedy's victory in the 1960 presidential election over Richard M. Nixon?

4. *Summarizing* What did the Civil Rights Act of 1964 accomplish?

5. **INFORMATIVE/EXPLANATORY** Write a short essay comparing and contrasting Kennedy and Johnson as presidents of the United States.

networks

There's More Online!

☑ **GRAPHIC ORGANIZER**
Freedom Rides

☑ **PRIMARY SOURCE**
Letter from
Birmingham Jail

☑ **SLIDE SHOW** Freedom Riders

☑ **TIME LINE** Civil Rights Movement

☑ **VIDEO**

Lesson 3
Civil Rights in the 1960s

ESSENTIAL QUESTION *How do new ideas change the way people live?*

IT MATTERS BECAUSE
The successes of the civil rights movement could not prevent tragedy and the spread of less peaceful protests.

The Growing Civil Rights Movement

GUIDING QUESTION *What leaders and groups emerged during the civil rights movement?*

The civil rights movement gained strength in the 1960s. Early activity targeted segregation in the South. Later, African Americans expanded their goal to fighting discrimination and racism in the North as well. In Northern cities, African Americans and whites often lived in different neighborhoods. As a result, many schools were all-white or all-African American.

High school and college students staged **sit-ins** in nearly 80 cities. A sit-in is the act of protesting by sitting down to block traffic and normal activities. It is a type of nonviolent protest. Protesters had sit-ins across the nation. Many took place in stores that did not serve African Americans. The sit-ins hurt business because the protests made it difficult for customers to shop. Gradually, many stores agreed to serve African Americans.

The sit-ins helped launch a new civil rights group, the Student Nonviolent Coordinating Committee (SNCC). Civil rights activist Ella Baker was one of SNCC's organizers. She had urged students to create the group instead of joining the NAACP. Baker told students that they had "the right to direct

(l)Bettmann/CORBIS, (cl) Bettmann/CORBIS, (cr) Flip Schulke/CORBIS,

Reading **HELP**DESK (CCSS)

Taking Notes: *Identifying*

As you read, use a diagram like this one to identify the major chain of events for the Freedom Riders in 1961.

Freedom Riders

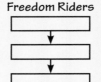

Content Vocabulary
• **sit-in**
• **interstate**

sit-in the act of protesting by sitting down, commonly used as a method of nonviolent protest

interstate moving between two or more states

their own affairs and even make their own mistakes." Earlier, Baker had played major roles in the NAACP and the Southern Christian Leadership Conference.

Freedom Riders Brave Violence

In 1960 the Supreme Court ruled that bus stations could not be segregated. The Congress of Racial Equality (CORE) decided to find out if officials in the South were enforcing the ruling. On May 4, 1961, a group of African Americans and white CORE members left Washington, D.C. Calling themselves Freedom Riders, they filled two buses bound for New Orleans. The trip went smoothly until it reached Alabama. There, angry whites stoned and beat the Freedom Riders.

The Freedom Riders pressed on. They met more violence in Birmingham and Montgomery, Alabama. In Jackson, Mississippi, police and Mississippi National Guard units met the buses. As the Freedom Riders tried to enter the whites-only waiting room at the bus station, they were arrested and jailed.

Despite the violence and arrests, more Freedom Riders kept coming all summer. In the fall, the federal government took steps to enforce the Supreme Court ruling. Officials issued new rules that banned segregation on **interstate** buses—those that crossed state lines—and in bus stations.

The Freedom Riders came under violent attack.

▶ **CRITICAL THINKING**
Summarizing What was the purpose of the Freedom Riders?

TEXT: Ella Baker/Ella Baker Center for Human Rights;
PHOTO: Bettmann/CORBIS

Civil Rights and Higher Education

African Americans continued to push for their civil rights. Their actions put pressure on President Kennedy to take a more active role in the civil rights struggle.

In 1962 a federal court ordered the University of Mississippi to enroll its first African American student, James Meredith. Mississippi Governor Ross Barnett and his state police kept Meredith from registering. Riots erupted when President Kennedy sent federal marshals to protect Meredith. A mob stormed a university building with guns and rocks. Marshals fought back with tear gas and nightsticks. Meredith did register, but two people died in the violence. Federal troops protected Meredith until he graduated in 1963.

State and federal power clashed again in June 1963 in Alabama. Governor George Wallace vowed to block the integration of the University of Alabama in Tuscaloosa. President Kennedy, acting on the advice of his brother, Robert, sent the Alabama National Guard to ensure the entry of African Americans to the university. Wallace backed down.

The Birmingham Connection

In spring 1963, Dr. Martin Luther King, Jr., and the SCLC began a protest to end segregation in Birmingham, Alabama. Police arrested hundreds, including Dr. King. Still, the protests continued. During Dr. King's two weeks in jail, he wrote the moving "Letter from Birmingham Jail." The letter was a response to criticism from a group of white church leaders. The leaders agreed with the need for greater civil rights. However, they favored a calm, orderly approach to making change. Dr. King forcefully defended his methods:

Dr. King's "Letter from Birmingham Jail" was written to address criticism of his use of civil disobedience.

▶ **CRITICAL THINKING**
Drawing Conclusions How did going to jail help Dr. King and his colleagues accomplish their goals?

PRIMARY SOURCE

❝ Perhaps it is easy for those who have never felt the stinging darts of segregation to say, 'Wait.' But when you have seen vicious mobs lynch your mothers and fathers at will and drown your sisters and brothers at whim; when you have seen hate filled policemen curse, kick, and even kill your black brothers and sisters . . . then you will understand why we find it difficult to wait. ❞

—Dr. Martin Luther King, Jr., "Letter from Birmingham Jail," 1963

TEXT: Letter from Birmingham Jail, Dr. Martin Luther King, Jr., April 16, 1963. Reprinted by arrangement with The Heirs to the Estate of Martin Luther King Jr., c/o Writers House as agent for the proprietor New York, NY. Copyright

Reading **HELP**DESK

Build Vocabulary: *Multiple Meaning Words*

Many words that are spelled the same may have multiple meanings. In the second paragraph under the heading "Civil Rights and Higher Education," notice the verb *stormed*. The verb *storm* can mean, as it does here, "to attack." It can also mean "to move about violently," "to be overly emotional," or "to rain, hail, or snow."

The protests continued. Horrified television viewers around the country watched as police set snarling dogs on unarmed demonstrators. They saw small children battered by powerful fire hoses. President Kennedy sent 3,000 troops to restore peace.

Then, on June 11, 1963, an NAACP leader named Medgar Evers was murdered in Jackson, Mississippi. The killing and the events in Alabama pushed President Kennedy to take a stand. He spoke on television about the "moral issue" facing the nation:

PRIMARY SOURCE

❝ It is not enough to pin the blame on others, to say this is a problem of one section of the country or another. . . . A great change is at hand, and our . . . obligation, is to make that revolution, that change, peaceful and constructive for all. Those who do nothing are inviting shame as well as violence. Those who act boldly are recognizing right. ❞

—President John F. Kennedy, televised speech, June 1963

Days later, the president sent new legislation to Congress. The bill aimed to give all Americans the right to be served in public places and to end discrimination in employment.

March on Washington

To rally support for Kennedy's civil rights bill, Dr. King and the SCLC called for a march on Washington, D.C. The date was set for August 28, 1963. More than 200,000 people of all colors and from all over the country arrived to take part in the event.

During the March on Washington in August 1963, huge crowds surrounded the reflecting pool between the Washington Monument and the Lincoln Memorial.

▶ **CRITICAL THINKING**
Analyzing Visuals How do you think images such as this affected attitudes about the civil rights movement?

Bettmann/CORBIS

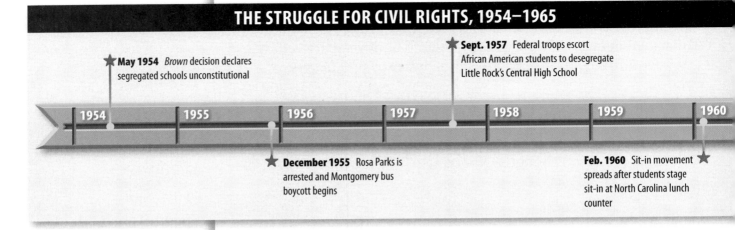

THE STRUGGLE FOR CIVIL RIGHTS, 1954–1965

May 1954 *Brown* decision declares segregated schools unconstitutional

Sept. 1957 Federal troops escort African American students to desegregate Little Rock's Central High School

| 1954 | 1955 | 1956 | 1957 | 1958 | 1959 | 1960 |

December 1955 Rosa Parks is arrested and Montgomery bus boycott begins

Feb. 1960 Sit-in movement spreads after students stage sit-in at North Carolina lunch counter

▶ **CRITICAL THINKING**
Identifying Central Issues Why was it important that federal troops helped desegregate the Little Rock schools?

The March on Washington was one of the high points of the civil rights movement. Nan Grogan Orrock, who would later serve in the Georgia Senate and House of Representatives, was a college student in 1963. She recalled her feelings on that August day:

PRIMARY SOURCE

❝ You couldn't help but get swept up in the feeling of the March. It was an incredible experience of this mass of humanity with one mind moving down the street. It was like being part of a glacier. You could feel the sense of collective [united] will and effort. ❞

—from *Mighty Like a Stream*

About 6,000 police officers watched. Yet all they did was direct traffic. No trouble occurred. Marchers walked peacefully through Washington. They carried signs urging Congress to act. They sang songs, including the one that became the movement's anthem: "We Shall Overcome." Later that day, Dr. King stood on the steps of the Lincoln Memorial. There, he delivered his "I Have a Dream" speech. Dr. King shared his vision of a changed country:

PRIMARY SOURCE

❝ I have a dream that one day this nation will rise up and live out the true meaning of its creed: 'We hold these truths to be self-evident; that all men are created equal.' . . . When we [let] freedom ring, . . . we will be able to speed up that day when all of God's children, . . . [will] join hands and sing in the words of the old . . . spiritual: Free at last! Free at last! Thank God Almighty, we are free at last! ❞

—from the "I Have a Dream" speech

TEXT: "I Have a Dream" by Martin Luther King, Jr., Reprinted by arrangement with the Estate of Martin Luther King Jr., c/o Writers House as agent for the proprietor New York, NY.

Reading **HELP**DESK **CCSS**

Academic Vocabulary

register to enroll; to sign up

Sept. 1962 James Meredith tries to register at University of Mississippi

Aug. 1963 Dr. King delivers "I Have a Dream" speech during March on Washington

July 1964 President Johnson signs Civil Rights Act of 1964 into law

Aug. 1965 Congress passes Voting Rights Act of 1965

| 1961 | 1962 | 1963 | 1964 | 1965 | 1966 |

May 1961 Freedom Riders brave violence to desegregate interstate bus travel

May 1963 Police use force to stop Birmingham marchers

March 1965 Dr. King leads march in Selma, Alabama, to build support for new voting rights law

Freedom Summer Campaign

President Kennedy did not live to see passage of his civil rights bill. He was assassinated in November 1963. After taking office, President Lyndon Johnson took up the challenge. He pushed Congress to pass the Civil Rights Act of 1964. The law outlawed discrimination in hiring. It ended segregation in stores, restaurants, theaters, and hotels. Yet even with this powerful new law, poll taxes and other laws kept African Americans from using their right to vote in many states.

In the summer of 1964, thousands of civil rights workers volunteered to work in the South. Their goal was to help African Americans **register,** or enroll, to vote. Freedom Summer workers faced strong, sometimes violent, opposition. The murder of three young civil rights workers in Mississippi deeply disturbed the nation.

Voting Rights

The next year, SNCC led a major protest in Selma, Alabama. The protest targeted the ongoing denial of African Americans' voting rights. Police attacked and beat demonstrators.

On March 15, 1965, President Johnson addressed the nation. He called for a new voting rights law. "[T]here can be no argument," he said. "Every American citizen must have an equal right to vote." Congress responded by passing the Voting Rights Act of 1965. In August, Johnson signed the historic act into law.

The law gave the federal government power to force local officials to let African Americans register to vote. This act led to dramatic changes in the South. In 1966 about 100 African Americans held elective office in all Southern states. By 1972 that number had increased tenfold.

Following the passage of the Voting Rights Act of 1965, African American voters joined whites waiting in line to cast their ballots in a small Alabama town.

After passage of the Voting Rights Act, the civil rights movement shifted its focus. It began to work on the problems of African Americans trapped in poverty and living in major cities.

☑ **PROGRESS CHECK**

Explaining What was the goal of the Freedom Riders?

Different Views

GUIDING QUESTION *Why did some African American leaders disagree with Dr. King's nonviolent protest?*

The Voting Rights Act was just one of the civil rights movement's many victories. Yet many African Americans were growing tired of the slow pace of change. Soon different voices began to compete for the attention of the African American community.

Malcolm X was born Malcolm Little in Omaha, Nebraska. He **emerged** as an important voice for African Americans at the height of the Civil Rights movement. Malcolm X was a leader in the Nation of Islam—also known as the Black Muslims. He criticized the civil rights goal of integration and said the best way for African Americans to achieve racial justice was to live apart from whites.

With this message, Malcolm X found many followers. By 1964, however, he began to soften his ideas. He called for "a society in which there could exist honest white-black brotherhood." Soon afterward, rival Black Muslims shot and killed him. Yet Malcolm X's fiery words and writings continued to influence people even after his death.

The Black Power Movement

Stokely Carmichael, who became the leader of SNCC, led the call for Black Power. This philosophy of racial pride encouraged African Americans to create their own culture. Carmichael and others called at times for a complete change of society through revolution.

Although rejected by groups such as the NAACP, Black Power had a great impact on the civil rights movement. It became popular in the poor city neighborhoods where many African Americans lived.

Stokely Carmichael voiced his beliefs for Black Power while participating in the Freedom March from Selma to Montgomery, Alabama.

Reading **HELP**DESK ⓒⓒⓢⓢ

Academic Vocabulary

emerge to rise up; to become

In Oakland, California, Huey Newton and Bobby Seale formed the Black Panther Party. The Panthers represented a growing frustration among urban African Americans. They were angry about poverty and a lack of jobs. The Panthers demanded reforms and armed themselves. They were involved in several clashes with the police.

Violent Clashes

The summer of 1965 brought major urban riots. A week of rioting in the Watts section of Los Angeles left 34 people dead. It took the National Guard to end the uprising.

Following Watts, racial violence hit major cities in 1965, 1966, and 1967. Protests, looting, and burning in Newark, New Jersey, led to 26 deaths and more than $10 million in property damage in 1967. A week later, an uprising in Detroit shut down the city for several days.

The Assassination of Dr. Martin Luther King, Jr.

On April 4, 1968, racial tension took another tragic turn. In Memphis, Tennessee, an assassin shot and killed Dr. Martin Luther King, Jr. His murder set off riots in more than 100 cities. Fires burned just blocks from the White House. A white racist named James Earl Ray went to prison for the crime.

Thousands attended Dr. King's funeral in Atlanta. Millions watched the service on television. All mourned an American hero who, just the night before, told his followers that God had "allowed me to go up to the mountain. … And I've seen the promised land. I may not get there with you. But … we, as a people, will get to the promised land!"

The Black Panthers represented the anger of many urban African Americans.

✓ PROGRESS CHECK

Explaining Why did some African Americans criticize integration?

LESSON 3 REVIEW (CCSS)

Review Vocabulary

1. Write a sentence describing what happens at a sit-in.

2. Describe the meaning of the word *interstate* and its significance to the civil rights movement.

Answer the Guiding Questions

3. ***Connecting*** Write a sentence describing what each leader or group is best known for in the civil rights movement: Ella Baker, Freedom Riders, President Johnson.

4. ***Describing*** What was James Meredith's contribution to the civil rights movement?

5. ***Identifying*** Who was Malcolm X, and what was his early philosophy?

6. **NARRATIVE** Imagine being present in Washington, D.C., to hear Dr. Martin Luther King, Jr., deliver the "I Have a Dream" speech. Write a letter to a friend describing the speech and its impact.

t.ex.: Dr. Martin Luther King, Jr., "I've been to the Mountaintop delivered April 3, 1968, Mason Temple. Reprinted by arrangement with The Heirs to the Estate of Martin Luther King Jr., c/o Writers House as agent for the proprietor New York, NY. Copyright 1968 Dr. Martin Luther King Jr; copyright renewed 1991 Coretta Scott King. PHOTO: David J. & Janice L. Frent Collection/Corbis

networks

There's More Online!

☑ **BIOGRAPHY**
 • Herman Badillo
 • Roberto Clemente

☑ **CHART/GRAPH**
 Gender Wage Gap

☑ **GRAPHIC ORGANIZER**
 Goals of Groups

Lesson 4
Other Groups Seek Rights

ESSENTIAL QUESTION *How do new ideas change the way people live?*

IT MATTERS BECAUSE

The civil rights movement inspired women and groups such as Latinos, Native Americans, and disabled Americans to organize and push for equal rights.

The Battle for Women's Rights

GUIDING QUESTION *How were American women influenced by the civil rights movement?*

The civil rights movement did more than expand freedom and opportunity for African Americans. It also helped women, Latinos, Native Americans, and people with disabilities. Women were the first to benefit. In 1963 Congress passed the Equal Pay Act. This law aimed to keep employers from paying women less than men for the same work.

Also in 1963, wife and mother Betty Friedan described the hopes of many women for greater opportunities in her book *The Feminine Mystique.* Three years later, **feminists**—activists for women's rights—created the National Organization for Women (NOW). NOW fought for equal rights for women in all **aspects** of life—jobs, education, and marriage. The "women's liberation" movement was underway.

In the early 1970s, NOW began a campaign for an Equal Rights Amendment (ERA) to the Constitution. The amendment stated, "Equality of rights under the law shall not be denied or abridged by the United States or by any state on account of sex." NOW members and others with similar views worked to pass the ERA. Leading the fight against the amendment was Phyllis

Reading **HELP**DESK ⓒⒸⓈⓈ

Taking Notes: *Describing*

As you read, use a diagram like this one to describe the goals of the different rights movements of this era.

Movement	Goals
Women	
Latinos	
Native Americans	
People with Disabilities	

Content Vocabulary
• **feminist**
• **Latino**

WOMEN'S PAY

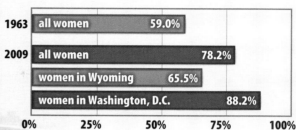

PERCENTAGE OF INCOME COMPARED TO THAT OF MEN

1963	all women	59.0%
2009	all women	78.2%
	women in Wyoming	65.5%
	women in Washington, D.C.	88.2%

0%   25%   50%   75%   100%

Source: www.census.gov/prod/2010pubs/acsbr09-3.pdf

In 1960 working women generally held lower-paying jobs with less status. Pilot Jerrie Cobb was an exception.

ECONOMICS SKILL

In the early 1960s, women who worked outside the home had limited job opportunities. In addition, women were paid less than men for the same work. When Congress passed the Equal Pay Act in 1963, full-time working women were paid 59 cents for every dollar men received.

Look at the bar graph to see how the situation has changed for women overall. The graph also includes figures for the state with the lowest estimated pay for women and for Washington, D.C., which has the highest estimated pay for women.

1 SPECULATING Why do you think pay in Washington, D.C., is higher than average for women?

2 CRITICAL THINKING
Summarizing How would you describe the changes in women's pay since 1963?

Schlafly. She warned that the ERA would upset men's and women's roles and damage the family. The amendment fell short of ratification.

Women's rights activists did win some victories. Women gained more job opportunities. A growing number of women rose to high-level jobs. More women than ever became doctors and lawyers.

Women also gained a greater voice in government. Women candidates won local and state political offices, seats in Congress, and appointments to the president's Cabinet. In 1981 President Ronald Reagan appointed Sandra Day O'Connor as the first female justice of the U.S. Supreme Court.

✓ PROGRESS CHECK

Explaining What was the purpose of the Equal Pay Act?

---

feminist activist for women's rights

Academic Vocabulary

aspect a particular phase or part of something

Build Vocabulary: *Word Parts*

One meaning for the suffix *-ist* is "one who believes in something." *Feminine* means "female," so a feminist is one who believes in and works for women and their rights.

AP Images

Lesson 4   **383**

Expanding Opportunities

GUIDING QUESTION *What other groups struggled for equality?*

The **Latino** (luh•TEE•noh)—or Hispanic—population sought equal rights in the 1960s as well. The term *Latino* refers to Americans with family backgrounds in Latin America or Spain. Although they share many aspects of culture and a language, Latinos are a **diverse** group with different histories.

In the last half of the 1900s, immigration from Mexico and other nations of Latin America rose sharply. The Latino population in the United States increased from 3 million in 1960 to about 50 million in 2010.

By far the largest Latino group in the United States comes from Mexico. Americans of Mexican background have lived in the United States since before the nation was founded. By 2010 more than 30 million Mexican Americans lived throughout the United States.

Latino Farmworkers Form Unions

The fight for rights started among Mexican American migrant farmworkers. These workers led difficult lives. They labored long hours in fields and orchards for low wages. In addition, they had to travel frequently, moving from farm to farm in search of the next job.

In the early 1960s, migrant workers formed unions to fight for better wages and working conditions. César Chávez (SHAH•vehz) organized thousands of workers into the United Farm Workers (UFW).

Chávez was familiar with the suffering of farmworkers. He had labored in the fields since age 10, when his family lost their Arizona farm during the Great Depression. Like thousands of other farmers, the Chávez family took to the road and became migrant workers.

After serving in World War II, Chávez took a paid job to win greater rights for Mexican Americans. In 1962 he returned to the fields and worked on his goal of organizing farmworkers into a union.

César Chávez talks with farmworkers in 1968. A migrant worker since childhood, Chávez had a keen understanding of the workers' plight.

Arthur Schatz/Time Life Pictures/Getty Images

Reading **HELP**DESK (CCSS)

Latino person with family background from Latin America or Spain

Academic Vocabulary

diverse containing many different elements

BIOGRAPHY

**Herman Badillo
(1929–)**

Herman Badillo (bah • DEE • yoh) was born in Puerto Rico. An orphan, he moved to New York City as a boy. He became a lawyer, then got involved in politics. In 1970 he became the first Puerto Rican to win election to Congress. He represented a district in New York City. Badillo later served as the city's deputy mayor.

**Roberto Clemente
(1934–1972)**

Baseball great Roberto Clemente (kluh • MEHN • tay) also came from Puerto Rico. He rose to fame while he was a player for the Pittsburgh Pirates. Clemente was a hero off the baseball diamond, too. He performed charity work in Latin America. In 1972 he died in a plane crash while delivering relief supplies to earthquake victims in Nicaragua.

▶ **CRITICAL THINKING**
Comparing and Contrasting How do you think the challenges Badillo and Clemente faced were similar? How were they different?

In his union work, Chávez followed the nonviolent philosophy of Mohandas Gandhi and Dr. Martin Luther King, Jr. In 1965 he asked Americans to boycott grapes until growers in the San Joaquin Valley of California signed union contracts. "To us," Chávez said, "the boycott of grapes was the most near-perfect of nonviolent struggles, because nonviolence also requires mass involvement." Some 17 million Americans responded to Chávez's call. "For the first time," Chávez said, "the farmworkers got some power."

Puerto Ricans and Cubans Migrate

Puerto Ricans, another Latino group, come from Puerto Rico. This island in the Caribbean is a commonwealth of the United States. People who live there are American citizens. Puerto Ricans have made major contributions to American history and culture.

Because Puerto Rico is not a wealthy island, many Puerto Ricans have migrated to American cities. They have come to places such as New York City in search of jobs. As with African Americans, Puerto Ricans have faced discrimination in the job market.

After Cuba's revolution in 1959, dictator Fidel Castro set up a Communist government. More than 200,000 people opposed to Castro fled to the United States in the 1960s. Thousands more came in the 1980s. These immigrants settled all over the United States. A large number settled in South Florida. There they have established a thriving community.

Build Vocabulary: *Word Origins*

The word *Latino* comes from the term *Latin America,* the part of North and South America south of the United States. This region is called Latin America because the people there speak languages—Spanish or Portuguese—that come from the Latin language.

Native Americans Organize

In the years after World War II, Native Americans in the United States experienced many changes. The federal government urged Native Americans to leave their reservations and to work in cities. Federal policy also tried to weaken the power of tribal government. These efforts did not improve the lives of Native Americans. Many could not find jobs in the cities. Those who were still living on reservations had few jobs or other opportunities. More than one-third of Native Americans lived below the poverty line.

Like other minority groups, Native Americans began to organize to improve their lives. In the 1960s, they began to demand political power and independence from the U.S. government. Native Americans stressed the teaching of their own histories, languages, and cultures in their schools. The National Congress of American Indians (NCAI) sought more control over Native American affairs.

In response, Congress passed the Indian Civil Rights Act of 1968. This law protected the constitutional rights of all Native Americans. The new law also recognized the right of Native American nations to make laws on their reservations. Supreme Court decisions in the 1970s supported the independence of tribal governments. These decisions also confirmed Native Americans' rights to land granted in treaties.

AIM—The American Indian Movement

Some younger Native Americans thought change was too slow in coming. In 1968 a group set up the American Indian Movement (AIM). AIM worked—and sometimes fought—for equal rights and improved living conditions. Clyde Bellecourt, Dennis Banks, and others founded the group, and Russell Means later became a key leader. In November 1969, AIM was among the Native American groups that took over Alcatraz Island, a former prison in San Francisco Bay. The protesters wanted to call attention to what they believed was the U.S. government's neglect of Native Americans' political and economic rights. The protest ended in June 1971 when the groups surrendered.

AIM was not finished with its protests. In the fall of 1972, AIM activists took over the Bureau of Indian Affairs in Washington, D.C. They demanded the lands and rights

In the 1973 takeover of Wounded Knee, American Indian Movement leaders Russell Means and Dennis Banks, along with others, protested the living conditions and treatment of Native Americans.

Reading **HELP**DESK (CCSS)

Reading Strategy: *Summarizing*

When you summarize a reading, you find the main idea of the passage and restate it in your own words. Read the first two paragraphs under the heading "AIM —The American Indian Movement." On a separate sheet of paper, summarize the reading in one or two sentences.

guaranteed under treaties with the United States. They surrendered the building after officials agreed to review their complaints.

Next, in February 1973, 200 members of AIM occupied Wounded Knee, South Dakota. This was the site on which federal troops massacred a group of Sioux in 1890. At the time of the AIM action, Wounded Knee was part of a Sioux reservation. The people there suffered from terrible poverty and ill health.

AIM leaders vowed to stay until the U.S. government agreed to review all Native American treaties and to investigate the treatment of Native Americans. After violence claimed several victims, AIM ended the protest. The event, however, focused attention on the living conditions of many Native Americans.

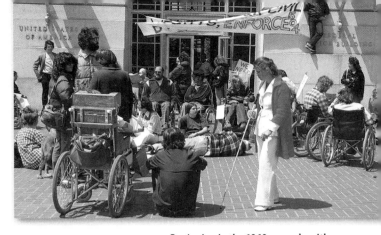

Beginning in the 1960s, people with physical disabilities demanded—sometimes through protest—better access to stadiums, restaurants, and other public buildings.

Americans With Disabilities

People with physical disabilities also sought equal treatment in the 1960s and the 1970s. Congress responded by passing a number of laws. One law required the removal of barriers that stopped some people from entering public facilities. Another law required employers to offer more opportunities in the workplace for people with disabilities.

The Education for All Handicapped Children Act (1975) stated that children with disabilities have the right to equal educational opportunities. Schools must now provide services to meet the needs of children with disabilities. As a result of these actions, people with disabilities enjoy more job opportunities, better access to public facilities, and a greater role in society.

 PROGRESS CHECK

Analyzing Why did the American Indian Movement form?

Bruce Kliewe

LESSON 4 REVIEW (CCSS)

Review Vocabulary

1. Write a paragraph that uses the following terms to describe events in the 1960s.

   a. feminist **b.** Latino

Answer the Guiding Questions

2. *Discussing* How did the civil rights movement lead to the Equal Rights Amendment?

3. *Explaining* What did César Chávez achieve for Latinos?

4. *Describing* What were the goals of the American Indian Movement?

5. **INFORMATIVE/EXPLANATORY** James Madison once wrote that "Equal laws, protecting equal rights, are . . . the best guarantee of loyalty and love of country." Write a paragraph explaining what you think Madison meant by his statement.

Write your answers on a separate piece of paper.

1 **Exploring the Essential Questions**

NARRATIVE Select a civil rights leader or a leader who achieved equal rights in other areas. Write an essay in which you describe the challenges and inequalities faced by that person in the years before protests began. Then describe the changes in society and the law that occurred during this period of protest. Finally, explain how that leader's life might have changed as a result.

2 **21st Century Skills**

COMMUNICATING Using the Internet, research and review images and other media, such as speeches and songs, that are associated with the civil rights era. Then, write a song or a poem that captures the spirit and goals of the movement. Present your poem or song to the class. Be prepared to explain how your work captures the spirit of the protests of this era.

3 **Thinking Like a Historian**

UNDERSTANDING CAUSE AND EFFECT The right to vote provides American citizens with an opportunity for civic involvement. Review the events related to voting rights in this chapter. Create a diagram, like the one to the right, that lists causes and effects related to voting rights. Be sure to include dates for important events. Begin with the restrictive laws and practices in the South that prevented African Americans from voting.

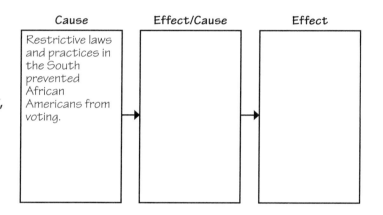

Cause	Effect/Cause	Effect
Restrictive laws and practices in the South prevented African Americans from voting.		

4 **Visual Literacy**

ANALYZING PHOTOGRAPHS This 1960 photo shows African Americans carrying out a sit-in protest at a "whites only" lunch counter in Greensboro, North Carolina. How would you describe the behavior and attitude of the four protesters in this photograph?

Jack Moebes/CORBIS

REVIEW THE GUIDING QUESTIONS

Choose the best answer for each question.

1 Who argued against "separate but equal" schools before the Supreme Court?

 A. Earl Warren

 B. James Farmer

 C. George Houser

 D. Thurgood Marshall

2 How did the Montgomery bus boycott achieve its goal?

 F. It damaged the city's buses.

 G. It hurt city businesses financially.

 H. It started riots all over the city.

 I. People boycotted shops that sold grapes.

3 How did President Johnson expand on President Kennedy's plans to help people with low incomes?

 A. by establishing Medicaid

 B. by setting up Model Cities

 C. by introducing the Job Corps

 D. by pushing through the Civil Rights Act

4 Why did some African American leaders disagree with Dr. King's methods?

 F. They believed his approach was too slow in bringing change.

 G. They didn't think African Americans should integrate.

 H. They believed that nonviolent protest was better.

 I. They thought he was too angry at white Americans.

5 The Indian Civil Rights Act of 1968 recognized Native American nations' rights to

 A. print their own currency.

 B. make laws on their reservations.

 C. elect representatives to Congress.

 D. live on Alcatraz Island in California.

6 What was the goal of the Equal Rights Amendment?

 F. to guarantee access to voting for disabled Americans

 G. to guarantee equality under the law for women

 H. to strengthen traditional roles of women

 I. to guarantee equality under the law for disabled Americans

DBQ ANALYZING DOCUMENTS

7 **Interpreting** This graph shows the changes in the Latino population since 1920.

Which is the largest group of Latinos in the U.S.?
A. Mexican Americans
B. Puerto Rican Americans
C. Cuban Americans
D. other Latino Americans

8 **Drawing Conclusions** Which of the following is the most reasonable conclusion to draw about Latino political influence?
F. Latinos continue to have little political influence.
G. Latino political influence is small because there are too many different Latino groups.
H. Latino political influence has grown because of the increase in population.
I. Latino political influence will probably decline in the coming years.

GROWTH OF LATINO POPULATION IN THE U.S.

POPULATION (MILLIONS)

❶ Mexicans
❷ Puerto Ricans
❸ Cubans
❹ Other Latinos
❺ Total Latinos

YEAR

Source: *Historical Statistics of the United States* and Pew Hispanic Center

SHORT RESPONSE

Betty Friedan wrote about the effects of a high birthrate.

"By the end of the fifties, the United States birthrate was overtaking India's. ... Where once [college women] had two children, now they had four, five, six. Women who had once wanted careers were now making careers out of having babies."

— from *The Feminine Mystique*

9 Why do you think Friedan specifically discusses the birthrate of college women?

10 Did Friedan approve or disapprove of the trend she described in the quote? Explain.

EXTENDED RESPONSE

11 **Informative/Explanatory** Write a short essay that reviews the areas where change occurred during the 1950s and 1960s. Which area has achieved the most lasting progress in equal rights? Which area has the farthest still to go? Give reasons for your opinions.

Need Extra Help?

If You've Missed Question	❶	❷	❸	❹	❺	❻	❼	❽	❾	❿	⓫
Review Lesson	1	1	2	3	4	4	4	4	4	4	1–4

The Vietnam Era

1960–1975

ESSENTIAL QUESTIONS · *What motivates people to act?*
· *Why does conflict develop?*

◀ *A Navy SEAL—which stands for "sea, air, and land"—prepares to do battle in Vietnam.*

Bettmann/CORBIS

The Story Matters . . .

The Navy SEAL creeps forward through the tangle of bushes, alert to every sight and sound around him. He moves silently, his uniform soaked with rain and his boots slippery with mud. Suddenly, he sees his leader raise a hand to signal his unit to stop. Something is out there—maybe the enemy, maybe a deadly booby trap. The SEAL's heart pounds as he readies himself to face the threat.

This SEAL was fighting a new type of war—one with difficult conditions and a clever enemy. In this chapter, you will learn about this war, its effects on the men and women who fought it, and the conflict it brought to the United States.

Place and Time: Southeast Asia 1960 to 1975

In the 1950s, Southeast Asia became a Cold War hot spot. Conflict erupted in Vietnam between the Communist North and the non-Communist South. In the early 1960s, the U.S. government sent troops to aid the South and became involved in a lengthy war. As American involvement increased, so did opposition to the war.

The Soviet-controlled government of East Germany built the Berlin Wall beginning in 1961 to stop East Germans from escaping to West Germany.

Step Into the Place

MAP FOCUS After World War II, Vietnam fought for independence from France. The nation was then divided into two separate countries: North Vietnam and South Vietnam.

By 1968 more than half a million U.S. troops were fighting in Vietnam.

1 PLACE What was the capital city of North Vietnam? What was the capital city of South Vietnam?

2 CRITICAL THINKING
Analyzing Visuals With which Vietnamese country did the United States have a close relationship? Explain your answer.

Step Into the Time

TIME LINE Look at the time line. Think about the challenges U.S. presidents faced during the Vietnam Era. Write a paragraph telling how a U.S. president might respond to a world event.

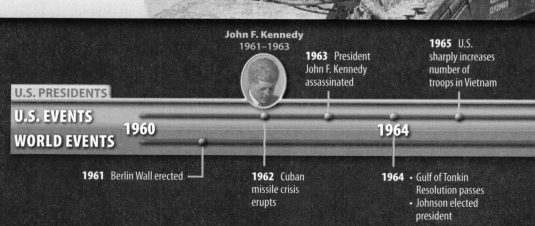

John F. Kennedy
1961–1963

U.S. PRESIDENTS

U.S. EVENTS

WORLD EVENTS

1960

1964

1963 President John F. Kennedy assassinated

1965 U.S. sharply increases number of troops in Vietnam

1961 Berlin Wall erected

1962 Cuban missile crisis erupts

1964
• Gulf of Tonkin Resolution passes
• Johnson elected president

(t)Popperfoto/Getty Images, (c)Bettmann/CORBIS, (b)White House Historical Association

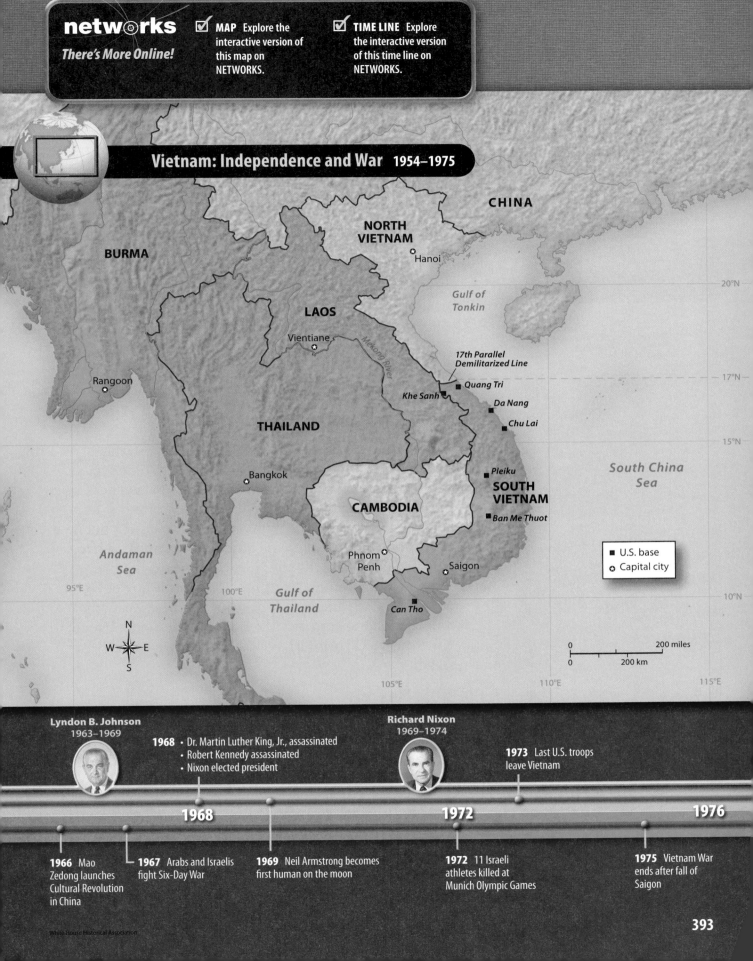

networks
There's More Online!

☑ **MAP** Explore the interactive version of this map on NETWORKS.

☑ **TIME LINE** Explore the interactive version of this time line on NETWORKS.

Vietnam: Independence and War 1954–1975

CHINA

NORTH VIETNAM

BURMA

Hanoi

Gulf of Tonkin

20°N

LAOS

Vientiane

Mekong River

17th Parallel Demilitarized Line

17°N

Quang Tri

Khe Sanh

Da Nang

Rangoon

Chu Lai

THAILAND

15°N

Pleiku

SOUTH VIETNAM

South China Sea

Bangkok

CAMBODIA

Ban Me Thuot

■ U.S. base
✧ Capital city

Andaman Sea

Phnom Penh

Saigon

95°E

100°E

Gulf of Thailand

Can Tho

10°N

N W E S

105°E

110°E

115°E

0   200 miles
0   200 km

Lyndon B. Johnson
1963–1969

1968 • Dr. Martin Luther King, Jr., assassinated
• Robert Kennedy assassinated
• Nixon elected president

Richard Nixon
1969–1974

1973 Last U.S. troops leave Vietnam

1968

1972

1976

1966 Mao Zedong launches Cultural Revolution in China

1967 Arabs and Israelis fight Six-Day War

1969 Neil Armstrong becomes first human on the moon

1972 11 Israeli athletes killed at Munich Olympic Games

1975 Vietnam War ends after fall of Saigon

☑ **GRAPHIC ORGANIZER**
Identifying Main Ideas

☑ **MAP**
Cuban Missile Crisis

☑ **PRIMARY SOURCE**
• Bay of Pigs Invasion
• "Ballad of the Green Berets"

☑ **SLIDE SHOW** Berlin Wall

Lesson 1
Kennedy's Foreign Policy

ESSENTIAL QUESTION *What motivates people to act?*

IT MATTERS BECAUSE
The fear of communism in the 1960s created tension around the world and greatly influenced America's foreign policy.

A New Leader

GUIDING QUESTION *Why did President Kennedy seek new ways to deal with the challenges and fears of the Cold War?*

John Kennedy became president in 1961. At that time, the American relationship with the Soviet Union was still unstable. The Cold War was the focus of much of the new president's effort. President Kennedy continued the anti-Communist foreign policy begun under Presidents Truman and Eisenhower, but he also brought some new ideas to the office. For example, during the presidential campaign, Kennedy led Americans to believe that the nation had fewer nuclear missiles than the Soviet Union. As president, Kennedy increased spending on these weapons. Meanwhile, he tried to convince the leader of the Soviet Union, Nikita Khrushchev (krush•CHAWF), to agree to a ban on nuclear testing.

A Flexible Response

One method Kennedy employed to deal with the challenges of the Cold War was to improve the country's ability to **respond** to threats abroad. In certain areas of the world, Communist groups fought to take control of their nations' governments. Many of these groups got help from the Soviet Union. They

Reading **HELP**DESK (CCSS)

Taking Notes: *Paraphrasing*
Find the main ideas and supporting details on these two pages. Then, paraphrase the information in a chart like this one.

Main Idea	Supporting Detail

Content Vocabulary
• guerrilla warfare
• flexible response
• blockade

did not wage war in the way armies had in World War II or in Korea. Instead, they used **guerrilla** (guh•RIH•luh) **warfare,** fighting with small groups of soldiers and using tactics such as ambush.

Needing a way to fight guerrilla wars, Kennedy introduced a plan called **flexible response.** It provided help to nations fighting Communist movements. This plan used special military units that were trained to fight guerrilla wars. One of these units was the Special Forces, known as the Green Berets (buh•RAYZ).

Foreign Aid

President Kennedy understood that poverty in the world's developing countries made the Communist promise of economic equality seem attractive. To weaken the appeal of communism, he decided to give aid to these poor countries. For example, Kennedy set up a 10-year plan called the Alliance for Progress to bring about economic growth in Latin America.

The Peace Corps, which is still active today, was another example of Kennedy's belief in stopping communism through foreign aid. At Kennedy's request, Congress created the Peace Corps in 1961. Peace Corps volunteers work for two years in other countries that ask for help. They serve as teachers, health care workers, and advisers in farming, industry, and government. By 1963 some 5,000 volunteers were working in more than 40 countries around the world. The Peace Corps is one of Kennedy's most enduring achievements.

President Kennedy called the green beret, worn by the Special Forces shown below, "a symbol of excellence, a badge of courage, a mark of distinction in the fight for freedom."

Horst Faas/AP Images

✔ PROGRESS CHECK

Describing What was the purpose of the Alliance for Progress?

---

guerrilla warfare fighting by small groups using tactics such as the ambush

flexible response President Kennedy's plan to help nations fighting Communist movements by providing special military units trained to fight guerrilla warfare

Academic Vocabulary

respond to reply with action

These Cuban exiles were taken prisoner during the failed Bay of Pigs invasion.

▶ CRITICAL THINKING
Drawing Conclusions Why was this event an embarrassment for President Kennedy?

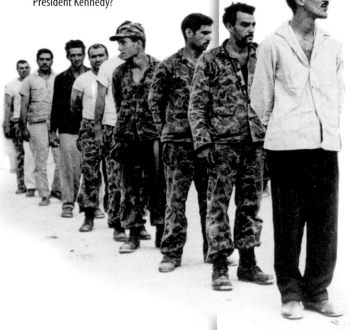

Cold War Crises

GUIDING QUESTION *How did the Kennedy administration respond to the Cold War crises in Cuba and Berlin?*

The Bay of Pigs

President Kennedy faced a serious challenge in Cuba, an island country in the Caribbean Sea. The challenge began during the last months of the Eisenhower administration. Rebel leader Fidel Castro had seized power in January 1959 and formed a new Cuban government. Castro soon set up a Communist dictatorship. Cuba also became an ally of the Soviet Union. Because Cuba lies only 90 miles (145 km) south of Florida, many Americans were worried about these actions.

While Eisenhower was still president, the Central Intelligence Agency (CIA) developed a plan to overthrow Castro. The CIA recruited Cuban exiles, many of whom had settled in the United States. These exiles had been forced to flee Castro's Cuba. The plan called for the exiles to land in Cuba and start an uprising. It was hoped that other Cubans would then join in a rebellion against Castro.

When Kennedy became president, he learned about the plan. Although he had doubts about it, he accepted the advice of military advisers and the CIA. The plan went forward.

The invasion began on April 17, 1961, when about 1,500 Cuban exiles landed at the Bay of Pigs on the south coast of Cuba. It did not go well. Many blunders **occurred.** At a key moment, Kennedy refused to provide American air support to back up forces on land. Within days Cuban forces crushed the invasion and captured the survivors.

The Bay of Pigs failure embarrassed Kennedy, who took the blame. The disaster had three effects. First, Kennedy no longer completely trusted military and CIA advice. Second, nations in Latin America lost trust in Kennedy. Third, Soviet leader Khrushchev came to think that Kennedy was not a strong leader and that he could be bullied.

Hulton Archive/Three Lions/Getty Images

Reading **HELP**DESK (CCSS)

Academic Vocabulary

occur to take place or happen

The Berlin Wall Divides Germany

By 1961 sixteen years had passed since the end of World War II. However, the wartime Allies still had not fully settled the status of Germany. West Germany became a full member of the Western alliance, but the Soviet Union continued to control East Germany.

Berlin's location—fully within East Germany—posed special problems. American, British, and French forces were still stationed in the western part of the city. This fact irritated the Soviet Union and led to conflict. In addition, people kept fleeing to West Berlin from Communist East Berlin, hoping to escape economic hardship and find freedom.

At a meeting in Vienna, Austria, in June 1961, Premier Khrushchev told President Kennedy that the West must move out of Berlin. He insisted on an agreement by the end of the year. Kennedy rejected Khrushchev's demand. To emphasize the West's right to stay in West Berlin, the United States later sent more troops to the city.

Later that summer, a large number of East Germans fled to West Berlin. In response, the East German government, with Soviet backing, closed the border between East Berlin and West Berlin on August 13. A huge wall of concrete blocks with barbed wire was built along the border. The Soviets posted armed guards along the wall to stop more East Germans from escaping to the West. As a result, the Berlin Wall cut most communications between the two parts of the city.

The Western Allies stayed in West Berlin. They could do little, however, to stop the building of the wall, which came to symbolize Communist repression.

✓ PROGRESS CHECK

Explaining What kind of government did Fidel Castro establish in Cuba?

Bettmann/CORBIS

Thinking Like a HISTORIAN

Drawing Inferences and Conclusions

To stop the flow of skilled workers, professionals, and intellectuals to the West, East Germany's Communist government began building the Berlin Wall on the night of August 13, 1961. The Berlin Wall stretched 28 miles (45 km) through the middle of Berlin and another 75 miles (120 km) around West Berlin. What did the need for the wall suggest about life in East Berlin? For more about drawing inferences and conclusions, review *Thinking Like a Historian.*

The Berlin Wall kept East Germans from crossing into West Berlin. It separated families and friends for many years.

▶ CRITICAL THINKING
Drawing Conclusions How might Khrushchev's view of Kennedy after the Bay of Pigs invasion have affected his decisions about Berlin?

The Cuban Missile Crisis

GUIDING QUESTION *Why did the United States force the Soviet Union to remove missiles placed in Cuba?*

The most dangerous Cold War crisis came in 1962. Once again, the setting was Cuba. In mid-October, an American spy plane flying over Cuba discovered that the Soviets were building launching sites for nuclear missiles on the island. Such missiles could reach the United States in minutes.

Over the next week, President Kennedy met with advisers to discuss how to handle the Cuban missile crisis. The ideas they explored included invading Cuba and bombing the missile sites. Then, new CIA photographs showed that work on the launch sites was moving quickly. Kennedy needed to reach a decision.

On October 22, 1962, President Kennedy appeared on national television. He revealed to the nation the "secret, swift, and extraordinary buildup" of Soviet missiles in Cuba. Kennedy responded to the buildup by ordering the U.S. Navy to **blockade,** or close off, Cuba until the Soviets removed their missiles. Kennedy threatened to destroy any Soviet ship that tried to break through the blockade.

GEOGRAPHY CONNECTION

By placing missiles in Cuba, the Soviet Union put a nuclear threat just 90 miles (145 km) from the Florida coast.

1 LOCATION How much of the United States would have been within range of intermediate-range ballistic missiles launched from Cuba?

2 CRITICAL THINKING
Analyzing Central Issues
What might have happened to the United States if troops had invaded Cuba or bombed the missile sites?

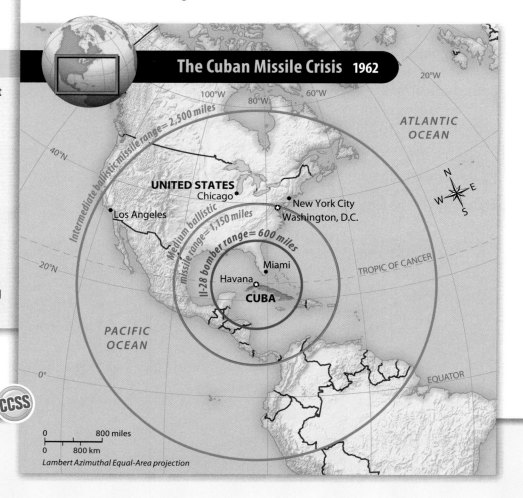

The Cuban Missile Crisis 1962

Intermediate ballistic missile range= 2,500 miles

Medium ballistic missile range= 1,150 miles

Il-28 bomber range= 600 miles

UNITED STATES
Chicago
Los Angeles
New York City
Washington, D.C.
Miami
Havana
CUBA

ATLANTIC OCEAN
PACIFIC OCEAN
TROPIC OF CANCER
EQUATOR

0   800 miles
0   800 km
Lambert Azimuthal Equal-Area projection

Reading **HELP**DESK (CCSS)

blockade to block or obstruct

The president warned that the U.S. would consider a nuclear attack from Cuba against a nation in the Western Hemisphere as an assault on the United States. The U.S. response, Kennedy stated, would be a nuclear attack against the Soviet Union.

Five days later, the Soviet ships turned back. The Soviets agreed to remove their missiles from Cuba, and the United States agreed not to invade Cuba. Nuclear war had been avoided.

With disaster averted, Kennedy and Khrushchev worked to build better relations. In 1963 a hot line was set up between Moscow and Washington for instant communication in times of crisis. The two nations also signed a treaty banning nuclear tests.

The Space Race

The rivalry between the two nations continued in space. In April 1961, Soviet pilot Yuri Gagarin (guh•GAHR•uhn) became the first person to orbit Earth. One month later, Alan Shepard, Jr., became the first American to make a spaceflight.

Kennedy then set the goal of landing a man on the moon by the end of the decade. Congress funded the National Aeronautics and Space Administration (NASA), which ran the space program. NASA expanded its Florida launching facility and built a control center in Houston, Texas.

Those efforts produced success. In February 1962, astronaut John Glenn became the first American to orbit Earth.

Then on July 20, 1969, television viewers around the world watched the spacecraft *Eagle* land on the moon. When astronaut Neil Armstrong took his first step on the moon, he announced, "That's one small step for man, one giant leap for mankind." By the end of the "Apollo" lunar program in 1972, another 10 Americans had landed on the moon.

President Kennedy (center) and Vice President Johnson (right) visited the Marshall Space Flight Center, located in Huntsville, Alabama, in 1962. Here, they tour the facilities with Wernher von Braun, director of the Center.

 **PROGRESS CHECK**

Explaining How was the Cuban missile crisis resolved?

Bettmann/CORBIS

 LESSON 1 REVIEW **CCSS**

Review Vocabulary

1. Explain the meaning of the terms *guerrilla warfare* and *flexible response* in the same sentence.

Answer the Guiding Questions

2. *Discussing* What new ideas did President Kennedy introduce for waging the Cold War?

3. *Explaining* How did the Kennedy administration respond to the Cold War crisis in Berlin?

4. *Describing* How did the United States force the Soviet Union to remove missiles placed in Cuba?

5. **INFORMATIVE/EXPLANATORY** Write a short essay describing the key foreign policy challenges the United States faced during the Kennedy administration.

networks

There's More Online!

☑ **CHART** A Soldier's Equipment

☑ **GRAPHIC ORGANIZER** American Involvement in Vietnam

☑ **MAP** Ho Chi Minh Trail

☑ **VIDEO**

Lesson 2
The Vietnam War

ESSENTIAL QUESTION *Why does conflict develop?*

IT MATTERS BECAUSE

The United States entered Vietnam in an attempt to fight the spread of communism in Southeast Asia.

The Conflict Begins

GUIDING QUESTION *How did Vietnam become a divided country?*

In the 1960s, the United States sharply increased its involvement in a conflict taking place in Southeast Asia. The conflict was a fight against the spread of communism in the region.

PRIMARY SOURCE

❝ We're at war with the most dangerous enemy that has ever faced mankind. . . . [I]t's been said if we lose that war, and in so doing lose this way of freedom of ours, history will record with the greatest astonishment that those who had the most to lose did the least to prevent its happening. ❞

—Ronald Reagan, "A Time for Choosing" 1964

The fight became known as the Vietnam War. The war, however, did not go as Americans intended.

Roots of Conflict

The roots of the Vietnam War can be **traced** back to World War II. In that war, Japanese forces captured the French colony of Indochina. The colony included what are today the nations

Reading **HELP**DESK (CCSS)

Taking Notes: *Identifying*

On a chart like the one shown, identify each president's main philosophy about involvement in Vietnam.

President	Philosophy
Eisenhower	
Kennedy	
Johnson	

Content Vocabulary

• **regime**
• **search-and-destroy mission**
• **napalm**
• **Agent Orange**

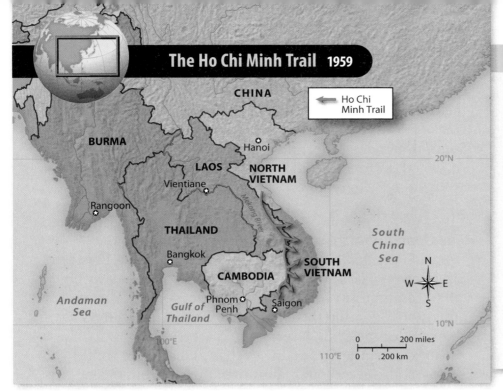

The Ho Chi Minh Trail 1959

CHINA

Ho Chi
Minh Trail

BURMA

Hanoi

LAOS   NORTH
            VIETNAM
Vientiane

Rangoon   20°N

THAILAND   South
                            China
Bangkok   Sea
          CAMBODIA   SOUTH   N
                      VIETNAM
Andaman   Phnom   W   E
Sea   Gulf of Penh Saigon
        Thailand   S
100°E   10°N
        110°E   0   200 miles
                0   200 km

GEOGRAPHY CONNECTION

In 1959 North Vietnam began to deliver supplies to Communist forces in South Vietnam. They used a network of paths and roads through the countries of Laos and Cambodia. This network became known as the Ho Chi Minh Trail.

1 MOVEMENT In which two directions do the red arrows on the map show movement?

2 CRITICAL THINKING
Drawing Conclusions Why do you think the North Vietnamese chose to travel through Laos and Cambodia instead of moving their supplies straight through South Vietnam?

of Cambodia, Laos, and Vietnam. Vietnamese forces led by Communist Ho Chi Minh (HOH CHEE MIHN) fought the Japanese.

Ho Chi Minh declared Vietnam's independence when Japan surrendered at the end of World War II. However, the French were unwilling to give up Vietnam and the other territories. They considered Indochina a valuable colony because it was rich in natural resources such as rice, rubber, and tin. Ho Chi Minh and his forces fought a long, bloody war against the French. They finally achieved victory in 1954 at Dien Bien Phu (dyehn byehn FOO).

The Geneva Accords

In 1954 the United States, France, Great Britain, the Soviet Union, China, and Vietnam met in Geneva, Switzerland. A peace agreement called the Geneva Accords divided Vietnam into two halves. Communist nationalists would control the North. Non-Communists—supported by the United States—would control the South. Then, in 1956, Vietnam would hold elections to decide the government for all of Vietnam. Although neither the United States nor South Vietnam signed the agreement, they did not oppose it. The United States, however, made clear that it would act if Communist North Vietnam attacked the South.

Academic Vocabulary

trace follow

In 1955 Ngo Dinh Diem (NOH DIN ZYEHM) became South Vietnam's leader. The Diem **regime** (ray•ZHEEM), or government, had the support of the United States. Diem ignored the Geneva Accords and refused to hold elections. He also cracked down on Communists in the South. Communists in the South responded by forming a group known as the Vietcong. In 1959 the Vietcong, on orders from Ho Chi Minh, began a war against the Diem regime.

The American Role Grows

The Communist threat in South Vietnam worried the United States. If Communists took South Vietnam, President Eisenhower once said, the countries of Southeast Asia would fall to communism like a row of dominoes—one right after the other. This "domino theory" helped shape American policy in Vietnam for the next 20 years.

To counter the Communist threat and support South Vietnam, the Eisenhower administration sent billions of dollars in aid. The United States also sent a few hundred soldiers to act as advisers to the South Vietnamese government and army.

Like Eisenhower, President Kennedy saw Vietnam as part of the global fight against communism. Kennedy sent U.S. Special Forces—the Green Berets—to train and advise South Vietnamese troops. Kennedy also pressured Diem to make reforms that would make communism less appealing to the people. Diem was urged to create a more democratic government and to help Vietnam's peasants. Diem did make some reforms, but they had little effect.

Meanwhile, Diem took away the rights of many people in South Vietnam. For example, he targeted members of the Buddhist religion, favoring Catholics like himself. Diem claimed that Buddhists were helping South Vietnam's Communists. As a result, he threw hundreds of Buddhists into prison and had many of them killed. Buddhists responded with protests, sometimes setting themselves on fire in public displays. These horrifying protests made it hard for Kennedy to continue to support Diem, and the United States withdrew its support in 1963.

In November 1963, the South Vietnamese army overthrew the government. They assassinated Ngo Dinh Diem. The United States supported the government takeover—but did not

Ho Chi Minh (below) and the Vietnamese fought to free themselves from Japanese and French domination.

UPI/Bettmann/CORBIS

Reading **HELP**DESK CCSS

regime a form of government, government in power, or period of rule

support the assassination of Ngo Dinh Diem. Days later, Kennedy was assassinated in Dallas, Texas. The question of what to do in Vietnam fell to the succeeding president, Lyndon B. Johnson.

✅ **PROGRESS CHECK**

Identifying Who was Ngo Dinh Diem?

The Conflict Deepens

GUIDING QUESTION *Why did the United States become involved in the war in Vietnam?*

In 1963, at the time of Kennedy's death, the United States had nearly 16,000 troops in Vietnam. They were serving as advisers. Secretary of Defense Robert McNamara told President Johnson that South Vietnam could not resist the Vietcong without more help from the United States. In a private May 1964 conversation, Johnson admitted doubts about the effort. "I don't think it's worth fighting for," he said, "but I don't think we can get out." Still, as Vietcong attacks continued, the United States took action to become more involved in the region.

President Johnson wanted Congress's support for expanding the American role in Vietnam. The chance to win that support came in August 1964 when it was reported that North Vietnamese patrol boats had attacked American ships in the Gulf of Tonkin near North Vietnam. Congress acted quickly. It passed a resolution that allowed the president to "take all necessary measures to repel any armed attack against the forces of the United States." The Gulf of Tonkin Resolution gave Johnson broad power to use American forces.

President Johnson began to **escalate** U.S. involvement in Vietnam in 1965. The increased involvement included greater numbers of ground troops as well as air attacks. Over the next three years, the number of American troops in Vietnam rose sharply. About 180,000 U.S. soldiers were in Vietnam by the end of 1965. Almost 400,000 were there by the end of 1966 and more than 500,000 by 1968.

The United States began a bombing campaign called Operation Rolling Thunder in March 1965. Planes attacked the Ho Chi Minh Trail, a network of roads, paths, and bridges from North Vietnam through Cambodia and Laos into South Vietnam. North Vietnamese troops used this route to bring equipment south. Other planes targeted bridges, docks, factories, and military bases in the North.

THEN

The Ho Chi Minh Trail, once a network of paths along which North Vietnam delivered supplies to Communist forces, is being transformed into a paved, multilane highway. It will reach all the way to the Chinese border. The project, which began in 2000 and is scheduled to be finished in 2020, is part of Vietnam's postwar recovery effort.

NOW

Predicting How might a new highway in the country contribute to Vietnam's economic growth?

Academic Vocabulary

escalate to increase

A U.S. patrol makes its way through a paddy, a flooded field used for growing rice.

From 1965 through 1968, bombing increased. During this time, American planes dropped more bombs on North Vietnam than they dropped on the Axis powers during World War II.

The Difficult Fight

On the ground, American troops found Vietnam to be a challenging environment in which to fight. Thick forests, muddy trails, swampy rice paddies, and the possibility of booby traps slowed troop movement. The Vietcong used guerrilla methods. They attacked, and then they hid among the Vietnamese population. American soldiers found it hard to tell friends and enemies apart. Soldiers described their discomforts and frustrations in letters home:

PRIMARY SOURCE

❝ My hands are covered with cuts. The jungles have thousands of leeches and mosquitoes of which I think I have gotten bitten almost all over my body. . . . Actually the fighting is not heavy yet, but the rumor is we're moving south. ❞

—from *Dear America: Letters Home from Vietnam*

To seek out and destroy Vietcong or North Vietnamese units, the American forces began **search-and-destroy missions.** Ground troops worked in cooperation with aircraft. Patrols on the ground radioed their location. Then, helicopter gunships roared to the scene to blast the enemy.

Americans bombed areas of South Vietnam. The goal was to drive guerrillas from their forest cover. Both sides used planes to drop **napalm** (NAY•pahlm), an explosive that burned intensely, to destroy jungle growth. North Vietnamese and Vietcong forces also used napalm in flamethrowers. These devices sprayed fuel or a burning stream of liquids.

To make it easier to see enemy troops in the forest, chemicals were sprayed to clear out leaves and tall grasses. One chemical, **Agent Orange,** is believed to have harmed many Americans and Vietnamese, causing serious health problems.

Growing Discontent

The American bombing did not stop the flow of troops and equipment from the North. Although the search-and-destroy missions killed thousands of North Vietnamese and Vietcong troops, the troops always seemed to be replaced. What Ho

PHOTO: Tim Page/CORBIS
TEXT: *Dear America: Letters Home from Vietnam*, by Bernard Edelman for the New York Vietnam Veterans Memorial Commission.

Reading **HELP**DESK ⓒⓒⓢⓢ

search-and-destroy mission mission by American forces to seek out and destroy North Vietnamese forces

napalm an intensely burning explosive used to destroy jungle growth

Agent Orange a chemical herbicide used to clear out forests and tall grasses

Chi Minh had said to the French became true again: "You can kill ten of my men for every one I kill of yours. But even at those odds, you will lose and I will win."

American soldiers grew frustrated. Philip Caputo, a young marine, recalled the changing attitude:

PRIMARY SOURCE

66 When we marched into the rice paddies on that damp March afternoon, we carried, along with our packs and rifles, the implicit convictions [beliefs] that the Viet Cong would be quickly beaten. ... We kept the packs and rifles; the convictions, we lost. 99

—from *A Rumor of War*

Confusion and Opposition in the United States

At first, as Communist losses grew, officials in the Johnson administration believed the United States could succeed and that victory in Vietnam was just a matter of time. As the war dragged on, some officials saw a gloomier picture. Secretary of Defense McNamara began to argue that the ground war and the air attacks had failed and that the war could not be won. Outside the nation's capital, opposition to U.S. involvement in Vietnam grew.

South Vietnamese civilians flee from advancing Vietcong troops.

☑ PROGRESS CHECK

Interpreting How did the soldier quoted in the Primary Source on this page feel about the possibility of defeating the enemy?

LESSON 2 REVIEW

Review Vocabulary

1. Examine the two terms below. Then write a sentence explaining what the terms have in common.

   a. napalm   **b.** Agent Orange

Answer the Guiding Questions

2. *Explaining* Which foreign countries did the Vietnamese fight in the 1940s and 1950s?

3. *Describing* What happened to Vietnam after its defeat of the French?

4. *Summarizing* What factors led the United States to become involved militarily in Vietnam?

5. NARRATIVE Write a letter home from the viewpoint of an American soldier arriving in Vietnam. In one or two paragraphs, describe the terrain you find yourself fighting in, and explain how it affects you as a soldier.

networks

There's More Online!

☑ **BIOGRAPHY**
Walter Cronkite

☑ **GRAPHIC ORGANIZER**
Events of 1968

☑ **MAP** Election of 1968

☑ **PRIMARY SOURCE**
Walter Cronkite on Vietnam

Lesson 3

The Vietnam Years at Home

ESSENTIAL QUESTION *What motivates people to act?*

IT MATTERS BECAUSE

The Vietnam War caused strain within the United States and between the United States and other nations.

Young People Protest

GUIDING QUESTION *How did the war in Vietnam lead to sharp divisions between Americans?*

The war in Vietnam led to severe divisions among Americans. Those for and against the war staged large public demonstrations to air their beliefs. They also attacked each other with growing anger. Antiwar protesters called President Johnson and war supporters "killers." Supporters of the war called protesters "traitors." The war seemed to split the country. Much of the division came from what people called the generation gap, a divide between the views of younger people and older people.

Opposition to the war increased as U.S. involvement increased. Some Americans wondered why the United States was involved in what appeared to be a civil war within Vietnam. Other Americans worried that the cost of the war was hurting programs in the United States. Still others viewed South Vietnam as a corrupt dictatorship. They believed that defending the country was unjust. All regretted the devastation of Vietnam's countryside and the lives lost in the war.

Some opposition to the war came from the **counterculture,** a movement that rejected traditional American values. Popular music played a role in communicating counterculture ideas. Some parents

(l) John Olson/Time Life Pictures/Getty Images, (cl) CBS/CBS Photo Archive/Getty Images (r) Charles H. Phillips/Time & Life Pictures/Getty Images

---

Reading **HELP**DESK **CCSS**

Taking Notes: *Evaluating*

As you read, use a chart like this to take notes on three key events of 1968 and how they changed life in the United States.

Event of 1968	How it changed life in U.S.

Content Vocabulary

• **counterculture**   • **credibility gap**
• **deferment**
• **conscientious objector**

were troubled by the music and other symbols of the counterculture—such as torn blue jeans and long hair for males.

A more serious challenge to traditional values came from some other parts of the counterculture. Some young people refused to follow long-standing roles of work and family. They rejected ideas such as the quest for personal success.

Students Protest the Draft

Students protested against the draft, the selective service system that supplied many of the soldiers for the war. The system required all men to register for the draft when they reached age 18.

Students had two major reasons for opposing the draft. Some believed that by ending the draft, they could halt the supply of soldiers needed to fight the war. Others called the draft unfair. Draft boards had the power to give men **deferments,** which excused them from the draft temporarily. Full-time students attending college received such deferments. Many college students were from the middle class or upper class. As a result, a large share of soldiers came from poor or working-class families. Many argued that deferments led to this unfair situation.

Some protesters became **conscientious** (kahn•shee•EHN•shuhs) **objectors,** claiming that their moral or religious beliefs prevented them from fighting. Other protesters showed their feelings by burning their draft cards.

Opposition Increases

Birds became the common symbols for the supporters and opponents of the war. Supporters of the Vietnam War were called hawks, because hawks are birds of prey. Opponents of the Vietnam War came to be called doves, because doves often symbolize peace.

As the war dragged on, more and more Americans became dissatisfied. Some thought the United States should not be fighting in Vietnam. Others opposed the way the government conducted the war. Both hawks and doves criticized the president for his handling of Vietnam. Johnson's approval rating dropped sharply.

Protests against the Vietnam War grew louder in the late 1960s.

An American nurse cares for an injured Vietnamese child.

counterculture a culture with values that differ from those of established society

deferment postponement of, or excuse from, military service

conscientious objector a person who refuses to serve in the armed forces or bear arms on moral or religious grounds

People who opposed the war did so for different reasons. Young protesters focused on what they saw as an unfair draft system for a war they did not believe in. The high number of minority soldiers dying in Vietnam also led to protests.

- In 1965 and 1966, more than 20 percent of those killed or wounded in combat were African American. At that time, about 13.5 percent of U.S. men between the ages of 19 and 25 were African American.

- The National Chicano Moratorium Committee was organized to make known the high rate of Chicano war casualties.

Based on these statistics, do you think the draft was unfair? To learn more about analyzing and interpreting information, review *Thinking Like a Historian*.

Over time, the size of antiwar protests grew. In October 1967, more than 50,000 people marched to the Pentagon, near Washington, D.C., to protest the war in Vietnam. The Pentagon is the headquarters of the Defense Department. Those who supported the war criticized the protesters for showing a lack of patriotism.

☑ **PROGESS CHECK**

Analyzing Why did some Americans feel that draft deferments were unfair?

1968—Year of Crisis

GUIDING QUESTION *How was 1968 a turning point in the Vietnam War and the nation's political life?*

As 1968 began, North Vietnam launched a series of major attacks in South Vietnam. Americans soon learned that 1968 would be a long and difficult year.

The Tet Offensive

The North Vietnamese and Vietcong began a series of attacks on January 31, 1968. The attacks began on Tet—the Vietnamese New Year. This Tet Offensive marked a turning point in the Vietnam War. The Communists attacked American military bases and South Vietnam's cities. Vietcong troops raided the United States embassy in Saigon, the capital. They also struck in Hue (hyoo•AY), the ancient capital of Vietnam.

On the battlefield, Tet was a disaster for the Communist forces. After a month of fighting, American and South Vietnamese soldiers had caused heavy enemy losses. However, the Tet Offensive turned many more Americans against the war and against President Johnson. The American people were shocked that an enemy supposedly close to defeat could launch such a massive attack. Major newspapers and magazines openly criticized the **conduct** of the war. Most Americans seemed to agree, believing that the army was losing ground. The Johnson administration developed a **credibility gap**—fewer people trusted what the administration said about the war.

Johnson Faces Opposition

President Johnson faced challenges in his own party as well as in the nation as a whole. One of those challenges came in 1967 from Democratic Senator Eugene McCarthy of Minnesota. He

Reading **HELP**DESK CCSS

credibility gap the difference between what is said and what people believe or know to be true

Academic Vocabulary

conduct to direct the course of

BIOGRAPHY

Walter Cronkite (1916–2009)

Walter Cronkite was a pioneer in television news. He hosted several TV news programs in the 1950s and 1960s. By 1968 he had become a familiar and trusted face to the American public. That year he went to Vietnam to report on the war. He had been a supporter of American actions there, but what he saw shook him. He helped give voice to the credibility gap when he said on the air, "We have too often been disappointed by the optimism of the American leaders, both in Vietnam and Washington, to have faith any longer in the silver linings they find in the darkest clouds."

announced that he would seek his party's nomination for the presidency. His act was a protest against the war. McCarthy, who was not well-known, seemed to have little chance of beating Johnson. In the March 12 primary in New Hampshire, however, McCarthy got 42 percent of the vote. Although Johnson won the primary, McCarthy's strong showing was a surprise. It indicated widespread opposition to the war.

Another antiwar candidate, Robert F. Kennedy, also entered the race for the Democratic nomination. Kennedy had served in Washington as attorney general during his brother's presidency and was now a senator from New York.

Johnson Reacts

President Johnson was disturbed by the events in Vietnam and the growing antiwar movement. The American commander in Vietnam, General William Westmoreland, asked for still more troops after the Tet Offensive. Instead of meeting Westmoreland's request, the president ordered a review of the war and U.S. involvement in the conflict. He also began to rethink his campaign for reelection.

On March 31, 1968, President Johnson went on television to announce a "new step toward peace." He planned to halt the bombing of North Vietnam's cities. He asked North Vietnam for a similar action so that peace talks could begin. Then, the president made a startling announcement: "I shall not seek, and I will not accept, the nomination of my party for another term as your president."

Violence and Unrest

Tragedy struck the nation a few days after Johnson withdrew from the presidential race. On the evening of April 4, 1968, a sniper in Memphis, Tennessee, shot Dr. Martin Luther King, Jr. The leader of the civil rights movement was dead.

▶ **CRITICAL THINKING**
Paraphrasing How would you paraphrase, or restate, what Walter Cronkite said in the quotation above?

TEXT: Walter Cronkite, CBS Evening News, February 27, 1968.
PHOTO: CBS/CBS Photo Archive/Getty Images

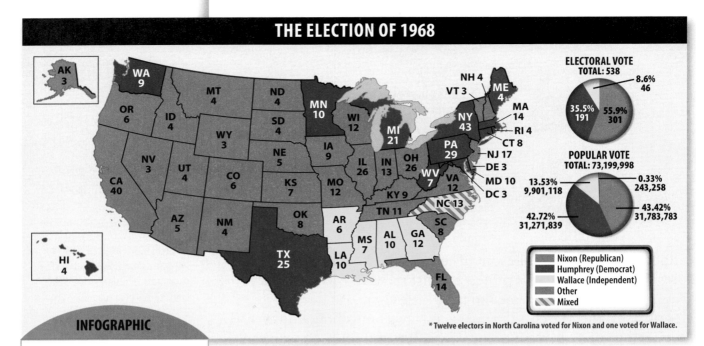

THE ELECTION OF 1968

ELECTORAL VOTE
TOTAL: 538
- 8.6% / 46
- 35.5% / 191
- 55.9% / 301

POPULAR VOTE
TOTAL: 73,199,998
- 13.53% / 9,901,118
- 0.33% / 243,258
- 42.72% / 31,271,839
- 43.42% / 31,783,783

Legend:
- Nixon (Republican)
- Humphrey (Democrat)
- Wallace (Independent)
- Other
- Mixed

* Twelve electors in North Carolina voted for Nixon and one voted for Wallace.

INFOGRAPHIC

The election of 1968 featured three candidates.

1 REGION Based on the map, in which parts of the country was Nixon's support the strongest?

2 CRITICAL THINKING
Calculating Would Humphrey have been able to win the election if he had received all of Wallace's electoral votes?

Across the country, people reacted to the assassination of Dr. King by rioting. Army troops were called on to control unruly crowds in some cities.

As the nation worried over unrest at home and war abroad, the race for president picked up speed. Joining McCarthy and Kennedy, Vice President Hubert H. Humphrey decided to seek the Democratic nomination. Humphrey avoided the primary elections. Instead, he tried to win support among Democratic Party leaders. These leaders would be key in choosing the nominee.

In June 1968, Kennedy and McCarthy faced each other in the primary election in California. Kennedy won. Moments after his victory speech, an assassin shot and killed him. The nation reeled with the shock of another assassination.

The Democratic Convention

Later that summer, the Democrats held their convention in Chicago. Humphrey seemed to have enough votes to win the nomination. As a supporter of civil rights and labor causes, Humphrey had much backing in the party. Humphrey was linked to Johnson's Vietnam policy, however. Antiwar Democrats felt angry and **excluded** from the convention.

Meanwhile, thousands of antiwar activists arrived in Chicago. They came to protest Humphrey's almost certain victory. Fearing violence, Chicago's mayor, Richard J. Daley, sent the police out in force. When antiwar protesters tried to march to the convention, police blocked their progress. The marchers began to throw sticks and bottles at the officers. The police responded quickly. The officers threw tear gas and charged in, hitting protesters with nightsticks. They chased those who fled, beating some and arresting many.

Even though Humphrey won the Democratic nomination, the violence—all shown on television—damaged his candidacy. Humphrey admitted, "Chicago was a catastrophe."

The Election of 1968

Most Americans longed for a return to law and order, and other presidential candidates responded to that longing. Third-party candidate Governor George C. Wallace of Alabama criticized the antiwar protesters. Wallace also opposed efforts to use busing as a tool for integration of the nation's schools. His tough stand on law and order and his appeal to racial fears won many voters. The Republican nominee was former Vice President Richard M. Nixon. Nixon claimed to stand for the conservative "silent majority" who wanted law and order and did not protest or demonstrate. Nixon also offered "peace with honor" in Vietnam. He gave no details, however, as to how this would be achieved.

The popular vote was close, with Nixon winning by about 500,000 votes. In the electoral vote, Nixon maintained a solid majority—winning 301 votes to Humphrey's 191. Nixon won the presidency with only 43.4 percent of the popular vote, but he and Wallace together won about 57 percent. It seemed that a definite majority of Americans wanted the government to restore order.

✓ PROGRESS CHECK

Summarizing What were the major "crisis" events that occurred in 1968?

On January 20, 1969, Richard Nixon took the oath of office on Capitol Hill.

▶ **CRITICAL THINKING**
Drawing Conclusions Why do you think Nixon's promise of return to order at home and "peace with honor" in Vietnam appealed to voters?

Charles H. Phillips/Time & Life Pictures/Getty Images

LESSON 3 REVIEW

Review Vocabulary

1. Use each of these terms in a complete sentence that will explain the term's meaning.

   a. counterculture
   c. conscientious objector
   b. deferment
   d. credibility gap

Answer the Guiding Questions

2. *Describing* In what ways did the Vietnam War divide the country?

3. *Listing* What were two reasons students opposed the draft?

4. *Summarizing* Why did the Tet Offensive trouble so many Americans?

5. **INFORMATIVE/EXPLANATORY** Identify three significant events from the year 1968 that would have received coverage in a newspaper. Write a headline for each newspaper story that reflects the event's significance and impact.

netw⊙rks

There's More Online!

☑ **GRAPHIC ORGANIZER**
Vietnam War Results

☑ **MAP** The Vietnam War

☑ **PRIMARY SOURCE**
A Soldier's Letter

☑ **SLIDE SHOW**
Vietnam War Protests

BURMA

Lesson 4
Vietnam in the Nixon Years

ESSENTIAL QUESTION *What motivates people to act?*

IT MATTERS BECAUSE

The Vietnam War took a heavy toll on America's soldiers and their families. It also changed the social and political climate in the United States.

Nixon Takes Office

GUIDING QUESTION *What steps did Nixon take to bring American forces home and end the Vietnam War?*

Richard Nixon took office in January 1969. He asked the country for calm: "We cannot learn from one another until we stop shouting at one another—until we speak quietly enough so that our words can be heard as well as our voices."

Nixon ran for president on a promise of "peace with honor" in Vietnam. Shortly after taking office, Nixon began working toward ending U.S. involvement in the war. As a first step, the president named Henry Kissinger as his National Security Advisor. Kissinger was given wide **authority** to use his skills in diplomacy to end the conflict. To that end, he launched a policy he called "linkage." This policy aimed at improving relations with the Soviet Union and China. These countries were top suppliers of aid to North Vietnam. Kissinger hoped to get the two Communist nations to reduce their aid and help end the war.

Nixon also wanted to begin pulling American forces out of Vietnam. He did not, however, want the withdrawal to be seen as a defeat. To achieve this "peace with honor," the president proposed three steps: (1) reforming the draft system, (2) giving South Vietnam a bigger role in fighting the war, and (3) expanding the bombing of enemy territory.

(l) AP Images, (cr) Leif Skoogfors/CORBIS, (r) Steve Raymer/CORBIS

Reading **HELP**DESK **CCSS**

Taking Notes: *Categorizing*

Use a chart like this one to record information about the Vietnam War in the proper category.

	Numbers of/Results to
Vietnamese civilians and soldiers killed	
American soldiers killed	
American soldiers wounded	
U.S. cost in dollars	

Content Vocabulary
- **Vietnamization**
- **martial law**
- **MIA**

COSTS OF THE VIETNAM WAR

A wounded soldier is loaded onto a helicopter.

WAR EXPENDITURES (IN MILLIONS)			
	Wartime Costs	Veterans' Benefits	Interest Payments
World War I	$23,700	$13,856	$11,100
World War II	$260,000	$65,231	$200,000
Korea	$50,000	$11,391	
Vietnam	$140,600	$13,173	

U.S. WAR DEATHS	
World War I	107,000
World War II	407,000
Korean War	35,500
Vietnam War	58,000

CHART SKILL

Although the Vietnam War took place in a small country on the other side of the world, it was expensive for the United States in terms of lives and money.

1 CALCULATING Based on the charts above, how do the human and financial costs of the Vietnam War compare with the costs of other wars of the 1900s?

2 CRITICAL THINKING *Analyzing* How do you think the costs of wars affect their acceptance by the public?

A New Vietnam Policy

At Nixon's urging, Congress made several changes to the draft system. These changes put an end to the practice of giving college deferments. They also ensured that only 19-year-olds could be called for service in Vietnam. Finally, draftees were now chosen by lottery on the basis of their birthdays. Protests against the draft faded with these reforms, in part because the government began drafting fewer young men. In addition, Nixon had promised to get rid of the draft in the future.

President Nixon also cut back the number of American troops in Vietnam. Known as **Vietnamization,** this plan called for the South Vietnamese to take a more active role in fighting. At the same time, Americans would become less involved. As South Vietnamese soldiers took over, American troops would be gradually withdrawn from the country. In June 1969, Nixon announced the removal from Vietnam of the first 25,000 American soldiers. These steps were based on his "Nixon Doctrine," which involved shifting some responsibility for fighting communism to other nations. "America cannot—and will not," Nixon said, "conceive all the plans, design all the programs, execute all the decisions and undertake all the defense of the free nations of the world."

AP Images

Vietnamization President Nixon's plan calling for the South Vietnamese to take a more active role in fighting and for Americans to become less involved

Academic Vocabulary

authority the power to command obedience or enforce laws

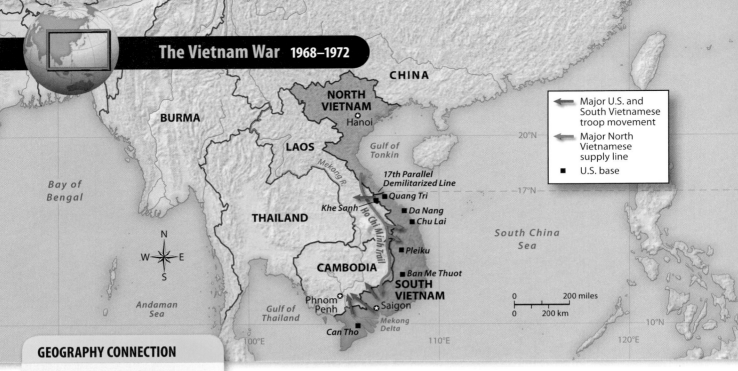

CHINA

NORTH VIETNAM
Hanoi

BURMA

LAOS

Gulf of Tonkin

20°N

Bay of Bengal

Mekong R.

17th Parallel Demilitarized Line

Quang Tri

17°N

Khe Sanh

Da Nang

Chu Lai

THAILAND

Ho Chi Minh Trail

Pleiku

South China Sea

CAMBODIA

Ban Me Thuot

SOUTH VIETNAM

Andaman Sea

Phnom Penh

Saigon

0   200 miles
0   200 km

Gulf of Thailand

Can Tho

Mekong Delta

10°N

100°E   110°E   120°E

Major U.S. and South Vietnamese troop movement

Major North Vietnamese supply line

■ U.S. base

GEOGRAPHY CONNECTION

This map shows some of the important events and locations of the Vietnam War from 1968 to 1972.

1 **LOCATION** Which U.S. base was closest to North Vietnam?

2 **CRITICAL THINKING**
Drawing Conclusions Why do you think the U.S. military built several of its bases along the coast?

In the third part of his Vietnam policy, Nixon stepped up the bombing campaign. Hoping to ease pressure on troops in South Vietnam, Nixon ordered the bombing of enemy supply routes and hideouts in neighboring Cambodia and Laos. He kept the bombing of Cambodia secret.

✓ PROGRESS CHECK

Analyzing In your opinion, was Henry Kissinger's "linkage" policy a good plan for ending the war in Vietnam?

The Protests Continue

GUIDING QUESTION *Why did new antiwar protests take place as Vietnamization moved forward?*

The growing desire by Americans to end the war was reflected in a new round of antiwar **demonstrations** beginning in late 1969. In October, more than 300,000 people took part in an antiwar protest in Washington, D.C.

The Nixon administration also tried to end the war through peace talks, held in Paris, with North Vietnam. Henry Kissinger represented the United States in the meetings. The United States had launched the bombing campaign to pressure the North Vietnamese to agree to peace terms.

Reading **HELP**DESK (CCSS)

Academic Vocabulary

demonstration protest gathering or march

The North Vietnamese, however, took a wait-and-see attitude. They believed that the growing strength of the antiwar movement in the United States would force the Americans to withdraw. North Vietnam's attitude, as well as the antiwar protests, alarmed President Nixon. In a speech in November, he appealed to the "silent majority" of Americans for support for his policy. "North Vietnam cannot defeat or humiliate the United States," he said. "Only Americans can do that."

The War Escalates

The war expanded elsewhere in Southeast Asia with a conflict that broke out between Communist and non-Communist forces in Cambodia. In April 1970, Nixon decided to send American troops to destroy Communist bases in Cambodia.

Americans were outraged by Nixon's decision to attack Communist bases in Cambodia. By sending U.S. troops to Cambodia, critics said, Nixon invaded a neutral country and overstepped his constitutional power as president.

Campus Protests

Americans who opposed the war saw the Cambodian invasion as a widening of the war. A storm of protests took place on college campuses across the nation. Most protests went peacefully. Two protests, however, ended in violence.

One of the protests that ended in tragedy took place at Kent State University in Kent, Ohio. In the protest, students burned a military building on campus. Ohio's governor declared **martial** (MAHR•shuhl) **law**—emergency military rule. He ordered 3,000 National Guard troops to Kent State. At noon on May 4, students gathered for a protest rally on the campus lawn. The National Guard told the protesters to leave. Some students threw rocks at Guard members. In response, Guard members fired their weapons. Four students died, and at least nine more were wounded.

The second tragic protest occurred on May 15. This time the site was Jackson State University in Jackson, Mississippi. Following a night of protests, two students were shot and killed.

A wave of student strikes followed the tragedies at Kent State and Jackson State. Hundreds of colleges and universities called off classes to avoid additional conflicts.

Americans were sharply divided about U.S. involvement in Vietnam. Failed peace talks and increased bombings sparked antiwar demonstrations across the nation, such as this one in Washington, D.C.

martial law emergency military rule

In 1982 the nation dedicated the Vietnam Veteran's Memorial in Washington, D.C. The memorial's walls of black granite bear the names of the more than 58,000 Americans killed or missing in Vietnam.

The Pentagon Papers

The Cambodian invasion cost Nixon much support in Congress. Many lawmakers were angry over the president's failure to tell them about the action. In December 1970, Congress repealed the Gulf of Tonkin Resolution. This resolution had given the president wide power in directing the war in Vietnam.

When Daniel Ellsberg, who had worked at the Defense Department, gave some secret papers to the *New York Times,* support for the war weakened further. These documents became known as the Pentagon Papers.

The Pentagon Papers showed that many Johnson administration officials questioned the war in private while supporting it in public. The papers gave details of decisions made by presidents and their advisers without the approval of Congress. They also showed how certain officials misled Congress and the public about Vietnam. The Pentagon Papers backed up what many Americans had long believed: The government had not been honest with them.

PROGRESS CHECK

Determining Cause and Effect Determine and list three cause-and-effect relationships described in the above paragraphs about the Pentagon Papers.

Peace and the War's Effects

GUIDING QUESTION *How did the peace talks lead to a withdrawal of all American forces in Vietnam?*

The Nixon administration worked to end the war, even as antiwar feelings swelled at home. The president sent Henry Kissinger to negotiate for peace, and in the fall of 1972 an agreement seemed close. South Vietnam, however, was against part of the deal allowing North Vietnamese forces to remain in its territory. As a result, the agreement collapsed.

The War Ends

In 1972 Nixon was reelected president in a landslide. After this victory, he unleashed American airpower against North Vietnam. In December 1972, the heaviest bombing of the war took place. North Vietnam returned to peace talks. Meanwhile, the United States pressured South Vietnam to accept peace terms. On January 27, 1973, all the sides reached an agreement.

Steve Raymer/CORBIS

Reading **HELP**DESK (CCSS)

MIA American soldier classified as missing during a war or other military action

The United States agreed to pull its troops out of Vietnam. The North Vietnamese agreed to return all American prisoners of war. American military involvement in Vietnam was at an end. The conflict, however, was not over. North Vietnam did not give up the goal of bringing all of Vietnam under its rule. In early 1975, the North launched a major offensive. Within a few weeks, its tanks were near Saigon. As North Vietnamese forces advanced, the last Americans left the country. Thousands of Vietnamese who had supported the Americans also fled to the United States. On April 30, 1975, Saigon fell to the Communists. Soon after, South Vietnam surrendered, and the long war was over.

The War's Impact

The Vietnam War took a staggering toll. More than 1 million Vietnamese died. More than 58,000 Americans were dead, and 300,000 more were wounded. Many were permanently disabled. The United States had spent more than $150 billion on the war.

About 2.7 million Americans served in Vietnam. Unlike the veterans of World War II, however, they found no hero's welcome when they returned home. Many Americans paid little attention to those who had fought and sacrificed in Vietnam.

Thousands of soldiers were missing in action—**MIA.** It was not known whether they were dead or alive. Families of the MIA demanded that the U.S. government press for information. The Vietnamese allowed American groups to search the countryside. As the years passed, the chance of finding anyone alive faded.

✓ PROGRESS CHECK

Distinguishing Fact From Opinion Is the following statement a fact or an opinion? "At the end of the Vietnam War, South Vietnam surrendered to the North and came under Communist control."

LESSON 4 REVIEW

Review Vocabulary

1. Use the following terms to write a paragraph about the Vietnam War.

   a. Vietnamization   **b.** martial law   **c.** MIA

Answer the Guiding Questions

2. ***Describing*** What did Nixon mean when he spoke of "peace with honor"?

3. ***Explaining*** What factors contributed to the growing protests in the war's final years?

4. ***Summarizing*** What were two factors that finally helped bring an end to the war in Vietnam?

5. **ARGUMENT** Write a letter telling Henry Kissinger how he should advise President Nixon about the Vietnam War. Make your opinions about the war clear, and use your writing skills to persuade Kissinger to take your advice to the president.

Write your answers on a separate piece of paper.

① Exploring the Essential Question

INFORMATIVE/EXPLANATORY Write an essay in which you tell the historical story of U.S. involvement in Vietnam. Trace the roots of the conflict to the World War II era, the Cold War, and the decisions of Presidents Eisenhower, Kennedy, Johnson, and Nixon.

② 21st Century Skills

SOCIAL AND CROSS-CULTURAL SKILLS Interview an individual who was an adult during the 1960s and has clear memories about the Vietnam War. Conduct an interview in which you ask questions about the person's feelings about the war and how those feelings might have changed over time. Write a report that summarizes your findings.

③ Thinking Like a Historian

MAKING COMPARISONS Working with a small group, research one of the armed conflicts in which the United States has been involved since the end of the Vietnam War, such as the Gulf War, the war in Afghanistan, and the war in Iraq. Create a graphic organizer to list similarities and differences between the recent conflict and the Vietnam War. Explore such features as the length and size of the conflict, the outcomes, public support, and major reasons for the conflict.

④ Visual Literacy

ANALYZING PHOTOGRAPHS After spending five years as a prisoner of war in North Vietnam, Air Force Lt. Col. Robert Stirm is reunited with his family. What conclusions can you draw from the photo? What questions do you have that are not answered in the photo or caption?

AP Photo/Sal Veder

REVIEW THE GUIDING QUESTIONS

Choose the best answer for each of the following questions.

1 President Kennedy tried to counteract the appeal of communism in poor areas of Asia, Africa, and Latin America by

A. creating the Peace Corps.

B. introducing Green Berets.

C. employing guerrilla warfare.

D. spending more on nuclear arms.

2 A result of the Cuban Missile Crisis was that

F. the United States resolved to invade Cuba.

G. Khrushchev formed an impression of Kennedy as a weak leader.

H. the United States and the Soviet Union agreed to create a hot line for dealing with crises.

I. Kennedy was assassinated.

3 President Eisenhower worried that if Vietnam fell to the Communists,

A. other countries would follow, like falling dominoes.

B. the Soviet Union would install missiles in the region.

C. France would lose its colony.

D. Japan would gain a foothold in the region.

4 When did President Johnson halt the bombing of North Vietnam's cities?

F. after the Tet Offensive

G. after Nixon's election

H. before the march on the Pentagon

I. during the Democratic Convention

5 Nixon provoked protests on campuses by

A. leaking the Pentagon Papers.

B. sending troops to Cambodia.

C. ending draft deferments for students.

D. having Kissinger seek a peace settlement.

6 Nixon used the bombing of Cambodia and Laos as a way to

F. conquer those nations.

G. establish a colony in the region.

H. pressure the North Vietnamese to reach a peace deal.

I. anger college students in the United States.

DBQ ANALYZING DOCUMENTS

In his book *In Pharaoh's Army,* Tobias Wolff talks about the beginning of the Tet Offensive.

"When the assault … first began we didn't know what was going on. … All the towns of the Delta … were full of [Vietcong]. Every town and city in the country was under siege. Every airfield had been hit. Every road cut. They were in the streets of Saigon, in the American embassy. All in one night."

7 **Making Inferences** According to this passage, what aspect of the Tet Offensive was most surprising to the Americans?

   A. Americans were shocked that a supposedly weak enemy could stage such a strong offensive.

   B. Americans were angry that military communications within Vietnam were so poor during the Tet Offensive.

   C. Americans were unhappy that taxes were raised to pay for better weapons and equipment after the Tet Offensive.

   D. Americans were shocked that U.S. troops were not ready for the attack.

8 **Drawing Conclusions** Reread the quote and notice the phrase "All in one night." Which statement best describes how the author felt about the Tet Offensive?

   F. He was relieved that the attack was over so quickly.

   G. He was shocked that such a huge attack happened in one night.

   H. He was surprised the enemy attacked by night instead of by day.

   I. Because it was dark, he did not know who was attacking.

SHORT RESPONSE

This political cartoon, titled "Our Position Hasn't Changed At All," appeared in the *Washington Post* on June 17, 1965.

Source: The Herb Block Foundation

9 What does the cartoon say about Johnson's policy in Vietnam?

10 In the cartoon, what is the significance of the escalator?

EXTENDED RESPONSE

11 **Informative/Explanatory** Using information from the primary sources and your knowledge of the era, write an essay explaining why the war was difficult for American soldiers and civilians and describing how support for U.S. involvement changed over time.

Need Extra Help?

If You've Missed Question	❶	❷	❸	❹	❺	❻	❼	❽	❾	❿	⓫
Review Lesson	1	1	2	3	4	4	3	3	2–3	2–3	2–4

A Troubled Nation

1968–1981

ESSENTIAL QUESTION   *How do governments change?*

The Story Matters . . .

John Young is commander of the Apollo 16 mission. As a child, he loved airplanes and rockets. Now, he is standing on the surface of the moon. Getting there has not been easy. Young has worked hard and made several space flights to prepare for this moment. This Apollo 16 mission was almost canceled because of engine trouble. Now, though, there is triumph and also pride in the great things Americans can do when they commit themselves to the task.

In the 1960s and 1970s, Americans everywhere got to share the pride of astronauts like John Young. The feeling helped the nation make it through a difficult time in its history.

◄ *John Young salutes the American flag as he jumps into the thin lunar air.*

CORBIS

421

Place and Time: The Middle East 1970s

Events in the Middle East complicated the foreign policy of the United States in this era. They also made things difficult at home, as sharp increases in the price of oil from the region created economic strain.

Step Into the Place

MAP FOCUS Although the United States is located far from the Middle East, events in this region affected the lives of Americans during the 1970s.

1 LOCATION Which nations are located nearest to Israel?

2 LOCATION What is the location of this region compared to the Soviet Union, the superpower rival of the United States in this era?

3 CRITICAL THINKING
Analyzing Why might the United States be interested in the political events in this region?

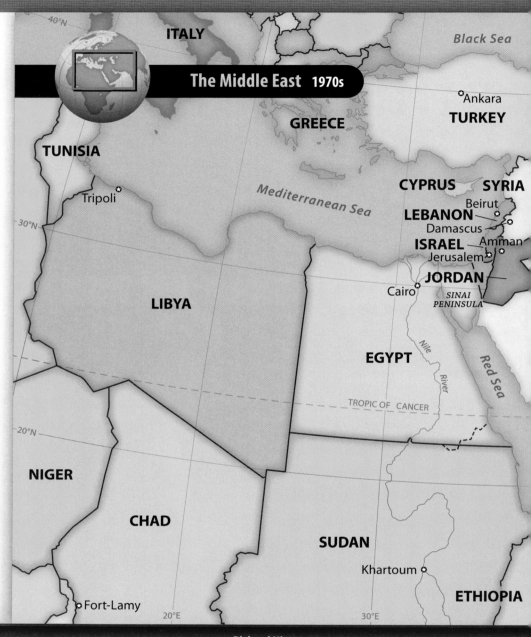

The Middle East 1970s

ITALY · Black Sea · GREECE · Ankara · TURKEY · TUNISIA · Tripoli · Mediterranean Sea · CYPRUS · SYRIA · Beirut · LEBANON · Damascus · ISRAEL · Amman · Jerusalem · JORDAN · Cairo · SINAI PENINSULA · LIBYA · EGYPT · Nile River · Red Sea · TROPIC OF CANCER · NIGER · CHAD · SUDAN · Khartoum · Fort-Lamy · ETHIOPIA

Step Into the Time

TIME LINE Look at the time line. For about how long did Iranians hold Americans hostage?

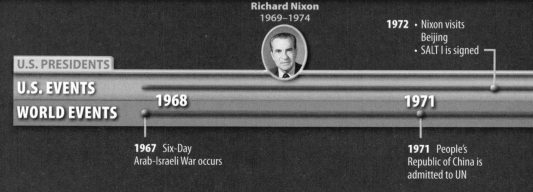

Richard Nixon
1969–1974

U.S. PRESIDENTS

U.S. EVENTS

WORLD EVENTS

1968

1971

1972 • Nixon visits Beijing
• SALT I is signed

1967 Six-Day Arab-Israeli War occurs

1971 People's Republic of China is admitted to UN

White House Historical Association

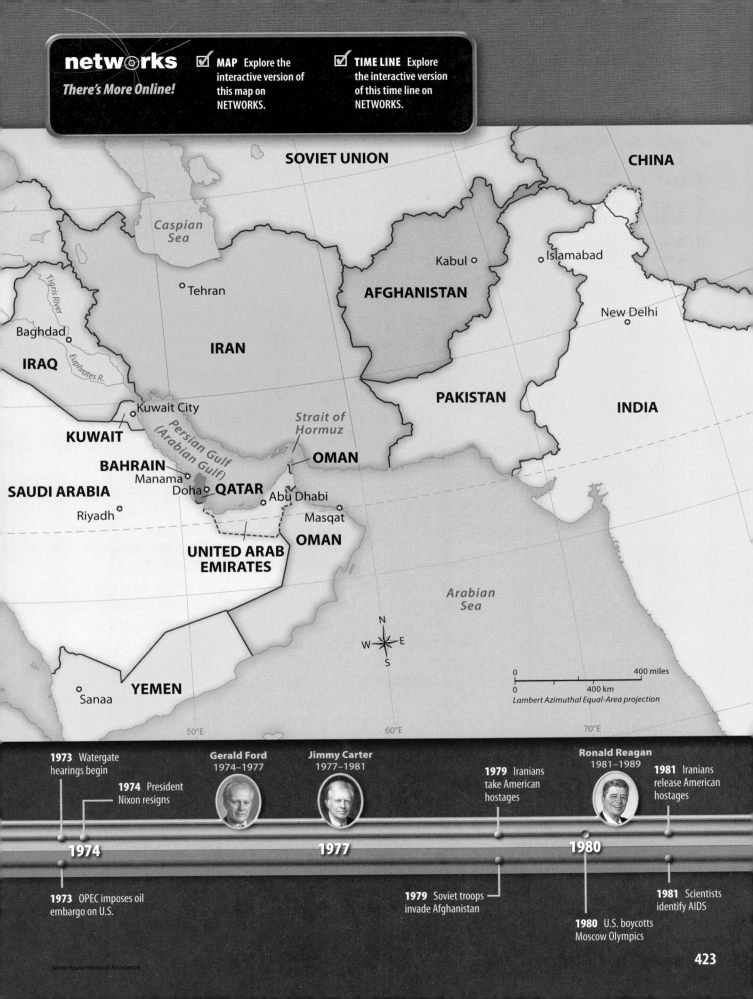

networks
There's More Online!

☑ **MAP** Explore the interactive version of this map on NETWORKS.

☑ **TIME LINE** Explore the interactive version of this time line on NETWORKS.

SOVIET UNION

CHINA

Caspian Sea

Kabul ⚬

Islamabad ⚬

Tehran ⚬

AFGHANISTAN

New Delhi ⚬

Tigris River

Baghdad ⚬

IRAN

Euphrates R.

IRAQ

PAKISTAN

INDIA

Kuwait City ⚬

Persian Gulf (Arabian Gulf)

Strait of Hormuz

KUWAIT

OMAN

BAHRAIN

Manama ⚬

SAUDI ARABIA

Doha ⚬ QATAR

Abu Dhabi ⚬

Masqat ⚬

Riyadh ⚬

UNITED ARAB EMIRATES

OMAN

Arabian Sea

N
W E
S

0   400 miles
0   400 km
Lambert Azimuthal Equal-Area projection

YEMEN

Sanaa ⚬

50°E   60°E   70°E

1973 Watergate hearings begin

Gerald Ford
1974–1977

Jimmy Carter
1977–1981

1979 Iranians take American hostages

Ronald Reagan
1981–1989

1981 Iranians release American hostages

1974 President Nixon resigns

1974

1977

1980

1973 OPEC imposes oil embargo on U.S.

1979 Soviet troops invade Afghanistan

1981 Scientists identify AIDS

1980 U.S. boycotts Moscow Olympics

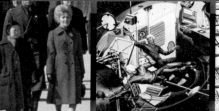

netw⊚rks

There's More Online!

☑ **BIOGRAPHY**
Henry Kissinger

☑ **CHART**
Soyuz Spacecraft

☑ **GAME**

☑ **GRAPHIC ORGANIZER**
Nixon's Foreign Policy

☑ **PRIMARY SOURCE**
Nixon and China

Lesson 1

Nixon's Foreign Policy

ESSENTIAL QUESTION *How do governments change?*

IT MATTERS BECAUSE

President Nixon's bold approach opened new doors in relations with China and the Soviet Union, though complicated problems still troubled the United States in other parts of the world.

A Thaw in the Cold War

GUIDING QUESTION *What did President Nixon do to improve relations with China and the Soviet Union?*

President Nixon hoped to build a more peaceful world. He made special efforts to reach out to the Soviet Union and the People's Republic of China. For example, in the summer of 1969 Nixon visited Romania. With the trip, he became the first president to go behind the iron curtain. Nixon wanted to find areas of common interest and cooperation with Cold War opponents.

To help shape his foreign policy, Nixon relied on his national security adviser, Henry Kissinger. Both men believed that peace would come through negotiation rather than through threats or force. Nixon followed a policy of **détente** (day•TAHNT)— attempts at **relaxing** international tensions. As détente replaced confrontation, Nixon hoped, the United States and Communist states could begin working to settle their disagreements.

Nixon realized that détente would work only if there were a balance of power. With a balance of power, rival countries or alliances have equal strength. "It will be a safer world and a better world," he declared, "if we have a strong, healthy United States, Europe, Soviet Union, China, Japan—each balancing the other, not playing one against the other."

Reading **HELP**DESK CCSS

Taking Notes: *Listing*

Create a diagram like this one to show the countries that were the focus of Nixon's foreign policy.

Countries ⟨

Content Vocabulary
• **détente**
• **embargo**

Academic Vocabulary
relax to ease

détente an attempt to ease international tensions

U.S. Relations With China

A first step toward détente was improving relations between the U.S. and China. Relations had been strained since 1949 when a Communist government seized power in China. The anti-Communist government of Chiang Kai-shek (JYAHNG KY·SHEHK) fled to the island of Taiwan. Both governments claimed to be the rightful government of all China. The United States refused to recognize the Communist People's Republic of China. Instead, it backed Chiang Kai-shek's government in Taiwan.

By 1970, however, both the U.S. and the People's Republic of China had good reasons to improve relations. Both countries shared a distrust of the Soviet Union. Since the 1960s, disagreements had divided China and the Soviets. Chinese and Soviet troops occasionally clashed along their borders.

Nixon hoped recognition of China would help end the war in Vietnam. He also hoped it would drive a deeper wedge between the Soviet Union and China. In the fall of 1970, Nixon told reporters he wanted to go to China. The Chinese responded by inviting a U.S. table tennis team to visit in April 1971. A week later, the United States announced the opening of trade with China.

While this "ping-pong" diplomacy went forward, U.S. and Chinese officials held secret talks. They discussed developing closer ties. Kissinger made a secret trip to China in July 1971. President Nixon then announced he would visit Beijing, the Chinese capital, "to seek the normalization of relations."

President Nixon made his historic trip to China in February 1972. Nixon and Chinese leader Chou En-lai (JOH EN·LY) agreed to allow more scientific and cultural exchange and promote trade. The U.S. did not make official diplomatic ties with China until 1979. Still, Nixon's trip marked the first formal U.S. contact with China in more than 25 years.

President Nixon's visit to China in 1972 advanced trade and improved relations between the U.S. and the People's Republic of China.

CORBIS

Détente led to the first joint space mission by the United States and the Soviet Union. The U.S. spacecraft *Apollo 18* and Soviet spacecraft *Soyuz 19* linked up in Earth's orbit on July 17, 1975.

U.S. Relations With the Soviet Union

After the China visit, Nixon traveled to Moscow, the Soviet capital, in May 1972. The Soviets welcomed a Cold War thaw. They wanted to prevent a U.S.-China alliance. They also hoped to buy United States technology. Nixon remarked, "There must be room in this world for two great nations with different systems to live together and work together."

While in Moscow, President Nixon and Soviet leader Leonid Brezhnev (BREHZH•nehf) signed the Strategic Arms Limitation Treaty (SALT I). In the treaty, the two sides agreed to set limits on some of their nuclear missiles. The United States and the Soviet Union also agreed to work together in trade and science. Nixon hoped that a new era of cooperation would help make the world more stable.

✓ PROGRESS CHECK

Identifying What is détente?

Middle East Tensions

GUIDING QUESTION *What was Nixon's foreign policy toward the Middle East?*

President Nixon's foreign policy aimed to maintain world stability without being drawn into conflicts. The president stated that the United States would help other nations. It would not, however, take "basic responsibility" for the future of those nations. A crisis soon arose in the Middle East that tested this policy.

Arab-Israeli Tensions

Since the Jewish state of Israel was founded in 1948, the United States supported Israel as it defended itself against attacks by its Arab neighbors. Fighting took place in that year, and again in 1956. These conflicts did little to resolve tensions in the region.

After Egypt closed a key waterway and massed its troops near Israel's border, Israel bombed Egyptian airfields on June 5, 1967. Within six days, Israel crippled the air forces of its Arab neighbors. Israeli troops moved west into the Gaza Strip, held by

Bettmann/CORBIS

Reading **HELP**DESK CCSS

embargo a ban on trade

Egypt since 1948. They also moved southwest into Egypt's Sinai Peninsula, and north into the Golan Heights part of Syria. Israel also captured the old city of Jerusalem and the West Bank, held by Jordan since 1948.

The "Six-Day War" of 1967 left Israel in control of these areas. When the fighting ended, the United Nations asked the Israelis to leave the captured territories. It asked the Arab nations to accept Israel's right to exist. The Arabs refused to negotiate, and Israel remained in the territories.

After the 1967 war, thousands of Palestinians lived in Israeli-held territory, and thousands more lived in neighboring Arab states. The Palestinians' demand for their own homeland became another source of tensions in the region.

Yom Kippur War

Tensions remained high between Arabs and Israelis. In 1973 Egypt and Syria attacked Israel to regain land lost in the 1967 war. Because this attack occurred on Yom Kippur, the most important Jewish holy day, the conflict became known as the Yom Kippur War.

Egypt's forces attacked Israel, hoping to recapture the Sinai Peninsula. In early battles, many Israeli planes were shot down. Egypt's troops crossed into the Sinai Peninsula, and Syria moved into the Golan Heights. With an American airlift of weapons, Israel struck back. The fighting raged until the United Nations negotiated a cease-fire. By this time, the Israelis had regained the land lost in the initial Arab advance.

Angered by the U.S. support of Israel, Arab oil-producing states placed an **embargo**—a ban on shipments—on oil sales to the United States and other "non-friendly" nations. At the time, the U.S. depended heavily on oil from the Middle East. The embargo led to an oil shortage in the United States. Long lines of cars formed at gas pumps as gas prices skyrocketed.

The fuel shortages caused by the 1973 oil embargo plunged the nation into a state of emergency. The Department of Energy considered different plans to save fuel. One plan was to close gas stations on Sundays.

▶ CRITICAL THINKING
Analyzing Political Cartoons What is the cartoon's message?

"*My text this morning is taken from Paragraph 15 of the President's message in regard to Sunday driving.*"

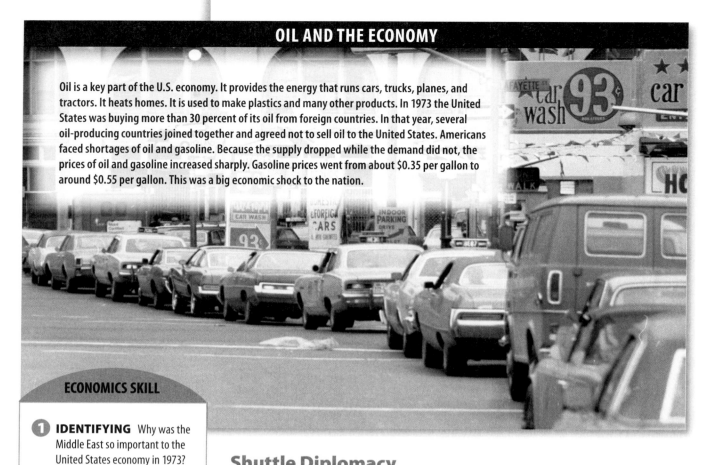

OIL AND THE ECONOMY

Oil is a key part of the U.S. economy. It provides the energy that runs cars, trucks, planes, and tractors. It heats homes. It is used to make plastics and many other products. In 1973 the United States was buying more than 30 percent of its oil from foreign countries. In that year, several oil-producing countries joined together and agreed not to sell oil to the United States. Americans faced shortages of oil and gasoline. Because the supply dropped while the demand did not, the prices of oil and gasoline increased sharply. Gasoline prices went from about $0.35 per gallon to around $0.55 per gallon. This was a big economic shock to the nation.

ECONOMICS SKILL

1 **IDENTIFYING** Why was the Middle East so important to the United States economy in 1973?

2 **CRITICAL THINKING**
Determining Cause and Effect What was the impact of the sudden drop in the supply of oil?

Shuttle Diplomacy

President Nixon sent Henry Kissinger to the Middle East. The goal was to gain Arab trust and to negotiate an agreement between Israel and its Arab neighbors. Kissinger engaged in "shuttle diplomacy"—traveling back and forth among Middle Eastern capitals in an effort to resolve the oil crisis and forge a lasting peace.

Early in 1974, Golda Meir, the prime minister of Israel, and Anwar el-Sadat (suh•DAT), the president of Egypt, agreed to separate Israeli and Egyptian forces in the Sinai Peninsula. Then, in March 1974, Kissinger persuaded the Arab nations to end the oil embargo. Diplomatic ties between the U.S. and Egypt—the most powerful Arab state—had been broken since 1967. Kissinger helped repair ties between the two nations by promising Egypt large amounts of foreign aid.

☑ PROGRESS CHECK

Summarizing What happened in the United States because of the oil embargo?

NY Daily News via Getty Images

Reading **HELP**DESK (CCSS)

Reading Strategy: *Sequencing*

To help you understand the complicated relationship between the United States and the nations of the Middle East, make a time line, and record key events along it.

Latin America

President Nixon wanted to prevent the spread of communism in Latin America. In 1970 the country of Chile elected Salvador Allende (ah•yehn•day) president. Allende was a socialist and follower of Karl Marx, the founder of communism. Allende became the first Marxist to gain power in the Americas through peaceful means.

Hoping to boost Chile's economy, Allende's government took over large businesses. It gave land to the poor and raised workers' wages. The economy grew, and the jobless rate went down. At the same time, the breakup of large farms led to a drop in food production. This caused food shortages. Also, higher wages led businesses to raise prices.

Allende's policies made him many enemies. His Marxist views frightened wealthy Chileans. Many took their money out of the country and invested it abroad where they believed it would be safe. Allende's takeover of American companies operating in Chile angered the United States. The Nixon administration decided to weaken the Allende government. To achieve that goal, the U.S. gave money to Allende's political opponents and promoted strikes. Labor strikes disrupted the country's economy. The U.S. also convinced foreign investors to stop loaning money to Chile. By 1972 Chile's economy was near collapse.

In 1973 Chile's military took action. With the knowledge of the Central Intelligence Agency, a group of Chilean military leaders under General Augusto Pinochet (pee•noh•CHEHT) overthrew the government. Allende died under uncertain circumstances. The United States immediately recognized the new military dictatorship and restored foreign aid to Chile.

☑ **PROGRESS CHECK**

Analyzing Why did the United States oppose Salvador Allende?

BIOGRAPHY

Henry Kissinger (1923–)

Henry Kissinger was born in Germany. He and his family moved to the United States in the 1930s to escape mistreatment by the Nazis. He grew up to become an expert in international affairs. In 1969 he became a top foreign policy adviser to President Nixon. He served throughout Nixon's presidency and in the presidency of Nixon's successor. In 1973 Kissinger shared the Nobel Prize for Peace with North Vietnam's Le Duc Tho for their efforts to end the Vietnam War.

▶ **CRITICAL THINKING**
Drawing Conclusions What qualities do you think are important for a diplomat and top presidential adviser to possess?

Corbis

LESSON 1 REVIEW

Review Vocabulary

1. Demonstrate your understanding of the terms *détente* and *embargo* by using each term in a sentence.

Answer the Guiding Questions

2. *Summarizing* What were President Nixon's goals in dealing with China and the Soviet Union?

3. *Identifying* What did President Nixon do to address problems in the Middle East?

4. *Describing* Why did the Nixon administration oppose the Allende government of Chile?

5. **INFORMATIVE/EXPLANATORY** Write a paragraph explaining how sports can improve relations between two nations.

networks

There's More Online!

☑ **BIOGRAPHY**
Barbara Jordan

☑ **GRAPHIC ORGANIZER**
Events of Watergate

☑ **MAP** 1972 Election

☑ **PRIMARY SOURCE**
• 1973 Rehabilitation Act
• Nixon's Resignation Address
• Ford Pardons Nixon

☑ **TIME LINE**
President Ford's Administration

☑ **VIDEO**

Lesson 2
Nixon and Watergate

ESSENTIAL QUESTION *How do governments change?*

IT MATTERS BECAUSE
Nixon's presidency and his plans to change the nature of government were overwhelmed by scandal.

Domestic Policies Under Nixon

GUIDING QUESTION *How did the role of the federal government change under Nixon?*

As a presidential candidate in 1968, Nixon pledged to bring back "law and order" to the country. He also vowed to reduce the role of government in people's lives.

Nixon's drive to restore law and order involved "cracking down on crime." He sought stiffer penalties for lawbreakers. Nixon also used federal money to help state and city police forces.

Federal Courts

President Nixon believed the federal courts should be tougher on criminals. "I believe some Court decisions have gone too far in weakening the peace forces against the criminal forces in our society," he said. During his presidency, President Nixon filled four seats on the Supreme Court. Warren Burger became chief justice. Nixon also named Harry Blackmun, Lewis Powell, and William Rehnquist justices. The president hoped that these justices would make decisions more in line with his own conservative thinking. The new justices did not always live up to Nixon's hopes.

Reading HELPDESK CCSS

Taking Notes: *Sequencing*

On a time line like this one, note major events that occurred during the Watergate crisis.

June 1972	May 1973	Oct. 1973	Aug. 1974
☐	☐	☐	☐

Content Vocabulary
• **revenue sharing**
• **affirmative action**
• **deficit**
• **executive privilege**
• **impeach**
• **amnesty**

Nixon's New Federalism

Nixon wanted to reduce government involvement in people's lives. He also aimed to cut federal spending. As president, he pledged to "reverse the flow of power and resources from the states and communities to Washington, and start power and resources flowing back … to the people." Nixon's plan was called New Federalism. One part of the plan was **revenue sharing**—giving states some of the money collected in federal taxes. States would then be free to use this money or give it to their cities and towns. Revenue sharing became law in 1972.

Nixon also promised to "quit pouring billions of dollars into programs that have failed." He sought to scale back many of President Johnson's Great Society programs. For example, Nixon closed the Office of Economic Opportunity, the agency that led Johnson's War on Poverty. Nixon did, however, create new agencies focused on popular concerns. The Occupational Safety and Health Administration (OSHA), for example, protected worker safety. The Environmental Protection Agency (EPA) helped protect the environment. These agencies still exist today.

On civil rights issues, Nixon tried to appeal to white voters. For example, Nixon opposed the use of forced busing to integrate schools. Under the order of state courts, students from some all-white or all-African American neighborhoods were sent by bus to schools in other areas. The goal was to produce racially mixed schools.

At the same time, Nixon worked to carry out federal court orders to integrate schools. Nixon also promoted **affirmative action,** an approach to hiring or promotion that favors disadvantaged groups. The Rehabilitation Act of 1973 was the first major legislation to outlaw discrimination against people with disabilities.

Economic Challenges

While in office, President Nixon had to deal with a number of weighty economic issues. The nation's manufacturers struggled against foreign competition.

Americans with disabilities protest for equal rights. The Rehabilitation Act of 1973 helped address some of their concerns.

Wally McNamee/CORBIS

---

revenue sharing a policy in which the federal government gives states some of its revenue to be used at state and local levels

affirmative action an approach to hiring or promotion that favors disadvantaged groups

Delegates at the 1972 Republican Convention, held in Miami Beach, Florida, nominated incumbents Richard Nixon for president and Spiro Agnew for vice president.

Inflation—an increase in the prices of goods and services—was a serious problem. Inflation was fueled by international competition for raw materials and the increasing cost of oil. The United States also faced slow economic growth and high unemployment.

President Nixon tried several ideas to fight inflation. He cut federal spending and raised interest rates to limit public borrowing. These actions did help drive down consumer prices. However, these measures also discouraged people from buying things. Businesses began to cut back, and production fell. The nation found itself in a difficult situation: Business activity was slow even as prices rose. Experts called the combination "stagflation."

Nixon then ordered a temporary freeze on wages and prices. He set guidelines for any future increases. The guidelines slowed inflation. Economic output, however, remained slow.

Later, Nixon tried a third approach. To stimulate the economy, he increased federal spending. This policy helped revive the economy for a short time. However, it created a budget **deficit**— that is, government spending was greater than government income.

None of Nixon's efforts restored the economy's health. Economic problems continued to trouble his presidency.

✓ PROGRESS CHECK

Analyzing What was the outcome of Nixon's efforts to improve the economy?

A Second Term—and Scandal

GUIDING QUESTION *Why was Nixon forced to resign during his second term?*

The troubled economy worried President Nixon as the 1972 presidential election neared. The ongoing war in Vietnam was another concern. These issues caused Nixon to have doubts about his chances for reelection.

In an effort to ensure victory at the polls, the president and his aides sometimes broke the law. In 1971, for example, Nixon asked his aides for an "enemies list." The list named people he thought were against his presidency. He ordered the FBI and the Internal Revenue Service (IRS) to investigate some of these

CORBIS

Reading **HELP**DESK ⒸⒸⓈⓈ

deficit when government spending is greater than government revenue, or income

people. This was an abuse of Nixon's presidential power. In addition, Nixon used some of his campaign money to pay for secret actions against his Democratic foes.

Nixon's Landslide Win

As it turned out, Nixon had little reason to fear any Democratic opponent. The Democratic Party was badly split. Several candidates were trying to win the party's nomination in 1972. They included former vice president Hubert Humphrey and senators Edmund Muskie of Maine and George McGovern of South Dakota. Former governor George Wallace of Alabama was also in the race.

Muskie and Humphrey could not gain wide support. Wallace's campaign ended in May 1972 when he was wounded in an assassination attempt. In the end, McGovern won the nomination. Many Democrats and labor union leaders, however, considered him to be too liberal. The failure of the party to unite behind McGovern hurt his campaign.

As the election neared, the economy and prospects for peace in Vietnam improved. These factors contributed to Nixon's landslide win. He won nearly 61 percent of the popular vote. The Republican victory in the Electoral College was even more lopsided—520 to 18.

The Energy Crisis

The surge in the economy did not last. During Nixon's second term, severe economic problems struck. A key blow was the 1973 oil embargo. Although the embargo was lifted in 1974, its economic effects continued. Oil prices shot up. The economy struggled. Many American companies laid off workers and others raised prices. Consumers complained about the rising prices and about the long lines at gas stations.

INFOGRAPHIC

President Nixon easily won reelection for a second term in 1972.

1 **PLACE** What was the only state Nixon failed to win?

2 **CRITICAL THINKING**
Drawing Conclusions What do you think are the reasons for Nixon's landslide victory?

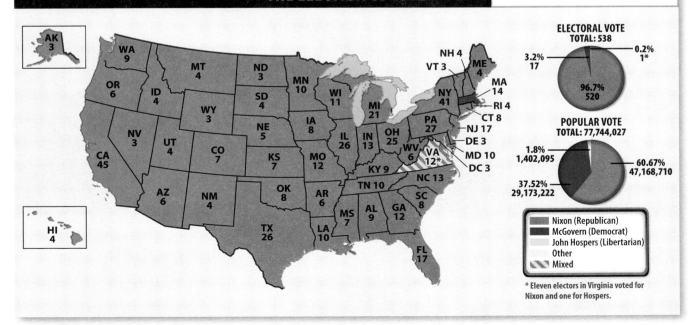

THE ELECTION OF 1972

ELECTORAL VOTE
TOTAL: 538

3.2% 17
0.2% 1*
96.7% 520

POPULAR VOTE
TOTAL: 77,744,027

1.8% 1,402,095
60.67% 47,168,710
37.52% 29,173,222

Nixon (Republican)
McGovern (Democrat)
John Hospers (Libertarian)
Other
Mixed

* Eleven electors in Virginia voted for Nixon and one for Hospers.

The president took steps to save oil. Nixon also urged Americans to conserve **energy** voluntarily. Congress lowered speed limits on highways because cars and trucks burn less fuel at lower speeds. There was also concern about the nation's reliance on imported oil. In response, Nixon urged development of American oil reserves. There was a special focus on Alaska, which had vast, untapped oil reserves.

Watergate Scandal

Nixon's second-term troubles were just beginning. What began as a newspaper story hardly anyone noticed eventually turned into a presidential crisis. This crisis had its roots in Nixon's reelection campaign.

Remember that Nixon had been worried about his chances for reelection in 1972. In June of that year, Nixon's reelection committee sent burglars to break into the Democratic Party's office in the Watergate building in Washington, D.C. The burglars hoped to steal information about the Democrats' campaign. They also planned to place listening devices—bugs—on the office telephones. These bugs would allow Nixon's team to listen in on the Democrats' phone calls. These actions, of course, were against the law.

Thanks to an alert security guard at the Watergate, police caught the burglars. Yet no one realized at first that the group was working for the Nixon campaign. The story captured little attention. In November, voters gave Nixon his landslide victory. There were few hints of the scandal about to unfold.

The Watergate complex in Washington, D.C., is best known as the site of the burglary that led to the Watergate scandal.

Brooks Kraft/Corbis

Reading **HELP**DESK (CCSS)

Academic Vocabulary

energy sources of usable power

Build Vocabulary: *Word Parts*

The suffix *-gate* today is added to ordinary words to suggest the presence of some type of scandal. For example, when the New England Patriots professional football team was caught spying on its opponents, the scandal was called "spygate."

The Investigation

Reporters at the *Washington Post* newspaper kept digging into the story of the burglary. Nixon denied any involvement, but reporters were able to link the burglary to the president's reelection campaign. Then, one of the burglars admitted that White House aides had lied about their involvement. In fact, the White House had pressured the burglars to plead guilty and remain silent.

In May 1973, the Senate began hearings on Watergate, as the scandal was now known. The hearings tried to find what the president knew about Watergate and when he knew it.

Investigators learned in July about a secret taping system that recorded the president's office conversations. They wanted to hear these tapes. President Nixon refused to hand them over. He claimed **executive privilege,** the principle that a president's conversations should remain private.

Archibald Cox, a special prosecutor who was investigating the administration, asked a court to force Nixon to hand over the tapes. Nixon refused. Nixon also ordered that Cox be fired. In protest, Nixon's attorney general and the attorney general's deputy quit. The event became known as the Saturday Night Massacre. Nixon's abuse of power shocked the nation.

Around this time, another scandal struck the administration. Vice President Spiro Agnew was charged with taking bribes while he was governor of Maryland. In October 1973, Agnew resigned. Nixon named House member Gerald R. Ford of Michigan as his new vice president.

Nixon Resigns

Public outrage was growing. As the pressure mounted, Nixon finally released some of the tapes. They were not, however, complete. Then, the Supreme Court ruled that the president had to turn over all of the tapes. Nixon obeyed this order.

Several days later, a House committee voted to **impeach** Nixon, or officially charge him with misconduct. The House of Representatives has the sole authority to impeach. If the House does so, the Senate holds a trial to decide on a president's guilt or innocence. Before the full House could vote on the committee's call for impeachment, investigators found clear evidence against the president. One tape revealed Nixon had ordered a cover-up of the Watergate break-in just days after it happened.

Bernard Golfryd/Premium Archive/Getty Images

BIOGRAPHY

Barbara Jordan (1936–1996)

Born in Houston, Texas, Jordan used education, keen intelligence, and a powerful speaking style to achieve success. After being one of just two women in her class to graduate from Boston University law school in 1959, she eventually returned to Texas and entered politics. Jordan became the first African American woman elected to Congress from a Southern state. In spite of suffering from multiple sclerosis, she won recognition as a strong voice for justice for her work on the House committee investigating Watergate. In 1976 she became the first African American woman to give a keynote address at a major party's national convention.

CRITICAL THINKING
Describing What are some of the barriers Barbara Jordan had to overcome to achieve success in her life?

---

executive privilege the principle that White House conversations should remain private

impeach to officially charge someone with misconduct in office

On August 8, 1974, Nixon resigned from the presidency, saying, "I would only say that if some of my judgments were wrong—and some were wrong—they were made in what I believed at the time to be the best interest of the nation."

▶ **CRITICAL THINKING**
Analyzing What do you think Nixon meant when he said he had acted in what he believed to be the best interest of the nation?

With this news, even Nixon's strongest supporters knew he would be impeached. To avoid this, Nixon resigned the presidency on August 9, 1974. Vice President Gerald Ford took the oath of office and became the nation's 38th president.

The Watergate crisis proved that the system of checks and balances worked. The legislative and judicial branches used their powers to check the abuses of the executive branch. Yet the scandal damaged the public's faith in its political leaders.

✓**PROGRESS CHECK**

Explaining How did Gerald Ford become president?

Healing the Nation

GUIDING QUESTION *How did Ford attempt to unite the nation after the Watergate scandal?*

After becoming president, Gerald Ford assured Americans, "Our long national nightmare is over." To fill the office of vice president, Ford selected Nelson Rockefeller, a highly respected former governor of New York.

More Upheaval

The public seemed pleased with Ford and the chance for a fresh start. Then, on September 8, 1974, Ford granted Richard Nixon a pardon for any crimes he may have committed as president. This meant that the former president could not be prosecuted for his part in Watergate.

Ford hoped the pardon would help heal the wounds of Watergate. Instead, the pardon stirred **controversy.** Many Americans asked why Nixon should escape punishment when others involved in the scandal had gone to jail. Some even accused Ford of making a bargain with Nixon. They speculated that Ford had offered Nixon the promise of a pardon in exchange for Nixon leaving the presidency. Ford insisted he had made no deal with Nixon. Still, the new president never fully regained the goodwill he enjoyed in his first weeks in office.

Yet another controversy arose when President Ford offered **amnesty,** or protection from prosecution, to those who illegally avoided military service during the Vietnam War. Ford promised these people would not be punished if they

Alex Webb/Magnum Photos, Inc.

Reading **HELP**DESK (CCSS)

amnesty protection from prosecution

Academic Vocabulary

controversy arguments between opposing viewpoints

pledged loyalty to the United States and performed some type of national service. Many people approved of amnesty. Others argued that "draft dodgers" and deserters should be punished.

Ford's Policies

Like Nixon, Ford worked for détente with the Soviet Union. In late 1974, Ford met with Soviet leader Brezhnev to discuss arms control. A year later, he traveled to Finland. There he signed the Helsinki Accords with the Soviet Union and other nations. The countries pledged to respect the human rights of their citizens. The accords also set new trade agreements.

Ford also worked to improve relations with China. When Chinese leader Mao Zedong (MOW DZUH·DUNG) died in 1976, a more moderate government came to power. China's new leaders wanted to increase trade with the United States.

Like Nixon, Ford faced a troubled economy. Inflation and unemployment remained high. Foreign competition led to factory closings and worker layoffs. Oil prices remained high.

To fight inflation, Ford launched voluntary wage and price controls. He called on Americans to save rather than spend money. He urged people to plant gardens to offset rising food prices. Ford also tried to cut government spending to control inflation. When this failed, the president asked Congress to pass a tax cut. This cut helped improve the economy, but it also reduced government revenue and helped lead to a budget deficit. Ford could not solve the nation's economic woes.

After his pardon of Nixon, President Ford faced many questions from the public and the press. Below, Ford defends his action at a press conference in September 1974.

☑ **PROGRESS CHECK**

Summarizing How did Ford attempt to put the Watergate scandal in the past?

Consolidated News Pictures/Hulton Archive/Getty Images

LESSON 2 REVIEW (CCSS)

Review Vocabulary

1. Write a paragraph about Nixon's presidency in which you use the following terms:

   a. revenue sharing   **b.** affirmative action

2. Explain the significance of:

   a. deficit   **b.** executive privilege
   c. impeach   **d.** amnesty

Answer the Guiding Questions

3. ***Explaining*** What was Nixon's view of the proper use of government power?

4. ***Analyzing*** Why was Nixon's presidency unable to survive the Watergate scandal?

5. ***Drawing Conclusions*** Why did President Ford's attempt to unite the nation after the Watergate scandal fail?

6. **ARGUMENT** Nixon's Watergate scandal and resignation was a terrible ordeal for the nation. Imagine you are an adviser to the new president, Gerald Ford. Write a memo in which you argue either for or against the granting of a pardon to Nixon.

netw⊙rks

There's More Online!

☑ **CHART/GRAPH**
- Retail Gas Prices
- President Carter's Accomplishments

☑ **GAME**

☑ **GRAPHIC ORGANIZER**
Issues of Carter Presidency

☑ **MAP** Election of 1976

☑ **PRIMARY SOURCE**
Hostage Diary

☑ **VIDEO**

Lesson 3
The Presidency of Jimmy Carter

ESSENTIAL QUESTION *How do governments change?*

IT MATTERS BECAUSE
President Carter's few successes were not enough for him to overcome the events that overwhelmed his presidency.

An Informal Presidency

GUIDING QUESTION *What problems did President Carter face?*

President Ford planned to seek election in 1976. First, though, he had to win the Republican nomination. In this race, Ford faced a strong challenge from Ronald Reagan, former governor of California. Reagan got the backing of many conservatives, but Ford overcame the challenge to win the nomination. He chose Senator Bob Dole of Kansas as his running mate.

Jimmy Carter won the Democratic Party's nomination. Carter stressed his **integrity,** or moral character, and his religious faith. A former Georgia governor, Carter had never worked in Washington, D.C. He was, therefore, seen as an "outsider." This was an appealing quality in the aftermath of Watergate. Senator Walter Mondale of Minnesota ran for vice president.

During the campaign, Ford ran on his record as president. Carter vowed to restore the faith of Americans in the federal government by making it more open and efficient. Carter won in a close election, gaining 50.1 percent of the popular vote. He owed his margin of victory in part to support from African American Southern voters.

Carter's presidency was less formal than many past presidencies. At his inauguration, Carter wore a basic business suit rather than more formal clothing. After the ceremony,

(cl)Corbis, (cr & r)Bettmann/CORBIS

Reading **HELP**DESK ⓒ**CCSS**

Taking Notes: *Listing*

On a chart like this one, record the major result of each issue of Carter's presidency.

Issue	Result
Panama Canal	
Camp David Accords	
Crisis in Iran	

Content Vocabulary
- **trade deficit**
- **human rights**
- **apartheid**
- **fundamentalist**

438 *A Troubled Nation*

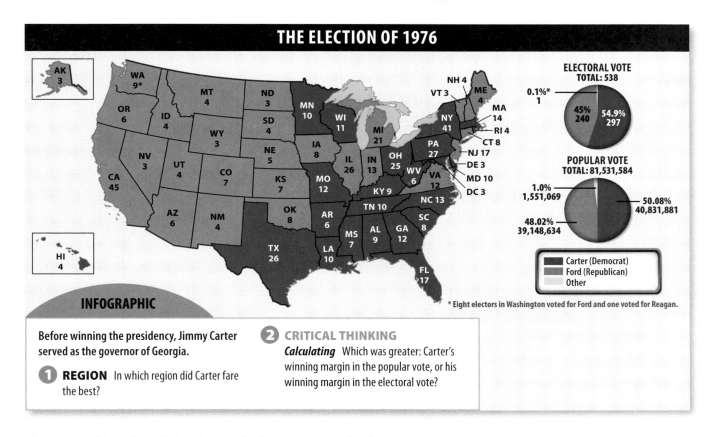

THE ELECTION OF 1976

AK 3

WA 9*
OR 6
ID 4
MT 4
ND 3
MN 10
WI 11
MI 21
NH 4
VT 3
ME 4
MA 14
NY 41
RI 4
CT 8
NV 3
UT 4
WY 3
SD 4
NE 5
IA 8
IL 26
IN 13
OH 25
PA 27
NJ 17
DE 3
MD 10
DC 3
CA 45
CO 7
KS 7
MO 12
KY 9
WV 6
VA 12
AZ 6
NM 4
OK 8
AR 6
TN 10
NC 13
SC 8
TX 26
LA 10
MS 7
AL 9
GA 12
HI 4
FL 17

ELECTORAL VOTE
TOTAL: 538
0.1%* 1
45% 240
54.9% 297

POPULAR VOTE
TOTAL: 81,531,584
1.0% 1,551,069
50.08% 40,831,881
48.02% 39,148,634

- Carter (Democrat)
- Ford (Republican)
- Other

* Eight electors in Washington voted for Ford and one voted for Reagan.

INFOGRAPHIC

Before winning the presidency, Jimmy Carter served as the governor of Georgia.

1 REGION In which region did Carter fare the best?

2 CRITICAL THINKING
Calculating Which was greater: Carter's winning margin in the popular vote, or his winning margin in the electoral vote?

Carter and his family broke with the custom of riding in a limousine from the Capitol to the White House. Instead, the Carters walked.

The Troubled Economy

Once in office, Carter tried to boost the economy. He cut taxes and increased spending. Unemployment went down, but inflation went up. Carter then called for spending cuts and a delayed tax cut. Carter's change of course made him seem weak and uncertain. As a Washington outsider, the president also had trouble gaining support in Congress.

Carter tried to address the country's energy problems. High energy costs made inflation worse. The high price of imported oil also led to a growing **trade deficit,** meaning that the value of foreign imports **exceeded** the value of American exports.

In April 1977, Carter presented a National Energy Plan to solve the energy crisis. Carter's plan included the creation of a Department of Energy to oversee energy policy. He called for more exploration of new sources of energy. He also wanted to collect taxes to increase oil production and energy conservation. Congress passed a weakened version of the plan in 1978.

Jimmy Carter, with his wife Rosalynn, addresses a crowd following his election victory in 1976.

Bettmann/CORBIS

trade deficit when the value of foreign imports is greater than the value of American exports

Academic Vocabulary

integrity moral character
exceed to be greater than

Rising energy prices were a major problem during Carter's presidency. As the table shows, prices continued to rise into the early 1980s. They later came down—but have risen sharply again in recent years.

PRICE OF REGULAR GASOLINE AT THE PUMP		
	PRICE PER GALLON	PRICE PER GALLON Adjusted for inflation
1971	$.36	$2.01
1981	$1.38	$3.38
1991	$1.10	$1.81
2001	$1.43	$1.80
2011	$3.70	$3.70

Source: United States Department of Energy

Nuclear Power

The United States first developed nuclear technology during World War II to make the atomic bomb. Scientists later learned how to use nuclear energy for peaceful purposes, such as make electricity. In the 1970s, nuclear power produced 10 percent of the nation's electricity.

In March 1979, a major accident took place at the Three Mile Island nuclear power plant near Harrisburg, Pennsylvania. Officials said there was little threat to the public from the event. Still, many people feared that this kind of accident could cause widespread harm. It could lead to a release of nuclear energy that might poison people and the land.

Public feeling against nuclear power grew. President Carter, however, did not want to halt the development of nuclear energy. Supporters argued that, with safeguards, nuclear power did not harm the environment.

✓ PROGRESS CHECK

Identifying What economic problems troubled Carter's presidency?

Carter's Foreign Policy

GUIDING QUESTION *What were some successes and challenges of President Carter's foreign policy?*

Carter based his foreign policy on human rights—the basic rights and liberties all people should have. He proposed that any nation that violated **human rights** should not receive support from the United States. For example, Carter condemned South Africa for its policy of **apartheid** (uh•PAHR•tayt), racial separation and discrimination against nonwhites.

The president's policy sometimes presented challenges for the United States. In 1980 Cuban dictator Fidel Castro allowed thousands of Cubans to leave Cuba by boat for Florida. This event came to be called the Mariel boatlift.

At first, the United States accepted the refugees. After all, the United States had long been critical of Cuban human rights violations. By the time Castro ended the boatlift five months later, about 125,000 Cubans had entered the United States. The United States had trouble absorbing so many immigrants in such a short time. A small number of the Cuban refugees were criminals and political prisoners that Castro had sent to the U.S.

Reading **HELP**DESK **CCSS**

human rights the basic rights and freedoms that all people should have

apartheid South African policy of racial separation and discrimination against nonwhites

on purpose. In the United States, public opinion turned against the Cuban refugees. Carter learned that a foreign policy based on a single issue—human rights—had limitations. Still, the president continued to work for human rights in other nations.

Panama Canal Treaties

President Carter took action to end Latin American bitterness over the Panama Canal. Over the years, U.S. control of the canal had caused friction between the United States and Panama. Carter signed two treaties with Panama in 1977. The treaties turned the Panama Canal over to Panama by the year 2000. They also ensured that the canal would remain a neutral waterway open to all shipping. Some Republicans in the Senate tried to block ratification of the treaties. They charged that Carter was giving away U.S. property. This effort failed. The Senate approved the treaties in 1978.

Middle East Summit

President Carter sought to bring peace to the Middle East. When talks between Israel and Egypt stalled in 1978, Carter invited Israeli prime minister Menachem Begin (muh•NAH•khuhm BAY•gihn) and Egyptian president Anwar el-Sadat to Camp David, Maryland, for a summit meeting. After nearly two weeks of talks, Begin and el-Sadat found common ground. The three leaders reached an agreement known as the Camp David Accords. The agreement led to an Egyptian-Israeli peace treaty signed at the White House in March 1979. The treaty marked the first time that Israel and an Arab nation had made peace.

President Carter, Anwar el-Sadat (left), and Menachem Begin (right) met at Camp David and reached a historic agreement.

Bettmann/Corbis

WELCOME BACK TO FREEDOM

Shortly after Ronald Reagan became president, Iran released the American hostages.

▶ CRITICAL THINKING
Drawing Conclusions How do you think the scenes of the hostages release affected public feeling toward the new president, Ronald Reagan?

Soviet-American Relations

Soviet human-rights abuses also came under criticism from President Carter. At the same time, Carter continued talks on arms control. In June 1979, President Carter and Soviet leader Brezhnev signed a second Strategic Arms Limitation Treaty, or SALT II. Critics in the Senate claimed that the treaty gave the Soviets an advantage over the United States. The Senate delayed ratifying it.

Any hope of Senate approval ended in December 1979, when the Soviets invaded the southwest Asian nation of Afghanistan. President Carter expressed the nation's outrage. The United States and other nations refused to take part in the Olympic Games scheduled to take place in the Soviet capital of Moscow. The decision to use the popular sporting event as a means of protest was controversial.

U.S. Hostages in Iran

In the 1970s, Iran was a major U.S. ally in the oil-rich Persian Gulf region. Iran's ruler, Shah Mohammad Reza Pahlavi, built a powerful military with U.S. aid. Many Iranians criticized corruption in the shah's government. Others disliked Western influences in Iran. They felt these influences weakened traditional Muslim values.

In January 1979, Islamic **fundamentalists**—people who believe in strict obedience to religious laws—forced the shah to flee Iran. The new ruler, Muslim leader Ayatollah Khomeini, was hostile to the United States for its support of the shah.

In November 1979, Iranian students, with government support, stormed the U.S. embassy in Tehran, the capital of Iran. The group held 52 Americans hostage. The United States was outraged. Diplomatic attempts to negotiate the release of the hostages failed. A daring desert rescue attempt ended in tragedy with the deaths of eight American soldiers. The hostage crisis dragged on and became a major issue in the presidential election of 1980.

The Election of 1980

As the election of 1980 approached, Carter's troubles mounted. Many Americans blamed him for a weak economy, which was experiencing both high inflation and high unemployment. They

Bettmann/CORBIS

Reading **HELP**DESK (CCSS)

fundamentalist someone who believes in strict obedience to religious laws or texts

also blamed him for not gaining the release of the American hostages. These issues seriously damaged the public's view of the president. His popularity among voters fell sharply.

President Carter was able to win the Democratic nomination in spite of opposition from Senator Edward Kennedy. The battle left the party deeply divided, however. The Republicans nominated Ronald Reagan as their candidate. Reagan—a former actor and governor of California—spoke of lower taxes, less government spending, strong defense, and national pride. His message had wide appeal to the voters.

Reagan easily won the election. He received 489 electoral votes while Carter received only 49. Republicans also gained control of the Senate for the first time since 1954.

The election and its aftermath were bitter for Carter. During the last weeks of his presidency, Carter worked to free the hostages taken by Iran, but he did not succeed. The Iranians finally did release the hostages—but only after Ronald Reagan took the oath of office. The hostages had been in captivity for 444 days.

☑ **PROGRESS CHECK**

Summarizing Why did the United States boycott the 1980 Olympics?

Ronald Reagan takes the oath of office to become the 40th president of the United States. His wife, Nancy Reagan, stands beside him while the Chief Justice of the United States administers the oath of office.

Bettmann/CORBIS

LESSON 3 REVIEW (CCSS)

Review Vocabulary

1. Use the following terms in a paragraph:

    a. human rights   **b.** apartheid

2. Use each of these terms in a sentence that explains the term's meaning.

    a. trade deficit   **b.** fundamentalist

Answer the Guiding Questions

3. ***Explaining*** How did President Carter try to revive the economy?

4. ***Evaluating*** Why did nuclear power become a major issue in the late 1970s?

5. ***Identifying*** List the key foreign policy achievements of Carter's presidency.

6. ***Drawing Conclusions*** Why did Ronald Reagan win the 1980 election?

7. **ARGUMENT** Write a letter to the editor of your local newspaper, expressing your opinion about the U.S. decision not to take part in the 1980 Olympic Games in Moscow.

Write your answers on a separate piece of paper.

1 **Exploring the Essential Question**

INFORMATIVE/EXPLANATORY How did the Watergate scandal affect Americans' view of the presidency? Write a summary essay that explores how the scandal affected American politics in the 1970s. Be sure to discuss how the scandal affected all the presidents of the decade.

2 **21st Century Skills**

INFORMATION LITERACY Using what you have read and Internet sources, create a two-tiered time line. On one side of the time line, record the key events in the Watergate scandal. On the other, place other events from the Nixon presidency, including foreign policy accomplishments and domestic achievements.

3 **Thinking Like a Historian**

COMPARING AND CONTRASTING Use a diagram such as the one at the right to compare and contrast the foreign policies of Nixon and Carter. Be sure to include examples of their successes and their failures.

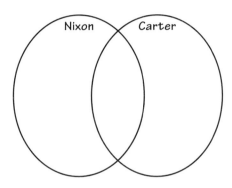

4 **Visual Literacy**

ANALYZING POLITICAL CARTOONS This cartoon shows President Nixon playing ping-pong with a Chinese official—while Chiang Kai-shek stands on the table between them. What do you think Chiang is trying to do? What is the meaning of the cartoon's caption?

High Lob

CHIANG

CHOU

HOW GRACEFUL

Pat Oliphant. *The Denver Post*, 1971.

REVIEW THE GUIDING QUESTIONS

Choose the best answer for each of the following questions.

1 Nixon improved U.S. relations with China by

   A. promising aid.

   B. resuming trade.

   C. signing SALT I.

   D. sharing technology.

2 What was an outcome of the 1967 Six-Day War?

   F. more Palestinians living under Israel's control

   G. shorter lines at U.S. gas pumps

   H. improved U.S. relations with Egypt

   I. Egyptian control of the Sinai Peninsula

3 Nixon reduced the involvement of the federal government in people's lives by

   A. introducing revenue sharing.

   B. promoting affirmative action.

   C. creating the Office of Economic Opportunity.

   D. enforcing orders to integrate schools.

4 What three things led to Nixon's landslide victory in the 1972 presidential election?

   F. the end of the Vietnam War, low unemployment, and poor Democratic candidates

   G. the end of the Iran hostage crisis, the end of the recession, and peace with China

   H. the Democrats' lack of unity, an upsurge in the economy, and the prospect of peace in Vietnam

   I. the improved relationship with Egypt, rising wages, and the Watergate scandal

5 Why were Ayatollah Khomeini and his supporters hostile to the United States?

   A. Carter ordered sanctions against Iran.

   B. U.S. policies were based on human rights.

   C. American leaders had supported the shah.

   D. Carter condemned the practice of apartheid.

6 Why were the Camp David Accords an important part of President Carter's administration?

   F. They limited the number of nuclear weapons the Soviet Union and the United States could have.

   G. They returned the Panama Canal to Panama.

   H. They led to the release of American hostages in Iran.

   I. They were the first peace agreement between Israel and an Arab nation.

DBQ ANALYZING DOCUMENTS

Henry Kissinger made this comment about the U.S. role in the overthrow of Chile's elected leader, Salvador Allende.

"I don't see why we need to stand by and watch a country go communist due to the irresponsibility of its own people."

Source: Tarak Barkawi, *War Inside the Free World*

7 **Making Inferences** What can you infer about Kissinger's attitude toward communism?

A. Kissinger believes that communism is an excellent system.

B. Kissinger supports the voters' right to choose communism.

C. Kissinger does not believe that responsible voters would ever choose communism.

D. Kissinger believes that Communists should not be allowed to vote.

8 **Drawing Conclusions** What led Kissinger to believe that Chileans were irresponsible?

F. Allende was elected president.

G. Allende was supported by all Chileans.

H. Pinochet had been allowed by the public to overthrow the government.

I. Pinochet ruined Chile's economy with the support of the people.

SHORT RESPONSE

This graph shows President Nixon's approval rating during parts of 1973 and 1974. Use this graph to answer questions 9 and 10.

9 Describe the general trend in Nixon's popularity.

10 Describe the events that would explain the extremes shown in this graph.

EXTENDED RESPONSE

11 **Narrative** Imagine you are a citizen living in the United States in the late 1970s. Write a letter to a friend in another country describing the mood of the nation and the reasons for that mood. Be sure to refer to specific events to explain the way you think people are feeling.

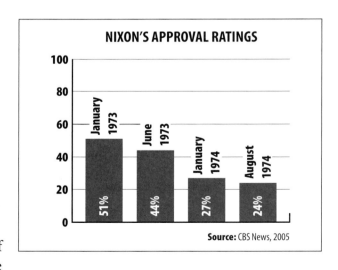

NIXON'S APPROVAL RATINGS

January 1973: 51%
June 1973: 44%
January 1974: 27%
August 1974: 24%

Source: CBS News, 2005

Need Extra Help?

If You've Missed Question	❶	❷	❸	❹	❺	❻	❼	❽	❾	❿	⓫
Review Lesson	1	1	2	2	3	3	1	1	2	2	2–3

New Challenges

1981 to Present

ESSENTIAL QUESTIONS • *What are the consequences when cultures interact?*
• *How do governments change?* • *Why does conflict develop?*
• *How do new ideas change the way people live?*

The Story Matters . . .

In his campaign for the presidency in 2008, Barack Obama promises "change." He is referring to the way he wants his administration to operate. Yet just by being on the ballot, Obama has already brought change to the nation. He is living proof that the United States is a different place than it was just a few decades ago.

As it always has, the United States is moving forward. With advancement come challenges. With the challenges come opportunity and the promise of a better future.

◀ *In 2008 Barack Obama became the first African American elected president of the United States. He was reelected to this office in 2012.*

U.S. Air Force

Place and Time: The World 1981 to Present

This map shows the share of total U.S. immigration by country. The years since 1981 have brought great change to the nation and the world, but one thing is still the same: The United States remains a land of hope and opportunity for people everywhere.

Step Into the Place

MAP FOCUS This map shows the parts of the world from which recent immigrants to the United States have come.

1 PLACE Based on the map, from which nation have the largest share of immigrants come?

2 MOVEMENT About what percentage of immigrants to the United States arrive from Canada?

3 CRITICAL THINKING
Analyzing Visuals A century ago, most immigrants to the United States were from Europe. How important is Europe as a source of immigration today?

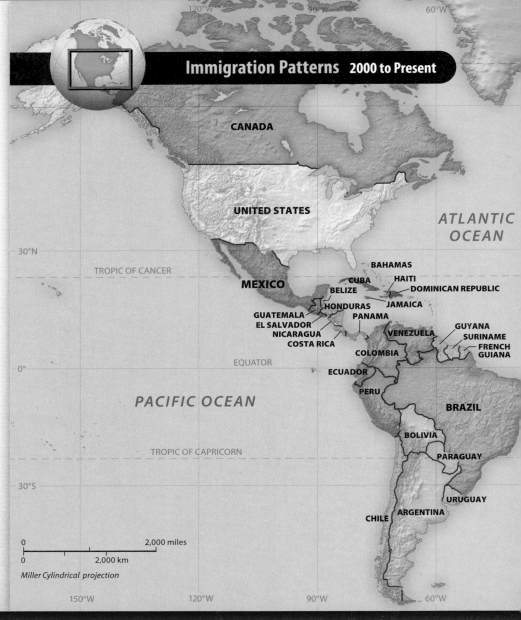

Immigration Patterns 2000 to Present

CANADA

UNITED STATES

ATLANTIC OCEAN

30°N

TROPIC OF CANCER

MEXICO

BAHAMAS
CUBA
BELIZE
HAITI
DOMINICAN REPUBLIC
HONDURAS
JAMAICA
GUATEMALA
PANAMA
EL SALVADOR
NICARAGUA
COSTA RICA
VENEZUELA
GUYANA
SURINAME
FRENCH GUIANA
COLOMBIA

EQUATOR
ECUADOR
PERU

PACIFIC OCEAN

BRAZIL

BOLIVIA

TROPIC OF CAPRICORN

PARAGUAY

30°S

URUGUAY
CHILE
ARGENTINA

0   2,000 miles
0   2,000 km
Miller Cylindrical projection

150°W   120°W   90°W   60°W

Step Into the Time

TIME LINE Look at the time line. Students in Beijing protested the Chinese communist government in 1989. What other events might indicate that communism was nearing its end?

Ronald Reagan
1981–1989

1983 U.S. troops invade Grenada

1987 President Reagan signs missile defense treaty with Soviet Union

1990 Americans with Disabilities Act passes

U.S. PRESIDENTS
U.S. EVENTS
WORLD EVENTS

1980   1986

1981 Egypt's president Anwar el-Sadat assassinated

1985 Mikhail Gorbachev becomes leader of Soviet Union

1989 Students protest at Tiananmen Square in China

1990 Nelson Mandela released from South African prison

White House Historical Association

networks

There's More Online!

☑ **MAP** Explore the interactive version of this map on NETWORKS.

☑ **TIME LINE** Explore the interactive version of this time line on NETWORKS.

Percentage of U.S. Immigrants by Country, 2000–2009

- < 1%
- 1–2.9%
- 3–4.9%
- 5–14%
- > 14%

George H. W. Bush 1989–1993

1995 Bomb kills 168 at Oklahoma City Federal Building

Bill Clinton 1993–2001

1998 President Clinton impeached

2001 War on terror begins

George W. Bush 2001–2009

2005 Hurricane Katrina strikes Louisiana and Mississippi

Barack Obama 2009–

2010 Healthcare Reform Act becomes law

1992

1998

2004

2010

1991 • Operation Desert Storm • Breakup of Soviet Union

1994 U.S., Mexico, and Canada agree to NAFTA

2004 Tsunami devastates Indonesia and surrounding region

2005 Terrorists bomb London subway system

2010 Haiti devastated by an earthquake

2011 Earthquake and tsunami strike Japan

(l, cl &cr)White House Historical Association, (r) U.S. Air Force

449

Total: $1.5 trillion

Lesson 1
The Reagan Revolution

ESSENTIAL QUESTION *What are the consequences when cultures interact?*

IT MATTERS BECAUSE
President Reagan helped bring about a conservative shift in the United States.

The Nation Changes Course

GUIDING QUESTION *How did President Reagan bring a new conservative approach to government?*

In the 1970s, a conservative movement gained strength in the United States. The movement was especially strong in the South and Southwest. In politics, conservatives favor tradition and moderation. They prefer a small government that has a limited reach into business and people's lives. Ronald Reagan's election to the presidency in 1980 was a key conservative victory. Reagan appealed to voters who were frustrated with the economy and worried that the United States had become weak internationally.

Ronald Reagan was a former actor with Illinois small-town roots. He had been a Democrat, but later switched to the Republican Party. Reagan served as governor of California from 1967 to 1975. During this time, state policies reflected his conservative views.

Reagan called for a return to what he called "traditional American values." These included ideas such as family life, hard work, respect for law, and patriotism. Reagan supporters shared the belief that the federal government made too many rules. They also thought that government collected too much in taxes and spent too much on social programs.

(l) CORBIS, (cl) Wally McNamee/CORBIS, (cr) The Herb Block Foundation, (r) Shepard Sherbell/CORBIS SABA

Reading **HELP**DESK **CCSS**

Taking Notes: *Defining*

Use a graphic organizer like this one to explain and define the basic principles of conservatism.

Conservatism

Content Vocabulary
• **deregulation**
• **federal debt**

Reagan also believed that the key to restoring America's strength was to get Americans to believe in themselves again:

66 I believe we, the Americans of today, are ready to act worthy of ourselves, ready to do what must be done to ensure happiness and liberty for ourselves, our children and our children's children. 99

—Ronald Reagan's First Inaugural Address, January 1981

Air Traffic Controllers' Strike

A few months after President Reagan took office, the nation's air traffic controllers went on strike. The strike was against the law, and the president ordered the controllers to go back to work. They refused. President Reagan acted quickly. He fired the controllers. Then, he ordered the military to oversee air traffic while new controllers were trained to do the work. Reagan's firm, swift action sent a message that he would use his power to carry out the policies in which he believed.

Less Government

President Reagan promised to "get the government off the backs of the American people." He believed a smaller, less involved government would be better. He worked toward a policy of **deregulation** (dee•reh•gyuh•LAY•shuhn)—removing rules and regulations that government places on businesses. For example, Reagan's Department of Transportation wrote new rules for automobile exhaust systems. The new rules were easier for carmakers to meet. However, they also weakened efforts to reduce pollution.

Reagan's Economic Policies

At the core of the "Reagan Revolution" was economic policy. Reagan called for less government spending. He also wanted to lower taxes. High taxes, Reagan argued, took too much money away from people and businesses. The president believed that if people and businesses paid less to the government, they would have more money to spend. Businesses would invest that money, helping the economy grow. A growing economy would create more jobs, helping everyone.

CORBIS

President Reagan leaves a building moments before he was seriously wounded in an assassination attempt. The shooting took place just weeks after Reagan took office as president in 1981.

deregulation the removal of rules and regulations

Reading Strategies: *Distinguishing Fact from Opinion*

Often, readers can tell an opinion from a fact by carefully reading for key words. For example, under Reagan's Economic Policies, the phrases *they believed* and *they felt* indicate that what follows is an opinion rather than a fact.

President Reagan and his supporters called this policy "supply-side economics." Reagan's critics labeled it "Reaganomics." They felt that it would help corporations and wealthy Americans, while only a little prosperity would "trickle down" to average Americans.

In President Reagan's first year in office, Congress cut taxes. It also cut federal programs such as student aid, welfare, and low-income housing. Supporters argued that these cuts would help everyone in the long run by boosting the whole economy.

While President Reagan wanted to cut many programs, he favored sharp increases in military spending. He believed that the Soviet threat made a military buildup necessary. With higher defense spending and lower taxes, the government spent more money than it collected. To make up the difference, the government borrowed money. This borrowing increased the **federal debt**—the amount of money owed by the government. Between 1970 and 1980, the federal debt grew from $381 billion to $909 billion. By 1990, the debt had jumped to $3.2 trillion.

Reagan's economic policy came into question when unemployment rose early in his presidency. However, the economy recovered a year later and began to grow. Businesses expanded and the high jobless rate went down. Investors showed confidence in the economy with a boom in stock trading.

A New Supreme Court

President Reagan favored judges who would **interpret** the Constitution strictly. He hoped to name justices to the bench who would put a conservative stamp on the Supreme Court. Reagan got several chances to achieve this goal. In 1981 he appointed Sandra Day O'Connor to the bench. She became the first woman ever to serve on the Supreme Court. In 1986 Chief Justice Warren Burger retired. Reagan promoted Justice William Rehnquist to take his place and lead the Court. Rehnquist was one of the Court's most conservative justices. To fill Rehnquist's old spot, Reagan selected the conservative Antonin Scalia. A year later, Justice Lewis Powell retired. The president chose another conservative judge, Anthony Kennedy.

☑ PROGRESS CHECK

Explaining What caused the federal debt to grow significantly in the 1980s?

Reading **HELP**DESK (CCSS)

federal debt the amount of money owed by the federal government

Academic Vocabulary

interpret to find the meaning of something based on individual judgment and knowledge

Foreign Policy Under Reagan

GUIDING QUESTION *Why did the Reagan administration take strong action to resist Communist influence overseas?*

Reagan had promised a tough stand against communism. He adopted a new foreign policy for the Cold War that replaced earlier policies of containment and détente. Reagan called the Soviet Union an "evil empire" and "the focus of evil in the modern world." He vowed that the U.S. would defeat it.

Strengthening the Military

President Reagan launched a massive buildup of the military. He increased the number of American tanks, ships, aircraft, and nuclear missiles. The Reagan military buildup was the largest peacetime buildup in American history. It cost about $1.5 trillion over five years.

The president also called for a system for destroying missiles launched against the United States. He called this the Strategic Defense Initiative (SDI). Others gave it the nickname "Star Wars." However, scientists failed to develop the technology for the SDI.

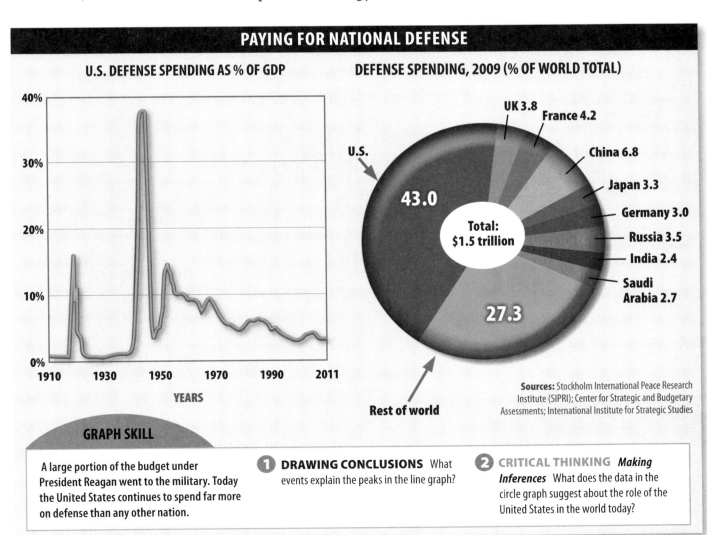

PAYING FOR NATIONAL DEFENSE

U.S. DEFENSE SPENDING AS % OF GDP

DEFENSE SPENDING, 2009 (% OF WORLD TOTAL)

UK 3.8
France 4.2
China 6.8
Japan 3.3
Germany 3.0
Russia 3.5
India 2.4
Saudi Arabia 2.7
U.S. 43.0
Total: $1.5 trillion
27.3
Rest of world

Sources: Stockholm International Peace Research Institute (SIPRI); Center for Strategic and Budgetary Assessments; International Institute for Strategic Studies

GRAPH SKILL

A large portion of the budget under President Reagan went to the military. Today the United States continues to spend far more on defense than any other nation.

1 **DRAWING CONCLUSIONS** What events explain the peaks in the line graph?

2 **CRITICAL THINKING** *Making Inferences* What does the data in the circle graph suggest about the role of the United States in the world today?

During his time in office, President Reagan held 42 news conferences, gave 47 major speeches, and made nearly 400 public appearances. His communication skills became the subject of political cartoons, like the one below. For more about analyzing political cartoons, review *Thinking Like a Historian.*

"CONSTANT DRUMBEAT"

▶ **CRITICAL THINKING**
Analyzing Political Cartoons Look at this cartoon and its title. What point is the cartoonist making about the president's communication with Americans?

Aid to Latin America

President Reagan also sent U.S. forces and aid to fight communism, especially in Latin America. In Nicaragua, rebels had overthrown the government. The rebels were called the Sandinistas. With aid from Cuba and the Soviet Union, they set up a Communist system in Nicaragua.

In the early 1980s, Reagan sent aid to the Contras, a group that was resisting the Sandinistas. The fighting in Nicaragua sparked disagreement between the president and Congress.

In 1983 President Reagan took military action against communism. Marxist rebels on the Caribbean island of Grenada staged an uprising. Reagan was concerned about the safety of American medical students on the island. He sent U.S. troops to rescue them and to set up an anti-Communist government.

The Middle East

Reagan's policies were less successful in the Middle East. In 1982 he sent marines to oversee removal of PLO guerillas from Lebanon. A car bomb killed more than 60 people at the U.S. embassy in April 1983. In October, terrorist attacks on U.S. and French military centers killed 299 people. Rather than deepen U.S. involvement, Reagan withdrew all U.S. forces.

✔ PROGRESS CHECK

Summarizing Why did Reagan take action in Grenada?

A Second Term

GUIDING QUESTION *What events occurred during Reagan's second term?*

By 1984 the American economy was strong again. President Reagan declared: "America is back—standing tall, looking [toward the future] with courage, confidence, and hope."

President Reagan and Vice President George H.W. Bush built their reelection campaign on this patriotic **theme.** The Democrats picked Walter Mondale, vice president under Jimmy Carter. For vice president, they chose Geraldine Ferraro, a member of Congress from New York. Ferraro became the first woman to win nomination for vice president from a major political party.

The 1984 election was one of the most uneven presidential elections in American history. Reagan won the electoral vote in a landslide, with 49 out of the 50 states.

The Herb Block Foundation

Reading **HELP**DESK (CCSS)

Academic Vocabulary
theme a subject or topic

The Iran-Contra Arms Deal

Despite Reagan's popularity, a scandal cast a shadow over his second term. Terrorists with ties to the government of Iran held Americans hostage in Lebanon. Hoping to gain the hostages' release, Reagan officials made a deal with Iran's leaders.

Members of Reagan's administration arranged a secret sale of weapons to Iran in return for help in freeing American hostages. Some of the officials decided to give money from this arms sale to the Contras, the group fighting the Sandinistas in Nicaragua.

News of these deals—which became known as the Iran-Contra scandal—created an uproar. Critics charged that these deals violated federal laws banning aid to the Contras. Congress held hearings to learn whether the president took part in breaking the law. However, Congress found no proof of Reagan's direct involvement.

Better Relations with the Soviets

Reagan's second term saw a major shift in Soviet-American relations. When Mikhail Gorbachev became the Soviet leader in 1985, he began a policy he called *glasnost*—allowing new ideas into Soviet society. He also introduced *perestroika* (pehr•uh•STROY•kuh), a policy reducing government control of the economy.

In 1987 Reagan and Gorbachev agreed to sign the Intermediate-Range Nuclear Forces (INF) Treaty. This treaty reduced the number of nuclear missiles in each country. The INF treaty was a big step toward reducing the threat of nuclear war.

President Reagan (right) and Soviet leader Gorbachev (left) made great progress in U.S.-Soviet relations in the late 1980s.

 **PROGRESS CHECK**

Summarizing What change in Soviet domestic policy took place in the 1980s?

Shepard Sherbell/CORBIS SABA

 **LESSON 1** REVIEW **CCSS**

Review Vocabulary

1. Use the following terms in a sentence about the Reagan presidency.

   a. deregulation **b.** federal debt

Answer the Guiding Questions

2. *Synthesizing* How might Reagan's background as an actor have helped him win support for his political career?

3. *Summarizing* Describe the basic features of President Reagan's economic policy.

4. *Evaluating* How did Reagan's view of communism affect his foreign policy?

5. *Making Inferences* What was the significance of the INF treaty?

6. NARRATIVE The year is 1984. Write a letter to the editor of a newspaper, explaining why you think people should vote for or against President Reagan for a second term.

netw⊙rks
There's More Online!

☑ **CHART/GRAPH**
- NATO Members
- Major Legislation of George H. W. Bush's Presidency

☑ **GRAPHIC ORGANIZER**
End of Cold War

☑ **MAP** Russia and Independent Republics

☑ **PRIMARY SOURCE**
Reagan at the Berlin Wall

Lesson 2
The First President Bush

ESSENTIAL QUESTION *What are the consequences when cultures interact?*

IT MATTERS BECAUSE
The end of the Cold War reshaped the world in new ways and left the United States as the only superpower.

The Cold War Ends

GUIDING QUESTION *What global events led to the end of the Cold War in the Bush presidency?*

George H. W. Bush, Reagan's vice president, won the 1988 presidential election. Bush gained 426 electoral votes compared to 112 for the Democratic Party candidate, Michael Dukakis. Bush's victory did not change the makeup of Congress. The Democrats **retained** control of the House and the Senate.

Changes in the Soviet Union

President Bush took office at a time of great change in the world. Soviet leader Gorbachev wanted to end the arms race so he could focus on reforming his country. In 1990 he and President Bush agreed on the Strategic Arms Reduction Treaty (START). For the first time, two nuclear powers agreed to destroy existing nuclear weapons.

Gorbachev's success in foreign affairs did not lead to support at home. Most Soviet citizens were more concerned about their own problems. They were less concerned with arms control. For years they had suffered shortages of food and basic items such as shoes and soap. These shortages were the result of the government's poor management and heavy defense spending. Gorbachev's plans aimed to solve the

(l)Tom Stoddart/Edit/Getty Images,
(cr)Sergei Guneyev/Time Life Pictures/Getty Images,
(r)Wally McNamee/CORBIS from Corbis

Reading **HELP**DESK ⓒⒸⓈⓈ

Taking Notes: *Determining Cause and Effect*

Create a graphic organizer like this one to list results of the end of the Cold War between the United States and the Soviet Union.

End of Cold War

Content Vocabulary
- **coalition**
- **downsize**
- **bankrupt**

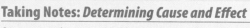

456 *New Challenges*

economic problems. However, change came slowly. Meanwhile, encouraged by Gorbachev's policy of glasnost, Soviet citizens began to openly express their unhappiness.

A Wave of Freedom

The changes in the Soviet Union were dramatic. As a result, the people of Eastern Europe felt free to demand change in their countries. In Poland in August 1980, shipyard workers won the right to form an independent labor union. This union was called Solidarity. Lech Walesa, the leader of Solidarity, became a symbol of resistance to Communist rule. Solidarity forced the government to hold open elections in June 1989.

In other Eastern European countries, demonstrators filled the streets of major cities. Public pressure combined with less Soviet control had a powerful effect. Long-closed national borders opened up. Across Eastern Europe, Communist governments began to collapse. By late 1989, the Iron Curtain that had divided Eastern and Western Europe since World War II was crumbling.

Freedom also came to East Germany. Protests raged, and thousands of East German citizens crossed the border into West Germany. On November 9, 1989, the Communist government opened the Berlin Wall. Germans brought hammers and chisels to chip away at the concrete barrier that had divided Communist East Berlin from the rest of the city. In 1990 East Germany and West Germany were finally reunited.

A group watches as a man helps knock down the Berlin Wall. The wall had for years divided the city of Berlin—and stood as a symbol of Europe's split into Communist and non-Communist areas.

The Soviet Union Collapses

As Eastern Europe was changing, Gorbachev faced rising opposition at home. Some reformers wanted him to move more quickly to change the country. At the same time, hard-line Communists resisted the changes he had already made. They feared the collapse of the Soviet empire.

In August 1991, a group of hard-line Communist officials and army generals tried to overthrow the government. They arrested Gorbachev and ordered soldiers to seize the Russian parliament building.

Tom Stoddart/Edit/Getty Images

Academic Vocabulary

retain to hold on to; to keep from changing

EUROPE

ESTONIA

Baltic Sea

LITHUANIA   LATVIA

BELARUS

UKRAINE

MOLDOVA

Black Sea

GEORGIA

ARMENIA

AZERBAIJAN

TURKMENISTAN

UZBEKISTAN

KYRGYZSTAN

TAJIKISTAN

ARCTIC OCEAN

Barents Sea

Kara Sea

Laptev Sea

ARCTIC CIRCLE

Sea of Okhotsk

RUSSIA

Lake Baikal

KAZAKHSTAN

Lake Balkhash

ASIA

Aral Sea

Caspian Sea

Volga R.

Kama R.

Ural R.

Ob R.

Yenisey R.

Irtysh R.

Lena R.

Amur R.

Border of Soviet Union (1990)
Russia after 1991
Independent Republics after 1991

0   800 miles
0   800 km
Lambert Conic projection

GEOGRAPHY CONNECTION

1 **PLACE** Based on the map, which of the former Soviet republics has the largest area after Russia?

2 **CRITICAL THINKING**
Speculating How might the collapse of the Soviet Union have affected peace and stability in Central Asia and Eastern Europe?

As the world watched, some 50,000 Russian citizens surrounded the building to protect it from the soldiers. People were used to harsh Soviet crackdowns of any uprising. The crackdown never came. Boris Yeltsin, president of the Russian republic, was an outspoken reformer. Standing on top of an army tank, he declared, "Democracy will win!" President Bush telephoned Yeltsin to express American support. On August 22, the coup fell apart. Gorbachev was freed.

The coup's failure triggered a tidal wave of democracy. In quick order, each of the 15 republics that made up the Soviet Union declared independence. Yeltsin banned the Communist Party in Russia. On December 25, 1991, Gorbachev made the stunning announcement that the Soviet Union no longer existed.

✔ **PROGRESS CHECK**

Determining Cause and Effect What did Solidarity accomplish in Poland?

Reading HELPDESK CCSS

Build Vocabulary: *Compound Words*

A compound word is a word made up of two words. *Classroom* and *sidewalk* are compound words. If you know the meaning of the shorter words that make up the compound word, you can figure out the meaning of the longer word.

Outspoken is a compound word made up of the two smaller words *out* and *spoken*. To be *outspoken* is to freely tell others your thoughts on a topic.

New Directions in Foreign Policy

GUIDING QUESTION *How did the Bush administration set out to develop a new foreign policy after the end of the Cold War?*

The Cold War was over, and a new era of hope—and challenge—began. The United States had to rethink its foreign policy goals. At the same time, President Bush faced crises in various parts of the world.

For example, in Panama, dictator Manuel Noriega led a corrupt government. In 1989 President Bush sent U.S. troops to overthrow Noriega. The troops seized the dictator and sent him to the United States to stand trial for drug trafficking. Panama then held elections and organized a new government.

China was another country of concern. In 1974 President Bush had served as the chief U.S. diplomat to the Asian nation. At that time, China's Communist government controlled the Chinese economy. In the coming years, however, China began making changes. Slowly, it gave Chinese citizens and businesses some freedom to make, sell, and buy goods and services.

China did not, however, make changes to its Communist political system. In May 1989, Chinese students and workers held protests calling for democracy. The protests took place in Tiananmen (tee·AHN·ahn·men) Square, in the center of the capital, Beijing (BAY·ZHING). On June 4, 1989, troops crushed the protest, killing several hundred protesters. Bush and other world leaders condemned the killings.

Chinese students gather in Tiananmen Square in Beijing, calling for democratic government. The Chinese government brutally crushed this demonstration to the horror of the democratic world.

Operation Desert Storm

Perhaps the most serious crisis facing President Bush came from the Middle East. In August 1990, Iraq's dictator, Saddam Hussein (hoo·SAYN), sent his army into Kuwait. This small country that borders southeastern Iraq is rich in oil.

President Bush vowed to stand up to Hussein. He persuaded other nations to join the U.S. in a **coalition** (koh·uh·LIH·shuhn), or a group united for action. President Bush demanded that Hussein withdraw his troops from Kuwait. Hussein refused.

American generals Colin Powell and Norman Schwarzkopf led the coalition forces. In January 1991, Operation Desert Storm began with missile attacks and bombing raids on Iraq. These destroyed military and civilian **sites.** Six weeks later, the coalition began a ground war. Within days, Kuwait was free and Iraq had accepted a cease-fire. American troops returned home to cheering crowds.

coalition a group formed for a common purpose

Academic Vocabulary

site a location or place

President George H. W. Bush's term in office was marked by great change around the world—and great challenges at home.

Conflict in the Balkans

Yugoslavia was another scene of post-Cold War conflict. This Communist country was made up of several republics. In the early 1990s, the republics of Slovenia (sloh•VEE•nee•uh), Croatia (kroh•AY•shee•uh), and Bosnia-Herzegovina (BAHZ•nee•uh hert•suh•goh•VEE•nuh) declared independence.

Within Croatia and Bosnia were many Serbs—people with cultural ties to the Yugoslav republic of Serbia. The Serbian government helped these Serbs fight for control of parts of Croatia and Bosnia. A terrible civil war followed, and thousands died. Reports of killings by the Serbs angered world leaders. NATO took military action to stop the bloodshed. Warring parties finally signed a peace plan in 1995 known as the Dayton Accords.

✓ **PROGRESS CHECK**

Explaining Why did President Bush send U.S. troops to the Middle East?

Bush and Domestic Policy

GUIDING QUESTION *What were the domestic challenges faced by the Bush administration?*

President Bush also faced major challenges at home. From the Reagan years, Bush inherited a growing federal debt and a slowing economy.

The Economy Stumbles

In 1990 the economy stopped growing—that is, it entered a recession. One cause was the end of the Cold War and the cuts in military spending that led to job losses in the defense industry. Companies also began to **downsize**—lay off workers—to become more efficient.

The government borrowing of the 1980s added to the economic trouble. The federal debt reached new highs, and business and personal debt also grew. The nation's debts made the recession worse. Individuals and businesses had borrowed heavily and now could not meet loan payments. They had to sell what they owned to pay their debts. Some were unable to pay off their debts and went **bankrupt.**

Wally McNamee/CORBIS

Many people urged the government to spend money. This spending, they hoped, would boost the economy. President Bush refused to increase federal spending. He did agree to extend benefits to the jobless. However, he opposed further government involvement.

A Banking Crisis

President Bush also faced a related financial crisis. President Reagan and Congress had cut regulations on savings and loan associations (S&Ls). These are financial institutions similar to banks. Many people banked and obtained home loans at S&Ls.

Under the new policies many S&Ls made risky loans. Then, borrowers could not repay their loans. Many S&Ls lost money and went out of business.

The government insured savings accounts in S&Ls. This means it had to pay out billions to customers of failed S&Ls. The government also bailed out struggling S&Ls. The total cost of the crisis was about $160 billion.

Bush's Achievements

While President Bush often disagreed with the Democrat-controlled Congress, the two sides worked together on some issues. The president and Congress improved the Clean Air Act and advanced civil rights. The Americans with Disabilities Act of 1990 banned job discrimination against people with disabilities. It created easier access to workplaces, transportation, and housing. The president also called for a war on illegal drugs. In 1989 he created the Office of National Drug Control Policy. This department oversees more than 50 federal agencies involved in the war on drugs.

✓ PROGRESS CHECK

Analyzing Why did many S&Ls fail in the 1980s?

LESSON 2 REVIEW

Review Vocabulary

1. Write a sentence to explain how *downsizing* could be related to *bankruptcy*.

Answer the Guiding Questions

2. *Describing* How did tearing down the Berlin Wall signal the end of the Cold War?

3. *Analyzing* What events suggest that the Soviet Union's weakness and collapse made Eastern Europe less stable?

4. *Making Connections* How did the policies of the Reagan administration affect the problems faced by President Bush?

5. **INFORMATIVE/EXPLANATORY** Write a short essay that explains how events in the Soviet Union led the peoples of Eastern Europe to challenge their Communist governments.

networks

There's More Online!

☑ **BIOGRAPHY**
Colin Powell

☑ **CHART**
Impeachment Process

☑ **GAME**

☑ **GRAPHIC ORGANIZER**
Clinton Legislation

☑ **MAP** Election of 2000

☑ **PRIMARY SOURCE**
Clinton Acceptance Speech

☑ **SLIDE SHOW**
2000 Presidential Campaign

Lesson 3
Toward a New Century

ESSENTIAL QUESTION *How do governments change?*

IT MATTERS BECAUSE
The presidencies of Bill Clinton and George W. Bush marked the shift from the twentieth century to the twenty-first century.

The Clinton Presidency

GUIDING QUESTION *What positive and negative events occurred in the Clinton administration?*

After the Persian Gulf War, the popularity of President George H. W. Bush soared. The troubled economy, however, hurt his reelection chances. Encouraged, a number of challengers entered the presidential race in 1992. The Democrats chose Arkansas governor Bill Clinton. Clinton picked Tennessee Senator Al Gore to run as his vice president. The Democratic campaign focused on the economy and the high unemployment rate.

Americans, meanwhile, were unhappy with "politics as usual." Many did not want to vote for either Bush or Clinton. Instead, they supported a **grassroots movement**—a popular movement organized at a local level—that put Texas business leader H. Ross Perot on the ballot as a third-party candidate. Perot called for an end to the government's **deficit spending,** or spending more money than it takes in.

The voters chose Clinton. He became the first candidate born after World War II to win the presidency. Clinton received 43 percent of the popular vote. Bush received 38 percent, and Perot got 19 percent. Perot's total was the highest percentage of popular votes for any third-party candidate since Theodore Roosevelt in 1912.

Reading HELPDESK (CCSS)

Taking Notes: *Identifying*
Use a diagram like this one to identify Clinton-sponsored legislation that passed into law.

Clinton Legislation

Content Vocabulary
- **grassroots movement**
- **perjury**
- **deficit spending**
- **gross domestic product**

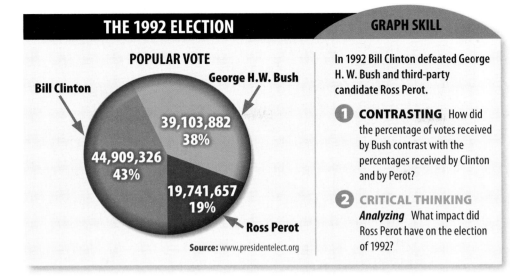

Clinton's Domestic Program

A key goal for the new president was to reduce the budget deficit—the gap between income and spending. To reach this goal, Clinton proposed cutting government spending and raising taxes for middle- and upper-income Americans. He also proposed tax credits to help the poorest Americans. President Clinton's plan narrowly passed in spite of Republican opposition.

Clinton had a bigger battle over his plan for health care reform. His goal was to control rising health care costs and provide **adequate** health insurance for every American. The president named First Lady Hillary Rodham Clinton to lead this effort to develop a health care plan.

Congress rejected Clinton's plan. Members believed it was too expensive and too reliant on government control. Later, Congress did pass measures that increased health care protection for the elderly, children, and other groups. An example was the 1997 Children's Health Insurance Program.

President Clinton won additional battles during his first term, including passage of the 1993 Brady Law. This law was named for press secretary James Brady, who was shot when a gunman attempted to assassinate President Reagan. The law required a waiting period and background check for people wishing to purchase a handgun. The 1994 crime bill banned 19 kinds of assault weapons and provided for 100,000 new police officers. Another successful Clinton proposal was the Family and Medical Leave Act of 1993. It allowed workers to take time off from their jobs for special family situations.

grassroots movement a movement made up of individuals and small groups in multiple locations around the nation who join together for a shared goal

deficit spending spending more money than is received and creating debt as a result

Academic Vocabulary

adequate enough for a specific purpose

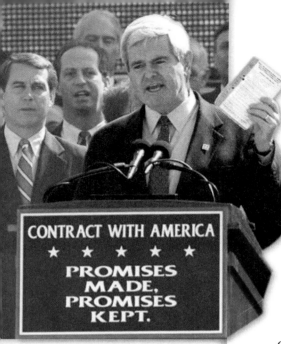

The Republican Plan

As the 1994 elections for Congress approached, House Republicans led by Newt Gingrich of Georgia created a plan. They called it the Contract with America.

In the contract, Republicans promised to reduce the size of federal government, balance the budget, lower taxes, and reform how Congress operates. They also pledged to reduce crime, reform welfare, and strengthen the family. The contract helped Republicans sweep to victory in the 1994 elections. For the first time in 40 years, they controlled both houses of Congress.

In 1995 the Republicans clashed with President Clinton over the new federal budget. As a result of the dispute, the federal government ran out of money. The government stopped providing many services for a total of 27 days. Congress and the president could see that compromise was needed.

The Republicans and President Clinton soon reached an agreement to balance the budget. The president pushed for an increase in the minimum wage and supported a welfare reform act. This measure set a work requirement for people receiving welfare. It also put a five-year time limit on how long a person could collect benefits.

Newt Gingrich helped lead a group of young Republican representatives in passing the Contract with America through the House.

A Second Term for Clinton

The year 1996 was a presidential election year, and the Republicans had high hopes. They chose Bob Dole to be their candidate. Dole had been the majority leader of the Senate. However, the economy was healthy and unemployment was at a 30-year low. President Clinton easily won reelection.

The economy continued to grow during President Clinton's second term. One measure of economic growth is the **gross domestic product** (GDP), the value of all the goods and services produced in a nation in a year. The GDP grew by about 4 percent per year in 1996 and 1997. These were among the highest growth rates since the boom that followed World War II.

As the economy grew, the government collected more taxes. At the same time, the president and Congress cut back the size of the federal budget. The 1998 budget year ended with a surplus of about $80 billion. This means the government took in $80 billion more than it spent. It was the first surplus in three decades.

AFP/Getty Images

Reading **HELP**DESK

gross domestic product the value of all goods and services produced in a nation in one year

Clinton's Impeachment

Thanks to the economy, President Clinton's popularity stayed high. However, scandals threatened his presidency. Clinton was accused of arranging illegal loans for a real estate company while he was governor of Arkansas. Former judge Kenneth Starr led the investigation.

Starr was unable to prove these charges. However, new charges arose of an improper relationship between the president and a White House worker. There was evidence that the president might have committed **perjury** (PUHR·juh·ree), or lied under oath, about the relationship. Starr widened the **scope** of the investigation. In September 1998, he sent a report to Congress. The report claimed that President Clinton had committed perjury and obstructed justice.

The House of Representatives began hearings on the scandal. In 1998 it voted, along party lines, to impeach the president. To impeach is to make a formal accusation of wrongdoing against a public official.

The case moved to the Senate. Under the Constitution, the Senate holds the trial in the case of impeachment. If the Senate finds the accused guilty of the charges, the individual is removed from office. It takes a two-thirds vote to convict and remove a president.

In February 1999, the Senate voted. President Clinton was found not guilty. He had survived the scandal, and he remained in office.

As details of his behavior became public, President Clinton faced increasingly difficult questions—and possible removal from office.

Foreign Policy Challenges

During Clinton's term, foreign affairs also presented challenges. The Cold War was over. Important decisions faced American leaders in defining the nation's new role in world affairs.

In 1993 Clinton persuaded Congress to ratify the North American Free Trade Agreement, or NAFTA. Under NAFTA, the United States, Canada, and Mexico agreed to drop trade barriers among the three nations. You may recall that countries sometimes use trade barriers to protect their businesses from foreign competition. NAFTA opponents feared a loss of U.S. jobs. Farmers also feared NAFTA. They worried that low-priced Mexican crops would hurt sales of U.S. crops. NAFTA supporters took a different view. They said that the treaty would lower prices for American consumers. It would also provide larger markets for American products.

perjury the act of lying after swearing to tell the truth

Academic Vocabulary

scope range or extent

Madeleine Albright became secretary of state in 1996—the first woman ever to hold that post and the highest-ranking woman in the history of American government to that point.

The Middle East continued to command attention. In September 1993, President Clinton invited Israeli Prime Minister Yitzhak Rabin and Yassir Arafat, head of the Palestine Liberation Organization (PLO), to the White House. There they signed a historic agreement. Israel recognized the PLO as the representative of the Palestinians, and the PLO recognized Israel's right to exist. The agreement created a plan for limited Palestinian self-government in certain areas.

The plan drew criticism from both sides, and violence in the area continued. In 1995 an Israeli extremist assassinated Prime Minister Rabin. Clinton continued peace efforts, but without success.

As you learned earlier, civil war had erupted in the former Yugoslavia. In Bosnia, Serbs engaged in ethnic cleansing—forcibly removing or killing members of the Muslim population. Clinton led the peace talks that produced the Dayton Accords, ending the crisis, in late 1995. Then, in 1998 Serbs tried to drive Muslims out of Serbia's Kosovo region. The United States and NATO launched air strikes against Serbia. This finally forced the Serbs to leave Kosovo and agree to negotiate.

✓ PROGRESS CHECK

Identifying What major trade agreement did Clinton make in 1993?

A New President for a New Century

GUIDING QUESTION *Why was the United States divided politically during a time of economic prosperity?*

As the Clinton presidency was coming to a close, questions lingered. How would he be remembered? The country had a balanced budget. The economy was strong. The impeachment trial, however, had left the country divided. Many people viewed Clinton's achievements favorably, but they had been disappointed by his personal behavior. As the 2000 election approached, the major parties looked for candidates with wide appeal.

The Parties Choose Their Candidates

The Republicans chose George W. Bush, son of George H. W. Bush, as their presidential candidate. George W. Bush was the governor of Texas. For his vice president, he chose Richard Cheney, who had been his father's Secretary of Defense.

United States Department of State

Reading **HELP**DESK

Reading Strategy: *Comparing and Contrasting*

When you compare and contrast, you look at how two or more things are the same and different. On a separate piece of paper, note issues on which candidates Bush and Gore agreed and those on which they did not.

The Democrats nominated Vice President Al Gore for president. They hoped that the popularity of Clinton's policies would mean votes for Gore. Gore made history by naming Senator Joseph Lieberman, from Connecticut, as his running mate. This marked the first time in U.S. history that a Jewish American ran on a national ticket.

Gore stressed protecting the environment and improving education. Bush also supported educational reform. Calling himself a "compassionate conservative," Bush favored local grassroots efforts to help the disadvantaged without large and costly government programs. A major campaign issue was what to do with the budget surplus. Gore and Bush agreed that Social Security and Medicare needed reform. They disagreed on the details. Both also supported tax cuts and plans to help seniors pay for medicines.

The 2000 race also included a third candidate—activist and consumer advocate Ralph Nader. He claimed there was little difference between Bush and Gore. Nader said, "Too much power in the hands of the few has further weakened our democracy." He ran as the nominee of the Green Party, which was known for its strong environmental views.

A Contested Election

The 2000 election results were extremely close. Gore won the popular vote. The electoral vote, however, was another matter. For five weeks the outcome remained uncertain. The key state was Florida. Without Florida's 25 electoral votes, neither Bush nor Gore had the 270 votes needed to win.

In Florida, the first count of ballots gave Bush a tiny lead— just a few hundred votes. Because the count was so close, state law required a recount. The state began to recount the votes in certain counties. Gore also asked for recounts in several other counties. A battle began over how and whether the recounts should be carried out. The issue ultimately reached the U.S. Supreme Court.

Americans learned more about the candidates' views in a series of three televised debates. Here presidential candidates Gore and Bush face off in the second debate, which took place on October 11, 2000 in Winston-Salem, North Carolina.

THE ELECTION OF 2000

AK 3
WA 11
OR 7
ID 4
MT 3
ND 3
MN 10
WI 11
MI 18
NH 4
VT 3
ME 4
MA 12
NY 33
RI 4
CT 8
NJ 15
DE 3
MD 10
DC 3*
SD 3
WY 3
NE 5
IA 7
IL 22
IN 12
OH 21
PA 23
WV 5
VA 13
NV 4
UT 5
CO 8
KS 6
MO 11
KY 8
NC 14
CA 54
AZ 8
NM 5
OK 8
AR 6
TN 11
SC 8
TX 32
LA 9
MS 7
AL 9
GA 13
FL 25
HI 4

ELECTORAL VOTE
TOTAL: 538
49.4% 266
50.4% 271

POPULAR VOTE
TOTAL: 105,417,475
3.74% 3,953,439
48.38% 51,003,926
47.87% 50,460,110

Bush (Republican)
Gore (Democrat)
Other

* One Gore elector from Washington, D.C., abstained from casting an electoral vote.

INFOGRAPHIC

The presidential election of 2000 was extraordinarily close.

1 **ANALYZING VISUALS** According to the map, in which parts of the country was Gore's support the greatest?

2 **CRITICAL THINKING**
Explaining Though Gore won in fewer than half the states, the election was very close. Why?

On December 12, in *Bush* v. *Gore,* the Court ruled that the recounts in selected places violated the Constitution. It further held that there was not enough time to conduct a fair recount. This ruling left Bush the winner in Florida.

A Second President Bush

George W. Bush was sworn in as the 43rd president of the United States on January 21, 2001. He called for the people of the United States to unite and get past their differences. The need for unity and cooperation was important in Congress as well. After the election the Senate was evenly split—50 Republicans and 50 Democrats.

In May 2001 Vermont Senator James Jeffords left the Republican Party and became an independent. This led to a historic switch in power. It shifted control of the Senate to the Democrats in mid-session. However, in the midterm elections of 2002, the Republicans regained control of the Senate. They also increased their majority in the House.

For his cabinet, President Bush wanted to reflect the country's diversity. He named people from different career and ethnic backgrounds. Bush appointed popular retired Army General

Reading **HELP**DESK CCSS

Reading Strategy: *Categorizing*

When you categorize, you place information in groups according to a shared characteristic. For example, baseball, soccer, and tennis can be categorized as sports that use balls.

List the people President Bush appointed to his cabinet on a separate piece of paper, and categorize them in at least two groups.

Colin Powell as secretary of state and Donald Rumsfeld as secretary of defense. Rumsfeld had served as secretary of defense during the Ford administration.

Bush's Domestic Policy

Once in office, President Bush focused on his domestic plans. These included cutting taxes, improving public education, and reforming Social Security and Medicare. He also favored strengthening the nation's defenses.

The new president's first task was to carry out his campaign pledge to cut taxes. Some critics argued that instead of cutting taxes, the government should use any budget surplus to pay off the national debt. Supporters claimed the cut would help the economy, which had gone into a slump during the election campaign. In June 2001, Congress passed and Bush signed a tax-cut bill.

Next, Bush proposed reforms in education. His plan called for public schools to hold yearly tests to measure student performance. It would also allow parents to use federal funds to pay for private schools if their public schools were doing a poor job. Congress refused to give federal funds to private schools. It did vote in favor of annual testing in public schools for grades 3 to 8. This law became known as the No Child Left Behind Act.

Foreign Affairs

In foreign affairs, Bush pushed for new military programs. One was a National Missile Defense System designed to shoot down incoming missiles. The president argued that missile defense was needed because hostile nations were developing long-range missiles.

Meanwhile, a horrifying event took place on September 11, 2001. A stunned nation realized that it was not immune to the dangers of a violent world. A new kind of war had begun.

Reuters/CORBIS

 PROGRESS CHECK

Summarizing What was George W. Bush's policy on education?

BIOGRAPHY

Colin Powell (1937–)

Born to immigrant parents, Colin Powell was raised in Harlem and the South Bronx of New York City. He attended public school and the City College of New York, where he studied geology and began military training. By the Persian Gulf War in 1991, he had risen to the role of chairman of the Joint Chiefs of Staff, the highest-ranking military position in the Department of Defense. He was the first African American to hold this post. After leaving the army, Powell went to work in 2001 for his fifth president, George W. Bush, as secretary of state. At the time, Powell was the highest ranking African American civilian in the history of the United States.

▶ **CRITICAL THINKING**
Comparing Which do you think is more impressive: Powell's success in the military or his success in the government? Explain your answer.

LESSON 3 REVIEW CCSS

Review Vocabulary

1. Use each of the following terms in a sentence that explains the term's meaning:

   a. grassroots movement **b.** deficit spending
   c. gross domestic product **d.** perjury

Answer the Guiding Questions

2. *Describing* What were the circumstances of Bill Clinton's first election to the presidency?

3. *Synthesizing* Explain why the Clinton presidency may be viewed both positively and negatively.

4. *Drawing Conclusions* Why do you think the vote in the 2000 election was controversial?

5. **ARGUMENT** How serious must a president's misdeeds be before he or she is forced from office? Write a short essay stating your opinion on this question.

What DoYou Think? (CCSS)

Should the United States Expand Domestic Oil Exploration?

Dependence on foreign oil concerns many Americans, but oil resources within the United States are limited. One source of oil is the ocean floor off the nation's coasts. However, drilling in these waters has long been controversial. The huge oil spill that occurred in the Gulf of Mexico in 2010 renewed the debate. Read what two U.S. senators had to say about offshore drilling.

No

PRIMARY SOURCE

❝ The simple truth is that we cannot drill our way to energy independence or lower gas prices. The U.S. uses roughly 25 percent of the world's oil, 7.5 bn [billion] barrels per year, but we have only 2–3 percent of the world's proven petroleum reserves. . . . [We should] reinstate a ban on new offshore drilling . . . and dramatically increase fuel efficiency for vehicles sold in America. Instead of saving three cents a gallon by 2030 by allowing wide open offshore drilling, we . . . will save consumers the equivalent of $1 per gallon of gas in 2030. . . . It also would eliminate the need for 3.9 m [million] barrels of oil per day, more than double the amount we now import from Persian Gulf nations such as Saudi Arabia. ❞

—"Oil Spill Shows Drilling is Not the Answer" by Bernie Sanders. Copyright Guardian News & Media Ltd 2010.

Proehl Studios/CORBIS

Obtaining energy from sources such as wind may help reduce dependence on oil.

Yes

66 In the wake of this accident, many are understandably concerned about the safety and environmental risks associated with offshore drilling. We are often quick to turn to reactionary and overly **stringent** public policy as a **stopgap** measure. Simply halting all offshore development will not address our energy needs and would immediately increase our dependence on foreign oil. This accident should not be used as an excuse to halt the gains the United States has made in developing domestic energy sources. 99

—Sen. Richard Shelby (R-AL)
Testimony to the U.S. Senate, May 11, 2010

Oil rigs fill the horizon off the coast of Santa Barbara, California.

Vocabulary

stringent
strict

stopgap
done in an emergency

What Do You Think? DBQ

❶ *Describing* According to these documents, what share of the world's oil does the United States use? What share does it own?

❷ *Comparing* On what problem do the two senators agree?

❸ *Contrasting* Contrast the solutions each senator proposes for the central problem.

networks

There's More Online!

- ☑ **CHART** President Obama's Supreme Court Choices

- ☑ **GRAPHIC ORGANIZER** September 11 Effects

- ☑ **MAPS**
  - Election of 2008
  - Election of 2012

- ☑ **PRIMARY SOURCE** Health Care Reform

- ☑ **SLIDE SHOW**
  - September 11 Attacks
  - Hurricane Katrina

Lesson 4
The Global War on Terror

ESSENTIAL QUESTION *Why does conflict develop?*

IT MATTERS BECAUSE

The September 11 terrorist attacks represented a new kind of warfare that challenged old ideas about how to defend the nation.

The Day That Changed the Nation

GUIDING QUESTION *What events occurred on September 11, 2001?*

Terrorism (TEHR•uhr•ih•zuhm) is the use of violence against civilians to reach a political goal, such as changing governments or their policies. Terrorists can be individuals or groups. They may act alone or with the support of some government.

On September 11, 2001, the United States suffered a devastating terrorist attack. Early that morning, terrorists hijacked four U.S. passenger planes. They then crashed two planes into New York City's World Trade Center. A third plane slammed into the Pentagon, headquarters of the Department of Defense, near Washington, D.C. The fourth plane was likely headed to another Washington, D.C., target. Instead, heroic passengers attacked the hijackers, and the plane crashed in the Pennsylvania countryside.

When the attacks were over, some 3,000 people were dead. The U.S. government quickly identified the evil plot as the work of a Saudi Arabian named Osama bin Laden and his terrorist organization, called al-Qaeda (al-KY•duh). Congress approved the use of force to fight the terrorists, and President Bush announced a war on terrorism.

(l)Max Whittaker/CORBIS, (cl, c & cr) AFP/Getty Images, (r) Chip Somodevilla/Getty Images News/Getty Images

Reading **HELP**DESK (CCSS)

Taking Notes: *Determining Cause and Effect*

Use a diagram like this one to identify the effects of the September 11 terrorist attacks at home and overseas.

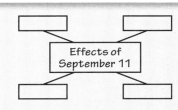

Effects of September 11

Content Vocabulary
- **terrorism**
- **bailout**
- **insurgent**
- **levee**

472 *New Challenges*

Terrorism Increases

Most of the world's 1 billion Muslims—followers of Islam—reject terrorism. However, some fundamentalists such as bin Laden do not. Muslim fundamentalists call for a return to traditional ways. Those who favor bin Laden's methods believe the need to create a pure Muslim society calls for drastic acts. Some Muslims feel that Western (U.S. and European) culture weakens traditional Muslim values. United States support for Israel is another factor behind strong anti-American feeling.

The War on Terrorism

Osama bin Laden had fought in Afghanistan in the 1980s against the Soviet invasion of that Muslim country. Using family wealth, he formed Al-Qaeda, which became a terrorist group dedicated to a fundamentalist Islamic vision.

Bin Laden was supported by the Taliban, a Muslim fundamentalist group that had gained control of Afghanistan's government in the 1990s. Bin Laden used Afghanistan as his base for planning the September 11 attacks.

After September 11, President Bush demanded that the Taliban turn over bin Laden and his followers and shut down all terrorist camps. When Taliban leaders refused, the U.S. military, aided by forces from several other countries, attacked. By December, the Taliban government had collapsed. The surviving Taliban fled into Afghanistan's mountains. Fighting with Taliban forces continued. Meanwhile, bin Laden escaped.

During the terrorist attacks of September 11, 2,752 people were killed in New York City alone. Here rescuers search for victims in the ruins of the World Trade Center.

Porter Gifford/CORBIS

Following the terrorist attacks of September 11, 2001, the United States began a military operation in Afghanistan that is ongoing today.

War in Iraq

The September 11 attacks raised fears that terrorists might get nuclear, chemical, or biological weapons. President Bush claimed that Iraq's leader Saddam Hussein had such weapons of mass destruction and might supply them to terrorists.

In 2003 a group of countries, led by the United States, invaded Iraq. Their forces quickly defeated the Iraqi army and drove Hussein from power. Hussein was later captured. The fighting did not end, however. **Insurgents** (ihn·SUHR·juhnts), or rebel groups, attacked the U.S.-led troops. The insurgents tried to defeat U.S. efforts. Some insurgents had ties to Saddam Hussein or al-Qaeda or other extremist groups.

Iraq also was torn by religious and ethnic divisions. Its Shia Muslims belong to one of the two main branches of Islam. Its Sunni Muslims belong to the second branch. Kurds are an ethnic minority who live mostly in northern Iraq. Hussein's fall sparked fighting among these groups.

As the conflict dragged on and more lives were lost, Americans' support for the war declined. Failure to find weapons of mass destruction led many to conclude the war was a mistake. Yet President Bush was determined to stay in Iraq to try to build a democracy. Iraq did in fact hold elections and establish a democratic government, though that government faced many challenges.

✓ PROGRESS CHECK

Describing Why did the United States invade Iraq?

A Second Bush Term

GUIDING QUESTION *Why did Bush lose support during his second term?*

President Bush sought reelection in 2004. However, the ongoing Iraq war began to erode his support. A growing national debt fueled by the war drained the country's economic strength.

Election of 2004

The Democrats chose Senator John Kerry of Massachusetts to run for president. North Carolina senator John Edwards was the party's choice for vice president.

President Bush claimed Kerry lacked the ability to carry on the war against terrorism. Kerry attacked Bush on the lack of success in Iraq and the weak economy. In a close race that

Max Whittaker/CORBIS

Reading **HELP**DESK (CCSS)

terrorism violence committed in order to frighten people or governments into granting demands

insurgent a person who revolts against a government or others in power

levee high walls or an embankment to prevent flooding in low-lying areas

hinged on a few key states, President Bush came out ahead. At the same time, Republicans were able to increase their hold on Congress.

Civil Liberties Issues

The war on terrorism raised questions about civil liberties. For example, Americans debated what to do with suspected terrorists captured in battle. The United States held many of these suspects at the American military base at Guantanamo Bay, Cuba. Bush officials claimed the prisoners were illegal enemy fighters who had very few rights.

The Supreme Court disagreed. In 2004 it ruled in *Rasul* v. *Bush* that these prisoners had some legal rights. Those rights included the right to appeal to a court. Bush then set up special military courts to hear each case. In 2006, however, in *Hamdan* v. *Rumsfeld*, the Court struck down this plan. It ruled that Bush's military courts violated U.S. military and international laws. Bush agreed to protect certain prisoner rights.

Other Issues at Home

President Bush had the opportunity to name two justices to the U.S. Supreme Court. First, he chose federal judge John J. Roberts, Jr., as chief justice. Later, Bush named federal judge Samuel Alito, Jr., to the bench. Both appointments strengthened the Court's conservative majority.

Disaster struck in August 2005: Hurricane Katrina slammed into the Gulf of Mexico coast. The storm left thousands homeless and at least 1,800 people dead. The city of New Orleans suffered great damage. Rising waters broke through **levees** (LEH•veez), or high walls along waterways, and flooded the city.

In August 2005, Hurricane Katrina destroyed whole neighborhoods in New Orleans. Many of the city's residents had to flee their homes, and a large number never returned.

▶ CRITICAL THINKING
Analyzing Explain how the loss of city residents after Katrina made recovery so challenging for New Orleans.

Many Americans wondered why national, state, and local governments failed to respond more quickly. As criticism mounted, President Bush promised federal funds to rebuild New Orleans.

The Elections of 2006

In 2006 voters made clear their unhappiness with President Bush's policies. The Democrats won control of both houses of Congress for the first time since 1992. House Democrats elected Nancy Pelosi to be the first female Speaker of the House of Representatives.

After the election, President Bush announced a "surge," or rapid increase, of some 20,000 more troops to Iraq. House Democrats criticized his new strategy. They called for him to set a **definite** timetable for pulling U.S. troops out of Iraq.

✅ **PROGRESS CHECK**

Summarizing What did the Supreme Court rule in *Hamdan* v. *Rumsfeld*?

A Historic Change

GUIDING QUESTION *Why did Americans choose Barack Obama as president in a historic election?*

As the presidential election of 2008 approached, candidates in both major parties jostled for position. The Iraq war and a weak economy were key issues.

Senator John McCain of Arizona won the Republican nomination. McCain was a Vietnam War hero and a reformer known for working with both parties. He named Alaska Governor Sarah Palin as his running mate. She became the first woman ever to run on a national Republican ticket.

Democrats seeking nomination included Senator Barack Obama of Illinois and former First Lady and current New York senator, Hillary Rodham Clinton. Senator Obama claimed the prize. He was the first African American ever nominated to run for president by a major party. He chose as his running mate Senator Joseph Biden of Delaware.

For a while, it appeared as if the campaign would be close. Then a severe financial crisis hit the nation in late September 2008. Voters seemed to blame Republican policies—and decided it was time for a change.

President Barack Obama and new First Lady Michelle Obama walk to the White House after his inauguration as president on January 20, 2009.

▶ **CRITICAL THINKING**
Drawing Conclusions What does the election of Obama say about the position of African Americans in U.S. society?

DOUG MILLS/AFP/Getty Images

Reading **HELP**DESK (CCSS)

Academic Vocabulary

definite specific or certain

Reading Strategy: *Summarizing*

When you summarize a reading, you find the main idea of the passage and restate it in your own words. Read the three paragraphs under the heading "A Historic Change." On a separate sheet of paper, summarize the reading in one or two sentences.

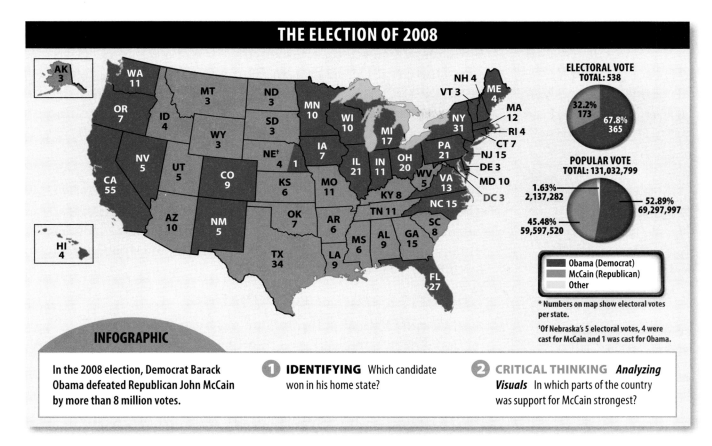

THE ELECTION OF 2008

AK 3

WA 11
OR 7
ID 4
MT 3
ND 3
MN 10
WI 10
MI 17
NH 4
VT 3
ME 4
MA 12
NY 31
RI 4
CT 7
NJ 15
DE 3
MD 10
DC 3

NV 5
UT 5
WY 3
SD 3
IA 7
IL 21
IN 11
OH 20
PA 21
WV 5
VA 13

CA 55
AZ 10
CO 9
NE† 4 1
KS 6
MO 11
KY 8
NC 15

NM 5
OK 7
AR 6
TN 11
SC 8
GA 15

HI 4
TX 34
LA 9
MS 6
AL 9
FL 27

ELECTORAL VOTE
TOTAL: 538

32.2% 173
67.8% 365

POPULAR VOTE
TOTAL: 131,032,799

1.63% 2,137,282
52.89% 69,297,997
45.48% 59,597,520

Obama (Democrat)
McCain (Republican)
Other

* Numbers on map show electoral votes per state.

†Of Nebraska's 5 electoral votes, 4 were cast for McCain and 1 was cast for Obama.

INFOGRAPHIC

In the 2008 election, Democrat Barack Obama defeated Republican John McCain by more than 8 million votes.

1 IDENTIFYING Which candidate won in his home state?

2 CRITICAL THINKING *Analyzing Visuals* In which parts of the country was support for McCain strongest?

The 2008 election brought the highest voter turnout since 1964—nearly 62 percent of eligible voters. Obama got 53 percent of the popular vote and 365 electoral votes to McCain's 173. In addition to the presidency, Democrats increased their majority in both the Senate and the House of Representatives.

The New President

Barack Obama was born in 1961 in Hawaii. His parents were a white American woman and a black man from Kenya, a country in East Africa. Obama had worked as a civil rights lawyer in the 1990s and taught law at the University of Chicago. **Prior** to his run for president, Obama served as a state senator in Illinois and then as a U.S. senator. In his inaugural address, he reminded Americans of what his election meant to the nation's ideals:

PRIMARY SOURCE

❝ This is the meaning of our liberty and our creed—why men and women and children of every race and every faith can join in celebration across this magnificent mall, and why a man whose father less than sixty years ago might not have been served at a local restaurant can now stand before you to take a most sacred oath. ❞

Academic Vocabulary

prior at an earlier time; before

In the first years of Obama's presidency, Supreme Court justices David Souter and John Stevens retired. Obama replaced these justices with Sonia Sotomayor (top) and Elena Kagan (bottom).

Domestic Issues

President Obama took office during the worst economic crisis since the Great Depression. In February 2009, he got Congress to pass a $787 billion spending bill to boost the economy. The bill included jobless benefits, tax cuts for workers, and funding to create jobs. Obama also approved money for **bailout**—a financial rescue of some companies.

One of the president's key goals was reforming the nation's health care system. He called on Congress to find ways to reduce the cost of health care. He wanted to make health insurance available to the 47 million Americans who had none. Congress finally agreed on a health care bill, which Obama signed into law in 2010.

The 2010 Congressional Elections

Critics said Obama's reforms added to a dangerously large national debt. Some gathered in protests called "tea parties." The name referred to the American colonists who protested British rule by throwing tea into Boston Harbor in 1773.

In the congressional elections of 2010, Republicans—with Tea Party support—won control of the House and captured more Senate seats. They vowed to overturn Obama's health care law and to make deep spending cuts. The law faced legal challenges but in 2012 was upheld by the U.S. Supreme Court.

President Obama's Foreign Policy

President Obama worked to improve relations with other nations. To assist him, he named former rival Hillary Rodham Clinton as secretary of state. In 2009 Obama received the Nobel Peace Prize for these efforts.

Obama's greatest challenge was the unpopular wars in Iraq and Afghanistan. Obama ended the U.S. military role in Iraq but kept troops longer in Afghanistan, where militants remained a threat. In 2011 U.S. forces at last located and killed Osama bin Laden in neighboring Pakistan. Obama planned to remove U.S. troops from Afghanistan by late 2014.

Meanwhile, uprisings toppled dictators in the Middle East. In Libya, dictator Muammar al-Qaddafi used force against his own people. Rebels overthrew Qaddafi with U.S. help. In Syria, Bashir Hassad's harsh rule led to a brutal civil war. World leaders pressured Hassad to step down, but he refused.

Reading **HELP**DESK CCSS

bailout a rescue, such as from financial ruin

(t) Tim Sloan/AFP/Getty Images;
(b) Chip Somodevilla/Getty Images News/Getty Images

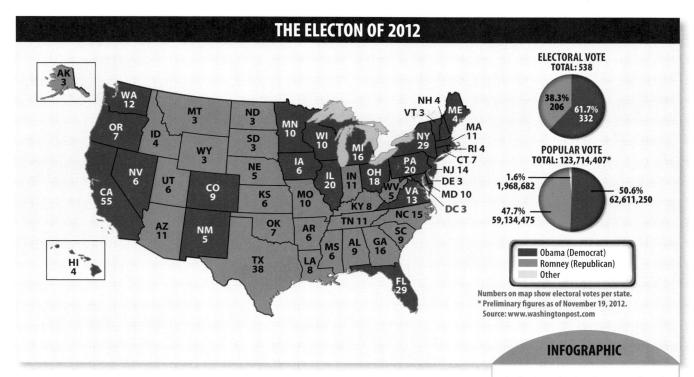

ELECTORAL VOTE
TOTAL: 538

38.3%
206

61.7%
332

POPULAR VOTE
TOTAL: 123,714,407*

1.6%
1,968,682

50.6%
62,611,250

47.7%
59,134,475

■ Obama (Democrat)
■ Romney (Republican)
□ Other

Numbers on map show electoral votes per state.
* Preliminary figures as of November 19, 2012.
Source: www.washingtonpost.com

The Election of 2012

The 2012 election saw voters deeply divided. President Obama ran for a second term, with Joseph Biden again his running mate. Their Republican challengers were former Massachusetts governor Mitt Romney and his running mate, Wisconsin Congressman Paul Ryan. Obama won by a narrow margin over Romney. Republicans kept control of the House, and Democrats, the Senate. It was not clear whether Obama and congressional Republicans could find common ground to tackle the debt and other national problems.

✔ PROGRESS CHECK

Describing What were major domestic issues the Obama administration had to face?

INFOGRAPHIC

In the 2012 election, Democrat Barack Obama defeated Republican Mitt Romney by about 2.6 million votes.

1 IDENTIFYING Which candidate won in Massachusetts, where Romney once was governor?

2 CRITICAL THINKING *Analyzing Visuals* Which states did Obama win in 2008 but not carry in 2012?

LESSON 4 REVIEW

Review Vocabulary

1. Use the following terms to write a short paragraph about the war on terror.

   a. terrorism   **b.** insurgent

2. Identify the significance of these words:

   a. levee   **b.** bailout

Answer the Guiding Questions

3. *Describing* How did the September 11 attacks affect President Bush's policies?

4. *Determining Cause and Effect* Why did the economy weaken during Bush's second term?

5. *Identifying* What event helped push Barack Obama to victory in the 2008 election?

6. **INFORMATIVE/EXPLANATORY** What challenges did Barack Obama face as president? What did he do to meet those challenges? Write a short essay that answers these questions.

networks

There's More Online!

☑ **CHART/GRAPH**
  • Leading Exporters/
    Importers
  • Proved Oil Reserves
    by Country
☑ **GRAPHIC ORGANIZER**
  Global Challenges
☑ **VIDEO**

Lesson 5

Twenty-First Century Challenges

ESSENTIAL QUESTION *How do new ideas change the way people live?*

IT MATTERS BECAUSE

Increased interdependence means that problems in one country—whether economic, environmental, or other—are often felt in countries in different parts of the world.

The Global Economy

GUIDING QUESTION *How did the global economy benefit from technology but suffer during the financial crisis?*

Today nations are **interdependent** (ihn·tuhr·dee·PEHN·duhnt)—that is, one country's economic well-being depends on the well-being of the others. Countries rely on one another for raw materials and for markets in which to sell goods. In other words, the nations of the world take part in a global economy.

Technology Drives Change

Key to the growth of the global economy has been the technology revolution. The machine that has driven this revolution is the computer. In the 1960s, scientists developed the integrated circuit, a small electronic device. A **decade** later, they came up with even more powerful circuits called microprocessors. These developments made it possible to make small, fast computers that store a lot of information.

A Global Financial Crisis

New technology helped the global economy grow in the 2000s. Technology created new opportunities to make money and to produce and buy more goods. In 2008, however, the

(l)Win McNamee/Getty Images News/Getty Images, (r) EPA/ASAHI SHIMBUN/Photolibrary

Reading **HELP**DESK (CCSS)

Taking Notes: *Making Connections*

Create a diagram like this one to identify global challenges. Then explain why each of these is a challenge.

Global Challenges

Content Vocabulary
• **interdependent**   • **free trade**
• **globalization**   • **outsourcing**
• **trade deficit**   • **acid rain**

bubble of prosperity burst. A major financial crisis hit the United States. The crisis also affected other nations around the globe.

Many experts trace the crisis to American banks and the practice of giving loans to people who were not able to repay them. The banks hoped that the economic growth would continue and that it would offset any effects of the risky loans.

Then, the economy started to sour unexpectedly. People began having trouble making house payments. Banks were hurt. They began loaning less money. Bank lending is key to the economy. Many businesses depend on loans to keep operating.

To ease the crisis, governments and banks tried different plans to encourage lending. The steps did not work quickly enough. The lack of money available for lending brought economies to the brink of collapse. Shoppers stopped buying products. Companies went bankrupt. People lost jobs, and goods became more expensive. Together, these events created the worst economic crisis since the Great Depression of the 1930s.

In the fall of 2008, the Bush administration agreed to a trillion-dollar bailout of many financial institutions. The government bought up "bad" debts in return for some control of U.S. banks. Upon entering office, President Obama extended government bailouts to struggling automakers and homeowners.

By 2012, the worst of the crisis seemed to be passed. The economy was growing. Yet unemployment remained high, and people in many areas were still struggling to recover.

Global Trade

The global financial crisis of 2008 showed that people and nations are closely linked. Technology has contributed to the rise of **globalization** (gloh·buh·luh·ZAY·shun), the linking of the world's economies and societies. Thanks to technology, the physical distance between countries does not always matter.

The United States's huge economy makes it a leader in world trade. The United States exports and imports a large number of goods and services. However, it spends hundreds of billions of dollars more on imports than it earns from exports. The result is a massive trade deficit. A **trade deficit** occurs when a country spends more on imports than it earns from exports.

The U.S. economy depends on selling American-made products. For this reason, Republican and Democratic presidents since World War II have supported free trade.

interdependent relying on each other
globalization the increasing economic interaction between people, companies, and governments of different nations

trade deficit what happens when the value of imports is greater than the value of exports

Academic Vocabulary

decade a period of ten years

Like most countries, the United States imports and exports many goods and services.

1 **DESCRIBING** As measured in dollars, does the United States import or export more goods and services?

2 **CRITICAL THINKING** *Calculating* In what way is the United States different from all the other countries shown in these graphs?

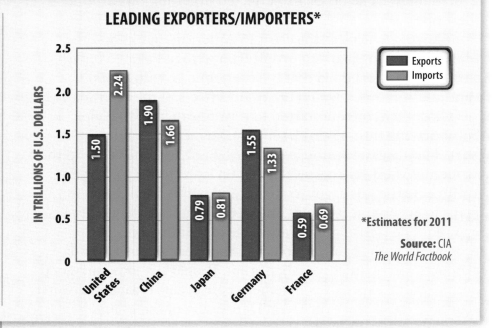

LEADING EXPORTERS/IMPORTERS*

IN TRILLIONS OF U.S. DOLLARS

■ Exports
■ Imports

United States — 1.50 / 2.24
China — 1.90 / 1.66
Japan — 0.79 / 0.81
Germany — 1.55 / 1.33
France — 0.59 / 0.69

*Estimates for 2011

Source: CIA
The World Factbook

Free trade means the removal of trade barriers so that goods flow freely among countries. The United States and other nations have been members of the World Trade Organization (WTO). It arranges trade agreements and settles trade disputes among countries.

Some experts believe that trade agreements such as NAFTA help spur economic growth. Others complain that they contribute to **outsourcing**—moving the production of U.S. goods and services to countries such as Mexico. Because workers are paid less in Mexico, the cost of goods may go down. Critics charge that the result is a loss of U.S. jobs. Free-trade supporters counter that the resulting economic growth means opportunities for more and better American jobs. They call for investments in education that will equip tomorrow's workers with the skills to prosper in the global economy.

Americans have debated trade policies since colonial days. Globalization ensures that this lively debate will continue.

☑ **PROGRESS CHECK**

Determining Cause and Effect What do analysts believe was the major cause of the financial crisis that began in 2008?

Reading **HELP**DESK (CCSS)

free trade the free flow of goods and services among countries through the removal of tariffs and other trade barriers

outsourcing the practice of moving production of goods or services to another location where the cost of labor is cheaper

acid rain rain containing high amounts of chemical pollutants from the burning of fossil fuels

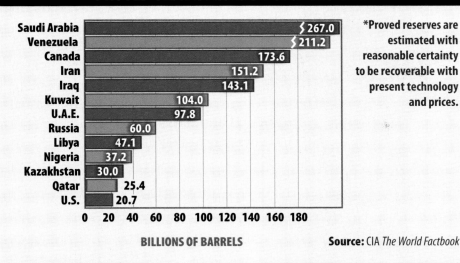

PROVED OIL RESERVES BY COUNTRY 2012*

GRAPH SKILL

Country	Billions of Barrels
Saudi Arabia	267.0
Venezuela	211.2
Canada	173.6
Iran	151.2
Iraq	143.1
Kuwait	104.0
U.A.E.	97.8
Russia	60.0
Libya	47.1
Nigeria	37.2
Kazakhstan	30.0
Qatar	25.4
U.S.	20.7

0 20 40 60 80 100 120 140 160 180

BILLIONS OF BARRELS

Source: CIA *The World Factbook*

*Proved reserves are estimated with reasonable certainty to be recoverable with present technology and prices.

This graph shows oil reserves that experts believe can be reached with current technology at a reasonable cost.

1 CALCULATING Where does the United States rank in terms of oil reserves?

2 CRITICAL THINKING *Explaining* Based on the information in the graph, what challenge is the U.S. facing?

Challenges for the Future

GUIDING QUESTION *What are the key environmental and social issues facing the U.S.?*

The trend toward globalization has made people **aware** of threats to the environment. Many fear that Earth's resources will soon be unable to support a rapidly rising population. The spread of human settlements into natural areas has already strained water and food resources and damaged wilderness areas.

Polluted Air and Water

Burning fossil fuels, such as oil, coal, and natural gas, pollutes the air. The pollution mixes with the air's water vapor to make **acid rain,** which is rain containing high amounts of chemical pollution. Acid rain harms trees, rivers, lakes, even the stone used in buildings. The United States has acted to reduce the volume of chemicals released into the air. Still, air and water pollution are serious problems in the U.S.

Most fossil fuels are made from petroleum, or oil. Petroleum is a natural resource that is limited in supply. People use oil for fuel and for making many other goods. The United States uses a lot of oil, but it does not have enough to meet its own needs.

Oil is found deep underground, or under the ocean floor. New technology has made it possible to get oil from very deep parts of the ocean. There are risks, however. In 2010 an oil-drilling rig in the Gulf of Mexico blew up, injuring and killing workers.

In 2010 an explosion at an offshore oil rig led to a massive oil leak in the Gulf of Mexico. The spill had a devastating impact on the people who depend on the Gulf for their livelihood and also on fish and wildlife in the area.

Win McNamee/Getty Images News/Getty Images

Academic Vocabulary

aware alert, having knowledge about something

A tsunami spawned by a powerful earthquake caused tremendous damage in coastal Japan in March 2011. The waves carried away cars, ships, and buildings, took thousands of lives, and triggered a nuclear crisis at a damaged power plant.

The blast caused a massive leak of oil into the Gulf of Mexico. Stopping the leak took nearly four months. Meanwhile, fish and wildlife and many natural habitats were choked with oil. The area affected ran along the coast from Louisiana to Florida. The spill was the largest in the history of ocean drilling.

Climate Change and Environmental Policies

Many scientists also think Earth's climate is undergoing a change. Average global temperatures seem to be rising. This threatens to change weather patterns. Results may include rain shortages in some places, melting ice in polar regions, and flooding in low-lying coastal areas. Many scientists think pollution is a cause of climate change, though others disagree.

In the United States, some state and local governments have tried to limit air pollution. The federal Environmental Protection Agency (EPA) also can make rules about environmental issues. For example, it can take steps to limit pollutants from cars.

President Obama agreed to have the EPA set limits on chemical pollutants. Obama also asked automakers to improve vehicle fuel efficiency by 2011 and to put a million electric cars on the road by 2015. Automakers now offer a "hybrid" gasoline-electric car that uses less gasoline and also all-electric models.

New Concerns About Nuclear Power

On March 11, 2011, a massive earthquake rocked the nation of Japan. The quake produced tsunamis—large ocean waves that slammed ashore, causing flooding and property damage.

The disaster left more than 25,000 dead or missing. It also damaged a nuclear power plant, crippling its system for cooling nuclear material. As a result, the plant released large amounts of radioactive material, some of which reached the United States.

The Japanese nuclear emergency raised anew questions about what role nuclear energy should play in the nation's energy future. How can people balance the need for reliable energy with the dangers different forms present? In addition, what can be

EPA/ASAHI SHIMBUN/Photolibrary

Reading **HELP**DESK (CCSS)

Taking Notes: *Word Origins*

The word *tsunami* comes from the Japanese language. *Tsu* means "harbor," and *nami* means "wave." The word was first used in 1897.

done to ensure the safety of the many nuclear plants already in operation around the world? These questions present a challenge as the nation works to find alternative energy sources.

A Changing Society

The U.S. population continues to change. Better health care has helped increase the number of older Americans. The foreign-born population is also growing. The number of Latinos—some of whom are immigrants, but most of whom were born in the U.S.—has risen sharply. Between 1980 and 2010, the Latino population soared from under 15 million to about 50 million.

Many immigrants have followed the nation's laws for entry to the United States. Currently, however, there are about 11 million immigrants who are in the United States illegally. Americans disagree about whether or not the U.S. should grant amnesty, or forgiveness, to immigrants already in the country illegally and allow them to become citizens. To prevent future illegal immigration, some Americans call for stronger border enforcement and a crackdown on those who hire illegal immigrants. In 2010 Arizona passed a law expanding police powers for identifying illegal immigrants in the state. The law sparked debate about how far the nation should go in combatting illegal immigration.

The debate about immigration is a familiar one that echoes throughout American history. While the issue represents a challenge, it also highlights a key fact: The United States remains a land of hope and freedom that draws millions to its shores.

☑ **PROGRESS CHECK**

Summarizing How is the population of the United States changing?

LESSON 5 REVIEW

Review Vocabulary

1. Write a short paragraph in which you use these vocabulary terms:

   a. interdependent **b.** globalization
   c. free trade **d.** outsourcing

2. Write two sentences that explain the significance of a *trade deficit* and *acid rain*.

Answer the Guiding Questions

3. *Analyzing* How has technology contributed to globalization?

4. *Identifying* What environmental concerns have become more serious issues in recent years?

5. *Identifying* Identify one key factor that is changing the nature of the U.S. population in recent years.

6. **INFORMATIVE/EXPLANATORY** Write an essay that describes how changes in U.S. society have made your life different from the lives of people who grew up 40 or 50 years ago.

Write your answers on a separate piece of paper.

1 Exploring the Essential Questions

INFORMATIVE/EXPLANATORY Think about the many changes and challenges the nation has experienced since 1980. Evaluate how well each of the presidents who has served since then has faced the events that confronted him during his terms. Cite specific events, actions, and policies in making your assessments.

2 21st Century Skills

INFORMATION LITERACY Create a graph of the following information: A worker spends $1,000 more than he or she earns each year for 10 years. In year 11, the worker gets a bonus of $6,000 and uses it to pay down the accumulated debt. Find the worker's debt at the end of the eleventh year. Then write a short essay that compares your graph with the spending policies of U.S. presidents and Congress in recent decades.

3 Thinking Like a Historian

MAKING COMPARISONS Research the debate about illegal immigration in the United States, including proposals of amnesty, or a path to citizenship, for illegal immigrants, as well as arguments in favor of stronger enforcement of immigration laws. Write an essay that describes the proposals and the arguments for and against them.

4 Visual Literacy

ANALYZING VISUALS This photo shows Vice President George H.W. Bush, President Reagan, and Soviet leader Mikhail Gorbachev sightseeing together in 1988. What makes this image a good symbol for the end of the Cold War?

Bettmann/CORBIS

REVIEW THE GUIDING QUESTIONS

Choose the best answer for each question.

1 Which of the following resulted from President Reagan's approach to government?

A. environmentally friendly cars

B. the growth of welfare programs

C. a military buildup

D. a sharp drop in the deficit

2 How did President Bush react to Iraq's attempt to take over Kuwait?

F. He convinced Saddam Hussein to withdraw his army.

G. He withdrew the U.S. from the United Nations.

H. He ordered the United States to bomb Kuwait.

I. He formed a coalition of forces to invade Iraq.

3 Which of President Clinton's goals went unrealized?

A. stricter gun control

B. health care for all Americans

C. family leave for workers

D. balancing the federal budget

4 Just weeks after the terrorist attacks of September 11, the United States did which of the following?

F. invaded Iraq

G. withdrew from the UN

H. attacked the Taliban and al-Qaeda in Afghanistan

I. sent UN forces to Kosovo

5 In general, the technology revolution has

A. isolated countries.

B. hurt world trade.

C. helped make countries interdependent.

D. caused widespread environmental harm.

6 What is the relationship between the deficit and the national debt?

F. When the deficit goes up, the national debt goes down.

G. When the deficit goes up, the national debt increases.

H. The deficit and the national debt are identical.

I. The deficit and the national debt are not related.

DBQ ANALYZING DOCUMENTS

7 **Analyzing Visuals** Which of the following best summarizes the information presented in these graphs?

A. Immigration has remained steady in its character over the decades shown.

B. Europe remains the main source of immigration.

C. Immigration from Latin America has risen greatly in recent decades.

D. Asia has faded from significance as a source of immigration today.

8 **Analyzing Visuals** Which region supplies the second-largest share of immigrants today?

F. Oceania   H. Europe

G. Asia   I. Latin America

FOREIGN-BORN POPULATION BY REGION OF BIRTH

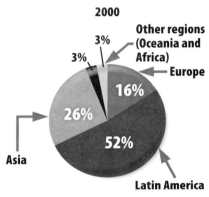

Source: Migration Policy Institute

SHORT RESPONSE

"An industry which burst onto the scene in the early days of the 20th century and became a vital part of our existence found itself crippled by too much regulation, too much government interference, and too much backseat driving by Washington. . . . So, we charted a new course to rebuild America from the bottom up. . . . It hasn't been easy . . . We weathered the storm together. . . . There was a time when Claycomo nearly had to shut down. . . . [Now] your industry and many others have begun to shape up. . . . I believe if Americans work together to improve quality, become more productive, hold down costs, and invest in tomorrow's technology, then we can out-compete, out-perform, and out-sell the pants off anybody."

—President Reagan, speech to the workers at Ford Motor Company's Claycomo Assembly Plant in Kansas City, Missouri, 1984

9 What does Reagan suggest was the reason this plant nearly shut down?

10 Which statement reflects Reagan's optimism? Explain your choice.

EXTENDED RESPONSE

11 **Argument** Write an essay in which you discuss what you think has been the biggest challenge facing the United States in recent decades, and what you think the biggest challenge is going forward. Use information from the chapter in formulating your essay.

Need Extra Help?

If You've Missed Question	**1**	**2**	**3**	**4**	**5**	**6**	**7**	**8**	**9**	**10**	**11**
Review Lesson	1	2	3	4	5	1, 3	5	5	1	1	1–5

THE DECLARATION of INDEPENDENCE

In Congress, July 4, 1776. The unanimous Declaration of the thirteen United States of America,

[Preamble]

When in the Course of human events, it becomes necessary for one people to dissolve the political bands which have connected them with another, and to assume among the Powers of the earth, the separate and equal station to which the Laws of Nature and of Nature's God entitle them, a decent respect to the opinions of mankind requires that they should declare the causes which **impel** them to the separation.

[Declaration of Natural Rights]

We hold these truths to be self-evident, that all men are created equal, that they are **endowed** by their Creator with certain unalienable Rights, that among these are Life, Liberty, and the pursuit of Happiness.

That to secure these rights, Governments are instituted among Men, deriving their just powers from the consent of the governed,

That whenever any Form of Government becomes destructive of these ends, it is the Right of the People to alter or to abolish it, and to institute new Government, laying its foundation on such principles and organizing its powers in such form, as to them shall seem most likely to effect their Safety and Happiness. Prudence, indeed, will dictate that Governments long established should not be changed for light and transient causes; and accordingly all experience hath shown, that mankind are more disposed to suffer, while evils are sufferable, than to right themselves by abolishing the forms to which they are accustomed. But when a long train of abuses and **usurpations,** pursuing invariably the same Object evinces a design to reduce them under absolute **Despotism**, it is their right, it is their duty, to throw off such Government, and to provide new Guards for their future security.

[List of Grievances]

Such has been the patient sufferance of these Colonies; and such is now the necessity which constrains them to alter their former Systems of Government. The history of the present King of Great Britain is a history of repeated injuries and usurpations, all having in direct object the establishment of an absolute Tyranny over these States. To prove this, let Facts be submitted to a candid world.

Words are spelled as originally written.

The Preamble The Declaration of Independence has four parts. The Preamble explains why the Continental Congress drew up the Declaration.

impel: force

Natural Rights The second part, the Declaration of Natural Rights, lists the rights of the citizens. It goes on to explain that, in a republic, people form a government to protect their rights.

endowed: provided

usurpations: unjust uses of power

despotism: unlimited power

List of Grievances The third part of the Declaration lists the colonists' complaints against the British government. Notice that King George III is singled out for blame.

Getty Images

He has refused his Assent to Laws, the most wholesome and necessary for the public good.

He has forbidden his Governors to pass Laws of immediate and pressing importance, unless suspended in their operation till his Assent should be obtained; and when so suspended, he has utterly neglected to attend to them.

He has refused to pass other Laws for the accommodation of large districts of people, unless those people would **relinquish** the right of Representation in the Legislature, a right **inestimable** to them and formidable to tyrants only.

He has called together legislative bodies at places unusual, uncomfortable, and distant from the depository of their Public Records, for the sole purpose of fatiguing them into compliance with his measures.

He has dissolved Representative Houses repeatedly, for opposing with manly firmness his invasions on the rights of the people.

He has refused for a long time, after such dissolutions, to cause others to be elected; whereby the Legislative Powers, incapable of **Annihilation**, have returned to the People at large for their exercise; the State remaining in the mean time exposed to all the dangers of invasion from without, and **convulsions** within.

He has endeavoured to prevent the population of these States; for that purpose obstructing the **Laws for Naturalization of Foreigners;** refusing to pass others to encourage their migrations hither, and raising the conditions of new Appropriations of Lands.

He has obstructed the Administration of Justice, by refusing his Assent to Laws for establishing Judiciary Powers.

He has made Judges dependent on his Will alone, for the **tenure** of their offices, and the amount and payment of their salaries.

He has erected a multitude of New Offices, and sent hither swarms of Officers to harass our people, and eat out their substance.

He has kept among us, in times of peace, Standing Armies without the Consent of our legislature.

He has affected to render the Military independent of and superior to the Civil Power.

He has combined with others to subject us to a jurisdiction foreign to our constitution, and unacknowledged by our laws; giving his Assent to their acts of pretended legislation: For **quartering** large bodies of troops among us:

relinquish: give up
inestimable: priceless

annihilation: destruction

convulsions: violent disturbances

Laws for Naturalization of Foreigners: process by which foreign-born persons become citizens

tenure: term

quartering: lodging

For protecting them, by a mock Trial, from Punishment for any Murders which they should commit on the Inhabitants of these States:

For cutting off our Trade with all parts of the world:

For imposing taxes on us without our Consent:

For depriving us in many cases, of the benefits of Trial by Jury:

For transporting us beyond Seas to be tried for pretended offences:

For abolishing the free System of English Laws in a neighbouring Province, establishing therein an Arbitrary government, and enlarging its Boundaries so as to **render** it at once an example and fit instrument for introducing the same absolute rule into these Colonies:

render: make

For taking away our Charters, abolishing our most valuable Laws, and altering fundamentally the Forms of our Governments:

For suspending our own Legislature, and declaring themselves invested with Power to legislate for us in all cases whatsoever.

He has **abdicated** Government here, by declaring us out of his Protection and waging War against us.

abdicated: given up

He has plundered our seas, ravaged our Coasts, burnt our towns, and destroyed the lives of our people.

He is at this time transporting large armies of foreign mercenaries to compleat the works of death, desolation and tyranny, already begun with circumstances of Cruelty & **perfidy** scarcely paralleled in the most barbarous ages, and totally unworthy the Head of a civilized nation.

perfidy: violation of trust

He has constrained our fellow Citizens taken Captive on the high Seas to bear Arms against their Country, to become the executioners of their friends and Brethren, or to fall themselves by their Hands.

He has excited domestic **insurrections** amongst us, and has endeavoured to bring on the inhabitants of our frontiers, the merciless Indian Savages, whose known rule of warfare, is an undistinguished destruction of all ages, sexes and conditions.

insurrections: rebellions

In every stage of these Oppressions We have **Petitioned for Redress** in the most humble terms: Our repeated Petitions have been answered only by repeated injury. A Prince, whose character is thus marked by every act which may define a Tyrant, is unfit to be the ruler of a free People.

petitioned for redress: asked formally for a correction of wrongs

Nor have We been wanting in attention to our British brethren. We have warned them from time to time of attempts by their legislature to extend an **unwarrantable jurisdiction** over us. We have reminded them of the circumstances of our emigration and settlement here. We have appealed to their native justice and magnanimity, and we have conjured them by the ties of our common kindred to disavow these usurpations, which, would inevitably interrupt our connections and correspondence. They too have been deaf to the voice of justice and of **consanguinity**.

unwarrantable jurisdiction: unjustified authority

consanguinity: originating from the same ancestor

We must, therefore, acquiesce in the necessity, which denounces our Separation, and hold them, as we hold the rest of mankind, Enemies in War, in Peace Friends.

[Resolution of Independence by the United States]

We, therefore, the Representatives of the united States of America, in General Congress, Assembled, appealing to the Supreme Judge of the world for the **rectitude** of our intentions, do, in the Name, and by Authority of the good People of these Colonies, solemnly publish and declare, That these United Colonies are, and of Right ought to be Free and Independent States; that they are Absolved from all Allegiance to the British Crown, and that all political connection between them and the State of Great Britain, is and ought to be totally dissolved; and that as Free and Independent States, they have full Power to levy War, conclude Peace, contract Alliances, establish Commerce, and to do all other Acts and Things which Independent States may of right do.

And for the support of this Declaration, with a firm reliance on the Protection of Divine Providence, we mutually pledge to each other our Lives, our Fortunes and our sacred Honor.

Resolution of Independence The final section declares that the colonies are "Free and Independent States" with the full power to make war, to form alliances, and to trade with other countries.

rectitude: rightness

Signers of the Declaration The signers, as representatives of the American people, declared the colonies independent from Great Britain. Most members signed the document on August 2, 1776.

John Hancock
    President from
    Massachusetts

Georgia
Button Gwinnett
Lyman Hall
George Walton

North Carolina
William Hooper
Joseph Hewes
John Penn

South Carolina
Edward Rutledge
Thomas Heyward, Jr.
Thomas Lynch, Jr.
Arthur Middleton

Maryland
Samuel Chase
William Paca
Thomas Stone
Charles Carroll
    of Carrollton

Virginia
George Wythe
Richard Henry Lee
Thomas Jefferson
Benjamin Harrison
Thomas Nelson, Jr.
Francis Lightfoot Lee
Carter Braxton

Pennsylvania
Robert Morris
Benjamin Rush
Benjamin Franklin
John Morton
George Clymer
James Smith
George Taylor
James Wilson
George Ross

Delaware
Caesar Rodney
George Read
Thomas McKean

New York
William Floyd
Philip Livingston
Francis Lewis
Lewis Morris

New Jersey
Richard Stockton
John Witherspoon
Francis Hopkinson
John Hart
Abraham Clark

New Hampshire
Josiah Bartlett
William Whipple
Matthew Thornton

Massachusetts
Samuel Adams
John Adams
Robert Treat Paine
Elbridge Gerry

Rhode Island
Stephen Hopkins
William Ellery

Connecticut
Samuel Huntington
William Williams
Oliver Wolcott
Roger Sherman

Bettmann/CORBIS

THE CONSTITUTION
of the UNITED STATES

The Constitution of the United States is truly a remarkable document. It was one of the first written constitutions in modern history. The Framers wanted to devise a plan for a strong central government that would unify the country, as well as preserve the ideals of the Declaration of Independence.

The entire text of the Constitution and its amendments follows. For easier study, those passages that have been set aside or changed by the adoption of amendments are printed in blue. Also included are explanatory notes that will help clarify the meaning of each article and section.

The Preamble introduces the Constitution and sets forth the general purposes for which the government was established. The Preamble also declares that the power of the government comes from the people.

The printed text of the document shows the spelling and punctuation of the parchment original.

Article I. The Legislative Branch
The Constitution contains seven divisions called articles. Each article covers a general topic. For example, Articles I, II, and III create the three branches of the national government—the legislative, executive, and judicial branches. Most of the articles are divided into sections.

Representation The number of representatives from each state is based on the size of the state's population. Each state is entitled to at least one representative. *What are the qualifications for members of the House of Representatives?*

Vocabulary

preamble: introduction
constitution: principles and laws of a nation
enumeration: census or population count

Preamble

We the People of the United States, in Order to form a more perfect Union, establish Justice, insure domestic Tranquility, provide for the common defence, promote the general Welfare, and secure the Blessings of Liberty to ourselves and our Posterity, do ordain and establish this **Constitution** for the United States of America.

Article I

Section 1

All legislative Powers herein granted shall be vested in a Congress of the United States, which shall consist of a Senate and House of Representatives.

Section 2

[1.] The House of Representatives shall be composed of Members chosen every second Year by the People of the several States, and the Electors in each State shall have the Qualifications requisite for Electors of the most numerous Branch of the State Legislature.

[2.] No person shall be a Representative who shall not have attained the Age of twenty five Years, and been seven Years a Citizen of the United States, and who shall not, when elected, be an Inhabitant of that State in which he shall be chosen.

[3.] Representatives and direct Taxes shall be apportioned among the several States which may be included within this Union, according to their respective Numbers, which shall be determined by adding to the whole Number of free Persons, including those bound to Service for a Term of Years, and excluding Indians not taxed, three fifths of all other Persons. The actual **Enumeration** shall be made within three Years after the first Meeting of the Congress of the United States, and within every subsequent Term of ten Years, in such Manner as they shall by Law direct. The Number of Representatives shall not exceed one for every thirty Thousand, but each State shall have at Least one Representative; and until such enumeration shall be made, the State of New Hampshire shall be entitled to chuse three; Massachusetts eight, Rhode-Island and Providence Plantations one, Connecticut five, New-York six, New Jersey four, Pennsylvania eight, Delaware one, Maryland six, Virginia ten, North Carolina five, South Carolina five, and Georgia three.

[4.] When vacancies happen in the Representation from any State, the Executive Authority thereof shall issue Writs of Election to fill such Vacancies.

[5.] The House of Representatives shall chuse their Speaker and other Officers; and shall have the sole Power of **Impeachment**.

Section 3

[1.] The Senate of the United States shall be composed of two Senators from each State, chosen by the Legislature thereof, for six Years; and each Senator shall have one Vote.

[2.] Immediately after they shall be assembled in Consequence of the first Election, they shall be divided as equally as may be into three Classes. The Seats of the Senators of the first Class shall be vacated at the Expiration of the second Year, of the second Class at the Expiration of the fourth Year, and of the third Class at the Expiration of the sixth Year, so that one third may be chosen every second Year; and if Vacancies happen by Resignation, or otherwise, during the Recess of the Legislature of any State, the Executive thereof may make temporary Appointments until the next Meeting of the Legislature, which shall then fill such Vacancies.

[3.] No Person shall be a Senator who shall not have attained to the Age of thirty Years, and been nine Years a Citizen of the United States, and who shall not, when elected, be an Inhabitant of that State for which he shall be chosen.

[4.] The Vice President of the United States shall be President of the Senate, but shall have no Vote, unless they be equally divided.

[5.] The Senate shall chuse their other Officers, and also a **President pro tempore**, in the Absence of the Vice President, or when he shall exercise the Office of the President of the United States.

[6.] The Senate shall have the sole Power to try all Impeachments. When sitting for that Purpose, they shall be on Oath or Affirmation. When the President of the United States is tried, the Chief Justice shall preside: And no Person shall be convicted without the Concurrence of two thirds of the Members present.

[7.] Judgment in Cases of Impeachment shall not extend further than to removal from Office, and disqualification to hold and enjoy any Office of honor, Trust or Profit under the United States: but the Party convicted shall nevertheless be liable and subject to **Indictment**, Trial, Judgment and Punishment, according to Law.

Electing Senators Originally, senators were chosen by the state legislators of their own states. The Seventeenth Amendment changed this, so that senators are now elected by the people. There are 100 senators, 2 from each state. The vice president serves as president of the Senate.

Impeachment One of Congress's powers is the power to impeach—to accuse government officials of wrongdoing, put them on trial, and if necessary remove them from office. *Which body has the power to decide the official's guilt or innocence?*

Vocabulary

impeachment: bringing charges against an official

president pro tempore: presiding officer of Senate who serves when the vice president is absent

indictment: charging a person with an offense

Section 4

[1.] The Times, Places and Manner of holding Elections for Senators and Representatives, shall be prescribed in each State by the Legislature thereof; but the Congress may at any time by Law make or alter such Regulations, except as to the Places of chusing Senators.

[2.] The Congress shall assemble at least once in every Year, and such Meeting shall be on the first Monday in December, unless they shall by Law appoint a different Day.

Section 5

[1.] Each House shall be the Judge of the Elections, Returns and Qualifications of its own Members, and a Majority of each shall constitute a **Quorum** to do Business; but a smaller Number may **adjourn** from day to day, and may be authorized to compel the Attendance of absent Members, in such Manner, and under such Penalties as each House may provide.

[2.] Each House may determine the Rules of its Proceedings, punish its Members for disorderly Behaviour, and, with the Concurrence of two thirds, expel a Member.

[3.] Each House shall keep a Journal of its Proceedings, and from time to time publish the same, excepting such Parts as may in their Judgment require Secrecy; and the Yeas and Nays of the Members of either House on any question shall, at the Desire of one fifth of those Present, be entered on the Journal.

[4.] Neither House, during the Session of Congress, shall, without the Consent of the other, adjourn for more than three days, nor to any other Place than that in which the two Houses shall be sitting.

Section 6

[1.] The Senators and Representatives shall receive a Compensation for their Services, to be ascertained by Law, and paid out of the Treasury of the United States. They shall in all Cases, except Treason, Felony and Breach of the Peace, be privileged from Arrest during their Attendance at the Session of their respective Houses, and in going to and returning from the same; and for any Speech or Debate in either House, they shall not be questioned in any other Place.

[2.] No Senator or Representative shall, during the Time for which he was elected, be appointed to any civil Office under the Authority of the United States, which shall have been created, or the **Emoluments** whereof shall have been encreased during such time; and no Person holding any Office under the United States, shall be a Member of either House during his Continuance in Office.

Congressional Salaries To strengthen the federal government, the Founders set congressional salaries to be paid by the United States Treasury rather than by members' respective states. Originally, members were paid $6 per day. In 2006, all members of Congress received a base salary of $165,200.

Vocabulary

quorum: minimum number of members that must be present to conduct sessions

adjourn: to suspend a session

emoluments: salaries

Section 7

[1.] All **Bills** for raising **Revenue** shall originate in the House of Representatives; but the Senate may propose or concur with Amendments as on other Bills.

[2.] Every Bill which shall have passed the House of Representatives and the Senate, shall, before it become a Law, be presented to the President of the United States; If he approve he shall sign it, but if not he shall return it, with his Objections to that House in which it shall have originated, who shall enter the Objections at large on their Journal, and proceed to reconsider it. If after such Reconsideration two thirds of that House shall agree to pass the Bill, it shall be sent, together with the Objections, to the other House, by which it shall likewise be reconsidered, and if approved by two thirds of that House, it shall become a Law. But in all such Cases the Votes of both Houses shall be determined by yeas and Nays, and the Names of the Persons voting for and against the Bill shall be entered on the Journal of each House respectively. If any Bill shall not be returned by the President within ten Days (Sundays excepted) after it shall have been presented to him, the Same shall be a Law, in like Manner as if he had signed it, unless the Congress by their Adjournment prevent its Return, in which Case it shall not be a Law.

[3.] Every Order, **Resolution**, or Vote to which the Concurrence of the Senate and House of Representatives may be necessary (except on a question of Adjournment) shall be presented to the President of the United States; and before the Same shall take Effect, shall be approved by him, or being disapproved by him, shall be repassed by two thirds of the Senate and House of Representatives, according to the Rules and Limitations prescribed in the Case of a Bill.

Section 8

[1.] The Congress shall have the Power To lay and collect Taxes, Duties, **Imposts** and Excises, to pay the Debts and provide for the common Defence and general Welfare of the United States; but all Duties, Imposts and Excises shall be uniform throughout the United States;

[2.] To borrow Money on the credit of the United States;

[3.] To regulate Commerce with foreign Nations, and among the several States, and with the Indian Tribes;

[4.] To establish an uniform Rule of **Naturalization**, and uniform Laws on the subject of Bankruptcies throughout the United States;

[5.] To coin Money, regulate the Value thereof, and of foreign Coin, and fix the Standard of Weights and Measures;

[6.] To provide for the Punishment of counterfeiting the Securities and current Coin of the United States;

[7.] To establish Post Offices and post Roads;

Where Tax Laws Begin All tax laws must originate in the House of Representatives. This ensures that the branch of Congress that is elected by the people every two years has the major role in determining taxes.

How Bills Become Laws A bill may become a law only by passing both houses of Congress and by being signed by the president. The president can check Congress by rejecting—vetoing—its legislation. *How can Congress override the president's veto?*

Powers of Congress Expressed powers are those powers directly stated in the Constitution. Most of the expressed powers of Congress are listed in Article I, Section 8. These powers are also called enumerated powers because they are numbered 1–18. *Which clause gives Congress the power to declare war?*

Vocabulary

bill: draft of a proposed law

revenue: income raised by government

resolution: legislature's formal expression of opinion

impost: tax

naturalization: procedure by which a citizen of a foreign nation becomes a citizen of the United States.

Elastic Clause

Elastic Clause The final enumerated power is often called the "elastic clause." This clause gives Congress the right to make all laws "necessary and proper" to carry out the powers expressed in the other clauses of **Article I.** It is called the elastic clause because it lets Congress "stretch" its powers to meet situations the Founders could never have anticipated.

What does the phrase **"necessary and proper"** in the elastic clause mean? Almost from the beginning, this phrase was a subject of dispute. The issue was whether a strict or a broad interpretation of the Constitution should be applied. The dispute was first addressed in 1819, in the case of *McCulloch* v. *Maryland*, when the Supreme Court ruled in favor of a broad interpretation.

Habeas Corpus A writ of habeas corpus issued by a judge requires a law official to bring a prisoner to court and show cause for holding the prisoner. A bill of attainder is a bill that punished a person without a jury trial. An "ex post facto" law is one that makes an act a crime after the act has been committed. *What does the Constitution say about bills of attainder?*

Vocabulary

tribunal: a court
insurrection: rebellion

[8.] To promote the Progress of Science and useful Arts, by securing for limited Times to Authors and Inventors the exclusive Right to their respective Writings and Discoveries;

[9.] To constitute **Tribunals** inferior to the supreme Court;

[10.] To define and punish Piracies and Felonies committed on the high Seas, and Offences against the Law of Nations;

[11.] To declare War, grant Letters of Marque and Reprisal, and make Rules concerning Captures on Land and Water;

[12.] To raise and support Armies, but no Appropriation of Money to that Use shall be for a longer Term than two Years;

[13.] To provide and maintain a Navy;

[14.] To make Rules for the Government and Regulation of the land and naval Forces;

[15.] To provide for calling forth the Militia to execute the Laws of the Union, suppress **Insurrections** and repel Invasions;

[16.] To provide for organizing, arming, and disciplining, the Militia, and for governing such Part of them as may be employed in the Service of the United States, reserving to the States respectively, the Appointment of the Officers, and the Authority of training the Militia according to the discipline prescribed by Congress;

[17.] To exercise exclusive Legislation in all Cases whatsoever, over such District (not exceeding ten Miles square) as may, by Cession of particular States, and the Acceptance of Congress, become the Seat of Government of the United States, and to exercise like Authority over all Places purchased by the Consent of the Legislature of the State in which the Same shall be, for the Erection of Forts, Magazines, Arsenals, dock-Yards, and other needful Buildings, —And

[18.] To make all Laws which shall be necessary and proper for carrying into Execution the foregoing Powers, and all other Powers vested by this Constitution in the Government of the United States, or in any Department or Officer thereof.

Section 9

[1.] The Migration or Importation of such Persons as any of the States now existing shall think proper to admit, shall not be prohibited by the Congress prior to the Year one thousand eight hundred and eight, but a Tax or duty may be imposed on such Importation, not exceeding ten dollars for each Person.

[2.] The Privilege of the Writ of Habeas Corpus shall not be suspended, unless when in Cases of Rebellion or Invasion the public Safety may require it.

[3.] No Bill of Attainder or ex post facto Law shall be passed.

[4.] No Capitation, or other direct, Tax shall be laid, unless in Proportion to the Census or Enumeration herein before directed to be taken.

[5.] No Tax or Duty shall be laid on Articles exported from any State.

[6.] No Preference shall be given by any Regulation of Commerce or Revenue to the Ports of one State over those of another: nor shall Vessels bound to, or from, one State, be obliged to enter, clear, or pay Duties in another.

[7.] No Money shall be drawn from the Treasury, but in Consequence of **Appropriations** made by Law; and a regular Statement and Account of the Receipts and Expenditures of all public Money shall be published from time to time.

[8.] No Title of Nobility shall be granted by the United States: And no Person holding any Office of Profit or Trust under them, shall, without the Consent of the Congress, accept of any present, Emolument, Office, or Title, of any kind whatever, from any King, Prince, or foreign State.

Section 10

[1.] No State shall enter into any Treaty, Alliance, or Confederation; grant Letters of Marque and Reprisal; coin Money; emit Bills of Credit; make any Thing but gold and silver Coin a Tender in Payment of Debts; pass any Bill of Attainder, ex post facto Law, or Law impairing the Obligation of Contracts, or grant any Title of Nobility.

[2.] No State shall, without the Consent of the Congress, lay any Imposts or Duties on Imports or Exports, except what may be absolutely necessary for executing its inspection Laws: and the net Produce of all Duties and Imposts, laid by any State on Imports and Exports, shall be for the Use of the Treasury of the United States; and all such Laws shall be subject to the Revision and Controul of the Congress.

[3.] No State shall, without the Consent of Congress, lay any Duty of Tonnage, keep Troops, or Ships of War in time of Peace, enter into any Agreement or Compact with another State, or with a foreign Power, or engage in War, unless actually invaded, or in such imminent Danger as will not admit of delay.

Article II

Section 1

[1.] The executive Power shall be vested in a President of the United States of America. He shall hold his Office during the Term of four Years, and, together with the Vice President, chosen for the same Term, be elected, as follows.

[2.] Each State shall appoint, in such Manner as the Legislature thereof may direct, a Number of Electors, equal to the whole Number of Senators and Representatives to which the State may be entitled in the Congress: but no Senator or Representative, or Person holding an Office of Trust or Profit under the United States, shall be appointed an Elector.

Limitations on the States Section 10 lists limits on the states. These restrictions were designed, in part, to prevent an overlapping in functions and authority with the federal government.

Article II. The Executive Branch Article II creates an executive branch to carry out laws passed by Congress. Article II lists the powers and duties of the presidency, describes qualifications for office and procedures for electing the president, and provides for a vice president.

Vocabulary

appropriations: funds set aside for a specific use

Previous Elections The Twelfth Amendment, added in 1804, changed the method of electing the president stated in Article II, Section 3. The Twelfth Amendment requires that the electors cast separate ballots for president and vice president.

Qualifications The president must be a citizen of the United States by birth, at least 35 years of age, and a resident of the United States for 14 years.

Vacancies If the president dies, resigns, is removed from office by impeachment, or is unable to carry out the duties of the office, the vice president becomes president. The Twenty-fifth Amendment sets procedures for presidential succession.

Salary Originally, the president's salary was $25,000 per year. The president's current salary is $400,000 plus a $50,000 nontaxable expense account per year. The president also receives living accommodations in two residences—the White House and Camp David.

[3.] The Electors shall meet in their respective States, and vote by Ballot for two Persons, of whom one at least shall not be an Inhabitant of the same State with themselves. And they shall make a List of all the Persons voted for, and of the Number of Votes for each; which List they shall sign and certify, and transmit sealed to the Seat of the Government of the United States, directed to the President of the Senate. The President of the Senate shall, in the Presence of the Senate and House of Representatives, open all the Certificates, and the Votes shall then be counted. The Person having the greatest Number of Votes shall be the President, if such Number be a Majority of the whole Number of Electors appointed; and if there be more than one who have such Majority, and have an equal Number of Votes, then the House of Representatives shall immediately chuse by Ballot one of them for President; and if no person have a Majority, then from the five highest on the List the said House shall in like Manner chuse the President. But in chusing the President, the Votes shall be taken by States, the Representation from each State having one Vote; A quorum for this Purpose shall consist of a Member or Members from two thirds of the States, and a Majority of all the States shall be necessary to a Choice. In every Case, after the Choice of the President, the Person having the greatest Number of Votes of the Electors shall be the Vice President. But if there should remain two or more who have equal Votes, the Senate shall chuse from them by Ballot the Vice President.

[4.] The Congress may determine the Time of chusing the Electors, and the Day on which they shall give their Votes; which Day shall be the same throughout the United States.

[5.] No Person except a natural born Citizen, or a Citizen of the United States, at the time of the Adoption of this Constitution, shall be eligible to the Office of President; neither shall any Person be eligible to that Office who shall not have attained to the Age of thirty five Years, and been fourteen Years a Resident within the United States.

[6.] In Case of the Removal of the President from Office, or of his Death, Resignation, or Inability to discharge the Powers and Duties of the said Office, the Same shall devolve on the Vice President, and the Congress may by Law provide for the Case of Removal, Death, Resignation or Inability, both of the President and Vice President, declaring what Officer shall then act as President, and such Officer shall act accordingly, until the Disability be removed, or a President shall be elected.

[7.] The President shall, at stated Times, receive for his Services, a Compensation, which shall neither be encreased nor diminished during the Period for which he shall have been elected, and he shall not receive within that Period any other Emolument from the United States, or any of them.

[8.] Before he enter on the Execution of his Office, he shall take the following Oath or Affirmation:—"I do solemnly swear (or affirm) that I will faithfully execute the Office of President of the United States, and will to the best of my Ability, preserve, protect and defend the Constitution of the United States."

Section 2

[1.] The President shall be Commander in Chief of the Army and Navy of the United States, and of the Militia of the several States, when called into the actual Service of the United States; he may require the Opinion, in writing, of the principal Officer in each of the executive Departments, upon any Subject relating to the Duties of their respective Offices, and he shall have Power to grant Reprieves and Pardons for Offences against the United States, except in Cases of Impeachment.

[2.] He shall have Power, by and with the Advice and Consent of the Senate, to make Treaties, provided two thirds of the Senators present concur; and he shall nominate, and by and with the Advice and Consent of the Senate, shall appoint Ambassadors, other public Ministers and Consuls, Judges of the supreme Court, and all other Officers of the United States, whose Appointments are not herein otherwise provided for, and which shall be established by Law: but the Congress may by Law vest the Appointment of such inferior Officers, as they think proper, in the President alone, in the Courts of Law, or in the Heads of Departments.

[3.] The President shall have Power to fill up all Vacancies that may happen during the Recess of the Senate, by granting Commissions which shall expire at the End of their next Session.

Section 3

He shall from time to time give to the Congress Information of the State of the Union, and recommend to their Consideration such Measures as he shall judge necessary and expedient; he may, on extraordinary Occasions, convene both Houses, or either of them, and in Case of Disagreement between them, with Respect to the Time of Adjournment, he may adjourn them to such Time as he shall think proper; he shall receive Ambassadors and other public Ministers; he shall take Care that the Laws be faithfully executed, and shall Commission all the Officers of the United States.

The Cabinet Mention of "the principal officer in each of the executive departments" is the only suggestion of the president's cabinet to be found in the Constitution. The cabinet is an advisory body, and its power depends on the president. Section 2, Clause 1 also makes the president—a civilian—the head of the armed services. This established the principle of civilian control of the military.

Presidential Powers An executive order is a command issued by a president to exercise a power which he or she has been given by the U.S. Constitution or by a federal statute. In times of emergency, presidents sometimes have used the executive order to override the Constitution and Congress. During the Civil War, President Lincoln suspended many fundamental rights, such as closing down newspapers that opposed his policies and imprisoning people who disagreed with him. Lincoln said that these actions were justified to preserve the Union.

Article III. The Judicial Branch The term judicial refers to courts. The Constitution set up only the Supreme Court, but provided for the establishment of other federal courts. The judiciary of the United States has two different systems of courts. One system consists of the federal courts, whose powers derive from the Constitution and federal laws. The other includes the courts of each of the 50 states, whose powers derive from state constitutions and laws.

Statute Law Federal courts deal mostly with "statute law," or laws passed by Congress, treaties, and cases involving the Constitution itself.

The Supreme Court A Court with "original jurisdiction" has the authority to be the first court to hear a case. The Supreme Court has "appellate jurisdiction" and mostly hears cases appealed from lower courts.

Vocabulary

original jurisdiction: authority to be the first court to hear a case

appellate jurisdiction: authority to hear cases that have been appealed from lower courts

Section 4

The President, Vice President and all civil Officers of the United States, shall be removed from Office on Impeachment for, and Conviction of, Treason, Bribery, or other high Crimes and Misdemeanors.

Article III

Section 1

The judicial Power of the United States, shall be vested in one supreme Court, and in such inferior Courts as the Congress may from time to time ordain and establish. The Judges, both of the supreme and inferior Courts, shall hold their Offices during good Behaviour, and shall, at stated Times, receive for their Services, a Compensation, which shall not be diminished during their Continuance in Office.

Section 2

[1.] The judicial Power shall extend to all Cases, in Law and Equity, arising under this Constitution, the Laws of the United States, and Treaties made, or which shall be made, under their Authority;—to all Cases affecting Ambassadors, other public Ministers and Consuls;—to all Cases of admiralty and maritime Jurisdiction;—to Controversies to which the United States shall be a Party;—to Controversies between two or more States;—between a State and Citizens of another State;—between Citizens of different States,— between Citizens of the same State claiming Lands under Grants of different States, and between a State, or the Citizens thereof, and foreign States, Citizens or Subjects.

[2.] In all Cases affecting Ambassadors, other public Ministers and Consuls, and those in which a State shall be Party, the supreme Court shall have **original Jurisdiction**. In all the other Cases before mentioned, the supreme Court shall have **appellate Jurisdiction**, both as to Law and Fact, with such Exceptions, and under such Regulations as the Congress shall make.

[3.] The Trial of all Crimes, except in Cases of Impeachment, shall be by Jury; and such Trial shall be held in the State where the said Crimes shall have been committed; but when not committed within any State, the Trial shall be at such Place or Places as the Congress may by Law have directed.

Section 3

[1.] **Treason** against the United States, shall consist only in levying War against them, or in adhering to their Enemies, giving them Aid and Comfort. No Person shall be convicted of Treason unless on the Testimony of two Witnesses to the same overt Act, or on Confession in open Court.

[2.] The Congress shall have Power to declare the Punishment of Treason, but no Attainder of Treason shall work Corruption of Blood, or Forfeiture except during the Life of the Person attainted.

Article IV
Section 1

Full Faith and Credit shall be given in each State to the public Acts, Records, and judicial Proceedings of every other State. And the Congress may by general Laws prescribe the Manner in which such Acts, Records and Proceedings shall be proved, and the Effect thereof.

Section 2

[1.] The Citizens of each State shall be entitled to all Privileges and Immunities of Citizens in the several States.

[2.] A Person charged in any State with Treason, Felony, or other Crime, who shall flee from Justice, and be found in another State, shall on Demand of the executive Authority of the State from which he fled, be delivered up, to be removed to the State having Jurisdiction of the Crime.

[3.] No Person held to Service of Labour in one State, under the Laws thereof, escaping into another, shall, in Consequence of any Law or Regulation therein, be discharged from such Service or Labour, but shall be delivered up on Claim of the Party to whom such Service or Labour may be due.

Section 3

[1.] New States may be admitted by the Congress into this Union; but no new State shall be formed or erected within the Jurisdiction of any other State; nor any State be formed by the Junction of two or more States, or Parts of States, without the Consent of the Legislatures of the States concerned as well as of the Congress.

[2.] The Congress shall have Power to dispose of and make all needful Rules and Regulations respecting the Territory or other Property belonging to the United States; and nothing in this Constitution shall be so construed as to Prejudice any Claims of the United States, or of any particular State.

Article IV. Relations Among the States Article IV explains the relationship of the states to one another and to the national government. This article requires each state to give citizens of other states the same rights as its own citizens, addresses admitting new states, and guarantees that the national government will protect the states.

New States Congress has the power to admit new states. It also determines the basic guidelines for applying for statehood. Two states, Maine and West Virginia, were created within the boundaries of another state. In the case of West Virginia, President Lincoln recognized the West Virginia government as the legal government of Virginia during the Civil War. This allowed West Virginia to secede from Virginia without obtaining approval from the Virginia legislature.

Vocabulary

treason: violation of the allegiance owed by a person to his or her own country, for example, by aiding an enemy

Republic Government can be classified in many different ways. The ancient Greek philosopher Aristotle classified government based on the question "who governs?" According to Aristotle, all governments belong to one of three major groups: (1) autocracy—rule by one person; (2) oligarchy—rule by a few persons; or (3) democracy—rule by many persons. A republic is a form of democracy in which the people elect representatives to make the laws and conduct government.

Article V. The Amendment Process Article V spells out the ways that the Constitution can be amended, or changed. All of the 27 amendments were proposed by a two-thirds vote of both houses of Congress. Only the Twenty-first Amendment was ratified by constitutional conventions of the states. All other amendments have been ratified by state legislatures. *What is an amendment?*

Article VI. National Supremacy Article VI contains the "supremacy clause." This clause establishes that the Constitution, laws passed by Congress, and treaties of the United States "shall be the supreme Law of the Land." The "supremacy clause" recognized the Constitution and federal laws as supreme when in conflict with those of the states.

Section 4

The United States shall guarantee to every State in this Union a Republican Form of Government, and shall protect each of them against Invasion; and on Application of the Legislature, or of the Executive (when the Legislature cannot be convened) against domestic Violence.

Article V

The Congress, whenever two thirds of both Houses shall deem it necessary, shall propose **Amendments** to this Constitution, or, on the Application of the Legislatures of two thirds of the several States, shall call a Convention for proposing Amendments, which, in either Case, shall be valid to all Intents and Purposes, as Part of this Constitution, when ratified by the Legislatures of three fourths of the several States, or by Conventions in three fourths thereof, as the one or the other Mode of **Ratification** may be proposed by the Congress; Provided that no Amendment which may be made prior to the Year One thousand eight hundred and eight shall in any Manner affect the first and fourth Clauses in the Ninth Section of the first Article; and that no State, without its Consent, shall be deprived of its equal Suffrage in the Senate.

Article VI

[**1.**] All Debts contracted and Engagements entered into, before the Adoption of this Constitution, shall be as valid against the United States under this Constitution, as under the Confederation.

[**2.**] This Constitution, and the Laws of the United States which shall be made in Pursuance thereof; and all Treaties made, or which shall be made, under the Authority of the United States, shall be the supreme Law of the Land; and the Judges in every State shall be bound thereby, any Thing in the Constitution or Laws of any State to the Contrary notwithstanding.

[**3.**] The Senators and Representatives before mentioned, and the Members of the several State Legislatures, and all executive and judicial Officers, both of the United States and of the several States, shall be bound by Oath or Affirmation, to support this Constitution; but no religious Test shall ever be required as a Qualification to any Office or public Trust under the United States.

Vocabulary

amendment: a change to the Constitution

ratification: process by which an amendment is approved

Article VII

The Ratification of the Conventions of nine States, shall be sufficient for the Establishment of this Constitution between the States so ratifying the Same.

Done in Convention by the Unanimous Consent of the States present the Seventeenth Day of September in the Year of our Lord one thousand seven hundred and Eighty seven and of the Independence of the United States of America the Twelfth. In witness whereof We have hereunto subscribed our Names,

Article VII. Ratification Article VII addresses ratification and declares that the Constitution would take effect after it was ratified by nine states.

Signers

George Washington, President and Deputy from Virginia

New Hampshire
John Langdon
Nicholas Gilman

Massachusetts
Nathaniel Gorham
Rufus King

Connecticut
William Samuel Johnson
Roger Sherman

New York
Alexander Hamilton

New Jersey
William Livingston
David Brearley
William Paterson
Jonathan Dayton

Pennsylvania
Benjamin Franklin
Thomas Mifflin
Robert Morris
George Clymer
Thomas FitzSimons
Jared Ingersoll
James Wilson
Gouverneur Morris

Delaware
George Read
Gunning Bedford, Jr.
John Dickinson
Richard Bassett
Jacob Broom

Maryland
James McHenry
Daniel of St. Thomas Jenifer
Daniel Carroll

Virginia
John Blair
James Madison, Jr.

North Carolina
William Blount
Richard Dobbs Spaight
Hugh Williamson

South Carolina
John Rutledge
Charles Cotesworth Pinckney
Charles Pinckney
Pierce Butler

Georgia
William Few
Abraham Baldwin

Attest: William Jackson, **Secretary**

Bill of Rights The first 10 amendments are known as the Bill of Rights (1791). These amendments limit the powers of government. The First Amendment protects the civil liberties of individuals in the United States. The amendment freedoms are not absolute, however. They are limited by the rights of other individuals. *What freedoms does the First Amendment protect?*

Amendment I

Congress shall make no law respecting an establishment of religion, or prohibiting the free exercise thereof; or abridging the freedom of speech, or of the press; or the right of the people peaceably to assemble, and to petition the Government for a redress of grievances.

Amendment II

A well regulated Militia, being necessary to the security of a free State, the right of the people to keep and bear Arms, shall not be infringed.

Amendment III

No Soldier shall, in time of peace be **quartered** in any house, without the consent of the Owner, nor in time of war, but in a manner to be prescribed by law.

Amendment IV

The right of the people to be secure in their persons, houses, papers, and effects, against unreasonable searches and seizures, shall not be violated, and no **Warrants** shall issue, but upon **probable cause**, supported by Oath or affirmation, and particularly describing the place, to be searched, and the persons or things to be seized.

Rights of the Accused This amendment contains important protections for people accused of crimes. One of the protections is that government may not deprive any person of life, liberty, or property without due process of law. This means that the government must follow proper constitutional procedures in trials and in other actions it takes against individuals. *According to Amendment V, what is the function of a grand jury?*

Amendment V

No person shall be held to answer for a capital, or otherwise infamous crime, unless on a presentment or indictment of a Grand Jury, except in cases arising in the land or naval forces, or in the Militia, when in actual service in time of War or public danger; nor shall any person be subject for the same offence to be twice put in jeopardy of life or limb; nor shall be compelled in any criminal case to be a witness against himself, nor be deprived of life, liberty, or property, without due process of law; nor shall private property be taken for public use without just compensation.

Vocabulary

quarter: to provide living accommodations

warrant: document that gives police particular rights or powers

probable cause: a reasonable basis to believe a person is linked to a crime

common law: law established by previous court decisions

bail: money that an accused person provides to the court as a guarantee that he or she will be present for a trial

Amendment VI

In all criminal prosecutions, the accused shall enjoy the right to a speedy and public trial, by an impartial jury of the State and district wherein the crime shall have been committed, which district shall have been previously ascertained by law, and to be informed of the nature and cause of the accusation; to be confronted with the witnesses against him; to have compulsory process for obtaining Witnesses in his favor, and to have the assistance of counsel for his defence.

Amendment VII

In Suits at **common law**, where the value in controversy shall exceed twenty dollars, the right of trial by jury shall be preserved, and no fact tried by a jury, shall be otherwise reexamined in any Court of the United States, than according to the rules of common law.

Amendment VIII

Excessive **bail** shall not be required, nor excessive fines imposed, nor cruel and unusual punishments inflicted.

Amendment IX

The enumeration in the Constitution, of certain rights, shall not be construed to deny or disparage others retained by the people.

Amendment X

The powers not delegated to the United States by the Constitution, nor prohibited by it to the States, are reserved to the States respectively, or to the people.

Amendment XI

The Judicial power of the United States shall not be construed to extend to any suit in law or equity, commenced or prosecuted against one of the United States by Citizens of another State, or by Citizens or Subjects of any Foreign State.

Rights to a Speedy, Fair Trial   A basic protection is the right to a speedy, public trial. The jury must hear witnesses and evidence on both sides before deciding the guilt or innocence of a person charged with a crime. This amendment also provides that legal counsel must be provided to a defendant. In 1963, the Supreme Court ruled, in *Gideon* v. *Wainwright*, that if a defendant cannot afford a lawyer, the government must provide one to defend him or her. *Why is the right to a "speedy" trial important?*

Powers of the People   This amendment prevents government from claiming that the only rights people have are those listed in the Bill of Rights.

Powers of the States   The final amendment of the Bill of Rights protects the states and the people from an all-powerful federal government. It establishes that powers not given to the national government—or denied to the states—by the Constitution belong to the states or to the people.

Suits Against States   The Eleventh Amendment (1795) limits the jurisdiction of the federal courts. The Supreme Court had ruled that a federal court could try a lawsuit brought by citizens of South Carolina against a citizen of Georgia. This case, *Chisholm* v. *Georgia*, decided in 1793, raised a storm of protest, leading to passage of the Eleventh Amendment.

Election of President and Vice President The Twelfth Amendment (1804) corrects a problem that had arisen in the method of electing the president and vice president. This amendment provides for the Electoral College to use separate ballots in voting for president and vice president. *If no candidate receives a majority of the electoral votes, who elects the president?*

Amendment XII

The electors shall meet in their respective states and vote by ballot for President and Vice-President, one of whom, at least, shall not be an inhabitant of the same state with themselves; they shall name in their ballots the person voted for as President, and in distinct ballots the person voted for as Vice-President, and they shall make distinct lists of all persons voted for as President, and of all persons voted for as Vice-President, and of the number of votes for each, which lists they shall sign and certify, and transmit sealed to the seat of the government of the United States, directed to the President of the Senate;—The President of the Senate shall, in the presence of the Senate and House of Representatives, open all the certificates and the votes shall then be counted;—The person having the greatest number of votes for President, shall be the President, if such number be a majority of the whole number of Electors appointed; and if no person have such majority, then from the persons having the highest numbers not exceeding three on the list of those voted for as President, the House of Representatives shall choose immediately, by ballot, the President. But in choosing the President, the votes shall be taken by states, the representation from each state having one vote; a quorum for this purpose shall consist of a member or members from two-thirds of the states, and a **majority** of all the states shall be necessary to a choice. And if the House of Representatives shall not choose a President whenever the right of choice shall **devolve** upon them, before the fourth day of March next following, then the Vice-President shall act as President, as in the case of the death or other constitutional disability of the President. The person having the greatest number of votes as Vice-President, shall be the Vice-President, if such number be a majority of the whole number of Electors appointed, and if no person have a majority, then from the two highest numbers on the list, the Senate shall choose the Vice-President; a quorum for the purpose shall consist of two-thirds of the whole number of Senators, and a majority of the whole number shall be necessary to a choice. But no person constitutionally ineligible to the office of President shall be eligible to that of Vice-President of the United States.

Vocabulary
majority: more than half
devolve: to pass on

Amendment XIII

Section 1

Neither slavery nor involuntary servitude, except as a punishment for crime whereof the party shall have been duly convicted, shall exist within the United States, or any place subject to their jurisdiction.

Section 2

Congress shall have power to enforce this article by appropriate legislation.

Amendment XIV

Section 1

All persons born or naturalized in the United States, and subject to the jurisdiction thereof, are citizens of the United States and of the State wherein they reside. No State shall make or enforce any law which shall **abridge** the privileges or immunities of citizens of the United States; nor shall any State deprive any person of life, liberty, or property, without due process of law; nor deny to any person within its jurisdiction the equal protection of the laws.

Section 2

Representatives shall be apportioned among the several States according to their respective numbers, counting the whole number of persons in each State, excluding Indians not taxed. But when the right to vote at any election for the choice of electors for President and Vice President of the United States, Representatives in Congress, the Executive and Judicial officers of a State, or the members of the Legislature thereof, is denied to any of the male inhabitants of such State, being twenty-one years of age, and citizens of the United States, or in any way abridged, except for participation in rebellion, or other crime, the basis of representation therein shall be reduced in the proportion which the number of such male citizens shall bear to the whole number of male citizens twenty-one years of age in such State.

Section 3

No person shall be a Senator or Representative in Congress, or elector of President and Vice President, or hold any office, civil or military, under the United States, or under any State, who, having previously taken an oath, as a member of Congress, or as an officer of the United States, or as a member of any State legislature, or as an executive or judicial officer of any State, to support the Constitution

Abolition of Slavery Amendments Thirteen (1865), Fourteen (1868), and Fifteen (1870) often are called the Civil War amendments because they grew out of that great conflict. The Thirteenth Amendment outlaws slavery.

Rights of Citizens The Fourteenth Amendment (1868) originally was intended to protect the legal rights of the freed slaves. Today it protects the rights of citizenship in general by prohibiting a state from depriving any person of life, liberty, or property without "due process of law." In addition, it states that all citizens have the right to equal protection of the law in all states.

Representation in Congress This section reduced the number of members a state had in the House of Representatives if it denied its citizens the right to vote. Later civil rights laws and the Twenty-fourth Amendment guaranteed the vote to African Americans.

Vocabulary
abridge: to reduce

Public Debt The public debt acquired by the federal government during the Civil War was valid and could not be questioned by the South. However, the debts of the Confederacy were declared to be illegal. *Could former slaveholders collect payment for the loss of their slaves?*

Right to Vote The Fifteenth Amendment (1870) prohibits the government from denying a person's right to vote on the basis of race. Despite the law, many states denied African Americans the right to vote by such means as poll taxes, literacy tests, and white primaries. During the 1950s and 1960s, Congress passed successively stronger laws to end racial discrimination in voting rights.

Election of Senators The Seventeenth Amendment (1913) states that the people, instead of state legislatures, elect United States senators. *How many years are in a Senate term?*

Vocabulary

emancipation: freedom from slavery

of the United States, shall have engaged in insurrection or rebellion against the same, or given aid or comfort to the enemies thereof. But Congress may by a vote of two-thirds of each House, remove such disability.

Section 4

The validity of the public debt of the United States, authorized by law, including debts incurred for payment of pensions and bounties for service in suppressing insurrection or rebellion, shall not be questioned. But neither the United States nor any State shall assume or pay any debt or obligation incurred in aid of insurrection or rebellion against the United States, or any claim for the loss or **emancipation** of any slave; but all such debts, obligations and claims shall be held illegal and void.

Section 5

The Congress shall have power to enforce, by appropriate legislation, the provisions of this article.

Amendment XV

Section 1

The right of citizens of the United States to vote shall not be denied or abridged by the United States or by any State on account of race, color, or previous condition of servitude.

Section 2

The Congress shall have power to enforce this article by appropriate legislation.

Amendment XVI

The Congress shall have power to lay and collect taxes on incomes, from whatever source derived, without apportionment among the several States and without regard to any census or enumeration.

Amendment XVII

Section 1

The Senate of the United States shall be composed of two Senators from each State, elected by the people thereof, for six years; and each Senator shall have one vote. The electors in each State shall have the qualifications requisite for electors of the most numerous branch of the State legislatures.

Section 2

When vacancies happen in the representation of any State in the Senate, the executive authority of such State shall issue writs of election to fill such vacancies: *Provided,* That the legislature of any State may empower the executive thereof to make temporary appointments until the people fill the vacancies by election as the legislature may direct.

Section 3

This amendment shall not be so construed as to affect the election or term of any Senator chosen before it becomes valid as part of the Constitution.

Amendment XVIII

Section 1

After one year from ratification of this article, the manufacture, sale, or transportation of intoxicating liquors within, the importation thereof into, or the exportation thereof from the United States and all territory subject to the jurisdiction thereof for beverage purposes is hereby prohibited.

Section 2

The Congress and the several States shall have concurrent power to enforce this article by appropriate legislation.

Section 3

This article shall be inoperative unless it shall have been ratified as an amendment to the Constitution by the legislatures of the several States, as provided in the Constitution, within seven years from the date of the submission hereof to the States by the Congress.

Amendment XIX

Section 1

The right of citizens of the United States to vote shall not be denied or abridged by the United States or by any State on account of sex.

Section 2

Congress shall have power by appropriate legislation to enforce the provisions of this article.

Prohibition The Eighteenth Amendment (1919) prohibited the production, sale, or transportation of alcoholic beverages in the United States. Prohibition proved to be difficult to enforce. This amendment was later repealed by the Twenty-first Amendment.

Woman Suffrage The Nineteenth Amendment (1920) guaranteed women the right to vote. By then women had already won the right to vote in many state elections, but the amendment put their right to vote in all state and national elections on a constitutional basis.

"Lame-Duck" Amendments The Twentieth Amendment (1933) sets new dates for Congress to begin its term and for the inauguration of the president and vice president. Under the original Constitution, elected officials who retired or who had been defeated remained in office for several months. For the outgoing president, this period ran from November until March. Such outgoing officials had little influence and accomplished little, and they were called lame ducks because they were so inactive. *What date was fixed as Inauguration Day?*

Succession This section provides that if the president-elect dies before taking office, the vice president-elect becomes president.

Amendment XX

Section 1

The terms of the President and Vice President shall end at noon on the 20th day of January, and the terms of the Senators and Representatives at noon on the 3d day of January, of the years in which such terms would have ended if this article had not been ratified; and the terms of their successors shall then begin.

Section 2

The Congress shall assemble at least once in every year, and such meeting shall begin at noon on the 3d day of January, unless they shall by law appoint a different day.

Section 3

If, at the time fixed for the beginning of the term of the President, the **President elect** shall have died, the Vice President elect shall become President. If a President shall not have been chosen before the time fixed for the beginning of his term, or if the President elect shall have failed to qualify, then the Vice President elect shall act as President until a President shall have qualified; and the Congress may by law provide for the case wherein neither a President elect nor a Vice President elect shall have qualified, declaring who shall then act as President, or the manner in which one who is to act shall be selected, and such person shall act accordingly until a President or Vice President shall have qualified.

Section 4

The Congress may by law provide for the case of the death of any of the persons from whom the House of Representatives may choose a President whenever the right of choice shall have devolved upon them, and for the case of the death of any of the persons from whom the Senate may choose a Vice President whenever the right of choice shall have devolved upon them.

Section 5

Section 1 and 2 shall take effect on the 15th day of October following the ratification of this article.

Vocabulary

president elect: individual who is elected president but has not yet begun serving his or her term

Section 6

This article shall be inoperative unless it shall have been ratified as an amendment to the Constitution by the legislatures of three-fourths of the several States within seven years from the date of its submission.

Amendment XXI

Section 1

The eighteenth article of amendment to the Constitution of the United States is hereby repealed.

Section 2

The transportation or importation into any State, Territory, or possession of the United States for delivery or use therein of intoxicating liquors, in violation of the laws thereof, is hereby prohibited.

Section 3

This article shall be inoperative unless it shall have been ratified as an amendment to the Constitution by conventions in the several States, as provided in the Constitution, within seven years from the date of the submission hereof to the States by the Congress.

Amendment XXII

Section 1

No person shall be elected to the office of the President more than twice, and no person who had held the office of President, or acted as President, for more than two years of a term to which some other person was elected President shall be elected to the office of the President more than once. But this Article shall not apply to any person holding the office of President when this Article was proposed by the Congress, and shall not prevent any person who may be holding the office of President, or acting as President, during the term within which this Article becomes operative from holding the office of President or acting as President during the remainder of such term.

Section 2

This article shall be inoperative unless it shall have been ratified as an amendment to the Constitution by the legislatures of three-fourths of the several States within seven years from the date of its submission to the States by the Congress.

Repeal of Prohibition The Twenty-first Amendment (1933) repeals the Eighteenth Amendment. It is the only amendment ever passed to overturn an earlier amendment. It is also the only amendment ratified by special state conventions instead of state legislatures.

Term Limit The Twenty-second Amendment (1951) limits presidents to a maximum of two elected terms. It was passed largely as a reaction to Franklin D. Roosevelt's election to four terms between 1933 and 1945.

Electors for the District of Columbia
The Twenty-third Amendment (1961) allows citizens living in Washington, D.C., to vote for president and vice president, a right previously denied residents of the nation's capital. The District of Columbia now has three presidential electors, the number to which it would be entitled if it were a state.

Abolition of Poll Tax   The Twenty-fourth Amendment (1964) prohibits poll taxes in federal elections. Prior to the passage of this amendment, some states had used such taxes to keep low-income African Americans from voting. In 1966 the Supreme Court banned poll taxes in state elections as well.

The Vice President   The Twenty-fifth Amendment (1967) established a process for the vice president to take over leadership of the nation when a president is disabled. It also set procedures for filling a vacancy in the office of vice president.

This amendment was used in 1973, when Vice President Spiro Agnew resigned from office after being charged with accepting bribes. President Richard Nixon then appointed Gerald R. Ford as vice president in accordance with the provisions of the Twenty-fifth Amendment. A year later, President Nixon resigned during the Watergate scandal and Ford became president. President Ford then had to fill the vice presidency, which he had left vacant upon assuming the presidency. He named Nelson A. Rockefeller as vice president. Thus individuals who had not been elected held both the presidency and the vice presidency.   *Whom does the president inform if he or she cannot carry out the duties of the office?*

Amendment XXIII

Section 1

The District constituting the seat of Government of the United States shall appoint in such manner as the Congress may direct:

A number of electors of President and Vice President equal to the whole number of Senators and Representatives in Congress to which the District would be entitled if it were a State, but in no event more than the least populous State; they shall be in addition to those appointed by the States, but they shall be considered, for the purposes of the election of President and Vice President, to be electors appointed by a State; and they shall meet in the District and perform such duties as provided by the twelfth article of amendment.

Section 2

The Congress shall have power to enforce this article by appropriate legislation.

Amendment XXIV

Section 1

The right of citizens of the United States to vote in any primary or other election for President or Vice President, for electors for President or Vice President, or for Senator or Representative in Congress, shall not be denied or abridged by the United States or any State by reason of failure to pay any poll tax or other tax.

Section 2

The Congress shall have power to enforce this article by appropriate legislation.

Amendment XXV

Section 1

In case of the removal of the President from office or his death or resignation, the Vice President shall become President.

Section 2

Whenever there is a vacancy in the office of the Vice President, the President shall nominate a Vice President who shall take the office upon confirmation by a majority vote of both Houses of Congress.

Section 3

Whenever the President transmits to the President pro tempore of the Senate and the Speaker of the House of Representatives his written declaration that he is unable to discharge the powers and duties of his office, and until he transmits to them a written declaration to the contrary, such powers and duties shall be discharged by the Vice President as Acting President.

Section 4

Whenever the Vice President and a majority of either the principal officers of the executive departments or of such other body as Congress may by law provide, transmit to the President pro tempore of the Senate and the Speaker of the House of Representatives their written declaration that the President is unable to discharge the powers and duties of his office, the Vice President shall immediately assume the power and duties of the office of Acting President.

Thereafter, when the President transmits to the President pro tempore of the Senate and the Speaker of the House of Representatives his written declaration that no inability exists, he shall resume the powers and duties of his office unless the Vice President and a majority of either the principal officers of the executive department or of such other body as Congress may by law provide, transmit within four days to the President pro tempore of the Senate and the Speaker of the House of Representatives their written declaration that the President is unable to discharge the powers and duties of his office. Thereupon Congress shall decide the issue, assembling within forty-eight hours for that purpose if not in session. If the Congress, within twenty-one days after receipt of the latter written declaration, or, if Congress is not in session, within twenty-one days after Congress is required to assemble, determines by two-thirds vote of both Houses that the President is unable to discharge the powers and duties of his office, the Vice President shall continue to discharge the same as Acting President; otherwise, the President shall resume the power and duties of his office.

Amendment XXVI

Section 1

The right of citizens of the United States, who are eighteen years of age or older, to vote shall not be denied or abridged by the United States or by any State on account of age.

Voting Age The Twenty-sixth Amendment (1971) lowered the voting age in both federal and state elections to 18.

Section 2

The Congress shall have power to enforce this article by appropriate legislation.

Amendment XXVII

No law, varying the compensation for the services of Senators and Representatives, shall take effect, until an election of representatives shall have intervened.

Congressional Pay Raises The Twenty-seventh Amendment (1992) makes congressional pay raises effective during the term following their passage. James Madison offered the amendment in 1789, but it was never adopted. In 1982 Gregory Watson, then a student at the University of Texas, discovered the forgotten amendment while doing research for a school paper. Watson made the amendment's passage his crusade.

▼ **Joint meeting of Congress**

Time & Life Images/Getty Images

GLOSSARY/GLOSARIO

- Content vocabulary are words that relate to American history content.
- Words that have an asterisk (*) are academic vocabulary. They help you understand your school subjects.
- All vocabulary words are **boldfaced** or **highlighted in yellow** in your textbook.

academy • anarchy

ENGLISH	A	ESPAÑOL

*academy a school or college for special training (pp. 54–55)

*academia escuela o universidad donde se brinda enseñanza especializada (págs. 54–55)

*accurate correct; precise (pp. 154–155)

*exacto correcto; preciso (págs. 154–155)

*achieve to accomplish (pp. 229–230)

*lograr completar (págs. 229–230)

acid rain rain containing high amounts of chemical pollutants from the burning of fossil fuels (pp. 482–483)

lluvia ácida lluvia que contiene grandes cantidades de contaminantes químicos provenientes de la quema de combustibles fósiles (págs. 482–483)

*adequate enough for a specific purpose (p. 463)

*adecuado apropiado para un propósito específico (pág. 463)

*adjust to become more suited to new conditions (p. 44)

*ajustarse hacerse más apropiado para una nueva condición (pág. 44)

*advocate to support; to publicly support something (p. 280)

*defender respaldar; apoyar en público algo (pág. 280)

*affect to have an impact on or to influence (pp. 128–129)

*afectar tener impacto o influencia (págs. 128–129)

affirmative action an approach to hiring or promoting that favors disadvantaged groups (p. 431)

acción afirmativa enfoque en la contratación o en la promoción que favorece a grupos desfavorecidos (pág. 431)

affluence having wealth (pp. 350–351)

opulencia tener riqueza (págs. 350–351)

Agent Orange a chemical herbicide used to clear out forests and tall grasses (p. 404)

Agente Naranja herbicida químico que se usa para limpiar bosques y eliminar los pastos altos (pág. 404)

*agrarian having to do with farming (p. 283)

*agrario relacionado con la agricultura (pág. 283)

airlift delivery of supplies by airplane (pp. 334–335)

aerotransporte entrega de provisiones por avión (págs. 334–335)

alliance system a system in which countries agree to defend each other or to advance common causes (p. 207)

sistema de alianza sistema por el cual los países acuerdan defenderse unos a otros o trabajar por causas comunes (pág. 207)

amnesty the granting of a pardon to a large number of persons; protection from prosecution (p. 43; p. 436)

amnistía perdón otorgado a un gran número de personas; protección de una acción judicial (pág. 43; pág. 436)

anarchist a person who believes there should be no government (pp. 238–239)

anarquista persona que cree que no debe haber gobierno (págs. 238–239)

anarchy disorder and lawlessness caused by lack of effective government (pp. 196–197)

anarquía desorden y caos ocasionados por la falta de un gobierno efectivo (págs. 196–197)

***annual** yearly (pp. 195–196)

anti-Semitism dislike of or discrimination against Jews as a religious, ethnic, or racial group (p. 295)

apartheid racial separation and economic and political discrimination against nonwhites (p. 440)

appeasement the policy of giving in to the demands of others in an effort to keep peace (pp. 296–297)

arbitration the process of resolving disputes between people or groups by agreeing to accept the decision of a neutral party (p. 165)

armistice a temporary agreement to end fighting (p. 192)

arms race competition between countries for stronger military power (p. 349)

***artillery** weapons (p. 275)

***aspect** a category, feature, or part of something (pp. 380–381)

assembly line a factory method in which work moves past stationary workers who perform a single task again and again (p. 106)

***assign** to appoint; to give the job to (p. 371)

assimilate to become part of a larger culture (p. 128)

assure to promise or to make sure (p. 345)

***attitude** a way of behaving, thinking, or feeling caused by one's opinions or beliefs (pp. 128–129)

***authority** the power to command; the power to enforce laws (pp. 412–413)

autocracy a government in which one person with unlimited power rules (p. 216)

***aware** alert; to have knowledge of (p. 483)

***anual** que ocurre una vez al año (págs. 195–196)

anti semitismo aversión o discriminación contra los judíos como grupo religioso, étnico o racial (pág. 295)

apartheid segregación racial y discriminación económica y política en contra de los no blancos (pág. 440)

apaciguamiento política de acceder a las demandas de otros como una medida para mantener la paz (págs. 296–297)

arbitraje proceso de resolución de disputas entre personas o grupos mediante la aceptación de la decisión de una parte neutral (pág. 165)

armisticio acuerdo temporal para finalizar una pelea (pág. 192)

carrera de armas competencia entre países por un poder militar más fuerte (pág. 349)

***artillería** armas (pág. 275)

***aspecto** categoría, característica o parte de algo (págs. 380–381)

cadena de montaje método de fábrica mediante el cual el trabajo pasa frente a trabajadores estacionarios quienes llevan a cabo una única tarea repetidas veces (pág. 106)

***asignar** nombrar; dar el trabajo (pág. 371)

asimilar incorporarse a una cultura más grande (pág. 128)

asegurar prometer o garantizar (pág. 345)

***actitud** manera de comportarse, pensar o sentirse ocasionada por la opiniones o creencias propias (págs. 128–129)

***autoridad** facultad de mandar; facultad de hacer cumplir las leyes (págs. 412–413)

autocracia gobierno en el que una persona gobierna con poder ilimitado (pág. 216)

***consciente** alerta; tener conocimiento (pág. 483)

B

bailout the rescue from financial ruin of a bank, company, or homeowner (p. 478)

sacar de apuros rescate de la ruina financiera de un banco, una compañía o un propietario de una casa (pág. 478)

balance of power an equality of power among different countries that discourages any group from acting aggressively (p. 207)

bankrupt a condition in which a person or business cannot pay its debts (p. 460)

barrio a Mexican neighborhood (pp. 174–175)

*****behalf** in the interest of (p. 153)

*****bias** prejudice, an unfair dislike of someone or something (p. 173)

black codes laws passed in the South just after the Civil War aimed at controlling freed men and women, and allowing plantation owners to take advantage of African American workers (pp. 46–47)

blitzkrieg violent, sudden attack used by Germans during World War II (p. 298; p. 300)

*****block** a large building used to house prisoners (p. 319)

blockade actions used to keep a country or area from communicating and trading with other nations or areas; to close off a country's ports (p. 398)

boycott to refuse to buy items in order to protest certain actions or to force acceptance of one's terms; to refuse to use (p. 366)

bureaucracy a system of government in which specialized tasks are carried out by appointed officials rather than by elected ones; a system of government marked by lots of rules and regulation (p. 275)

balance de poder igualdad de poder entre países diferentes que disuade a cualquier grupo de actuar de manera agresiva (pág. 207)

bancarrota condición en la cual una persona o negocio no puede pagar sus deudas (pág. 460)

barrio vecindario mexicano (págs. 174–175)

*****en nombre de** en el interés de (pág. 153)

*****parcialidad** prejuicio, aversión injusta por alguien o algo (pág. 173)

códigos negros leyes aprobadas en el Sur después de la Guerra Civil, cuyo objetivo era controlar a los hombres y mujeres libertos, y permitir a los dueños de las plantaciones aprovecharse de los trabajadores afroamericanos (págs. 46–47)

ataque relámpago ataque violento y repentino usado por los alemanes durante la Segunda Guerra Mundial (pág. 298; pág. 300)

*****bloque** edificio grande que se usa para albergar prisioneros (pág. 319)

bloqueo acción que evita que un país o zona se comunique y comercie con otras naciones o zonas; cierre de los puertos de un país (pág. 398)

boicot negarse a comprar productos para protestar contra ciertas acciones o con el fin de presionar para que acepten las condiciones de una persona; negarse a perder (pág. 366)

burocracia sistema de gobierno en el cual algunas tareas especializadas son realizadas por funcionarios designados, no elegidos; sistema de gobierno marcado por muchas reglas o normas (pág. 275)

C

calendar a system for breaking time into units and keeping track of those units (pp. 5–6)

capital human-made goods that people use to produce goods and services; money or other resources used to create wealth (p. 23)

censure to formally criticize (p. 338)

*****challenge** something that is difficult (pp. 5–6)

calendario sistema usado para dividir el tiempo en unidades y hacer un seguimiento de esas unidades (págs. 5–6)

capital bienes hechos por el ser humano que se usan para producir bienes y servicos; dinero y demás recursos usados para generar riquezas (pág. 23)

censurar críticar formalmente (pág. 338)

*****desafio** algo que es difícil (págs. 5–6)

chronology order of dates in which events happen (pp. 5–6)

*civil having to do with citizens and their government (p. 363)

civil defense protective measures taken in case of attack (p. 306)

civil disobedience refusing to obey laws considered unjust (p. 366)

closed shop practice of businesses hiring only union members (p. 341)

coalition a group formed for a common purpose (p. 459)

cold war a war in which two enemies do not fight in combat but instead compete and conflict in other ways (p. 336)

*collapse a sudden fall or failure of something, such as a structure or the value of money (p. 264)

collective bargaining discussion between an employer and union representatives of workers over wages, hours, and working conditions for the union membership as a whole (p. 115)

*commission a group of officials chosen for a specific responsibility (p. 57)

*communication the exchange of messages or information (p. 184)

*concentrate to focus (p. 310)

concentration camp large prison camp used to hold people for political reasons (p. 315)

*conclude to figure out or decide (pp. 346–347)

*conduct to direct the course of (p. 408)

*conflict a war; prolonged struggle (pp. 324–325)

conscientious objector a person who refuses to serve in the armed forces or bear arms on moral or religious grounds (p. 407)

*consent to agree (p. 222)

cronología orden de fechas en las que suceden los hechos (págs. 5–6)

*civil perteneciente o relativo a los ciudadanos y su gobierno (pág. 363)

defensa civil medidas de protección que se toman en caso de un ataque (pág. 306)

desobediencia civil negativa a obedecer las leyes que se consideran injustas (p. 366)

empresa de sindicación obligatoria práctica por la cual las empresas solo contratan a miembros del sindicato (pág. 341)

coalición grupo que se forma con un propósito en común (pág. 459)

guerra fría guerra en la que dos enemigos no pelean en combate, sino que compiten y entran en conflicto de otras maneras (pág. 336)

*colapso caída repentina o falla de algo, como una estructura o el valor de la moneda (pág. 264)

negociación colectiva discusión entre un empleador y representantes del sindicato de trabajadores acerca de los salarios, las horas y las condiciones laborales para los miembros del sindicato como un todo (pág. 115)

*comisión grupo de funcionarios escogidos para una responsabilidad específica (pág. 57)

*comunicación intercambio de mensajes o información (pág. 184)

concentrar enfocar (pág. 310)

campo de concentración campo de prisión grande que se usa para detener personas por razones políticas (pág. 315)

*concluir determinar o decidir (págs. 346–347)

*conducir dirigir el curso (pág. 408)

*conflicto guerra; lucha prolongada (págs. 324–325)

objetor de conciencia persona que se niega a servir en las fuerzas armadas o portar armas debido a razones morales o religiosas (pág. 407)

*acceder acordar (pág. 222)

conservation protection and preservation of natural resources (p. 166)

conservación protección y preservación de los recursos naturales (pág. 166)

*__consist__ to be made up of; to include (pp. 372–373)

*__constar__ estar conformado por; incluir (págs. 372–373)

consolidation the practice of combining different companies into one (pp. 98–99)

consolidación práctica de unir diferentes compañías en una (págs. 98–99)

*__consult__ to seek information or advice (p. 187)

*__consultar__ buscar información o consejo de una persona o un recurso (pág. 187)

*__consume__ to use (p. 225)

*__consumir__ usar (pág. 225)

containment policy of holding back or stopping communism (p. 334)

contención política de frenar o detener el comunismo (pág. 334)

*__controversy__ arguments between opposing viewpoints (p. 436)

*__controversia__ argumentos entre puntos de vista opuestos (pág. 436)

convoy a group of ships that escort and protect other ships (pp. 218–219)

convoy grupo de barcos que escoltan y protegen a otros barcos (págs. 218–219)

*__cooperate__ to agree to work together (p. 334)

*__cooperar__ estar de acuerdo en trabajar juntos (pág. 334)

cooperative enterprise owned by and operated for the benefit of a certain group (p. 88)

cooperativa empresa que es propiedad de cierto grupo y funciona para su beneficio (pág. 88)

corporation type of business or organization owned by many people but treated by law as though it were a person (p. 109)

corporación tipo de negocio u organización de propiedad de muchas personas, pero que la ley trata como si fuera una persona (pág. 109)

corruption dishonest or illegal actions (p. 53)

corrupción acciones deshonestas o ilegales (pág. 53)

counterculture a culture with values that differ from those of established society (pp. 406–407)

contracultura cultura con valores que difieren de los que establece la sociedad (págs. 406–407)

credibility gap the difference between what is said and what people believe or know to be true (p. 408)

pérdida de credibilidad diferencia entre lo que se dice y lo que la gente cree o sabe que es cierto (pág. 408)

*__credit__ a loan; money borrowed to pay for goods or services at a future time (p. 54)

*__crédito__ préstamo; dinero que se toma prestado para pagar bienes o servicios en un futuro (pág. 54)

*__crucible__ a vessel used to melt things (pp. 130–131)

*__crisol__ recipiente que se usa para fundir cosas (págs. 130–131)

*__currency__ money (pp. 88–89)

*__moneda__ dinero (págs. 88–89)

D

dawdle waste time (p. 157)

entretenerse perder tiempo (pág. 157)

*__decade__ a period of ten years (pp. 480–481)

*__década__ periodo de diez años (págs. 480–481)

Glossary/Glosario

*decline** to drop or go down steadily (p. 263)

default to fail to meet an obligation, especially a financial one (pp. 264–265)

deferment postponement of, or excuse from, military service (p. 407)

deficit when government spending is greater than government revenue, or income (p. 432)

deficit spending spending more money than is received and creating debt as a result (pp. 462–463)

*definite** specific or certain (p. 476)

demilitarized zone a region where military forces are not allowed (p. 344; p. 346)

*demonstration** a protest gathering or march (p. 414)

*deny** to refuse to grant, agree, or believe (p. 172)

deport to expel from a country (p. 239)

deregulation the removal of rules and regulations (p. 451)

desegregate to end the system of separating races (pp. 342–343)

*detect** to notice (p. 243)

détente an attempt to ease international tensions (p. 424)

*device** equipment (p. 251)

dictator leader who has absolute power and rules a nation by force (pp. 294–295)

*dimension** the level on which something exists or takes place (pp. 210–211)

disarmament giving up military weapons (p. 302)

discrimination unfair treatment based on prejudice toward a certain race, ethnic group, religion, age group, or gender (pp. 170–171; p. 363)

dissent to disagree with or oppose an opinion; disagreement or opposition (p. 226)

*diverse** containing many different elements (p. 384)

*decadencia** decaer o declinar a ritmo constante (pág. 263)

mora no cumplir una obligación, especialmente una financiera (págs. 264–265)

aplazamiento postergación o excusa del servicio militar (pág. 407)

déficit cuando los gastos del gobierno son mayores que sus rentas o ingresos (pág. 432)

exceso de gasto público gastar más dinero del que se recibe y, como resultado, crear una deuda (págs. 462–463)

*definitivo** específico o seguro (pág. 476)

zona desmilitarizada región donde las fuerzas militares no están permitidas (pág. 344; pág. 346)

*manifestación** reunión de protesta o marcha (pág. 414)

*negar** rechazo a reconocer, estar de acuerdo o creer (pág. 172)

deportar expulsar de un país (pág. 239)

desregulación eliminación de las reglas y regulaciones (pág. 451)

desegregación dar por terminado el sistema de separación racial (págs. 342–343)

*detectar** notar (pág. 243)

distensión intento de disminuir las tensiones internacionales (pág. 424)

*aparato** equipo (pág. 251)

dictador líder que tiene poder absoluto y gobierna una nación por la fuerza (págs. 294–295)

*dimensión** nivel en que algo existe u ocurre (págs. 210–211)

desarme entregar las armas militares (pág. 302)

discriminación trato injusto basado en un prejuicio hacia una raza determinada, grupo étnico, religión, grupo etario o género (págs. 170–171; pág. 363)

discrepar no estar de acuerdo u oponerse a la creencia o práctica establecida o ampliamente aceptada (pág. 226)

*diverso** que contiene muchos elementos diferentes (pág. 384)

dividend a stockholder's share of a company's profits, usually as a cash payment (p. 109)

dollar diplomacy the policy of using economic investment to protect U.S. interests abroad (p. 198)

*****domestic** having to do with the home or the home country (p. 340)

downsize to lay off workers to make a company smaller (p. 460)

dry farming a farming method that depends on plowing after every rain and snow to trap moisture in the soil in dry, non irrigated land (p. 78)

due process procedures the government must follow that are established by law and guaranteed by the Constitution (p. 31)

*****dynamic** energetic; forceful (p. 240)

dividendo participación que tiene un accionista sobre las ganancias de una compañía, generalmente como un pago en efectivo (pág. 109)

diplomacia del dólar política de usar la inversión económica para proteger los intereses estadounidenses en el exterior (pág. 198)

*****doméstico** relacionado con el hogar o el país de origen (pág. 340)

reducir práctica de despedir trabajadores para disminuir el tamaño de una compañía (pág. 460)

agricultura en sitios secos método agrícola que depende de arar después de cada lluvia y nevada para atrapar la humedad en el suelo en terrenos secos y no irrigados (pág. 78)

debido proceso procedimientos establecidos por la ley y garantizados por la Constitución que el gobierno debe seguir (pág. 31)

*****dinámico** enérgico; fuerte (pág. 240)

E

*****economy** the overall system by which goods are made, distributed, and used (p. 349)

ecosystem a community of living beings and the surroundings in which they live (p. 19)

elevation the height of an area above sea level (p. 15)

*****eliminate** to get rid of (pp. 195–196)

embargo a prohibition or blocking of trade with a certain country; a ban on trade (pp. 426–427)

*****emerge** to rise up; to become (p. 380)

emigrate to leave one's homeland to live elsewhere (p. 125)

*****energy** sources of usable power (p. 434)

*****enormous** huge (p. 251)

*****ensure** to make certain (p. 82)

entrepreneur a person who starts a new business, introduces a new product, or improves a management technique (p. 23; p. 109)

*****economía** sistema general por el cual se producen, se distribuyen y se usan bienes (pág. 349)

ecosistema comunidad de seres vivos y el entorno en el cual viven (pág. 19)

elevación altura de un área sobre el nivel del mar (pág. 15)

*****eliminar** deshacerse de (págs. 195–196)

embargo prohibición o bloqueo del comercio con un país determinado; suspensión del comercio (págs. 426–427)

*****emerger** levantarse; salir a la superficie (pág. 380)

emigrar dejar la tierra natal para vivir en otro lugar (pág. 125)

*****energía** fuentes de energía utilizable (pág. 434)

*****enorme** inmenso (pág. 251)

*****garantizar** asegurar (pág. 82)

empresario persona que inicia un nuevo negocio, introduce un producto nuevo o mejora una técnica de administración (pág. 23; pág. 109)

Glossary/Glosario

*environment the physical surroundings (p. 20); a person's surroundings (p. 116)

*equip to outfit (pp. 210–211)

*escalate to increase (p. 403)

espionage spying (pp. 336–337)

ethnic group people who share a common culture or heritage (p. 125)

*eventual later (pp. 193–194)

evolution scientific theory that humans and other species changed and developed over long periods of time (pp. 252–253)

*exceed to be greater than (p. 439)

*exclude to prevent from being involved in something; to shut out (p. 48; p. 410)

executive privilege the principle that White House conversations should remain secret to protect national security (p. 435)

expansionism the practice of spreading a nation's territorial or economic control beyond its borders (pp. 181–182)

expatriate someone who chooses to live in another country (p. 251)

*expert a person with advanced knowledge (pp. 246–247)

*exploit to make use of (p. 188)

*extract to remove or take out with force (pp. 68–69)

*medioambiente entorno físico (pág. 20); entorno de una persona (pág. 116)

*equipar preparar (págs. 210–211)

*escalar aumentar (pág. 403)

espionaje espiar (págs. 336–337)

grupo étnico personas que comparten una cultura común o herencia (pág. 125)

*final posterior (págs. 193–194)

evolución teoría científica que explica que los seres humanos y otras especies cambian y se desarrollan durante largo tiempo (págs. 252–253)

*exceder ser mayor que (pág. 439)

*excluir evitar involucrarse en algo; dejar fuera (pág. 48; pág. 410)

privilegio ejecutivo principio por el cual las conversaciones en la Casa Blanca deben permanecer en secreto para proteger la seguridad nacional (pág. 435)

expansionismo práctica de extender el control territorial o económico de una nación más allá de sus fronteras (págs. 181–182)

expatriado alguien que escoge vivir en otro país (pág. 251)

*experto persona que tiene conocimiento avanzado (págs. 246–247)

*explotar hacer uso de (pág. 188)

*extraer remover o retirar con fuerza (págs. 68–69)

F

*factor a contributing cause (p. 76)

factors of production the resources used in the production process, including natural resources, labor, and capital (p. 109)

Fair Deal a program aimed at solving some of the nation's economic problems after World War II (p. 340)

*factor causa que contribuye (pág. 76)

factores de producción recursos que se usan en el proceso de producción, entre ellos los recursos naturales, la mano de obra y el capital (pág. 109)

Fair Deal programa dirigido a resolver algunos de los problemas económicos de la nación después de la Segunda Guerra Mundial (pág. 340)

fascism a political philosophy that stresses the glory of the state over the individual and that favors dictatorship (p. 280)

federal debt the amount of money owed by the federal government (p. 452)

federal system the sharing of power between the national government and state and local governments (p. 31)

feminist an activist for women's rights (pp. 382–383)

*****final** last (pp. 229–230)

flapper a carefree young woman of the 1920s (pp. 250–251)

flexible response President Kennedy's plan to help nations fighting Communist movements by providing special military units trained to fight guerrilla warfare (p. 395)

free enterprise system economic system in which people and businesses are free to own the means of production and to compete for profit with a minimum of government interference (p. 25)

free trade the free flow of goods and services among countries through the removal of tariffs and other regulations (p. 482)

fundamentalist someone who believes in strict obedience to religious laws (p. 442)

*****funds** money (p. 302)

fascismo filosofía política que enfatiza la gloria del Estado sobre el individuo y favorece la dictadura (pág. 280)

deuda federal cantidad de dinero que debe el gobierno federal (pág. 452)

sistema federal poder compartido entre el gobierno nacional y los gobiernos esatales y locales (pág. 31)

feminista activista de los derechos de las mujeres (págs. 382–383)

*****final** último (págs. 229–230)

flapper mujer joven y despreocupada de los años 1920 a 1930 (págs. 250–251)

respuesta flexible plan del presidente Kennedy para ayudar a las naciones a pelear contra los movimientos comunistas mediante el suministro de unidades militares especiales entrenadas para combatir a la guerra de guerrillas (pág. 395)

sistema de libre empresa sistema económico en el cual las personas y las empresas son libres de poseer los medios de producción y competir para obtener lucro con una mínima interferencia del gobierno (pág. 25)

libre comercio flujo libre de bienes y servicios entre países gracias a la remoción de aranceles y otras regulaciones (pág. 482)

fundamentalista alguien que cree en la obediencia ciega a las leyes religiosas (pág. 442)

*****fondos** dinero (pág. 302)

G

*****generate** to produce or make something exist (p. 272)

genocide killing an entire ethnic group (p. 314)

globalization an increasing worldwide economy in which many countries become interdependent through policies like free trade (p. 481)

globe a round model of the Earth (p. 14)

grandfather clause part of southern state constitutions after the Civil War that placed high literacy and property requirements for voters whose fathers and grandfathers did not vote before 1867 (p. 60)

*****generar** producir o hacer que algo exista (pág. 272)

genocidio matar a todo un grupo étnico (pág. 314)

globalización aumento de la economía global en la que muchos países se vuelven interdependientes mediante políticas de libre comercio (pág. 481)

globo terráqueo modelo redondo de la Tierra (pág. 14)

cláusula del abuelo parte de las constituciones estatales sureñas después de la Guerra Civil que fijaba exigentes requisitos de alfabetismo y propiedad a los electores cuyos padres y abuelos no votaban antes de 1867 (pág. 60)

grassroots movement small groups of people in multiple locations around the nation who join together for a shared goal (pp. 462–463)

gross domestic product the value of all goods and services produced in a nation in one year (p. 464)

gross national product the total value of all goods and services produced by a nation (pp. 246–247)

*guarantee to promise that something will take place (p. 30)

guerrilla warfare fighting by small groups using tactics such as the ambush (p. 395)

movimiento *grassroots* grupos pequeños de personas en diferentes ubicaciones de la nación que se unen con un objetivo en común (págs. 462–463)

producto interno bruto valor de todos los bienes y servicios que se producen en una nación en un año (pág. 464)

producto nacional bruto valor total de todos los bienes y servicios que produce una nación (págs. 246-247)

*garantizar prometer que algo ocurrirá (pág. 30)

guerra de guerrillas combatir en grupos pequeños usando tácticas como la emboscada (pág. 395)

H

Holocaust the name given to the mass slaughter of Jews by the Nazis during World War II (p. 314)

homestead to earn ownership of land by living on it (p. 76)

human rights the basic rights and freedoms that all people should have (p. 440)

Holocausto nombre dado al exterminio masivo de judíos por los nazis durante la Segunda Guerra Mundial (pág. 314)

colonizar tener propiedad de la tierra por vivir en ella (pág. 76)

derechos humanos derechos básicos y libertades que todas las personas deben tener (pág. 440)

I

*identify to show or prove who someone is; to recognize someone or something (p. 114)

impeach to formally charge a public official with misconduct in office (p. 50; p. 435)

imperialism the policy of extending a nation's rule over other territories and countries (p. 183)

*income money received (p. 28)

*individual a single person (p. 99)

inflation increase in price of goods or services (pp. 339–340)

*initiate to begin (p. 84)

initiative the right of voters to place an issue on the ballot in a state election (pp. 154–155)

injunction a court order to stop something from happening (pp. 116–117)

*identificar mostrar o probar quién es alguien; reconocer a alguien o algo (pág. 114)

recusar denunciar formalmente a un funcionario público por mala conducta en el ejercicio de su cargo (pág. 50; pág. 435)

imperialismo política de extender el gobierno de una nación sobre otros territorios y países (pág. 183)

*ingresos dinero recibido (pág. 28)

*individuo una sola persona (pág. 99)

inflación aumento en el precio de bienes o servicios (págs. 339–340)

*iniciar comenzar (pág. 84)

iniciativa derecho de los votantes de hacer una propuesta en la votación en una elección estatal (págs. 154–155)

interdicto judicial orden judicial para evitar que algo ocurra (págs. 116–117)

*inspect to examine carefully in order to judge quality (p. 166)

installment buying purchasing products by making small payments over a period of time (p. 247)

insurgent a person who revolts against a government or others in power (p. 474)

integrate to unite, or to blend into a united whole; to bring races together (pp. 54–55; p. 364)

integration whites and African Americans living side-by-side (pp. 240–241)

*integrity moral character (pp. 438–439)

*intelligence the ability to learn facts and skills and apply them (p. 159)

interdependent relying on each other (pp. 480–481)

internment camp camp where Japanese Americans were kept during World War II (pp. 308–309)

*interpret to explain the meaning of something (p. 452)

interstate across state lines (pp. 374–375)

*intervene to get involved (pp. 244–245)

invest to commit money in the hopes of making more money in the future (pp. 262–263)

iron curtain symbolic division between East and West in Europe during the Cold War (p. 333)

island hopping a strategy used during World War II that called for attacking and capturing certain key islands and then using these islands as bases from which to attack others (p. 322)

*isolate set apart or cut off (p. 139)

isolationism the belief that a nation should stay out of the affairs of other nations (pp. 182–183)

isthmus a narrow strip of land connecting two larger bodies of land (pp. 195–196)

*inspeccionar examinar con cuidado para juzgar la calidad (pág. 166)

compra a plazos comprar productos haciendo pagos pequeños durante un tiempo (pág. 247)

insurgente persona que se subleva en contra de un gobierno u otros en el poder (pág. 474)

integrar unir o mezclar en una unidad; juntar razas (págs. 54–55; pág. 364)

integración blancos y afroamericanos viviendo uno al lado de otro (págs. 240–241)

*integridad carácter moral (págs. 438–439)

*inteligencia capacidad de aprender hechos y destrezas y aplicarlas (pág. 159)

interdependiente que dependen uno del otro (págs. 480–481)

campo de concentración campo donde se mantenía a los japonesamericanos durante la Segunda Guerra Mundial (págs. 308–309)

*interpretar explicar el significado de algo (pág. 452)

interestatal más allá de la frontera estatal (págs. 374–375)

*intervenir involucrarse (págs. 244–245)

invertir asignar recursos con la esperanza de producir más dinero en el futuro (págs. 262–263)

cortina de hierro división simbólica entre el Este y el Oeste en Europa durante la Guerra Fría (pág. 333)

saltos de rana estrategia usada durante la Segunda Guerra Mundial en la que era preciso atacar y capturar ciertas islas clave, y luego usarlas como base desde donde podían atacar a otras (pág. 322)

*aislar apartar o cortar (pág. 139)

aislacionismo creencia de que una nación debe permanecer por fuera de los asuntos de otras naciones (págs. 182–183)

istmo franja angosta de tierra que conecta dos masas grandes de tierra (págs. 195–196)

Glossary/Glosario

Glossary/Glosario

J

jazz an American musical style combining work songs, gospel music, spirituals, and African rhythms (pp. 142–143)

jazz estilo musical estadounidense que mezcla canciones, música evangélica, cantos religiosos y ritmos africanos (págs. 142–143)

K

Kaiser German emperor (pp. 222–223)

káiser emperador alemán (págs. 222–223)

kamikaze during World War II, a Japanese suicide pilot whose mission was to crash into his target (p. 322)

kamikaze durante la Segunda Guerra Mundial, un piloto suicida japonés cuya misión era estrellarse contra su objetivo (pág. 322)

knell sound of a bell rung slowly as an indication of the end of something (p. 319)

doblar sonido de una campana que toca lentamente como indicio del final de algo (pág. 319)

L

*labor to work or try hard (pp. 98–99)

*trabajo trabajar o intentar con esfuerzo (págs. 98–99)

labor union organization of workers who seek better pay and working conditions (p. 114)

sindicato organización de trabajadores que buscan mejorar su salario y sus condiciones laborales (pág. 114)

laissez-faire a belief that government should have as little involvement in private life as possible (p. 243)

laissez-faire creencia de que el gobierno debe tener la menor participación en la vida privada como sea posible (pág. 243)

landform natural feature of the Earth's land surface (p. 14–15)

accidente geográfico característica natural de la superficie de la Tierra (págs. 14–15)

land-grant college college funded by the Morrill Acts of 1862 and 1890 (p. 138)

universidad en concesión de tierra universidad fundada según la Ley Morrill de 1862 y 1890 (pág. 138)

Latino or Hispanic family background from Latin America or Spain (p. 384)

latinoamericano o hispano origen familiar de Latinoamérica o España (pág. 384)

lease to rent (p. 243)

arrendar alquilar (pág. 243)

levee high walls or an embankment to prevent flooding in low-lying areas (pp. 474–475)

dique paredes altas o un malecón que previenen la inundación de zonas bajas (págs. 474–475)

literacy test a method used to prevent African Americans from voting by requiring prospective voters to read and write at a specific level (p. 60)

prueba de alfabetismo método usado para evitar que los afroamericanos voten exigiendo que los posibles electores lean y escriban a un nivel específico (pág. 60)

*locate to settle at a place; to exist at a place (p. 75)

*localizar asentarse en un lugar; existir en un lugar (pág. 75)

long drive a trip of several hundred miles on which ranchers led their cattle to railroads and distant markets (p. 75)

viaje largo viaje de varios cientos de millas en el que los ganaderos conducían su ganado hacia los ferrocarriles y mercados distantes (pág. 75)

lynching putting to death by the illegal action of a mob (p. 60)

linchar provocar la muerte mediante la acción ilegal de una turba (pág. 60)

M

*major important; significant (pp. 132–133)

*principal importante; significativo (págs. 132–133)

map a flat drawing of all or part of the Earth's surface (p. 14)

mapa dibujo plano de toda la superficie terrestre o parte de ella (pág. 14)

market economy economic system in which individuals and businesses own the factors of production, and buyers and sellers choose to do business with those who satisfy their needs and wants best (p. 24)

economía de mercado sistema económico en el cual los individuos y las empresas son propietarios de los factores de producción, y los compradores y vendedores eligen hacer negocios con aquellos que mejor satisfacen sus necesidades y deseos (pág. 24)

martial law emergency military rule (p. 415)

ley marcial emergencia militar (pág. 415)

mass media forms of communication that can reach millions of people (pp. 250–251)

medios de comunicación social formas de comunicación que pueden llegar a millones de personas (págs. 250–251)

mass production factory production of goods in large quantities (p. 106)

fabricación en serie producción en fábricas de bienes en grandes cantidades (pág. 106)

materialism focus on collecting money and possessions (pp. 354–355)

materialismo centrar la atención en reunir dinero y posesiones (págs. 354–355)

*maximize make as large as possible (p. 28)

*maximizar hacer tan grande como sea posible (pág. 28)

*mechanism a set of moving or working parts in a machine or other device (p. 105)

*mecanismo conjunto de partes móviles o que trabajan en una máquina u otro aparato (pág. 105)

Medicaid health insurance program for low-income people (pp. 372–373)

Medicaid programa de seguro médico para las personas de bajos recursos (págs. 372–373)

Medicare health insurance program for all elderly people (pp. 372–373)

Medicare programa de seguro médico para todas las personas mayores (págs. 372–373)

merger the combining of two or more businesses into one (p. 112)

fusión unión de dos o más negocios en uno (pág. 112)

MIA American soldier classified as missing during a war or other military action (pp. 416–417)

MIA (sigla en inglés) soldado estadounidense clasificado como desaparecido durante una guerra u otra acción militar (págs. 416–417)

middle class social class occupied by comfortable but not wealthy people (p. 133)

clase media clase social ocupada por personas con comodidades, pero no ricas (pág. 133)

migrant worker a person who moves from place to place to find work (p. 278)

trabajador migrante persona que se mueve de un lugar a otro para encontrar trabajo (pág. 278)

*migrate to move from one place to another to live or work (p. 278)

*emigrar desplazarse de un lugar a otro para vivir o trabajar (pág. 278)

militarism celebration of military ideals, and a rapid buildup of military power (p. 207)

militarismo celebración de los ideales militares, y una rápida concentración del poderío militar (pág. 207)

*minor of lesser importance (p. 134)

*menor de importancia secundaria (pág. 134)

mobilization the gathering of resources and troops in preparation for war (pp. 224–225)

movilización reunión de recursos y tropas en preparación para la guerra (págs. 224–225)

Model T early Ford car (p. 105)

modelo T carro marca Ford antiguo (pág. 105)

monopoly a market where there is only one provider of a good or service (p. 111)

monopolio mercado en el que solo hay un proveedor de un bien o servicio (pág. 111)

muckrakers investigative reporters who exposed corruption (p. 154)

muckrakers periodistas investigadores que denuncian la corrupción (pág. 154)

mumblety-peg game in which players throw or flip a jackknife in various ways so that the knife sticks in the ground (p. 157)

mumblety-peg juego en el que los jugadores lanzan una navaja de bolsillo de varias formas de manera que la hoja se clave en el suelo (pág. 157)

*mutual shared in common (p. 90)

*mutuo que se tiene en común (pág. 90)

mutualista Mexican American aid group (pp. 174–175)

mutualista grupo mexicano-estadounidense de ayuda (págs. 174–175)

N

napalm an intensely burning explosive used to destroy jungle growth (p. 404)

napalm explosivo que arde intensamente usado para destruir el crecimiento en la selva (pág. 404)

nationalism a strong sense of devotion to one's country; a feeling of intense loyalty to a country or group (pp. 206–207)

nacionalismo fuerte sentido de devoción al país propio; sentimiento de lealtad intensa a un país o grupo (págs. 206–207)

National Grange a network of local farmers' groups (p. 88)

National Grange red de grupos de agricultores locales (pág. 88)

national self-determination the right of people to decide how they should be governed (p. 228; p. 230)

autodeterminación nacional derecho de las personas a decidir cómo deben ser gobernadas (pág. 228; pág. 230)

nativism belief that native-born Americans are superior to foreigners (p. 252)

nativismo creencia de que los indígenas nacidos como estadounidenses son superiores a los extranjeros (pág. 252)

nativist anti-immigrant (pp. 128–129)

nativista anti-inmigrante (págs. 128–129)

naturalization the legal process of becoming a citizen (p. 30)

naturalización proceso para hacerse ciudadano (pág. 30)

nomadic moving from place to place in a fixed pattern (pp. 80–81)

nómada que se desplaza de un lugar a otro siguiendo un patrón fijo (págs. 80–81)

*normal like what people are used to (pp. 238–239)

*normal como a lo que la gente está acostumbrada (págs. 238–239)

*nuclear atomic, relating to a weapon whose power comes from a nuclear reaction (p. 349)

*nuclear atómico, relacionado con un arma cuyo poder proviene de una reacción nuclear (pág. 349)

Glossary/Glosario

O

obtain to gain (p. 296)

occur to take place or to happen (p. 396)

oligopoly a few large companies that control prices for an entire industry (p. 153)

opportunity cost the cost of the next best use of time and money when choosing to do one thing or another (p. 23)

outcome the effect or result of an action or event (p. 58)

outsourcing the practice of moving production of goods and services to another location where the cost of labor is cheaper (p. 482)

override to reject or defeat something that has already been decided (p. 47)

overseas across the ocean (p. 306)

obtener ganar (pág. 296)

ocurrir tener lugar, pasar (pág. 396)

oligopolio pocas compañías grandes que controlan los precios de toda la industria (pág. 153)

costo de oportunidad costo de la mejor alternativa de tiempo y dinero cuando se elige haver una cosa u otra (pág. 23)

resultado efecto o producto de una acción o un evento (pág. 58)

subcontratación práctica de trasladar la producción de bienes y servicios a otra localidad en donde el costo de la mano de obra es más barato (pág. 482)

anular rechazar o derrotar algo que ya se ha decidido (pág. 47)

ultramar del otro lado del océano (pág. 306)

P

pacifist(s) a person who is opposed to the use of violence (p. 226)

partner a person who takes part in an activity with others, especially in the operation of a business (p. 110)

pension a sum paid regularly to a person, usually after retirement (pp. 284–285)

perjury the crime of lying under oath; the act of lying after swearing to tell the truth (pp. 336–337; p. 465)

perceive to view; to become aware of by observing (pp. 226–227)

philosophy a set of ideas or beliefs (p. 138)

poll tax a tax a person must pay in order to vote (pp. 58–59)

pool a group sharing in some activity, for example, among railroad barons who made secret agreements and set rates among themselves (pp. 100–101)

populism an appeal to the common people (pp. 88–89)

pacifista(s) persona que se opone al uso de la violencia (pág. 226)

socio persona que toma parte en una actividad con otros, especialmente en el funcionamiento de un negocio (pág. 110)

pensión suma que se paga regularmente a una persona, por lo general después de su retiro (págs. 284–285)

perjurio crimen de mentir bajo juramento; el acto de mentir después de jurar decir la verdad (págs. 336–337; pág. 465)

percibir ver; volverse consciente mediante la observación (págs. 226–227)

filosofía conjunto de ideas o creencias (pág. 138)

impuesto al sufragio impuesto que una persona debe pagar para votar (págs. 58–59)

consorcio grupo que comparte cierta actividad, por ejemplo, entre los magnates del ferrocarril quienes hicieron acuerdos secretos y fijaron tasas entre ellos (págs. 100–101)

populismo llamado a la gente común (págs. 88–89)

*pose to offer (p. 334)

poverty line the minimum income needed to live (pp. 372–373)

*primary an election in which a political party chooses its candidates (p. 168)

*prior at an earlier time; before (p. 477)

*proceed to continue (p. 220)

productivity the degree to which resources are being used efficiently to produce goods and services (pp. 246–247)

*professional showing a high degree of specialized skill (pp. 158–159)

prohibition laws that banned making or selling alcohol; a total ban on the manufacture, sale, and transportation of liquor throughout the United States, achieved through the Eighteenth Amendment (pp. 162–163; p. 252)

*promote to help the progress of something (p. 272)

propaganda ideas or information intentionally spread to harm or help a cause; information used to influence opinion (p. 213)

protectorate a country under the control of a different country (p. 193)

provisional government temporary government (p. 187)

public works projects such as the building of highways, parks, and libraries built with public funds for public use (p. 266)

*plantear ofrecer (pág. 334)

línea de pobreza ingreso mínimo necesario para vivir (págs. 372–373)

*primaria elección en la que un partido político escoge a sus candidatos (pág. 168)

*previo en un momento anterior; antes (pág. 477)

*proceder continuar (pág. 220)

productividad grado al cual los recursos se usan de manera eficiente para producir bienes y servicios (págs. 246–247)

*profesional que muestra un alto grado de destreza especializada (págs. 158–159)

prohibición leyes que vedan la fabricación y venta de alcohol; prohibición total de la producción, la venta y el transporte de licor en Estados Unidos, lograda mediante la Decimoctava Enmienda (págs. 162-163; pág. 252)

*promover ayudar al progreso de algo (pág. 272)

propaganda ideas o información que se difunden intencionalmente para perjudicar o apoyar una causa; información que se usa para influir en la opinión (p. 213)

protectorado país bajo el control de un país diferente (pág. 193)

gobierno provisional gobierno temporal (pág. 187)

obras públicas proyectos como la construcción de autopistas, parques y librerías construidos con fondos públicos para uso público (pág. 266)

Q

*questing seeking, on a quest (p. 283)

*quota number or share assigned to a group (p. 131)

quota system an arrangement setting the number of immigrants (pp. 252–253)

*quote to repeat words written or spoken by another person (p. 452)

*buscar indagar, en una búsqueda (pág. 283)

*cuota cantidad o participación asignada a un grupo (pág. 131)

sistema de cuotas arreglo que dispone el número de inmigrantes (págs. 252–253)

*citar repetir palabras escritas o dichas por otra persona (pág. 452)

R

*__radical__ extreme (p. 43)

__ragtime__ a type of music characterized by syncopation in the melody (pp. 142–143)

__railroad baron__ a powerful business leader who controlled a major railroad (p. 99)

__ration__ to limit use; to make scarce items available to people on a limited basis (p. 225; p. 306)

__rebate__ a discount or return of part of a payment (p. 100)

__recall__ the right of voters to remove incompetent elected officials from office (pp. 154–155)

__recession__ an economic downturn (pp. 246–247)

__Reconstruction__ after the Civil War, the period of rebuilding the South and readmitting the former Confederate states into the Union (pp. 42–43)

__recruit__ to hire people for jobs (p. 128)

__referendum__ the right of voters to accept or reject laws (pp. 154–155)

__regime__ a form of government in power, or period of rule (p. 402)

*__register__ to enroll; to sign up (pp. 378–379)

*__relax__ to ease (p. 424)

__relief__ changes in elevation of the Earth's surface (p. 15); aid for the needy; welfare (p. 266)

__reparation__ payment for damages caused during a war (pp. 229–230)

*__research__ the careful collection of information (p. 4, 6)

__reservation__ an area of land set aside for use by a group (p. 81)

*__respond__ to reply with action (pp. 394–395)

*__retain__ to hold on to; to keep from changing (pp. 456–457)

*__radical__ extremo (pág. 43)

__tiempo rasgado__ tipo de música caracterizado por la síncopa de la melodía (págs. 142–143)

__magnate del ferrocarril__ líder poderoso de negocios que controla un ferrocarril importante (pág. 99)

__racionar__ limitar el uso; hacer que elementos escasos estén a disposición de las personas de manera limitada (pág. 225; pág. 306)

__rebaja__ descuento o devolución de una parte del pago (pág. 100)

__revocatoria__ derecho de los votantes para retirar de sus cargos a los funcionarios elegidos incompetentes (págs. 154–155)

__recesión__ descenso económico (págs. 246–247)

__Reconstrucción__ después de la Guerra Civil, el periodo de reconstrucción del Sur y la readmisión de los antiguos estados confederados en la Unión (págs. 42–43)

__reclutar__ contratar personas para desempeñar trabajos (pág. 128)

__referendo__ derecho de los votantes para aceptar o rechazar leyes (págs. 154–155)

__régimen__ forma de gobierno en el poder, o periodo de gobierno (pág. 402)

*__inscribir__ matricular (pág. 378–379)

*__relajarse__ aliviar (pág. 424)

__relieve__ cambios en la elevación de la superficie de la Tierra (pág. 15); __auxilio__ ayuda para los necesitados; asistencia social (pág. 266)

__reparación__ pago por los daños causados durante una guerra (págs. 229–230)

*__investigación__ recolección cuidadosa de información (pág. 4, 6)

__reservación__ área de tierra dispuesta para ser usada por un grupo (pág. 81)

*__responder__ contestar con una acción (págs. 394–395)

*__retener__ aferrarse; evitar que cambie (págs. 456–457)

revenue sharing a policy in which the federal government gives states some of its revenue to be used at state and local levels (p. 431)

*****revolution** a war to overthrow a government (p. 216)

participación en los ingresos fiscales política mediante la cual el gobierno federal da a los estados de sus ingresos para que se usen a niveles estatales y locales (pág. 431)

*****revolución** guerra para derrocar a un gobierno (pág. 216)

S

scalawag a name given by former Confederates to Southern whites who supported Republican Reconstruction of the South (p. 53)

*****scheme** a plan or arrangement for doing or organizing something (pp. 284–285)

*****scope** the range or extent of something (p. 465)

search-and-destroy missions a mission by American forces to seek out and destroy North Vietnamese forces (p. 404)

*****secure** to gain control of (p. 322)

segregation the separation or isolation of a race, class, or group; separation of one group from another (p. 60; p. 172)

settlement house place in large cities where people get assistance with social problems and challenges related to urban life (p. 134)

sharecropping system of farming in which a farmer works land for an owner who provides equipment and seeds and receives a share of the crop (pp. 54–55)

shareholder a person who invests in a company by buying stock (p. 109)

*****shift** to move (p. 305)

siege military blockade (p. 312)

*****site** a location or place (p. 459)

sit-in the act of protesting by sitting down, commonly used as a method of nonviolent protest (p. 374)

*****skein** yarn or thread loosely wound around a spool (p. 131)

skyscraper a very tall building (p. 135)

slum highly populated, poor, run-down urban area (p. 133)

bribón nombre dado por los antiguos confederados a los blancos sureños que apoyaban la Reconstrucción republicana del Sur (pág. 53)

*****esquema** plan o disposición para hacer u organizar algo (págs. 284–285)

*****alcance** rango o extensión de algo (pág. 465)

misiones de búsqueda y destrucción misión mediante la cual las fuerzas estadounidenses buscaban y destruían a las fuerzas vietnamitas (pág. 404)

*****asegurar** obtener el control (pág. 322)

segregación separación o aislamiento de una raza, clase o grupo; separación de un grupo de otro (pág. 60; pág. 172)

hogar comunitario lugar en las ciudades grandes donde las personas obtienen ayuda con problemas sociales y desafíos relacionados con la vida urbana (pág. 134)

aparcería sistema en el cual un agricultor trabaja la tierra para un propietario que suministra el equipo y las semillas y recibe una parte de la cosecha (págs. 54–55)

accionista persona que invierte en una compañía comprando acciones (pág. 109)

*****correr** mover (pág. 305)

sitio bloqueo militar (pág. 312)

*****emplazamiento** ubicación o lugar (pág. 459)

sentada acto de protesta al permanecer sentado que por lo general se usa como método de protesta no violenta (pág. 374)

*****madeja** hilo o hebra suelta alrededor de un carrete (pág. 131)

rascacielos edificio muy alto (pág. 135)

barrio bajo altamente poblado, pobre, área urbana deprimida (pág. 133)

socialist a person who believes industries should be publicly owned (p. 226)

sodbuster name given to Great Plains farmers (p. 78)

spectator sport a sport played for the entertainment of spectators (p. 141)

sphere of influence section of a country in which a foreign nation enjoys special rights and powers (p. 188)

Square Deal Theodore Roosevelt's promised program of fair and equal treatment for all (p. 165)

***stable** unchanging (pp. 339–340)

stalemate a situation in a conflict in which neither side can make progress against the other (pp. 208–209)

standard gauge 4 feet 8.5 inches, the distance between rails agreed upon by all railroad companies (p. 100)

standard of living necessities and comforts enjoyed by an individual or group (pp. 350–351)

steerage quarters for low-paying passengers below the deck of a ship (p. 126)

***stock** shares of ownership a company sells in its business (p. 109)

stock exchange a place where shares in corporations are bought and sold through an organized system (pp. 262–263)

stopgap measure carried out in an emergency (p. 471)

***stress** to call attention to (p. 213)

strikebreaker person hired to replace a striking worker in order to break up a strike (p. 116)

stringent strict (p. 471)

subsidy money or goods given by a person or government to support a project that benefits the public; grant of money, often from the government, to a person or company for an action intended to benefit the public (pp. 70–71; pp. 270–271)

suburb residential area outside a city center (p. 133)

socialista persona que cree que las industrias deben ser públicas (pág. 226)

rompeterrón nombre dado a los agricultores de las Grandes Llanuras (pág. 78)

deporte espectáculo deporte que se jugaba para entretener a los espectadores (pág. 141)

esfera de influencia sección de un país en la cual una nación extranjera disfruta de derechos y poderes especiales (pág. 188)

Trato Justo programa en el que Theodore Roosevelt prometió un trato justo e igual para todos (pág. 165)

***estable** sin cambio (págs. 339–340)

punto muerto situación en un conflicto en la que ningún lado puede hacer un progreso en contra del otro (págs. 208–209)

medida estándar 4 pies 8.5 pulgadas: la distancia entre los rieles que acordaron todas las compañías ferrocarrileras (pág. 100)

nivel de vida necesidades y comodidades que disfruta un individuo o un grupo (págs. 350–351)

tercera clase habitaciones debajo de la cubierta de un barco para los pasajeros que pagan poco (pág. 126)

***ganado** el término en inglés "stock" también significa "acción", participación en la propiedad de una compañía que esta vende (pág. 109)

bolsa lugar en donde las acciones de las corporaciones se compran y se venden mediante un sistema organizado (págs. 262–263)

medida provisional medida que se implementa en una emergencia (pág. 471)

***acentuar** llamar la atención (pág. 213)

esquirol persona contratada para reemplazar a un trabajador huelguista con el fin de finalizar una huelga (pág. 116)

riguroso estricto (pág. 471)

subsidio dinero o bienes que el gobierno o una persona da para apoyar un proyecto que beneficia al público; donación de dinero, con frecuencia del gobierno, a una persona o compañía para una acción que beneficia al público (págs. 70–71; págs. 270–271)

suburbio zona residencial ubicada fuera del perímetro de la ciudad (pág. 133)

subversion attempts to overthrow or undermine a government by working secretly within that government (pp. 366–367)

suffragist person who fought for woman suffrage, or women's right to vote (p. 160)

***sum** total amount (pp. 68–69)

summit meeting of heads of government (p. 349)

surplus an amount left over (p. 349)

***suspend** to temporarily set aside or stop operation of something (p. 50)

sweatshop a shop or factory where workers work long hours at low wages under unhealthy conditions (pp. 113–114)

subversión intentos para derrocar o debilitar un gobierno con personas que trabajan de manera secreta en ese gobierno (págs. 366–367)

sufragista persona que luchó por el sufragio femenino, o por el derecho de las mujeres a votar (pág. 160)

***suma** cantidad total (págs. 68–69)

cumbre encuentro entre los jefes del gobierno (pág. 349)

excedente cantidad que sobra (pág. 349)

***suspender** dejar de lado o detener temporalmente el funcionamiento de algo (pág. 50)

sweatshop almacén o fábrica en donde los trabajadores trabajan durante largas jornadas bajo condiciones insalubres (págs. 113–114)

T

***target** object of an attack (p. 298; p. 300)

tariff a tax on imports (p. 27)

***technique** a method for accomplishing a task (p. 247)

tenement a type of residence that is often run-down and crowded (p. 133)

***tense** anxious (p. 312)

territory area completely controlled by a country (p. 193)

terrorism violence committed in order to frighten people or governments into granting demands (p. 472; p. 474)

***theme** a subject or topic (p. 454)

time zone a geographic region in which the same standard time is used (pp. 72–73)

totalitarian seeking to control all aspects of life through dictatorial control (p. 295)

***trace** follow (pp. 400–401)

***objetivo** blanco de un ataque (pág. 298; pág. 300)

arancel impuesto a las importaciones (pág. 27)

***técnica** método para realizar una tarea (pág. 247)

inquilinato tipo de residencia que con frecuencia está deteriorada y llena de gente (pág. 133)

***tenso** ansioso (pág. 312)

territorio área completamente controlada por un país (pág. 193)

terrorismo violencia cometida para asustar a las personas o los gobiernos de manera que cedan a lo que se exige (pág. 472; pág. 474)

***tema** sujeto o tópico (pág. 454)

huso horario región geográfica en la que se usa el tiempo estándar (págs. 72–73)

totalitario que busca controlar todos los aspectos de la vida mediante el control dictatorial (pág. 295)

***rastrear** seguir (págs. 400–401)

trade deficit when the value of foreign imports is greater than the value of American exports; the sum result of importing more goods than are exported in a given year (p. 439; p. 481)

*transcendent most important (p. 275)

transcontinental going across a continent (pp. 70–71)

*transmit to send a message by electronic signal; to pass from one person or place to another (pp. 102–103)

*trend a general direction of events (p. 112)

*trigger to cause an event to happen (p. 191)

trust a combination of firms or corporations formed by a legal agreement, especially to reduce competition (p. 110)

trustbuster a government official who investigates and combats alliances formed to control competition and prices (p. 165)

déficit comercial cuando el valor de las importaciones extranjeras es mayor que el valor de las exportaciones estadounidenses; la suma que resulta de importar más bienes de los que se exportan en un año dado (pág. 439; pág. 481)

*trascendental muy importante (pág. 275)

transcontinental que atraviesa un continente (págs. 70–71)

*transmitir enviar un mensaje mediante una señal electrónica; pasar de una persona a otra o de un lugar a otro (págs. 102–103)

*tendencia dirección general de los eventos (pág. 112)

*desencadenante algo que hace que ocurra otro evento (pág. 191)

trust unión de compañías o corporaciones formadas mediante acuerdo legal, especialmente para reducir la competencia (pág. 110)

trustbuster empleado del gobierno que investiga y combate las alianzas que se forman para controlar la competencia y los precios (pág. 165)

U

U-boat a German submarine (pp. 210–211)

unemployment insurance payments by the government for a limited period of time to people who have lost their jobs (p. 286)

*unify to join together (pp. 296–297)

urban of or like a city (pp. 132–133)

U-boat submarino alemán (págs. 210–211)

seguro de desempleo pagos que hace el gobierno, durante un periodo limitado de tiempo, a las personas que han perdido sus empleos (pág. 286)

*unificar unir (págs. 296–297)

urbano de una ciudad o parecido a una (págs. 132–133)

V

vaquero a cowhand, particularly a Mexican cowhand (p. 75)

vaudeville a type of theatrical show, with dancing, singing, comedy, and magic acts (p. 142)

Vietnamization President Nixon's plan calling for the South Vietnamese to take a more active role in fighting and for Americans to become less involved (p. 413)

*vision an imagined plan of action (p. 184)

*voluntary done by choice (p. 34)

vaquero ganadero, en especial un ganadero mexicano (pág. 75)

vodevil tipo de representación teatral con danza, canto, comedia y actos de magia (pág. 142)

vietnamización plan del presidente Nixon para que Vietnam del Sur asumiera un papel más activo en la lucha, de manera que los estadounidenses estuvieran menos involucrados (pág. 413)

*visión plan de acción imaginario (pág. 184)

*violuntario que se puede elegir libremente (pág. 34)

Glossary/Glosario

W

*welfare the good wealth, happiness, and comfort of a person or group; care for the health and safety of a group (p. 286)

work relief programs that give needy people jobs (pp. 270–271)

*bienestar riqueza, felicidad y comodidad de una persona o grupo; el término en inglés "welfare" también significa "asistencia social", cuidado de la salud y seguridad de un grupo (pág. 286)

trabajo de auxilio programas que dan empleo a las personas necesitadas (págs. 270–271)

Y

yellow journalism a type of journalism based on sensational stories (p. 140)

periodismo amarillo tipo de periodismo basado en historias sensacionalistas (pág. 140)

Glossary/Glosario

The following abbreviations are used in the index: m=map, c=chart, p=photograph or picture, g=graph, crt=cartoon, ptg=painting, q=quote

Index

Index